Queens and Queenship
in Medieval Europe

The image, status and function of queens and empresses, regnant and consort, in kingdoms stretching from England to Jerusalem in the European Middle Ages, are the focus of these studies. They confront many of the central issues in the study of women's authority and power in medieval societies and raise questions about the perception of women rulers in contemporary records (and modern historical writing). Did queens exercise real or counterfeit power? Did the promotion of the cult of the Virgin enhance or restrict their sphere of action? Is it time to revise the early feminist view of women as victims? Important papers on Emma of England, Margaret of Scotland, coronation and burial ritual, Byzantine empresses and Scandinavian queens, among others, clearly indicate that a reassessment of 'women's work' and the role of women in the world of medieval dynastic politics is under way.

Queens and Queenship
in Medieval Europe

PROCEEDINGS OF A CONFERENCE HELD
AT KING'S COLLEGE LONDON
APRIL 1995

EDITED BY

Anne J. Duggan

THE BOYDELL PRESS

First published 1997
The Boydell Press, Woodbridge

ISBN 0 85115 657 6

The Boydell Press is an imprint of Boydell & Brewer Ltd
PO Box 9, Woodbridge, Suffolk IP12 3DF, UK
and of Boydell & Brewer Inc.
PO Box 41026, Rochester, NY 14604–4126, USA

A catalogue record for this book is available
from the British Library

Library of Congress Cataloging-in-Publication Data
Queens and queenship in medieval Europe : proceedings of a conference
held at King's College London, April 1995 / edited by Anne J. Duggan.
    p.   cm.
Includes bibliographical references and index.
ISBN 0–85115–657–6 (alk. paper)
    1. Queens – Europe – Congresses.   2. Middle Ages – History –
Congresses.   I. Duggan, Anne.
0107.3.Q44   1997
940.1 – DC21   97–917

This publication is printed on acid-free paper

Printed in Great Britain by
St Edmundsbury Press Ltd, Bury St Edmunds, Suffolk

Contents

III. Images of Queenship

IV. Queens and Culture

Illustrations

Contributors

Professor János M. Bak
Central European University, Budapest

Professor George Conklin
Department of History, Northwestern State University of Louisiana

Dr Paul Crossley
Courtauld Institute of Art, London

Dr Anne J. Duggan
Department of History, King's College London

Professor Dr Volker Honemann
Germanistisches Institut, Westfälische Wilhelms-Universität Münster, Germany

Professor Steinar Imsen
Historisk Institutt, University of Trondheim, Norway

Dr Liz James
School of European Studies, University of Sussex

Professor Dr Kurt-Ulrich Jäschke
Historisches Institut, Universität des Saarlandes, Saarbrücken

Ms Sarah Lambert
Goldsmiths College, London

Professor Janet L. Nelson
Department of History, King's College London

Professor John C. Parsons
Department of History, University of Toronto

Dr Karen Pratt
Department of French, King's College London

Dr Dion Smyth
Prosopography of the Byzantine Empire Project, King's College London

Professor Pauline Stafford
Department of Humanities, University of Huddersfield

Professor Mary Stroll
Department of History, University of California, San Diego, California

Ms Valerie Wall
Institute of Historical Research, London

Dr Diana Webb
Department of History, King's College London

Abbreviations

AASS	*Acta Sanctorum*, edd. J. Bolland and G. Henschen, 70 vols (Antwerp/Brussels, 1643–1944)
BO	J. F. Böhmer, *Die Regesten des Kaiserreichs unter den Herrschern aus dem Saechsischen Hause 919–1024*, ed. E. von Ottenthal, *Regesta Imperii, ii/1 (Innsbruck, 1893; repr. with supplement, Hildesheim, 1967)*
BMik	J. F. Böhmer, *Die Regesten des Kaiserreichs unter Otto II. 955–983*, ed. H. L. Mikoletzky, *Regesta Imperii*, ii/2 (Graz, 1950)
c.; cc.	capitulum; capitula
c.	*circa*
ch.	chapter
HJL	*Hessisches Jahrbuch für Landesgeschichte*
EHD	*English Historical Documents*
JDG	*Jahrbücher der Deutschen Geschichte*, ed. Historische Commission bei der Königlichen Academie der Wissenschaften (Munich/Berlin/Leipzig, 1863–)
JL	P. Jaffé, *Regesta Pontificum Romanorum ad annum 1198*, edd. W. Wattenbach, S. Loewenfeld, F. Kaltenbrunner, and P. Ewald, 2 vols (Leipzig, 1885–8)
Lex. des MA	*Lexikon des Mittelalters* (Munich/Zürich, 1979–)
LThK	*Lexikon für Theologie und Kirche*, edd. M. Buchberger *et al.*, 10 vols (Freiburg im Breisgau, 1930–38; 2nd edn, + Index, 1957–65; 3rd edn, 1993–)
Mansi	*Sacrorum Conciliorum nova et amplissima collectio*, ed. J. D. Mansi, cont. I. B. Martin, L. Petit, 53 vols (Florence/Venice, 1759–98; Paris, 1901–27; repr. Graz, 1960–61)
Medieval Queenship, ed. Parsons	*Medieval Queenship*, ed. J. C. Parsons (London, 1993)
MGH	*Monumenta Germaniae Historica:*
Constitutiones	*Constitutiones et acta publica imperatorum et regum*, 8 vols (Hanover/Leipzig, 1893–1927) = *MGH Leges*, Sectio IV
DRG	*Diplomata regum et imperatorum Germaniae*, 8 vols (Hanover/Leipzig/Berlin/Weimar, 1879–1959; repr. 1956–57)

Epp.	*Epistolae*, 8 vols (Berlin, 1887–1939)
Fontes	*Fontes iuris Germanici antiqui in usum scholarum ex Monumentis Germaniae historica separatim editi*, 10 vols (Hanover/Leipzig, 1869–1984)
Libelli	*Libelli de lite imperatorum et pontificum saec. XI et XII conscripti*, 3 vols (Hanover, 1891–97; repr. 1957)
Poet. Lat.	*Poetae Latini aevi Carolini*, i–ii, ed. E. Dümmler, iii, ed. V. Traube (Berlin, 1881–86) = *Poetae latini medii aevi*, i–iii
SRG	*Scriptores rerum Germanicarum in usum scholarum ex Monumentis Germaniae historica separatim editi*, 61 vols (Hanover, etc., 1839–1935; variously re-edited and reprinted)
SRG, NS	*Scriptores rerum Germanicarum*, New Series (Berlin, 1922–)
SS	*Scriptores* (in folio), 32 vols in 34 (Hanover, 1826–1934)
NglL	*Norges gamle Love*, iii (Christiania/Oslo, 1849)
pd	printed
PL	*Patrologiae cursus completus, series latina*, ed. J. P. Migne, 234 vols (Paris, 1844–1955)
RS	Rolls Series: *Rerum Britannicarum medii ævi scriptores: Chronicles and Memorials of Great Britain and Ireland during the Middle Ages*, published under the direction of the Master of the Rolls (London, etc., 1858–1911)
repr.	reprint
SCH	*Studies in Church History*
s.a.	*sub anno*
s.v.	*sub vocabulo*
TRHS	*Transactions of the Royal Historical Society*

Preface

The papers in this volume were presented at the Second International Conference held under the auspices of the Centre for Late Antique and Medieval Studies at King's College London in the Great Hall of the College on 19–21 April 1995. The theme was 'Queens and Queenship in the Middle Ages', and the Conference was planned to enable comparisons to be made across time, from the fifth to the early sixteenth century, and between very different monarchical structures in the Middle Ages, embracing regions as diverse as England (before and after the Norman Conquest), France, Hungary, Scotland, the Romano-German empire, Scandinavia, Byzantium, and the Latin Kingdom of Jerusalem. Central and northern Italy did not have a monarchy during the greater part of the medieval period, but it was not without its powerful symbols of queenship. Lacking human queens, the papacy, some Italian city-states, and many confraternities adopted the Virgin Mary as their queen and protectress, and her image as Queen of Heaven became one of the most pervasive and potent images of queenliness in the Middle Ages. It was therefore appropriate that one of the highlights of the Conference was a performance of music in honour of Maria *Regina*, presented in the College Chapel by the Clerks' Group, under the direction of Mr Edward Wickham.

Our grateful thanks are due to the British Academy, the Goethe Institute, and the Humanties Research Committee of King's College London, all of whom provided financial or other assistance for various aspects of the Conference; and to the Isobel Thornley Bequest, whose generous grant made possible the publication of this volume. At the same time, the Centre for Late Antique and Medieval Studies wishes to record its gratitude to King's College London for the splendid facilities which were made available for the Conference and to the Dean who allowed us to use the College Chapel for the Marian concert.

For permission to reproduce photographs from materials in their charge, the authors wish to thank the following:

Florence	Bargello Museum
Fredriksborg	Nationalhistoriske Mueseum
London	British Library
	British Museum
	Courtauld Institute of Art
Lübeck	Museum für Kunst & Kulturgeschichte der Hansestadt
Merseyside	National Museums and Galleries
New York	Art Resource
	Metropolitan Museum of Art

Pierpont Morgan Library
Paris Bibliothèque Nationale
Rome Bibliotheca Apostolica Vaticana
Bibliotheca Hertziana, Max-Planck-Institut

AJD
King's College London
3 July 1996

This book is produced with the assistance of
a grant from Isobel Thornley's Bequest to
the University of London

Introduction

Anne J. Duggan

The study of medieval queens is beset by problems. In addition to their virtual invisibility in many narrative sources, there is the presumed or actual bias of the predominantly male commentators. How objective, for example, is Michael Psellus's depiction of Byzantine empresses in the eleventh century or William of Tyre and his continuators' versions of events in the Latin Kingdom of Jerusalem in the twelfth, where five queens inherited the crown of that most military of military societies in the twelfth-early thirteenth century? Alternatively, there is the suspicion that even positive images of royal women are didactic programmes, not authentic portrayals of real women. How historically valid are the portrayals of holy queens and empresses? How far are we dealing with accounts of female power specifically constructed to channel and confine the feminine according to male-centred ideas of what is right and proper conduct for a woman? Is it possible to extract a true history of royal and imperial women from the stereotypes – negative and positive – which pictorial image, narrative history, and literary *topoi* have constructed? There are genuine difficulties in interpreting such material, but in emphasising the female stereotypes is there not a tendency to overlook the powerful effect of male stereotypes in the same sources?

In attempting to answer some of these questions, the papers in this volume reflect the wide range of current thinking on the subject of female rule. At one end of the spectrum, János Bak portrays queens as convenient scape-goats, easy targets of narrow-minded local nobilities, traduced by chauvinist historians, and some-times physically abused or even murdered, while Sarah Lambert's analysis of the history of the Latin Kingdom of Jerusalem exposes a changing cocktail of uncertainty and hostility to the rule of queens. At the other end of the spectrum, Liz James's study on early Byzantine empresses and Pauline Stafford's work on the late Anglo-Saxon queen Emma both propose a re-interpretation of the conven-tional images and a re-valuation of the status and function of female consorts and rulers. While not discounting the bias of the sources, they ask new questions and suggest new ways of looking at the evidence.

Central to their approach is a re-interpretation of the surviving pictorial images. Liz James allows that the representations of Byzantine empresses can be read as images of isolation and sequestration; but she proposes an alternative reading. Whether it be the anonymous empress (pl. 7), or the consular diptych of Flavius Taurus Clementinus (pl. 8), with its twin images of Anastasios I and Ariadne, or

Theodora in her splendour in the famous mosaic in Ravenna (pll. 9, 14), these are all images of the exalted status and power of an empress. These imperial women are officially set apart from and above the rest of society. Dignified with the title of Augusta, crowned and bejewelled, they are paired with corresponding images of the emperor. The Theodora image can be seen as a splendid depiction of female isolation (she is surrounded by her household, occupying her own cloistered space), but it can also be read as a counterbalance to that of Justinian, who approaches the altar from the other side of the apse. What is emphasised here and in the diptych is the sharing of imperial power and dignity. The male and female images are balanced and complementary.

In an equally arresting manner, Pauline Stafford reassesses the significance of the two surviving depictions of Queen Emma of England. In the first (pl. 1), she finds not so much the subordination of a wife and queen to her husband as a sharing of royal status in a formal act. The queen, identified by her Anglo-Saxon name of Ælfgifu, stands on one side of an altar bearing a cross while King Cnut, drawn to the same scale, stands on the other; moreover, and not without significance, Emma stands beneath an image of the Virgin Mary, the mother of God, whose gestures she imitates, while Cnut stands beneath that of St Peter. The vertical pairing of the queen with the Virgin thus places her in the primary position, to the right of the altar. These are not chance associations. The picture thus 'stresses the special status of a king's wife, as queen, that is as a consecrated person, and as an office-holder'.

The difficulty of correctly interpreting such images derives partly from the application of modern norms and values to late antique and medieval constructs, partly from the ambiguous or polysemic character of the images themselves, and partly from the paradox which the images were intended to portray. The manifold images of the Virgin Mary, virgin-mother of God, Queen of Angels, Queen of Heaven, Mother of Mercies, Salvation of the Roman people, type of *Romana ecclesia*, etc., etc., present a bewildering range of possibilities and ambiguities. At the level of the pictorial representation, Mary is very much a queen, often clothed in imperial dress, crowned and enthroned. Hers indeed was the most widely-disseminated image of queenship, its iconographical form derived in part from the iconic representations of Byzantine empresses. She was, however, simultaneously Mother of God and archetype of obedience to God. Her obedience, expressed in the 'fiat' of the Annunciation, reversed the disobedience of Eve (and Adam) in the garden of Eden, and her position as Mother of God depended on that submission. Hers was a sublime example of the paradox of Christian abnegation: 'he who humbles himself shall be exalted' (Lk 14:11). Either the supreme elevation or the supreme self-abnegation can be emphasised. The cult of the Virgin from the fifth century onwards and the progressive construction of her queenly status can be seen as enhancements of queenly office – and were so appropriated by earthly queens (like Blanche of Castile, pl. 27), but that 'Marianizing tendency' could also, it is argued by Parsons and others, represent not so much an elevation as a confinement of the feminine, in which the queen's image was constructed as a 'paradigmatic figure of the completely perfect and totally absent woman upon whom the moral and social order depended'. Mary's acceptance of the role required of her could be read as an image of female submission to and dependence on male authority, since her queenship of heaven was the consequence of her submission on earth. But her submission was to God not to her husband Joseph, who is usually depicted in the guise of protector of the Virgin and her Child, and it paralleled Christ's, who was 'made obedient to his father unto death, even death on the cross', in a reversal of the original disobedience of Eve and Adam.

Those who see the Virgin as a paradigm of womanly submission suppress both the universal application of her model to men and women alike and the implications of her sublime elevation. The Virgin was associated with her Son not only in the salvation of the whole human race but in His eternal rule. His Ascension was paralleled by her Assumption, and she took her place beside Him in heaven. The iconographical transformation of the Virgin into the Queen of Heaven, traced by Mary Stroll, tilted the balance from 'humble handmaid' to *co-adiutrix* (though without eliminating it), and it was in this guise that she was adopted by the papacy and adorned some of the great Roman basilicas erected in her honour.

This Queen of Heaven was her Son's spouse as well as His mother, enjoying a unique position of dignity and power to which no man could aspire. The duality of her position in relation to Christ thus made her an ideal model for queens, as wives and mothers of kings. It was an image which both elevated their role and differentiated it from that of male rulers, in that it emphasised the queenly and womanly virtues of mercy, benevolence, kindness and intercession. (It was as protectress and intercessor that some leading Italian city-states adopted her as a kind of surrogate queen.)[1] While kings inspired awe and fear, queens represented the milder aspects of the ruler's responsibility for widows, orphans, and the unprivileged. Feeding the hungry, visiting the sick, visiting the imprisoned were all practical expressions of active Christianity – and the traditional activities of Christian widows since the days of the early Church. The activities of the Byzantine empresses discussed by Liz James and Dion Smythe and of the German empresses and queens discussed by Kurt-Ulrich Jäschke and Volker Honemann all fit this pattern, and Christine de Pizan, writing for a young French princess, was still emphasising these duties in the mid-fourteenth century.

These aspects of the consort's role can be written off as historically insignificant varieties of 'women's work', safe side-lines, marginalisations of female talent; but it may be argued equally that these activities were not only socially respected but dynastically and politically important. Liz James's question about the relative importance in the Byzantine world of an emperor's success in battle and an empress's endowment of a church might with advantage be extended to the whole of the medieval Christian West. It might be argued also that to discount or de-value the role of queens and empresses in the social, charitable, and religious aspects of the life of their societies constitutes the real marginalisation of the feminine.

And what weight should be given to the crucial role of royal women in the sphere of family and dynastic politics? If family is narrowed to the domestic sphere of house-management, then the role of women within it is diminished. But if the

---

[1] See Diana Webb, ch. 11.

family is re-valued, as many of the papers in this volume suggest that it should be, then the place of women is correspondingly enhanced. As monarchy became progressively dynastic and legitimate birth an essential requirement in the transmission of the right to rule, royal women, as daughters, wives, mothers and grandmothers – and hence as princesses and queens – played a crucial role in the creation and protection of the legitimacy upon which male rulers depended for the transmission of the throne to their lawful offspring. Emma in England and Margaret in Scotland are two outstanding examples of this activity; but the key role of royal women in the area of dynastic continuity recurs again and again in this volume; and it is a role which extended far beyond the purely biological acts of conception and birth. Jäschke's study of Romano-German empresses and queens from the tenth to the fourteenth century shows their pre-eminent importance as continuators and transmitters of the dynastic claim, protectors of minor children, framers of family policy, and preservers of family tradition and reputation. To dismiss the familial, religious or cultural role of women, royal or otherwise, is to suffer the same myopia as the chroniclers whose bias is condemned.

Most queens-consort were foreigners in a foreign land, sometimes betrothed in the cradle and sent to the households of their prospective husbands to learn the language and customs which would shape their lives.[2] The isolation and vulnerability produced by this almost universal practice of royal exogamy is discussed by János Bak. Like the Irish princess Iseut in Beroul's *Tristran* (cited by Karen Pratt) their foreign origins made them easy targets for criticism or attack, whether contemporary or retrospective. It would, nevertheless, be misleading to erect a general thesis of queen-baiting on the basis of these exceptional examples. For most of the queens discussed in this book, the protective envelope of royal status and territorial endowment counterbalanced the negative features described by Professor Bak. Marriage treaties were carefully negotiated to ensure that the queen was properly maintained. The incomes bestowed on Henry II's daughter Joanna when she married William II of Sicily in 1177 were minutely recorded, for example,[3] and Philip II of France insisted on an appropriate endowment for his sister Margaret when she married Béla III of Hungary in 1186.[4] Queens had their own households, their own estates and incomes, their own seals, and their own powers of patronage, direct and indirect. Even the unfortunate Ingeborg of Denmark, discussed by George Conklin, was able to live in some state and make significant pious and charitable donations in her widowhood, and during Philip II's life, her crowned and anointed status afforded her some protection against the French king who had repudiated her on the day after their wedding.

The role of royal women in the cultivation of the courtly arts of music, poetry,

---

2 Cf. Elizabeth of Hungary, below, p. 265.
3 *Gesta Regis Henrici Secundi Benedicti Abbatis*, ed. W. Stubbs, 2 vols, RS 49 (1867), i, 172–4.
4 Z. J. Kosztolnyik, *From Coleman the Learned to Béla III (1095–1106): Hungarian Domestic Politics and their Impact on Foreign Affairs*, East European Monographs (Boulder, 1987), p. 212.

and modes of courtly conduct, as well as their patronage of painters and artists, needs to be examined further. Paul Crossley, for example, links the rapid spread of French Gothic style through central and eastern Europe to the family connections of St Elizabeth of Thuringia, enshrined in a new-style Gothic church at Marburg. Daughter of Andrew II of Hungary and Gertrude of Andechs-Meranien[5] and widow of Landgrave Henry IV of Thuringia, her network of relations embraced the royal houses of Hungary and France as well as the Piasts of Lower Silesia in Poland. For nearly every queen of the Middle Ages a similar network of international connections could be established. A 'foreign queen in a foreign land' may in some circumstances have suffered suspicion and isolation, but by her very presence she attested the international standing of the family into which she married. Awareness of their elevated family connections is evident in the elaborate tombs of Eleanor of Castile and Philippa of Hainault (queens respectively of the English kings Edward I and Edward III), the one displaying armorial bearings proclaiming Eleanor's distinguished ancestry and the other adorned with statuettes of Philippa's kin and the king's.[6]

But did queens- and empresses-consort exercise any real power? The answer to this question will depend upon the meaning given to the term, but if one accepts Pauline Stafford's definition of power as 'the ability to take part in the events . . . to have the means of strategic action', then most queens had it, to a greater or lesser extent. Her study of Queen Emma challenges both Enright's view of queens as powerless women confined to 'family politics' and Wallace-Hadrill's picture of queens as 'honorary men'. Neither stereotype fits Emma. Despite being a foreigner (Norman), this queen-consort was the richest woman in England, with the power to take independent action and to intervene forcefully in the turbulent political events of her time. It was through her that the legitimacy of the Old English royal house was passed from Æthelred to Cnut and then to the sons which she had borne for them. If Emma demonstrates the possibilities for a queen even in difficult circumstances, so too does Margaret of Scotland, whose life was constructed by her biographer Turgot to project an image of dynastic purity at a crucial moment in the evolution of the Scottish kingdom. In her case, legality, legitimacy, and conformity with reformed marriage codes helped to establish her claims. Despite being Malcolm III's second wife, neither crowned nor anointed (for Scottish kings were inaugurated in an ancient ceremony outside the church at Scone), the Scottish regnal lists from the late twelfth century emphasise her position rather than Malcolm's as the fount of dynastic legitimacy, the king being described merely as 'the husband of St Margaret the Queen'!

Even more striking examples of the effective exercise of authority are found in the Byzantine world. Pulcheria exercised imperial power from 414–53, first in the name of her brother Theodosios and then with her husband Marcian (450–3);

---

5 For her sister Agnes, see below, p. 271.
6 See Parsons, ch. 16. Similar consciousness of personal rank and status is evident in the seals of Queen Blanche of Norway and Sweden and Queen Philippa of Norway, Sweden, and Denmark (fig. 12).

Ariadne, eldest daughter of Leo I and Verina, transmitted the imperium first to her son Leo II, who died in childhood, and then to two husbands in succession (Zeno and Anastasios I), successfully resisting the determined efforts of her own mother to hold on to power; Zoe, likewise, in the eleventh century, succeeded her father and legitimised her three husbands. If these actions did not constitute effective exercise of power, one might ask, what did?

In the later Middle Ages, the queens of Norway, Sweden, and Denmark (discussed by Steinar Imsen) demonstrated the remarkable powers that could be exercised by queens consort and regnant. In his estimation, their territorial endowment, for which he has invented the telling term of 'queendom', was constructed not merely to provide an income for the queen but to support the position of the monarchy. The complementarity between kings and queens-consort which Pauline Stafford finds in the New Minster image of Emma and Cnut (pl. 1) could scarcely go further. Among these remarkable women, Queen Margaret of Norway (d. 1412), is described by Imsen as 'without any doubt the ablest Scandinavian ruler of the period'; her adopted daughter-in-law Philippa (daughter of Henry IV of England and wife of King Eric: 1406–30), played a full role in political affairs throughout his reign, even to the extent of equipping and organising a naval expedition to Stralsund. So too did Dorothea (d. 1495) and Christina (d. 1521). These queens-consort and -regnant were certainly not powerless adornments of their husbands' courts nor were their activities contained within a narrow stereotype of 'women's roles'.

Nevertheless, while the position of the queen- or empress-consort was fairly well defined in custom and in law, that of the queen regnant presented conceptual and legal difficulties. Queenship had been constructed as a status complementary to that of the male ruler, not powerless, as we have seen, but not in itself the source of power. A queen regnant was therefore anomalous and in the usual run of events exceptional. Moreover, her position was complicated by the elevation of her husband to the throne. The intrusion of a non-dynastic male might engender hyper-criticism, envy, and conflict among the nobility. The choice for the queen lay between marrying within the kingdom, and disturbing the balance of power between noble alliances and factions, or marrying a foreign prince, who might be unpopular, or submitting to a choice made by the leading barons of her realm. In the early modern period, England's Queen Elizabeth avoided these pitfalls by remaining unmarried, whereas her contemporary Mary Queen of Scots paid a heavy price for her choice of husbands. In the Middle Ages, England's 'Empress' Matilda suffered for the unpopularity of her husband (and from the uncertainty about the rules for succession to the crown).

For the Latin Kingdom of Jerusalem in the twelfth century, the related problems associated with female rule and the marriage of reigning queens gravely disturbed the political equilibrium of the state. How far these difficulties were a consequence of misogyny or of self-centred exploitation by the nobility or of the military crisis faced by the kingdom, or a combination of all three, is open to debate; and in recording the crises, chroniclers could construct the story according to their own political programmes. They could choose to blame the queens, their husbands, or self-seeking baronial factions for the resulting disarray, but it was lack of clear laws for female succession and the absence of precedents for the position of a king-by-marriage which created the problem. In a reversal of the principles applied to male rulers, husbands of regnant queens and empresses became kings and emperors, were crowned, and occupied the throne with them. As the nobles said to Jocaste in the *Roman de Thèbes*: 'Everyone wishes him to have the kingdom; and you, my lady, will be his wife; may you have the kingdom along with him.' But the rights of the king-by-marriage were ill-defined.

How exceptional were the woman rulers discussed in these pages? Certainly, some of them were women of exceptional character and foresight: Emma of England, Margaret of Scotland, Melisende of Jerusalem, Margaret of Norway, the western empresses Adelaide, Theophanu, Cunigunde, the Byzantine empresses Verina, Ariadne, Theodora, Zoe; but without the status they enjoyed and royal or imperial office they exercised, they would not have been able to affect the fate of dynasties and nations in the way that they did. That their methods and circumstances varied with time and location is not surprising; but there is a fundamental consistency in the foundations of their power and status. What they had in common was participation in a culture of dynastic power in which their elevated positions were marked by styles and titles, enhanced by ceremonial coronation and in many cases by sacred anointing, which ordained them for a specific function as sharers in royal government, responsible with the king for good rule. With few exceptions (e.g. Theodora), queens- or empresses-consort were women of high rank in their own right: daughters of royal or princely families, destined from birth to marry kings or princes. The position of a porphyrogenita princess, born in the porphyry chamber of the imperial palace in Constantinople, was exalted and exclusive, just as the dignity of being a king's daughter (*filia regis*) conferred special status. They were educated in a courtly milieu which accustomed them to the exercise of power. Their marriages were matters of political and dynastic significance, and their position, dignity, and economic welfare were defined in their marriage contracts. Liz James is probably right to lay more stress on the potentialities of the office than on the individual capacity of the office-holder and to argue that the effective exercise of power by Byzantine empresses was less exceptional than traditional historiography was prepared to allow. The same might be said of other royal consorts in other periods and places.

If a conclusion is to be drawn from this wide spectrum of female rule, it is that queens- and empresses-consort were not merely bearers of royal children and adornments of the court. In many kingdoms they were anointed for their office in ceremonies traceable to the ninth century and earlier (J. L. Nelson). That their role in the government and in the state was different from that of kings and emperors does not cancel out the fact that they played an important part in the maintenance of dynastic rule, in the cultivation of the arts, and in the maintenance of the *memoria* of their families. These women were powerful figures, even if, as Stafford emphasises, their effectiveness waxed and waned with their life-cycle and the opportunities of the time and place. They may not have been able to enter the male hierarchy upon which political and clerical power depended, but they could often exercise not only influence but authority over both by reason of their official status. As the king, alone of the secular hierarchy, transcended the distinction between lay and clerical in consequence of his special office, so the queen, by virtue of her office, transcended the boundaries between male and female as well as between lay and clerical. Equally, however, just as the king did not become a priest or bishop, so the queen did not become a king. Aspects of the clerical office remained beyond the capacity of the king; and aspects of male rule were absent from the government of queens. The complementarity which characterised spiritual and secular office in Christian society characterised also the relationship between male and female authority. Nevertheless, queens and empresses discharged an office which enabled them to exercise authority over these male hierarchies. Except in France, where a particular crisis gave rise to a particular anti-female solution, the lawful inheritance and transmission of the crown by women was not ruled out *a priori*, and the position of the queen-consort waxed and waned not so much according to the operation of prejudice as to the circumstances and conditions of the time. The requirements of political stability and dynastic continuity overcame the prejudices of political society. In Byzantium, in Jerusalem, in the later medieval Scandinavian kingdoms, as well as in Castile in the fifteenth century and England and Scotland in the sixteenth, women did inherit and exercise in their own right the supreme power in the state.

I

Queens and Empresses
in the West

1

Emma: The Powers of the Queen in
the Eleventh Century [1]

Pauline Stafford

Queen Emma, wife of Æthelred II and Cnut, mother of Harthacnut and Edward the Confessor, is the first and only early English queen whom we can *see*. There are two contemporary images of her (pll. 1 and 2). The fact that we have two pictures of Emma is in itself significant. It reflects the increased depiction of royalty in general in the late Saxon period, and the possible influence on English iconography of continental representations of Ottonian and West Frankish royal women.[2] It is surely also an indication of her importance during her own lifetime, some index of her power and a sign of the sympathetic attitude towards her of some of the clerical image-makers of the first half of the eleventh century. It is instructive to begin a consideration of her and of the powers of an eleventh-century English queen with these pictures. The images are, I shall suggest, ambiguous and difficult to read; but consideration of those difficulties points towards some of the problems posed when we consider women's power in general and the queen's powers in particular.

The first of these images (pl. 1) presents her alongside her second husband Cnut as queen and wife. It is the frontispiece to the *Liber Vitae* of New Minster Abbey, Winchester.[3] It is a portrayal of Emma in a friendly source; I shall have cause to return to Winchester in Emma's story, but it is not clear whether we should read it as a representation of a powerful woman, or of a powerless one. It shows Emma

---

1 Much of the research on which this paper is based was made possible through my tenure of a British Academy Research Readership, 1994–96. Earlier versions of this paper were given at the universities of Glasgow and Liverpool and to Historical Association audiences in Hull and London. I am grateful to all those who asked questions, raised problems, and made suggestions, as well as to fellow participants in the 1995 conference on Queens and Queenship at King's College London.
2 See e.g. P. E. Schramm, *Die deutschen Kaiser und Könige in Bildern ihrere Zeit*, 2 vols (Leipzig, 1928); W. Cahn, 'The Psalter of Queen Emma', *Cahiers archéologiques*, xxxiii (1985), 73–85, and R. Deshman, '*Christus Rex et magi reges*: Kingship and Christology in Ottonian and Anglo-Saxon Art', *Frühmittelalterliche Studien*, x (1976), 367–405, and '*Benedictus Monarcha et monachus*: Early Medieval Ruler Theology and the Anglo-Saxon Reform', *ibid.*, xxii (1988), 204–40.
3 London, British Library, MS Stowe 944, fol. 1r; pd *Liber Vitae: Register and Martyrology of New Minster and Hyde Abbey Winchester*, ed. W. de Gray Birch, Hampshire Record Society, 5 (1892).

and Cnut making a gift to the church of New Minster, Winchester, jointly. Emma married Cnut, the Danish conqueror, in 1017, after he had defeated her first husband, the English king Æthelred, and taken over the kingdom. The image seems to stress her marriage; the fillet around her head is a symbol of a married woman, the veil dropped by an angel on her head is possibly a symbol of her royal marriage.[4] It is, by contrast, a royal crown which is brought from heaven for Cnut. She is called in the picture not *Emma*, the name given her in her native Normandy, but *Ælfgifu*, the name she took, or was given, at her first marriage to Æthelred in 1002, the name of his saintly grandmother. The whole image could thus be read as one of the queen as secondary to the king, as king's *wife*, with the role of wife, secondary and contingent, so much so that her own identity is submerged in the symbolic name-change. The marriage to Æthelred if not to Cnut could be read as a case of woman as pawn of men's politics, passively transacted by others, not acting herself; either marriage producing a partnership which is no partnership – she is wife, he is king. He grasps the cross, she gestures towards it.

But the image could be read differently. She may not grasp the cross, but she is clearly involved in the gift, gesturing actively towards it; she is as large and as prominent as her husband in the picture, and size is significant in an early eleventh-century image. Moreover a first marriage which gave her an English name had added an English identity to her Norman one, both important to her new husband, Cnut, major reasons for the second marriage and possibly factors in her increasing importance during his reign. And she is a queen; she is called *regina*. She has become a woman associated, like the king, with the sacred. Her name change links her to the only sainted queen in recent English history, whilst the artist who drew this picture has paralleled her with the Virgin Mary herself, whose figure stands above Emma, very like her;[5] indeed her association with Mary has placed her, not Cnut, on the right hand side of the cross, on the right-hand side of Christ.[6] So if the image suggests the contingency and secondary status of a woman like Emma in marriage, it also points to the partnership, and to the new identity as an opportunity as much as a diminution. And it stresses the special status of a king's wife, as queen, that is as a consecrated person, and as an office-holder.

The second picture (pl. 2) is again of Emma, but now some twenty years or more later; this time it is a picture not of Emma and her husband, but of Emma and her sons. It is the frontispiece to the manuscript of a work now known as the *Encomium Emmae*,[7] a highly political work which Emma herself commissioned.

---

4   See the discussion of this in G. R. Owen, 'Wynflæd's Wardrobe', *Anglo-Saxon England*, viii (1979), 195–222.
5   M. Clayton, *The Cult of the Virgin Mary in Anglo-Saxon England* (Cambridge, 1990), p. 167.
6   T. A. Heslop, 'The Production of *de luxe* Manuscripts and the Patronage of King Cnut and Queen Emma', *Anglo-Saxon England*, xix (1990), 151–95, at p. 157 n. 16.
7   London, British Library, MS Addit. 33241, fol. 1v. The work is untitled in the manuscript. It was known as *Gesta Cnutonis* in the late Middle Ages. The view of it as an 'Encomium Emmae' dates from Duchesne's edition of 1619. It is edited by A. Campbell, Camden Third Ser., 72 (1949).

Emma is shown as large, prominent, and now crowned. Her sons, by contrast, are marginal, secondary, subservient, or at least duly cognisant of her importance, peeping in at the side. And she is enthroned. Lay people are rarely shown enthroned in mid-eleventh-century England; enthronement is usually confined to Christ or other heavenly figures, the king himself is only just beginning to be shown enthroned at this date.[8] Here surely is an image of power, of a patroness, of a mother, powerful in crowned and enthroned maternity, fronting a book in which she has put forward her own picture of eleventh-century politics.[9] That book ends with a verbal picture which echoes the pictorial image which fronts it.

> Mother and both sons (Harthacnut and Edward the Confessor), having no disagreement between them, enjoy all the ready goods of the kingdom. Here faith is held among those who share rule, here the bond of maternal and fraternal love thrives indestructibly. All these things Jesus Christ maintained for them. He who makes those who live in one house of one mind, the Lord of all things, for whom, abiding in the Trinity, rule flourishes unfading.[10]

Mother and sons, bound by family affection, rule together in a trinity of power which comes close to being compared with that of the Trinity itself. Here, then, is Emma as a crowned queen, but powerful especially as a mother, and as a mother of the king, *mater regis*.

But the Encomiast seems almost to invite consideration of the disagreement there might be between them, to invite us to see this image as merely a maternal pipe dream or, perhaps, spindle fantasy. This was a trinity of power, an alliance of mother and sons which crumbled almost immediately, as alliances of mothers and sons so often do; held together by family bonds which are as fraught and fragile as strong and binding. The images enclose a book in which Emma arguably tried desperately to do the impossible, to justify the actions of a politically active woman in a situation in which she could not win.[11] The crown on the head of motherhood could be merely a sick mockery of the inadequacy of maternity as a source of

---

8 See discussion in B. B. Rezak, 'The King Enthroned, a New Theme in Anglo-Saxon Royal Iconography: The Seal of Edward the Confessor and its Political Implications', *Kings and Kingship*, ed. J. Rosenthal, *Acta*, 11, 1984 (Binghamton, New York, 1986), pp. 53–88, and T. A. Heslop, 'English Seals from the Mid-Ninth Century to 1100', *Journal of the British Archaeological Association*, ciii (1980), 1–16. This may be the earliest representation of an enthroned lay royal figure in an English associated manuscript – the manuscript was probably produced at St Omer.

9 For discussions of the Encomium and its nature see the Introduction to Campbell's edition; E. John, 'The *Encomium Emmae reginae*: A Riddle and a Solution', *Bulletin of the John Rylands Library*, lxiii (1980–81), 58–94; M. M. Campbell, 'The *Encomium Emmae Reginae*: Personal Panegyric or Political Propaganda?', *Annuale mediaevale*, xix (1979), 27–45; F. Lifshitz, 'The *Encomium Emmae Reginae*: A Political Pamphlet of the Eleventh Century?', *Haskins Society Journal*, i (1989), 39–50.

10 *Encomium Emmae*, ed. Campbell, p. 52.

11 I have discussed Emma's dilemmas and problems here in more detail in e.g. 'The Portrayal of Royal Women in England, Mid-Tenth to Mid-Twelfth Centuries', in *Medieval Queenship*, ed. Parsons, pp. 143–67, at pp. 163–5.

power, and of the limitations of any office which is no more than a consecrated female role. The message of the situation which these images represent might surely be that neither office nor role were able to overcome the flux of events, the strains of dynastic politics, the limitations on female political activity or the inexorable unfolding of the female lifecycle.

These images raise many questions about Emma as a powerful woman. Is she a wife, mother or queen *(regina)*? How do these three affect each other? How far do any of them bring power or authority? And why do these images suggest not merely power, but ambiguity and limitation?

But it is not merely ambiguous and limited power, but power which fluctuated and changed over time which the second picture, read in context, suggested. That picture of flux and of the inexorable female lifecycle is underlined by Emma's career. Emma was the daughter of the duke of Normandy. She was married first to the English king Æthelred the Unready, and then in 1017 to his Danish conqueror Cnut. Her say in the first marriage was probably nil, and it is difficult to be certain how much control she had over the second one. She had sons by both marriages, sons with claims on the English throne. Her importance during Æthelred's reign was limited; but at the side of Cnut she was recognised as a powerful queen, perhaps even as a regent. Her most dramatic years followed the death of Cnut in 1035. His death was followed by a dispute over the succession to the throne which involved Emma's sons by both husbands in a struggle against another son of Cnut by an earlier wife. Emma seized the royal treasury, seems to have taken control of Cnut's mercenary forces and attempted to secure the throne for one of her own sons. It was probably she who orchestrated a campaign of defamation against her principal rivals, Cnut's first wife and her son.[12] By 1037 her efforts had collapsed – largely as a result of Earl Godwine changing sides. Emma went into exile in Flanders. There she called on Harthacnut from Denmark and Edward from Normandy to put together a plan for the recovery of the English throne. Harthacnut responded with an invasion fleet in 1040. It came first to Flanders to collect his mother, and the two together set out for England. Emma had what must have been the great personal satisfaction of seeing the English nobility, who had deserted her cause, falling over themselves to welcome their new king, and the return of their queen. By 1041 Harthacnut had invited his half-brother Edward back to England, and associated him in rule. Emma now commissioned the work of self-presentation and apologia, the *Encomium Emmae*, whose frontispiece we have been considering. In 1042 Harthacnut died and Edward became king. Before the end of 1043 he had attacked his mother and deprived her of much of her treasure. Although she was partially restored, her position at court was never again strong. She seems to have spent the last decade or so of her life in quiet dowager retirement in Winchester.

These dramatic ups and downs are reflected more soberly in the witness lists

---

[12] The wife, Ælfgifu of Northampton, was labelled as a concubine; the son's paternity, even his maternity were doubted – the famous stories of the baby in the bedpan and the concubine and the cleric started here; see *Encomium*, pp. 38–40.

of charters and other similar documents. Emma appears only irregularly in Æthelred's reign.[13] She is much more prominent during Cnut's reign.[14] The joint role she is given in some documents now is even more marked in the few which have survived from the reign of her son Harthacnut and from the first year of Edward's reign.[15] She then slips almost from view in the 1040s. In fact we hardly hear of her until the chronicle mentions her death in 1052: 'In this year died the old Lady, the mother of King Edward and Harthacnut.'[16]

The titles used to describe her extend this picture of fluctuation by suggesting changing contemporary perceptions of her position and its bases. During Æthelred's reign she is called *conlaterana regis*[17] and occasionally *regina*.[18] She is almost invariably *regina* in the period of her marriage to Cnut,[19] but almost invariably *mater regis* during the reigns of Harthacnut and Edward.[20] In vernacular documents, she is always the Lady/*Hlæfdige*.[21] These titles, formalised as they are,

---

13 In P. Sawyer, *Anglo-Saxon Charters: An Annotated List and Bibliography*, Royal Historical Society (1968) (= S), 902 (1002); S 910 and 911 (1005); S 915, etc. (1007), she appears in virtually all charters of this year, and cf. S 918, dated 1008, but with a witness list of 1007 (see S. Keynes, *The Diplomas of King Æthelred 'the Unready', 978–1016* [Cambridge, 1980], p. 263), S 923 (1011), S 926 (1012). Note the association with the year of her marriage and possible organisation of her court and lands, 1002; the birth of her son Edward in 1005, and possibly that of Alfred in 1011/12 – he appears for the first time in a witness list in 1013. 1007 may have marked the birth of her daughter, Godgifu, but this was a significant year for the reorganisation of the court and kingdom seeing, for example, the spectacular rise of Eadric. Her witness in this year may relate to the involvement of the royal family at such a critical moment – see below.

14 She is an almost invariable witness of his charters from her first appearance in 1018 onwards. Her position in the witness lists is very prominent, never lower than immediately following the archbishops, and by the 1030s almost always immediately after the king. In two Old Minster, Winchester, charters, S 970 and 972, she witnesses first jointly with the king – perhaps one of several indications of her regency.

15 E.g. S 982, 993–95, 998–1002, 1006, some of which are of very doubtful authenticity.

16 *Anglo-Saxon Chronicle*, MS C, *s.a.* 1051, in *English Historical Documents*, ii, ed. D. C. Douglas and G. Greenaway, 2nd edn (1981), p. 116 where 'seo ealde hlæfdige' is translated as 'the queen mother'.

17 S 902, 915, 918 – all from the Abingdon archive; S 943, Thorney archive, but involving lands in Oxfordshire near to Abingdon, and S 923, a Burton archive charter.

18 S 926, 910, 911 and 916; S 910 and 991 belong to 1005, the year of Edward's birth, and S 926 may belong to that of Alfred. The choice of titles may relate to some stress on their legitimacy or claims, but she is also *regina* in S 916, 1007, a St Alban's archive charter which seems to have no such connection with the birth of her sons. This may be a preference of the scriptorium – it may be significant that it is only in a St Alban's charter, S 888, that Ælfthryth is given the title *regina* in the 990s. The possibility that the title is used in Emma's early years for the benefit of her sons could be a reminder how far the office was from escaping the biological bases of the queen's power and authority – see below.

19 *Regis conlaterana* in a New Minster archive charter, S 956 (1019), and in two Abingdon charters, S 964 and 967, where the title had commonly been used of her during Æthelred's reign; but she is *regina* in an Abingdon charter from the end of the reign, S 973 (1034).

20 The exceptions are S 996, Horton/Sherborne archive, where she is *regina*, and the spurious S 995, a Bury archive charter, in which she is *regina, mater* but also *Ymma*, a name which she is given in few if any English sources before 1066.

21 See e.g. S 1423, 981, 1465, 1391, 1471, etc.

are nonetheless instructive. *Conlaterana regis* here means 'king's wife', or literally 'she who stands beside and aids the king'; *regina* and *mater regis* obviously mean 'queen' and 'king's mother' respectively. Such titles root Emma's position in family roles, yet suggest an official status which sometimes seems to eclipse them. They are perceptions of her importance, but of an importance whose nature could be seen by contemporaries in some ways to change over time, whilst in others to retain the unvarying superiority of office, *regina*, and class status, *domina*, Lady. The fluctuations in her career, the dramatic reversals, the extent to which it is tied to husbands and sons, the thematic variations of her titles raise their own questions about her power to set alongside the paradoxes of the pictures. It is scarcely surprising that historians have found the power of the queen a problem.

Some have been tempted to deny power altogether to early medieval queens like Emma. Michael Enright has questioned whether they should be seen as powerful at all.[22] The court and comitatus was an essentially masculine world in which the queen functioned only in a secondary way, 'The Lady with the mead cup', a defuser of tension, a reinforcer of hierarchy. When we see her acting we should interpret her as a pawn of faction rather than a personal agent,[23] a flexible instrument of others, a passive symbol rather than an actor. She is confined to the world of 'family politics',[24] which Enright, whilst allowing them a role in Germanic political theory, seems to deprive of real political substance. Thus Emma has no secure position; in 1037 she seems to fall when the great noble Godwine deserts her cause; she is a pawn of marriage politics, her whole career appears within the confines of family; even at her death she is remembered as the mother of kings. It is not difficult to see where Enright gets his view of a helpless pawn of noble faction trapped in family politics. His interpretation certainly gives important insight into the role of a queen at court, but his solution downplays the signs of power, paradoxical and contradictory though they may be.[25] Whilst it accommodates, for example, Emma's comings and goings in the witness list, it is less successful at explaining the more remarkable fact that she is there at all. She is the only early eleventh-century woman to appear in the witness lists of English royal charters.

Full recognition of such a fact could lead to another solution to the problem of the power of these early queens. J. M. Wallace-Hadrill, for example, suggested that the early Frankish queen should be seen as an 'honorary man', who takes part in the world of politics, but does so by 'transcending the care for her household';[26] by implication, though he does not spell this out, by passing from the private to the public world. Wallace-Hadrill's solution recalls the strange masculine titles occasionally given to some of Emma's continental near contemporaries – *dux* or

---

[22] In M. J. Enright, 'Lady with a Mead Cup: Ritual, Group Cohesion and Hierarchy in the Germanic Warband', *Frühmittelalterliche Studien*, xxii (1988), 170–203.

[23] *Ibid.*, pp. 199–200.

[24] *Ibid.*, p. 203.

[25] Though he allows for a 'qualified' role for her 'borrowed power', see *ibid.*, pp. 202–3.

[26] J. M. Wallace-Hadrill, *The Frankish Church* (Oxford, 1983), p. 404.

imperator, duke or emperor.[27] Such titles certainly suggest that the fullness of power and authority could be seen in some circles as masculine; that a woman who came close to exercising it was thereby degendered or regendered. Wallace-Hadrill's solution captures much of this, as it captures the lonely eminence of a woman like Emma in the charter witness lists. But it distracts us from the very gendered roles of wife and mother which were the bases of the position of all these women. The titles *dux* and *imperator* are masculine, but they described women who ruled as regents for sons, through the gendered role of mother. Emma herself was never called *rex* – her titles are invariably *regina, mater regis, conlaterana regis*. No English source denied the female origins and nature of her position. And the continental sources which denied them to her close contemporaries are very much in a minority, and may be as interested in overriding as in denying those female origins.[28] Wallace-Hadrill's solution gives the queen power, but only at the price of making power masculine by definition, and of demarcating and depoliticising a private feminine domain.

Those strange titles, even though not used of Emma, merit further thought. They suggest that the offices and powers they describe, whilst in some ways masculine, were seen as also detachable from the male bodies which usually filled them; that the emperor or duke had a second official body which could be filled by a woman. In other words that the potential for a *rex femineus*, a female king, a woman filling a male or degendered office, was already there. But these titles do not describe

27 *Imperator* used of Empress Theophanu in *Ottonis III. Diplomata, MGH DRG*, ed. T. von Sickel, 2 vols (Hanover, 1893; repr. 1956), ii/2, 876–7: Theophanu 2, 1 April 990, Ravenna, for John of Farfa, 'Theophanius gratia divina imperator augustus . . . anno vero imperii domni Theophani imperatoris'. *Dux* used of Beatrice in Gerbert d'Aurillac, *Correspondance*, edd. P. Riché and J. P. Callu, 2 vols (Paris, 1993), nos 32, 55, 61, 63, 101, and *MGH DRG*, ii/1, Otto II, no. 308, June 983, not long after the death of Frederick. She is *ductrix* in a diploma of Otto III, *MGH DRG*, ii/2 no. 2, 984. That female form was in use in the late tenth and especially the early eleventh century, see J. F. Niermeyer and C. Van Kieft, *Mediae Latinitatis Lexicon Minus* (Leiden, 1976) with references to the German chancery of Henry II, Thietmar, Ekkehard of St Gall, etc.

28 Gerbert's letter and Otto II's charter may represent first attempts to grapple with the fact of a woman regent. It is at times of change, doubt and uncertainty, when faced with novel situations, or at politically sensitive moments, that the titles and formulae chosen by chancery scribes or notaries can be most informative. There are other possible explanations. Theophanu's two imperial charters (one as *imperator*, the other as *imperatrix*, but issued in her own name) belong to the period immediately after her setting up of a new Italian chancery in 988 (see J. Fleckenstein, 'Hofkapelle und Kanzlei unter der Kaiserin Theophanu', *Kaiserin Theophanu*, edd. A. von Euw and P. Schreiner (Cologne, 1991), ii, 305–10, at p. 310), and to her first serious direct interventions in Italy. Given the reluctance of the Pavian scribes to date by Otto's German regnal years, the charter of 990 is arguably attempting to give a description of the situation which would maximise Otto's power in Italy. It needed an imperial regnal date, and the scribe chose the only one available, that of Theophanu herself. Clearly this is no simple description of Theophanu as an emperor; but the political sensitivity of the situation merely underlines the importance of giving her the title. Cf. J. M. Bak, 'Roles and Functions of Queens in Arpádian and Angevin Hungary (AD 1000–1386)', *Medieval Queenship*, ed. Parsons, pp. 13–24, esp. p. 21 on *rex foemineus* at a later date as an attempt to reconcile woman's incapacity with the fact of her rule.

reges feminei, women who ruled as kings by descent. They describe women who, like Emma, ruled as wives and mothers, and who are normally called *regina*, *ductrix*, *imperatrix*. With these early queens we are dealing not with female kingship, but with queenship. Queen or empress in their case is not a female king; she is the wife or mother of one. Her position derives from an intimate relationship with the king's body, a body which itself can be twofold, a physical and an official body, king and kingship. This duality combined in a single person makes the public/private distinction a difficult one to hold on to, if indeed it does not confound that distinction on which both Enright and Wallace-Hadrill depend, even render it misleading and inapplicable. It is through her relationship to the physical body of the king, through family politics, and I deliberately do not call these private politics, that Emma gained some of her powers and her limitations. And it is through her relationship to the official body of the king that she comes close to acquiring an official body herself, close to queenship – though as I shall suggest, not quite close enough.

The way forward is by recognising and exploring the paradoxes and ambiguites of the queen's powers. The masculine titles might themselves be seen as in some ways a recognition of such ambiguity, of the difficulty in describing what were nonetheless the real powers of such women. This involves a recognition of the dichotomy noted by John Parsons:[29] the queen is a woman, with the powers and limitations of the roles of at least noble women in her own society, including and especially those of wife and mother; but at the same time she is the king's wife or mother, whose intimate relationship is with the body of the ruler himself. I want, thus, to suggest that Emma as an eleventh-century queen had power, even authority. Or rather, that she had a complex configuration of powers. This configuration was affected by lifecycle, elements of it changing or accumulating; some elements of it were unambiguous and unvarying, others contested, only ambiguously socially accepted. These powers were realised in combination and in the context of critical historical events. It was a configuration in many of its elements gender neutral, in others gender specific: one peculiar to a woman who was *domina*, wife, mother *and* queen.

Any discussion of the power of the queen, or of any women, must begin with more thought on the definition of power itself.[30] Power has been given a range of

---

29 J. C. Parsons, 'Ritual and Symbol in the English Medieval Queenship to 1500', *Women and Sovereignty*, ed. L. O. Fradenburg (1992), pp. 60–77, especially at p. 60.

30 The following discussion is based on a range of work, including M. Weber, 'Power' and 'The Social Psychology of World Religions', *From Max Weber: Essays in Sociology*, edd. H. H. Gerth and C. Wright Mills (1948); S. Lukes, 'Power and Authority', *A History of Sociological Analysis*, edd. T. Bottomore and R. Nisbet (1978), pp. 633–76; R. S. Peters and P. Winch, 'Authority', *Political Philosophy*, ed. A. Quinton (Oxford, 1967), pp. 83–111; 'Political Power and Necessity', in G. Balandier, *Political Anthropology*, trans. A. M. Sheridan Smith (1972); the discussion in H. Moore, *Feminism and Anthropology* (Oxford, 1988); the Introduction to *Women and Power in the Middle Ages*, edd. M. Erler and M. Kowaleski (Athens, Ga, 1988), pp. 1–17. I have been especially influenced by M. Strathern's discussion in *The Gender of the Gift* (Berkeley, Ca, 1988), particularly in the doubt it raises about the power of persons as a constant, rather than as something which is temporarily

definitions. It is the ability or chance to realise our own will, if necessary against the resistance of others. It is efficacy, that is the ability to act effectively, to produce effects, with some definitions stressing coercion, threat and force. Feminist anthropologists, concerned with this overemphasis on coercion and force, prefer to stress that power is the ability to have and follow a strategy, to be a social actor, to have long- and short-term aims and to be able to follow them – with the emphasis on strategy and pursuit rather than primarily on successful outcome. If we take this idea, of what we might call power as process, Emma had it, and in ways which parallel those of male actors. Emma certainly had a strategy. She worked to get one of her sons on the throne. That necessarily involved gaining the support of others – like Godwine; to be powerful does not mean to be able to work alone. But it was *her* strategy, and she continued it after her exile, when such support was temporarily lost. She *was* exiled – but that does not mean she was not powerful. Godwine himself was exiled; both he and Emma effected a successful return. The sheer unpredictability of the turn of events is one reason why outcomes are a bad way of judging power. Emphasis on capacity for strategic action is a definition of power which allows for but also stresses the uncertainty of events, the uncertainty of all power – male or female. *It is the ability to take part in the events*, to have the *means at your disposal to give some chance of success* in them which constitutes power on this definition – i.e. the means of strategic action. And Emma had those means.

Power may be both competitive (involved in a situation where our own desires come up against those of others) and relational (the power of one person over another may be the result of a permanent or semi-permanent relationship between them). It may be conceived economically; power is the ability to convert the labour of others into our own prestige or status. If the first definition emphasised the process, these stress the bases of power. Emma certainly had relational power. Behind the drama of succession politics lay a constant. Emma, we can be fairly certain, was the richest woman in England until her transition to dowagerhood in 1043. She held extensive lands in, for example, the East Midlands and Wessex, she had a major stake in the towns of Exeter and Winchester, and jurisdiction over the whole of West Suffolk.[31] The lands she controlled meant that she had tenants and officials dependent on her, who included nobles of considerable wealth. Her jurisdiction in West Suffolk, for example, was controlled by one Ælfric son of Wihtgar; his own son in Domesday appears as one of the richest men in East

exercised in certain situations. My discussion is in some respects a critique of some feminist definitions of power which almost exclude women by definition. It has certainly been influenced by Simone De Beauvoir, *The Second Sex* (Penguin edition, 1972) and her emphasis on the project rather than simply the outcome, though I would not agree entirely with her existentialist emphasis on the individual, nor with her exclusion of many traditional female activities from the realm of possible projects.

31 A full discussion of her lands will be given in my book, *Queen Emma and Queen Edith. Queenship and Women's Power in Eleventh-Century England* (Oxford, 1997).

Anglia.[32] We are not well enough informed about the line-ups in and after 1035 to know what role such men played; but it seems unlikely that they had no part in events. In these lands Emma was a *domina*, a lady, with the relational powers of her class. Her estates and her position at court enabled her to turn the labour of others into her own prestige. She was, for instance, sought after and is remembered as one of the great patrons of the eleventh century. She commissioned *de luxe* illuminated manuscripts, many from Peterborough, an abbey with which tenth- and eleventh-century English queens in general and Emma in particular had long-term links.[33]

These bases of action again show the similarities with, but now also some of the differences from, eleventh-century male power, and from the power of other noble women. As a *domina*/Lady, Emma was like other nobles; but unlike a noble*man* her landholding fluctuated during her lifetime as a result of the lifecycle which changed wife to dowager. She was liable not only to the sort of exile which paralleled her career with that of Godwine, but to the deprivation of land in 1043 which was an attack specifically on a dowager who had attempted to retain lands beyond her widow's status. Yet she is not merely another noble woman, even though she shares with such women the female life-cycle. Emma may be a *Hlæfdige*, a Lady, but no other *domina*, no other noble woman, appears in the witness lists. It is as a lady, but as the Lady Mother of the king, or his Lady Wife, that Emma appears. *Lady* acquired a specific meaning as the title of the queen in tenth- and eleventh-century England. Its most normal meaning was as a mistress of servants or followers; but it was as a noble mistress that Emma appeared, as mistress of a *royal* household, a position she acquired as wife and mother. It is the witness lists' record of the royal *familia*, as family and household, which includes the queen. If Godwine's and Emma's careers converged on the uncertain strategies and underlying stabilities of the noble courtier, they begin to diverge on office and even more markedly on the bases of her power in marriage and maternity; all of which are not merely roles involving power, but legitimate power sanctioned by authority.

Power may be legitimate, or illegitimate; there are ways of exercising it which are or are not acceptable. And with the question of legitimacy we move from power towards authority. If many definitions of power stress the *ability* to act, authority stresses the *right* to act. It is, if you like, a sort of short circuit around the system of power. Authority induces obedience without the need for force, payment or argument. A person with authority can command simply by the position they are in. Authority is 'socially sanctioned power'; power sanctioned by the gods, by age, by gender, by status, wealth, military prowess. It can reside in office. It usually rests on tradition, though traditions can grow very quickly. Emma had the author-

---

[32] P. Clarke, *The English Nobility under Edward the Confessor* (Oxford, 1994), pp. 357–63, for details of his son's estate; and S 1084 for reference to Ælfric as Emma's official.

[33] See T. A. Heslop, 'The Production of *de luxe* Manuscripts and the Patronage of King Cnut and Queen Emma', *Anglo-Saxon England*, xix (1990), 151–95

ity: of a female office, with a developing tradition behind it, that of queen; perhaps of a wife, and certainly of a mother.

The more formal role of a West Saxon/English queen developed in the tenth century, and in the late tenth century especially. By the end of that century, an English queen was anointed and not merely anointed to be the occupant of the royal bed. The titles used for late tenth- and eleventh-century English queens only twice speak of her as 'consecrated to the royal bed'.[34] The ritual used for the consecration of a queen did not stress the fertility of the queen, or her role as king's bedfellow. It was not derived from the marriage ritual. Its derivation was from the ritual for the making of an abbess,[35] itself an ambiguous female office but a female office nonetheless. After her consecration, the queen feasted separately from her husband, and at least in 973 not just in a feast of women but with the abbesses and abbots,[36] one of the constituent orders of the kingdom. At least one eleventh-century English manuscript of the queen's coronation *ordo* speaks of share in ruling.[37] If we are to read this symbolism as meaning anything, it suggests that the queen was seen as exercising a specific role in the kingdom, and one associated with the king in rule, a fact underlined by her involvement in areas like East Anglia and the East Midlands where West Saxon rule was being extended.[38]

This earthly development was paralleled by the development of the idea of Mary Queen of Heaven, which was also growing strongly in late tenth-and early eleventh-century English ecclesiastical circles.[39] The presentations of Mary not only stress her queenship, but give an idea of the dignity which could be attached to it in contemporary eyes. Plate 3 shows Mary as part of what has been called a heavenly Quinity;[40] not the traditional trinity of father, son and holy spirit, but a fivesome where the usual three are joined by Mary and her infant. Mary is shown crowned; she was a *queen*. This image, like the one of Emma with which I began, was produced at New Minster, Winchester.[41] Churchmen, especially at

---

34 S 909, St Frideswide's 1004; S 955, 1019 Shaftesbury cartulary, for minister Agemund.
35 See J. L. Nelson, 'The Second English *Ordo*', *Politics, Law and Ritual in Early Medieval Europe* (London, 1986), pp. 361–74 at p. 367 and n. 22; and in this volume.
36 See *Vita Oswaldi*, in *Historians of the Church of York and its Archbishops*, ed. J. Raine, 3 vols, RS 7 (1879–94), i, 8.
37 See the Third Ordo in Cambridge, Corpus Christi College, MS 44, pd J. Wickham Legg, *Three Coronation Orders*, Henry Bradshaw Society, 19 (1900), p. 61. The final blessing prayer over her states, 'Benedictionis suae dominus omnipotens ancille suae videlicet regine nostrae conferat largitatem, qui regalis imperii te voluit esse participem . . .'.
38 I have discussed her role in the kingdom in greater detail in my *Queen Emma and Queen Edith*.
39 On this development in general see M. Clayton, *The Cult of the Virgin Mary in Anglo-Saxon England* (Cambridge, 1990), pp. 159–67.
40 See E. Kantorowicz, 'The Quinity of Winchester', *Art Bulletin*, xxix (1947), 73–85; J. Kidd, 'The Quinity of Winchester Reconsidered', *Studies in Iconography*, vii–viii (1981–82), 21–33, and J. O'Reilly, 'St John as a Figure of the Contemplative Life: Text and Image in the Art of the Anglo-Saxon Benedictine Reform', *St Dunstan, his Life, Times and Cult*, edd. N. Ramsay, M. Sparks and T. Tatton Brown (Woodbridge, 1992), pp. 165–85, especially pp. 174–82.
41 London, British Library, MS Cotton Titus D.xxvii, fol. 75v, the prayerbook of Ælfwine,

Winchester, were producing some very positive pictures of queens at the turn of the eleventh century. It was at Winchester that Emma was represented as a parallel of the heavenly queen in the *Liber Vitae* (pl. 1); that image was probably produced by the same artist who drew the Quinity.[42]

Emma, or those who wished to justify her, could use a strong tradition of holy queenship; and an actual tradition of some very powerful women, like her mother-in-law Ælfthryth, and before her Eadgifu, who seems to have ruled alongside her sons in the 940s much as Emma did a century later.[43] And Queen Emma drew on an ideology with its own material bases and expressions: the queen's lands and household, with its own opportunities for preferment, an alternative route to success for individual nobles. At least one priest attached to Emma's household became a bishop.[44]

All of this gave an eleventh-century English queen access to the authority of a sacrally sanctioned office, and of a tradition of queenly activity. The queen was the only woman to exercise something which we can recognise as a secular office in eleventh-century England. This office placed her, in the eyes of those who drew up the witness lists of charters, not with ealdormen and king's thegns, but with bishops and abbots, often next to the king himself in the hierarchy of the kingdom. There are important questions here about the drafting of charters, about how far the witness lists record everyone present at the royal court, too large to broach here.[45] What can be asserted, however, is that the witness lists give some idea, however circumscribed and partial in the perspective they represent, of the recognition and perception of relative power. Power is always social; it exists and grows in its recognition. The witness lists record primarily office-holders.[46] They enshrine a perception of the kingdom as a series of groups, of office-holders in relation to the king. It is thus arguably office, with its capacity to degender and regender, which is the root of the queen's power. The fact of being the only secular female office-holder would seem to account for her unique position.

But nothing about the queen's position was so simple or straightforward. Comparison with the development of another female office in the tenth century, that of abbess, suggests some important aspects of the queen's office. There can be no doubt of the importance of the nunneries over which the tenth- and eleventh-century abbesses presided; little doubt either that abbesses came on

---

dean, later abbot, of New Minster, pd *Ælfwine's Prayerbook*, ed. B. Günzel, Henry Bradshaw Society, 108 (1993).

[42] *Ibid.*, p. 12.

[43] On these women see e.g. my 'The King's Wife in Wessex, 800–1066', *Past and Present*, xci (1981), 3–27.

[44] It is very likely that Stigand was so attached – see further discussion of the queen's household in my book, *Queen Emma and Queen Edith*.

[45] Cf. for example S. Keynes, *The Diplomes of King Æthelred 'the Unready', 978–1016* (Cambridge, 1980), pp. 130–4 and pp. 154–62.

[46] I think this even extends to the *ministri*, many of whom were officials at the royal court or local royal servants; cf. K. Mack, 'The Stallers: An Administrative Innovation in the Reign of Edward the Confessor', *Journal of Medieval History*, xii (1986), 123–34.

occasion to court.[47] But after a few brief appearances in mid tenth-century witness lists[48] abbesses disappear from view, whilst the abbots go on to secure a recognised position in the hierarchy of the kingdom. The abbess failed to gain recognition in the eyes of those who drew up the witness lists, in spite of her sacral office. Yet earlier abbesses had achieved very different recognition in the witness lists of late seventh- and eighth-century charters. In the first flush of conversion the capacity of their office to degender may have been at its height. But equally their office may not so much have overcome gender, as combined with it in particular family situations to empower these early abbesses; as royal daughters and widows. Christian office was enhanced by the fact of royal origins, even as that office extinguished some of the limitations of gendered roles. Earlier abbesses witnessed, as abbesses, but also as members of the royal family; their witnessing seems to indicate that it is some combination of family position and office which accounted for their prominence or lack of it. Although tenth-century abbesses were still of high birth, there were aspects of tenth-century English monasticism which were inimical to the open recognition of their family connections.[49] Perhaps also the nature of the kingdom had changed, and the royal family which ruled it.

Tenth-century churchmen were by contrast favourable to the development of the office of the queen. Their recognition of it in witness lists indicates the specific place they accorded it in views of the body politic, seen both as a series of offices, and as an extension of the king's own body through time. A narrowing of the royal family from the ninth to the eleventh centuries with its emphasis on the queen as legitimate wife and mother, as well as an emphasis on office, may have underpinned these ideas.

Comparison between the queen and the *æthelings*, or princes, is particularly instructive here. They sometimes appear when the court has a peculiarly military nature,[50] and when Emma, by contrast, tends to be absent; a fact which emphasises the continuing importance of general gender constructions of masculinity and

---

47 See e.g. the evidence of the admittedly late life of Æthelflæd, abbess of Romsey, London, British Library, MS Lansdowne 435, fols 44v–45r.

48 S 1178 (966) a Croyland charter, has Merwenna abbess of Romsey after the abbots and before the duces; S 1179 (966), also Croyland, has Merwenna and Wulwina *Mercamensis* (? Werhamensis). Both charters are highly suspect. But it is very strange for a forger to include abbesses, who so rarely appear in witness lists, and I am tempted to suggest that these were taken from some list or lists he was adapting. The witness of the abbess/magistra of Wilton, Ælfgyth, S 582, AD 955 is far more secure.

49 See E. John, 'The King and the Monks in the Tenth-Century Reformation', *Orbis Britanniae* (1966), pp. 154–80; but cf. for a more nuanced discussion A. Williams, '*Princeps Merciorum Gentis*: The Family, Career and Connections of Ælfhere, Ealdorman of Mercia', *Anglo-Saxon England*, x (1982), 143–72.

50 In the reign of Æthelred, e.g. after 1008, when the queen is virtually absent. Possible links between the Viking invaders and Normandy could not have helped Emma's position in these years, see below. Responsibility for young children may have kept her from court – but cf. the prominence of continental queens like Gerberga and Theophanu when their children were small. Young children would not have prevented her appearance at the occasional great courts and festivals.

femininity in the status of royal family members. But in other ways they parallel the queen. Like her, their position, as recognised in the witness lists, fluctuates considerably. They appear in the witness lists as potential heirs, and as potential male heirs,[51] thus in relation to the king's body, but in the context of narrower notions of inheritance which relegated other family members, and all daughters (and thus abbesses). Those same notions of inheritance forefront the legitimate wife and mother of the king. They appear especially at times of crisis.[52] And here, in contrast to the military courts, the queen is often with them.[53] Crisis in the royal family involved all those seen to have a say in its future; and as wife and especially mother the queen is there. Political crisis in the tenth and eleventh centuries often involved, indeed often centred on, the royal family. It often involved faction and grouping *within* that family, bringing in the wives and mothers of rival princes. The problem of separating family and politics, private and public, in such a society is clear.

That problem is underlined by some of the most interesting appearances of the princes. In a series of charters of the 990s they are recorded as witnesses, even though they were children, in some cases probably no more than infants.[54] Children as a group were as incapable in their own way as women; age can be just as important a division as gender. Yet these charters, which normally also include the dowager queen Ælfthryth, record them. The charters in question are of exceptional interest. They articulate almost a political theory, a view of kingship and of the kingdom, of the relation of king and people and of the nature of kingship itself.[55] And that nature includes, indeed centres on, the idea of an undying body united across the generations by blood. There were other notions of the body politic in England *c.* AD 1000, most notably that view of a series of offices each with their duties put forward by Archbishop Wulfstan in his *Institutes of Polity, Civil and Ecclesiastical*;[56] but it is important for the queen that one of those current was the idea of a narrow descent group of the royal family itself as the undying body of the king. That notion included the under-age sons, seems to many to have excluded the daughters, but brought in the legitimate wife and mother of the king. Such notions enhanced and encouraged a definition of queenship itself. It is possible

---

[51] See discussion of the meaning of the terms *ætheling* and *clito* in D. Dumville, 'The Ætheling: A Study in Anglo-Saxon Constitutional History', *Anglo-Saxon England*, viii (1979), 1–33.

[52] See e.g. the appearance of Eadwig and Edgar at the end of Eadred's reign when the question of the succession must have been to the fore, and especially of Edgar in the first year of Eadwig's reign, which extended the succession crisis.

[53] Thus Eadgifu reappears with her young grandsons in the last years of Eadred's reign, as does Ælfthryth in the 990s.

[54] S 876, 896, 891, 878, 879, 893.

[55] The charters in question are S 876, 896, 891 and the undated S 937; the king's own lifecycle, specifically the transition from youth to maturity, is placed in the longer perspective of the actions of his predecessors and the future actions of his successors. This extension of the king's body through time seems to be one version of the notion of a kingship which transcends the individual king. I hope to return to a detailed discussion of these important charters elsewhere.

[56] Trans. M. Swanton, *Anglo-Saxon Prose* (1975), pp. 125–38.

that some of those responsible for writing those charters of the 990s may also have been responsible for the rapid development of the office and idea of queenship.

In the history of the tenth-century royal family and kingdom, and in the theory which accompanied it, the office of the queen developed strongly, sufficiently to be the underlying theme in perceptions of Emma's position. But its development linked her, as it linked the princes, to the body of the king. Neither she nor they had assured recognition apart from that proximity. Emma may have been queen, the lands and influence attached to the position hers, but only until the death of husband or the marriage of son made her a dowager. The resources of her office were thus affected by the cycle of family life; they are tied to her roles of wife and mother. The fluctuating tradition of female power that she inherited had been related to the crises of the tenth-century royal family rather than to some unchanging notion of queenly office. Her titles had changed over time. *Regina* is the one which recurs; and it is especially the one which is used to describe her when she exercises the full powers of a wife alongside Cnut. It was clearly an important one, one which described a special power and authority, acquired once at consecration. But at critical stages of her career it was eclipsed by *mater regis*; and some at least of its resources passed from widow to wife in the cycle of family life.

In the late tenth and early eleventh centuries some churchmen worked hard at the idea of queenship as office, perhaps even hinting at the idea of a second body of queenship itself. Kantorowicz suggested that the two natures of Christ, presented in the Quinity (pl. 3), were an important model for the two bodies of the king.[57] And here is Mary enthroned and crowned in relation to both. But the overwhelming message of this image is of the motherhood which gives Mary contact with the power of the Godhead. Queenship, even as office, had crowned rather than overcome the limitations and potential of motherhood. Queenship in the eleventh century was an office which only achieved full power and authority when coupled with a ruling husband or son who was sympathetic, or with political crises which forefronted the royal family or with the dominance of the woman's natal family. The office of queen *c.* 1000, unlike that of abbess, remained closely connected to the family roles of women, a complication which rendered it more ambiguous than other offices, a limitation of its capacity to degender, but also a reinforcement of its potential. In this combination lie many of the sources of the paradoxes and fluctuations I began with. To understand the queen's power, we thus need to consider not merely office, but also women's family roles more generally.

A queen was a consecrated and crowned wife. This was a powerful role, but a problematic one; the picture of Emma as Cnut's wife was the more ambiguous one. Sacred role models, developed for the queen as Maria *Regina*, were thin on the ground for wives; Mary had been Christ's mother, not the Holy Ghost's wife. Old Testament wives, were either intercessors par excellence, like Esther, or like Jezebel, expressed the evil face of conjugal power. But Esther should not be too

---

[57] See E. Kantorowicz, 'The Quinity of Winchester', *Art Bulletin*, xxix (1947), 73–85, and cf. *idem, The King's Two Bodies: A Study in Mediaeval Ruler Theology* (Princeton, NJ, 1957), section III.

readily dismissed. Commentary on her was favourite reading for many queens; the Empress Judith in the ninth century had commissioned a commentary on her.[58] Intercession merits further consideration; it stands both inside and outside the process of power. From the point of view of the supplicant, the intercessor is approachable, yet at the same time sufficiently a part of the mechanisms of power to be efficacious. Negotiation, patronage and mercy are all aspects of intercession. The king's wife was a straddler of boundaries rather than a marginal figure.

A wife was always some other man's daughter or sister. Her role involved being a guarantor of peace and friendship between families, one of the most traditional of all the functions of political marriages. It was a difficult one. She was a comer-in to any family, unskilled in its ways, an object of suspicion – a situation exacerbated when relations between the two families which she joined were strained. For Emma these limitations and problems of being a wife were most prominent in the political circumstances of Æthelred's reign. We cannot even be certain Emma could speak English when she arrived in 1002.[59] Her marriage sealed an alliance with Normandy, which was harbouring Viking invaders of England. Her followers fell under suspicion of treachery.[60] Emma appears far less important during the reign of her first husband than during that of her second, and this is one reason why. This woman descended of Danes on both sides could hardly be an effective symbol of peace in the troubled last years of Æthelred's reign. Yet this position of a wife as a lateral link could be a source of strength in other conditions. In the reign of the Danish conqueror Cnut, when her husband was anxious for good relations with Normandy, its Viking origins had a new meaning; Emma's relationship to the counts of Normandy could now contribute to her high status.

Once married, a wife was controlled to some extent by her husband; she might be a *domina*/lady to others, but he was her *dominus*/lord.[61] Contemporary notions of marriage no doubt facilitated her secondary status during Æthelred's reign. But a wife was also a *conlaterana regis*, a partner, intimate counsellor and aid[62] of the king, an accepted adviser of her husband, with important functions in the management of a large household. To hold these positions for any time was to gain the

---

[58] On Judith see E. Ward, 'Caesar's Wife: The Career of the Empress Judith 819–29', in *Charlemagne's Heir: New Perspectives on the Reign of Louis the Pious*, edd. P. Godman and R. Collins (Oxford, 1990), pp. 205–27.

[59] No direct evidence exists here, and since the marriage may have been planned as early as 991/2 there could have been preparations, including language instruction.

[60] See e.g. the emphasis in the *Anglo-Saxon Chronicle*, MS C, *s.a.* 1003, in *English Historical Documents*, i, ed. and trans. D. Whitelock, 2nd edn (1979), on her followers' involvement in the fall of Exeter.

[61] See the usages of *dominus* in Niermeyer, where its primary meanings are 'used by any dependent, even personally free, to indicate a "lord" and "husband" '; and *hlaford* in T. N. Toller and A. Campbell, *Supplement* to J. Bosworth, *An Anglo-Saxon Dictionary* (Oxford, 1972) with four major meanings: a master of servants, a male head of household, a ruler, an owner/proprietor, a husband.

[62] See meanings given in R. E. Latham, *Dictionary of Medieval Latin from British Sources* (1981), and cf. Niermeyer, under *collaterare, collaterales*, and Du Cange, *Glossarium Mediae et infimae latinitis* under *conlaterana* and *collateralis*.

advantages of the informal power and knowledge, the links of patronage accumulated by someone involved in the household and in the management of family property.

Emma might have accumulated such power over time. But in her case, there is a particular transformation in her position after the accession of Cnut and her marriage to him, a transformation too marked to be simply explained as a gradual accumulation of power. Perhaps she was of particular importance to her conquering foreign husband because of the expertise she had to offer him in English politics. A foreign king who spent much of his time out of the country needed a regent; he might see his wife as the best choice, his partner and aid, yet as a woman unable to challenge his rule, indeed reliant on its continuance for her own.

The eleventh-century English queen was also a crowned and consecrated mother. This was how Emma was shown in the *Encomium*. It was how Mary was shown in the Quinity, and a contemporary sermon calls Mary *hlæfdige*/lady because she gave birth to a king.[63] In this society, steeped in Old Testament traditions, it is not surprising that it is the queen mother who is the figure of power and authority. The Chronicles of ancient Israel were dated by the year of a king and his mother; it was to his mother Bathsheba, not his wife, that Solomon bowed and it was she whom he seated on his right hand.[64] Early eleventh-century English motherhood had power and authority; in its representation it seemed the least problematic of female roles. Yet its power was often only fully realised at the vulnerable stage of widowhood, and its representations mask tensions and contradictions.

Widows appear as the most powerful group of eleventh-century women, if we judge that power by visibility, action and landholding.[65] But widows were also uniquely vulnerable. Their rights were carefully protected because they were so exposed. A widow needed to act to protect them, usually with the help of a male patron or of her son. Emma pursued her most visible and active political careers as a widow. But she was in a sense forced into such action by her very situation as a widow who now had to protect and attempt to prolong her own power or lose it. Emphasis on her capacity for action has to be balanced by recognition of her vulnerability.

Widowhood extends the role of wife; *uxor* in eleventh-century England meant wife or widow.[66] And as a widow after 1035 Emma experienced not merely the

63 See M. Clayton, *The Cult of the Virgin Mary in Anglo-Saxon England* (Cambridge, 1990), pp. 247–8.

64 See e.g. II Chronicles 13:2; 22:2; 24:1; 25:1; 26:3 etc; I Kings 2:19 and cf. I Kings 1:31 where Bathsheba *as a wife* bowed to David.

65 Cf. T. J. Rivers, 'Widows' Rights in Anglo-Saxon Law', *American Journal of Legal History*, xix (1975), 208–15; M. A. Meyer, 'Land Charters and the Legal Position of Anglo-Saxon Women', *The Women of England from Anglo-Saxon Times to the Present*, ed. B. Kanner (Hamden, Connecticut, 1979), pp. 57–82, and my 'Women in Domesday', *Medieval Women in Southern England*, ed. K. Bate, *et al.*, Reading Medieval Studies, 15 (Reading, 1989), pp. 75–94.

66 It occurs regularly with both meanings in the pages of Domesday Book, for example.

realisation of motherhood in the context of the vulnerability of widowhood, but the tensions *between* the roles of mother and wife in the context of early eleventh-century English politics. A queen may be a crowned wife and mother; but wife and mother can be at odds within the same woman. A wife was expected to look to her husband's interests, a mother to care for those of her children, especially her sons. If the two clash, as they often can, and especially at a time of serial marriage, the result is a situation of great difficulty for the woman concerned. When, as in Emma's case, the second husband is also the conqueror of the father of her older sons the tension between the roles was impossible. Emma as mother of sons by Æthelred had different interests from Emma as wife of the conqueror Cnut. And Emma as mother of sons by Cnut had conflicts with Emma as mother of sons by Æthelred. These tensions were at the root of her difficulties after 1035. That most unambiguous of queens, Mary Queen of Heaven, was a virgin mother, with one son and no husband. Emma might have envied her the fact that the Holy Ghost never proposed marriage.

As Emma's problems suggest, the ideology of motherhood could be ill-suited to the real life situations of mothers. The unspoken contradictions and ambiguities of early English notions of motherhood offer us a final insight into the paradoxes of her situation. Those contradictions are arguably found in a literary source, the poem *Beowulf*. Whatever the date of the composition of this poem, the surviving manuscript dates from *c.* 1000,[67] which would suggest it was still seen as relevant in the eleventh century. The *Beowulf* poet was interested in queens, and particularly in queens as deriving power from and exercising power in the royal household. The good queen is the 'Lady with a mead cup', sower of household peace, bridge between king and followers, smoother of domestic discords. She is a link between hostile peoples united by marriage; the poet is very aware of how far this makes her a living reminder of past defeats, of kinsmen killed, of the kind of situation that faced Emma during Æthelred's reign. As the mother of princes, as the wife of the king she has a say in the succession. Enright[68] saw in all this the peculiar position of the queen in a world of men, in it but not of it, the cement, the mediator, and argued from this for a limited role of real queens. But this is only a partial projection, of the *acceptable* face of queenship; a fantasy of queenship which renders it unproblematic. This partial reading underestimates the power of the queen, and her problems.

These are signalled in one of the bad queens in *Beowulf*, the monster Grendel's

---

[67] On the vexed question of the dating of Beowulf, see e.g. *The Dating of Beowulf*, ed. C. Chase (Toronto, 1981); K. Kiernan, 'The Eleventh-Century Origin of Beowulf and the Beowulf Manuscript', *ibid.*, pp. 9–21, is inclined to link the poem with Cnut's reign, as is R. Frank in the same volume, though Kiernan's discussion of the manuscript is contested by L. Boyle, 'The Nowell Codex and the Poem of Beowulf', *ibid.*, pp. 23–32. It is not essential for my argument that the poem's composition be dated now, though an association with the court where Emma was queen would be interesting to say the least.

[68] Above, n. 21.

mother.[69] She rules her household alone, without a man, defends it herself, takes her own vengeance. She is 'husbandless and son-obsessed'.[70] She operates by night, in secret, has her home in the depths of the mere. There were limits in the minds of many as to what a woman could and should do in the traditionally sanctioned roles of wife and mother. Grendel's mother as the active independent woman transgressed them. The poet portrays the paradoxical position of powerful women, not with sympathy, but with fear. As a mother her commitment to her children becomes a disruptive force. She is not merely the mistress of her household but its active defender, to the death if necessary. Her secrecy and night-time action, like that of Grendel himself, suggest the fear of the backstairs manipulative power which is exercised in all courts, by men and women alike.

The poem pinpoints some of the sources of female power, articulates some of the unease in the face of accepted and sanctioned female power, that of queen, mother and wife, and provides no resolution. I doubt whether the poet or his audience were fully aware of the ambiguities which emerge; it would have been easier for a queen like Emma if they had been. The poet divides the acceptable and unacceptable faces of queenly action between his good and bad queens. The Lady with the mead cup is as much a partial fantasy as Grendel's mother. His failure to combine them is a final indication of the difficulties faced by flesh and blood powerful women and the problem of presenting them unambiguously.

The power and authority of Emma, and of queens like her, was real. She was no simple victim, certainly not of men, many of whom were important, for example, in the promotion of the image of queenship. Nor was she weak and men powerful. In important ways her powers compare with those of a man like Godwine, and have parallels with the position of princes. Although some of the sources of her power and authority were gender-specific, others were gender-neutral. Indeed the questions which consideration of her raise about power could fruitfully be extended to eleventh-century men, since they beg the question whether there are any powerful *persons*, as opposed to powerful actions, roles, temporary identities which the individual assumes, passes through or performs.[71]

A woman like Emma played roles written for her by tradition, and the representations of those traditions often mask the essentially contested nature of the power and authority they possess. But I do not wish to reduce her to a collection of roles. They were in themselves sufficiently complex, she played so many of them, and circumstances and context varied sufficiently, for an individual script.

---

69 See here J. Chance, 'The Structural Unity of *Beowulf*: The Problem of Grendel's Mother', *New Readings on Women in Old English Literature*, edd. H. Damico and A. Hennessey Olsen (Bloomington, Ia, 1990), pp. 248–61, whose ideas I have built upon. I do not wish to suggest that this view of Grendel's mother exhausts the rich potential meanings of the monster – merely that this was one of them which would certainly have resonated in the court-society for which the poem was probably written. I am very grateful to Professor J. Cross for discussion of this point, though I would not wish to implicate him in my interpretation.
70 Chance, p. 252.
71 On which see especially M. Strathern, *The Gender of the Gift* (Berkeley, Ca, 1988).

Just as succession crisis released the potential for action inherent in notions of motherhood and its responsibilities, so foreign rule and the need for regents transformed the possibilities which a wife's established role entailed. Ironically in both cases the notion that *regimen femineum* was impossible, that a woman could not herself rule, the gendered limitations of queenship, made a woman an obvious choice as regent for husband or son. The extent to which the female lifecycle accumulated identities as wife, widow and daughter was a source of strength as well as weakness for Emma. As daughter of a duke of Normandy, widow of an English king, and as an English queen Emma was an attractive wife to the conquering Cnut, a choice which opened a new and high-profile period of her career.

Around about the year 1000 if not before, in England and in Europe, the idea was growing that the king had two bodies:[72] the magisterial, undying body of kingship, and the body of a human male. As it developed, the magisterial body of the king would eventually allow for another sort of powerful woman, the *rex femineus*, the female king. But that was far in the future, and it is with *regina*, the queen, not *rex femineus*, that I have been dealing here. What I have proposed could serve as a model of that queenship. It is paradoxical because it combines the roles of mother, wife, mistress of the household, and the relationships of each to the physical body of the king, with an official role. It must be studied in relation to changing notions of motherhood, wifely activity, the household/domestic domain, family structure, as well as to notions of office and the state, the structure of the court and household, and to the nature of power. It is possible to argue that the late tenth and first half of the eleventh century in England saw a particularly favourable conjunction in this model. That at a period when the domestic domain was still not fully separated from the political, when the charters of the 990s could present the undying body of the king as a catalogue of his ancestors, as his blood family extended through time, the particular combination of familial and official which the queen embodied had enormous potential. It could be argued that this moment would pass; it must be left to those studying other times and places to suggest whether or not it did.

But it may be that the situation was also more complex. Circumstances are crucial; the variables in the model are numerous and their interactions offer many possibilities. The separation of the public and private is often, if not always, a normative statement rather than a simple description of reality; and as long as kings ruled in person it is a very contentious one. I doubt whether the opportunities for queenly power closed after the eleventh century, though I suspect that analysis of them will continue to be dogged by the paradoxes and limitations with which I began.

To return finally to that rich image of the Quinity. It is, of course, primarily an image of Christ's two natures, human and divine. Kantorowicz suggested that the

---

[72] See Kantorowicz, *The King's Two Bodies*, section III.

king's two bodies grew in some ways out of the two natures of Christ, whose vicar the king was on earth. Mary's position is anomalous. Like the queen, she is only there because she is the mother of Christ's human, male body. But that relationship brings her into contact with the Godhead itself, the fount of all authority. We could wish for no clearer picture of the ambiguity and potential of an early eleventh-century English queen – perhaps of all queens.

Plate 1 Emma (Ælfgifu) and Cnut, from the *Liber Vitae* of New Minster Abbey, Winchester, British Library, Stowe MS 944, fol. 6 (reproduced by permission of the British Library)

Plate 2 Emma and her sons and the author, frontispiece of the
Encomium Emmae, London, British Library, Additional MS 33241,
fol. 1v (reproduced by permission of the British Library)

Plate 3 The so-called Quinity, from the prayer book of Ælfwine, abbot of the New Minster, London, British Library, Cotton Titus D xxvi and xxvii, fol. 75v (reproduced by permission of the British Library)

2

Queen Margaret of Scotland (1070–93): Burying the Past, Enshrining the Future

Valerie Wall

Queen Margaret, second wife of Malcolm III, became the progenitrix of the Scottish royal dynasty on the accession of her son Edgar in 1097. Her importance is clear from the Scottish regnal lists of the late twelfth century onwards which apply to her husband the epithet *Hic fuit vir Sanctae Margaretae (reginae)*, implicitly excluding the descendants of Duncan II, Malcolm's son by his first marriage to Ingibiorg, repudiated wife or daughter of Thorfinn, earl of Orkney.[1] A paucity of contemporary Scottish sources leads to a tendency to judge his relationship with Margaret through the cult of personalities and in the light of her canonisation in 1250.[2] However, it was possibly only as a result of the succession crises precipitated by their deaths in 1093 that she became, by default, a mother of kings.

From the mid-tenth century, there had been strenuous efforts by Scottish kings to limit the succession to the descendants of one lineage.[3] In the absence of a son, Malcolm III's great-grandfather, Malcolm II, had secured the throne for his grandson Duncan I by representational succession through his daughter Bethoc, achieved by the slaying of all adult male opposition and entering into mutually advantageous anti-Danish alliances with the English kings. One important heiress emerged from this, Gruoch, the daughter or granddaughter of a king of a rival dynasty in Fife. Her first marriage to Gillacomgain, mormaer of Moray had represented a threat to Malcolm, and her husband was slain possibly at his instigation, leaving her a widow with a young son Lulach. Her father Boite and her brother or nephew had suffered similar fates. In 1040 Duncan I was killed in battle by Gillacomgain's cousin Macbeth, who took the kingship. He married his cousin's widow Gruoch, and entered into an alliance with Thorfinn. In 1054 Edward the Confessor authorised an attack on Macbeth led by Siward earl of

---

[1] See the Scottish regnal lists F, K and N in M. O. Anderson, *Kings and Kingship in Early Scotland* (Edinburgh, 1973), pp. 276, 289, 291.

[2] M. Lynch, *Scotland: A New History* (London, 1991), p. 78. Some stereotype images of her 'forceful' personality are gathered by D. Baker, ' "A Nursery of Saints": St Margaret of Scotland Reconsidered', *Medieval Women*, SCH (Oxford, 1978), pp. 119–41.

[3] For what follows, see generally A. A. M. Duncan, *Scotland: The Making of the Kingdom* (Edinburgh, repr. 1992), pp. 88–132. More specifically, V. Wall, 'Macbeth King of Scots: an eleventh-century pilgrim to Rome', *Early Medieval Europe* (forthcoming).

Northumbria on behalf of Duncan's son Malcolm (III), whilst at the same time sending Ealdred bishop of Worcester to Cologne to negotiate the return from Hungary of his half-brother Edmund Ironside's surviving son, Edward the Exile, his wife Agatha, the half-niece of the emperor Henry III, and their children Margaret, Christina and Edgar.[4] Malcolm III finally gained the throne in 1058, after slaying Macbeth and his successor Lulach, and with the connivance possibly of Thorfinn, a point unacknowledged by English sources.[5]

It is not the place here to analyse the interaction between these bewildering strands, but what is pertinent within this framework of violence is the role of women as daughters, wives, widows and mothers in the transmission of kingship. It is an axiom that the politics of succession are fundamental to the study of status and influence of medieval women. The circumstances that produced and influenced the power of women arose from their traditional role within the family and court politics that were central to personal monarchies.[6] On the other hand, the idealised behaviour of wife, mother and daughter, conceived from a largely male viewpoint, failed to recognise or resolve the contradictory expectations of wife and mother in a patriarchal family, or the specific problems of women as stepmothers and second wives in a polygamous society.[7] This is no more clearly demonstrated than in the primary source for Margaret, the *Vita S Margaretae Scotorum Reginae*, written by Turgot, prior-archdeacon of Durham, and dedicated to her daughter Matilda, wife of Henry I of England, and which is regarded as a role model for Matilda – a Mirror for a Princess.[8] The *Vita* forms part of a corpus of material produced at Durham in the early twelfth century in defence of the rights and lands of the Patrimony of St Cuthbert, which had often been harried by the English, Scots and Scandinavians.[9] The process of peaceful co-operation with the

---

4   *Anglo-Saxon Chronicle* [= *ASC*], ed. D. Whitelock with D. C. Douglas and S. I. Tucker (London, 1961), D, *s.a.* 1054. For this family's fortunes before 1057, see G. Ronay, *The Lost King of England* (Woodbridge, 1989), and N. Hooper, 'Edgar the Ætheling, Anglo-Saxon Prince, Rebel and Crusader', *Anglo-Saxon England*, xiv (1985), 197–200.

5   *Annals of Ulster (to AD 1131)*, ed. and trans. S. Mac Airt and G. Mac Niocaill (Dublin, 1983), *s.a.* 1058, confirms that Lulach was slain *per dolum*.

6   P. Stafford, 'The Portrayal of Royal Women in England, Mid-Tenth to Mid-Twelfth Centuries', *Medieval Queenship*, ed. Parsons, p. 144.

7   *Ibid.*, p. 145.

8   The various versions of the *Vita* have most recently been discussed by L. L. Huneycutt, 'The Idea of the Perfect Princess: The Life of St Margaret in the Reign of Matilda II (1100–18)', *Anglo-Norman Studies*, xii, ed. M. Chibnall (Woodbridge, 1990), 81–97. The longer version of the Life is extant in a late twelfth-century manuscript, London, British Library, Cotton Tiberius D.iii, fols 179b–186, which represents the earliest version datable to 1104–7. For this paper, I have used the printed edition in *Symeonis Dunelmensis Opera et Collectanea*, ed. J. Hodgson Hinde, Surtees Society, 51 (1868), pp. 234–54, hereafter cited as Turgot: page references are from that edition.

9   For this and what follows, see V. Wall, 'Malcolm III and the Foundation of Durham Cathedral', *Anglo-Norman Durham 1093–1193*, edd. D. Rollason, M. Harvey and M. Prestwich (Woodbridge, 1994), pp. 325–37. For praise of peace in England under kings Edgar and Edward the Confessor, see Turgot, pp. 234 and 237.

Scottish royal family had been acknowledged publically when Malcolm laid one of the foundation stones of the new cathedral on 11 August 1093, and with the *conuentio* drawn up probably at the same time, in which spiritual benefits were promised to him, Margaret and their children. Turgot stresses the close relationship between Durham and Margaret's foundation of the church of the Holy Trinity at Dunfermline, asserting that he acted as her sacrist there and as her confessor.[10] The priest who brought the news of Margaret's death to Durham took the habit of a monk to serve St Cuthbert.[11] Turgot displays little interest in Scotland, mentioning only Dunfermline and St Andrews in Fife by name. Unlike the author of the *Encomium Emmae* who presents Ælfgifu of Northampton as a rival to Emma and denigrates her status and that of her sons, Turgot does not acknowledge the existence of Malcolm's first wife, Ingibiorg, yet there is no evidence to suggest that Malcolm intended to overlook their son Duncan's rights to the kingship.[12] What other Durham sources do is simply disguise the fact that he was Ingibiorg's son.[13] His charter in favour of Durham in 1094, whilst referring to his father, wife and children, does not mention his mother.[14] His name appears in the Durham *Liber Vitae* immediately after Malcolm and Margaret, implicitly as one of their sons.[15] One of the most important purposes of Turgot's writing was posthumously to place Margaret firmly in control of family and court, moving her centre stage as the wife and the queen of Malcolm and the mother of kings of Scots, rather than a second wife whose sphere of influence might have been confined to southern Scotland. According to Turgot, Margaret had begged him to take care of her sons and daughters after her death, because her prophetic powers had led her to fear for the kingdom, when Malcolm embarked on his final, fatal military expedition against her advice.[16] The work is a justification of Turgot's role as kingmaker and a defence of Durham's interference in the Scottish succession in the years

---

[10] *Ibid.*, pp. 239, 250–1.

[11] *Ibid.*, p. 252.

[12] Two further sons by Ingibiorg or another liaison were Donald, who was *ri Alban* in Moray until his death in 1085 (*Annals of Ulster, s.a.* 1085) and Malcolumb who was a witness to Duncan's Durham charter of 1094.

[13] A. J. Piper, 'The Durham Cantor's Book', *Anglo-Norman Durham 1093–1193*, p. 87, has drawn attention to a Countess Ingibiorg in the Martyrology in Durham, Cathedral Library, MS B.IV.24, whom he suggests is Malcolm's first wife. If this identification is correct, the status accorded to Ingibiorg is interesting. F. Lifshitz, 'The "Encomium Emmae Reginae": A "Political Pamphlet" of the Eleventh Century?', *Haskins Society Journal*, i (1989), 40–1 notes the exclusion of references to Emma's association with the West Saxon dynasty, implying that her sons Edward and Alfred by her first husband Æthelred were by her second husband Cnut.

[14] A. C. Lawrie, *Early Scottish Charters* (Glasgow, 1905), no. 12, p. 10.

[15] *Liber Vitae Ecclesiae Dunelmensis*, Surtees Society, 136 (1923), fol. 12r.

[16] Turgot, pp. 251–2. There are striking similarities between the roles cast for Emma, Edith and Margaret as peacemakers. See for example E. Searle's interpretation of the *Encomium Emmae Reginae* in 'Emma the Conqueror', *Studies in Medieval History presented to R. Allan Brown*, ed. C. Harper-Bill (Woodbridge, 1989), p. 286.

1093–97.[17] With these criteria firmly in mind, I wish to return to the circumstances of her marriage.

Edward the Exile had eventually arrived in England in 1057, but he had died almost immediately.[18] The Confessor provided a home for Agatha, Margaret, Christina and Edgar at court, raising the children as if they were his own.[19] However, the family lacked an independent power base. Agatha was a widow in England, but she was not an Anglo-Saxon widow. She had no proprietary rights and her legal status was insecure.[20] There is no evidence of any associations with religious or lay institutions, but Edgar was still young, and by the eleventh century women other than the queen were virtually absent from the witness lists of royal charters.[21] Edgar and Christina alone held lands in England, but only post Conquest.[22] Nevertheless, a possible betrothal between Malcolm and the fourteen-year-old Margaret, arranged at a meeting between himself and the Confessor at Gloucester in 1059, suggests that Edward may have been using one of the daughters in a political alliance.[23] However, in the light of 1066, the circumstances of the marriage in *c.* 1070 were entirely different. The family had fled north, seeking sanctuary in Scotland. The *Anglo-Saxon Chronicle* and Turgot both suggest that Margaret was unwilling to marry, having promised herself to God.[24] The imagery is of Margaret as the bride of Christ, determined to preserve her virginity, but by divine appointment doing God's work on earth by turning the Scottish king and his people away from paths of error and vice. However, Margaret was about twenty-four years of age at the time of her marriage. A woman could enter a nunnery of her own free will at the age of sixteen.[25] There is no way of knowing whether she had ever considered that course of action, but once married, she showed no interest in the cloister, except as a place for the education of her daughters, not as nuns, but as marriageable commodities. She founded no

---

17 For the charters of Duncan and Edgar in favour of Durham, see J. Donnelly, 'The Earliest Scottish Charters?', *Scottish Historical Review*, lxviii (1989), 1–22.

18 *ASC* D, *s.a.* 1057; Hooper, pp. 201–2.

19 F. Barlow, *Edward the Confessor* (London, repr. 1979), p. 218.

20 The literature on Anglo-Saxon widows is extensive. See most recently P. Stafford, 'Women and the Norman Conquest', *TRHS*, 6th Ser., iv (1994), 221–49. The rights of widows feature in the law codes, see *English Historical Documents* [= *EHD*], i, ed. D. Whitelock (London, 1955), no. 50, II Cnut 73 and 74.

21 Stafford, 'Women and the Norman Conquest', p. 226.

22 Hooper, p. 204 n. 37 for Edgar. For Christina, see *Domesday Book*, xiv (Oxfordshire), ed. J. Morris (Phillimore, 1978), no. 54 and xxiii (Warwickshire), ed. Morris (Phillimore, 1976), no. 42, and B.2.

23 *Annales Lindisfarnenses et Dunelmenses*, ed. G. H. Pertz, *MGH SS*, xix (Hanover, 1866), 508; *Willelmi Malmesbiriensis Monachi Historiae Novellae*, ed. W. Stubbs, 2 vols, RS 90 (1887–9), ii, 528–9. The timing and reasoning behind Henry I's claim, and the fact that the *Annales* are a late twelfth-century compilation, should be borne in mind.

24 Turgot, p. 238; *ASC* D, *s.a.* 1067. For the dating of this northern recension, and its influence on Turgot, see Whitelock, *ASC*, pp. xvi and 146 nn. 1 and 6; S. Hollis, *Anglo-Saxon Women and the Church* (Woodbridge, 1992), p. 218 n. 63.

25 A. L. Klinck, 'Anglo-Saxon Women and the Law', *Journal of Medieval History*, viii (1982), 119 n. 7.

nunneries in Scotland. Her interest in the cause of women was as a mother, within the family, of her six sons and two daughters, and of her people, widows and orphans.[26] Turgot's identification of Margaret with the Queen of Heaven, fully embodied in the work, is embryonically evident in the portrayal of Emma in the *Encomium Emmae* and of Edith in the *Vita Ædwardi regis*.[27] The Marian image of the queen as consort to the king and co-protector of the church cannot be applied to Margaret as mother of nuns, although it is apparent in Turgot's description of the circumstances of her marriage, which embraces the ambiguities of chastity and motherhood:

> While . . . she meditated in the law of the Lord day and night and, like another Mary, sitting at His feet, she delighted to hear his Word, by the desire of her friends rather than by her own, yes, rather by the appointment of God, she was married to Malcolm son of Duncan the most powerful king of the Scots.[28]

A letter written by Lanfranc to Margaret after her marriage confirms the belief that she had been raised to be queen. Her letter is not extant, but the sense of his reply suggests that she was manipulating her noble birth and the partnership of her marriage.

> It is as a result of Christ's teaching here that you who are born of a royal line, brought up as befits a queen and nobly wedded to a noble king, are chosing me as your father, an alien of neither birth nor worth . . . and you ask me to accept you as my spiritual daughter . . . I am sending your glorious husband and yourself our very dear brother dom Goldwin as you asked me to, and two other brothers with him . . . for he could not accomplish single handed what is required in God's service and your own . . . I beg you to strive to complete the work that you have begun for God and your souls' welfare as quickly and effectively as you can.[29]

It is possible that Margaret had known Brother Goldwin as a teacher or confessor, so it is worth considering what images of women would be projected in her learning, within the intellectual ambience of late Anglo-Saxon England.[30]

---

26 Turgot, pp. 240, 246, and 248.
27 Hollis, pp. 118, 177–8, 208–12.
28 Turgot, p. 238.
29 *The Letters of Lanfranc, Archbishop of Canterbury* (Oxford, 1979), no. 50, pp. 160–3. This request for Benedictine monks from Canterbury for Dunfermline forms the basis for the important debate on Margaret's role in church reform in Scotland. See G. W. S. Barrow, *The Kingdom of the Scots* (London, 1973), ch. 6. For an opposing view, see G. Donaldson, 'Bishops' Sees before the Reign of David I', *Scottish Church History* (Edinburgh, 1985), pp. 11–24. Turgot naturally ignores these rival Benedictines, but he does claim that Margaret corrected abuses in the Scottish church, pp. 243–5.
30 Space precludes consideration of German and Hungarian influence on Margaret and her family, and on Turgot. For images of queenship here, see P. Stafford, 'Portrayal of Royal Woman', esp. p. 162; *idem, Queens, Dowagers and Concubines: The King's Wife in the Early Middle Ages* (London, 1983), pp. 3 and 27; Ronay, *The Lost King of England*.

An archetypal woman was that of her namesake, St Margaret of Antioch, whose legend was well known in England.[31] Margaret may have seen a vernacular version in a Canterbury manuscript dated post-1031, which perhaps was used as a teaching tool.[32] Importantly, three saints in the litany are given equal status by the use of capitals in their names – St Margaret of Antioch, St Augustine of Canterbury and St Dunstan.[33] The Legend is a stock Christian martyr story of a fifteen-year-old girl who was determined to preserve her virginity in the name of Christ. Enduring a catalogue of tortures for rejecting the pagan prefect Olibrius, she was eventually beheaded. It could have acted as a model for a girl of the same name and age, encouraged to see herself as the bride of Christ, yet foregoing this role through divine intervention. In the context of this paper, an important aspect of the Legend is the relationship between concubinage and unfree status.[34] In the Old English version, Olibrius says that if she is free, he will take her for his wife, but if she is a slave he will give money for her, and she will become his concubine.[35] Only in this particular Old English text is *cyfes* (concubine) synonymous with slave.[36] The relationship between free status and a Christian in the OE version is only implicit.[37] In the Latin *Passio S Margaretae*, the *exemplum* for the Old English version, the relationship is explicit. In response to Olibrius, she replies 'I am free and a Christian.'[38]

The contents of this manuscript reflect the preoccupations of churchmen of late Anglo-Saxon England, who in the wake of Scandinavian conquest sought to equate loose sexual practices with viking heathenism.[39] Anglo-Saxon women exemplified by both the legendary and contemporary Margaret became chaste heroines. In contrast, Malcolm's first wife, Ingibiorg, was the repudiated wife, concubine, widow or possibly daughter of Thorfinn earl of Orkney, and she is the first recorded Scandinavian queen of the Scots. It became a useful argument, when stressing the legitimacy of Margaret's sons as kings of Scots, to suggest that Ingibiorg's

---

[31] See most recently M. Clayton and H. Magennis, *The Old English Lives of St Margaret* (Cambridge, 1994).

[32] London, British Library, MS Cotton Tiberius A.iii. It contains also the *Regula S Benedicti*, the *Regularis Concordia*, and works by Ælfric and Wulfstan. For Ælfric's vernacular collection of Lives of Roman Virgin Martyrs, see Hollis, pp. 73 and 87 n. 69; Clayton and Magennis, p. 82, quoting M. Gibson, *Lanfranc of Bec* (Oxford, 1978), pp. 126–7, suggest that if Margaret were betrothed to Malcolm III as early as 1059, the importance at the English court of the Legend would be heightened at that point. The naming of Margaret and her sister Christina may reflect their parents' knowledge of the cult of these two saints in Bolsena on the pilgrimage route (Clayton and Magennis, pp. 7–23). See also V. Ortenberg, *The English Church and the Continent in the Tenth and Eleventh Centuries* (Oxford, 1992), pp. 119–21.

[33] Clayton and Magennis, p. 85.

[34] M. Clunies Ross, 'Concubinage in Anglo-Saxon England', *Past and Present*, cviii (1985), 23.

[35] Clayton and Magennis, pp. 114–15.

[36] Clunies Ross, p. 23 n. 74.

[37] Clayton and Magennis, pp. 116–17.

[38] *Ibid.*, pp. 198–9.

[39] C. Fell, *Women in Anglo-Saxon England* (London, 1984), pp. 66 and 138.

marriage was not *de more Christiano*, relegating it to the status of a concubine.[40] Concubinage was a sexual union, without betrothal or dowry. It lacked legal protection for women and children, although a concubine did have customary privileges and her children could inherit if acknowledged by their father.[41] However, the regulation of marriage customs, condemnation of concubinage, divorce and adultery increasingly featured in the Anglo-Saxon law codes, as the church sought to remove the privileges of concubines by redefining the relationship as illegal and immoral.[42] Children were thus illegitimate and barred from inheritance.[43] Concubinage could now be a term to blacken the opposition, although in fact marriage *more Danico* did not suggest a lowly position.[44] In the belief that Margaret would not have consented to a marriage in the first place if there were irregularities with Malcolm's first union, it is further suggested that Ingibiorg was dead by 1070.[45] In fact, we have no knowledge of her death. She may have remained active further north in Scotland and a situation similar to that of Cnut, Ælfgifu of Northampton and Emma may well have existed. Margaret might have been pious, but she was hardly politically inept. If the cause of her brother were weak or lost, she took over the responsibility as head of her family, preserver of the lineage and defender of the status of her children. A betrothal in 1059 and marriage in 1070 could be accommodated, but sensitive to the climate of change, she and her encomiasts would be anxious to raise the status of her marriage and establish it as legitimate and Christian, to ensure that she was classed neither as concubine nor adultress. The *Anglo-Saxon Chronicle* stressed the legality of the union. Her brother Edgar and friends were approached, but only with reluctance did they and she eventually give their consent. Any shortcomings, such as the intimation of coersion placed on them as fugitives, were dealt with by the intervention of Divine Providence and the nobility of her ancestry.[46] In the context of the Legend, this latter point has one further important implication – that of slavery. Symeon of Durham carefully distinguished between the noble status of Margaret and her family, and the circumstances of their arrival in Scotland in friendship, with that of the innumerable English captives taken into Scotland in slavery.[47] The contrast is also apparent in Turgot, where he recounts that Margaret restored many of these slaves to freedom by paying their ransom.[48]

---

40 See W. D. H. Sellar, 'Marriage, Divorce and Concubinage in Gaelic Scotland', *Transactions of the Gaelic Society of Inverness*, li (1981), 476.

41 Stafford, *Queens, Dowagers and Concubines*, p. 63; Clunies Ross, pp. 6 and 34.

42 Fell, p. 66; *EHD*, i, no. 50, II Cnut 54.1 and 55.

43 Clunies Ross, p. 6.

44 E. Searle, 'Women and the Succession at the Norman Conquest', *Anglo-Norman Studies*, ii (Woodbridge, 1981), 161–2, 168–9 and 226 n. 8, discusses the status of Harold Godwineson's wife Edith Swan-neck and Cnut's wife Ælfgifu of Northampton, both wives *more Danico*.

45 Sellar, 'Marriage, Divorce and Concubinage', p. 476.

46 *ASC* D, *s.a.* 1067.

47 *Symeonis monachi Opera omnia*, ed. T. Arnold, 2 vols, RS 75 (1882–5), ii, *Historia Regum*, *s.a.* 1070.

48 Turgot, p. 247. See *EHD*, i, no. 50, II Cnut 54 for condemnation of sexual union with slaves,

It is perhaps illogical to define Margaret's status purely in terms of English customs which might have little relevance in Scotland. We need to understand the customs which regulated marriage in that kingdom.[49] There was Scandinavian influence in Scotland.[50] In contemporary Scandinavian society, concubinage was accepted and the ceremony of *aettleithing* could bring 'illegitimate' sons into the family.[51] Given the strong Irish background, the question could be set in the context of the Irish Law Codes.[52] Irish society was polygamous, and the law tracts made distinction between, but also provision for the first wife (*cétmuinter*) and the second wife (*adaltrach*), who was also betrothed, and whose children could inherit.[53] Concubinage and divorce were permitted.[54] We could also draw a comparison with Anglo-Saxon England where kingship was more institutionalised and kin-groups and feud less developed.[55] Paradoxically, however, customs in eleventh-century Britain were remarkably similar, and I have already said that there is no evidence to suggest that Duncan was in any way ineligible for the throne. Sellar has drawn attention to the continuing influence of Irish marriage customs in Gaelic Scotland.[56] However, Margaret's legacy to her children was to capture the mood of reform, providing the basis on which they could deny the claims of the descendants of Duncan and of Lulach. Lanfranc's above quoted letter to Margaret stressed the nobility of her marriage. This should be contrasted with his letter of 1074 to Turlough O'Brien, king of Munster, concerning the marriage customs of his people.[57] Taken a stage further, the marriage practices of the Irish kings remained the same as their people, whereas in Scotland they did not. Alexander and David, the youngest of Margaret's six sons, were alone in marrying, each only once.

There was one difference compared with England, and that was an absence of any distinguishing ritual in queen-making in Scotland. Scottish kings were not crowned, but inaugurated in a ceremony which took place outdoors near the cross in the cemetery at the east end of the church at Scone.[58] The king was seated on

the relevance of which may be seen in Emma's suggestion that Ælfgifu of Northampton's son Harold by Cnut was the child of a 'certain concubine' and a man of unfree status, *Encomium Emmae Reginae*, ed. A. Campbell, Camden Third Series, 72 (London, 1949), p. 41, and pp. 33–4, for the emphasis on the legitimacy of Emma's marriage to Cnut, and of their children. See also F. Kelly, *A Guide to Early Irish Law* (Dublin, 1988), pp. 95–8.

49 Turgot, p. 245, claims that Margaret corrected marital abuses in Scotland – the unlawful marriage of a man with his stepmother or with a widow of his deceased brother.

50 The difficulty of defining the status of Viking women in Britain and Scandinavia is discussed by Fell, pp. 128–36.

51 Sellar, 'Marriage, Divorce and Concubinage', p. 491 n. 48; Clunies Ross, p. 16.

52 Sellar, 'Marriage, Divorce and Concubinage', pp. 464–93.

53 *Crith Gablach*, ed. D. A. Binchy (Dublin, 1941), pp. 80–1.

54 Sellar, 'Marriage, Divorce and Concubinage', pp. 466, 470.

55 H. R. Lloyn, 'Kinship in Anglo-Saxon England', *Anglo-Saxon England*, iii (1974), 197–209.

56 Sellar, 'Marriage, Divorce and Concubinage', p. 487.

57 *Ibid.*, pp. 470–1.

58 The first detailed account is of the ceremony for the nine-year-old Alexander III on 13 July 1250: *Johannis de Fordun Chronica Gentis Scotorum, Gesta Annalia, The Historians of Scotland*, ed. W. F. Skene, i (Edinburgh, 1871), 294–5.

the mound of his predecessors and married to the earth goddess, a union which led hopefully to fertility in all senses – his own family, the crops, the well being of his people.[59] Its strong sexual overtones excluded a queen. Scottish kings were not anointed, so neither were their queens. Margaret could not be a partner to her husband in what was becoming an essential element of queen-making elsewhere.[60] It could not set her apart from Ingibiorg, nor raise her status above that of a second wife. However, as with Turgot's list of queenly virtues, there is a danger of imposing images or symbols of power on a system where they are irrelevant. They add nothing to our understanding of court politics. Donaldson suggested that Malcolm III suffered from two excessively pious wives and that he offset the oppressive piety of his household by four times invading the north of England.[61] One could place various interpretations on this, but it serves as an important reminder that Ingibiorg's first husband or father Thorfinn Sigurdsson was a second generation Christian, who had travelled to Rome in 1050, building the first cathedral at Birsay on his return. Part of the earldom of Orkney lay not only within the diocese of Hamburg-Bremen, but also within the overlordship of the king of Norway. Malcolm may indeed have had two wives, each being manipulated by, and themselves manipulating, conflicting political and ecclesiastical affiliations and kin-groups, and with whom he had to find a *modus vivendi*. On the other hand, not only do we not know whether Ingibiorg was dead or alive, but her son Duncan had been absent from Scotland since 1072 when he was given as hostage to William I at Abernethy. On his release and knighting by Robert duke of Normandy in 1086, he had remained at the court of William Rufus. All we can say that into this possible vacuum of opposition, there is some positive evidence for the practical exercise of queenship on Margaret's part.

Her marriage to Malcolm took place in Dunfermline, and according to Turgot, was celebrated by her immediate foundation there of the church of the Holy Trinity, as an eternal monument of her name and devotion, for the redemption of Malcolm's soul, for the good of her own and to obtain prosperity in this life and the next for her children.[62] At its inception, Dunfermline may have been a personal expression of her marriage and family, or an assertion of Malcolm's authority over Fife. It was possibly also intended as a family mausoleum. Margaret gave a fine cross and other precious treasures to Dunfermline.[63] The unlocated native hermits who Margaret venerated were probably the culdees of St Serfs, Loch Leven in Fife, to whom she and Malcolm made grants.[64] She recognised the importance of the patronage of the cult of native saints. Her son, Æthelred, was given the lay

[59] K. Hughes, *The Church in Early Irish Society* (London, 1966), pp. 28–30; Duncan, *Scotland*, pp. 115–16.

[60] J. L. Nelson, ch. 15, below.

[61] G. Donaldson, *A Northern Commonwealth: Scotland and Norway* (Edinburgh, 1990), p. 61.

[62] Turgot, pp. 238–9. For a recent assessment of the buildings and tombs, see E. Fernie, 'The Romanesque Churches of Dunfermline Abbey', in *Medieval Art and Architecture in the Diocese of St Andrews*, ed. J. Higgitt, British Archaeological Association (1994), pp. 25–37.

[63] Turgot, p. 239.

[64] *Ibid.*, p. 247; Lawrie, *ESC*, no. 8, p. 7.

abbacy of Dunkeld, where some of the relics of Columba were housed, and which was closely associated with Malcolm's dynasty.[65] Malcolm's grandmother, Bethoc, had been married to Crinan, a previous lay abbot. The development of the cult of St Andrew, and the building of the church of St Rule to house his relics, which has be dated to Malcolm's reign, is still open to debate.[66] However, although here again the king's intention may have been to free the site from its previous dynastic connections, Margaret did provide ferries, and houses of shelter and rest on either side of the Forth, for the devout who flocked to St Andrews from all sides.[67] These places are preserved as Queensferry North close to Dunfermline and Queensferry South close to Edinburgh, two extended centres of royal power, providing an important bridgehead between Fife and Lothian, where the build-up of the influence of this second family lay, and which could provide a springboard for further expansion. Malcolm had probably been planning to grant Lothian, that part of the patrimony which lay between the Forth and the Tweed, as an apanage to his eldest son Edward by Margaret and this hypothesis is borne out by the subsequent divisions. It is significant that in 1094 it was not confirmed to Duncan, but possibly held back for the sons of Malcolm's second marriage.[68] However, following his laying of a foundation stone at Durham, Malcolm travelled to Gloucester for his pre-arranged meeting on 24 August with William Rufus, but he was publically humiliated when the English king refused to speak to him.[69] Goaded into making an old-fashioned ravaging attack across the Tweed, he was ambushed at Alnwick on 13 November by Robert de Mowbray, earl of Northumbria, an event which resulted in his death and that of his son Edward. Margaret died in Edinburgh three days later, barely a widow and never a dowager queen. Her body was transported across the Forth to Dunfermline to be buried at her request before the high altar.[70] Malcolm's body lay at Tynemouth Abbey, to be recovered by his son Alexander and reinterred at Dunfermline.[71] The manner of Malcolm's death led to a succession dispute, until his son Edgar entered Scotland in 1097 with an army

---

[65] See Æthelred's grant to the culdees of St Serfs, Loch Leven, witnessed by his brother Edmund at Dunfermline, made probably on the death of their mother – copy extant in National Library of Scotland, Adv. Lib., MS 34.6.24, p.16. Confirmatory *notitia* printed Lawrie, *ESC*, no. 14, pp. 11–12. Dunkeld was included in an Anglo-Saxon list of saints' resting places: see D. W. Rollason, 'Lists of Saints' Resting Places in Anglo-Saxon England', *Anglo-Saxon England*, vii (1978), 62, 64, 72, 87.

[66] See most recently, M. Ash and D. Broun, 'The Adoption of St Andrew as Patron Saint of Scotland', *Medieval Art and Architecture . . . St Andrews*, ed. Higgitt, pp. 16–24, and S. Heyward, 'The Church of St Rule, St Andrews', *ibid.*, pp. 38–46.

[67] Turgot, p. 247. There may have been a family mausoleum at St Andrews for the rival dynasts of Gruoch's ancestors, Constantine II, his son Indulf and grandson Culen; cf. *Prophecy of Berchan* in *Chronicles of the Picts and the Scots*, ed W. F. Skene (Edinburgh, 1867), pp. 92–5. According to Turgot, p. 239, Margaret also gave a fine cross to St Andrews.

[68] Wall, 'Malcolm III', pp. 329, 335–6. Space precludes any in depth discussion of the complex issue of Lothian.

[69] *Ibid.*, pp. 333–4.

[70] Turgot, p. 254. For queens' burial requests, see J. C. Parsons, ch. 16, below.

[71] A. O. Anderson, *Early Sources of Scottish History AD 500 to 1286*, 2 vols (repr. Stamford, 1990), ii, 86–7.

led by his English uncle Edgar the Ætheling and deposed his Scottish uncle Donald III.[72]

Despite the trauma of these events, Margaret had laid the foundation on which her family could build their future security when they returned as kings. For Dunfermline, the first extant authentic charter is that of her son David soon after his accession in 1124, when he not only began work on a larger abbey church, but confirmed the previous gifts of his parents, his brothers Duncan, Æthelred, Edgar, and Alexander and his wife Sibylla, and which was made with the assent of his own wife Maud and son Henry, before adding grants of his own.[73] He made over thirty grants and mandates concerning the rights of Dunfermline.[74] Royal patronage continued to Alexander III.[75] Familial continuity is expressed through repeated concern for the souls of the donors and of their ancestors and successors. Kings Edgar, Alexander I and David were buried at Dunfermline, so also Malcolm IV.[76] After the establishment of this family as kings and the development of Dunfermline as the national royal mausoleum, the Scottish regnal lists added a standard formula, introducing Iona as an autonomous burial site for earlier Scottish kings of all dynasties.[77] The dichotomy of *interfectus est* to describe the deaths of previous kings and *mortuus est* for the descendants of Malcolm and Margaret contributes to the image of the queen as peaceweaver, and what appears to be a peacefully unopposed line of kings.[78]

In conclusion, Margaret's power emanated from an ability to grasp at opportunities presented to her. Whilst women could work only within a 'palette of images', they could manipulate the arguments which provided legitimate authority and power.[79] Before her marriage and after her death, her family were victims of fluid succession practices, shifting patterns of kin-group relationships and multiple marriages. They were a high status family whose blood was either a blessing or a curse. In the intervening years, Margaret had attached herself to two institutions which could provide hope of stability and permanence – a legally-defined marriage and the Church. Donaldson stated that as the mother of eight children, Margaret's

---

72 Wall, 'Malcolm III', p. 329.
73 *Registrum de Dunfermelyn (Liber Cartarum Abbatie Benedictine SS Trinitatis et B Margarete regine de Dunfermelyn)*, Bannatyne Club, 74 (Edinburgh, 1842), pp. 3–7. The foundation charter of Malcolm, printed by Lawrie, *ESC*, no. 10, pp. 8–9, is spurious; see *Registrum*, pp. xx–xxi, but the lands mentioned therein are confirmed by all subsequent grants.
74 *Ibid.*, pp. 8–18.
75 *Ibid.*, pp. 19–47. The link was re-established by Robert I after 1306.
76 See Anderson, *Kings and Kingship*, pp. 264–91, Regnal Lists F, G. I, K, N.
77 *Ibid.*, Regnal Lists D, F, G, I, K, N. The dynasty faced challenges from the descendants of Lulach and Duncan II.
78 For the influence both on Margaret and her descendants, this could be placed in the context of royal burials elsewhere in this period. See E. M. Hallam, 'Royal Burial and the Cult of Kingship in France and England, 1060–1330', *Journal of Medieval History*, viii (1982), 359–80; E. Mason, 'Westminster Abbey and the Monarchy between the Reigns of William I and John (1066–1216)', *Journal of Ecclesiastical History*, xli (1990), 199–216.
79 Stafford, 'Portrayal of Royal Women', p. 146.

achievement was uncommon in a saint.[80] Images of female power were predominantly Christian and familial.[81] They were not, however, gender specific. Margaret's legacy to her sons and daughters was to ensure that they also had the ability to manipulate these images.

---

[80] Donaldson, quoted by Baker, ' "A Nursery of Saints" ', p. 127.
[81] Stafford, 'Portrayal of Royal Women', p. 144.

3

Ingeborg of Denmark, Queen of France, 1193–1223 *

George Conklin

When Ingeborg cried out her fateful words of appeal *Mala Francia, mala Francia; Roma, Roma* at the divorce proceedings of Compiègne (5 November 1193), little did she realise that she would be creating for herself one of the legendary cases of annulment and spousal abuse in the Middle Ages.[1] There is no question today and was little then that the actions of this council were a farce. Pope Innocent III later termed it a *ludibrii fabula*.[2]

After 1193, her life was not her own. Thenceforth, everything she did was constrained by political, legal, religious, or royal considerations. Indeed, as far as we know, the very marriage itself was not of her making. Certainly the annulment was not, and the consequent events presented few opportunities for her to do little more than react. When opportunity did come her way she responded, however, with steadiness of purpose and with steadfastness in the rightness of her position as true wife and queen of France. Perhaps one could argue that for her to waver was to do so to her own peril, but even people in peril have second thoughts and question their decisions. Ingeborg seems never to have done so. Even at her lowest

---

* This affords me an opportunity to acknowledge two debts of gratitude, especially to Professor Laurent Mayali, Director of the Robbins Collection of Civil and Religious Law, University of California, Berkeley who has generously extended to me over the course of the years access to that collection and to Northwestern State University, Natchitoches, Louisiana, without whose generous financial support my travels and research for this article would not have been possible.

1 *Gesta Innocentii III* (*PL*, ccxiv), xlix.95, 'Quae cum reginae per quemdam exponeretur interpretem, illa, ultra quam dici posset admirans, flens et ejulans, exclamavit: Mala Francia, mala Francia; et adjecit: Roma, Roma.' The proceeding at Compiègne declared Philip legally separated from Ingeborg. Even though the medieval term for such a separation was divortium, what Philip sought was an annulment, that is, a separation with the right to remarry following a decree of nullity of the first marriage, not a divorce in the modern sense.

2 Innocent III, *Regesta*, *PL*, ccxiv, 746–7, 'Licet enim bonae memoriae Coelestinus papa praedecessor noster sententiam illam divortii, quin potius illius ludibrii fabulam, de fratrum consilio duxerit penitus irritandam, diligenter eum admonens et frequenter ut praedictam reginam reciperet in gratiam conjugalem'; *PL*, ccxv, 1497, 'Nos autem nec unum archiepiscopum deposuimus. Remensem videlicet, avunculum tuum, qui sententiam divortii seu potius ludibrii fa[b]ulam promulgavit.' *Gesta Innocentii III*, liii.100, '. . . quaesivit ab avunculo suo, Remensi archiepiscopo, qui sententiam divortii promulgaverat, utrum verum esset quod sibi dominus papa scripserat, videlicet, quod illa non erat divortii dicenda sententia, sed ludibrii fabula nominanda.'

point in 1205 she called upon Pope Innocent III to ignore any renunciation of the marriage she might make under duress.

From the outset Ingeborg insisted on the legality of her marriage to King Philip II of France on 14 August 1193 (vigil of the Assumption of the Blessed Virgin Mary).[3] At best their sexual relations lasted until the next day (the Assumption) when during their double coronation Philip 'by the devil's suggestion, began to be horrified, to tremble and turn pale at the sight of her. He was so deeply disturbed that he could scarcely restrain himself until the end of the ceremony which had just begun.'[4] Thereupon Philip disavowed her and had her imprisoned. His sudden aversion still remains a mystery, its cause subject to all manner of speculations.

The French chronicler Rigord attributed Philip's affliction to diabolical machinations and alleged sorcery, but the English chronicler William of Newburgh preferred more earthy causes – 'this shameful levity is variously described, some say because of the fetid smell of her breath, others that it was because of some hidden deformity that [Philip] repudiated her, and still others because he did not find her a virgin'.[5] The most recent modern explanation for Philip's strange behaviour has attributed it to an illness he contracted on the Third Crusade, called *arnoldia* by the English chroniclers, a form of sweating sickness.[6] Whatever may have been its cause, Ingeborg steadfastly proclaimed that she and Philip had consummated the marriage, while the king strove for twenty years (1193–1213) to have the marriage annulled. The prolonged dispute evoked a goodly amount of correspondence between king, popes, prelates, and lawyers.[7] A fresh scrutiny of

---

[3] R. Davidssohn, *Philipp II. August von Frankreich und Ingeborg* (Stuttgart, 1888), p. 32; *Die Register Innocenz' III. 1. Pontifikatsjahr, 1198/1199*, edd. O. Hageneder and A. Haidacher (Graz-Cologne, 1964), p. 10n incorrectly gives *15* August 1193.

[4] *Gesta Innocentii III*, xlviii.93–4, 'Sed, inter ipsa coronationis solemnia, suggerente diabolo, ad aspectum ipsius coepit vehementer horrescere, tremere ac pallere, ut nimium perturbatus, vix sustinere posset finem solemnitatis incoeptae.'

[5] *Oeuvres de Rigord et de Guillaume le Breton: Historiens de Philippe-Auguste*, ed. H.-F. Delaborde, 2 vols (Paris, 1882), i, 124–5, 'Sed mirum! eodem die, instigante diabolo, ipse rex, quibusdam, ut dicitur, maleficiis per sorciarias impeditus, uxorem tam longo tempore cupitam, exosam habere cepit'; *Chronicles of the Reigns of Stephen, Henry II, and Richard I*, ed. R. Howlett, 4 vols, RS 82 (London, 1884–89), i, 369, 'Causa sane pudendae levitatis hujus varie assignatur. Dicunt enim quidam, quod propter foetidum oris spiritum, alii, quod propter latentem quandam foeditatem repudiaverit eam, vel quia non invenit eam virginem.' The phrase 'latentem quandam foeditatem' has usually been taken to mean physical ugliness, but as there is testimony to her beauty maybe more weight should be given to 'latens' and the possibility that Philip knew something that no one else did. Rigord described Canute VI's sister as 'Ingeburgem sororem suam pulcherrimam' (Rigord, c. 92, p. 124). Stephen of Tournai's description of her is presented below.

[6] J. Baldwin, *The Government of Philip Augustus: Foundations of French Royal Power in the Middle Ages* (Berkeley, 1986), pp. 357 and 568 n. 2.

[7] It is an easy temptation to write about all those who surrounded Ingeborg, as Robert Davidssohn did in his still standard 1888 dissertation on the queen. Davidssohn's work retains its value, however, because he unravels the intricacies of royal manoeuvering and tactics, discusses the political circumstances surrounding the case, examines the implications and repercussions of the annulment for France and its neighbours, and resolves the legal question of affinity, to which some recent scholars would have done well to refer: cf.

the letters (to, from, and about her) is offered here in the hope of giving voice to the historical Ingeborg.[8]

One of the best and earliest portrayals of Ingeborg appeared in a letter written by a sympathiser, even perhaps a confidant, after Philip first imprisoned her at Cysoing in the diocese of Tournai.[9] There the kindly bishop and renowned canonist Stephen of Tournai took up her cause and in 1194 wrote on her behalf to Archbishop William of Reims.

In writing to his episcopal colleague, Stephen of Tournai knew he was remonstrating with the leading French prelate, the king's uncle, and the chief engineer of Ingeborg's ruin in the council at Compiègne. He was also addressing an invaluable patron and lifelong friend and ally. It must have been a difficult letter to compose. The bishop began his letter to the archbishop with an appearance of great deference. He likened William to the sculptor, himself to the clay; the archbishop was the potter and he was the pot.[10] This exceeds even Stephen's customary humility formulas and leads one to suspect that through *litotes* he intended to convey dissent from the decisions recently taken. He extolled Ingeborg as a precious pearl which had been crushed by men – and no doubt Stephen considered William among the main crushers.[11] Stephen proclaimed her worthy of the royal treasury, the royal palace, of heaven itself, and since she merited such supernatural reward then certainly she deserved her earthly due as queen of France.[12] Indeed without any qualification or hesitation, Stephen called her queen (*reginam dico*), which so soon after the proceedings at Compiègne was surely an affront to the council's decision. As one of the leading canonists in France, his displeasure at that decision and avowal of her status as queen would have carried legal weight in the Gallican church and at the papal *curia*. And what had the queenship brought her? – imprisonment, poverty, and exile.[13]

In describing Ingeborg, Stephen reminded William that she was of noble parentage and royal stock (*puella illustris regum natalibus*). In keeping with her high birth, she was a woman of comparable virtue in both senses of the term: in terms of her upright character (*insignis moribus*) and pure in deed (*operibus vere*

Baldwin, *Philip Augustus*, p. 478 n. 16, where he criticises M.-B. Bruguière ('Le mariage de Philippe Auguste et d'Isambour de Danemark: aspects canoniques et politiques', *Mélanges offerts à Jean Dauvillier* [Toulouse, 1979], pp. 135–56) for ignoring German scholarship, namely Davidssohn, on their relationship.

8 The question of her authorship of her letters will be considered below.

9 *Lettres d'Etienne de Tournai*, ed. J. Desilve (Valenciennes/Paris, 1893), *ep.* 213, pp. 263–5. Stephen's letter says 'apud Cysonium', but most scholars argue that she lived in the priory of Beaurepaire (dioc. Arras); cf. Davidssohn, *Philipp II*, pp. 47–8; E. de Moreau, *Histoire de L'Église en Belgique*, 3 vols (Brussels, 1940–45), iii, 107.

10 *Ibid.*, p. 263, 'non abiciet me plastes lutum suum, vasculum suum figulus, artifex opus manuum suarum'.

11 *Ibid.*, p. 264, 'Est apud nos preciosa margarita, que conculcatur ab hominibus.'

12 *Ibid.*, 'honoratur ab angelis, digna thesauro regio, digna palatio, digna celo'.

13 *Ibid.*, 'reginam dico, que apud Cysonium quasi ergastulo clauditur, paupertate premitur, exilio relegatur'.

munda).[14] Though she possessed a lovely face, like Ambrose's virgin, her true beauty lay in her faith.[15] Despite her youth (eighteen at the time of the marriage), she was mature in spirit (*animo cana*, a good Ambrosian phrase). The theme is a feminised version of the *puer-senex* topos.

Mindful of writing to a friend, colleague, and superior, Stephen chose to develop Ingeborg's character through a remarkable display of biblical erudition. He cast her as almost more mature than Sarah, wiser than Rebecca, kinder than Rachel, more devout than Anna, and purer than Susanna.[16] Sarah was also renowned for her great beauty even in her advanced years (Genesis 12:14). The reference to Rebecca, wife of Isaac, who tricked Isaac into giving Jacob the blessing of the firstborn, alluded to Ingeborg's intelligence. Her patience was that of the long-suffering Rachel, wife of Jacob. Her piety excelled that of Anna, patiently awaiting the arrival of the Messiah (1 Timothy 5:5). The allusion to Susanna contained an admonition to his archiepiscopal friend. In the Book of Daniel, the beautiful and pious Susanna spurned two lustful elders, who then accused her of adultery. Daniel intervened just before her execution (Daniel 13:1–64). Through the story, Stephen was urging Archbishop William to reverse course (which he later did) and become Ingeborg's Daniel.

In remarking upon Ingeborg's physical beauty – no uglier than Helen of Troy – Stephen perhaps hoped to counter the charge, echoed in William of Newburgh, that she was too ugly for the king to consummate the marriage.[17] But Stephen had more in mind than this. If one lays out each of Ingeborg's virtues, physical and moral, and imagines their opposite, then what appears is Stephen the lawyer going through the charges laid against her and rebutting them.

As for her daily routine Stephen informed William that she spent her days in prayer, reading, and manual labor. These are of course the duties of a religious. The reference to her reading is probably of most interest, since with a few exceptions, notably Heloise, we have little information on the literacy and learning of twelfth-century women. Unfortunately, we are not told what Ingeborg read. The close of the letter records what purport to be Ingeborg's actual words: 'my friends and relations like strangers have abandoned me; my one and only refuge is my lord archbishop of Reims, who has favoured, nourished, and fed me generously from the beginning of my adversity'.[18] The paraphrase from the Book of Job expressed her sense of forlornness before the great archbishop as Job had been before God.

Ingeborg sent her first letter to Pope Celestine III in 1196.[19] She relates to him

14 *Ibid.* Her father was King Waldemar I (1157–82).
15 *Ibid.*, 'cum Ambrosiana virgine pulchra facie, sed pulchrior fide'.
16 *Ibid.*, 'pene dixerim Sara maturior, Rebeca sapientior, Rachele gracior, Anna devocior, Susanna castior'.
17 *Ibid.*, 'nec deformior Helena'.
18 *Ibid.*, 'Amici mei et proximi mei, quasi alieni, recesserunt a me; unicum refugium meum dominus meus Remensis archiepiscopus, qui me ab initio adversitatis mee liberaliter fovit, aluit et nutrivit.' Cf. Job 19:13, 'et noti mei quasi alieni recesserunt a me'.
19 Celestine III, *PL*, ccvi, 1277–8. In his handling of the case, Celestine has never come off

that three years had elapsed since the king of France had married her. She noted that 'as nature required [Philip] had rendered the marital debt to her'.[20] In effect, Ingeborg was proclaiming to the pope that the marriage had been fully consummated and that no valid canonical grounds for separation remained.[21] Ingeborg then gave her own appraisal of Philip's motives for the disavowal. She cited the incitement of the devil (*instigatione diabolica*), but then sober-mindedly introduced the evil princes (*malitiosorum principum persuasione seductus*), who seduced (her word) the king into taking Agnes of Meran as wife (*filiam ducis S.* [recte *B*] *superinduxit et retinet pro uxore*).[22] For good measure Ingeborg added that 'Philip made a decree of a wish, a law of wilfulness, and a passion out of desire'.[23] The queen had now levelled the same charge of diabolical intervention against Philip that he had alleged against her in 1193.

As for her attack on Agnes, Ingeborg employed a phrase that she may have intended to resonate with another marital irregularity in the French royal family. Ingeborg described Agnes as *filiam Ducis S.* [recte *B*], whom the king *superinduxit*. This phrase, though common terminology for a mistress, also echoed Abbot Suger's description of King Philip I's second wife, the *superducta Andegavensi[s] comitissa Bertrada*.[24] If Ingeborg intended to recall to Pope Celestine the bigamous marriage of her husband's great grandfather, it was a subtle reminder of the troubles his eleventh-century predecessors had on that account. Whatever the case may be, Ingeborg certainly did not recognise the marriage between Philip II and Agnes and if Celestine did, she implied, he too was condoning bigamy.

When Ingeborg characterised her incarceration, she described how she lived as one proscribed (*proscripta dego*), which in Roman law was to live both as an outlaw and in exile.[25] She may have also had in mind the very real possibility that she could meet the same fate as other famous proscribed personages, since she ended the letter with the warning that 'unless you [Celestine] take mercy upon me I may die in the near future'.[26] Despite her imprisonment, she told the pope that

well with modern historians; nonetheless, Ingeborg's letter gives no hint of dissatisfaction with him.

20 *Ibid.*, col. 1278, 'jam enim triennium est elapsum quod rex Franciae me in aetate nubili desponsavit . . . prout naturalis ordo requirit, debitum reddidit maritale'.

21 The pope had already (13 May 1195) rejected Philip's argument for nullity on grounds of affinity (*PL*, ccvi, 1095–8 nos 212–14), but the cardinal legates Censius and Melior were unable to secure the adhesion of the French bishops, who were too timid to act against the king (Paris, 7 May 1196): Baldwin, *Philip Augustus*, pp. 83–4, 478 n. 17.

22 Agnes was the daughter of Duke Bertold of Andechs-Meranien; she married Philip on 1 June 1196.

23 *PL*, ccvi, 1278, 'sed facit de voluntate decretum, de pertinacia legem et de voluptate furorem'.

24 Suger, *Vie de Louis VI le Gros*, ed. H. Waquet (Paris, 1964), p. 10.

25 A. Berger, *Encyclopedic Dictionary of Roman Law* (Philadelphia, 1953), p. 658, cites Sulla's *Lex Cornelia de proscriptione* for outlawry and the subsequent imperial legislation on exile (*Corpus iuris civilis*, edd. P. Krueger and T. Mommsen, 3 vols [1877, repr. Dublin and Zurich, 1973], ii, 393 [*Codex Iustinianus* 9.49]).

26 *PL*, ccvi, 1278, 'Unde nisi vestra misericordia mihi misereri dignetur, morti succumbam in proximo temporali.'

she still weeps for her king, whom she said was contemptuous of the orthodox faith. Philip rejected all religious counsel and she artfully ranked the order of those whom he refused to obey, beginning with the pope: he did not fear to spurn his, Celestine's letters; he refused to hear the commands of the cardinals (the legates Censius and Melior); and he disobeyed the pronouncements of the archbishops, bishops, and other religious.[27] In effect, she declared Philip had thumbed his nose at the religious nation at home and abroad, which was indeed true.

The entire letter reveals a firmness of resolve stiffened by knowledge of the law. The queen knew precisely where her case rested legally and what the law required. From the outset, consummation formed the gravamen of Ingeborg's case that there had been a valid and complete marriage. She also boldly accused Philip of adultery and bigamy, even calling him an evil example to all Christians and to all his realm.[28] These were not the words of a meek, submissive, twenty-one-year-old girl. She was going to fight for the marriage and her rightful place as queen of France. Philip sooner than anyone realised this. Pope Celestine III certainly found out in 1193. In 1198 it was to be Pope Innocent III's turn.

From Ingeborg's point of view, the accession of Innocent III must have given rise to new hopes, and indeed one of his first acts instructed Philip to restore her to his marital affection and readmit her as queen into the fullness of his royal grace – *in plenitudinem gratiae regalis*.[29] This phrase fittingly reverberated with *in plenitudine potestatis*, a term Innocent would much develop later.[30]

Philip declined to restore Ingeborg and Innocent III imposed an interdict on France on 13 January 1200, carefully avoiding, however, excommunicating Philip and Agnes.[31] A few months later, in September 1200, Philip managed to get the

---

[27] *Ibid.*, 'Proh dolor! spernere vestrae sanctitatis litteras non formidat, audire cardinalium jussa recusat, archiepiscoporum et praesulum dicta contemnit, et admonitiones religiosorum quorumlibet aspernatur.'

[28] *Ibid.*, 'Christianis et universis de regno suo exemplum tribuit malignandi.'

[29] Innocent III, *Regesta*, *PL*, ccxiv, 4, 'Rogamus igitur fraternitatem tuam, monemus et exhortamur in Domino, ac per apostolica tibi scripta mandamus, quatenus eumdem regem ex parte nostra diligentius moneas et inducas, et in remissionem ei peccatorum injungas ut praedictam reginam in plenitudinem gratiae regalis admissam maritali studeat affectione tractare'; cf. *Die Register Innocenz III. 1. Pontifikatsjahr*, pp. 9–12. Gratian interpreted marital affection as a habitual attitude of respect, deference, and consideration toward one's spouse that differentiated a marital relationship from casual cohabitation: Gratian, *Decretum*, ed. Ae. Friedberg, *Corpus Iuris Canonici*, i (Leipzig, 1879; repr. Graz, 1959), D. (distinctio) 34, d.p.c. (dictum post capitulum) 3; C. (causa) 32, q. (questio) 2, d.a.c. (dictum ante capitulum) 6; C. 32, q. 5, d.p.c. 16. In the words of J. Noonan, 'Marital Affection in the Canonists', *Studia Gratiana*, xii (1967), 489–509, esp. p. 502, it was the will to treat the other spouse as a spouse. See also C. M. Rousseau, 'The Spousal Relationship: Marital Society and Sexuality in the Letters of Pope Innocent III', *Mediaeval Studies*, lvi (1994), 89–110.

[30] There are numerous works on the term *plenitudo potestatis*, but see J. A. Watt, *The Theory of Papal Monarchy in the Thirteenth Century: The Contribution of the Canonists* (New York, 1965) and K. Pennington, *Pope and Bishops: The Papal Monarchy in the Twelfth and Thirteenth Centuries* (Philadelphia, 1984).

[31] Baldwin, *Philip Augustus*, pp. 85, 178–9. Innocent reminded Philip of this in 1208 (*PL*, ccxv,

interdict lifted. With the complicity of the cardinal-legate Octavian, he engineered a sham rapprochement with Ingeborg.[32] It is now that Philip's case enters its second phase. Before 1200, it revolved around the validity of the flimsy decree of separation on grounds of affinity pronounced at Compiègne.When this became untenable, he turned, after 1200, to claiming non-consummation *per maleficium*.[33] Thereafter, impotence through sorcery was the chief argument emanating from the *curia regis*. Davidssohn[34] believed that Philip could from the first have sought an annulment on grounds of impotence – on the basis of a recent decretal of Celestine III[35] – if he had he not been in such a rush to remarry, since the decretal permitted annulment, where impotence was proven, after three years of marriage. But there is no evidence that the decretal was known in France as early as 1193, having been sent to Acre in the first year of Celestine's pontificate (1191–92),[36] and moreover, a successful plea of impotence in one marriage constituted a diriment impediment

---

1497), 'Nos autem, etsi protulerimus sententiam interdicti, non quidem in totum regnum, sed in partem aliquam regni tui, non tamen te vel superinductam excommunicationi subjecimus.'

32 He was supposed to persuade Philip to obey the interdict, to banish Agnes, and to take Ingeborg back as wife and queen (*PL*, ccxiv, 882).

33 H. Tillmann, *Pope Innocent III*, trans. W. Sax (Amsterdam, 1980), p. 342; Davidssohn, *Philipp II*, p. 209; Baldwin, *Philip Augustus*, p. 206. Gratian, C. 33, q. 1, d.p.c. 3 allowed for divorce on grounds of non-consummation. Drawing on this text, the Bolognese canonist Rufinus distinguished between congenital impotence and temporary impotence and considered impotence *de maleficiis* (which Philip claimed in 1202) as temporary. Although Rufinus accepted congenital impotence as grounds for annulment, he was hesitant about temporary impotence, and required reconciliation of the couple if the impotent party regained sexual capacity: *Die Summa decretorum des Magister Rufinus*, ed. H. Singer (Paderborn, 1902), pp. 496–7: C. 33, q. 1, *ante*; in contrast, Stephen of Tournai allowed a decree of nullity on grounds of temporary impotence, because there was a defect in the original consent to marry: *Die Summa des Stephanus Tornacensis über das Decretum Gratiani*, ed. J. F. von Schulte (Giessen, 1891), pp. 245–6: C. 33, q. 1 *ante*. In the decretal legislation, Alexander III (*Liber Extra* or *Decretals of Gregory IX* [= *X*], ed. Friedberg, *Corpus Iuris Canonici*, ii [Leipzig, 1881; repr. Graz, 1959], 4.13.2) likewise allowed annulment on grounds of non-consummation. For a discussion of Alexander's marriage decretals see C. Brooke, *The Medieval Idea of Marriage* (Oxford, 1989), pp. 169–72, who reconsiders (briefly) C. Donahue, 'The Dating of Alexander the Third's Marriage Decretals: Dauvillier Revisited after Fifty Years', *Zeitschrift der Savigny-Stiftung für Rechtsgeschichte: Kanonistische Abteilung*, lxviii (1982), 70–124. The general decretal treatment of impotence *per maleficium* occurs in *X*, 4.15.1–7. In general on the indissolubility of marriage see J. Gaudemet, 'L'Interprétation du principe d'indissolubilité du mariage chrétien au cours du premier millénaire', *Sociétés et Mariage* (Strasbourg, 1980), pp. 230–89; and M. Maccarrone, 'Sacramentalità e indissolubilità del matrimonio nella dottrina di Innocenzo III', *Lateranum*, xliv (1978), 449–514.

34 *Philipp II*, pp. 36–7.

35 *X*, 4.15.5.

36 *Laudabilem* introduced the three-year trial period into the official legislation of the church. For its address, date, and transmission through the early decretal collections, see W. Holtzmann, *Studies in the Collections of Twelfth-Century Decretals*, ed., rev., and trans. C. R. Cheney and M. G. Cheney, Monumenta Iuris Canonici, Series Collectionum, 3 (Vatican City, 1979), pp. 173, 175, 195, 229, 265, 274, 288, 294, 316 (I am grateful to Dr Charles Duggan for this reference). For a discussion of the triennial period see P. A. D'Avack, *Cause di nullità e di divorzio nel diritto matrimoniale canonico* (Florence, 1952), pp. 526–31.

to a subsequent marriage. This explains why Philip claimed impotence *per maleficium* (not discussed in Celestine's decretal) as grounds for nullity in 1202, since such impotence was regarded as temporary. Philip hoped to tie the case up into a thirteenth-century version of 'he says' – 'she says', which he did. Then as now law was a very blunt instrument for discovering the truth of the matter in cases involving sex. Philip turned the law's inadequacy to his own advantage and he had as an ally Pope Innocent III's own mixed motives.[37]

In November 1200, Innocent wrote to Ingeborg. Angry though he was at Octavian for too quickly raising the interdict, Innocent did not think he could re-impose it and so had to put the best face on what was a done deal. The pope likened the interdict to the oil and wine which the Good Samaritan used to soothe the wounds of the man by the wayside.[38] Knowing its lifting offered nothing soothing to Ingeborg, Innocent could only promise that she would never be put aside without judgement of the church, meaning the *ecclesia Romana*.[39] He reiterated his demand that Philip restore her as wife and queen and treat her with marital affection.[40] But then came a blow. Innocent left the door open for a new trial.[41] We do not know Ingeborg's immediate reaction, but we can gauge something of the bitter disappointment from a letter she sent to the pope in 1203.

Ingeborg opened with a reference to herself as the least of Innocent's daughters (*filiarum eius minima*) and queen of France in name only (*Franciae, nomine solo, regina*).[42] Despite her years of bitterness, Philip remained for her a 'perpetual bundle of myrrh, who may yet abide between her breasts'.[43] Then in a skilfully worded passage, Ingeborg employed two terms important for the expression of papal power: *vicarius Christi* and *gladius spiritus*.[44] With Innocent, *vicarius Christi* became the new term of art for the pope and it is found together with the

---

[37] This is not the place to discuss Innocent and this case, but historians are divided over his intentions. Among his political concerns was a complicated German policy of trying to separate Philip II from Philip of Swabia in the years 1200–1204 (Tillmann, *Innocent III*, pp. 333–4). Innocent had to weigh such concerns with his role as guardian and keeper of ecclesiastical law and morality. His political designs prevented him from taking as severe punitive measures against Philip as he would have liked, and his convictions concerning marriage would not allow him to dispose of the politically inconvenient Ingeborg. Tillmann regards Innocent as a pope realistically trying to make the best of a difficult situation, while Davidssohn tends to judge him as duplicitous.

[38] Innocent III, *Regesta*, PL, ccxiv, 881–2, 'tandem vulneribus fotis oleo, vinum cum Samaritano duxerimus infundendum, in terram regis ipsius interdicti sententiam proferentes'.

[39] *Ibid.*, col. 882, 'et praeter Ecclesiae judicium non dimittet'.

[40] *Ibid.*, 'ut idem rex te in gratia retineat conjugali et maritali affectione pertractet'.

[41] *Ibid.*, col. 883. 'Noverimus autem et habeas pro constanti quod nos, dante Domino, in tua tibi non deerimus ratione, licet, regi postulanti justitiam, non potuerimus nec velimus audientiam denegare.'

[42] *PL*, ccxv, 86–8.

[43] *Ibid.*, col. 86, 'fasciculum myrrhae mihi factum, inter ubera commorantem sustineo'.

[44] Innocent III, *Regesta*, PL, ccxv, 86–7, 'remedium amaritudinis, per vos Christi vicarium, desiderans obtinere. Vos siquidem per Dei gratiam estis successor Petri, collega Pauli, qui Corinthium gladio spiritus trucidare minime formidavit.'

older *successor Petri*.[45] *Gladius spiritus* is the ancient predecessor to the more common *gladius spiritualis*, emerging from Bernard's *De Consideratione* and canonistic writings of the twelfth century as a metaphor for the relations of *regnum* and *sacerdotium*.[46] If Ingeborg was indeed using these terms as they were currently construed in the papal curia, then they point to a remarkable keenness for papal rhetoric on her part.

The letter proceeded to recount to Innocent her physical and emotional distress. Through the solitude of imprisonment, the king sought to destroy her youth. Philip blushed at nothing, she lamented, to gain her consent to the annulment against the rights of matrimony and the law of Christ (*contra matrimonii jura et legem Christi*). The worst of all to endure were the royal henchmen sent daily to curse, slander, and threaten her (*opprobriis et calumniis per suos satellites me irritare non cessat*). They were most likely clerics, since Ingeborg scorned them as the forerunners of the Antichrist, who while they kept the appearance of religion (*speciem pietatis*) in reality lacked its substance (*virtutem eius abnegant*). She also complained of not being bled (*si volo minuere mihi sanguinem, facere non possum*), which ironically was probably the one benefit of her imprisonment.

Perhaps more significant to Innocent were the reports that Ingeborg could not receive the ministrations of the church. She could not confess, rarely heard Mass, and never heard the Office. The final plea to the pope reflected her near total despair. She entreated him to ignore any renunciation of the marriage if she should succumb out of female weakness to a tortured confession.[47] Whatever judicial and political considerations may have been on Innocent's mind at this moment, as a priest he could hardly have resisted such an appeal as this. For all the display of biblical and legal erudition, the letter reached beyond law and politics to a very basic level of simple human decency. Ingeborg had personalised the consequences of her separation to Innocent III in a way no other person could or did.[48]

The year 1205 should be considered the nadir of Ingeborg's marital life. In July, Innocent wrote to inform her of his intention to grant Philip a new trial on the

---

45 Innocent III, *Sermo 2 in consecratione*, PL, ccxvii, 657–8, as cited in C. Morris, *The Papal Monarchy: The Western Church from 1050 to 1250* (Oxford, 1989), p. 431. The standard treatment is still M. Maccarrone, *Vicarius Christi: storia del titolo papale* (Rome, 1952).

46 On the change from the use of *gladius spiritus* to *gladius spiritualis* see W. Levison, 'Die mittelalterliche Lehre von den beiden Schwerten', *Deutsches Archiv*, ix (1951), 21ff. There are numerous studies on the two-sword metaphor, but see especially the work of E. Kennan, 'The *De consideratione* of St Bernard of Clairvaux and the Papacy in the Mid-Twelfth Century: A Review of Scholarship', *Traditio*, xxiii (1967), 73–115, and A. Stickler, 'De ecclesiae potestate coactiva materialis apud magistrum Gratianum', *Salesianum*, iv (1942), 2–23; *idem*, 'Il gladius negli atti dei concili e dei RR Pontifice sino a Graziano e Bernardo di Clairvaux', *Salesianum*, xiii (1951), 414–45; *idem*, 'Sacerdozio et regno nelle nuove richerce ai secoli XII e XIII', *Miscellanea historiae pontificiae*, xviii (1954), 1–26.

47 Innocent III, *Regesta*, PL, ccxv, 88, 'et rogans et protestans, quod, si minis ac terroribus compulsa, feminea fragilitate, contra jura matrimonii mihi aliquid proposuero, non sit in praejudicium praenominati matrimonii, et a vobis qui persecutor estis confessionis extortae, nequaquam recipiatur'.

48 This raises the question of whether Ingeborg herself wrote the letter, which will be considered below.

grounds of affinity and sorcery.[49] The news of a new trial must have come as a bitter but not unexpected blow to Ingeborg. Innocent declared that he had done everything humanly possible to rekindle Philip's love for her, but because of sin (*peccatis exigentibus*) the king could not be induced to restore her to his marital affection.[50] Even so powerful a pope as Innocent III had to allow that the royal affections belonged to God's province.[51]

After much legal and diplomatic wrangling, Philip was finally prepared to admit in 1212 that intercourse had occurred, but he argued there had been no insemination. Innocent dispensed with this bit of legal *legerdemain* in a letter sent in the same year to Brother Guérin:

> Through some wicked adulators he [Philip] has been induced into errors of truth and justice. He believes that he can rightly swear that he has not carnally known his wife because [he argues] even though there was commingling of the sexes in carnal intercourse, there was not a subsequent commixture of seed in the female vessel.[52]

Philip's effort to convince the pope that while he did have intercourse, he did not inseminate her, went nowhere. Innocent was not that innocent. In his letter to Guérin, Innocent recorded that he himself was exhorting Philip 'to avert his hearing from insanities of this kind'.[53]

The last letter of Innocent III to Ingeborg dates from May 1210.[54] It openly acknowledged her bitterness in the same terms in which she had revealed it to him seven years before.[55] Innocent explained that the misery of the human condition is a universal one from which none is immune.[56] Perhaps an echo of his *De miseria conditionis humanae* (*c.* 1196), more commonly known as the *De contemptu mundi*, Innocent's resignation could only have dimmed rather than brightened her hopes:

---

[49] Innocent III, *Regesta, PL*, ccxv, 680. The new strategy also appears in the *forma in qua consulit dominus papa de divortio celebrando* (*ibid., PL*, ccxvii, 68–9) and is dated either 1205 (Tillmann, *Innocent III*, p. 338) or 1207 (Davidssohn, *Philipp II*, pp. 214ff).

[50] Innocent III, *Regesta, PL*, ccxv, 680, 'non potest aliquatenus inclinari, neque nos eius animo amorem possumus inspirare'.

[51] *Ibid.*, 'cum hoc solus Deus facere possit, in cuius manu cor regis existit'.

[52] *Ibid.*, col. 618, 'Cum ergo per quosdam adulatores veritatis et justitiae inimicos in eum sit errorem inductus ut credat se licite posse jurare quod reginam uxorem suam carnaliter non cognovit, pro eo forte quod etsi commistio sexuum in eorum carnali commercio intercesserit, commistio tamen seminum in vase muliebri non extitit subsecuta.'

[53] *Ibid.*, 'per nostras eum litteras exhortamur ut suum de caetero ab huiusmodi falsis insaniis avertat auditum'.

[54] *Ibid.*, coll. 258–9.

[55] Compare Ingeborg's letter to Innocent (*PL*, ccxv, 86), 'Pater sanctissime recogitabo vobis omnes annos meos in amaritudine animae meae' with Innocent's to Ingeborg (*PL*, ccxvi, 258), 'Super amaritudine in qua es paterno tibi compatientes affectu'.

[56] *PL*, ccxvi, 258, 'Attendens quod universa quae in miseriae huius mundo a quocumque penduntur, quasi quaedam necessaria sunt humanae vitae tributa, quorum immunitatem nemo poterit cum effectu vel petere vel sperare.'

Therefore console yourself about your fate, dearest daughter in Christ, and in assuming a bold spirit, do not retreat from its steadfastness, so that having as it were bewailed your own fate, you may bemoan the fact that you have not seen what is happening to you also befalling many less worthy.[57]

He then proceeded to instruct her that 'without an adversary virtue weakens' (*cum enim sine adversario virtus marceat*). He admonished her to be patient, to incline herself to God's wishes and in so doing the Holy Spirit, who is the true husband of the faithful and who would reward her well-tested patience. Be assured, he concluded, that in whatever way was fitting and right, he would never withdraw his apostolic favour from her.[58]

In one sense Innocent was vindicated, because her patience was rewarded in 1213 when, as inexplicably as he separated from her, Philip took her back. Sadly, however, Ingeborg's restoration was never more than *pro forma*. When she died in 1237/8, she had been restored as queen in name only. Whatever happened that fateful night between this royal couple, most likely it had nothing to do with Philip's sudden physical revulsion from his new wife, nor his lack of sexual capacity – as the children from Agnes of Meran later revealed.[59] With regard to Philip's continued aversion, perhaps Roger of Howden and William of Newburgh are correct to tie it to his disappointment over lack of Danish support for an invasion of England.[60] Their suggestion of a political motive for the king's subsequent treatment of Ingeborg might have some merit. Even so there is another element to consider. The king may have discerned or provoked in his new bride a degree of wilfulness that he realised he could not control, that he would not or could not tolerate. On the other hand, Ingeborg may have said or done or requested something to provoke Philip's wrath, which became so immediately deep-seated that even on the wedding night he was prepared to wreck his life's work.[61] Without new evidence, what provoked Philip's anger and Ingeborg's resolve can remain only a matter for speculation, but clearly strong feelings on both sides were already in play on the night of their wedding. After the farce of Compiègne, Ingeborg's opposition to Philip's insistence on an annulment would only have increased his ire, hardened his measures against her, and stiffened his determination to be rid of her. His irascibility over the subject of his wife became apparent at a meeting of the French clergy in 1197, where Rigord records that the French prelates were like

---

57 *Ibid.*, coll. 258–9, 'Quapropter, charissima in Christo filia, de tua te consolare fortuna, et animum induendo virilem, ab ipsius constantia non recedas, ut quasi de proprio fato conquesta, illud tibi gemas accidere quod multis indignioribus non videris evenire.'

58 *Ibid.*, col. 259, 'tuam remuneret patientiam, verum etiam gratia sui (Spiritus), qui verus sponsus est fidelium animarum, exspectationis tuae angustiam recompenset, secura de nobis quod in quibus oportuerit et decuerit, nequaquam tibi suffragium favoris apostolici subtrahemus'.

59 Innocent legitimised Philip's children from Agnes on the basis of the doctrine of putative marriage. See Peter Lombard, *Sententiae libri quattuor*, iv. 41, 3 (*PL*, cxcii, 939–40) and Brooke, *Medieval Idea of Marriage*, p. 52.

60 Davidssohn, *Philipp II*, pp. 21–2, 35n.

61 Baldwin, *Philip Augustus*, p. 118.

'mute dogs not able to bark because they feared for their skins. So they did nothing.'[62] It is not a very good comment on the French clergy when the king can intimidate them in this fashion. As Ingeborg dug in her heels, Philip grew more determined to crush her. He, however, could only go so far. Ingeborg understood perfectly well her status as crowned queen and royal consort. Medieval political marriages were a welter of public and private, personal and institutional considerations and Ingeborg adroitly exploited the boundaries between the queen as a political figure and legal wife to thwart Philip's machinations. In the end she outlasted him and in the interim outmanoeuvred him, albeit not without the complicity of a sometimes reluctant Pope Innocent III.

But when it is said that she did this, how much was truly her own work and how much was the work of others on her behalf? Philip outmatched Ingeborg in the political realm, but in the judicial arena she could meet him on something like a level playing field.[63] It was here that she could combine her political station as crowned queen with her legal status as wife to save herself, her marriage, and her position. With so much at stake, one would think that Ingeborg would naturally want to play as large a role in the conduct of the case as possible. What her role was, however, is not easy to ascertain. The only area where her hand can possibly be seen is in the composition of her letters. The assumption, however, is that her advisers composed them on her behalf.[64] Who these advisers were – Ingeborg's circle so to speak – has never been examined, though it is known that some of the king's *familiares* (most importantly Brother Guérin) were also her's.[65]

Those who advocate Ingeborg's authorship bear the burden of proof. It is assumed that she could not have written the letters sent in her name because as a woman she would not have possessed the requisite learning to compose them. Medieval women, even highborn ones, were not usually literate in learned Latin. Moreover, without access to formal legal training, she could not have constructed the sophisticated legal arguments the letters exhibit; nevertheless, several points should be considered before entirely rejecting her authorship.

Stephen of Tournai attests that Ingeborg could read, and while it is not known what she read, it is not implausible that she gained a respectable degree of knowledge of the canon law of marriage either from her own reading or from being read to. Stephen himself would have been a likely candidate for instructor since he was visiting her with some regularity. To eliminate *a priori* Ingeborg's authorship on the grounds that she lacked any knowledge of marriage law is not warranted. Moreover, the heading of Stephen of Tournai's letter notes that he was writing on her behalf, which if composed by him would suggest he wanted to

---

[62] Rigord, c. 92, p. 125, 'Sed quia facti sunt canes muti non valentes latrare, timentes etiam pelli sue, nihil ad perfectum deduxerunt.' Davidssohn dates the council to 1196, but W. Janssen dates it to 1197 in his *Päpstlichen Legaten in Frankreich vom Schisma Anaklets II. bis zum Tode Coelestins III. (1130–1198)* (Cologne, 1961), pp. 149–51.

[63] To Innocent III's credit he kept the field fairly level, no doubt for his own reasons.

[64] Raised in discussion by Dr David Carpenter.

[65] Brother Guérin was one of the executors of Ingeborg's will (Baldwin, *Philip Augustus*, p. 118). Davidssohn, *Philipp II*, pp. 256–8, discusses him and Ingeborg.

distinguish his writings for her from her own.[66] Finally, her letters contain a skilful blend of legal argument and personal touch, which sets them apart from all other correspondence. They convey the impression of a single pen enduring over the course of the entire correspondence, when it is known that her advisers changed.

Even though this amounts to an argument *ex silentio*, further investigation in two directions may strengthen it: more consideration of the assumptions concerning the Latin correspondence by twelfth-century women, that is, further investigation into what has come to be called a 'female discourse'; and secondly, re-examination of Ingeborg's letters and charters in the light of that discourse. With respect to the first, the correspondence cautions that the role of secretaries, scribes, counsellors, and advisers in the composition of letters for females is too greatly stressed, while for males it is the opposite. This is not without warrant in general, but the generalisation does not remove the call for questioning of assumptions in this particular case. As regards the letters themselves, they deserve the same scrutiny to discover her authorial voice as has been done for her contemporaries. The case for Ingeborg composing her own letters is not made here, but it is reopened.

Obviously Ingeborg was not a queen in any normal sense of the term. Her life was too conditioned by the political exigencies of the pope and king and the personal whims of her husband for that to be possible. Cut off from the usual avenues of influence (family and court) and imprisoned, she lost virtually all independence. And unlike Eleanor of Aquitaine she had no sons through whom to operate. As queen in name only, Ingeborg was less able than almost any other medieval queen to fulfil her office. And what of the office itself. How did she conceive of it? Again it is difficult to say, but we can glean something of her concept of queenship after her restoration.

Philip restored Ingeborg in 1213 as inexplicably as he had disavowed her. Though a recrudescent queen in his (not her) eyes, she was not permitted to assume any queenly duties. It is also doubtful whether Philip allowed Ingeborg to have anything like a court or chancery of her own during the remainder of his reign. She did not live in Paris with him and so was only a nominal wife.[67] Between her restoration and Philip's death we know of only one act: she sent to the church of St-Maclou in Bar-sur-Aube one of three teeth of St Maclou, which she had discovered in a reliquary in the royal castle at Pontoise.[68]

After Philip's death, it becomes possible, however, to form something of an image of Ingeborg as an active queen. In other words, it becomes possible to draw a distinction between her status as queen, which she certainly had a strong

---

66 On the other hand it is a commonplace device in letter collections for the copyists to identify letters written for others, so that the distinction may turn out to be of no significance. I am indebted to Professor Anne Duggan for this observation.

67 She probably lived near Orléans, where she had dower lands. At one point she was called *Regina Aurelianensis* (Davidssohn, *Philipp II*, p. 274).

68 Cited in Davidssohn, *Philipp II*, pp. 321–2, who mentions that the seal of the charter has survived, but does not discuss it or even say it is her seal; cf. *ibid.*, p. 262 for his discussion of the gift.

conception of, and the office of queen, which she had no practical opportunity to exercise. Freed from her husband's tyranny in 1223, Ingeborg acquired a considerable amount of independence.[69] In no small measure this was owing to her own fortitude. Having suffered and endured as she did, a lesser person might have given vent to rancour, but Ingeborg remained true to Philip's memory. Partly in gratitude for her loyalty to him, but perhaps also out of remorse for her suffering, both her stepson Louis VIII and her step-grandson Louis IX treated her well and gave her considerable latitude to devote her remaining years to pious deeds as a benefactress to churches, churchmen, and hospitals. She bestowed upon the church of St Aignan in Orléans a house and a vineyard;[70] she founded the chapel of St Vaast in the royal castle at Pontoise;[71] she dispensed alms, evidenced by gifts to Master Gilbert of St Jacob,[72] to the abbey of Cour Dieu,[73] and by her will.[74] She was particularly generous to the Cistercians, whose general chapter in 1228 ordered that she be commemorated in prayer along with popes, the church and kingdom, papal legates, the king, his family, and the Cistercian order.[75] She came to the attention of Pope Honorius III for her endowment of thirteen priests in the hospital church of Corbeil.[76] Whether these charitable deeds after 1223 indicate how she would have behaved before will never be known, but they are certainly in keeping with her character and were acts expected of a queen. Ingeborg well understood her status as queen; arguably, had she been allowed she would have exercised the duties attached to that status.

Although Ingeborg could not make herself an active political queen in the customary sense of the term, she did not allow herself to be marginalised into oblivion. Her strength and resolve ensured that she was always a factor in the calculations of her political masters and so she reminds us that the force of personality should never be divorced from events. In the end Ingeborg upheld her station as queen despite being denied the office, and so fashioned a degree of mutual reinforcement and protection between the office and herself as the office-holder. For Ingeborg, the reciprocity assured her survival.

---

[69] *Ibid.*, pp. 268–90 and esp. p. 278.

[70] *Ibid.*, p. 262.

[71] *Ibid.*, p. 262n, citing a charter from 1281, 'capella, vulgariter nuncupata capella regis apud Pontisaram in castello regis'.

[72] *Ibid.*, p. 276. Charter printed in *Recueil des historiens des Gaules et de la France* (Paris, 1880), xix, 325.

[73] Cited in Davidssohn, *Philipp II*, p. 327; discussed, *ibid.*, pp. 277–8.

[74] *Ibid.*, pp. 263–5.

[75] *Ibid.*, p. 272.

[76] 'Ingeburgis dei gratia Francorum regina . . . statuimus pro anima inclite recordationis karissimi viri nostri Ph. gloriosi Francorum regis et antecessorum et successorum suorum . . . tredecim presbyteros in ecclesia hospitalis de Corbolio ibidem in perpetuum permansuros et divina celebraturos ita, quod nos uniquique illorum duodecim libratas reddituum parisiensis monete ad eorum sustentationem assignare debemus', as cited in Davidssohn, *Philipp II*, p. 326; cf. pp. 272–3 for his dicussion. Honorius placed Ingeborg under papal protection (*ibid.*, p. 276).

4

Late Medieval Scandinavian Queenship

Steinar Imsen

During most of the period from 1319 to 1523 the Scandinavian kingdoms shared kings; firstly Norway and Sweden until 1363, secondly Norway and Denmark from 1380, and thirdly all three kingdoms from 1388/1396. Consequently nearly all late medieval Scandinavian queens can be regarded as 'union-queens'. They include a long list of able and competent women, who played active roles in society and politics, and one of them, Queen Margaret of Norway, is without any doubt the ablest Scandinavian ruler of the period. She was architect of the union of the three monarchies, the so-called *Kalmarunion*, which she ruled uncontestedly to her death in 1412. As a group the 'union-queens' are indeed impressive when compared to their sister queens in other ages of Scandinavian history. In the following we will focus on the political importance of the 'union-queens', and try to find out what conditioned their unique position in the Scandinavian political system in the late Middle Ages. But first of all; who were they?

The 'union-queens'

They were six in number, five if we restrict ourselves to consorts. Queen *Margaret* of Norway (1353–1412) was never married to a 'union-king'.[1] Her use of the title *Queen of Sweden* expressed a pretension rather than a reality. Although her husband King Håkon VI of Norway had been formally accepted as Swedish king in 1362, he never ruled in Sweden. In fact Håkon and his father Magnus Eriksson were expelled from that country in 1363, the very year in which Håkon married Margaret in Copenhagen. Later, now a widow, and first as the mother and guardian of a child king and then as the adopted mother of an elected heir, Margaret ruled

---

1 According to contemporary definition a queen was the lawful wife of a king. The Scandinavian word *dronning/drottning* (queen) comes from old Scandinavian *dróttning* (f.), which is derived from *drótt/dróttinn* (m.), i.e. lord or prince. Dronning in its original meaning then should be translated as 'lady' or 'princess', but the title of drottning was reserved for the king's spouse by the end of the viking age. In the Nordic languages the terms drott and drottning are probably older than the term of king, and we should notice that there is no Scandinavian feminine equivalent to king, like the German *Königin*. Queen in the meaning of monarch does not appear in Scandinavian usage during the Middle Ages. It is characteristic that the Norwegian law of succession to the throne of 1302 says 'En su er hin siaunda erfd er dotter konongs skilgeten hin ælzsta ein tekar konongsdomer' ('This is the seventh heir that the King's eldest lawful daughter, and she alone, takes the Kingdom'): *NglL*, iii, 47.

the three northern monarchies as *fullmektig frue og rette husbonde* (plenipotentiary mistress and lawful householder) for almost twenty-five years.[2]

Margaret's Norwegian marriage was not primarily conditioned by Norwegian concerns, but reflected rather a combination of Norwegian-Swedish dynastic interests and King Valdemar's ambition to re-establish Danish dominance in Scandinavia and the Baltic.[3] However, the immediate reason for the marriage was Magnus Eriksson's urgent need for support to put down the aristocratic revolt which in any case cost him his Swedish crown. The other five 'union-queens' are Blanche (*c.* 1320–63), Philippa (1393–1430), Dorothea (*c.* 1430–95), Christina (1461–1521), and finally Isabella (1501–26), or Elizabeth as she was called in Scandinavia.

Blanche, Margaret's mother-in-law, was daughter of John of Namur and Mary of Artois. We do not know what political motives – if there were any – which made King Magnus go to Flanders in 1334 to find a wife. As Blanche descended from the counts of Flanders as well as from the royal houses of France and Luxemburg, her distinguished ancestry can in itself explain Magnus' choice.[4] The royal couple celebrated their marriage at the Norwegian castle of Tønsberghus in 1335, and in 1336 they were crowned king and queen of Norway and Sweden in Stockholm. Blanche's youngest son Håkon (b. 1340) was designated by his father and formally approved by the Norwegian estates as hereditary king of Norway in 1343, while his elder brother Eric (b. 1339), who according to the law was heir to the Norwegian throne, was designated successor to the Swedish throne. Eric died in 1359 after having joined his father's adversaries, and the influential noblewoman

---

2 The Norwegian letter of election (1388) says: 'a hafuom vi allæ fyrnæmfdir, erkibiskop, biskopa, profaster, riddara oc swæina, vppa vara vægna ok vppa ganska rikissens j Noreghe endrekteligha anamat, wtualt oc vnfanget med godhom vilia a høghborna forstinno, frw Margareta drothnengh . . . til ganska rikissens j Noreghe mæktugha frwa oc rettan husbonda, oc at ænnæ fyrnæmfd drothnengh Margareta skal fulmæktugh væra at firirstanda ok raadha rikit j Noreghe mæktuligha oc valdeligha j allum stykkium ifuir ganska rikit' ('then all of us, the archbishop, bishops, deans of the royal chapters, knights, and squires have unanimously elected the highborn princess, Queen Margaret to be plenipotentiary mistress and lawful householder of the realm of Norway, and the same Margaret shall rule the realm of Norway with all powers and rights . .)' (*NglL*, 2nd ser., i, 4). For a contemporary likeness, see pl. 4.

3 The marriage of Margaret's elder sister Ingeborg to Henry, younger son of Albert, duke of Mecklenburg, in 1362, is also seen as an element in Valdemar's strategy for extending Danish power in Scandinavia. (In 1360 and 1361 respectively Valdemar had reconquered Scania and occupied Gotland.) The new Swedish king from 1364, Albert of Mecklenburg, was the eldest son of Eufemia, sister of King Magnus Erikson. King Albert and the Norwegian king Håkon were cousins. From 1375 onwards these two very closely related dynasties competed for the same political goal, namely the dynastic unification of the three Scandinavian kingdoms. K. Erslev, *Dronning Margrethe og Kalmarunionens Grundlæggelse* (Copenhagen, 1882), p. 34; cf. K. Hørby, *Tiden fra 1340 til 1523*, *Danmarks historie*, ed. Aksel E. Christensen *et al.*, ii/1 (Copenhagen, 1980), 48.

4 H. Koht, 'Magnus Erikssons giftemål med Blanche av Namur', *Historisk Tidsskrift* (Norway), 5th ser., v (1924). Cf. W. Paravicini, 'Das Haus Namur im Ostseeraum', *Mare Balticum. Beiträge zur Geschichte des Ostseeraums in Mittelalter und Neuzeit: Festschrift zum 65. Geburtstag von Erich Hoffmann*, edd. W. Paravicini *et al.* (Sigmaringen, 1992).

Figure 1 Seal of Queen Blanche (1364), with coat-of arms of Norway, Namur, France and the Swedish dynasty of 'the Folkunger': 'SBLANC (he: dei: gracia regi)NE: SUECIE: NORWEGIE: ET: SCANIE' (*Norske Konge-Sigiller og andre Fyrste-Sigiller fra Middelalderen* [Kristiana/Oslo, 1924], pl. 16)

Birgitta Birgersdatter (St Birgitta) accused the queen of having poisoned her son. In many ways Blanche was made a political scapegoat by the noble opposition in Sweden, and it was Blanche the murderess and the evil spirit of the royal family who survived in Swedish tradition and historiography. As a matter of fact Blanche's innocence was not finally proved until the advent of modern critical historiography at the end of the eighteenth century. Because of the political situation in Sweden Blanche preferred to live in Norway from the end of the 1350s.

Philippa was the youngest daughter of Henry IV of England and Mary Bohun. She married Eric of Pomerania, Margaret's adopted heir to the three Scandinavian crowns, in 1406.[5] It was King Henry who in 1401 took the initiative in proposing

---

5   Eric was the son of Duke Vratislav VII of Pomerania and Mary of Mecklenburg, daughter of Margaret's sister Ingeborg.

an English-Scandinavian double marriage, in which Philippa would be given to King Eric and Eric's sister Catherine would marry the Prince of Wales. According to the Danish historian Kristian Erslev Henry's marriage plans were motivated by his need for international recognition. The negotiations proved complicated, partly because Margaret would not enter into an alliance against France, and partly because the English negotiators claimed hereditary rights to the crowns of Norway, Denmark and Sweden for children born of the marriage between Henry's son and Catherine. This claim was incompatible with the elective constitutions of Sweden and Denmark, and the planned double marriage was abandoned.[6] Nevertheless, on 8 December 1405 Henry IV proclaimed Philippa queen of Norway, Denmark and Sweden, and on 26 October 1406 she was formally married to Eric at the Danish archbishop's palace in Lund (Scania). Later on, Catherine was married to Count John of Neunburg-Oberpfalz, titular duke of Bavaria, probably after rec-ommendations from Henry IV, whose eldest daughter had been married to the eldest son of the German king Rupert. Philippa and Eric did not have any children.

Dorothea (pl. 5), daughter of John of Brandenburg and Barbara of Saxony, belonged to the German dynasty of Hohenzollern. She was married to King Christopher of Bavaria in 1443.[7] After Christopher's sudden death in January 1448 the Swedes broke out of the Union, electing their own 'national' king, Karl Knutsson Bonde. Dorothea's claim to her Swedish morning-gift would be one of the main issues in the ensuing struggle between Sweden and Denmark, not least because in 1449 Dorothea married the new Danish king, Christian I of Oldenburg, who claimed to be the lawful successor of the 'union-kings'. In 1450 Christian was crowned king of Norway, and in 1457 he was elected king of Sweden, but his rule there was effective only for short periods after 1463. From then on the Swedish Council of the Realm prevented Dorothea from enjoying her Swedish morning-gift, and for the rest of her life she fought bitterly, but in vain, for her rights in Sweden. Dorothea was also involved in a feud with her uncle, Prince Elector Albert Achilles, over the inheritance from her father, and she even obtained papal support for her claims in Brandenburg and Sweden.[8] Her first marriage was childless, but

---

6   Erslev, *Dronning Margrethe*, p. 366: 'By Eric's English marriage as well as Catherine's German, Margaret had beforehand turned away any idea that the Scandinavian kingdoms would be involved in struggles on the continent, and in fact these family connections never influenced Scandinavian politics'; cf. *ibid.*, p. 363 and L. Daae, 'Erik af Pommerns, Danmarks, Sveriges og Norges Konges, Giftermaal med Philippa, Prindsesse af England', *Historisk Tidsskrift* (Norway), 2nd ser., ii (1880); L. Hamre, *Norsk historie frå omlag 1400* (Oslo, 1968). However, we should notice that in 1393 Margaret had turned to Richard II for help in finding a wife for her stepson Eric (E. Haug, 'Erik av Pommerns norske kroning', *Historisk Tidsskrift* [Norway, 1995]).

7   Christopher of Bavaria was son of Catherine, Eric of Pomerania's sister, and John of Neunburg-Oberpfalz. He succeeded his uncle Eric as king of the three Scandinavian kingdoms 1439–42.

8   Dorothea's nephew, son of her sister Barbara of Mantua, being a cardinal, advocated her interests at the Roman Curia (J. Lindbæk, 'Dorothea, Kristiern den førstes dronning, og familien Gonzaga', *Historisk Tidsskrift* [Danish], iii [1900–2], 461, 490, 505); cf. J. E. Olesen, *Unionskrige og stændersamfund 1450–1481* (Århus, 1983), p. 374; G. Carlsson,

Figure 2 Seal of Philippa, Queen of Norway, Sweden and Denmark, showing the coat-of-arms of Denmark, Sweden, Norway, Pomerania, France and England: 's' .philippe.dei.gracia.dacie.suecie.noruegie.schlaourum. gotorumque.regine.et dua' pomeranie' (*Norske Konge-Sigiller og andre Fyrste-Sigiller fra Middelalderen* [Kristiana/Oslo, 1924], pl. 19)

she bore four sons for Christian. The elder two, Olav and Knut, died at an early age, while John (Hans), the third, succeeded his father as Scandinavian 'union-king' in 1483, and Frederick, the youngest and his mother's favourite, became duke of Slesvig and Holstein. Much later, Frederick (I) was elected King of Denmark (1523) and Norway (1524), following the flight of his nephew Christian II.

Christina (pl. 6) was daughter of Prince Elector Ernst of Saxony and Elizabeth of Bavaria. She married Crown Prince John in Copenhagen in 1478, and became queen of Denmark and Norway in 1483. In 1499 she was also crowned queen of Sweden. Their son Christian (II) was elected king of Denmark and Norway in

'Drottning Dorotheas svenska morgongåfva', *Historisk Tidskrift* (Swedish), 1911 (Stockholm, 1912), 238–68.

1513. He was also duly elected king of Sweden, but the Swedish opposition effectively resisted his claims on the throne until 1520.

Isabella of Habsburg, the last Scandinavian 'union-queen', was daughter of Archduke Philip of Burgundy and Queen Joan of Spain. She married Christian II in Copenhagen in 1515, after long and troublesome negotiations with Emperor Maximillian, Isabella's grandfather, initiated on Christian's behalf by his uncle, Prince Elector Frederick of Saxony, in 1513. The marriage treaty, which guaranteed Isabella a dowry amounting to 250,000 guilders, was concluded in Enns on 29 April 1514, but when the royal envoy arrived in Brussels in the early summer of 1515 to bring the child-queen to her new homeland, her brother Archduke Charles protested. He and his councillors would not let Isabella go unless Christian sent away his mistress Dyveke.[9] The archbishop of Trondheim, Eric Valkendorf, who was leader of the embassy, solved the delicate problem by promising to persuade Christian to abandon Dyveke (which he never did). Archbishop Eric, the former royal favourite, ended his life as a refugee in Rome. Unlike her predecessors Isabella took no part in politics, and at the age of twenty-two (in 1523) she was driven into exile with her husband.

If we consider our list of 'union queens' in a longer medieval perspective stretching back to the Vikings, they provide clear evidence of a significant shift in the foreign relations of the Scandinavian monarchies. Where they had previously directed their attention and ambitions towards each other and their Baltic and West European neighbours, in the fifteenth century they turned towards Germany. It is no exaggeration to state that from the reign of Christian I, Scandinavian royal politics were thoroughly enmeshed in the world of German territorial princes. Our list of queens also gives clear evidence of the preponderance of Danish interests in union affairs and in its external relations once we move into the fifteenth century.

'Union-queenship'

The cases of the queens Margaret Sambiria of Denmark (d. 1282) and Ingeborg Eriksdatter of Norway (1244–87) show that the combined role of widow and king-mother could bring women to the top in politics and government in the high Middle Ages. Also the Swedish duchess Ingeborg, daughter of the Norwegian king Håkon V and mother of the 'union-king' Magnus Eriksson, based her aggressive dynastic foreign politics in the early 1320s on her status as widow and guardian of her son. Margaret, too, dowager-queen of Norway, and King Valdemar's daughter, legitimised her political positions in Denmark and Norway from 1376 to 1387 on the guardianship of her minor son Olav, and after 1380 on being the only adult representative of the united dynasties of Norway-Sweden and Denmark.[10] Even though she ruled the Scandinavian kingdoms in her own name from

---

[9] *Diplomatarium Norvegicum* (= *DN*), XVII no. 1177, cf. C. F. Allen, *De tre nordiske Rigers Historie under Hans, Christiern den Anden, Frederik den Forste, Gustav Vasa, Grevefeiden, 1497–1536*, 5 vols (Copenhagen, 1864–72), ii, 102.

[10] H. Nielsen, 'Formynderstyre', *Kulturhistorisk leksikon for nordisk middelalder* (= *KLNM*), iv (Copenhagen, 1959), col. 494.

1387 to 1396, she acted in fact as a kind of stepmother for the Norwegian king Eric after 1389. It may well be argued that her political 'stepmothership' continued until 1412, and that Margaret's status as progenitor of the new dynasty of Norway from 1388 gave her a dynastic platform for ruling the Union after 1396/97, though of course not in any legal sense.[11] Margaret always referred to her own position in dynastic terms, i.e. as queen (wife and mother), daughter or heir.[12]

Though basically dynastic Margaret's position from 1387 onwards was formally that of an elected regent, a unique political construction in Scandinavia. In Denmark and Sweden her regency was intended to be of an interim nature, to be terminated the moment that an acceptable male candidate had been found for the empty thrones. In Norway, on the other hand, Queen Margaret was elected regent for life and was empowered to renew the dynasty through the adoption of an heir of her choice. This irregular proceeding must be assumed to have been adopted as a way out of the problem which arose when her son, King Olav, died. The next in line of succession was Albert of Mecklenburg, King of Sweden. Margaret adopted her sister's grandson Eric and had him proclaimed hereditary king of Norway. This solved the legal problem posed by the Mecklenburg succession in Norway, and it gave Margaret a head start when the search for alternatives to the Mecklenburgers was on in both Sweden and Denmark. Margaret's status as Norwegian sovereign for life was altered on the accession of Eric in 1389. Her position was normalised, and her regency in Norway was then defined as interim. This turn of events clearly indicates the objective of the legal constructions brought about by the crisis of 1387–8.

Margaret's special status in Norway is evidence of a close and trusting relationship between King Håkon's widow and the Norwegian nobility, who from all the evidence seem to have supported her loyally through all these dynastic manoeuvres.[13] One of the leading members of the Norwegian Council of the Realm, Håkon Jonsson, even renounced his own hereditary rights to the crown.[14] Regardless of her shifting formal status, from 1387/88 Queen Margaret ruled all three kingdoms, united in her hands, and with full royal powers.

The documents from the meeting of the Scandinavian grandees at Kalmar in 1397 to crown Eric clearly presume Margaret's immediate retirement. However, as we have already seen, she continued to rule the lands of the three crowns effectively long after Eric came of age (around 1400) and up to her death. We have no evidence that Eric resented this state of affairs, but rather that he saw himself as a loyal apprentice in statecraft.

After 1397 Margaret started the process of turning the Union into something more than a personal union. Although she did not succeed in establishing a lasting

[11] *NglL*, 2nd ser., i, 1; cf. *ibid.*, p. 7.
[12] A. E. Christensen, *Kalmarunionen og nordisk politik 1319–1439* (Copenhagen, 1980), pp. 114, 116.
[13] S. Imsen, *Arv-annammelse-valg. En studie i norsk tronfølgerett i tidsrommet 1319–1450* (Oslo, 1972), pp. 26–31.
[14] *NglL*, 2nd ser., i, 9.

Scandinavian federation, she nevertheless did achieve a substantial political strengthening of the Union. She worked hard to build a core of effective political and administrative institutions through which the Union monarchy could govern its enormously extensive lands more effectively, and she took particular care to establish good personal relations with some leading members of the 'national' nobilities.[15] On the other hand, she systematically gave fiefs and offices in Norway and Sweden to Danes and Germans, people who were dependent on her favour alone. Margaret also developed close relations with the Roman Curia, which gave her complete control over appointments to bishoprics and ecclesiastical benefices. As the bishops were *ex officio* members of the Councils of the Realms, she thereby ensured a permanent group of loyal counsellors inside the national representations. The church also contributed to the financing of the queen's political projects.

Better than any official document, her masterly way of tackling people and situations, her political genius so to say, is exemplified in the secret instruction she gave to King Eric, then about twenty-three years old, before a visit to Norway in 1405:

'When you meet the Norwegians you must give them a drink of the good German beer which I have sent in advance,' she begins, and continues, 'At the first meeting it is important to create a friendly atmosphere. If Sir Ogmund or somebody else invites you to be his guest, you should eat with them, and if anyone, man or woman, young or old, wants to give you a gift, you must receive it thankfully, even if the gift be very humble; people might misunder-stand a rejection and become angry . . . You must also remember to pray to the Lord and be his servant, late as well as early, and mind your words; don't say too much, neither in anger nor needlessly, as this can cause great damage to yourself as well as to others . . . You should also summon the members of the Council of the Realm and do your best to establish friendly relations with them. Ask for their advice, but remember never to summon all members of the Council at once . . . If the Norwegians ask you to return the Great Seal you can answer that this will have to wait until we have found a qualified keeper . . . Nevertheless you should tell the counsellors who in your opinion might be an actual candidate, and if they protest against him, say that . . . nobody should be critical until our man has proved if he is able or not. I believe that you will never find a more competent candidate for the position of chancellor . . . Don't let anybody move you to deprive our candidate of his benefices, that is a question for us and God alone. You should know that there are a lot of people who do not like our man, partly because he is a foreigner, and partly because he stands firm on the rights of the Crown . . . And finally remember to read this instruction carefully.'[16]

---

[15] For instance Ogmund Finnson, chairman of the Norwegian Council of the Realm, who was married to Margaret's closest girlfriend Catherine, granddaughter of St Birgitta. After King Håkon's death, Ogmund took care of the internal affairs of the realm on behalf of the royal house, while Maragaret dealt with the kingdom's interests abroad (*NglL*, iii, 213, cf. *DN*, i, no. 469). In 1406 Catherine was appointed fostermother and Mistress of the Robes for Queen Philippa (Hamre, *Nòrsk historie*, p. 37).

[16] *NglL*, 2nd ser., i, 72. This is a short extract from a comprehensive and revealing document.

Margaret's politics merged the political goals of the Swedish-Norwegian dynasty (the *Folkunger*) and that of the Danish royal house. Married into the Norwegian royal family she followed up her husband's and father-in-law's struggle to re-conquer the Swedish throne. As daughter of King Valdemar she was committed to his mission of restoring the Danish monarchy and winning back Slesvig, which had been all but lost to the German counts of Holstein before 1340.[17]

Although Philippa and Dorothea were both designated future guardians and regents in case of minor kings,[18] Queen Margaret was the last to base her political career on the role of mother or stepmother. Blanche, Philippa, Dorothea, and Christina show that queens did not necessarily have to lean on a minor king to obtain political influence and position.

Throughout Magnus Eriksson's reign Queen Blanche is often seen participating in government together with her husband. They issued charters of freedom for people who had committed homicide, so-called *landsvistbrev*, they granted donations and signed treaties with foreign princes. Blanche also contracted loans with the Curia on behalf of the king and, in 1346 and 1347, together with her husband, she laid the economic foundation of the future Bridgettine convent in Vadstena (Sweden).[19] In addition to sharing in public business with her husband Blanche

---

17 The literature about Margaret is vast. The best modern survey is A. E. Christensen, *Kalmarunionen*. See also, Erslev, *Dronning Margrethe*, which is the classic work on Margaret; E. Lönnroth, *Sverige och Kalmarunionen 1397–1457* (Gothenburg, 1934); J. Rosén, 'Drottning Margaretas svenska räfst', *Scandia, Tidskrift för historisk forskning*, xx (Lund, 1950); H. Koht, *Dronning Margareta og Kalmarunionen* (Oslo, 1956); L. Hamre, *Norsk historie frå omlag 1400* (Oslo/Bergen/Tromsø, 1968); M. Linton, *Drottning Margareta. Fullmäktig fru och rätt husbonde* (Gothenburg, 1971). Cf. E. Albrectsen's review in *Historisk Tidsskrift* (Denmark), lxxvii (1977); B. Losman, 'Drottning Margaretas ekonomi och donationspolitik', *Scandia*, xxxviii (Lund, 1972); E. Albrectsen, *Herredømmet over Sønderjylland 1375–1404* (Copenhagen, 1981); E. Haŭg, *Provincia Nidrosiensis i dronning Margretes unions- og maktpolitikk* (Trondheim, 1996).

18 A. E. Christensen, *Kalmarunionen*, pp. 184–8; Olesen, *Unionskrige*, p. 129. Cf. *Diplomatarium Christierni Primi* (= *DCP*), p. 84.

19 G. A. Blom, 'Svensk og norsk i Magnus Erikssons og dronning Blancas andre testamente av 15. juli 1347', *Studier i äldre historie tillägnade Herman Schück 5/4 1985* (Stockholm, 1985). In her capacity as 'Mistress of the Robes' to the young queen the noblewoman Birgitta Birgersdatter advised the king and his queen in matters of matrimony. It is said that her advice in sexual matters provoked strong resentment from the royal couple, although it was primarily political controversies which led to the break between Magnus/Blanche and Birgitta, who after 1350 became the 'ideological leader' of the noble opposition against the king. Nevertheless, Magnus and Blanche, and after them Margaret continued to support Birgitta's plans for a Scandinavian monastic order for both men and women, especially of noble descent. At the age of twelve Queen Margaret had been sent for upbringing in the house of Birgitta's eldest daughter, Merete Ulfsdatter, and Merete's daughters Ingegerd and Catherine were Margaret's closest girlfriends. Ingegerd became a nun in Vadstena in 1374 and later abbess of the convent, and Catherine was, as we have already mentioned, appointed 'Mistress of the Robes' for Queen Philippa in 1406. It was also Margaret who brought about the final canonisation of Birgitta in 1391; she gave large donations to the Bridgettines, and was even registered as a lay sister in Vadstena. Margaret's support for the Brigittine

also ruled parts of the kingdoms herself, partly on behalf of her husband, partly in her own name. From 1358 she resided at the castle of Tønsberghus, one of the strongest fortresses in Norway, as Magnus Eriksson's personal representative in the country, administering his fiefs of Vestfold and Skienssysla. (Their youngest son Håkon had by this time come of age and had assumed his powers as king of Norway.)

In 1423 King Eric left his kingdoms for a sojourn in Italy and Germany, and for two years Queen Philippa ruled all three Scandinavian kingdoms alone, which she did with skill and authority. In Norway these years were marked by considerable social unrest and political discontent. From the Orkneys in the west to Borgarsysla in the east Philippa received supplications and written complaints. To restore order and peace and to establish relations of trust with her subjects she appointed commissions to hold public inquiries throughout the country.[20] She negotiated peace with the Hanseatic League, with which Eric had been at war for years, and she even concluded a currency convention between the Union and Lübeck.[21]

However Philippa had taken part in governmental business before Eric left his kingdoms, as in 1422, when she together with members of the Swedish Council of the Realm arbitrated a dispute between prominent members of the Swedish nobility, and Eric's return did not bring Philippa's political career to an end. In 1426 she was sent to Sweden to secure help to repulse an attack by the Hansa on Copenhagen. Philippa also received and audited Swedish county accounts during this stay, and the year after, when she had returned to Denmark, she equipped and organised a naval expedition to Stralsund.[22] She was on a public commission when

movement was motivated by pious as well as political interest. As a religious order which especially appealed to the Scandinavian nobility, the Bridgettines might forward political integration. Eric and Philippa too supported Vadstena by donations and by establishing new convents in Finland, Norway and Denmark. When the Council of Constance in 1418 questioned the validity of Birgitta's canonisation as well as the privileges which the Order had obtained in Rome during the Great Schism, King Eric, Queen Philippa and her brother King Henry V of England intervened, saving both Birgitta's canonisation and the privileges. Philippa too was registered as lay sister in Vadstena, where she died in 1430 (J. E. Olesen, 'Kongemakt, birgittinere og Kalmarunion', *Birgitta, hendes værk og hendes klostre i Norden*, ed. Tore Nyberg [Odense, 1991]). Cf. Anders Fröjmark, *Mirakler och helgonkult. Linköpings biskopsdöme under senmedeltiden*, Studia Historica Upsaliensia, 171 (Uppsala, 1992), pp. 22, 173, 190, 195. Because of Christopher's early death he did not have time to establish the same close relations with Vadstena as his predecessors, although he seem to have intended to do so. Queen Dorothea visited Vadstena in 1446, but after the first separation of Denmark and Sweden in 1448 the Bridgettines lost most of their former influence in Scandinavian politics. Dorothea, and after her Christina, instead committed themselves to the Fransiscans at home in Denmark, and neither Danish nor Norwegian bishops or noblemen were present at the enshrinement of Catherine, Birgitta's daughter, in 1489. This event was celebrated as a national Swedish one.

20 *DN*, i, 697. See also S. Imsen, *Norsk bondekommunalisme fra Magnus Lagabøte til Kristian Kvart. Del I: Middelalderen* (Trondheim, 1990), p. 173.

21 *Sverges Traktater méd främmande Magter*, iii (Stockholm, 1895), 86.

22 C. G. Styffe, *Bidrag till Skandinaviens Historie ur utländska Arkiver*, 4 vols (Stockholm,

she died in Vadstena in 1430. Queen Philippa is said to have been the only one of the 'union-monarchs' ever to have achieved popularity among the Swedes.

Queen Dorothea was also an effective manager of affairs when her husband was absent, which he often was, and she proved to be a very able administrator and a tough politician.[23] 'The queen is in Malmö now; I hope she will not come closer, but I fear she will visit Falsterbo', the local commissioner for Lübeck wrote in 1466. He was reporting to the city council about a dispute with local Danish authorities over tolls and taxes.[24] As in the case of Philippa Dorothea's participation in state affairs was not restricted to the periods of her husband's absence. All through her long public life she regularly took part in negotiations with the Hansa and with foreign princes; like Philippa she was sent to Sweden to secure military support, and she also organised on occasion the equipping of warships. She negotiated peace with the Swedes on behalf of her husband; she mediated between the Hanseatic League and the king; she instructed royal officers and commanders, collected taxes, received and audited county-accounts, etc.[25] But above all Dorothea's political talents were deployed in Slesvig.

When in 1460 her second husband Christian I was elected count of the German principalities Holstein and Stormarn and duke of the old Danish province Slesvig, these territories were dynastically united to the Danish Crown in a personal union. But Christian's lordship in the united Slesvig-Holstein could not be made effective until he had paid off all his creditors. His debts in Slesvig-Holstein were to be a major political issue in the following two decades, and it was Queen Dorothea who finally secured victory, both over the king and his creditors.

Dorothea was an outstanding economic manager. Slowly but steadily she accumulated her resources, lent out money to Christian in return for collateral security in fiefs, benefices, and royal offices, which in her hands proved very profitable – contrary to what had been her husband's experience. In the 1460s she was already redeeming mortgages in Slesvig-Holstein, and around 1470 she virtually controlled the greater part of the southern principalities. Her position there was massively strengthened during the 1470s, and in 1479 and 1480, just before Christian died, he was forced to pawn his lordship in Slesvig-Holstein to the queen. Since Holstein was German territory, this transaction was confirmed by the German emperor Frederick III.[26]

Dorothea continued to rule her principalities even after the accession of her elder son John in 1483. Contrary to the interest of the realm and the new king,

1859–75), ii (1864), xcviii; cf. *ibid.*, nos 88–9. K. Erslev, *Erik af Pommern, hans Kamp for Sønderjylland og Kalmarunionens Opløsning* (Copenhagen, 1901), p. 190. Cf. E. Jørgensen and J. Skovgaard, *Danske Dronninger* (Copenhagen, 1910), p. 65.

23 W. Christensen, *Dansk Statsforvaltning i det 15. Århundrede* (Copenhagen, 1903), p. 10. Cf. Olesen, *Unionskrige*, p. 370.

24 J. Skovgaard, 'Dorothea', *Dansk Biografisk Leksikon*, ii (Copenhagen, 1933).

25 *Missiver fra Kongerne Christiern I's og Hans's Tid* (Copenhagen, 1912–14), i, 11, 13, 21, 23, 25, 30, 38, 43, 46; ii, 67, 68, 85. Cf. Olesen, *Unionskrige*, pp. 78, 84, 146, 180, 190, 203, 213, 275, 355–9.

26 *DCP*, nos 231, 233, 240–1; cf. nos 158, 192, 227.

Dorothea now planned for the transfer of the lordship of Slesvig-Holstein to her younger son Frederick. We should notice that the old queen in this conflict with the king gave priority to the dynasty. Dorothea and John did not reach a compromise until 1487, when the lordship was split between the king and his brother Duke Frederick.[27]

Like Philippa, Christina in many of her years as 'union-queen' had to live in the shadow of an active and impressive mother-in-law. Her husband's journeys abroad were short and infrequent, and we have no evidence that she ever functioned as regent in his absences, although she was entrusted with the management of some regions. The Danish historian William Christensen, who has written the standard work on Danish administration in the fifteenth century, nevertheless holds the view that as a rule the queens of this century regularly acted as regents during the king's absence, which is confirmed by the case of Queen Isabella, Christina's daughter-in-law. Even though Isabella never interfered with or was involved in politics, she nevertheless was – at least nominally – entrusted with the government of Denmark and Norway in 1520 while her husband was busy conquering Sweden.[28] Only on one occasion do we see Christina playing a role in important politics, namely from September 1501 to May 1502, when she defended the besieged castle of Stockholm. After the surrender she was taken into custody by her husband's Swedish adversaries, and she was not released until late in the autumn of 1503.[29]

Christina had the management of her fiefs as well as counties which she had received from the king in return for loans; and she husbanded her domains very competently indeed. Her fiscal administration is better documented than that of her husband. In addition to an abundance of county accounts she has left a series of very carefully drawn household accounts for the period 1496–1520.[30] Thus Queen Christina appears to be a women of the same character as her mother-in-law, as well as her successors – queens of Denmark after 1536, namely Christian III's consort Dorothea of Saxony-Lauenburg and Frederick II's spouse Sophia of Mecklenburg-Schwerin.[31]

---

[27] For Dorothea's position in Slesvig and Holstein, see E. Arup, 'Den finansielle side af erhvervelsen af hertugdømmerne', *Historisk Tidsskrift* (Danish), 7th ser., iv, 318, 322, 332, 361–70, 373, 415, 416, 420–2, 427, 430–8, 455–75, 480, 482. Cf. Olesen, *Unionskrige*, p. 289; *idem*, 'Det danske rigsråd', p. 31.

[28] W. Christensen, *Dansk Statsforvaltning*, p. 12; *NglL*, 2nd ser., iv, 140.

[29] Allen, *De tre nordiske Rigers*, i, 292–308.

[30] W. Christensen, *Dronning Christines Hofholdningsregnskaber* (Copenhagen, 1904), pp. i–iii.

[31] S. Imsen, *Våre dronninger* (Oslo, 1991), pp. 65–71; cf. M. Mackeprang, 'Dronning Sofie og livgedinget. Et stykke dansk landbrukshistorie fra tiden 1600', *Historisk Tidsskrift* (Danish), 7th ser., iii (1900–02).

The economic foundation of 'union-queenship'

To fully understand the position of the 'union-queens' we must look closer at their economic situation. Basically their position was similar to that of their sisters – wives in the propertied classes. The main components of their economy were the dowry and the morning-gifts.[32] The system of wedding-gifts was primarily intended to secure subsistence if the wife were to survive her husband, and also to secure for her a proportioned share of her husband's estate.[33] Although in Scandinavian law dowry and morning gifts were regarded as the particular estate of the wife, she could not claim full and free possession and use of these as long as her husband lived.

The marriage treaty between King Eric Magnusson of Norway and Margaret daughter of Alexander III of Scotland concluded in Roxburgh on 25 July 1281, specified a dowry of 14,000 marks sterling for Margaret, and in return the Norwegian crown guaranteed morning-gifts amounting to 1400 silver marks per annum in rents from landed estates.[34] This is the oldest Scandinavian treaty of this kind which we know in detail. The treaty confirms what we have suspected for the preceding centuries, that morning-gifts as a rule were assigned in the form of rents from landed property, and that the king disposed of his wife's means.[35]

In our series of queens, Blanche would seem to mark a turning point. The institution of the morning-gift had until then functioned as a personal insurance for the queen. It now became much more; to some degree it became an active share in the powers and prerogatives of the Crown: it became separate property, separately administered by the queen.

Originally Blanche was enfeoffed with the castle of Tønsberghus, the town of Tønsberg and the districts belonging to the jurisdiction of Tønsberghus, i.e. Vestfold and Skiensysla at the western side of Oslofjord. In Sweden she was enfeoffed with the bailiwick of Lödöse and the castle of Linholm at Hisingen, near the mouth of the border-river Götaelv. In 1353 her Norwegian fiefs and benefices were exchanged from the western part of Oslofjord to the eastern, i.e. she surrendered the castle of Tønsberghus to her husband acquiring instead the very important border-castle of Båhus, including the jurisdiction of the town Marstrand and the counties of Båhus len (Elvesysla, Ranrike, Vetteherred) and Borgarsysla, in other words the region between Oslo and present day Gothenburg. It is possible

---

[32] A. Taranger, *Udsigt over den norske Rets Historie, IV Privatrettens Historie* (Kristiania/Oslo, 1917), p. 319; cf. L. Carlsson, S. Iuul, L. Hamre, J. Rosén, 'Morgongåva', *KLNM*, xi, col. 695–703; L. Carlsson, 'Medgift', *KLNM*, xi, cols 517–19; H. Nielsen, 'Livgeding', *KLNM*, x, cols 639–40.

[33] Taranger, *Udsigt over den norske Rets Historie, iv*, 322; cf. *KLNM*, xi, col. 520.

[34] *DN*, xix, no. 305.

[35] Even though the economic base of the queens' households as a rule was generally secured by income from crown lands, they were also assigned a share of taxes and other royal revenue. A case in point is the Danish princess Ingeborg, who in 1261 married the Norwegian heir, the later Magnus Håkonsson of Norway (H. Koht, *Norske dronningar* [Oslo, 1926], p. 34).

SCANDINAVIA IN THE LATE MIDDLE AGES

- • Towns from which queens enjoyed royal revenues.
- △ Castles held by queens
- —— Provinces ruled by queens
- --- Provinces with morning-gift towns, estates, etc.

Figure 3

that she also acquired the Swedish territories of Dalsland and Värmland on this occasion, and which she certainly possessed in 1358.[36] From now on Blanche in fact was ruler of a Norwegian-Swedish domain – we could call it a 'queendom' of her own. In addition to this her husband had granted her in 1341 an annual rent of 2 marks of gold, and in 1346 he added an annual sum from the royal revenues of the Scania fair.[37]

At the very latest Blanche took charge of her 'queendom' from 1353. As we see, the queen's morning-gifts changed radically from being a life insurance to becoming a political guarantee for the royal house, a sort of dynastic demesne under queenly rule, so to say. As I have already mentioned she also took over the administration of the castle and bailiwick of Tønsberghus on behalf of her husband. In fact Blanche and Magnus controlled all Eastern Norway south of Oslo, including the adjacent Swedish regions.

When Queen Margaret arrived in Norway, she was duly accorded these queenly domains, so strategically placed on both sides of the Swedish-Norwegian border.[38] During her reign, these lands were to become the bridgehead for the reconquest of Sweden and a laboratory for her greatest project, the union of the three Scandinavian crowns. In 1376, when her son Olav also became king of Denmark and she regent, these queenly domains were extended southwards to include the Danish border province of Halland with the castle of Varberg. From now on she ruled as her personal 'queendom' a Scandinavian union in miniature.

The political role of the 'queendom' did not cease with the unification in 1397. On Eric's accession in 1389 Margaret was guaranteed her Norwegian domains. When he was elected king of Sweden in 1396, she was enfeoffed with the greater part of Western Sweden as a sort of delayed recognition of her pretended status as Swedish queen. When Eric was duly crowned in Kalmar in 1397, her possession of all these castles, fiefs and domains was confirmed, and to them were now also added (for her lifetime) the extensive Danish domains which had been her father's gift to her. In other words, an arrangement which had originally served as security for dowager-queens had been transformed into an imperial instrument, a territorial basis for the dynastic unification of the three kingdoms with their dependencies. The decision about Margaret's 'queendom' fits perfectly well into what was decided about her and Eric's political rights as stated in the great charter which concluded the Kalmar-meeting: Hereafter Margaret and Eric should have all castles, fiefs and offices in the united kingdoms at their unrestricted disposal, not only for their own lifetime, since they were also granted the right to dispose of them in advance for their successors.[39]

As the real 'union-queen' Margaret kept full control over the whole of this

---

[36] *Regesta Norvegica* (= *RN*), v, 25, *DN*, ii, 319; cf. *RN*, v, 207, 208, vi, 431; *DN*, xviii, 21.

[37] *DN*, ii, 239, *DN*, vi, 177.

[38] The deposition of Magnus and Håkon as kings of Sweden did not affect the Swedish parts of Blanche's 'queendom', which could be transferred intact to Margaret in 1365.

[39] *NglL*, 2nd ser., i, 14, 29, 35; cf. *KLNM*, x, col. 609; xi, col. 702.

queenly demesne until her death. There was no reason to make a separate 'queendom' for Philippa, being the nominal 'union-queen'. It is uncertain whether Philippa received a dowry from her father; but she was splendidly equipped when she left England in 1406.[40] Her morning-gift-domains were not aggregated into a block like Margaret's, neither did Philippa manage her properties herself. This changed from about 1420 when the possibility that the marriage might be childless became real, and consequently the question of succession to the throne became acute. To secure the succession of Eric's Pomeranian nephew Bugislav as Scandinavian king, it was decided to establish a new 'queendom' concentrated on Central Sweden, including Stockholm and Uppsala.[41] The hold on Sweden was regarded as crucial for implementing the plans of hereditary succession to the 'union-throne'. Though Eric's dispositions were in accordance with what had been decided in Kalmar in 1397, he rightly foresaw strong resistance from the Swedes against any steps which might threaten the elective principle of succession to the throne in their country.[42] Philippa's regency for an eventual minor king was part of the arrangement for her Swedish 'queendom'.

Dorothea received a morning-gift-demesne in 1445 containing elements of the former 'union-model' of Blanche's and Margaret's 'queendoms'. In Denmark she was enfeoffed with central parts of Sjælland (Zealand), including the town of Roskilde. In Sweden her domains included the town Örebro including jurisdiction over the territories of Närke and Värmland, stretching from the Norwegian border into central parts of Sweden. The Norwegian contribution to her dowry was Jemtland and Herjedalen, a county bordering on Sweden and close to Dalarna (Dalcarlia).[43]

We have already indicated that Queen Dorothea's Swedish enfeoffments and domains would prove politically troublesome when Sweden opted out of the union in 1448.[44] The Swedish Council of the Realm confirmed Dorothea's morning gift

---

[40] Daae, *Erik af Pommerns*, p. 363; *DN*, xix, 840–59, 875. Cf. *ibid.*, nos 671, 673–9, 681, 685, 686a, b, 689, 691, 694–700, 702a, b, 709.

[41] Originally Philippa's morning-gift domains were the province of *Romerike* in Norway, *Örebro* castle with town and county in Sweden, and *Nesbyhoved* castle and the town of *Odense* in Denmark. According to the 1420 arrangement her new morning-gift-demesne should consist of *Örebro* castle, town and county, the county of *Närke* with mines, the town of *Arboga* with mines, the hundreds of *Lagalösekjöping* and *Snevinga*, *Västerås* castle, town and county, *Uppsala* town and county, *Stockholm* castle with town and county, the county of *Östhammar*, and *Tälje* castle, town and county, all in the central province of *Uppland*, Sweden. Until this arrangement could be implemented she should enjoy all royal revenues from Sjælland, including castles and towns.

[42] *NglL*, 2nd ser., i, 90–105; cf. Erslev, *Erik af Pommern*, p. 114; Olesen, *Unionskrige*, p. 229. Cf. *idem*, 'Det danske rigsråd, kong Hans og Kalmarunionen', *Struktur og funktion. Festskrift til Erling Ladewig Petersen* (Copenhagen, 1994), p. 28.

[43] *NglL*, 2nd ser., i, 266; G. Carlsson, 'Drottning Dorotheas morgongåfva', *Historisk Tidskrift* (Swedish), 1911 (Stockholm, 1912), p. 230.

[44] Olesen, *Unionskrige*, pp. 9, 23, 64, 120, 135, 139, 229, 267, 359, 392; *idem*, 'Die doppelte Königswahl 1448 im Norden', *Mare Balticum*; Olesen, 'Det danske rigsråd', p. 34.

of 1445 when they recognised Christian I as king of Sweden in 1457. In the years that followed, up to 1464 when Christian was deposed in Sweden, Dorothea was in full and effective possession of her various Swedish, Norwegian and Danish domains. For the rest of her life Dorothea fought fiercely for her rights in Sweden, but in vain. She even managed to get Sten Sture, the Swedish regent, excommunicated by the pope.

In the marriage treaty between Ernest of Saxony and King Christian I, Christina's morning-gift was stipulated as an annual payment of 4000 guilders.[45] We do not know if any new arrangements was made in regard to Christina's morning-gifts after her elevation as queen. However, as dowager queen, free from a domineering mother-in-law, we see her in possession of central towns and rural domains in Fyn and Jylland.[46] We know very little if anything about her possessions in Norway.[47] At her coronation in Uppsala in 1499 Christina was granted the very same morning-gift-domain which her mother-in-law had fought for over decades. The Swedish letter of donation stated that the queen should dispose freely of all her possessions from the first day. That this did not happen can be read from the so-called Kalmar-sentence of 1505, which confirmed Christina's rights in Sweden.[48]

During the second half of the fifteenth century the 'Union' changed from being a dynastic confederation to become an instrument for Danish supremacy in Scandinavia, which the Swedes successfully managed to resist. After Queen Dorothea's death the political content of a separate 'queendom' as territorial guarantor of the dynastic union of Scandinavia seems to have lost all meaning. In spite of her Swedish coronation, Christina was in fact a Danish-Norwegian queen only. After her time, and after the dissolution of the Union in 1523, the Scandinavian queenship was deprived of its former political significance.

We may draw some clear conclusions from this sketchy review of Scandinavia's queens in the late Middle Ages. The unification of Norway, Denmark, and Sweden invested the queens with a key role. This role had important economic and political dimensions, and gave these women unprecedented possibilities to deploy political and administrative talent and even statecraft. Those who filled these roles include a group of extraordinarily gifted women. However, it was not their talents which opened up the political field to these queens, but rather a unique situation, lasting from the second half of the fourteenth century until about 1500, combined with the dynastic framework of Scandinavian politics in the late Middle Ages. The

---

[45] *DCP*, no. 220.

[46] In Denmark, Christina possessed *Trankær* (Langeland), *Rougsø herred* (Jylland), *Ribe* (Jylland), *Kolding* (Jylland), *Varde* (Jylland), *Randers* (Jylland), *Viborg* (Jylland), *Odense* (Fyn), *Svendborg* (Fyn), *Nesbyhoved* (Fyn), *Assens* (Fyn), *Bogense* (Fyn), *Kerteminde* and *Købing* at Mors (Jylland): W. Christensen, *Dansk Statsforvaltning*, p. 18.

[47] Olesen, 'Det danske rigsråd', p. 31.

[48] In Sweden Christina was granted *Örebro* castle with town and county, the provinces of *Närke, Värmland,* and *Dalsland,* and the mines of *Nordskog: Sverges Traktater,* iii, 510, 703; cf. Allen, *De tre nordiske Rigers,* i, 357.

processes which went into the forming of the modern state in Scandinavia can be traced back to 1520s. This development deprived the queens of a significant political role, and relegated them to the sphere of court intrigues and the closed circle of private (albeit royal) family life.

Plate 4 Margaret, Queen of Norway, Sweden, and Denmark (daughter of Valdemar IV of Denmark). At the age of twelve, in 1365, she moved from her foster mother Merete Ulfsdatter, St Birgitta's daughter, to live with her 25-year-old husband Håkon VI in Oslo. The royal couple had only one child, Olav, born at Akershus castle in 1370. Margaret made her début as politician after her father's death in 1375, fighting for Olav's candidature to the Danish throne. Olav was elected king of Denmark in 1376, and succeeded his father as hereditary king of Norway in 1380, when he also claimed to be the lawful king of Sweden. It was his sudden death in 1387 which led to the election of Margaret as regent of Denmark and Norway, and somewhat later in Sweden as well. (Museum für Kunst & Kulturgeschichte der Hansestadt Lübeck)

Plate 5

Plate 6 Queens Christina and Isabella, and Christina's daughter Elisabeth, married to the electoral prince of Brandenburg. Queen Christina settled in Odense in her old age, devoting much of her time to pious work, especially for the Franciscans. She also spent a lot of money on art and artists. This altarpiece was commissioned for the Franciscan convent of Odense. Today it can be seen in the church of St Knut in Odense. The sculptor was Claus Berg, who was in Christina's service. Claus's son Frants, named after St Francis, was later appointed Lutheran superintendant (bishop) in Oslo. (F. Beckett, *Danmarks Kunst. Annen Del: Gotiken* [Copenhagen, 1926], p. 231; cf. *ibid.*, pp. 168, 202–205, 209, 218–21)

Plate 5 (opposite) Dorothea of Brandenburg, Queen of Denmark, Norway and Sweden, here portrayed on a copy of an altarpiece which she commissioned at Christian I's death in 1481. The copy can be seen in the castle of Fredriksborg in Denmark. (Nationalhistoriske Mueseum på Fredriksborg)

5

From Famous Empresses to Unspectacular Queens: The Romano-German Empire to Margaret of Brabant, Countess of Luxemburg and Queen of the Romans (d. 1311)

Kurt-Ulrich Jäschke*

General trends in the history of queens in the Romano-German empire

Anyone looking at the history of queens and empresses in the medieval empire from Ottonian times onwards will be struck by the very great contrasts between the renowned women of the earlier period and the pale shadows who were their thirteenth- and fourteenth-century successors. In the great age there were seven distinguished imperial women. From the tenth century come Adelheid, second wife of Otto I, and her daughter-in-law Theophano. Recently called 'the holy mother of kings',[1] Adelheid has enjoyed popular fame since Gertrud Bäumer's novel *Adelheid – Mother of the Kingdoms*,[2] which opens with a quotation attributed to Gerbert, 'It is manifest, to be sure, that you have been until now the most famous lady and mother of the kingdoms' (988),[3] while Theophano is famous for her regency for her son Otto III, which culminated in the issue of diplomas in her

---

* This paper could not be printed as read at the conference and as offered by the author in July 1995. Rearrangements, abbreviations, summaries and changed emphases are due to Anne Duggan and Janet Nelson.

1 K. Schreiner, 'Hildegard, Adelheid und Kunigunde. Leben und Verehrung heiliger Herrscherinnen im Spiegel ihrer deutschsprachigen Lebensbeschreibungen aus der Zeit des späten Mittelalters', *Spannungen und Widersprüche. Gedenkschrift für František Graus*, edd. S. Burghartz, H.-J. Gilomen *et al.* (Sigmaringen, 1992), p. 41, title for ch. 2, 'Adelheid, die heilige Mutter von Königen'. Cf. the epithet *Genetrix regum* applied to the second wife of Charlemagne (d. 783): *MGH, Poet. Lat*, i/2 (1881), 59 no. 22.

2 *Adelheid – Mutter der Königreiche* (Tübingen, 1936; 1962: 106,000).

3 'Certe clarissimam dominam ac matrem regnorum vos hactenus fuisse manifestum est': *Die Briefsammlung Gerberts von Reims*, ed. F. Weigle, *MGH, Die Briefe der deutschen Kaiserseit* (Weimar/Boehlau/Berlin, 1949–), ii (1966), 156 no. 128 (the sender was probably Archbishop Adalbero of Reims, not Gerbert). Weigle compares this text with *ibid.*, p. 105 (from 986) and even with p. 43 (from 984). The heading in 'M, D' also has *mater regnorum* (*ibid.*, p. 155), which, from this letter alone, has been registered in the index, *ibid.*, p. 276, though it is the editors' supposition only. Dated 987 by Bäumer; but cf. *Lettres de Gerbert 983–997*, ed. J. Havet, Collection de textes, 6 (Paris, 1889), pp. lxxiii, 115 n. 7, which dates it Aug. 988.

own name, some of which used the masculine style. 'Theophanius gratia divina imperator augustus' and 'anno vero imperii domni [!] Theophanii imperatoris' are the intitulation and part of the dating formula of a diploma issued from Ravenna on 1 April 990.[4] From the eleventh century come Cunigunde, acclaimed co-foundress of the bishopric of Bamberg (1007), venerated as an officially canonised saint from 1200; Gisela, praised by Wipo as the most important counsellor of her third husband, Conrad II;[5] and Agnes, widow of the Emperor Henry III, regent for her son Henry IV, whose guardianship she spectacularly lost in the 'royal kidnap of Kaiserswerth' in 1062.[6] And from the twelfth century come the self-styled Empress Matilda, more widely known for her position in England and Normandy than for her period as the wife of Emperor Henry V, and Constance I, whose marriage to the future emperor Henry VI brought the Staufen to Sicily.[7] Compared with these, the wives of the later Romano-German kings – styled 'kings of the Romans' (*reges Romanorum*) in their own times – seem virtually unknown. Who, even among medieval specialists, knows much about Yolande of Aragon (d. 1300), wife of Alfonso of Castile, or Sancha of Provence (d. 1261) and Beatrice of Valkenburg (d. 1277), wives of Richard of Cornwall, or even of Gertrude of Hohenberg (d. 1281), Agnes of Burgundy (d. 1323),[8] Imagina of Isenburg-

---

4 D Theophano, 2 in *Ottonis III. Diplomata*, ed. T. Sickel, *MGH DRG*, ii/2 (1893), 876–7.
5 Cf. K.-U. Jäschke, '*Tamen virilis probitas in femina vicit.* Ein hochmittelalterlicher Hofkapellan und die Herrscherinnen – Wipos Äußerungen über Kaiserinnen und Königinnen seiner Zeit', *Ex Ipsis Rerum Documentis. Beiträge zur Mediävistik. Festschrift für Harald Zimmermann zum 65. Geburtstag*, edd. K. Herbers, H. H. Kortüm and C. Servatius (Sigmaringen, 1991), p. 435; *idem, Notwendige Gefährtinnen. Königinnen der Salierzeit als Herrscherinnen und Ehefrauen im römisch-deutschen Reich des 11. und beginnenden 12. Jahrhunderts*, Historie und Politik, 1 (Saarbrücken-Scheidt, 1991), p. 53, *et passim*; *Wiponis Gesta Chuonradi II. imperatoris*, c. 4, ed. H. Breßlau, *Wiponis opera*, 3rd edn, *MGH SRG*, lxi (1915; repr. 1965), 25–6: 'ex consensu et peticione principum consecrata necessaria comes regem sequebatur. Haec de regina interim breviavi.'
6 Cf. K.-U. Jäschke, *Zu Königinnen und Kaiserinnen der Salierzeit*, Forschungen zur Geschlechterdifferenz, 1–2 (Würzburg, 1992), pp. 8–11, 46–7. Now a northern suburb of Düsseldorf, Kaiserswerth was an island in the Rhine with collegiate church and imperial palace; cf. T. Struve, 'Kaiserswerth', *Lex. des MA*, v/4 (1990), 860–1.
7 See the novel by 'H. Benrath' (pseudonym for A. H. Rausch, 1882–1949), *Die Kaiserin Konstanze. Ein heroisches Frauenleben aus der zweiten Hälfte des 12. Jahrhunderts* (Stuttgart, 1935; Munich, 1979; Stuttgart, 1986). Rausch specialised in the lives of reigning women: *Die Kaiserin Galla Placidia* (Stuttgart, 1937; repr. Munich, 1990), *Die Kaiserin Theophano. Historischer Roman* (Stuttgart, 1940; 2nd edn Munich, 1978; repr. Stuttgart, 1991). Cf. M. Stratmann, 'Nachleben und Popularisierung', in *Kaiserin Theophanu. Begegnung des Ostens und Westens um die Wende des ersten Jahrtausends. Gedenkschrift*, ii, edd. A. von Euw and P. Schreiner (Cologne, 1991), p. 423 and nn. 51–2, where the dates 1935 and 1937 for the novels are interchanged, and 'Rauch' and 'Theophan*u*' are misprints.
8 For the various forms of her name, see W. K. Prinz von Isenburg, *Stammtafeln zur Geschichte der europäischen Staaten*, ed. (2nd) Frank Baron Freytag von Loringhoven, i (Marburg, 1953), table 6, 'Agnes'; F.-R. Erkens, 'Rudolf I.', *Lex. des MA*, vii/5 (1994), 1072, 'Isabella/Elisabeth'; K.-F. Krieger, *Die Habsburger im Mittelalter. Von Rudolf I. bis [zu] Friedrich III.*, Urban-Taschenbuch, 452 (Stuttgart, etc., 1994), p. 63, 'Isabella'; p. 238 (genealogical table), 'Agnes (Isabella)'.

Limburg (d. 29 September, after 1313), Elizabeth of Görz-Tyrol (d. 1313), or Margaret of Brabant (d. 1311)?

The English reader will consult the *New Encyclopaedia Britannica* in vain;[9] the German reader will find no mention of Yolande, Sancha, Beatrice, Agnes or Imagina in the Brockhaus *Enzyklopädie*,[10] where Gertrude of Hohenburg occurs only in the genealogical table of the Habsburgs.[11] The latest edition of Brockhaus includes a new article on Elizabeth of Görz-Tyrol, emphasising her efficient defence of her children's inheritance after the death of her husband Albert I in 1308[12] – perhaps echoing on a grand scale the efforts of Empress Theophano after Otto II's death in 984.[13] But Margaret of Brabant, 'Queen of the Romans' (*regina Romanorum*),[14] has not benefited from this new attitude of the Brockhaus editors towards Elizabeths[15] and Margarets[16] during the last twenty years. Although the art historian knows Margaret from the sculpture by Giovanni Pisano in Genoa,[17] she does not appear in the index of what is still the most useful handbook of

[9] See the index to the 1988 impression of the 15th edn, *s.vv.* Yolande, Sancha and Beatrice, Gertrude, Agnes/Elizabeth/Isabella, Imagina, Elizabeth, and Margaret; cf. also *s.v.* Richard of Cornwall, *ibid.*, x (1988), 44–5.

[10] Cf. vol. xxv of the 2nd edn, 24 vols (Mannheim, 1986–94); there was no index to the 1st edn, 20 vols (Wiesbaden, 1966–74).

[11] Brockhaus, 2nd edn, ix (1989), 334.

[12] Brockhaus, 2nd edn, vi (1988), 312, not to be found in *idem*, 1st edn, v (1968), 461; cf. below n. 86. Anna, eldest daughter, m. (1) Hermann of Brandenburg (d. 1308) 1295, (2) Henry VI of Silesia-Breslau 1310 (*Die Habsburger. Ein biographisches Lexikon*, ed. B. Hamann, [Vienna/Munich, 1988; 3rd edn 1993], pp. 51–2); Agnes, 'eldest daughter' [!], m. Andrew III of Hungary (d. 1301) 1296 (*ibid.*, p. 29); Elizabeth m. Frederick [I]V of Lorraine (d. 1328[/29]) 1307 (*ibid.*, pp. 82–3); Catherine m. Charles of Calabria 1316 (*ibid.*, p. 232); Guta-Jutta m. Louis IV of Oettingen 1319 (*ibid.*, p. 160). The articles in Hamann's *Lexikon* have their authors' initials, but Winfried Stelzer (Vienna) has expressed reservations about the handling and presentation of his articles. I therefore generally omit the authors' names when citing this dictionary.

[13] Sophia, abbess of Gandersheim (1002–39) and Essen (1011–39); Adelheid, abbess of Quedlinburg (999–1043), Frohse, Vreden, Gernrode (1014–43), and Gandersheim (1039–43): W. Glocker, *Die Verwandten der Ottonen und ihre Bedeutung in der Politik. Studien zur Familienpolitik und zur Genealogie des sächsischen Kaiserhauses*, Dissertationen zur mittelalterlichen Geschichte, 5 (Cologne/Vienna, 1989), pp. 295, 424. Mathilda (d. 1025) m. Ezzo, count palatine of Lotharingia: before Theophano's death (15.vi.991) according to M. Parisse, 'Ezzo', *Lex. des MA*, iv/1 (1987), 197; possibly after her death, according to Gerhard [!] Althoff, 'Mathilde', *ibid.*, vi/2 (1992), 392; Glocker (*Verwandten der Ottonen*, p. 295) dates the marriage *c.* 993.

[14] Cf. *Urkunden- und Quellenbuch zur Geschichte der altluxemburgischen Territorien bis zur burgundischen Zeit*, ed. C. Wampach, vii (Luxemburg, 1949), 448 no. 1370 (15.v.1311), Cremona (or.), etc.

[15] Brockhaus, v (1968), 461–4 contained eighteen dynastic women of this name; 2nd edn, vi (1988), 312–14 only sixteen.

[16] Brockhaus, xii (1971), 131–2 has separate articles on nine of them; the 2nd edn, xiv (1991), 193–4 also contains nine, but Margaret Rose, countess of Snowdon, is omitted in favour of Queen Margarete II of Denmark (1972–).

[17] *Giovanni Pisano a Genova*, ed. M. Seidel (Genoa, 1987).

German history, and in the text she is confused with her aunt,[18] while Newcomer's study on 'the Grand Duchy of Luxemburg' does not even mention her name.[19] Modern official Luxemburg knows Margaret quite well, however. Her marriage to Henry VII in 1292 was an element in the spectacular reconciliation between Brabant and Luxemburg after the Limburg war, and her unexpected death at Genoa in 1311 is recorded as a grievous loss on her husband's journey to Rome.[20]

Margaret of Brabant is usually presented as the second of three German queens crowned at Aachen, the first being Gertrude of Hohenberg (1273) and the third being King Sigismund's second queen in 1414.[21] But Thietmar of Merseburg's succinct summary of Widukind's profuse narrative of the events at Aachen in 936 records that Otto I had his English wife Edith[22] consecrated shortly after himself,[23] presumably in the same place,[24] if not in the same liturgical ceremony.[25]

---

18 B. Gebhardt, *Handbuch der deutschen Geschichte*, 9th edn, ed. H. Grundmann, i (Stuttgart, 1970), 876; Grundmann, 'Wahlkönigtum, Territorial- bewegung und Ostbewegung im 13. und 14. Jahrhundert, 1198–1378', *ibid.*, pp. 507–8, '. . . hatte Heinrich VII. die Schwester [!] des siegreichen Herzogs Johann [I.] von Brabant geheiratet', which remains uncorrected in the paperback edition (1973; 8th edn 1985), p. 145.

19 J. Newcomer (Lanham, 1984), pp. 87, 337 [index].

20 G. Trausch, 'Die Verlockung eines großen Reiches. Die politischen Verflechtungen des Hauses Luxemburg im Europa des 13. und 14. Jahrhundert[s]', *Voilà Luxembourg*, vii (Luxemburg, 1995), 35, 37. The date '5 May 1288' (p. 34) should read '5 June'. For the date of her death, see Wampach, *UQB*, vii (1949), 473–6 no. 1389 (14.xii.1311); H. Thomas, 'Margarete von Brabant', *Lex. des MA*, vi/2 (1992), 235. A. Mussatus, *Historia Augusta* [*Albertini Mussati Paduani . . . de gestis Heinrici VII. caesaris Historia Augusta*], v. 4, ed. L. A. Muratori, *Rerum Italicarum Scriptores*, x (Milan, 1727), 404 has 13.xii, cited by Böhmer, *Regesten Heinrichs VII*, p. 298. But the arguments in *Die Romfahrt Kaiser Heinrichs VII. im Bildercyclus des Codex Balduini Trevirensis*, ed. G. Irmer (Berlin, 1881), pp. 60–1, point to her death *in crastino sancte Lucie*.

21 The following statistics correct the last sentence in Jäschke, *Notwendige Gefährtinnen*, p. 240, which rashly relied on Irmer, *Romfahrt*. He names Sigismund's queen as 'Eleonore' (p. 22); but she is usually called 'Barbara' and was born a countess of Cilli; cf. Isenburg, *Stammtafeln*, i, table 6; Freytag von Loringhoven, *Europäische Stammtafeln*, iii (Marburg, 1956), table 108; and the articles on 'Barbara von Cilli' in *ADB*, ii (1875), 48; *NDB*, i (1953), 581; *Lex. des MA*, i (1980), 1433. Irmer may have confused Sigismund's queen and Empress Barbara (d. 1451) with Eleonore of Portugal (d. 1467), whom Frederick III married in 1452; cf. *ibid.*, iii (1986), 1804.

22 *Widukindi monachi Corbeiensis Rerum gestarum Saxonicarum libri III*, ii.1–2, 5th edn, ed. P. Hirsch and H.-E. Lohmann, *MGH SRG*, lx (1935), 63–7, devastatingly analysed by J. Fried, *Der Weg in die Geschichte. Die Ursprünge Deutschlands bis 1024*, Propyläen Geschichte Deutschlands, 1 (Berlin, 1994), pp. 481–6.

23 Cf. the separate *ordo* in *Ordines coronationis imperialis*, ed. R. Elze, *MGH Fontes*, ix (1960), 6–9 no. 3 (*c.* 900 from West Frankia); cf. new paragraphs from the second half of the tenth century in no. 4b (*ibid.*, p. 12).

24 *Die Chronik des Bischofs Thietmar von Merseburg*, ii.1, ed. R. Holtzmann, *MGH SRG*, NS, ix (1935; repr. 1955), 38: 'ad Aquasgrani proficiscuntur. Quo . . . Confortatus in Deo tunc et in regno sceptriferorum maximus Otto coniugem suam Editham, Ethmundi regis Anglorum filiam [!] bene timoratam, quam patre suo adhuc vivente duxerat, consecrari precepit.' The modern analytical narrative is H. Beumann, *Die Ottonen*, Urban-Taschen-bücher, 384 (Stuttgart, etc., 1987; 2nd edn 1991), pp. 53–5.

25 Cf. picture 4b for 6.i.1309 in Irmer, *Romfahrt*, opposite p. 20; *Kaiser Heinrichs Romfahrt*.

Nineteenth-century scholars were disinclined to accept Thietmar's testimony, on the grounds that he had committed retrospective adulteration by tainting past with present practice.[26] But Thietmar was familiar with the custom of separate consecrations for queens. The only consecration of a Romano-German queen during his lifetime had been that of Cunigunde, wife of Henry II. This had been a wholly separate ceremony. Henry II had been chosen and consecrated at Mainz in June, 1002, but the double consecration of the queen and an Ottonian abbess took place at Paderborn in August.[27] Thietmar described these events without reservation or ambiguity. He would presumably have described Edith's consecration in the same way, if he had been aware of a wholly separate ceremony.[28]

Separate ceremonies for queens were normal practice up to and including the consecration of Richenza,[29] wife of Lothar III, in 1125. He was consecrated at Aachen on Sunday, 13 September, and she at Cologne at some later but unrecorded date.[30] Thereafter, when one finds exceptions, one should look for special political circumstances which required *joint* ceremonies of legitimation.[31] The coronation of the rival king Conrad III on the feast of SS Peter and Paul at Monza in 1128 may be thought of as one such example.[32] A further case was the Roman consecration of Emperor Henry VII in 1313.[33] Yet others are the two consecrations

Die Bilderchronik von Kaiser Heinrich VII. und Kurfürst Balduin von Luxemburg 1308–1313, ed. F.-J. Heyen (Boppard, 1965; slightly changed = dtv.1358, Munich 1978), p. 59; *Il Viaggio di Enrico VII in Italia*, ed. M. Tosti-Croce (Città di Castello, 1993), p. 79.

26 R. [A.] Köpke/E. Dümmler, *Kaiser Otto der Große*, JDG, 9 (Leipzig, 1876), pp. 38–9 n. 2, 41–2; BO 55h, p. 34. Cf. H. Vollrath, 'Die Landnahme der Angelsachsen nach dem Zeugnis der erzählenden Quellen', *Ausgewählte Probleme europäischer Landnahmen des Früh- und Hochmittelalters*, i, ed. M. Müller-Wille and R. Schneider, Vorträge und Forschungen, 41/i (Sigmaringen, 1993), 336; P. E. Schramm, *Kaiser, Könige und Päpste. Gesammelte Aufsätze zur Geschichte des MA*, iii (Stuttgart, 1969), 80, 119; G. Wolf, 'Königinnen-Krönungen des frühen Mittelalters bis zum Beginn des Investiturstreits', *ZRG*, cvii, *Kan. Abt.*, lxxvi (1990), 70–1; Jäschke, *Notwendige Gefährtinnen*, p. 44 (relying on Schramm). Some constitutional historians conceded the possibility of separate ceremonies: G. Waitz, *Deutsche Verfassungsgeschichte*, 2nd edn, vi (Berlin, 1896), 258 no. 3. First crowned queen in Germany: M. Kirchner, *Die deutschen Kaiserinnen in der Zeit von Konrad I. bis zum Tode Lothars von Supplinburg*, Historische Studien, ed. E. Ebering, 79 (Berlin, 1910), p. 115; P. Krull, 'Die Salbung und Krönung der deutschen Königinnen und Kaiserinnen im MA', Phil. Diss. Halle-Wittenberg (Halle, 1911), p. 22. Possibly anointed: F.-R. Erkens, 'Die Frau als Herrscherin in ottonisch-frühsalischer Zeit', in *Kaiserin Theophanu*, ii, 258. Some of the following arguments for Edith's consecration are voiced by K. Leyser, 'Die Ottonen und Wessex', *Frühmittelalterliche Studien*, xvii (1983), 81–2 (trans. 'The Ottonians and Wessex', in Leyser, *Communications and Power in Medieval Europe. The Carolingian and Ottonian Centuries*, ed. T. Reuter [London, 1994], ch. 5).
27 *Regesta Imperii*, ii/4 (1971), nos 1483yy and 1496a.
28 Thietmar, *Chronicon*, v. 13 (p. 243).
29 Kirchner, *Deutsche Kaiserinnen*, pp. 116ff; Krull, *Salbung und Krönung*, pp. 22–3 and 27–33.
30 *Regesta Imperii*, vi/1/i (1994) no. 93 p. 62.
31 H. Decker-Hauff, 'Das Staufische Haus', Catalogue, *Die Zeit der Staufer*, iii (Stuttgart, 1977), p. 350 in no. 37; Krull, *Salbung und Krönung*, p. 63 was sceptical.
32 *Regesta Imperii*, vi/1/i (1994), no. 166, not mentioning Gertrud of Comburg.
33 *Regesten Heinrichs VII.*, ed. J. F. Böhmer in *idem*, ed., *Regesta Imperii inde ab anno*

of Irene-Mary Angelos and Philip of Suabia, at Mainz on Lady Day in September, 1198[34] and again at Aachen on the Epiphany, 1205.[35] The same place and highly significant feast-day were chosen by Margaret of Brabant and Henry VII in 1309.[36] Other examples are the Aachen coronations of Richard of Cornwall and Sancha of Provence in 1257;[37] of Rudolf I of Habsburg and Gertrude-Anna of Hohenberg in 1273;[38] of Imagina of Isemburg-Limburg and Adolf of Nassau in 1292;[39] of Henry VII and Margaret of Brabant in 1309;[40] and of Beatrix of Glogau and Lewis of Bavaria in 1314.[41] One might add to these Aachen statistics the fact that Henry (VII, *der Klammersiebente*),[42] son of Frederick II, had his wife demonstatively consecrated at Aachen in 1227.[43]

This general picture is readily explained by reference to the intricate connection between queens and kings and by the constitutional, political and economic position of kingship in the Romano-German empire. That connection is to be understood as a legal dependence of the queen, in her role as the king's wife, mother or grandmother only. As such she lost overriding influence, though not necessarily individual command of local and personal loyalties, when her husband died and when there was no son under age to be looked after – or if he was taken away from her. The position of Empress Adelheid, the *mater regnorum* of 988, cited above, reflected these conditions. Her young grandson Otto III was nominally on the Romano-German throne, while Emma, her daughter (d. 989 at the earliest)

MCCXLVI usque ad annum MCCCXIII, 1 vol. + 2 supplements (Stuttgart, 1844–57), p. 302; K.-U. Jäschke, 'Imperator Heinricus' (= Beiheft [1] zu Hémecht, Luxemburg 1988), pp. 81–8, commenting on *ibid.*, pp. 123–4 §15.

34 *Regesta Imperii*, v/1 (1881), no. 19a and *ibid.*, v/2 (1882), no. 5528f (8.ix.1198); Decker-Hauff, 'Staufisches Haus', p. 356 in no. 70; H. Grotefend, *Taschenbuch der Zeitrechnung des deutschen MA. und der Neuzeit*, 12th edn, ed. Jürgen Asch (Hanover, 1982), p. 159, table 8; *ibid.*, p. 113: 'gekr. Sept. 5' (a misprint).

35 *Regesta Imperii*, v/1, no. 89a and v/2, nos 5528f; Decker-Hauff, 'Staufisches Haus', p. 356 in no. 70.

36 Böhmer, *Regesten Heinrichs VII.*, p. 258.

37 *Regesta Imperii*, v/2 no. 5253f (17.v.1257); Krull, *Salbung und Krönung*, p. 41.

38 *Regesta Imperii*, vi/1 (1898), no. 4d, p. 18 (Tuesday, 24.x.1273); Grotefend/Asch, p. 181, table 19.

39 *Regesta Imperii*, vi/2 (1848), nos 28 and 1048 (24.vi.1292).

40 Cf. in addition picture 4b in Irmer, *Romfahrt*, opposite p. 20; *Kaiser Heinrichs Romfahrt*, p. 59; *Il Viaggio*, p. 79.

41 H. Thomas, *Ludwig der Bayer 1282–1347* (Regensburg/Graz, 1993), pp. 68–9 (the date 27 Nov. in Brockhaus, 2nd edn, xiii [1990], 574 is a misprint). Frederick the Fair of Austria was crowned at Bonn on the same day, but without his spouse Isabel-Elizabeth of Aragon, who was consecrated at Basle at Pentecost, 1315: Cf. Hamann, p. 146 with *ibid.*, p. 83; Thomas, *Ludwig der Bayer*, p. 75.

42 G. Wolf, 'Heinrich VII., Wimpfen, Worms und Heidelberg', *ZGO*, 137, NS 98 (1989), pp. 468 and 471, turns against the traditional parenthesis around the number, but risks confusion with the Luxemburg king and emperor Henry VII.

43 Krull, *Salbung und Krönung*, p. 40; Decker-Hauff, 'Staufisches Haus', p. 364 in no. 87 and p. 369 in no. 106; Grotefend/Asch (1982), p. 184, table 21 for 28 March. The coronations of Anna I (1349), Anna II (1354), and Joan (1376) are further included among Aachen ceremonies by Krull, *Salbung und Krönung*, pp. 45–6, 56.

by her first husband King Lothar of Italy (d. 950), was living as widow of King Lothair in West Frankia (d. 986) and mother of his successor Louis V (d. 987).[44] But from 1125 at least, however, the *reges Romanorum* owed their constitutional position rather more to election than to heredity, and that minimised the queen's claim to power in widowhood. But so-called regencies of queen (grand-) mothers, relatively common earlier, came to an end with Empress Constance II (d. 1222).

The political emergence of territorial princes after the Investiture Contest meant that the queen's territorial background assumed greater importance. This can be observed in the cases of Empress Beatrice (d. 1184) in relation to Burgundy and of Empress Constance I (d. 1198) in relation to Sicily. The erosion of the king's demesne and of royal property since at least the struggle for the throne between the Staufen and the Welfs in 1198–1218 deprived queens, too, of central resources and threw them back on their territorial bases, if they had any.

Queens and the *memoria* of their families

Romano-German queens shared partly in their husband's rank and status, being crowned like them and consecrated for their position as partners and coadjutors of the monarch. But examination of the sources reveals that these noble women also played a special role in maintaining the *memoria* of their families – and in this respect the unspectacular queens could rival their more renowned imperial predecessors. In Carolingian times it was already a familiar idea that a virtuous wife of the king would not only be useful in many aspects of everyday life and rule, but also for the salvation of her husband's soul. In the 'Book on Christian Governors' by Sedulius Scottus, from which this summary is taken,[45] St Paul's original words 'The unbelieving man is sanctified by the believing wife'[46] (which applied to the practical life on earth) were made rather more urgent by the alteration from 'sanctified' to 'will be redeemed'.[47] Nevertheless, the shift from 'female ruler of the people', as envisaged by Sedulius,[48] and from the queen, responsible for the appearance and internal administration of the king's household, as presumably described by Adalhard of Corbie (d. 826)[49] and propagated by Hincmar of Reims,[50]

---

[44] K. F. Werner, 'Die Nachkommen Karls des Großen bis um das Jahr 1000, 1.–8. Generation', in *Karl der Große. Lebenswerk und Nachleben*, ed. W. Braunfels, iv (1967), pp. 403–82, gen. table, nos vii.69, viii.40 and 81 [with misprints in some numbers, concerning Emma]; O. G. Oexle, 'Emma', *Lex. des MA*, iii (1986), 1887.

[45] *Liber de rectoribus Christianis*, v, ed. S. Hellmann, *Sedulius Scottus*, Quellen und Untersuchungen zur lateinischen Philologie des Mittelalters, i/1 (Munich, 1906), pp. 34–7.

[46] I Corinthians 7:14a; cf. *Biblia Sacra iuxta vulgatam versionem*, ed. R. Weber, 2 vols, 2nd edn (Stuttgart, 1975), p. 177, 'Sanctificatus est enim vir infidelis per mulierem fidelem', with the textual note for 7:14.

[47] *Sedulii Liber*, c. 5, p. 35, 'unde et apostolus ait, quoniam vir infidelis salvabitur per mulierem fidelem'.

[48] *Ibid.*, p. 37, 'Princeps et rectrix populum si rite gubernant.'

[49] Cf. Hincmar, *De ordine palatii*, iii §12, ed. T. Gross, trans. R. Schieffer, *MGH, Fontes*, iii (1980), 11 and 54; B. Kasten, 'Hl. Adalhard', *LThK*, 3rd edn, i (1993), 132–3.

[50] Hincmar, *De ordine palatii*, iv §13 (p. 56); v §§19, 22 (pp. 68, 72, 74).

to the queen responsible for her husband's salvation even after his death, was already in the offing.

Mathilda, second wife of King Henry I, appeared as the foundress of convents after her husband's death in 936 to secure liturgical commemoration (*memoria*) for him and for dead relatives and friends.[51] Thietmar of Merseburg, whose chronicle is the most comprehensive narrative source for the so-called 'rise of the First Reich',[52] insisted on the good example, famous and worthy of imitation, which she had given by her deeds after the death of her lord,[53] and devoted the longest and most detailed description of the first queen of the Ottonian kingdom to these pious works. For Thietmar and his hearers and readers, it was very important that the queen-widow should help her deceased husband, and those memorable deeds consisted of feeding not only the poor but also birds, and of establishing a female convent at Quedlinburg, *ex sua proprietate*, on the thirtieth day after his death, *in die tricesima*.[54] From the first, Thietmar had insisted on her usefulness to her husband in divine and human things, as well as on her physical attraction. She was desired by Henry, while he was still married to Hatheburg, his first wife, because of her beauty and her riches.[55]

Queen Mathilda's activities did not end in Quedlinburg, although she died and was buried there beside her husband, in accordance with her own preparations in 968.[56] It is difficult to establish how far she helped to secure the continued survival of the Quedlinburg canons after her husband's death,[57] but the collegiate church in the valley had secured its material possessions by 961, though dependent on the future abbess on the hill, and the intervention of Mathilda is explicitly mentioned in royal diplomas as securing the salvation of the souls of members of the royal family.[58] In the meantime, she had founded two or three further houses: Enger in the diocese of Osnabrück, before 947,[59] Pöhlde, south-west of the Harz Mountains,

---

[51] Althoff, 'Mathilde', p. 391.

[52] This is the title of the introduction to *Germany in the Tenth Century*, ed. B. H. Hill, Jr (New York, etc., 1969).

[53] Thietmar, *Chronicon*, i.21 (p. 26), 'Et inclita venerabilis gesta Machtildis, quae post excessum senioris sui sumopere fecit, equidem paucis comprehendam ad imitationem bonam . . .'.

[54] Thietmar, *Chronicon*, i.21 (p. 26), 'domna Machtildis, viro suimet, vinculo momentaneae mortis depresso, succurrit, non solum pauperibus, verum eciam avibus victum subministrans. Congregationem quoque [*this word in Thietmar's own hand*] sanctimonialium in die tricesima in supra memorata urbe statuit'; *ibid.*, p. 28, 'ex sua proprietate'.

[55] Thietmar, *Chronicon*, i.9 (p. 14), 'et mens regis ab amore uxoris decrescens, ob pulcritudinem [!] et rem cuiusdam virginis, nomine Mathildis, secreto flagravit . . . coniunctaque ei tam in divinis quam in humanis profuit'. Cf. Glocker, *Verwandte der Ottonen*, pp. 46–8 and 263–4.

[56] Thietmar, *Chronicon*, ii.18 (p. 60).

[57] *Die Lebensbeschreibungen der Königin Mathilde*, ed. B. Schütte, *MGH SRG*, lxvi (1994), 127 n. 129, commenting on the *Vita Mathildis antiquior*, c. 8 (xi).

[58] BO 302 from Quedlinburg (15.vii.961), model for BMik 575 from Wallhausen (25.vii.961).

[59] Contrary to E. Karpf, 'Stift Enger', *Lex. des MA*, iii (1986), 1923 ['Damenstift']; cf. B. Schütte, *Untersuchungen zu den Lebensbeschreibungen der Königin Mathilde, MGH, Studien und Texte*, 9 (Hanover, 1994), p. 35 with n. 142: 'Kanonikerstift' – thus K. Schoppe,

established between 946 and 950,[60] and, comparatively late, in 961, a second collegiate house for noble women in the castle of Nordhausen 'on the southern slopes of the Harz mountains' and in the north-western part of the fertile lowland known as the 'Golden Meadows' ('Goldene Aue').[61] Her husband had developed the castle in a prominent spur-position on the hill since *c.* 910.[62] In contrast with the Christmas palace of Pöhlde and the so-called abbey there, Nordhausen was not mentioned by Thietmar of Merseburg (d. 1018).[63] In recent research, nevertheless, Nordhausen sometimes appears the centre of Mathildine propaganda. Both Lives of Mathilda were said to have been written in the house,[64] in 973/4 and 1002/03 respectively, but the latest editor has proposed a different provenance for both. The *Vita antiquior* has been ascribed to a canoness or cleric from Quedlinburg;[65] the *Vita posterior* to the circle of the Bavarian duke Henry IV, who had recently become King Henry II. 'His' author used the older Life, but did not repeat its 'emphatic glorification of the fatherland of the Saxons (*patria Saxonum*)'.[66]

The *Vita posterior* tries to make propaganda for Henry II as the only legitimate heir to the Ottonian throne,[67] and that a *vita Mathildis* is a convenient means for this aim, is striking in itself. The reputation of this 'holy Mathilda' and 'queen' as Thietmar calls her, even in the year of her death (968),[68] could help to make one of her later descendants acceptable to the Saxons, even though his line had built up its duchy in Bavaria. And not only for hagiographers, but also in the presentation by Thietmar, it was her spiritual virtues and merits that saved an ill-begotten son from the devil's clutches[69] and caused the proficiency of the elder son to flower:[70]

'Enger', *LThK*, 2nd edn, iii (1959), 881. Enger in Westphalia lies 8 km WNW of Herford, 38 km due ESE of Osnabrück; *Stielers Handatlas*, 10th repr. of 9th edn (Gotha, 1921), map 9 D5.

60 Schütte, *Lebensbeschreibungen*, p. 127 n. 128, commenting on *Vita antiquior*, c. 8 on the basis of *Vita Mathildis posterior*, c. 15, *ibid.*, pp. 172–3; Thietmar, *Chronicon*, v. 38 (p. 264), 'Weihnachtspfalz'; cf. Karl Heinemeyer, 'Pöhlde', *Lex. des MA*, vii/1 (1994), 39. Pöhlde lies 25 km ESE. of Northeim, 28 km ENE of Göttingen: *Muir's Historical Atlas: Medieval and modern*, 11th edn, ed. R. F. Treharne and H. Fullard (London 1969), map 10 Dc, index pp. 10 and 17 prints 'Nordheim' and 'Pohlde'.

61 *New Enc. Brit.*, viii (1988), 759.

62 K. Blaschke, 'Nordhausen', *Lex. des MA*, vi (1993), 1236 – but cf. *New Enc. Brit.*, viii (1988), 759, 'First mentioned in 927 as the site of a royal castle'.

63 For this statement I rely on the indices of Thietmar, *Chronicon* (ed. Holtzmann) and *Thietmar von Merseburg. Chronik*, trans. W. Trillmich, Ausgewählte Quellen zur deutschen Geschichte des Mittelalters. Freiherr vom Stein-Gedächtnisausgabe, 9 (Darmstadt, 1957), p. 504.

64 Thus Althoff, 'Mathilde', p. 391.

65 Schütte, *Lebensbeschreibungen*, pp. 10ff.

66 *Ibid.*, pp. 43–4.

67 *Ibid.*, pp. 76, 79–82, 85–93 and 110.

68 Thietmar, *Chronicon*, ii.18 (p. 60), 'cum egrotantis regine finem Mahtildis [!] expectaret . . . Post haec sancta Mahtildis II. Id. Marcii migravit ab hoc exilio'. Against this interpretation Trillmich, *Thietmar . . . Chronik*, p. 55 insists on 'pious' only: 'fromme Mathilde'.

69 Thietmar, *Chronicon*, i.24 (pp. 30, 32).

70 *Ibid.*, ii.4 (p. 42), 'Venerabilis autem regina Mahtiltis . . . fideli erga Deum servito promeruit, quod virtus filii in omnibus floruit.'

respectively the later Duke Henry I of Bavaria and the later Emperor Otto I. Even more interesting is Thietmar's explanation for Otto I's election to the throne after the death of his father Henry I: 'Raising their hands, all the princes of the state elected Otto according to the decree and the petition of his father, because they wanted to mitigate the heavy grief of Queen Mathilda.' It is with this statement that Thietmar opens Book II of his chronicle,[71] which is devoted to Otto I – small wonder, then, that among the causes for Emperor Otto I's own grief in 968, because of the irreparable damage done to the state, first place was taken by the death of his mother,[72] although it was not the first in time and did not occupy the first place in the narrative sequence.[73] Neither Mathilda's interventions in the diplomas of her time, which are counted by modern historians to measure a queen's influence in numerical terms,[74] nor her debatable influence on the royal succession in 936 were Thietmar's main concern, but rather her merits in securing the *memoria* and the success of her eldest son, both connected with a new collegiate institution in the Church.[75]

When a copy of Thietmar's chronicle was written at Corvey in Westphalia in about 1120, an addition drawing on local experience was made to the description of Henry I's fortifications and churches. Henry had had the altar of the martyr-saint Guy or Vitus, Corvey's principal saint, wonderfully decorated with gold and precious stones, and the interpolator added that the initiative of Mathilda, the king's wife, lay behind it.[76] No surviving royal diploma records this action, but the late note concerning her generosity towards the oldest and most noble abbey in Saxony is supported by the fact that the first of Mathilda's six or seven known interventions during the reign of Henry I (919–36)[77] is found in diplomas for

---

[71] 'Omnes rei publicae principes magnum reginae Mathildis [!] merorem lenire cupientes, Ottonem, filium eius, patris sui decreto ac peticione uno ore in regem sibi et dominum elegerunt, elevatis dextris': *ibid.*, ii.1 (p. 38), first sentence.

[72] 'Imperator autem, comperta lugubri matris et filii caeterorumque nece principum, gravi queritur merore invincibile tocius rei publicae damnum': *ibid.*, ii.20 (p. 60).

[73] *Ibid.*, ii.18–19 (pp. 58, 60) places the deaths in the following sequence: 3.ii, Bishop Bernard of Halberstadt; 2.iii, Archbishop William of Mainz; 14.iii, 'sancta Mahtildis' (all 968); Gero's son Siegfried (959); 20.v, Marcher Count Gero I (965).

[74] Cf. Kirchner, *Deutsche Kaiserinnen*, pp. 7–8 n. 11, 11 n. 7, 17 n. 24, etc.; Erkens, 'Frau als Herrscherin', pp. 246–8.

[75] Even the blossoming of Otto I's 'virtue' was connected with Quedlinburg: 'Mahtildis, constructo, ut predixi [= Thietmar's reference in his own statement in i.21; cf. above n. 53], in Quidilingeburg monasterio congregationeque sanctimonialium ibi collecta, fideli erga Deum servitio promeruit': Thietmar, *Chronicon*, ii.4 (p. 42), partly quoted above in n. 70.

[76] 'Hic in Nova Corbeia aram sancti Viti martiris auro et gemmis variis mirifice ornavit, hortatu Mahtildis, coniugis sue' is an addition to Thietmar, *Chronicon*, i.18, in the Corvey version only, p. 25.

[77] The others are BO 16 and 51 for Herford; BO 22 for a ministerial woman, but transmitted in the archives of Quedlinburg; BO 29 for St Maximin of Trier and BO 48 for Neuenheerse. BO 29 = D.H.I. 24 seems not to have been discarded as one of the notorious fabrications of St Maximin: cf. T. Kölzer, *Studien zu den Urkundenfälschungen des Klosters St. Maximin vor Trier, 10.–12. Jahrhundert*, Vorträge und Forschungen, Sonderband 36 (Sigmaringen, 1989), pp. 20, 23.

Corvey.[78] Her interventions continued after her husband's death, though they were not very numerous and were distributed through the more than thirty-one years of her remaining life: six occur in diplomas of her son and a further three in those of her grandson.[79] They are, furthermore, concentrated very much on Quedlinburg.[80] This marked reduction in Mathilda's recorded activities after the Quedlinburg foundation(s) of 936 has been explained by a disagreement between the queen and her sons, because – as they thought – she gave too much for pious causes.[81] Her sons would concede only her lifetime's usufruct from her endowment (*dos*).[82]

According to modern research, free ownership was different from the so-called constrained property ('gebundenes Eigentum'), which resulted from gifts according to Teutonic law ('Schenkung nach germanischem Recht'). *Dos* donations belonged to the latter category, so that the successors of kings who had endowed their wives with *dos* from royal property, could and did handle this widow's property. Thus the character and substance of royal property ('Reichsgut') was not changed by its donation as *dos*.[83] Mathilda had first relied on her *dos* when financing her *memoria*-activities. There was also a difference between jointure ('Wittum, Leibgedinge') and dower, the latter being mere usufruct by the widow, irrespective of its origin as morning-gift. It was precisely the connection of a queen's endowment with the office of her husband that might arouse suspicion as to the nature of her property. But in the end all this was a question of political enforcement and, therefore, of personality and power, not of status, let al.one of something like a queen's department. It is highly revealing that, after the first for Quedlinburg in 937, further interventions by Mathilda occurred only after the death of her daughter-in-law Edith,[84] her rival at court and, as we shall see later, in holiness, too.

More than three hundred and fifty years later, something of these traditions can be found in the activities of Elizabeth of Görz-Tyrol and her daughter Agnes. In 1274, Elizabeth married Albert, later King Albert I, whom she survived by five years after his murder in 1308.[85] Historical accounts of her life are confused and

---

78 BO 4 and 5 no. 5 not mentioned in *Sächsische Zeit 919–1024. Register*, ed. H. Zimmermann, *Regesta Imperii*, ii/6 (Cologne/Vienna, 1982), 251, *s.v.* 'Mathilde'.

79 The last three are neglected by Kirchner, *Deutsche Kaiserinnen*, p. 8 n. 11. But see BMik 575, 576 and 585 in the next note! The whole group 'after 936' is not considered by Erkens, 'Frau als Herrscherin', p. 247 n. 27.

80 BO 74 (937) for St Servatius at Quedlinburg; BO 187 (950)[!] for Engern; BO 238, 253 and 302 for St Servatius at Quedlinburg; BO 404 (965) from Quedlinburg for the bishopric of Osnabrück. BMik 575 (961) for St Servatius at Quedlinburg; BMik 576 for Hadmersleben; BMik 585 for [St Jacob and] Wigbert, in the suburb of Quedlinburg. Cf. above at n. 57.

81 BO 101a, pp. 58–9.

82 Althoff, 'Mathilde', col. 391.

83 G. Althoff, 'Probleme um die dos [!] der Königinnen im 11. und 12. Jahrhundert', in *Veuves et veuvage dans le Haut Moyen Âge*, ed. M. Parisse (Paris, 1993), p. 128.

84 BO 101a, p. 59; cf. Leyser, 'Ottonen und Wessex', p. 83.

85 Cf. [J.] Loserth, 'Elisabeth', *ADB*, vi (1877), 8–9; G. Frieß, 'Königin Elisabeth von Görz-Tirol', *Blätter des Vereins für Landeskunde von Niederösterreich*, NS 24 (1890); A. Gauert, 'Elisabeth', *NDB*, iv (1959), 440–1; K. Bosl, 'Elisabeth', *Biographisches*

confusing: general opinion has her marrying *King* Albert (although he did not succeed his rival Adolf of Nassau until 1298) and securing the rulership for her children before her retirement to Königsfelden,[86] although neither succeeded in her lifetime. Nevertheless, before and after her husband's death, this 'ancestress of all [later] Habsburgs' played a crucial role not only 'as the leader of Habsburg politics after the murder of her husband on May 1, 1308,' but also as promoter of Hallstatt salt production and intermediary in her husband's many 'conflicts with his territorial barons and with the princes of the empire'.[87] And it was only after she had secured the territorial position of her sons that she retired to the monastery of Königsfelden,[88] of which she was co-foundress. This double monastery for Poor Clares and Franciscans was established on the very spot where Albert I had been murdered,[89] and after Elizabeth's death her daughter Agnes, widowed queen of Hungary, secured its further existence.[90]

Although clearly established as a memorial to a slaughtered king, and often described as the family mausoleum of the Habsburgs, until its subordination to Bern from 1415 onwards,[91] there is good reason to question whether Königsfelden ever played that role. Albert's own body was not interred there. It was moved on 29 August 1309 from its temporary grave in Wettingen[92] to Speyer cathedral, the

Wörterbuch zur deutschen Geschichte, i, 2nd edn (1973), cols 615–16. Many references in A. Lhotsky, *Geschichte Österreichs seit der Mitte des 13. Jahrhunderts, 1281–1358*, Österreichische Akademie der Wissenschaften. Veröffentlichungen der Kommission für Geschichte Österreichs, 1 (Vienna, 1967), p. 383 [index].

[86] Brockhaus, 2nd edn, vi, 312, 'heiratete im Nov. 1274 König Albrecht I. . . . Nachdem sie die Herrschaft für ihre Kinder gesichert hatte, zog sie sich . . . zurück.'

[87] J. Riedmann, 'Elisabeth – deutsche Königin', *Lex. des MA*, iii (1986), 1831–2, 'Stammutter aller Habsburger' und 'Konflikte . . . mit Landherren [!] und Reichsfürsten'; cf. *idem*, 'Mittelalter', in J. Fontana, P. W. Haider, *et al.*, *Geschichte des Landes Tirol*, 2nd edn, i (Bozen, etc., 1990), 427.

[88] Riedmann, 'Elisabeth', col. 1832.

[89] The charter of *Elyzabeth quondam Romanorum regina* dates from Brugg, 6.xii.1309; *Codex diplomaticus Alemanniae et Burgundiae Trans-Juranae intra fines dioecesis Constantiensis*, ed. T. Neugart, ii (St Blasien, 1795), 369–70 no. 1073. Brugg, site of a bridge on the Aare with a bridge-tower of the twelfth century, had grown into a Habsburg-founded town by the first third of the thirteenth century (Brockhaus, iii [1967], 348). It received free-city status in 1284 (*ibid.*, 2nd edn, iv [1987], 46). Brugg lies 3 km WNW of Königsfelden: *Stielers Handatlas*, map 14 C6.

[90] Cf. B. Degler-Spengler, 'Königsfelden', *Lex. des MA*, v (1991), 1327.

[91] G. Boner, 'Königsfelden bei Brugg', *LThK*, 2nd edn, vi (1961), 452, 'im 14. Jahrhundert Erbbegräbnis der Habsburger'; *Denkmale der deutschen Könige u. Kaiser*, edd. P. E. Schramm *et al.*, Veröffentlichungen des Zentralinstituts für Kunstgeschichte in München, 7 (Munich, 1978), ii, 52 no. 8; F. Laubenberger, 'Grablegen der Habsburger und St. Blasien', *Zeitschrift des Breisgau-Geschichtsvereins*, cii (1983), 27ff.

[92] Despite the assertion in the *Chronica Mathiae de Newenburg*, ed. A. Hofmeister, *MGH SRG*, NS, iv (1924–40, repr. 1955), c. 36, pp. 72 and 344, where the Habsburg mausoleum conception is already manifest. The Königsfelden church was begun only in 1310: Brockhaus, 2nd edn, xii (1990), 262. The assertion, *ibid.*, x (1970), 427, that the important glass windows come from the thirteenth century, is a misleading misprint. The rich Cistercian monastery of Wettingen had existed since 1227: K. Spahr in *LThK*, 2nd edn, x (1965), 1080. *Denkmale*, ed. Schramm, ii, 52 no. 7, 114 no. 7 for the sarcophagus at Wettingen.

mausoleum of the Salian-Staufens, where his father Rudolf I (d. 1291) had been laid to rest;[93] and Albert's second son, Frederick the Fair (d. 1330), was entombed in the Carthusian house of Mauerbach west-north-west of Vienna.[94] Furthermore, after his death in Vienna in 1358, Duke Albert II was entombed in the Carthusian house of Gaming in Lower Austria, about one hundred kilometres due west-south-west of Vienna,[95] and his eldest brother Rudolf IV (the Founder), having died at Milan in 1365, was buried not at Königsfelden but 'in the princes' vault of St Stephen's at Vienna'.[96]

The burial of Elizabeth at Königsfelden in 1313,[97] even before the church was consecrated,[98] suggests rather the clinging to a foundress than an attempt to establish a new centre for family burials. There is no evidence that the remains of earlier members of the family were transferred there. There was no repetition in favour of Königsfelden of the transfer of Albert I's body from Wettingen to Speyer. Nevertheless, two of Queen Elizabeth's sons, Dukes Leopold I the Glorious (d. 1326) and Henry the Friendly (d. 1327),[99] their wives, Catherine of Savoy (d. 1336) and Elizabeth of Virneburg (d. 1343),[100] and three of her daughters[101] were buried there, including Agnes (d. 1364), widow from 1301 of King Andrew III of

---

93 On 29 August 1309: Böhmer, *Regesten Heinrichs VII.* (1844/1849/1857), p. 268. This is confirmation of the *Chronica Mathiae*, c. 37 (pp. 80 and 348f), 'uno die Albertum et Adolphum, Romanorum reges occisos, Heinricus rex Spire in sepulcris regiis sepelivit: Alberto in uxoris olim Friderici imperatoris, Adolpho vero in eiusdem filie sepulcris sepultis'. These are the graves of Empress Beatrix (d. 15.xi.1184), and her daughter Agnes (d. 8.x.1184), recently betrothed to Prince Richard of England, later Richard I. According to Decker-Hauff, 'Staufisches Haus', pp. 352 no. 44 and 356 no. 67, the graves were situated side by side. He still rests there, and not at St Paul in the Lavant valley as recently advertised by M. Hawlik-van de Water, *Die Kapuzinergruft. Begräbnisstätte der Habsburger in Wien*, 2nd edn (Freiburg/Basle/Vienna, 1993), p. 327 (with photograph of the church); correctly, *ibid.*, p. 329.
94 Hamann, p. 145; cf. below at n. 249.
95 W. Maleczek, 'Albrecht II.', *Lex. des MA*, i/2 (1978), 321; Hawlik-van de Water, *Kapuzinergruft*, p. 324, with photograph.
96 Hamann, p. 407, 'in der Fürstengruft von St. Stephan (zu) Wien'; Hawlik-van de Water, *Kapuzinergruft*, p. 322, photograph of the so-called cenotaph.
97 Hamann, p. 81; Laubenberger, 'Grablegen', p. 28, has Vienna for her death in 1313, and 1316 for her burial at Königsfelden.
98 Brockhaus, 2nd edn, xii (1990), 262.
99 Hofmeister, p. 72 n. 7, commenting on *Chronica Mathiae*, c. 36: 'In quo loco occisionis [*sc.* Alberti Romanorum regis] sollempne monasterium Kúngesvelt ordinis Minorum est constructum, in quo rex primo sepultus, Spiram postea est translatus; in quo eciam loco plures filiorum suorum sunt sepulti; in quo postea filia regis.'
100 Krieger, *Die Habsburger*, p. 239 [genealogical table]. Catherine and Elizabeth d. 1337 according to Laubenberger, 'Grablegen', p. 37 n. 9; but cf. Hamann, pp. 233 and 83. Neither are all the dates nor all the (eleven) names in Laubenberger's note convincing.
101 Guta-Jutta (d. 1329), Elizabeth (d. 1352), widow of Duke Frederick IV of Lorraine (killed in battle, 1328/29; Hamann, p. 83; Krieger, *Die Habsburger*, p. 238: 1328; for 22.iv.1329, cf. M. Parisse, 'Friedrich V./Ferri IV.', *Lex. des MA*, iv/5 [1988], 953), and Agnes (d. 1364): see Hamann, pp. 160, 82, and 29. Elizabeth's burial at Königsfelden is particularly significant, for although she died at Nancy, she was not interred beside her husband at the Cistarcian monastery of Beaupré, 5 km SE of Lunéville (diocese of Toul, now Nancy).

Hungary, who had maintained a small court beside the monastery until her death at the age of eighty-three or eighty-four, and is regarded at least as co-foundress.[102] This cluster of burials, together with the interment in 1386 of Elizabeth's grandson, Duke Leopold III of Austria,[103] might seem to give support to the family mausoleum theory, but it will not survive close examination.

It was only after an earlier interment in a Friars' Minor church, either at Bruck in Upper Styria,[104] where he had died in 1327, or in Styria's most important town Graz,[105] that Duke Henry the Friendly's remains had been transferred to Königsfelden by his widow, Elizabeth of Virneburg,[106] presumably in agreement with his sister, ex-Queen Agnes of Hungary, who is thought to have had a special liking for her second youngest brother.[107] Leopold III's burial almost certainly owed more to convenience than to mortuary policy, for he was killed in the battle of Sempach,[108] only thirty-five kilometres south of the church where his grandmother and a group of uncles and aunts already lay (and his body probably remained there until 1770, not 1415).[109] The chronology of these burials points in the same direction: seven of the nine occurred within thirty-nine years, 1313 to 1352, and the last two (of Agnes and Duke Leopold III, 1364 and 1386, respectively) are explained by special circumstances. Agnes had spent the greater part

---

[102] G. Boner, 'Agnes von Ungarn', *LThK*, 2nd edn, i (1957), 199; T. von Bogyay, 'Agnes von Österreich', *Lex. des MA*, i/1 (1977), 313 – both with 128*1* to 1364. An alternative date of birth (1280) is given in Brockhaus, i (1966), 194, with reference to H. von Liebenau, *Lebensgeschichte der Königin Agnes* (Regensburg, 1868); *Hundert Urkunden zu der Geschichte der Königin Agnes von Ungarn* (Regensburg, 1869), and repeated (without references) in the 2nd edn, i (1986), 216 and xxv (1994), 18; and also in T. Zotz, 'Agnes von Ungarn', *LThK*, 3rd edn, i (1993), 238, with reference to Hamann, pp. 29–30.

[103] He rested there until 1770: W. Stelzer, 'Leopold III.', *Lex. des MA*, v (1991), 1902; Hamann, p. 244.

[104] 'St Mary in the Forest', founded 1272: Hamann, p. 162; *Reclams Kunstführer Österreich*, 5th edn (Stuttgart, 1981), ii, 60.

[105] A house of Friars Minor founded *c.* 1240: *Johannis abbatis Victoriensis Liber certarum historiarum*, ed. F. Schneider; H. Ebner, 'Graz', *Lex. des MA*, iv (1989), 1661; *Reclams Kunstführer Österreich*, ii, 154: first mentioned in 1239.

[106] *MGH SRG*, 36/ii (1910), ii, 96–7 and 128 = v. 8 (version A) and v. 6 (version B, D, A 2), respectively; A. Huber, 'Herzog Heinrich von Österreich und Steiermark', *ADB*, xi (1880), 558.

[107] Before his marriage to Elizabeth of Virneburg (contracted to secure the vote of Henry of Virneburg, archbishop of Cologne for his brother Frederick the Fair: Huber, 'Herzog Heinrich', p. 558; Lhotsky, *Geschichte Österreichs*, p. 225 n. 255 together with the correction, *ibid.*, pp. 403 and 300), Agnes had considered him an appropriate husband for her Arpad stepdaughter Elizabeth (Lhotsky, *Geschichte Österreichs*, pp. 299–300), later confined to the Dominican house of Töss, where her patient life under harsh conditions resulted in a local cult: see V. Honemann, ch. 6, below. The dates of her residence at Töss are controversial (*ibid.*, n. 11).

[108] Brockhaus, x (1970), 427 with reference to E. Maurer, *Das Kloster Königsfelden*, Die Kunstdenkmäler der Schweiz, Kanton Aargau, 3 (Basel, 1954). This detail (and the literature) is missing in Brockhaus, xii (2nd edn, 1990), 262, but the consecration of the nave in 1320 is noted. For the 'cenotaph' and 'Tumba', see *Denkmale*, ed. Schramm, ii, 114 no. 8 and p. 52.

[109] Hamann, pp. 29, 81, etc.; Laubenberger, 'Grablegen', pp. 29–33, 37 n. 6, 38 n. 22.

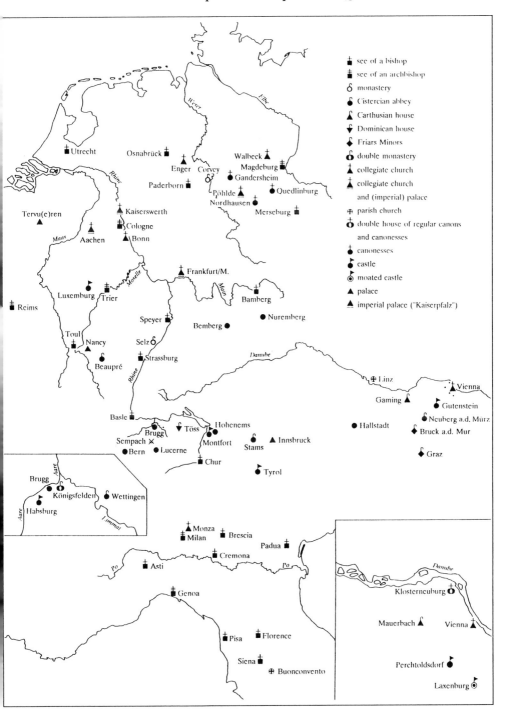

Figure 4 Important centres in the Romano-German Empire

of her widowhood in a small court beside the monastery, and Duke Leopold had been killed in the vicinity. Moreover, from the second half of the fourteenth century onwards, the Habsburgs tended to concentrate their burials first in the Carthusian house at Gaming[110] in lower Austria, very roughly half-way between Salzburg and Vienna, and then at St Stephen's in Vienna. For both places, the initiative came from reigning dukes.

The influence of ex-Queen Elizabeth and ex-Queen Agnes, then, consisted in concentrating the memorial services for members of the Habsburg family in one newly-built double monastery of a relatively modern order at Königsfelden. But the effects of their initiative did not last beyond their own lifetime. Even at the height of their influence, alternative sites were being developed at Gaming and Vienna (and from 1409, Stams, the burial church of the rulers of Tyrol, was also used);[111] and when Otto 'the Debonnaire' died in 1339 on a journey from Graz to Vienna, he was buried first with the Augustinians in Vienna and then transferred to the Cistercian house at Neuberg in the Mürz valley (Upper Styria),[112] which he himself had founded,[113] and where his first two wives were already interred[114] and his two sons Frederick II and Leopold II were later entombed in 1344, even though Frederick II had been educated by ex-Queen Agnes at Königsfelden.[115]

To summarise. There were at least nine Habsburg burials at Königsfelden between 1313 and 1386. Other monasteries had smaller numbers in the fourteenth century: at Mauerbach, only Frederick the Fair in 1330, though he was not only a rival king, but in his last years, a Romano-German co-king as well; at Neuberg in the Mürz valley, six members of Otto the Debonnaire's family, from 1330 to 1344; at Gaming, three burials from 1351 to 1373; at Vienna's Stephansdom there were at least eleven medieval entombments from 1362 to 1493.[116] The imperial vault at the Capuchin church in Vienna was used only from 1633 onwards. All of them honoured their foundresses and founders. The ideas of a founder's burial and of a family vault were present side by side with the dynastic concentration suggested by the ex-queens Elizabeth and Agnes.

---

[110] 'Mary's Throne' with its church of the 'Assumption of the Blessed Virgin'. See Appendix I.

[111] See Appendix I.

[112] Hamann, pp. 377, 378 [W. Stelzer]; A. Fink, 'Neuberg an der Mürz', *LThK*, 2nd edn, vii (1962), 891.

[113] Hamann, pp. 377 and 378. According to Neuberg tradition, Duke Albert II was persuaded by dreams to transfer his brother's remains there, although Otto is said to have requested burial at Neuberg: *Continuatio Novimontensis ad 1339, codex episcopalis*, ed. W. Wattenbach, *MGH SS*, ix (1859), 671–2; Fink, 'Neuberg an der Mürz', col. 891, calls them 'Annales Novimontenses'.

[114] Elizabeth of Lower Bavaria, d. Vienna, 1330; Anne of Luxemburg, d. 1338: Hamann, pp. 84 and 52.

[115] Hamann, pp. 147 and 244.

[116] Hawlik-van de Water, *Kapuzinergruft*, p. 322, cautiously omits Catherine (d. 1387) and Beatrix of Zollern (d. 1414); cf. Appendix I, below.

Holy queens of the Romano-German empire: from interventions to religious cult

When Henry I died in 936 the role of first woman at the king's court had fallen to the Anglo-Saxon Edith, wife of Otto I since 929[117] or 930.[118] Otto had already had a liaison with a noble Slav, becoming as late as 929 the father of a son, named William – later archbishop of Mainz,[119] – and Edith might have been slightly older than Otto's seventeen years in 929,[120] if she was born between 905 and 912.[121] But Otto had been completely captivated by her. The story of their meeting reads like a chapter in one of the Sagas. In response to Henry I's request for a wife from Europe's oldest royal family for his eldest son, King Athelstan, the Anglo-Saxon king had sent two of his half-sisters, and Otto had chosen the elder![122] Presumably a separate court was established for the couple at Magdeburg,[123] in the lands given to the future queen by her father-in-law and bridegroom.[124] Mathilda now had a daughter-in-law possibly only about ten years younger than herself; and she hastened to secure her position by having earlier donations to herself declared as her jointure, settled on her by a husband[125] who was her elder by about twenty years.[126]

Otto duly approved the settlement of the jointure, as he had already approved the donations to his mother two years earlier,[127] and lived with his spouse. Edith's son (b. 930) and daughter (b. 931) were given Liudolfing names, Liudolf and Liutgard.[128] The contrasting choice of 'William'[129] for the Slav's son in 929 may

---

117 G. Waitz, *Jahrbücher des Deutschen Reichs unter König Heinrich I.*, 3rd edn, *JDG*, 8 (1885), p. 133 and n. 2; BO 23h = 54d; Glocker, *Verwandte der Ottonen*, p. 270 no. 3.

118 *Two of the Saxon Chronicles*, ed. C. Plummer, ii (Oxford, 1899), 121–2; G. Althoff and H. Keller, *Heinrich I. und Otto der Große. Neubeginn und karolingisches Erbe*, 2 vols (continuous pagination), Persönlichkeit und Geschichte, 122–1 (Göttingen/Zürich, 1985), pp. 105–6, 107–8. 929/30: K. Schmid, 'Edgith', *Lex. des MA*, iii/8 (1985), 1572; *Handbook of British Chronology*, edd. E. B. Fryde, D. E. Greenway et al., Royal Historical Society, Guides and Handbooks, 3rd edn (London, 1986), 24–5; T. Struve, 'Otto I., d.Gr.', *Lex. des MA*, vi (1993), 1563.

119 Köpke/Dümmler, *Otto der Große*, p. 8; Glocker, *Verwandte der Ottonen*, p. 278 no. 3.

120 His birthday 23.x.912 in BO 55c is a misprint only regarding the day of the month; comparison with *ibid.*, g p. 2 results in 23.xi.912, as known since Köpke/Dümmler, pp. 6–7 at the latest.

121 Glocker, *Verwandte der Ottonen*, p. 270 no. 3, based on Köpke/Dümmler, pp. 11–12.

122 Köpke/Dümmler, p. 9; BO 23h; *Handbook of British Chronology*, p. 24 *s.v.* 'Aelfgifu'.

123 Cf. hints by Köpke/Dümmler, pp. 10 and 63–4 [Edith] and by Althoff/Keller, p. 111 [Otto].

124 BO 23h and 70; Kirchner, *Deutsche Kaiserinnen*, p. 10 and no. 5.

125 Cf. BO 17 (13.v.927) to 24 (16.ix.929), Quedlinburg. Althoff/Keller, pp. 102–3, referring to the articles by K. Schmid, *ibid.*, p. 251.

126 Glocker, *Verwandte der Ottonen*, p. 263 no. 3, where the misprint 'born 994/97' for Mathilda should be corrected to 894.

127 BO 24 and 17 respectively, cf. *ibid.* p. 33.

128 Glocker, *Verwandte der Ottonen*, pp. 278–9 nos 4–5.

129 Brockhaus, 2nd edn, xxiv (1994), 201; xxv (1994), 1020, *s.v.* 'Wilhelm von Aquitanien'. His most famous namesake was the saint of Gellone (d. after 806), a former count of Toulouse.

have been for the benefit of the Anglo-Saxon allies, by way of reassurance that he would not be considered throneworthy: a further slim argument for dating the 'royal wedding', as Widukind of Corvey called it,[130] to 929, the year of William's birth.

It was the importance of the Anglo-Saxon connection that minimised the influence of Mathilda, and, having lost her eldest son to the daughter-in-law, the queen might have clung all the more to her youngest son Henry, late as the explicit evidence for this is,[131] especially as he married only after the accession of his elder brother to the throne.[132] Widukind of Corvey intimates that Mathilda's intercession influenced Otto's decision to raise Henry to the duchy of the Bavarians.[133] This took place in December 947[134] at the earliest,[135] that is nearly two years after the death of Queen Edith on 26 January 946.[136]

To some extent, the rivalry between Mathilda and her daughter-in-law Edith may have restricted the latter's involvement in royal affairs. On the other hand, it was only with Adelheid (d. 999),[137] Edith's successor – now frequently called *consors regni*[138] – that queens and empresses began to feature increasingly frequently in royal diplomas. By the time of Cunigunde, such interventions occurred in one third of the imperial diplomas issued by Henry II (d. 1024),[139] and with little of the regional restrictions which had characterised the small number of interventions of Mathilda and Edith. Mathilda's most southerly intervention was St Maximin of Trier,[140] and only one of the seven known interventions of Edith involved a recipient outside of Saxony (the episcopal church of Utrecht). Moreover, three of Edith's interventions were with her son, who was only six years old at the time of the first example.[141]

---

[130] Widukind, i. 37 (p. 54), 'nuptiae regales'.
[131] *Vita Mathildis posterior*, c. 6 (p. 156); cf. Thietmar, *Chronicon*, i.21 (p. 28). Thietmar had used this Vita, according to Schütte, *Lebensbeschreibungen*, pp. 48–9.
[132] Glocker, *Verwandte der Ottonen*, pp. 273–4 no. 5 (*c.* 937/40).
[133] Widukind, ii.36 (p. 95), 'monitu et intercessione sanctae matris eius recordatus est multis laboribus fatigati fratris prefecitque eum regno Baioariorum'.
[134] Glocker, *Verwandte der Ottonen*, p. 273 no. 5.
[135] BO 157a, p. 79: winter 947/48.
[136] BO 131a.
[137] Kirchner, *Deutsche Kaiserinnen*, p. 17 with n. 26; Erkens, 'Frau als Herrscherin', p. 247.
[138] T. Vogelsang, *Die Frau als Herrscherin im hohen Mittelalter. Studien zur* consors regni *Formel* [!], Göttinger Bausteine zur Geschichtswissenschaft, 7 (Göttingen, etc., 1954), pp. 22–4 and, more often, Erkens, 'Frau als Herrscherin', pp. 248–51, with references to research hitherto published.
[139] Kirchner, *Deutsche Kaiserinnen*, p. 25 n. 8; Jäschke, *Notwendige Gefährtinnen*, p. 37.
[140] BO 29; cf. at nn. 77–80 above.
[141] BO 59 for Corvey (17.x.936), with Liudolf; BO 61 for the bishopric of Utrecht, with Giselbert; BO 63 for the bishopric of Halberstadt, with Liudolf; BO 69 for the archbishopric of Hamburg, with Thiethar, bishop of Hildesheim (cf. *Regesten der Erzbischöfe von Bremen 1, 787–1306*, ed. O. H. May, Veröffentlichungen der historischen Kommission für Hannover, Oldenburg, Braunschweig, Schaumburg-Lippe und Bremen, 11 [Hanover/Bremen, 1937], no. 100; 8.viii.937); BO 80 for Herford, with Bishop Tuto of Paderborn; BO 83 for Corvey, without the queen's name, though unequivocally *interventu coniugis nostre dilecte*: Diploma Ottonis I (*MGH DRG*, i/1–2), no. 27 (936/40); BO 126 for two lay persons, with

Such a display of dynastic continuity[142] and motherly care and education[143] would be extended to a child of merely sixteen months, when Henry IV first appeared in a diploma of his father Henry III, dated March 1052, and it was a glimpse of reality, not merely dynastic propaganda, that the first place in this formula was taken by Empress Agnes, the mother, with the additional title of *consors*.[144] Later interventions by the boy, from the age of three onwards, followed the same pattern: mother first[145] and never without her,[146] whereas 'separate' interventions of Queen and then Empress Agnes occurred both before and after her first son's birth on 11 November 1050,[147] generally alone rather than with her infant son at the beginning,[148] but always linked with 'King Henry IV' after Henry III's second journey to Rome.[149] Thus the propaganda of royal dominance ('königliche Herrschaftspropaganda') did not go as far as presenting a one- to five-year-old child or child-king (Henry was elected king in 1053 and consecrated Henry IV as early as 1054)[150] as the necessary means to approach the sovereign's presence and gain his favour. The 'roles' changed only *pro forma* from the first diploma of Henry IV (then aged six): the child-king 'reigned' according to the

Liudolf (11.vi.945). Cf. Erkens, 'Frau als Herrscherin', p. 247 n. 27. Kirchner, *Deutsche Kaiserinnen*, p. 11 n. 7, and Leyser, 'Ottonen und Wessex', p. 83, counted only six. BO 83 is also missing from *Regesta Imperii*, ii, Index, p. 196 *s.v.* 'Edith'.

142 This is emphasised by T. Struve, 'Die Interventionen Heinrichs IV. in den Diplomen seines Vaters. Instrument der Herrschaftssicherung des salischen Hauses', *Archiv für Diplomatik*, xxviii (1982), 215–19, 222.

143 Thanks are due to P. Corbet (Nancy), who generously provided me with a pre-publication version of his richly annotated essay 'Les impératrices ottoniennes et le modèle marial. Autour de l'ivoire du Château Sforza de Milan', *Comprendre Marie? Réflexions historiques*, edd. D. Iogna-Prat, E. Palazzo et D. Russo (Paris, forthcoming), at n. 48.

144 *Die Regesten des Kaiserreiches unter Heinrich IV.*, first instalment, ed. T. Struve [= J. F. Böhmer, *Regesta Imperii*, iii/2/i (Cologne/Vienna, 1984) = Böhmer/Struve], no. 8, Kaiserswerth (5.iii.1052), on the basis of *DHIII* (Diploma Heinrici III) in *Die Urkunden Heinrichs III.*, edd. H. Bresslau and P. F. Kehr, *MGH DRG*, v (1926–31), no. 283, 'ob interventum thori ac regni nostri consortis, scilicet Agnetis imperatricis auguste, simulque dilectissime prolis nostre Heinrici'.

145 Böhmer/Struve, no. 16 (29.v.1054); nos 17, 20, 24, 28, 31, 46 (14.xii.1055), etc. should be compared with *DDHIII* nos 322, 323, 328, 331, 335, 340 and 361, etc. respectively, because of the sometimes ambiguous wording 'intervenes with his mother' in the single 'Regesten'.

146 Cf. the list of thirty-nine [!] *DDHIII* in Struve, 'Interventionen', pp. 192–6, ranging from *D* 283 to *D* 381 = Böhmer/Struve, nos 8–69, this of 28 September 1056.

147 Böhmer/Struve, no. 1; *DHIII* 114 (29.xi.1043) for the monastery of Leno; *D* 120 p. 151; *D* 121 p. 152; etc., to *D* 250 p. 334; *D* 254 (3.viii.1050).

148 *DHIII* 261 (10.ii.1051); *D* 266 p. 355; etc., to *D* 327 (17.xi.1054).

149 *DHIII* 361 (14.xii.1055), 'ob interventum regni thorique nostri consortis Agnetis imperatricis nec non dilectissimi filii nostri Heinrici regis Quarti'; *D* 363 p. 495, etc., the last being *D* 381 (28.ix.1056), 'per interventum carissimae contectalis nostrae, scilicet Agnetis imperatricis augustae, nostrique filii dilectissimi Heinrici Quarti regis'. The last *DHIII* is a royal mandate; *DD* 383–409 are medieval falsifications.

150 Böhmer/Struve, nos 13 and 18. The term 'children's king' ('Kinderkönig') is preferred by T. Kölzer, 'Das Königtum Minderjähriger im fränkisch-deutschen Mittelalter. Eine Skizze', *Historisches Zeitschrift*, ccli (1990), 291 *et passim*.

intitulation, but the mother-guardian intervened, generally in the first position,[151] until March 1062,[152] just before the kidnap of the twelve-year-old king at Kaiserswerth, mentioned above.[153]

The received standard was the intervention of the king's or emperor's wife, and this was made public by every recital of a king's or emperor's diploma,[154] regardless of her actual influence,[155] though reflecting her real presence at the royal or imperial court.[156] Most recipients of Ottonian diplomas were ecclesiastics or ecclesiastical institutions. Lay recipients, including the queen and king, accounted for only 5% of the total, even at the end of the period.[157] Although the number of lay recipients trebled during Henry III's reign,[158] the overall impression remains that written documents were coveted – and preserved – primarily by the men and institutions of the Church. They needed protection by kings to keep their landed property, and the help of the queens and empresses was very welcome to mediate such protection. The recital of their names in diplomas guaranteeing secular estates provided a positive picture of those 'venerable matrons', as they would be called by Lupold of Bemberg in 1341/42.[159]

Furthermore, they were foundresses and co-foundresses of ecclesiastical institutions. To the examples mentioned above might be added Queen Edith for St Maurice at Magdeburg[160] and Empress Adelheid for her burial monastery of Selz (French: Seltz) in the northern part of the diocese of Strassburg,[161] and Empress Cunigunde for Kaufungen, her residence-monastery in widowhood, east of Cassel, dedicated on the first anniversary of her husband's death.[162] Small wonder that pious queens and empresses are presented as saints. And so legends grew, probably sometimes during their life-time, but usually soon after their death. These legends transmitted stories about miracles wrought by them or at their graves. All this resulted in a cult of their relics and in the appellation 'holy' applied to them by contemporaries and later authors. Mathilda, Adelheid, and Cunigunde were all

---

[151] Böhmer/Struve, nos 84 (5.xii.1056), 85, 87, 92, 96, etc.
[152] *Ibid.*, no. 247 (19.iii.1062).
[153] *Ibid.*, no. 252; cf. above at n. 6.
[154] Cf. Struve, 'Interventionen', pp. 217–19.
[155] Jäschke, *Notwendige Gefährtinnen*, p. 104.
[156] Cf. the formula *propter incrementum* for Henry IV, when not at court, Struve, 'Interventionen', pp. 199–200, 205, 207–10.
[157] There are twenty-six authentic texts among the 510 authentic numbers in the *DDHII*.
[158] There are fifty-five authentic diplomas for lay persons or their communities among the 382 authentic numbers in the *DDHIII*.
[159] *Libellus de zelo*, or *Germanorum veterum principum zelus et fervor in Christianam religionem Deique ministros*, printed for Jacob Wimpfeling by Johannes Bergmann von Olpe (Basle, 1497), fol. xix^b, 'de zelo Christianae religionis venerabilium matronarum Mechtildis . . .'. For the author, 'Lupoldus Bebenburgius', see fol. i^a. My thanks are due to the Badische Landesbibliothek, Karlsruhe, for a microfilm of the tract, and to G. Hoffmann of the 'Fernleihe', University Library at Saarbrücken, who secured it for me.
[160] BO 70. Thietmar, *Chronicon*, ii.3 (p. 40); cf. below n. 191.
[161] A. Hauck, *Kirchengeschichte Deutschlands*, 3rd/4th edn, iii (Leipzig, 1906), 1024; K. Schmid, 'Adelheid', *LThK*, 3rd edn, i (1993), 157.
[162] Emphasised by Lupold of Bemberg, *Libellus de zelo*, fol. xx^b, lines 33f.

called 'holy'. Of these, however, only Cunigunde[163] and Adelheid[164] secured formal canonisation.

The evidence for Mathilda's reputation for sanctity is ambiguous. *Lives* of Mathilda have been in existence since 973/74 and 1002/03 respectively;[165] but an authorised cult seems to have been approved only since the nineteenth century, and then only on a local level.[166] Widukind of Corvey described her as *mirae sanctitatis femina*, whose soul was carried up to heaven together with that of Bishop Bernard of Halberstadt, who had died in 968, nearly six weeks before the queen.[167] Since Bernard was never considered a saint, one should ask whether Widukind's text really means 'a woman of wonderful sanctity', as translated by modern medievalists,[168] and not simply 'of remarkably good piety',[169] or even 'of astonishing moral virtue'.[170] The sketch which Widukind devoted to her, presumably for the period of her life after her husband's death, does not call for veneration of her relics and records no miracles that would speak for themselves, although he gives the precise day of the month for her death.[171] Widukind's use of *sanctus* and

---

163 Promoted by Bishop Thimo of Bamberg (1196–1202) and the Bamberg Chapter: Kirchner, *Die deutschen Kaiserinnen*, pp. 164–5, among other references on the basis of *Regesta Imperii*, v/2,3 (1892) no. 570[5] of 3.iv.1200 from Pope Innocent III = P. 1000.

164 The 'Staufen' bishop Otto of Strassburg (1082/84–1100) fulfilled the wishes of Selz and instigated the formal canonisation of Adelheid by Pope Urban II in 1097: *Regesten der Bischöfe von Straßburg bis zum Jahre 1202*, ed. P. Wentzcke, Regesten der Bischöfe von Straßburg, i/2 (Innsbruck, 1908), nos 335 and 357; R. Folz, *Les saintes reines du moyen âge en Occident, VIe–XIIIe siècles*, Subsidia Hagiographica, 76 (Brussels, 1992), pp. 77 and 176–7 (table); cf. Vogelsang, *Frau als Herrscherin*, p. 38. The cult remained local, confined to Alsace, although Hugo of Flavigny (d. *c.* 1114 or *c.* 1140) recognised 16 December as the day for remembrance of 'the holy empress Adelheid, mother of Otto II', 'Necrologium' preceding *Chronicon Hugonis, monachi Virdunensis et Divionensis, abbatis Flaviniacensis*, ed. G. H. Pertz, *MGH SS*, viii (1848), 287, 'XVII. Kal. Ian. Adeleidae, imperatricis sanctae, obitus recolitur, matris Ottonis II'. Folz's reference to the 'mère d'Otton III', *Saintes reines*, p. 78 is a misprint. For Hugh of Flavigny, see P. Bourgain, *Lex. des MA*, v/1 (1990), 171; *Tusculum-Lexikon griechischer und lateinischer Autoren des Altertums und des Mittelalters*, 3rd edn, edd. W. Buchwald, A. Hohlweg and O. Prinz (Munich, 1982), p. 353.

165 Schütte, *Lebensbeschreibungen*, pp. 10, 42–3; cf. above at n. 64.

166 Folz, *Saintes reines*, pp. 65, 177 (table).

167 H. Jakobs, 'Mathilde/Mechthild', *LThK*, 2nd edn, vii (1962), 168; Widukind, iii. 74, p. 150. Bernard died 2 Feb., Mathilde 14 March 968: Thietmar, *Chronicon*, ii.18 (pp. 58–60); Hauck, *Kirchengeschichte*, iii, 985. The bishop is omitted from Folz's translation from Widukind, iii.74 (*Saintes reines*, p. 64).

168 *Quellen zur Geschichte der sächsischen Kaiserzeit*, edd. and trans. A. Bauer and R. Rau, Ausgewählte Quellen zur deutschen Geschichte des Mittelalters und der Neuzeit, Series A, 8 (Darmstadt, 1971), p. 179. *Widukind von Corvey. Res gestae Saxonicae/Die Sachsengeschichte*, edd. and trans. E. Rotter and B. Schneidmüller, [Reclams] Universal-Bibliothek, 7699 (Stuttgart, 1981), p. 229, 'eine Frau von wunderbarer Heiligkeit'.

169 'Frömmigkeit': Georges, *Handwörterbuch*, ii (1918), 2477–8 *s.v.* 'sanctitas'.

170 'Moral purity, virtue, probity': *Oxford Latin Dictionary*, vii (1980), 1686.

171 14 March: Widukind, iii.74 (p. 151).

the like ranged from a quality of God[172] down to men, things[173] and attitudes[174] devoted or sacred to God or belonging to His saints. The Old Testament priest, judge and prophet Samuel is 'holy',[175] Pope Gregory I is 'most' or 'very holy', through comparison with other men of his times.[176] But *sanctus* could even be merely the opposite of perjury.[177] When used directly and attributively of Queen Mathilda, modern translators shun the term 'holy mother'[178] and regard her as 'venerable'.[179]

The two persons, besides Mathilda, who earned the praise *mirae sanctitatis* in Widukind's narrative were Archbishop Hildibert of Mainz (927–37)[180] and Abbot Warin of Corvey (826–56).[181] According to Widukind, Hildibert became known for his prophetic spirit;[182] Warin, the first regularly chosen abbot of Corvey, was remembered for his translation of the relics of St Vitus to Corvey in the ninth century.[183] That was good company, and we know that, following the translation of 836, Corvey became a destination for pilgrims ('Wallfahrtsziel').[184] But there is no hint of a received cult of either Hildibert or Warin during the Middle Ages.[185]

We need to emphasise this because Widukind of Corvey used the earlier life of St Mathilda in his chapter on Queen Edith's death.[186] His description of Edith is not very dissimilar. He praised her as highly for her saintly religion as for her royal descent, and also recorded the precise day of her death;[187] her younger contemporary Hrotsvita of Gandersheim emphasised her descent from the holy king and martyr Oswald.[188] The Ottonian house may have played a role in promoting St Oswald's cult on the Continent from the tenth century onwards,[189] but there was something akin to a popular cult of St Edith, evident since Thietmar of Merseburg, who had stressed Edith's help in public and hidden things for Otto I, as he had for Mathilda and Henry I.[190] It was her 'intercession' that mattered, and since this was connected with divine help for the king and with the attribute 'most holy' for

---

172 *Ibid.*, i.38 (p. 55), quoting Psalm 144:17.
173 Widukind, i.33 (p. 46); i.38 (p. 55); ii.1 (p. 66).
174 *Ibid.*, ii.41 (p. 100).
175 *Ibid.*, i.31 (p. 44).
176 *Ibid.*, i.8 (p. 10).
177 *Ibid.*, ii.10 (p. 74).
178 *Ibid.*, ii.36 (p. 95); quoted above in n. 133.
179 Bauer/Rau, p. 117; Rotter/Schneidmüller, p. 149.
180 Hauck, *Kirchengeschichte*, iii, 27, 83, 981.
181 K. Honselmann, 'Warin', *LThK*, 2nd edn, x (1965), 957.
182 Widukind, ii.1 (p. 65).
183 *Ibid.*, iii.2 (p. 106).
184 Honselmann, 'Warin', col. 957; H. H. Kaminsky, 'Corvey I', *Lex. des MA*, iii/2 (1984), 295.
185 Warin (d. 20.ix.856) is called blessed ('selig') by Honselmann, 'Warin', col. 957.
186 Schütte, *Lebensbeschreibungen*, pp. 16–18.
187 Widukind, ii.41 (p. 100): 26 Jan., 'Haec nata ex gente Anglorum non minus sancta religione quam regali potentia pollentium stirpe claruit.'
188 *Gesta Ottonis*, cc. 85–97, esp. 94–7, in *Hrotsvithae Opera*, ed. P. von Winterfeld, *MGH SRG*, xxxiv (1902), 207.
189 Cf. V. Ortenberg, *The English Church and the Continent in the Tenth and Eleventh Centuries* (Oxford, 1992), p. 77.
190 Cf. above at n. 55.

Edith,[191] we may understand it as reference more to her prayer than to her political abilities. The king might have been influenced by her 'prayers' in building the cathedral of Magdeburg, which Thietmar related next, before coming to the climax. Edith possessed so many virtues that after her death miracles occurred,[192] presumably at her tomb in Magdeburg.[193] Thietmar insists, furthermore, that Otto began building the new Magdeburg cathedral over the place where the holy Edith rested, and that he wanted to be buried next to her, even though he had recently married Queen Adelheid,[194] who was nearly twenty years his junior.[195] At Magdeburg itself, it was recorded that Otto's new church was built 'over the bones of blessed Queen Edith'.[196] Odo of Magdeburg, writing in 1212/18,[197] implied that Edith had been added to Magdeburg's Theban Legion patrons as a new saint.[198] In the later Middle Ages, her anniversary seems to have been celebrated only at the cathedral and at the collegiate church of St Sebastian in Magdeburg,[199] but there was a wider knowledge of St Edith connected with Magdeburg. Two miracle stories from the first part of the twelfth century at the latest can be reconstructed from a common stock in the *Annalista Saxo* for the year 936 and in the so-called *Annales Palidenses* for 935.[200]

Further references to the holiness of Queen Edith were spread by various versions of the Duke Ernest plot in Middle High German verse and in medieval Latin prose and even in Old Czech verse. Version B from the first decade or from the beginning of the thirteenth century[201] offers a picture of Emperor Otto's wife

---

191 Thietmar, *Chronicon*, ii.3 (p. 40), 'Quaecumque ei publice vel occulte provenere nocentia, divinae miserationis gratia ac intercessione suimet sanctissimae contectalis Aedithae assidua securus evasit. Cuius instinctu . . .', follows the account of the building of Magdeburg. Cf. above at n. 160.

192 Thietmar, *Chronicon*, ii.3 (pp. 40–2), 'quae innumera virtute predita, ut signis post obitum claruit, inducias vitae istius sibi concessas Deo hominibusque accepte perduxit'. Cf. Folz, *Saintes reines*, p. 66.

193 *Gesta archiepiscoporum Magdeburgensium*, i, ed. W. Schum, *MGH SS*, xiv (1883), 376, 'testantur ad tumulum eius post modicum divinitus ostensa miracula'.

194 Cf. Thietmar, *Chronicon*, ii.5 (pp. 42, 44) with ii.11 (p. 50), '[Rex] incipiens aecclesiam mirum in modum in loco, ubi sancta requiescit Aedith et iuxta quam post obitum suimet pausare desideraverat ipse'. Thietmar added *suimet* with his own hand.

195 Glocker, *Verwandte der Ottonen*, pp. 270–1: born *c.* 932.

196 *Gesta archiepiscoporum Magdeburgensium*, c. 6, p. 379, 'pius imperator . . . super ossa beate Edith regine, que obiit anno Dominicae incarnationis 947 [!] . . . monasterium . . . edificavit'.

197 Cf. H.-J. Behr, 'Odo von Magdeburg', *Die deutsche Literatur des Mittelalters. Verfasserlexikon*, 2nd edn, vii/1 (1987), 18, and B. Gansweidt, 'Odo von Magdeburg', *Lex. des MA*, vi (1993), 1359 – who adjusts her slightly earlier dating to 1205–32 and probably 1205/06 in *Der Ernestus des Odo von Magdeburg. Kritische Edition mit Kommentar eines lateinischen Epos aus dem 13. Jahrhundert*, Münchener Beiträge zur Mediävistik und Renaissance-Forschung, 39 (1989), pp. 19–22.

198 *Ernestus*, i.229–42, pp. 40–1.

199 Folz, *Saintes reines*, p. 66.

200 *Annalista Saxo*, ed. G. Waitz, *MGH SS*, vi (1844), 600; *Annales Palidenses*, ed. G. H. Pertz, *ibid.*, xvi (1859), 62.

201 H.-J. Behr, 'Die Rückkehr des Verbannten. Reflexe alter consors-regni-Vorstellungen im

Ottegebe (Edgifu/Edith) as a Mary-like and blessed woman, for whose sake God wrought miracles.[202] She was simply treated as a saint.[203] It cannot be excluded that this passage had already belonged to version A of the text, which is transmitted only in fragments. These point to an origin between 1170/76 and 1180/81.[204] The *Gesta Ernesti ducis de Saxonia* [!] say of Edhilda-Odogeve that she had been famous no less for her holiness than for her royal power;[205] this version was known in the west of Germany by the first half of the thirteenth century.[206] In version C,[207] *Ottegeba* is no more than a pious woman, for whose soul the emperor had earnestly prayed after her death, in spite of her flowering virtues during her lifetime.[208] The passages about the emperor's wife in version D seem to be incomplete;[209] but their meaning can be established for the second half of the thirteenth century,[210] though from an Old Czech recast of the first part of the fourteenth century only.[211] In this *Vévoda Arnošt* reference is made to reliable reports that God is working wonderful miracles through the (relic of) this desirable empress, who (in her lifetime) had been magnificent, at *Maidburk*.[212] Edith herself is called *Diana*.[213] Facts and

Herzog Ernst?', *Sprache und Recht. Festschrift für Ruth Schmidt-Wiegand*, i (Berlin/New York, 1986), 45; cf. *idem*, 'Herzog Ernst', *Lex. des MA*, iv (1989), 2194.

[202] 'Herzog Ernst-B', lines 234–56: *Herzog Ernst*, ed. K. Bartsch (Vienna, 1869), p. 19.

[203] Slightly misleadingly, *Herzog Ernst. Ein mittelalterliches Abenteuerbuch*, trans. B. Sowinski, [Reclams] Universal-Bibliothek, 8352–7 (Stuttgart, 1970), pp. 365f, commenting on 'Herzog Ernst-B', line 244: by this Ottegebe 'is raised to the rank of holiness'.

[204] H.-J. Behr, *Herzog Ernst. Eine Übersicht über die verschiedenen Textfassungen und deren Überlieferung*, Litterae. Göppinger Beiträge zur Textgeschichte, 62 (Göppingen, 1979), p. 9; *idem*, 'Rückkehr', p. 45.

[205] *Gesta Ernesti ducis*, ed. P. Lehmann, Abhandlungen der Bayerischen Akademie der Wissenschaften, Philosophisch-philologische und historische Klasse, 32, treatise 5 (Munich, 1927), p. 10, 'Otto Mangnus [!] . . . uxorem de gente Anglorum duxit, quam alii Edhildam, alii Odogeven nominant. Que anno XI., ex quo regni consorcia tenuit, obiit in Christo, non minus sanctitate quam regali potencia clara.'

[206] *Gesta Ernesti*, p. 8; cf. Behr, *Herzog-Ernst . . . Überlieferung*, p. 25, commenting on 'Herzog Ernst Erf[urt]'.

[207] Known as a 'Latin prose of the thirteenth century', Behr, 'Herzog Ernst', col. 2194.

[208] 'Herzog Ernst', ed. R. F. M. Haupt, *Zeitschrift für deutsches Alterthum*, vii (1849), 194, lines 22–33.

[209] *Herzog Ernst D, wahrscheinlich von Ulrich von Etzenbach*, ed. H.-F. Rosenfeld, Altdeutsche Textbibliothek, 104 (Tübingen, 1991), pp. 5–6, concerning verses after lines 136 and 166.

[210] Behr, 'Herzog Ernst', col. 2194.

[211] Cf. H. Szklenar, 'Herzog Ernst', *Verfasserlex.*, iii (1981), 1175, with *Herzog Ernst D*, ed. Rosenfeld, p. xxviii.

[212] 'Vévoda Arnošt', lines 233–6 and 229–30. I have been following the New High German translation by E. von Schreiber and W. Baumann in *Herzog-Ernst-D*, ed. Rosenfeld, p. 185: 'In Maidburk . . ./ wurde sie begraben, in diesem Bistum,/ das der Kaiser selb(er) angelegt/ und mit Reichtum ausgestattet hatte./ Hier berichten sichere Nachrichten,/ daß Gott wunderbare Wunder tut/ durch die Gestalt [!] dieser begehrenswerten/ Kaiserin, die früher prächtig war.'

[213] 'Vévoda Arnošt', line 226, trans. in *Herzog-Ernst-D*, ed. Rosenfeld, p. 185.

names suggest Magdeburg traditions,[214] but Rudolf of Hohenems (about 1220)[215] included *St Ottegebe the Pure* in his verse novel 'The Good Gerhard'.[216] Rudolf of Hohenems belonged to the ministerial following of the counts of Montfort in Vorarlberg (5 km south-west of Hohenems), and the work was commissioned by Rudolf of Steinach, who belonged to the ministerial following of the bishops of Constance.[217] Rudolf insisted that the archbishopric of Magdeburg had been founded by the imperial couple with the active participation of 'the noble and the pure' empress,[218] and implies that the new church was dedicated to the highest empress, the Virgin Mary.[219] This mistaken belief may have sprung from confusion between the Ottonian cathedral and the later archiepiscopal foundation of the collegiate church of Our Lady at Magdeburg (*Liebfrauenstift*),[220] but no one on the spot would have made that mistake, since there was always a clear distinction between the cathedral and the collegiate church.[221]

Queen Edith seems to have been widely acknowledged as a holy queen during the High and Late Middle Ages. This is borne out by the treatise on 'the zeal and enthusiasm of the ancient German princes for the Christian religion and the servants of God', composed by the highly esteemed jurist and later bishop of Bamberg (1353–63) Lupold of Bemberg in the years 1341/42 to demonstrate the well-proven faith of German kings and emperors, and their wives, which had been acknowledged by the popes.[222] That the thirteenth chapter, 'On the zeal for the Christian religion of certain ancient German queens or empresses and on the miracles wrought through their merits', was written with St Mathilda, St Edith, Adelheid, Cunegund and Radegund in mind, is demonstrated by the notes inserted into the margins of the incunabulum of the treatise by Jacob Wimpfeling in 1497.[223] There was no process of canonisation, but Edith's holiness was known, nevertheless, though not recognised to the extent of giving her 'the honours of the altars' ('Ehre der Altäre'). There seem to be no altars, let alone churches dedicated to St Edith of Magdeburg. Nevertheless, considering that the first canonisation by a

---

214 Cf. *Gesta archiepiscoporum Magdeburgensium*, ii, 377 with *Annales Magdeburgenses, s.a.* 938, ed. G. H. Pertz, *MGH SS*, xvi (1859), 143: 'Diana'. *Die Magdeburger Schöppenchronik*, i, ed. C. Hegel, *Die Chroniken der deutschen Städte vom 14. bis ins 16. Jahrhundert*, vii (Leipzig, 1869), 7: 'godinne Diane'.

215 Cf. W. Walliczek, 'Rudolf von Ems', *Verfasserlex.*, viii/2 (1991), 324 with N. H. Ott, 'Rudolf von Ems', *Lex. des MA*, vii/5 (1994), 1084.

216 *Der guote Gêrhart von Rudolf von Ems*, ed. J. A. Asher, *Altdt. Textbibl.*, 56, 3rd edn (Tübingen, 1989), p. 5: 'Sante Ottegebe diu reine'.

217 Ott, 'Rudolf von Ems', cols 1083–4.

218 Asher, *Der guote Gêrhart*, p. 8 'diu edel und diu reine'.

219 *Ibid.*, p. 6.

220 *Urkundenbuch des Klosters Unser Lieben Frauen zu Magdeburg*, ed. G. Hertel, Geschichtsquellen der Provinz Sachsen und angrenzender Gebiete, 10 (Halle, 1878).

221 Cf. M. Kintzinger, 'Magdeburg A II', *Lex. des MA*, vi/1 (1992), 75.

222 Cf. K. Colberg, 'Lupold von Bebenburg', *Verfasserlex.*, v (1985), 1076. Modern Bemberg lies nearly 20 km SW of Rothenburg o.d.T., nearly 5 km E of Gerabronn.

223 Hain/Copinger, no. 2725, here fol. xix[a]–xxi[a], subtitle fol. xix[a], 'De zelo Christianae religionis quarundam veterum reginarum seu imperatricum Germanarum ac de miraculis per merita quarundam ex eis facta.'

pope occurred in 997, one should be cautious about accepting too readily the latest conclusion that 'Edith's canonisation was stalled from the start'.[224]

Such a statement has more validity in relation to Margaret of Brabant. It was in September, 1315, that a delegation from Lombardy arrived at the court of King John of Bohemia and presented five documents on miracles wrought at the tomb of Queen Margaret at the Friars Minors of Genoa.[225] The first miraculous healing occurred on the seventh day after the queen's death in December 1311. The notarial document, by which it was attested, is dated on 10 April 1313.[226] Two other miracles were attested in the same year, the first of these in the archiepiscopal palace at Genoa itself,[227] and there was another in 1315, which numbered the local archbishop among the witnesses.[228] The fifth healing also took place in 1313.[229] At least two of these events took place while the widower Emperor Henry VII was still alive, and we know from accounts of his Italian expedition that he held his wife in high esteem. Albertinus Mussatus, famous as the first Poet Laureate of modern [!] times,[230] and an occasional eye-witness of the transactions at the royal court,[231] is explicit in giving her a prominent role in consultations and decisions at court.[232] Mussatus even insists on her gift of eloquence, whereas her husband appeared to be slow and chary of words.[233] The king did not hesitate to demand for her a share of money or other gifts, when he took payments from a Lombard town like Padua[234] or Asti or Genoa.[235] He even allowed her to have her own, though not always separate, court, and some financial dealings of her own. The accounts of Giles, clerk of Madame the Queen of the Romans, are preserved for a period of eight and a half months in 1310/11,[236] and it is clear that the queen's court had to be heavily subsidised by the king.[237] The establishment of the queen's *curia* may have been a temporary expedient, since there is no trace of a steward

---

224 Fried, *Ursprünge Deutschlands*, p. 515: 'Ediths Kanonisation blieb im Ansatz stecken'.

225 *Chronica Aulae Regiae*, i.123, ed. J. Emler, Fontes rerum Bohemicarum, 4 (Prague, 1884), pp. 219–20.

226 *Ibid.*, p. 220, 'Actum in domo fratrum Minorum Ianuensium anno Domini MCCCXIII., indiccione duodecima [!], die decimo Aprilis, presentibus fratre Bonifacio Epynola, fratre . . .'.

227 *Ibid.*, p. 221 no. 2 (28 June 1313), 'Actum Ianue in palacio archiepiscopali sancti Silvestri anno Domini MCCCXIII⁰, indiccione undecima [correct], die vicesima octava Iunii, presentibus Rostagno'; *ibid.*, p. 222 no. 4 (1313, without day of the month).

228 *Ibid.*, pp. 221–2 no. 3 (13.vi.1315), 'in presencia fratris Porcheti, archiepiscopi Ianuensis, Iohannis Turci de Claresco'.

229 *Ibid.*, 222 no. 5; the instrument has no dating clause.

230 M. Picone, 'Albertino Mussato', *Lex. des MA*, vi/5 (1992), 971: crowned at Padua with ivy and myrtle, 25.xii.1315.

231 Mussatus, *Historia Augusta*, ii.7, ed. Muratori, *Scriptores*, x, 351–2, etc.

232 *Historia Augusta*, i.8, cols 329–30; ii.5, col. 349; iii.4, col. 364; etc.

233 *Ibid.*, i.13, col. 340.

234 *Ibid.*, iii.6, col. 372.

235 F. Prowe, 'Die Finanzverwaltung am Hofe Heinrichs VII. während des Römerzuges', Phil. Diss. Berlin (Berlin, 1888), p. 14 n. 2.

236 'Contes Gile, clerc madame la royne des Romains', ed. J. Schwalm, 'Apocha rationis camerae reginae', *MGH Constitutiones*, iv/2 (1909–11), 1150–52 no. 1151 [!].

237 Cf. Prowe, *Finanzverwaltung*, p. 14.

of her household, whereas *magistri curię* (regalis) are hinted at since King Rudolf I of Habsburg in 1290,[238] King Adolf of Nassau in 1293[239] and King Albert I in 1300,[240] and the office is firmly established under King Henry VII in 1309,[241] allegedly because of its success at the head of princely households during the second half of the thirteenth century.[242] When the difficulties in Lombardy required firm action, the queen's court was united with the king's on the eve of Trinity Sunday, 1311[243] to prepare for the famous siege of Brescia.

This queen had died too early to accompany her husband to the imperial consecration at Rome. We know from Henry VII that he and the pope had planned to celebrate this exactly 350 years after the imperial consecration of Otto I, that is on Candlemas (2 February), 1312. Henry VII's policy and that of his court, including the queen, aimed not only at a revival of the Staufen emperorship, but also, after several generations of monarchs had not gone to Italy, at an imitation of an Ottonian king who had. In the context of those ambitions there was room even for an attempt to imitate the four Ottonian queens and empresses in sanctity. But constitutional and religious developments were no longer helpful to the central powers in the Romano-German empire, and queens were not spared the effects of these developments. They lost any overriding stature and became, at best, important for their territorial connections and for local traditions.[244]

Appendix I

a. Habsburg burials at Gaming and Vienna

1. Gaming. 'Mary's Throne', the Carthusian monastery at Gaming, with its church of the 'Assumption of the Holy Virgin'[245] was founded in 1330 by Duke Albert II of Austria and settled with Carthusians from Mauerbach

---

238 *MGH Constitutiones*, iii (1904–06), 427 no. 445; cf. *Regesta Imperii*, vi/1 (1898), no. 2379 (21.x.1290) without a name.

239 Knight Raimund of Cologne in *Regesta Imperii*, vi/2 (1948), 83 no. 233 (2.v.1293).

240 *MGH, Constitutiones*, iv/1 (1906), 71 no. 93 (26.ii.1300): Nicholas of Wartenfels, this 12 km N of Kulmbach; *Stielers Handatlas*, map. 13 C4/5.

241 John of Braunshorn: *MGH Constitutiones*, iv/1, 250 no. 287 (1.iv.1309); p. 290 no. 336 (3.xii.1309); etc. – Geoffrey of Leiningen: *ibid.*, p. 815 no. 813 (30.vi.1312); p. 817 no. 815 (4.vii.1312), etc. Cf. *Kaiser Heinrichs Romfahrt*, p. 141 no. 81; *Il Viaggio*, p. 152 no. 23. Braunshorn on the Hunsrück lies 16 km WSW of St Goar.

242 Cf. W. Rösener, 'Hofämter an mittelalterlichen Fürstenhöfen', *Deutsches Archiv*, xlv/2 (1989; appeared 1990), 549 with reference to the royal court, only to 1309.

243 'Apocha rationis', p. 1152.

244 Everything that sounds like English in this paper is due to the painstaking efforts of Dr Anne Duggan and Mr Martin Jones (King's College, London), and to the typing of Renate Weich (Saarbrücken); the stubborn Germanisms are my own.

245 'Marienthron, Klosterkirche Mariä-Himmelfahrt', *Handbuch der deutschen Kunstdenkmäler*, ed. G. Dehio, *Niederösterreich*, 5th edn (1976), p. 70.

(Allerheiligental),[246] 16 kilometres due west of Vienna, which had been founded in 1313[247] or 1316 by Albert II's next eldest brother Frederick the Fair (who was buried there after his death in January 1330 at Gutenstein, Lower Austria, 50 kilometres due south-west of Vienna).[248] Originally planned for a location near Lucerne, the foundation-stone of the church was laid at Gaming in 1332; the church was consecrated in 1342[249] and all the buildings were completed in 1358.[250] A double-sized house of twenty monastic cells,[251] it was the largest Carthusian house in the German province of the order. The preparations for the ducal burial ostensibly pointed to a transfer of the concentration of power into the Austrian lands;[252] indeed, Albert II buried his wife Joan of Pfirt in Gaming in 1351,[253] but after his own entombment in 1358, there was only one further Habsburg burial there, that of his daughter-in-law Elizabeth (d. 1373),[254] first wife of Albert III and daughter of Charles IV. The 'duke's vault' at Gaming[255] thus contained only one duke, one wife and one daughter-in-law!

2. Vienna, St Stephen's. When Rudolf IV, 'the Founder', died at Milan in 1365, he was buried not at Gaming but in the 'dukes' vault' of St Stephen's in Vienna.[256] Imitating the kings of old, he had been re-modelling the Viennese parish church into an 'archduke's church' in the style of Gothic cathedrals from 1359 onwards, and he crowned this demonstration of ducal dominion with a series of kinglike statues and the specially-constructed ducal burial chamber.[257] St Stephen's was not raised to the status of a collegiate church until 1365,[258] but even before Archduke Rudolf's interment in that year, his next younger brother Frederick, who had died in Vienna in 1362, was buried there.[259] It is therefore no surprise that Rudolf IV's wife Catherine of Bohemia also received her final resting place in St Stephen's, following her death in Vienna in 1395. A daughter of the late Emperor Charles IV, she was also known as Catherine 'of Luxemburg'.[260]

---

246 H. Paulhart, 'Gaming', *LThK*, 2nd edn, iii (1960), 511.
247 Dehio, *Niederösterreich*, p. 207.
248 F. Loidl, 'Mauerbach', *LThK*, 2nd edn, vii (1962), 185; Hamann, p. 145; Stieler's *Hand-Atlas* (1921), map 17 E6.
249 Hamann, p. 34; Dehio, *Niederösterreich*, p. 70.
250 Paulhart, 'Gaming', col. 511.
251 Dehio, *Niederösterreich*, p. 70: 'Doppelkartause mit 20 Mönchszellen'.
252 Cf. Hamann, p. 34, 'Schwerpunktverlagerung auf die österreichischen Lande'.
253 Paulhart, 'Gaming', col. 511; Hamann, p. 179.
254 A. A. Strnad, 'Albrecht III.', *Lex. des MA*, i/2 (1978), 321–2; Hamann, p. 84; Krieger, *Die Habsburger*, p. 239. The date of her death is given as 1378 in Paulhart, 'Gaming', col. 511: a misprint?
255 Hamann, p. 84, 'Herzogsgruft'.
256 Hamann, p. 407; cf. above at n. 96.
257 Hamann, p. 409: 'Programm der Fürstenfiguren und der herzoglichen Grabpflege ['grave care'] (als) Höchstmaß an herrscherlicher Repräsentation [!]'.
258 W. Stelzer in Hamann, p. 409.
259 Hamann, p. 148; Hawlik-van de Water, *Kapuzinergruft*, p. 322.
260 Hamann, p. 234; Krieger, *Die Habsburger*, p. 238 (genealogical table, p. 239, but not repeated below).

The burial-place of the reigning duke was clearly more important than that of less elevated members of the family. Although Albert III's first wife was buried at Gaming,[261] and his younger brother Leopold III (d. 1386) at Königsfelden,[262] Albert himself (known as the Duke with the Pigtail)[263] was interred in St Stephen's Vienna,[264] having died at Laxenburg Castle in Lower Austria, 16 kilometres due south of Vienna,[265] and so were his son Albert IV the Patient (d. 1404),[266] who died at Klosterneuburg[267] and his daughter-in-law, Joan Sophie of Bavaria (d. 1410).[268] Small wonder that the search is now on for the tomb of Albert's second wife, Beatrix of Zollern[269] or of Nuremberg.[270] She died in 1414 at Perchtoldsdorf in Lower Austria, 13 kilometres south-south-west of Vienna,[271] and her grave has never been found; equally, the tomb of his sister Catherine, who died in 1387 as abbess of St Clara, Vienna, remains unidentified.[272]

Since Duke William the Friendly (d. 1406) and his brother Duke Leopold IV the Fat (d. 1411) were also interred in St Stephen's,[273] it is likely that from that time onwards special circumstances explain when a reigning member of the Habsburg dynasty of Austria was not entombed in St Stephen's, Vienna, or directly in its princes' vault ('Fürstengruft des Stephansdoms'),[274] nominal cathedral church since 1469.[275] This impression is reinforced by the conveyance of Frederick

---

261 See above, n. 254.
262 Cf. above at nn. 103 and 108.
263 'Albrecht III. mit dem Zopfe', Hamann, p. 36; Krieger, *Die Habsburger*, p. 239. The nickname points to his foundation of a knights' company and the emblem of its members; cf. Strnad, 'Albrecht III.', col. 322; Hamann, pp. 36–7 (with illustration).
264 Strnad, 'Albrecht III.', col. 321.
265 'Schloß Laxenburg': Strnad, 'Albrecht III.', col. 321, Hamann, p. 36. But 'das Alte Schloß' at Laxenburg, in the possession of the Habsburgs from the fourteenth century onwards, was a moated castle: Brockhaus, xi (1970), 220, 'Wasserburg'. This historical note is omitted from the 2nd edn, xii (1990), 163. The term 'Wasserburg' is missing in L. Villena and others, *Glossaire. Burgenfachwörterbuch des mittelalterlichen Wehrbaus* (Frankfurt am Main, 1975), p. 193 [Index]; cf. *Stielers Handatlas*, map 17 D7.
266 Krieger, 'Habsburger', p. 238.
267 Hamann, p. 38; F. Röhrig, 'Klosterneuburg', *Lex. des MA*, v (1991), 1225–6: duke's castle, double monastery ('Doppelstift'), and central place for the cult of the holy Babenberg duke Leopold III.
268 Hamann, p. 180; Krieger, *Die Habsburger*, p. 238.
269 Hamann, p. 65.
270 Krieger, 'Habsburger', p. 238. The form 'Nuremburg' as English for 'Nürnberg' seems to be a misprint in *Muir's Historical Atlas*, map 31 B.
271 Hamann, p. 65; *Stielers Handatlas*, map 17 D7. The castle was already a ruin by the fifteenth century: Brockhaus, xiv (1972), 366. This historical note is missing from the 2nd edn, xvi (1991), 662 and ascribed to the fifteenth–sixteenth centuries in Dehio, *Niederösterreich*, p. 246.
272 Hamann, pp. 233–4.
273 Hawlik-van de Water, *Kapuzinergruft*, p. 322.
274 Hamann, pp. 36, 38, 407, etc.
275 Cf. 'Stephansdom', Brockhaus, xviii (1973), 85, with F. Loidl, 'Wien 1–3', *LThK*, 2nd edn, x (1965), 1112. Contrary to the *New Encyclopædia Britannica*, xi (1988), 248, there is no article 'Stephansdom' in the 2nd edn of Brockhaus, xxi (1993), 164, and the notice *s.v.*

the Fair (d. 1330) from Mauerbach to St Stephen's in 1789,[276] comparable to the transportation to St Stephen's of Elizabeth, widowed queen of France (d. 1592) from her foundation Mary Queen of Angels, Vienna,[277] and of Empress Eleonora (d. 1655) from her foundation for Carmelite sisters in Vienna, both in 1782.[278] But all these facts are misleading. The last of the Habsburg emperors to be buried immediately at the Stephansdom was Frederick III (d. 1493), and then only in part: his heart and entrails found their rest at the parish church of Linz, where he had died.[279]

3. **Vienna, St Mary of the Angels – the Capuchin vault.**   It was only from 1633 onwards that the Habsburgs finally had their imperial vault, and that under the church of St Mary of the Angels in Vienna, built for Capuchin friars in 1622–32.[280] Emperor Matthias (d. 1619) is said to be 'the first Habsburg sovereign who was entombed in the Capuchin vault, [allegedly] established by his consort'.[281] Empress Anna of Tyrol, 'the foundress of the Capuchin vault',[282] had died in 1618, three months before her husband.[283] In her last will she had, together with her husband, founded not only the Capuchin house at Vienna, but also the later imperial vault. Neither was consecrated until 1632, and the imperial couple lay provisionally in the Poor Clares' monastery of Mary Queen of Angels until 1633, when they were ceremonially transferred to the Capuchin vault.[284] Although the 'Vault of the Angels' ('Engelsgruft') was small and built for the founders only,[285] Habsburg burials were habitually celebrated there from that time onwards, from the empresses Mary Anne (d. 1646)[286] and Mary Leopoldine (d. 1649)[287] and their husband Emperor Ferdinand III (d. 1657)[288] to Archduke Leopold, died at Willimantic in Connecticut in 1958,[289] and Empress Zita, who died at St John's

---

'Wien' (*ibid.*, xxiv [1994], 171) does not contain the information used above, neither does the *New Enc. Brit.*, xxix (1988), 510, *s.v.* 'Vienna'.

[276] Hamann, p. 145. Hawlik-van de Water, *Kapuzinergruft*, p. 322.

[277] Hamann, pp. 87, 88 [Marianne Rauchensteiner].

[278] Hamann, pp. 78 and 79: 'Siebenbüchnerinnenkloster [in der Sterngasse]' for 'Karmelit<er>innen'. The facts are confused in Hawlik-van de Water, '*Kapuzinergruft*', p. 322.

[279] Hamann, p. 149. Hawlik-van de Water, *Kapuzinergruft*, p. 325, has for Linz 'bone and heart' – or is it '[one] leg and heart' ('Bein und Herz')?

[280] Dehio, *Wien*, 6th edn (1973): p. 28, 'Kapuziner-Kirche heilige Maria zu den Engeln'; p. 29, 'Kaisergruft'; cf. pp. [222–3] no. 6 ['Wein I, Südwestviertel'].

[281] V. Press, 'Kaiser Matthias', *NDB*, xvi (1990), 405, 'als erster habsburgischer Herrscher in der von seiner Gemahlin errichteten [!] Wiener Kapuzinergruft beigesetzt'.

[282] 'Die Gründerin der Kapuzinergruft': caption in Hamann, p. 58.

[283] Hamann, pp. 57, 353.

[284] Hamann, p. 58, 'provisorisch im Königin-Kloster' [R. Neck]; Hawlik-van de Water, *Kapuzinergruft*, p. 28.

[285] Hawlik-van de Water, *Kapuzinergruft*, p. 28.

[286] Hamann, pp. 289–90.

[287] *Ibid.*, pp. 328–9.

[288] *Ibid.*, p. 112.

[289] *Ibid.*, pp. 263–4.

collegiate church at Zizers in Graubünden (Switzerland),[290] 10 kilometres north of Chur,[291] and was entombed in the Capuchin vault, some two weeks after her death in 1989.[292]

b. Burials at Stams

The Cistercian abbey of Stams had been founded by Count Meinhard II of Görz-Tyrol and his wife Elizabeth of Bavaria, widow of the Staufen king Conrad IV (d. 1254), to serve as the burial church of Tyrolian territorial princes. The year was 1273 at the latest (because ex-Queen Elizabeth died in this year)[293] and not 1284,[294] which was the year of the consecration. 5 November 1284[295] was a Sunday, and St Malachy's day, as celebrated by the Cistercians.[296] Since Malachy was renowned for successfully introducing Cistercian monasticism into Ireland, starting with Mellifont (west-north-west of Drogheda, county Louth),[297] one may deduce from the choice of 'his' Sunday in 1284 that the celebrations at Stams were signalling a Malachy-like role for the founder[298] and a Mellifont-like position for the foundation. Meinhard II and Elizabeth of Bavaria and Stams introduced Cistercian monks into Tyrol, as Malachy and Mellifont had introduced their fellow-brethren into Ireland.

Neither had the date been left to chance, nor was it the casual result of building activities on the site since 1273. That may be surmised from the fact that the celebrations were attended not only by Meinhard, but also by seven bishops, and

---

[290] Brockhaus, 2nd edn, xxiv (1994), 572: 14 March 1989; cf. *ibid.*, xxv (1994), 1045. That she found her last rest at Vienna may be surmised from the 16 lines in *Archiv der Gegenwart*, ed. W. Zürrer, lix (St Augustin, 1989), 33142, which omit her place of death, day of entombment, and burial church.

[291] *Stielers Handatlas*, map 14 D9. There had been a royal villa at Zizers long ago, which had been given to Bishop Hartbert of Chur in 955: BO 241, 249; *Regesta Imperii*, ii, Index (1992), p. 327.

[292] Confirmed by W. Stelzer (Vienna) and K. Andermann (Karlsruhe), to whom I owe the reference to Hawlik-van de Water, *Kapuzinergruft*, pp. 309 and 312: entombed 1 April 1989 at 3 pm., the hour of her husband's death in Madeira on 1 April 1922 (1992 is a misprint).

[293] K. Spahr, 'Stams', *LThK*, 2nd edn, ix (1964), 1008; Decker-Hauff, 'Staufisches Haus', p. 364 no. 89.

[294] This is suggested by H. Dopsch, 'Meinhard IV.', *Lex. des MA*, vi/3 (1992), 474.

[295] Riedmann, 'Mittelalter', p. 604; W. Köfler, 'Die Gründung von Stift Stams', in *Eines Fürsten Traum. Meinhard II. – Das Werden Tirols*, Exhibition catalogue, edd. J. Riedmann *et al.* (Tyrol/Innsbruck,1995), p. 337.

[296] Grotefend/Asch, pp. 76, 181 table 19. Malachy had died in the arms of St Bernard at Clairvaux on 1/2 November 1148, and the Latin Church generally celebrated his feast on 2 (later 3) Nov. (cf. D. H. Farmer, *The Oxford Dictionary of Saints*, 3rd edn (1992), p. 315). His first Life had been written by St Bernard himself: A. Gwynn, 'Malachias', *LThK*, 2nd edn, vi (1961), 1322–3.

[297] Gwynn, 'Malachias', 1322–3; *idem* and R. N. Hadcock, *Medieval Religious Houses: Ireland* (London, 1970), pp. 116, 139–40; D. Ó Cróinín, 'Malachias', *Lex. des MA*, vi/1 (1992), 160.

[298] Köfler, 'Gründung', p. 339.

that the monks moved from their temporary wooden buildings to the new structures more than two weeks later, on 21 November 1284.[299] In connection with those purely Cistercian connotations there is room for additional motives: if not for a general Staufen memorial foundation (*staufische Gedächtnisstiftung*)[300] then perhaps for a 'memorial foundation of Conrad-Conradin', through his mother Elizabeth of Bavaria, pointing back to her first marriage with the last-but-one Staufen king, Conrad IV. Conrad-Conradin had been supported by her second husband, although Meinhard II had not followed his stepson to the disastrous battle of Tagliacozzo, let alone to execution in the market place of Naples on 29 October 1268.[301] Stams was founded by Conrad-Conradin's mother and stepfather within five years, and the anniversary of his death fell on the octave before the consecration day of 5 November! But if there was such a deliberate memorial plan, why was it not recorded at the time?

Local tradition[302] and modern scholarship uphold the concept of a connection between Conrad-Conradin and Stams. But it is a deduction of later historiography, starting only with Wolfgang Lebersorg (d. 1646),[303] to connect the monastery of Stams with the death of Conrad-Conradin in 1268, as if Stams had been a memorial foundation by his mother Elizabeth[304] for the last male Staufen. The remarkable generosity of Meinhard II (d. 1295) and his wife in establishing this Cistercian house should be connected with the wish both to establish a spiritual centre for the newly emerging 'land' and also to create a respectable burial place for the princely dynasty. Elizabeth and Meinhard, and their descendants, were buried there,[305] among them Henry VI, duke of Carinthia and count of Tyrol from 1295, king of Bohemia and Poland 1307–10, who died at the castle of Tyrol in 1335.[306] The 'success' of this foundation had been in some respects prepared by Meinhard II, when he had the remains of his ancestors transferred from the castle of Tyrol[307] to Stams.

The idea of a burial church for the dynasty in the sense of the mausoleum of

---

[299] *Ibid.*, pp. 337ff.
[300] Cf. *ibid.*, p. 339.
[301] H. M. Schaller, 'Konradin', *NDB*, xii (1980), 557, 559; P. Herde, 'Konradin', *Lex. des MA*, v (1991), 1368.
[302] Köfler, 'Gründung', p. 340. In a lecture on 'Meran und das Stift Stams aus historischer Sicht' (City Library of Meran, 2 June 1995), J. M. Köll, abbot of Stams, was quite convinced that the tragic end of Conrad-Conradin had been the impulse, though indirect, for the foundation of the monastery.
[303] Köfler, 'Gründung', p. 340.
[304] Against Laubenberger, 'Grablegen', p. 37 n. 7, who even talks of 'Kaiser Konrad IV.'; cf. Riedmann, 'Mittelalter', p. 427, and *idem, Eines Fürsten Traum*, pp. 342 and 344, commenting on nos 12.2 and 12.10 respectively.
[305] Laubenberger, 'Grablegen', p. 37 n. 7 conveniently refers to Oswald Graf Trapp, 'Die Grabstätten der Landesfürsten und ihrer Familienmitglieder in Tirol', *Jahrbuch der Vereinigung katholischer Edelleute in Österreich* (Innsbruck/Vienna/Munich, 1933); Riedmann, 'Mittelalter', p. 431.
[306] H. Dopsch, 'Heinrich VI.', *Lex. des MA*, iv (1989), 2070.
[307] Riedmann, 'Mittelalter', p. 431.

the territorial princes (*Mausoleum der Landesfürsten*)[308] was acknowledged as territorially useful, when Duke Frederick IV of Austria-Tyrol (Friedl 'with the Empty Pocket') was buried in Stams as the first of the Habsburgs in 1439.[309] Whether he had himself prepared for this event by commissioning life-size monumental statues to embellish the grave monument at Stams seems doubtful, for it was his son Sigismund 'Rich-in-Coins' who in 1475 made the contract with the Augsburg sculptor Hans Radolt.[310] 'Friedl with the Empty Pocket' had been married twice, and both his wives, together with three young children, had been entombed in the so-called Frederick's vault at Stams: Elizabeth of the Rhenish Palatinate in 1409 and Anne of Brunswick-Lüneburg in 1432.[311] Friedl's only surviving son Duke Sigismund 'Rich-in-Coins' buried his first wife Eleanor of Scotland, after she had died at Innsbruck in 1480, in a new vault in the western part of the church of the monastery of Stams, and he himself was entombed there also, having died at Innsbruck in 1496.[312]

The burial church of Tyrol at Stams was thus re-used by the Habsburgs from 1409. How far this had been the intention of the two founders in 1273 is difficult to establish. But it is surely not without significance that Elizabeth of Görz-Tyrol, daughter of Elizabeth and Meinhard II, was about twelve years old when she left her family to be married to King Rudolf's son Albert in 1274, and it was she who wanted to be known as (co-)foundress of Königsfelden, which functioned for a time as a Habsburg memorial monastery.[313] When in 1309 she set out the duties of Königsfelden's Poor Clares, she required that the abbess and convent should always intercede with the Divine Clemency for herself and her dead husband as well as for all her ancestors and her children, living or dead.[314]

---

308 This term is used for 1273 already: *Geschichte Tirols. Zur Ausstellung auf Schloß Tirol*, edd. J. Nössing and H. Noflatscher, 2nd edn (Bozen, 1991), p. 40 [K. Wolfsgruber].

309 *Reclams Kunstführer Österreich*, ii, 739; Riedmann, 'Mittelalter', p. 482, 484–6; Maleczek, 'Friedrich IV.', *Lex. des MA*, iv/5 (1988), 954; Hamann, p. 148; P. Rainer in *Geschichte Tirols*, edd. Nössing/Noflatscher, pp. 35 and 48.

310 Riedmann, 'Mittelalter', p. 616: Frederick IV; G. Ammann, 'Die Stiftskirche [Stams] als Grablege der Tiroler Landesfürsten', in *Eines Fürsten Traum*, pp. 449–50, 451 no. 17.5: Sigismund.

311 Hamann, pp. 85 and 52; Ammann, 'Die Stiftskirche', pp. 449 and 451 no. 17.3.

312 Hamann, pp. 74 and 418, 'Sigmund "der Münzreiche" '; Ammann, 'Die Stiftskirche', pp. 449–50. His second wife Catharine of Saxony left the Habsburg lands for her new husband Duke Erich of Brunswick in 1496/97 and was buried at Minden, after she had died at the new residence of Calenberg (south of Hanover), in 1524: Hamann, p. 235; cf. *Stielers Handatlas*, map 9 D8 and D6 respectively.

313 See above, at nn. 97–103.

314 According to her charter's arenga, 'Elyzabeth, quondam Romanorum regina' frees the convent from temporal needs, so that 'valet omnipotens Dominus devotorum suorum preces exaudiens pro nostre salutis augmento confidentius exorari'. Her most intense wishes are, 'nostre ac dive recordacionis domini Alberti, Romanorum regis, thori nostri consortis karissimi, nec non progenitorum nostrorum animarum saluti felicius intendere'. The convent's duty is, 'ut pro nobis et prefato domino nostro ac marito necnon pro vivis et defunctis nostris liberis ac progenitoribus universis divinam clementiam iugiter interpellent'; therefore 'curiam nostram Rinvelden . . . tradimus': *Codex diplomaticus Alemanniae*, ii, 369 no. 1073 (1309).

Appendix II

Queens and Empresses in the Romano-German Empire to 1324

Mathilda (d. 968)	m.	Henry I (d. 936)
Edith (d. 946)		
Adelheid (d. 999)	m.	Otto I (d. 973)
Theophano (d. 991)	m.	Otto II (d. 983)
Cunigunde (d. 1033)	m.	Henry II (d. 1024)
Gisela (d. 1043)	m.	Conrad II (d. 1039)
Gunhild-Cunigund (d. 1038)	m.	Henry III (d. 1056)
Agnes (d. 1077)		
Berta (d. 1087)	m.	Henry IV (d. 1106)
Eupraxia-Praxedis-Adelheid (d. 1109)		
Mathilda (d. 1167)	m.	Henry V (d. 1125)
Richenza of Nordheim (d. 1141)	m.	Lothar III (d. 1137)
[Gertrude of Comburg (d. 1130/31)]	m.	Conrad III (d. 1152)
Gertrude of Sulzbach (d. 1146)		
Adele of Vohburg (d. after 1187)	m.	Frederick I (d. 1190)
Beatrice of Burgundy (d. 1184)		
Constance I (d. 1198)	m.	Henry VI (d. 1197)
Isabella-Elizabeth-Yolante of Brienne (d. 1228)	m.	Frederick II (d. 1250)
Bianca Marchioness Lancia (d.1233/4)		
Isabella-Elizabeth of England (d. 1241)		
Margaret of Austria (d. 1267)	m.	Henry (VII; d. 1242)
Elizabeth of Bavaria (d. 1273)	m.	Conrad IV (d. 1254)
Beatrice of Brabant (d. 1288)	m.	Henry Raspe (d. 1247)
Elizabeth of Brunswick (d. 1266)	m.	William of Holland (d. 1265)
Yolante-Violante of Aragon (d. 1300)	m.	Alfonso X of Castile (d. 1284)
Sanch(i)a of Provence (d. 1261)	m.	Richard of Cornwall (d. 1272)
Beatrice of Valkenburg (d. 1277)		
Gertrude-Anne of Hohenberg (d. 1281)	m.	Rudolf I of Habsburg (d. 1291)
Agnes-Elizabeth-Isabella of Burgundy (d. 1323)		
Imagina of Isenburg-Limburg (d. after 1313)	m.	Adolf of Nassau (d. 1298)
Isabella of Görz-Tyrol (d. 1313)	m.	Albert I of Habsburg (murdered 1308)
Beatrice of Glogau (d. 1322)	m.	Lewis the Bavarian (d. 1347)
Margaret of Holland (d. 1356)		
Isabella-Elizabeth of Aragon (d. 1266)	m.	Frederick the Fair (d. 1330)

6

A Medieval Queen and her Stepdaughter: Agnes and Elizabeth of Hungary

Volker Honemann

Almost seven hundred years ago, on the first day of May in the year of Our Lord 1308, Albert I, king of the Romans, was on his way to meet his queen. Together with his household, he had spent the last days of April in one of his favourite resorts, Baden on the Limmat. When news arrived that his wife, Queen Elizabeth, had left Kleinbasel to see her husband, Albert went to meet her. On his way he and his entourage had to cross the river Reuß near the village of Windisch. Boarding a boat, Albert was separated from his men – there were just three Swiss noblemen and his nephew John with him. Having arrived on the other side of the river, the king rode on – and was all of a sudden attacked by his four companions with daggers and swords. Several dagger thrusts pierced his breast, a heavy sword stroke split his face and his skull. Realising that they had achieved what they wanted the murderers fled. The bishop of Straßburg who was the first to arrive at the scene of horror found Albert covered in his blood, dying. Within a short time, the queen arrived, accompanied by members of her family. It is likely that Princess Agnes, former queen of Hungary was among them. Somehow Queen Elizabeth and the other members of the family overcame the terrible shock. In deep desperation the body of the murdered king was brought to the nearby town of Brugg, and later on to the monastery of Wettingen.[1]

The murder of King Albert on 1 May 1308 was one of the great catastrophes of German history in the Middle Ages. The causes of this crime need not concern us here – Albert's nephew John, soon called *Parricida*, felt himself cheated of his inheritance. Seeing no future for himself, he conspired against his uncle – successfully, as we have seen. Far more interesting are the consequences which this crime had for the German Reich and for the Hapsburg family. As for the Reich, a development which would have led to a strong kingship based upon a solid

---

1 See A. Hessel, *Jahrbücher des Deutschen Reiches unter König Albrecht I. von Habsburg* (Munich, 1931), pp. 222–7; B. Meyer, 'Studien zum habsburgischen Hausrecht. I. Die Ermordung Albrechts in Windisch', *Zeitschrift für Schweizerische Geschichte*, xxv (1945), 153–76; and A. Nevsimal, 'Königin Agnes von Ungarn. Leben und Stellung in der habsburgischen Politik ihrer Zeit', dissertation (Vienna, 1951), pp. 87–90, who discusses a number of chronicles which state that Agnes stayed at least in the 'Vorlande' at the time of the murder. Together with her mother, Queen Elizabeth, she was present at the burial of Albrecht I in Speyer.

'Hausmacht' was abruptly halted. Within a short time the evils of particularism which repeatedly damaged the development of the Reich could again be seen everywhere. Even more important was the impact of the murder on the Hapsburg family. From one moment to the next, the focal point of the family no longer existed, and the life and fate of Agnes and her stepdaughter Elizabeth, the two royal women who are the subject of this paper, were completely changed by this catastrophe.[2]

Agnes, second daughter of Albert I and his wife Elizabeth of Görz-Tyrol, one of no less than twelve surviving children of this couple, was born in 1280. Several marriage-projects organised by her father failed,[3] but in 1296 Agnes was married to Andrew III, king of Hungary, the last of the kings from the dynasty of the Arpads. Five years later, on 14 January 1301, the king died. The marriage seems to have been an unhappy one – Andrew was a notorious womaniser – and there were no children apart from one daughter from the king's first marriage with Fenena of Kujawia, a child, called Elizabeth, born around 1293. After the death of her husband, Agnes left Hungary. An Austrian military expedition, led by Agnes's brother Duke Rudolf III and the renowned Herman of Landenberg had made its way to Ofen; after lengthy talks with the Hungarian magnates, Agnes was permitted to leave – and somehow managed to take with her her stepdaughter Elizabeth, now about eight years of age. In addition to all that, she also took with her 'very considerable treasures'.[4] Because of her enormous dowry, she had been regarded as the wealthiest bride in Europe – but now she seems to have become truly rich. A few years later, in 1304, in an agreement with the new king of Hungary, Charles Robert of Anjou (who had been supported by the Hapsburgs) Duke Rudolf succeeded in safeguarding the whole of Agnes's widow's estate.[5] Back in Vienna, Agnes decided to live in the midst of the great Hapsburg domestic circle. She never married again. Shortly after her father had been murdered, she and her mother founded a monastery for Franciscan nuns and friars, called Königsfelden. It was built at the place where the murder had been committed. By the side of the monastery, Agnes had a small residential complex built for herself – and there she lived for more than fifty years, dying in 1364.

As for her stepdaughter Elizabeth, we know very little about her.[6] At a very

---

2 For details see A. Lhotsky, *Geschichte Österreichs seit der Mitte des 13. Jahrhunderts* (Vienna, 1967), pp. 155–64. Because of the close relationship between them, most historical sources and studies treat Agnes and Elizabeth together. Due to the considerable political influence she had, Agnes always gets the lion's share; see for example the (unpleasantly patriotic) book of H. v. Liebenau, *Hundert Urkunden zu der Geschichte der Königin Agnes von Ungarn* (Regensburg, 1869), with 'Regesten' of historical sources mentioning Agnes, Nevsimal, 'Königin Agnes', Lhotsky, *Geschichte Österreichs*, and the excellent studies of G. Boner: 'Die Gründung des Klosters Königsfelden', *Zeitschrift für schweizerische Kirchengeschichte*, xlvii (1953), 1–24, 81–112, 181–209; 'Königin Agnes von Ungarn', *Brugger Neujahrsblätter*, lxxiv (1964), 3–30.
3 Lhotsky, *Geschichte Österreichs*, p. 119.
4 *Ibid.*, p. 121; Nevsimal, 'Königin Agnes', pp. 121–2.
5 Liebenau, *Hundert Urkunden*, p. 24; Nevsimal, 'Königin Agnes', p. 77.
6 See n. 2 above and *Das Leben der Schwestern zu Töß beschrieben von Elsbet Stagel samt*

early age she was engaged to Wenzel III, heir to the crown of Bohemia. This meant that at the moment of King Andrew's death, Wenzel was one of the candidates for the Hungarian throne – and that makes it clear why the Hapsburgs were very eager to take Elizabeth, this 'precious pledge', with them.[7] The last thing they could possibly want was a union of the kingdoms of Bohemia and Hungary – with large parts of the Hapsburg domains in between. When it became clear that Elizabeth had left Hungary and was living in the Hapsburg household, Wenzel lost interest. In 1305 he married a daughter of the duke of Teschen. But what were Agnes's and the Hapsburg family's plans concerning Elizabeth? Based on the life of Elizabeth in the *Lives of the Nuns of Töss*,[8] Lhotsky tells us that Agnes intended to marry Elizabeth to the brother she loved most, Duke Henry of Austria.[9] But one can assume that from the moment when the Hapsburgs decided to support the aspirations of Charles Robert of Anjou to the Hungarian throne – in order to prevent a Hungaro-Bohemian union – the 'precious pledge' could no longer be used. For the following years, we know nothing about Elizabeth's fate; apparently she continued to live in the Hapsburg circle. In 1308, at the age of fifteen, she seems to have entered the renowned Dominican convent of Töss, near Winterthur. After several decades of an almost saintly life she died there in 1336.[10]

These are the bare facts – but how have they been interpreted? Here the problems start. If one looks at the medieval sources (there is a wealth of them concerning Agnes but only relatively few dealing with Elizabeth) the image is contradictory to a very high degree.[11] And if one looks at modern interpretations one will find the same. Brigitte Hamann's Hapsburg-dictionary, for example, paints a rather unpleasant picture. It is 'under disgraceful circumstances' that Agnes (forcibly) puts her stepdaughter into the convent of Töss – this seems to be the classic case of an evil stepmother and a victimised stepdaughter. As for Agnes, we are told that under the pretext of piety she developed a bigoted cleverness in

---

der Vorrede von Johannes Meier und dem Leben der Prinzessin Elisabet von Ungarn, ed. F. Vetter, Deutsche Texte des Mittelalters, 6 (Berlin, 1906), pp. xvii–xxi, 98–122, and M.-C. Däniker-Gysin, *Geschichte des Dominikanerinnenklosters Töß 1233–1525*, Neujahrsblatt der Stadtbibliothek Winterthur (Winterthur, 1958), pp. 31–2, 98.

7   Lhotsky, *Geschichte Österreichs*, p. 121.

8   See *Das Leben der Schwestern*, p. 102, and Däniker-Gysin, *Dominikanerinnenklosters Töß*, p. 31. According to the life, Elizabeth was already a nun in the convent of Töss when Duke Henry intended to marry her.

9   *Ibid.*, pp. 299–300.

10   It is not quite clear at which date Elizabeth came to Töss. Nevsimal, 'Königin Agnes', pp. 103–6 assumes that she entered the convent as late as *c.* 1316, based on the fact that on 8 August 1318 Agnes gave 200 marks of silver as a 'Leibgeding' for 'swester Elsbeten', living in the convent of Töss (see Liebenau, *Hundert Urkunden*, pp. 38–9 no. 21, and *Urkundenbuch der Stadt und Landschaft Zürich*, edd. J. Escher, P. Schweizer *et al.*, ix [Zürich, 1915], xiii [Zürich, 1957], no. 3566). On the other hand, the inscription on Elizabeth's gravestone, quoted by Johannes Meyer's manuscript of the life of Elizabeth (see below), states that dying in 1336 she had lived in Töss for twenty-eight years – which brings us back to the year 1308. To make things even more complicated the Töss chronicle gives the day of Elizabeth's death as 6 May 1338: see Nevsimal, 'Königin Agnes', p. 106.

11   See the sources discussed by Boner, 'Die Gründung', pp. 1–17, and Meyer.

worldly affairs, exercising a far-reaching and strict control over her brothers and nephews. Notions like these stem from respected historians – in this case Heide Dienst and Winfried Stelzer – and therefore they cannot easily be discarded.[12]

If we go back into the nineteenth century, the picture becomes even darker. Here we see a queen of Hungary who without any mercy persecutes the murderers of her father – their families and their men – and who, after the slaughter of the whole garrison of one of the castles of her enemies, exclaims that walking in their blood gives her no less joy than walking in the dew of May.[13] This is, to give just one example, the picture painted by the famous Swiss writer Conrad Ferdinand Meyer in his ballad 'Lady Agnes and her nuns'. It is supported by important Swiss historians of earlier times. Aegidius Tschudi in his sixteenth-century *Chronicon helveticum* asserts that in avenging the murder of her father, Agnes had ordered the execution and expulsion of almost a thousand people; altogether she had been 'much harder and sharper' ('vil strenger und scherpffer') than her brothers. Consequently, the founding of the Königsfelden monasteries and Agnes's own almost monastic life now becomes an act of expiation for her own evil doings.[14]

If we finally look at contemporary sources, chronicles of the fourteenth century, we get a wholly different picture of Agnes's personality and actions, and also of her relationship with her stepdaughter Elizabeth. The mid-fourteenth-century *Königsfelden Chronicle*[15] shows us a princess who from her early days onwards is pious, tries to avoid the society of men and seeks God, who dislikes the worldliness of courtly life (in particular tournaments) but enjoys listening to sermons or other discourse about God, and who is an example of modesty: because she is very small, she always wears clothes cut from the dresses her sisters no longer want. Married to the king of Hungary, she explains to him that she wants to remain a virgin – and is therefore loved by him even more. After his death she leads the chaste and modest life of an exemplary widow. After the death of her father, she moves to Königsfelden and builds for herself a 'small and modest house, which looked more like a hermit's cell than the lodgings of a queen'.[16] The life she leads there, a life full of prayer and spiritual exercises, does not differ very much from the life of the nuns, who love their benefactress deeply and always pray for her. As for her stepdaughter Elizabeth, we are told that Agnes always looks after her and 'honestly manages her life' ('besorget si erlichen ir leben'), 'making' her a nun in the convent of Töss ('macht sy ein closterfrowen ze Töss'),[17] where she visits her daughter (*sic*) Elizabeth frequently. After a long life of exemplary

---

[12] H. Dienst and W. Stelzer, 'Agnes, Königin von Ungarn', *Die Habsburger. Ein biographisches Lexikon*, ed. B. Hamann, 3rd edn (Munich, 1988), pp. 29–30.

[13] Boner, 'Die Gründung', p. 14.

[14] K. Ruh, 'Agnes von Ungarn und Liutgart von Wittichen. Zwei Klostergründerinnen des frühen 14. Jahrhunderts', *Philologische Untersuchungen gewidmet Elfriede Stutz zum 65. Geburtstag*, ed. A. Ebenbauer (Vienna, 1984), pp. 374–91 at pp. 375–6; Boner, 'Die Gründung', pp. 12–13.

[15] *Ibid.*, pp. 103–10.

[16] *Ibid.*, p. 106.

[17] *Ibid.*, p. 109.

piety, Agnes, the 'beloved mother not only of the nuns and monks of Königsfelden, but of the whole country and in particular of the poor' dies a good death.[18]

The contradiction between the two images is obvious – and leads to a number of questions: what do we really know about Agnes's personality, about her life and deeds, about her political role as a queen and queen dowager, and, finally, about her relationship with her princely 'daughter' Elizabeth? For Agnes, and to a minor extent for Elizabeth, there is an exceptional range of sources. First of all, many important chronicles of the fourteenth and fifteenth centuries, dealing with things Austrian, tell us about Agnes: for example, John of Viktring, Matthew of Neuenburg and Ottokar in his Austrian Rhyme chronicle.[19] In general, the story of her Hungarian marriage and her years as queen of Hungary are related only in brief. Rather more emphasis is given to the circumstances of her return to Austria after the death of her husband. Her part in the founding of Königsfelden and her pious life there are described in some detail. The different recensions of John of Viktring's *Liber certarum historiarum*, for instance, declare that 'Lady Agnes ['domina'], widow of the deceased King Andrew of Hungary and daughter of King Albert, lived there [in Königsfelden] a religious and devout life, producing sixtyfold fruit, and like a second Tabitha doing many good deeds and always giving alms.[20] Like the widow Anne she never left the temple of God, by day and night serving her creator.[21] Her praise need not be sung here, because Sidonius [*recte* Symmachus] says: To praise the excellent is as superfluous as to use a torch in full sunshine.'[22]

Apart from the chronicles dealing with the history of Austria or of the Reich in general, there is one chronicle which is of particular importance for us. Some time in the later fourteenth century, the special *Chronicon Koenigsveldense* mentioned above was produced – certainly in one of the two Königsfelden convents. Today, we have only a fifteenth-century German version of it, but it is very likely that the Latin text originated shortly after Agnes's death in 1364. This Latin original was extensively used by later chroniclers. The German version has eight pages describing Agnes's life and death in great detail.[23] Almost everything we know about her comes from this source: details, such as that she was small, sturdy and not pretty, that after the premature death of her husband she gave an enormous amount in alms and managed (by her own and her friends' incessant prayers) to liberate his soul from purgatory, that – late in her life – the emperor Charles IV came to see her several times and called her a second Esther, no other woman in Christianity being so wise. Altogether, one could call the Königsfelden chronicle a text written to praise the pious life of Agnes. Kurt Ruh[24] has rightly called it a 'hagiographical

---

18 *Ibid.*, p. 110.
19 See in particular Boner, 'Die Gründung', pp. 5–7.
20 Iohannis abbatis Victoriensis, *Liber certarum historiarum*, ed. F. Schneider, *MGH SRG*, i–ii (Hanover/Leipzig, 1909–10); cf. Acts 9:36.
21 Luke 2:36–7.
22 II, 7.
23 *Chronicon Koenigsveldense*, pp. 103–10.
24 Ruh, 'Agnes von Ungarn', p. 377.

document' – it borders on a saint's life, developing the image of a woman who from early childhood onwards leads a saintly life, who seems to be destined to become the foundress and benefactress of Königsfelden. Her direct contact with God (several times she is informed by celestial voices about the outcome of one of her undertakings) and her saintly death intensify this impression. One could well imagine that this chronicle-cum-saint's life was written in Königsfelden shortly after her death in order to initiate some sort of veneration for the beloved foundress.

In addition to the special – and extremely influential – case of the *Koenigsfelden Chronicle*, there is a second special case, this time a whole group of texts, early Swiss historical writings, starting with the chronicle of Heinrich Gundelfinger and continuing with those of Brennwald, Stumpf, Tschudi and Bullinger.[25] It is here that the image of Agnes as the merciless avenger of her father's death emerges, culminating in Bullinger's picture of Agnes walking in blood as in the dew of May. Twentieth-century research has shown that all this is wholly wrong: Agnes may have supported harsh revenge for the murder of her father, but when it took place, she was not around. What we see here has rightly been called a 'historical forgery committed by rabid anti-Hapsburg Swiss historians'.[26]

Apart from the chronicles, there are the charters – and there is a surprisingly high number of them. Theodor von Liebenau, in addition to producing a *Life of Queen Agnes of Hungary*, collected more than one hundred charters dealing with Agnes or issued by her. To give just a few examples: on 8 August 1318, she gives two hundred marks of silver for the dowry ('Leibgeding') of her stepdaughter in Töss and to mark the anniversary of the death of Elizabeth's father;[27] on 29 September 1329, she fixes regulations for the celebration of different anniversaries in 'our monastery of Königsfelden' – which sounds as if she treated the Königsfelden convents like an 'Eigenkloster';[28] on 2 February 1330, she pre-scribes what has to be done with the land she has acquired for Königsfelden.[29]

In addition to this wealth of pious acts, the charters show us a wholly different aspect of this complex personality: apparently Agnes's personal standing was so great that she was asked time and again to act as an intermediary or arbitrator in cases of conflict. In February 1333, she manages to establish a treaty for a five-year peace between Austria and a number of Swiss towns and regions.[30] On 25 February 1351, she settles a dispute between Basel and Berne.[31] On 12 October in the same year, she resolves a conflict between Duke Albert of Hapsburg and the Swiss Confederation[32] – and here one could go on.[33] If one takes this sort of activity into

---

[25] Late fifteenth–sixteenth century: see Boner, 'Die Gründung', pp. 8–17.
[26] *Ibid.*, p. 376.
[27] Liebenau, *Hundert Urkunden*, pp. 38–9 no. 21.
[28] *Ibid.*, p. 46 no. 29.
[29] *Ibid.*, pp. 47–8 no. 30.
[30] *Ibid.*, pp. 58–9 no. 38.
[31] *Ibid.*, p. 110 no. 72.
[32] *Ibid.*, p. 116 no. 76.
[33] For further details see Nevsimal, 'Königin Agnes', pp. 151–61.

consideration, it becomes clear that, despite living far away from Vienna or Innsbruck and virtually leading the life of a nun, Agnes managed to be politically active. The same impression emerges when we see that her brothers, the governing dukes of Austria, meet her frequently to ask her for advice.[34] Altogether, it looks as if after the death of her mother Agnes was in many ways the 'head' of Hapsburg politics – and it becomes understandable why an emperor with the standing of Charles IV called her a 'second Esther'.[35]

In addition to chronicles and charters, we have literary texts prompted by Agnes or addressed to her. When Agnes's mother, Queen Elizabeth of Austria died in 1313, she asked the famous Cistercian Philipp of Ratsamhausen, bishop of Eichstätt (who was present at the funeral) to give her spiritual advice concerning the governance of the two Königsfelden convents. Soon afterwards, Philipp sent her a *Life of Saint Walburg*.[36] Far more important – and difficult – is the second text. Master Eckhart, the most famous German mystic of the Middle Ages, addressed his *Book of Divine Consolation* (including his *Sermon on the Noble Man*) to Agnes. Modern research has shown that it is very likely that this book was not written immediately after the death of Albert, that Master Eckhart never met Agnes, and that his book offers consolation only in a very general way.[37] Nevertheless, the very existence of this text demonstrates the importance of Agnes and the fame her pious and withdrawn life had brought her.

And there is still more. According to a relatively old tradition, she owned for some time a twelfth-century Latin-German prayer book, known nowadays as the *Prayers and Benedictions of Muri*[38] – a very interesting collection of spiritual texts, combining prayers and benedictions (for example, for happiness in matrimony, for good luck while travelling, morning- and evening prayers), many of them with a strong magical accent. Moreover, we know certainly that Agnes owned a German bible[39] – which seems to have disappeared – and we have an enormous wealth of relics and ornaments owned by her or given by her to convents and churches. In 1357, for example, she drew up a long list of all the ornaments that members of the Hapsburg family had donated to the monasteries of Königsfelden.[40]

---

34 See examples given by Lhotsky, *Geschichte Österreichs*, pp. 189, 208, 228.

35 See Fryger, Clevi (?), *Chronicon Koenigsfeldense*, ed. M. Gerbert, *De translatis Habsburgo-Austriacorum principum eorumque coniugum cadaveribus* (St Blasien, 1772), pp. 87–113 at p. 109. Nevsimal, 'Königin Agnes', pp. 151–2, rightly points out that Agnes was never formally instituted with the administration of the Austrian 'Vorlande', but that her power was very important.

36 See L. L. Hammerich, 'Das Trostbuch Meister Eckeharts', *Zeitschrift für deutsche Philologie*, lvi (1931), 69–98 at p. 94, and the editor's introduction to Philipp's text, Philipp von Rathsamhausen, *Vita sanctae Walburgis*, AASS, 3 Feb., 3rd edn (Paris/Rome, 1865), pp. 558–68.

37 G. Théry, OP, 'Le *Benedictus Deus* de Maître Eckhart', *Mélanges Joseph de Ghellinck* (Gembloux, 1951), ii, 905–35 at pp. 912–17; K. Ruh, *Meister Eckhart. Theologe, Prediger, Mystiker* (Munich, 1985), pp. 115–35.

38 A. Masser, 'Gebete und Benediktionen von Muri', *Verfasserlexikon*, ii (1980), cc. 1110–12.

39 Liebenau, *Hundert Urkunden*, p. 137.

40 *Ibid.*, pp. lxxxxviij, 133–4.

If we now proceed from the stepmother to the stepdaughter, the picture changes. Elizabeth, princess of Hungary, daughter of King Andrew III, is mentioned only very briefly in the late medieval chronicles – and almost always in combination with her stepmother Agnes. The *Königsfelden Chronicle*, talking about Agnes, states rather bluntly, 'She had a stepdaughter who was the child of King Andrew of Hungary by a different woman. This stepdaughter she brought with her from Hungary into this country and made her a nun in Töss.'[41] We have no charters issued by Elizabeth, and we know nothing of her personal belongings. But we do have a document of particular importance. The last of the *Lives of the Nuns of Töss*, the so called *Tösser Schwesternbuch*, consists of a 'Life of sister Elizabeth, daughter of King Andrew of Hungary, who was a nun of the Dominican order in the monastery of Töss in the German province'[42] – it is by far the longest of the lives. We do not know exactly when this life was written, but it must have been at some time during the later fourteenth century.[43] In contrast with the other lives, this one starts with a quotation from the Bible, 'Be faithful until death and I shall give you the crown of life.' At the end of the text, when several miracles worked by Elizabeth after her death have been reported, we are told that some people felt uneasy about the text, people who had seen only the human weakness in Elizabeth's monastic life but not her spiritual merits. This unease is dispelled by a vision experienced by one of the nuns of Töss: after mass she sees in the choir of the church a bishop reading from the life of Elizabeth of Hungary to the whole convent, and at the end exclaiming, 'Everything which is written here is true, and still much more which has not been said about her.'[44] The exceptional nature of the life of Elizabeth of Hungary is furthermore confirmed by the fact that one of the manuscripts of the *Tösser Schwesternbuch*, produced by the famous Dominican reformer Johannes Meyer,[45] has a different ending. Here the narrator goes back to the beginning of the text, pointing out the enormous difference between the worldly status of Elizabeth ('such a young, beautiful, delicate sister, daughter of a powerful, noble king, lawful heiress to all the countries of the kingdom of Hungary')[46] and her life of poverty in Töss, full of pain, which she suffered patiently: she had really been faithful until death. Right at the end, as a quotation from the Latin inscription on Elizabeth's tomb in the church of Töss, the date of her death is given as 31 October 1336. A part of the tomb still exists, and for some

---

[41] *Chronicon Koenigsveldense*, p. 109.

[42] *Leben der Schwestern*, ed. Vetter, pp. 98–102.

[43] Research about the *Tösser Schwesternbuch* is unanimous that the life of Elizabeth of Hungary was *not* written by Elsbeth Stagel, who died around 1360: see A. Haas, 'Stagel (Staglin), Elsbeth OP', *Verfasserlexikon*, ix (1993), pp. 223–4. If we take into consideration what this life has to say about Agnes (see below) it is also unlikely that it was written before Agnes's death, which occurred in 1364.

[44] *Leben der Schwestern*, ed. Vetter, p. 1209.

[45] See *Das Leben der Schwestern*, p. xiii, and W. Fechter, J. Meyer, OP, *Verfasserlexikon*, vi (1987), p. 483.

[46] *Das Leben der Schwestern*, ed. Vetter, pp. 121–2.

time Elizabeth was venerated in Töss, but her cult has not been acknowledged by the Church.

If we read the life of 'Queen Elsbeth' in the *Tösser Schwesternbuch*, we can see where the notion of Agnes as an evil stepmother comes from. Immediately after the death of King Albert, we are told, Agnes built the monastery of Königsfelden and started to live a spiritual life, forcing Elizabeth to become a nun like her. Elizabeth is shown all the monasteries in Suabia and finally decides to enter the convent of Töss.[47] On the next pages of the life, things get even worse. After a mere fifteen weeks of life as a novice, Agnes forces the convent of Töss to permit Elizabeth to take her final vows – much before the legitimate time! In spite of the fact that Elizabeth is the right and lawful heiress to the throne of Hungary, Agnes gives her a lady in waiting ('hofmeisterin') who is extremely rude. When Elizabeth falls ill, she is sent to Baden. Because she is so poor, members of the local nobility give her many presents. Agnes, her stepmother, acts differently. She invites Elizabeth to Königsfelden and shows her all the treasures, once belonging to King Andrew, Elizabeth's father, which she has brought from Hungary, but she keeps everything for herself. People in Zürich, both laymen and clergy, want to see Elizabeth, knowing that she is the most noble nun in the whole country – she goes there and is very much honoured. When she returns to Töss, she explains that if this had not happened, she would certainly have fallen into a very grave illness because of the perfidy of her stepmother. After a life of exceptional suffering and exceptional grace (Saint Elizabeth of Thuringia appears to her and she performs several miracles) Elizabeth dies. Eight days later, her stepmother comes to Töss; by night, Elizabeth appears to Agnes – the ladies in waiting can see her but cannot hear what stepmother and stepdaughter are saying. From now onwards until the time of her death, the narrator declares, Agnes gave much more to the convent of Töss than before.[48]

Modern historical research has regarded the image of the relationship between Agnes and Elizabeth developed by the life of Elizabeth of Hungary as plain truth.[49] In my opinion, we should be cautious. The life of Elizabeth of Hungary is in many ways comparable to the life of Agnes, contained in the *Königsfelden Chronicle*. As far as I can see, we do not have much information corroborating the statements of the life concerning Agnes. And we have to acknowledge that these statements fit very well into the life of a medieval nun. To have such a wicked stepmother is first of all a spiritual trial for the royal nun, it adds to her suffering and makes her even more pious, it advances her along the road to holiness. Some lines of her life even seem to have political – that is anti-Hapsburg – undertones. It is with disgust

---

47 *Ibid.*, p. 100.
48 *Ibid.*, pp. 101–17.
49 In 1855, Jacob Burckhardt gave a lecture 'On the Nature of Queen Agnes of Hungary' ('Über den Charakter der Königin Agnes von Ungarn') which has not been published; for the contents see W. Kaegi, *Jacob Burckhardt. Eine Biographie*, iii (Basel/Stuttgart, 1956), 620–4. Burckhardt paints a very colourful picture, showing an arrogant, inhumane and physically ugly stepmother who constantly pesters her beautiful, devout and princely stepdaughter.

and anger that the author describes how miserably royalty is treated.[50] Insisting on the fact that Elizabeth is the lawful heiress to the Hungarian throne, he seems to point out that she could have become queen of Hungary, had she not been tucked away in the convent of Töss.[51]

How far is it possible to draw conclusions from these contradictory accounts? As far as Agnes is concerned, things seem to be relatively clear. At the centre of her attention is always the well-being and promotion of the affairs of her family. All her political actions and many of her spiritual doings point in this direction. Her decision to set up a sort of residence in Königsfelden, in an area of the Hapsburg Reich which was endangered by the Swiss aspirations to independence, was a significant aspect of Hapsburg politics for more than half a century. Important factors in this context were Agnes's wealth – if necessary, she could pay to achieve what she wanted – and her enormous longevity – she far outlived all her brothers and sisters, most of them by several decades. The career of Agnes is of interest in the context of what a woman could achieve in the later Middle Ages, even without holding the official position of a reigning queen or duchess. For many years, Agnes seems to have been one of the focal points of Hapsburg politics – the fact that her brothers sought her advice time and again makes that clear. As for her spiritual life, we should avoid modern judgements. First of all, her spiritual life cannot be separated from her secular activities. Buying land for Königsfelden is at one and the same time a pious and a political act. On the other hand, the enormous number of her endowments (be they in the form of money, relics or ornaments) demonstrates that Agnes was pious in the ordinary late medieval sense, using money to buy herself into heaven – and in this sense she was *very* pious. Furthermore, it was not only her own spiritual welfare she wanted to promote. As we have seen, she also tried to obtain her husband's release from purgatory, and we can assume that the same applies to her father and the many members of the Hapsburg family whose deaths she experienced from the days of her youth onwards. How she managed to survive all these catastrophes (for example, the battle of Morgarten in 1315 and the early death of Frederick the Fair and his wife in 1330) we do not know. Her relationship with her stepdaughter Elizabeth we cannot really judge. One can be sure only that it was dominated by Agnes's concern for the well-being of her own family – and that could mean taking harsh measures against a young girl who could become politically dangerous to the Hapsburgs.

As far as Elizabeth is concerned, we have to admit that the surviving historical evidence about her seems to be very meagre. Therefore, it would be wise to err on the side of caution. What one can assume is that, once her fiancé Wenzel had lost the battle for the Hungarian throne and had dissolved the betrothal, the Hapsburgs were no longer much interested in Elizabeth. When Charles Robert of Anjou had established himself firmly on the throne of Hungary (with considerable help from the Hapsburgs!), the danger from Elizabeth dwindled. Was that danger still great enough to put her into a nunnery and to rely on the fact that – as a medieval woman

---

[50] *Das Leben der Schwestern*, ed. Vetter, p. 121.
[51] *Ibid.*, pp. 102, 121.

– she would regard a nun's vow as binding her for the whole of her life? We do not know for sure. What we can see from her 'Life' makes me doubt that she was nothing but the victim of Hapsburg family politics and an evil stepmother. In any case, we should take into consideration that by leading a life of exemplary devotion and piety, Elizabeth of Hungary followed the pattern of life of many thousands of women in the later Middle Ages, a pattern that – in contemporary eyes – guaranteed altogether the most 'successful' life one could live, leading her much further along the way to holiness than most of her contemporaries.

II

Image and Reality
in the East

7

Goddess, Whore, Wife or Slave:
Will the Real Byzantine Empress Please Stand Up? *

Liz James

In 1975, Sarah B. Pommeroy published her book, *Goddesses, Whores, Wives and Slaves: Women in Classical Antiquity*.[1] The book was the first book in English to attempt a social history of women in the Greek and Roman worlds. Written at a time when feminism as a political movement was beginning to make a significant impact on academic studies, Pomeroy introduced her text by asking 'what women were doing while men were active in all the areas traditionally emphasised by classical scholars?'[2] Her title suggests the ways in which she sought to answer this question. Woman was either a goddess, a whore, a wife or a slave.

Her opening concern, 'What were women doing while men were active?', is still a relevant issue in the study of women in history. As was the case with the Classical woman in the 1970s, so it is with the Byzantine empress in the 1990s. There is no book on 'the empress'. Indeed, in the most recent book on Byzantine women, Gillian Clark's 1993 publication, *Women in Late Antiquity*, there is no entry for empresses in the index. Deaconesses, midwives, widows, virgins and even lesbians are all present; empresses, other than named individuals, are not.[3] This absence in the literature seems to derive from two sources: partly it is a result of the almost unspoken belief that empresses are unique women and so we, as historians, should focus on women who are not exceptional; partly it is a legacy of feminist scholarship which has remained concentrated on the working class woman above all others, leaving those of us who do not work on the nineteenth and twentieth centuries to feel slightly guilty when we study élite women.

The other aspect of Pomeroy's work that interests me are her four categories – goddess, whore, wife, slave – and what these say about the perception of women. All four can, and indeed, have, been applied to Byzantine empresses. In place of the pagan goddess is St Helena. The mother of Constantine the Great, the first

*   The original conference paper aimed to raise questions rather than answering them; this written version suffers from the same flaw and may appear overly sweeping in some of its generalisations. My thanks to Dion Smythe and Shaun Tougher for their advice and encouragement.

1   New York, 1975.
2   Pomeroy, *Goddesses*, ix.
3   Oxford, 1993.

Christian emperor, she may have played a part in both his conversion to Christianity and in the court politics of the period; she was also revered for her discovery of the True Cross. Further, Leslie Brubaker has already shown how the role of 'New Helena' was a key one for Byzantine empresses.[4] For whores, look no further than the one Byzantine empress everyone has heard of, the ex-circus performer, Theodora, whose career was so graphically detailed by Procopios.[5] Wife: what is the empress but the wife of the emperor? In the case of Aelia Flacilla, wife of Theodosios I, Kenneth Holum has argued that she derived her status purely from her success as mother of Theodosios's children.[6] And finally slave: very simply, a woman's place in the Late Antique world was as the property of her husband.[7] Yet none of these descriptions entirely answer the question of what a Byzantine empress was. What did it mean to be an empress and how was this role defined? What is this concept of 'queenship' and what does it tell us about female power and authority? If there is more to women's history than goddesses, whores, wives and slaves, then is it possible that our own prejudices as historians have blinded us to what might have been going on in the past with regard to the role of powerful women?

What was a Byzantine empress?[8] The *Oxford Dictionary of Byzantium* defines her in this way: 'Empress. Legally, the empress depended on the emperor, but in favourable circumstances late Roman empresses such as Pulcheria, Ariadne, Theodora or Sophia might wield great power, especially through a regency.'[9] These two key points – first that the empress depended on the emperor and second that exceptional women might, in exceptional circumstances, wield power – have formed the basis of historians' understanding of what an empress was. This paper will begin to explore the validity of these claims.

'Legally the empress depended on the emperor.' In legal terms, the emperor was placed above the laws and had no legal position; he was responsible to no one for his legislative and administrative acts and no organ of state had a right to control him. He was bound only by the unwritten principles of government. Indeed, as

[4] L. Brubaker, 'Patterns in Byzantine Matronage: Aristocratic and Imperial Commissions, Fourth Century to Sixth Century', *Byzantine Studies Conference Abstracts*, xvi (1990), 27–8.

[5] In the *Secret History*, esp. ix.10–25 and xv.17–35.

[6] K. Holum, *Theodosian Empresses* (Berkeley, 1982), ch. 1.

[7] See e.g. C. Galatariotou, 'Holy Women and Witches: Aspects of Byzantine Concepts of Gender', *Byzantine and Modern Greek Studies*, ix (1984/5), 55–94, and F. Goria, *Studi sul matrimonia dell' adultera nel diritto giustinianeo e bizantino* (Turin, 1975), pp. 182–5 and 228–51, for evidence of this. I am grateful to Charles Barber for this last reference.

[8] For the purposes of this paper, I am thinking of empresses in the fourth, fifth and sixth centuries, the period from Constantine the Great to Justin II. For an earlier approach to many of the issues raised here, see S. Runciman, 'Some Notes on the Role of the Empress', *Eastern Churches Review*, iv (1972), 119–24.

[9] *Oxford Dictionary of Byzantium*, ed. A. Kazhdan (Oxford, 1991), *s.v.* 'Empress'. This is the traditional view, upheld by scholars from the nineteenth century on. See, for example, the approach of J. B. Bury, 'The Constitution of the Late Roman Empire', no. 8 in *Selected Essays*, ed. H. Temperley (Amsterdam, 1964), pp. 99–125, esp. 110–12, and L. Bréhier, *Les Institutions de l'empire byzantin* (Paris, 1970).

divinely promoted through God's agency, human laws could not restrict him.[10] If the emperor had no place in law, where did that leave his consort? Either related by blood or by marriage to God's emperor, was she also bound by human laws? What little evidence there is for the claim that her position depended on him comes in the *Digest*, the legal compilation produced in the reign of Justinian.[11] As a sixth-century compilation, this text raises an historical problem: how far did it merely reiterate the *status quo* and how far did it make concrete things which had not been concrete before? In fact, no legal text pays much attention to empresses, just as little is paid to emperors.[12] Whether this proves that she was legally dependent on him is not so straightforward.

By suggesting that the empress depended on the emperor, the implication seems to be that the empress was merely the wife of the emperor and without him was nothing. The careers of several empresses suggest a different version of events. On the death of the emperor Arcadios in 408, his son, Theodosios II, succeeded to the throne at the age of seven. Pulcheria, Theodosios's sister, assumed imperial power in 414 at the age of fifteen, wresting authority away from the praetorian prefect, and ruling on behalf of her brother. When he died in 450, Pulcheria married the *domestikos* Marcian, but continued to rule the empire until her death in 453. Clearly, her position was not legitimised by her husband; rather, her father and her brother were the more significant figures. Pulcheria's power depended on dynastic succession, on the dynastic legitimisation of power. Just as Theodosios II himself was legitimised as emperor by virtue of being his father's son, so too was his sister.

This pattern of inheritance can be seen again in the case of the empress Ariadne. Born before 457, she was the eldest daughter of Leo I and his wife Verina; the couple had no surviving sons. On Leo's death in 474, Ariadne's son became emperor; when he died at a young age, her husband, Zeno, took power. On Zeno's death in 491, Ariadne remarried, choosing Anastasios, a relatively unimportant court official, who then succeeded to the throne. Ariadne's power did not depend upon her husbands; rather, she legitimised them. Her power did depend on an emperor, her father, Leo I, whose legitimate successor she was, in the same way that a son – and indeed, her own son – would be perceived. This same situation recurred in the eleventh century when the empress Zoe ascended to the throne as the legitimate heir of her father, another emperor without sons, and legitimised her three husbands.[13] These are all instances where the emperor's succession depended on the empress, when power was transferred through female inheritance and by female will, where, perhaps, the emperor's succession depended on the empress.

10 Bury, 'Constitution', p. 113.

11 *Digest* I.3.31.

12 J. Beaucamp, 'La Situation juridique de la femme à Byzance', *Cahiers de civilisation médiévales*, xx (1977), 149, makes this clear. Her *Le Statut de la femme à Byzance (4e–7e siècle). 1. Le droit impérial* (Paris, 1990) contains next to nothing on empresses because there is so little primary data.

13 For Zoe, see B. Hill, L. James, D. Smythe, 'Zoe: The Rhythm Method of Imperial Renewal' in *New Constantines*, ed. P. Magdalino (Aldershot, 1994), pp. 215–30.

It is in this context that we should perhaps consider the question of why the Byzantines never felt the need to introduce an equivalent to the Salic Law.

The case of the late sixth-century empress Sophia, the wife of Justin II, is slightly different. After Justin's death, she nominated his two successors and endeavoured to rule through them without marrying either. Justin had succeeded his childless uncle, Justinian, to the throne; Sophia was Theodora's niece. This raises the intriguing question of whether her position derived from her status as imperial widow or as legitimate heir through her relationship with the previous empress. It may have been a mixture of both. Throughout Byzantine history, there are many examples where the empress survived her husband and the passing of power depended in large part on her. How far this is a case merely of the empress's power depending on the emperor and how far it is a reflection of the empress's own position is an issue that has yet to be satisfactorily explored.

In this context, the question as to why these women needed to marry or to nominate male co-rulers is a key one. The answer is both practical and ideological. In practical terms, it is as simple as the need for a military presence. The one drawback to a woman's rule was that it was impossible for her ever to command an army in the field. This opened her to the risk of being overthrown by a successful general. The way round this problem was surely to marry a general or appoint a loyal general or, as Eirene did, to appoint eunuchs as generals. It has been suggested that these imperial women remarried because they could not live without the love of a good man.[14] Love is an irrelevance; power, and the retention of power, are more plausible motives.

In ideological terms, the issue is harder to disentangle. It is another truism of Byzantine history that in this period, people were unhappy with the idea of a female ruler. Like most truisms, there is some validity in this view, but it also does not entirely reflect the actual political situation. Women did rule in Byzantium: Pulcheria, Ariadne, Sophia, to name but three. The way in which they ruled was, however, different from the way in which men – emperors – ruled; it is this difference in power that marks the boundaries between an emperor and an empress. This is the point made elsewhere in this volume by Pauline Stafford. She moves away from the conventional definition of power as producing an effect or achieving a result, as wielding authority and influencing international affairs, to seeing it as the ability to act, to take part in events, to have a strategy and to pursue it, without necessarily succeeding, and to be in a position to influence others and to use their labours for one's own prestige. Authority gives one the right to act, gaining obedience without force. Where Bury said that the empress was never in the position to exercise independent sovereign power, though she might be her husband's consort,[15] Stafford's approach allows us to suggest that sovereign power is only one version of power, and even that Bury's definition of 'sovran power'

---

[14] It has been suggested that passion was part of Sophia's motivation in choosing Tiberios as Justin II's successor. See A. M. Cameron, 'The Empress Sophia', *Byzantion*, xlv (1975), 5–21.

[15] Bury, 'Constitution', p. 112.

may not be the only definition possible. The empress's power may not be the same as the emperor's but this is not to say that she is without power or that her power does not come from her office. It is a different power, which may operate and be manifested differently.

This leads me back to the second half of the *Dictionary of Byzantium*'s definition of empresses, that 'in favourable circumstances late Roman empresses ... might wield great power'. The Appendix lists the women married to Eastern Roman emperors between the early fourth century and the late sixth century. Twenty-two women are listed, including the empress-mother Helena. Of these twenty-two, there are fourteen whom we actually know did wield power and influence events to a greater or lesser extent; of the remaining eight, we know next to nothing about their activities.[16] This suggests either that 'favourable circumstances' were in fact a commonplace for empresses in Late Antiquity or that we have seriously underrated the real power of the empress. It is plausible that the office of empress, like that of emperor, was rather more than nominal, and had its own duties and functions connected with it. Comments from the sources certainly suggest an official position for imperial women. Kenneth Holum cites the case of Justa Grata Honoria, the sister of the Western emperor Honorios, who was forced to 'forfeit the sceptre' after her affair with her steward. As Holum points out, if women did not share in the rule of empire, how could Justa Grata forfeit the sceptre?[17] There is also some evidence for the actions of empresses. Eudoxia earned the wrath of Chrysostom for her role in affairs of state; Pulcheria and Eudocia both sought to rule the empire; Theodora is reported as interviewing ministers, ecclesiastics and foreign ambassadors.[18]

It is not as if the Roman world did not offer some standing to outsiders. As a parallel case to the woman with power, there are the barbarian generals so powerful in the fourth and fifth centuries in both Eastern and Western empires. No historian has seriously tried to claim that they held power by force of personality alone or through 'favourable circumstances'; their positions within the Roman governmental structure and their respect for Roman titles suggest that official positions also counted for something. If it works for barbarian generals, why not also for imperial Roman women?

Imperial titles serve as one significant pointer in assessing the position of imperial women. Titles were of great significance in Byzantium: in Paul Magdalino's

---

16 Some intriguing evidence does survive for some of these eight. Valentinian's first wife, Marina Severa, was banished from court, but reappears there later in his reign and second marriage; Valen's wife, Domnica, was said to have converted him to Arianism; Basiliscus had the image of his wife, Zenonis, placed on coins with the title Augusta.

17 Holum, *Theodosian Empresses*, pp. 2–3.

18 *Ibid., passim* on the actions of imperial women from Flacilla to Pulcheria; Procopios, *Secret History*, xv.21–2; xvi.17–22, and A. M. Cameron, *Procopius* (London, 1985), pp. 73–4; W. H. C. Frend, 'The Mission to Nubia: An Episode in the Struggle for Power in Sixth Century Byzantium', *Etudes et Travaux*, viii (1975), 10–16, deals with the rival embassies of Justinian and Theodora sent to convert the Nubians.

phrase, not the icing on the cake but the essence of government.[19] So how were these women officially described?[20] Of the twenty-two imperial women, twelve are given the title of Augusta.[21] *The Dictionary of Byzantium* remarks that 'In the Late Roman period the status of empress was granted only grudgingly to imperial women.' However, twelve out of twenty-two does not seem a negligible number, nor necessarily grudging. These figures break down more significantly. Of the ten women married to the first six emperors, two bore the title Augusta; of the eleven women married to the last twelve emperors in this period, all but one have the title. This suggests a change in the use and perception of the title, an aspect of nomenclature that the *Dictionary*'s definition fails to take into account. In her examination of the different titles used by imperial women and the ways in which these change, Barbara Hill has made it very clear that imperial titles confer status and that status conveys power.[22] Although Hill's work focuses on the twelfth century, the issues she raises are significant for earlier empresses. What were these women called and what significance did these titles hold? What did 'Augusta' mean in Early Byzantium and what were imperial women called if they did not have the title Augusta?[23]

By questioning the assumption that it was only in favourable circumstances that empresses had power, it becomes possible to open up the ways in which female imperial power might be reflected. The careers of Helena, Eudocia, Pulcheria, Ariadne, Theodora and the rest of the influential imperial women suggest that in reality the empress was a figure of considerable power within the empire and, moreover, that her power did not simply derive from her personality alone, as historians have seemed eager to stress, but rather from her position, as empress. By removing this potentially patriarchal bias about female character and its role as the dominant force in any woman's actions, it may prove possible to re-read the

---

[19] P. Magdalino, 'Innovations in Government', in *Alexios I Comnenos*, edd. M. E. Mullett and D. C. Smythe (Belfast, 1996), pp. 147–8.

[20] L. Bréhier, 'L'Origine des titres impériaux à Byzance', *Byzantinische Zeitschrift*, xv (1906), 161–75, makes no mention of female titles. E. Bensammer, 'La Titulature de l'imperatrice et sa signification', *Byzantion*, xlvi (1976), 243–91, is the only article dealing specifically with the empress's titles. For a detailed critique of this, see B. Hill, 'Patriarchy and Power in the Byzantine Empire from Maria of Alania to Maria of Antioch, 1080–1180', unpublished Ph.D. thesis, Queen's University Belfast, 1994, ch. 2.

[21] According to Jordanes, *Romana*, 314, Domnica was also styled Augusta, bringing the number of empresses to hold that title in this period to thirteen. For details of the style of these imperial women, see A. H. M. Jones, J. R. Martindale, J. Morris, *The Prosopography of the Later Roman Empire, I, AD 260–365* (Cambridge, 1971), and J. R. Martindale, *The Prosopography of the Later Roman Empire, II, AD 395–527* (Cambridge, 1980).

[22] For the crucial importance of titles and the relevance of female titles, see Hill, *Patriarchy and Power*. She compares the three titles of Augusta, basilissa and despoina, pointing out that Augusta was the title by which the woman who had been crowned was addressed and which carried with it the visible functions and honours of being imperial.

[23] Holum, *Theodosian Empresses*, p. 29, argues that the title of 'Augusta' afforded influence, not power, but elsewhere suggests that empresses had power when their husband's authority was weak (e.g. Eudoxia, wife of Arcadios, p. 48). This contradictory stance raises again the question of the difference between power and influence.

evidence from the perspective of Byzantine society and the organisation of that society. What happens when both images and texts are reconsidered from this changed perspective?

The classic study of imperial ideology in Byzantine art is André Grabar's *L'empereur dans l'art byzantin*.[24] Grabar argued that imperial art had one basic function: to magnify the supreme power of the emperor. It carried with it the weight afforded by its official nature, its sacred/divine connotations and its links with the imperial mystique. These aspects might be portrayed in various ways, from the victorious emperor triumphant above his barbarian enemies, to the emperor receiving gifts and homage, the emperor making offerings to God and being blessed by God, the emperor being crowned, and through the use of a whole range of historical, biblical and mythological analogies.

However, within this framework, Grabar did not specifically discuss female imperial iconography. For him, this functioned as a sub-set of imperial iconography, a pendant to images of the emperor, reiterating the messages of male iconography. How images of empresses might do this was never really examined; indeed, it did not exist as a concern.[25] It is clear, however, that many of the standard analogies for the emperor, such as Christ or King David, and the place of the emperor as the instrument of divine and imperial victory are problematic at least and frequently irrelevant if applied to a woman. This raises several fundamental questions. Should female imperial iconography be examined in the same terms as male? If so, then how does the empress relate to God? Was she perhaps constructed as a type of the Virgin Mary? Grabar's basic premise is that imperial imagery is about the public display and affirmation of imperial power. It is designed to magnify the supreme power of the emperor. How does that work for empresses?

Male imperial images are interpreted on two levels: the individual, the specific emperor; and the official, the emperor as emperor. However, images of female imperial figures tend to be discussed only in terms of the individual. Debate about the Trier ivory, for example, has focused around a discussion of which empress is shown, rather than what her presence may signify; discussion of anonymous female sculptured heads centres on the question of identity; the Theodora mosaic in San Vitale, Ravenna, is said to magnify Theodora in order to play down her Procopian past.[26] Little emphasis has been placed on what sort of a picture of

---

[24] Paris, 1936. For a recent critique of some aspects of Grabar's work, see T. Mathews, *The Clash of Gods* (Princeton, 1993).

[25] In similar fashion, Rostovtzeff noted only two un-enfranchised classes in ancient Greece, neither of which were women: M. I. Rostovtzeff, *Greece* (Oxford, 1963), p. 176, cited in Pomeroy, *Goddesses*, xii.

[26] For the Trier ivory, see S. Spain, 'The Translation of Relics Ivory, Trier', *Dumbarton Oaks Papers*, xxxi (1977), 279–304; K. G. Holum and G. Vikan, 'The Trier Ivory, Adventus Ceremonial and the Relics of St Stephen', *ibid.*, xxxiii (1979), 113–33; J. Wortley, 'The Trier Ivory Reconsidered', *Greek, Roman and Byzantine Studies*, xxi (1980), 381–94; for female imperial sculpture, see the discussion of R. R. R. Smith, 'Roman Portraits: Honours, Empresses and Late Emperors', *Journal of Roman Studies*, lxxv (1985), 209–21; for Theodora, see C. Barber, 'The Imperial Panels at San Vitale: A Reconsideration', *Byzantine and Modern Greek Studies*, xiv (1990), 19–42.

female imperial power these images might provide. Identity is only a small part of what such images are about. Just as with male imperial images, there is scope to interpret these as images not only of a person but also of an office and of power. When read in this light, a different view of the significance of the Byzantine empress is apparent.

Plate 7 illustrates the small late fifth-/early sixth-century ivory plaque from the Bargello Museum in Florence, an object very similar to a panel in the Kunst-historisches Museum in Vienna. Both ivories show an empress, a standing figure in the Florence ivory, a seated in the Viennese, wearing elaborate imperial robes, crowned with a diadem, holding the *globus cruciger*, and, in the Florence plaque, a sceptre. Both empresses are positioned within curtained niches, above which are placed eagles supporting wreaths. In both cases, the empress's robes bear a *tablion* with an imperial portrait on it. The traditional interpretation of these two images of imperial power is that the ivories show an empress, lavishly dressed and with symbols of power to stress her position; the emperor's bust on her robe, however, underlines her dependence on him. They reflect the static, almost private, nature of imperial women, screened away behind curtains, placed in niches to stress their apartness as women and to underline their special status.[27] Moreover, the two panels can be compared to the Barberini ivory, which is dated to the same late fifth-/early sixth-century period.[28] Here, the victorious, horse-borne warrior-emperor is displayed in his majesty; at his feet, subject races pay homage; above his head, Christ sends down his blessing and approval. The Barberini ivory portrays all the triumphal glory of empire; the Florence and Vienna panels display the secluded world of the imperial woman. The emperor is active, the empress passive, or, as John Berger once suggested, men act and women appear.[29] Indeed, since one interpretation of the Barberini emperor is as Anastasios, and since the empress ivories are usually interpreted as Ariadne, the two pieces form a contrasting display of family imperial power.[30]

Such an interpretation certainly fits with the belief that the empress depended on the emperor. It also fits with Holum's description of the female imperial virtues as piety, humility, philanthropy and wifely love, essentially passive, or even domestic, virtues.[31] However, in contrast, one might prefer to recall the triumphal entry of Constantius II into Rome in 357, as described by Ammianus

---

[27] As is suggested in Barber, 'Imperial Panels', pp. 22, 36–7.

[28] For the most recent description of the Barberini ivory, see *Byzance*, catalogue of an exhibition at the Louvre 1992–1993 (Paris, 1992), pp. 63–6.

[29] J. Berger, *Ways of Seeing* (London, 1972), p. 47.

[30] The image is identified as Ariadne on two grounds: the dating of the ivory; and its similarity to a variety of other imperial images, some identified (e.g. the Clementius diptych), others anonymous. K. Weitzmann, *Age of Spirituality: Late Antique and Early Christian Art*, catalogue of an exhibition at the Metropolitan Museum of Art 1977–78 (New York, 1977), p. 31, suggests that the remarkable number of extant portraits ascribed to Ariadne can be explained by her position as sole heiress of imperial office which she conferred on her consorts.

[31] Holum, *Theodosian Empresses*, p. 22.

Marcellinus.[32] Here, the historian emphasises another aspect of imperial dignity: the stress placed on imperial gravity, solemnity, lack of movement, all of which serve to mark the emperor out as suprahuman. These qualities remain important imperial qualities throughout the Byzantine period. They are also qualities portrayed in the Florence ivory. As the curtains are drawn away, the full-frontal empress is revealed. Solemn, grave, motionless, she appears almost like a deity in a shrine, a totem, niched and marked out not only as more than woman, but as more than human.

Even if it were the case that men act and women appear, appearing may itself be a powerful form of action, a presenting and re-presenting, a being something, an embodiment of power in being present, a force just through presence.[33] Further, it is surely the woman's imperial status not her sex which is stressed. As for the emperor's portrait on her robe, if we go along with the belief that this is a representation of Ariadne, then it may serve as a reminder that her husbands gained their imperial power through her, that she legitimised them, not the other way round. Both the Florence and the Vienna ivories are felt to be central panels in five-part imperial diptychs; if these are the central panels, where is the emperor positioned in these pieces, and what happened in the other four panels? With the Barberini ivory and the Florence and Vienna pieces, surely what we have are two ways of representing different sets of imperial virtues and qualities, rather than a 'his 'n' hers' of imperial representation.

A consular diptych now in the Liverpool Museum (pl. 8) also seems to offer some access to female imperial power.[34] The scene portrayed is virtually the same in both panels of the diptych: the consul sits on a lion-headed throne, wearing his triumphal toga; in his left hand he holds a *mappa*, in his right a sceptre surmounted by a bust. He is supported by personifications of Constantinople and Rome, whilst below two youths pour out largesse. Above the inscriptions are two roundels with the busts of an emperor and an empress. The left hand leaf names the consul as Flavius Taurus Clementinus, which enables it to be dated precisely to 513. Consequently, the imperial busts at the top can only be Anastasios I and Ariadne. These busts display two different forms of imperial costume: the crowns are different, and the emperor wears a cloak pinned at the shoulder in the manner of Justinian at Ravenna, whilst the empress has an elaborate collar, like Theodora at Ravenna. By including a depiction of the empress on a piece commemorating accession to high office, such diptychs suggest that the empress had a status which made her presence on official objects significant. I do not mean at any point to suggest that the empress is ever as important as the emperor, merely that she too has a role in validating official acts. If she did not matter in power terms, would it be necessary to include her? In similar vein, how often does the presence of Prince

---

32 Ammianus Marcellinus, *History*, 16, x.9–11.
33 I am grateful to the anthropologist Liz Tonkin for this suggestion.
34 For a full description of this piece, see M. Gibson, *The Liverpool Ivories* (London, 1994), no. 8, pp. 19–22 and plates VIIIa and b.

Philip add to the regal significance of our Queen and how often is his portrait included as a part of official imagery?[35]

A similar message is offered by the Trier ivory. This small panel, once the side of a box or casket, portrays a procession in an architectural setting. The figures move towards a female imperial figure standing in front of a church which is still in the process of construction. This empress dominates the proceedings; the male imperial figures are shown smaller and rather less important. Although debate has focused on the identity of the empress and the date of the ivory itself, regardless of this, one thing is clear. The empress is important enough to receive the procession into the church alone. She is the significant figure on this ivory.

My next example is perhaps one of the best known of all pieces of Byzantine art, the monumental mosaic panel from the church of San Vitale in Ravenna depicting the empress Theodora (pl. 9). Much work has gone into interpreting the possible connotations and ramifications of this piece. In all of it, stress has fallen in two ways. Either the panels are examined from the personal angle, as representations of Justinian and Theodora, or from the point of view of imperial iconography, in which female imperial iconography functions, as it did with Grabar, as a sub-set of male iconography with the same values and meanings.[36] More recently, it has been recognised that gender plays a role in these panels, but here, emphasis has only lain on the separate, private aspects of the Theodora panel and the place of the empress as a special woman. It is her sex, not her position that has been emphasised.[37]

Though important, this is not the whole story. The image is still the image of an empress, an official figure. In Grabar's terms, as an imperial image, it is a part of the public display and affirmation of imperial power. For that display and affirmation to be complete, the empress needs to be included, for just as the emperor has a powerful public role, so too does the empress.[38] One vital point about this panel makes this clear: the empress's actions.[39] The empress carries the communion chalice. This is a startling depiction. Women in Orthodox worship could only participate in the lay parts of the liturgy – the responses, the creed and

---

[35] The fifth-century usurper Basiliscus certainly thought the Augusta a significant enough figure to include on his coinage and, by the ninth century, the position of Augusta was being represented as an essential element of empire. Shaun Tougher reminds me that Leo VI justified his third marriage on these grounds. See S. F. Tougher, 'The Reign of Leo VI (886–912): Personal Relationships and Political Ideologies', unpublished Ph.D. thesis, University of St Andrews (1994), ch. 5, esp. pp. 117–19.

[36] See, for example, the analysis by O. von Simson, *Sacred Fortress: Byzantine Art and Statecraft in Ravenna* (Chicago, 1948), pp. 28–33, where the panels are only discussed in terms of Melchizedek, Moses and the mission of the emperor.

[37] Barber, 'Imperial Panels', pp. 26–7, 34–40, stresses the elements that mark out Theodora as an empress and argues for the empress's position as a special woman.

[38] On this, see Galatariotou, 'Holy Women and Witches'; Barber, 'Imperial Panels'; Clark, *Women in Late Antiquity.*

[39] I owe this observation to Kellie Gratten, formerly of the Queen's University, Belfast.

certain chants and prayers.[40] Their chances of getting near the communion chalice, never mind holding it and processing with it, were non-existent. In reality, this action could never have happened. In this way, it is a deed which stresses Grabar's point about the ways in which imperial imagery marks out the sacred nature of rulership in Byzantium and elevates it to a suprahuman status. This is not an image of a woman but of an empress; as such, she too is raised above the rank of normal humanity, not by exceptional circumstances but by her position of power. Only thus can she hold the Eucharistic vessel.

One final image-based piece of evidence for the importance of the office of empress is a rather more mundane type of object, the counterweight, that is the weight placed on a steelyard to act as a balance (pl. 10). Over seventy examples of surviving counterweights are in the form of empress's heads, making them the commonest image on counterweights.[41] Emperors are also used. After the third century, in fact, it seems that imperial personages are virtually the only image found on these weights. A good case can very easily be made for the use of the emperor's image; it acts as an official stamp and guarantee, as it does on coins. Again, however, where does such an interpretation leave the image of the empress? The current model of the empress's power and position has her dependent on the emperor and on exceptional circumstances; this offers no real solution. Only if the empress is allowed some sort of official position and role do these objects begin to make some sense.

Not only is a reinterpretation of images possible, but a re-reading of texts from this changed perspective can also produce some interesting results. Of all these early empresses, apart from the sainted Helena, one name recurs in a variety of Byzantine sources, from histories and world chronicles to poems, oracles and encyclopaedic compilations. It is not, as one might expect, *pace* Procopios, the empress Theodora, but rather the fifth-century empress Verina, wife of Leo I, a figure one might describe as the lost empress.

Verina married Leo I at some point before 457 and bore two daughters and a son who died in infancy. After Leo's death, she hoped to rule through her grandson, Leo II, but the child's father, Zeno, was proclaimed emperor and the boy Leo died eleven months into his reign. Verina then intrigued against Zeno and, between 475 and her death in *c.* 484, plotted continuously to regain power, playing off a variety of figures, including Zeno and her own brother Basiliscus, against each other, but, according to conventional versions of events, without actually achieving anything.

Nevertheless, the figure of Verina appears in a surprisingly wide range of sources. She is mentioned in most Byzantine histories and chronicles which deal with the fifth century. In the sixth-century chronicle of John Malalas, for example,

---

40 J. Herrin, ' "Femina Byzantina": The Council in Trullo on Women', *Dumbarton Oaks Papers*, xlvi (1992), 100.

41 For a recent catalogue of these, see N. Franken, *Aequipondia. Figürliche Laufgewichte römischer und frühbyzantinischer Schnellwaagen* (Alfter, 1994), pp. 171–81. I am grateful to Christopher Entwhistle for this reference and his advice on this topic.

she is the first empress to whom he gives the title 'Augusta'.[42] Elsewhere, the eighth-century *Parastaseis Syntomai Chronikai*, a 'brief historical guide' to the monuments of Constantinople, describes two statues of her. One was erected in the lifetime of her husband; the other when she 'crowned her brother . . . to the acclamations of the Green faction: "Long life to Verina the orthodox Helena". For she was very orthodox.'[43] How accurate an acclamation this might have been is a subject for debate, but we should note that the memory of Verina was such as to warrant her remembrance in this text, both here and in several other places.[44] This particular passage is repeated, virtually identically in the tenth-century *Souda* lexicon, an encyclopaedic compilation, which makes little reference to other imperial luminaries such as Theodora and Sophia.[45] Other texts also make reference to Verina's piety. In the tenth-century poem by Constantine Rhodios on the church of the Holy Apostles, she appears as 'the most pious empress'.[46] She again appears as exceptionally pious in an unpublished tenth-century manuscript which describes the discovery of the Virgin's robe and also the translation of the relics of the Virgin by herself and Leo I.[47] Even the church of the Virgin Pege, built by Justinian, is ascribed to Leo and Verina in later Byzantine sources. A novella by Justinian underlines her reputation for pious building activities: the building of a church in the Chalkoprateia dedicated to the Virgin and containing her girdle is credited to Verina.[48]

However, another, very different tradition about Verina has also survived. In contrast to this picture of a pious, orthodox, new Helena, Chapter 89 of the *Parastaseis* reveals an alternative figure. Here, she is said to have 'bewitched' an island for no apparent reason. Elsewhere, in the tenth-century *Oracles of Baalbek*, she is recalled as Scylla, the many-headed monster of classical mythology.[49]

It is not common for two such contrasting impressions of one figure to survive in the historical record. Nevertheless, despite surviving to some effect in Byzantine memory as both 'pious' and 'a witch', Verina is virtually overlooked in modern histories of Byzantium.[50] This, I would suggest, depends in part upon what one constructs as important in history: in traditional historical terms, Verina is an

---

[42] John Malalas, *Chronicle*, xiv.44.
[43] *Constantinople in the Early Eighth Century: The Parastaseis Syntomoi Chronikai*, edd. A. M. Cameron and J. Herrin (Leiden, 1984), p. 92.
[44] *Parastaseis*, chs 29, 40, 61, 89.
[45] *Suida Lexicon*, ed. A. Adler (Leipzig, 1928), p. 469, *s.v.* 'Berina'. Overall, the *Souda* contains relatively few references to historical figures.
[46] Constantine the Rhodian, ed. E. Legrand, 'Description des oeuvres d'art et de l'église des saints apôtres à Constantinople', *Revue des Études Grecques*, ix (1896), lines 108–9.
[47] A. Wenger, 'Notes inédites sur les empereurs Théodose I, Arcadius, Théodose II, Léon I', *Revue des Études Byzantines*, x (1952), 54–7.
[48] See M. Jugie, 'L'Église de Chalcopratia et le culte de la ceinture de la Sainte Vierge à Constantinople', *Échos d'Orient*, xvi (1913), 308.
[49] P. J. Alexander, *The Oracle of Baalbek* (Washington, 1967), pp. 82, 110.
[50] G. Ostrogorsky, *History of the Byzantine State* (Oxford, 1954), makes no mention of her; A. M. Cameron, *The Mediterranean World in Late Antiquity* (London, 1993), offers two glancing references.

unimportant, relatively powerless figure; she does not achieve anything of great significance, being just a failed rebel. Yet, for some reason, she was a significant figure in Byzantine memory.

In this context, the traditional definition of power again handicaps our reading of the past. In extending the definition, as Stafford suggests, it becomes possible to ascribe more weight to imperial women. Not only that, the pendant to the definition of power as the ability to take part in events or pursue ambitions is to question what these events or ambitions might be. Our twentieth-century definition of what events are important is very different from the events we think the Byzantines saw as crucial. To us, dedicating a church or founding a monastery does not necessarily carry the same weight as losing a battle or treating with an enemy. But Byzantium was a God-dominated society, God's empire on earth, and the emperor was God's regent. So dedications to God, interrelationships between imperial figures and God were, in some ways, as indicative of power as interrelatonships between imperial figures and men. In Byzantium, which action says more about power: an emperor meeting an envoy or an empress building a church? In defining imperial virtues in terms of victories, foreign policies, economic reforms, aspects such as piety and philanthropy have, to some extent, been played down. Rather than the *Dictionary of Byzantium*'s 'exceptional circumstances', what we might have are different sets of imperial virtues and different spheres of imperial activity.[51] In looking for signs of female power, I suggest that we may not always have looked in the right places. The role of the Byzantine empress is more complicated than scholars have allowed for; when we categorise women as goddess, whore, wife, slave, mother, virgin, we box in that suprahuman figure, the empress, and restrict her undoubted power.

Appendix

Byzantine Empresses of the Fourth to Sixth Centuries

Empresses in bold type are those whose activities are relatively well-documented.

				Helena Augusta	mother of Constantine
son of	Constantine	= (1)	Minervina		
Constantine Chlorus		= (2)	**Fausta Augusta**		
son of Constantine	Constantius	= (1)	Anonyma		cousin of Constantius
		(2)	**Eusebia**		
		(3)	Faustina		
cousin of Constantius	Julian	=	**Helena**		sister of Constantius

---

51 Often enough, traditional male virtues are castigated as female vices: reward becomes partiality, vengeance, personal vindictiveness. See P. Stafford, *Queens, Concubines and Dowagers: The King's Wife in the Early Middle Ages* (Athens, Georgia, 1983), pp. 24–5.

	Jovian	=	Charito	
	Valentinian	=	Marina Severa	
			Justina	
brother of Valentinian	Valens	=	Domnica Augusta	
	Theodosios I	=	**Aelia Flacilla Augusta**	
			Galla	daughter of Valentinian
son of Theodosios I	Arcadios	=	**Eudoxia Augusta**	
son of Arcadios	Theodosios II	=	**Athenais/ Eudocia Augusta**	
son-in-law of Arcadios	Marcian	=	**Pulcheria Augusta**	sister of Theodosios II
	Leo I	=	**Verina Augusta**	
grandson of Leo I	Leo II:		Unmarried (died aged 7)	
son-in-law of Leo I	Zeno	=	**Ariadne Augusta**	daughter of Leo I
uncle-in-law of Zeno	Basiliscus	=	Zenonis Augusta	
	Zeno	=	**Ariadne Augusta**	
son-in-law of Leo I	Anastasios I	=	**Ariadne Augusta**	
	Justin I	=	**Lupercina/ Euphemia Augusta**	
nephew of Justin	Justinian I	=	**Theodora Augusta**	
nephew of Justinian	Justin II	=	**Sophia Augusta**	niece of Theodora

Plate 7 Ivory panel of an empress (Bargello Museum, Florence)

Plate 8 Ivory diptych of the consul Flavius Taurus Clementinus (by kind permission of the National Museums and Galleries on Merseyside)

Plate 9 Mosaic panel of the empress Theodora (photo: author)

Plate 10 Bronze empress counterweight (British Museum, MLA 1980, 6–2, 13) (by courtesy of the Trustees of the British Museum)

8

Behind the Mask:
Empresses and Empire in Middle Byzantium

Dion C. Smythe

There were no queens in Byzantium and therefore no concept of 'queenship', but the careers of Byzantine empresses in the period 1025–1180 present interesting comparisons with those of queens in the West and in the Latin Kingdom of Jerusalem.[1]

The best-known image of a middle-Byzantine empress is the mosaic panel of the empress Zoe (regnant 1028–50).[2] The 'Zoe panel' in Aghia Sophia, the Church of the Holy Wisdom of God, the cathedral church of Constantinople, shows the earthly rulers, identified by labels as Zoe and Constantine IX Monomachos (1042–55).[3] Together with the later John II-Eirene panel,[4] it was intended to record imperial donations to the cathedral church and to legitimise the reign of the rulers depicted. In each case, the paired rulers flank a sacred person (Christ in the Zoe panel and the Θεοτόκος – the Virgin Mary – in the John and Eirene panel); each emperor carries an ἀποκόμβιον (money bag) and the empresses carry scrolls representing the decrees which detailed the imperial donations to the Great Church. In each case, too, the female ruler is set in a position of visual equality with the male ruler, but Zoe's representation is highly problematical.[5] It shows the

---

1 Here I draw on my work for the *Prosopography of the Byzantine Empire*, a British Academy funded project based at King's College London (working in co-operation with the Berlin-Brandenburg Akademie der Wissenschaft's *Prosopographie der mittelbyzantinischen Zeit*), whose aim is to create an on-line database of all Byzantine persons for the period 641–1261. The criticism of concentration on career-line analysis of individuals who may be the exception, due to their position at the apex of the social pyramid, comes from J. C. Parsons, 'Family, Sex and Power: The Rhythms of Medieval Queenship', *Medieval Queenship*, ed. Parsons, p. 1.

2 For Zoe's right to be viewed as the empress of Byzantium in the second quarter of the eleventh century, see L. James, B. Hill and D. Smythe, 'Zoe: The Rhythm Method of Imperial Renewal', *New Constantines*, ed. P. Magdalino (Aldershot, 1994), pp. 215–29.

3 N. Oikonomides, 'The Mosaic Panel of Constantine IX and Zoe in Saint Sophia', *Revue des Études Byzantines*, xxxvi (1978), 219–32; R. Cormack, 'Interpreting the Mosaics of Saint Sophia at Istanbul', *Art History*, iv (1981), 141–6.

4 This panel, showing John II Komnenos (1118–43) and his wife Eirene Komnene, was put up in the south gallery of Aghia Sophia near the Zoe panel probably in the 1120s.

5 The heads of the three figures (Constantine IX Monomachos, Zoe and the central figure of Christ) – as well as the inscriptions bearing the name of Constantine Monomachos – have

immobile features of a young woman, whereas Zoe was sixty-four years old at the time of the scene apparently depicted in the panel. This seeming contradiction between image and reality, combined with the 'mask-like' quality of Eirene Komnene's depiction in the companion mosaic[6] suggests that material sources, like texts, provide images behind which the realities of empresses and βασίλεια (empire) in middle Byzantium may be concealed. How far can we penetrate behind the mask?

Although the remark *graecae sunt, non leguntur* alerted some medieval Latin readers to the difficulty of reading Greek letters, it is important in the context of public status to emphasise the particular forms of the titles bestowed on Byzantine empresses.[7] The Byzantine titles which may be regarded as the equivalents of the Western 'queen' are three in number.[8] The first, αὐγούστα (augousta), was the usual formal title of the wife of the reigning emperor, in effect the empress-consort

all been changed; moreover, the representation of Zoe shows a young woman, although she was sixty-four years old when she married Constantine IX Monomachos in 1042. More than fifty years ago, Whittemore solved part of the puzzle by demonstrating that the emperor's name originally contained only seven letters, with the initial cross, so that the image commemorated Romanos III Argyros (1028–34), Zoe's first husband, rather than her second husband Michael IV (1034–41) or even Michael IV (1041–2), her adopted son, and nephew of Michael V. Whittemore therefore dated the original fabrication of the panel to between 1028 and 1034 (T. Whittemore, *The Mosaics of Haghia Sophia at Istanbul, Third Preliminary Report: Work Done in 1935–8: The Imperial Portraits of the South Gallery* (Oxford, 1942), pp. 19–20). Whittemore suggested two reasons for the changes: firstly, that after her marriage to Constantine IX Monomachos Zoe wished to record her new husband, and took the opportunity of adding a more pleasing portrait of herself; or secondly, that in 1042 when Michael V attempted to depose and exile Zoe, he or his supporters may have ordered the destruction of her image as a *damnatio memoriae*. But neither of these explanations accounts for the alterations made to the figure of Christ, with the possible exception of the rather weak appeal to 'stylistic unity'. Furthermore, if the alteration were to be seen as an attempt at *damnatio memoriae*, why was the inscription above Zoe's head left intact? Oikonomides suggests that that alteration of the Zoe and Romanos III panel to show Zoe and Constantine IX may have been made because the donation by Constantine IX far outweighed that of Romanos III. The location in the south gallery (the usual location of the Holy Synod at this time) suggests to Oikonomides that the patriarch was the patron, and if that were so, the known thrift of Michael Kerularios, patriarch from 1043 to 1058, may explain why, instead of making a new panel, the Romanos III panel was re-worked to commemorate Constantine IX's benefactions. Oikonomides suggests that the explanation for the replacement heads for Zoe and Christ may be re-use of an older mosaic, destroyed in the fire of 1043 or 1044 in Aghia Sophia. This interpretation has the benefit at least of removing the need to have recourse to Zoe's supposed vanity to explain the mosaics of the Great Church (Oikonomides, 'The Mosaic Panel', pp. 221–30).

6 'Mask-like, without a blemish': Whittemore, *Mosaics of Haghia Sophia*, pp. 22–4. This description is an echo of Michael Psellos's descriptions of the empress Zoe, *Chronographia*, vi.6 (ed. E. Renauld [Paris, 1926], i, 120).

7 The basic matter of terminology is also addressed, for the Islamic world, by F. Mernissi, *The Forgotten Queens of Islam*, trans. M. J. Lakeland (Cambridge, 1994), pp. 9–36.

8 E. Bensammar, 'La Titulaire de l'imperatrice et sa signification', *Byzantion*, xlvi (1976), 243–91. See also B. Hill, 'Patriarchy and Power in the Byzantine Empire from Maria of Alania to Maria of Antioch, 1080–1180' (Ph.D. thesis, Queen's University of Belfast: 1994), ch. 2, pp. 44–79.

(with on occasion the additional qualification of having produced a male heir).[9] It is a Greek feminine form derived from the Latin *augustus*, and so has strong imperial connections. However, it was not the obvious female counterpart to the standard emperor's title (αὐτοκρατώρ καὶ βασιλεύς) in the middle period, and indeed the law codes seem to make explicit this differentiation. The emperor as the vice-gerent of God was the living embodiment of the law (νόμος ἔμψυχος) and was therefore above the law; the status of the αὐγούστα, by contrast, was dependent on the emperor and as αὐγούστα, she was subject to the law.[10]

The second title is strictly speaking a pair of words: ἡ βασιλίς or ἡ βασιλίσσα.[11] These are the femine forms of one of the emperor's standard titles (βασιλεύς), employed from the reign of Heraklios (610–41) onwards. In usage, however, especially in literary sources, the term βασιλίς/βασιλίσσα was employed to express not merely a title of honour but the concept of a woman at the pinnacle of political power. These words were used to refer to empresses-regnant, but could also be applied to consorts and regents as well as to women with tangential connection with the reigning emperor.

The final title is δέσποινα, with its variant form δεσπότης. Because of its connotations of mastery, δέσποινα (mistress, lady), could be used of an empress in the same way that the emperor was master of all his subjects. Describing an empress as 'Mistress' frequently expressed her power in relation to the powerless.[12] The use of δέσποινα also drew the parallel between the woman as ruler of the empire and the woman as ruler of her household, an interesting reflection of a development in the governmental structure in Byzantium's 'long twelfth century'.[13]

If these are the titles of the 'queens-equivalent', what can be said of the institution, of its role and functions? Curiously, given the possession of a bureaucracy with differentiated function open to advancement by merit, the 'office' of empress in Byzantium can hardly be said to exist. Parsons points out some common threads that can be observed in treatments of the office of Western medieval queens: the familial context in which they operated; the role of the queen's household, when frequently the king's household served as the government, and finally the role of the queen in the bedchamber, not least as the producer of male heirs.[14] Two of these roles are very familiar from the history of Byzantium in the

---

9   Bensammar, 'La Titulaire', pp. 272–8.

10 *Ibid.*, p. 272. As an example of the way in which the empress was dependent on the will of the emperor, see the treatment of the elevation and subsequent deposition of Anna Dalassena as vice-*reine* in B. Hill, 'Alexios I Komnenos and the Imperial Women', in *Alexios I Komnenos*, edd. M. Mullett and D. Smythe (Belfast, 1996), pp. 50–2.

11 Bensammar, 'La Titulaire', pp. 278–84.

12 *Ibid.*, pp. 284–8. See Anna Komnene, *Alexiade*, III.ii.7, ed. B. Leib (Paris, 1938–45), i, 110, for Anna Dalassena's use of this title.

13 A. P. Kazhdan and A. W. Epstein, *Change In Byzantine Culture in the Eleventh and Twelfth Centuries* (London, 1985), pp. 69–73 and 99–119, esp. p. 71, for the criticism of Alexios I Komnenos by Zonaras for 'conceiving and calling the empire his own house'.

14 Parsons, 'Family, Sex and Power', pp. 2–6.

eleventh and twelfth century: the familial context[15] and the function as progenitrix of male heirs. The notion of the 'queen's household', however, with its developed and complex bureaucracy,[16] is one that properly belongs in the medieval West. In Byzantium, residence in Constantinople, 'the Queen of Cities', was a vital assertion of imperial legitimacy, and although in the course of the twelfth century the practice began to weaken under the Komnenoi, for the emperors residence in the capital meant residence in the Sacred Palace. Given the political importance of the Imperial Palace,[17] it should come as no surprise that the Byzantine bureaucracy had officials charged with ensuring its safety for the emperor. The role of the queen as governor of the royal household was not a function of the Byzantine empress; that role resided in the office of παπίας of the Great Palace.[18]

Similarly the centralised economy of the empire – even granting the 'feudalising' tendency of the twelfth century[19] – limited the empress's economic role. Empresses could and did distribute money from the imperial treasuries (and, like the empress Zoe, were criticised for doing so),[20] but there were no dower estates to be administered and governed as distinct entities. Since no household accounts survive, evidence for empresses' financial activity must be drawn largely from their roles as patrons: as founders or restorers of monasteries; as patrons of holy men; or as literary patrons.[21]

The fourteen imperial women who exercised authority in Byzantium in the eleventh and twelfth centuries can be examined in three broad categories: two empresses-regnant (with one empress-regent); nine empresses-consort, and two empresses-*manquées*.

---

[15] For a comprehensive footnote on the lack of need to demonstrate the reality of Komnenian family government, see M. Mullett, 'Alexios I Komnenos and Imperial Revival', in *New Constantines*, p. 261 n. 11.

[16] On the imperial administration, see M. Angold, *The Byzantine Empire, 1025–1204: A Political History* (London, 1984), pp. 126–33; J. B. Bury, *The Imperial Administrative System in the Ninth Century* (London, 1911); P. Magdalino, *The Empire of Manuel I Komnenos 1143–1180* (Cambridge, 1993), pp. 208–15; N. Oikonomides, *Les Listes de préséance byzantines des IXe et Xe siècles* (Paris, 1972), pp. 80–234.

[17] Cf. Anna Komnene's record in *Alexiad*, xv, of John Komnenos racing from his father's death bed to seize the imperial palace with the account given by Niketas Choniates of Manuel I Komnenos sending his trusted servant John Axouch to take the palace on his behalf after the suspicious death of John II Komnenos in Cilicia. See Mullett, 'Alexios I Komnenos and Imperial Revival', pp. 263–7; and R. Browning, 'Death of John II Komnenos', *Byzantion*, xxxi (1961), 229–35.

[18] Bury, *Imperial Administrative System*, pp. 126–8.

[19] A. Harvey, *Economic Expansion in the Byzantine Empire, 900–1200* (Cambridge, 1989).

[20] One of the causes of Zoe's dissatisfaction with Romanos III as a husband, in addition to the fact that he came to avoid intercourse with her, was that he denied her access to the imperial treasury: Psellos, *Chronographia*, iii.6 (ed. Renauld, i, 36). When wooing the future Michael IV, Zoe is described as covering him with gold (*ibid.*, iii.20, ed. Renauld, i, 46). Psellos criticises Zoe for her generosity during the period of her joint rule with Theodora (*ibid.*, vi.5, ed. Renauld, i, 119–20), but this must be viewed together with the positive attribute of imperial generosity ascribed to the ruling sisters by Psellos in the preceeding paragraph.

[21] Hill, 'Alexios I Komnenos and the Imperial Women', pp. 48–9.

Empresses-regnant

The eleventh century in Byzantium can be viewed as Byzantium's century of the empress. The early eleventh century should be seen as the reign of the empress Zoe, rather than the successive reigns of her husbands and adoptive son.[22] Zoe was the second daughter of Constantine VIII (1025–28) and thus was the niece of the emperor Basil II the Bulgarslayer (976–1025). She was born in 976 and died in Constantinople in 1050. As her elder sister Eudokia had already entered a nunnery, Zoe was by default the heir to the Macedonian dynasty, since Basil II had never married and had no heirs of the body.[23] She was married with a certain amount of unseemly haste to Romanos Argyros as her father Constantine VIII lay dying, and Romanos succeeded to the throne on his father-in-law's death as the husband of Zoe in 1028.[24] Even though she was past child-bearing age when she married, Zoe and Romanos III hoped for children and an heir, but when recourse even to supernatural aid proved ineffective, Romanos III abandoned Zoe and ignored her affairs.[25] It was through one of these affairs, with the future Michael IV, brother of John the Orphanotrophos, that Romanos III met his end, poisoned and then drowned with at least the connivance of Zoe, as gossip related by Michael Psellos records.[26] Following the accession of Michael IV in 1034, Zoe's position was more closely prescribed by the new emperor and his brother John the Orphanotrophos, and she was constrained to adopt their nephew Michael to secure the succession within their family.[27] On the death of Michael IV in 1041, Michael V came to the throne by virtue of his connection to Zoe.[28] He attempted to oust Zoe in 1042 but his unpopular policies provoked a rebellion by the populace, who clamoured for Theodora, not trusting Zoe to keep Michael V from power.[29] For several months in 1042 Zoe and Theodora ruled jointly as empresses-regnant with no male associated on the throne, but in 1042 Zoe married Constantine IX Monomachos, and he became emperor and Theodora was excluded once more from power.[30] Zoe pre-deceased her third husband, Constantine IX Monomachos, and when he died in 1055 he was succeeded by Theodora, the last representative of the dynasty. She ruled alone for one year, and on her death-bed agreed to the succession of Michael VI Stratiotikos (1057–58).[31]

The third and final representative of this century of empresses-regnant in

---

22 James, Hill, and Smythe, 'Zoe: The Rhythm Method of Imperial Renewal', pp. 215–29.
23 Psellos, *Chronographia*, ii.4–5 (ed. Renauld, i, 27–8); M. Arbagi, 'The Celibacy of Basil II', *Byzantine Studies/Études byzantines*, ii (1975), 41–5.
24 Psellos, *Chronographia*, ii.9 (ed. Renauld, i, 30).
25 *Ibid.*, iii.5–6 (ed. Renauld, i, 34–5).
26 *Ibid.*, iii.26 (ed. Renauld, i, 51–2).
27 *Ibid.*, iii.15–16 (ed. Renauld, i, 61–2).
28 *Ibid.*, v.4–5 (ed. Renauld, i, 87–8).
29 *Ibid.*, v.17–21, 36 (ed. Renauld, i, 96–8, 108).
30 *Ibid.*, v.51 and vi.11 (ed. Renauld, i, 116 and 122).
31 *Ibid.*, VI Theodora, 1–2, 19–21 (ed. Renauld, ii, 72, 82–3).

Byzantium is Eudokia Makrembolitissa, who reigned briefly in 1067 as the widow of Constantine X Doukas and regent for her son Michael VII Doukas and then again after the capture of her second husband Romanos IV Diogenes at Manzikert in 1071.[32] However, she was ousted when her son came into his own with the support of the Varangian guard.[33] Eudokia's position is slightly different from that of Zoe or Theodora, since she ruled as regent, instead of being herself the source of dynastic legitimacy.

Empresses-consort

In addition to these three empresses-regnant/regent, there were nine empresses-consort. The first example of an empress-consort is Helena, wife of Constantine VIII. Psellos, in *The Chronographia*, introduces Helena as Constantine's wife, then as the daughter of Alypios, and finally as the mother of three daughters. She is described merely as coming from one of the most noble and revered families, being beautiful in elegance and good in spirit. Conveniently – in the patriarchal view – having given birth to the three daughters of Constantine VIII, she died.[34]

Sklerina, the second empress-consort, was Constantine IX Monomachos's 'other woman'. She attained the title of 'Augousta', the formal Byzantine title of 'empress', during the life of Constantine's wife Zoe (who was after all the source of legitimacy for his rule), and according to Psellos, Sklerina had her position officially recognised and ratified in a curious 'peace treaty' acclaimed by the senate, and the *ménage à trois* was made manifest in the domestic arrangements of the Great Palace.[35] She died in about 1044, and Constantine IX was buried beside her in the Monastery of the Mangana eleven years later.[36] The manner in which Constantine IX Monomachos was able to introduce his mistress into the imperial palace and grant her a style and title which was the equivalent of the purple-born Zoe confirms that the status of 'empress' depended entirely on the emperor, when there was one. Autarky for the office of empress became effective only when there was no emperor.

More regularly in the category of empresses-consort is Aikaterine, wife of Isaak Komnenos (1057–59). The daughter of John Vladislav of Bulgaria, Aikaterine was particularly scathing in her attack on her husband, when he determined to retire to a monastery rather than dying in the purple in 1059, describing in very bleak terms the life of an empress whose husband had abdicated, as she was likely to become the plaything of those seeking the succession.[37] In this, the position of the

---

[32] *Ibid.*, VII Konstantinos, x.6 (ed. Renauld, ii, 141); and VII Eudokia, 1–3 (ed. Renauld, ii, 152–3); and VII Romanos, iv.25 (ed. Renauld, ii, 163–4).

[33] *Ibid.*, VII Romanos, iv.30–1 (ed. Renauld, ii, 166).

[34] *Ibid.*, ii.4 (ed. Renauld, i, 27).

[35] *Ibid.*, vi.50–9 (ed. Renauld, i, 142–5).

[36] *Ibid.*, vi.202 (ed. Renauld, ii, 71).

[37] *Ibid.*, VII Isaak Komnenos, 82 (ed. Renauld, ii, 133).

Byzantine widow empress is comparable with the situation in the West, although there at least feudal usage provided some protection in the dower.[38]

There then follows a run of strong empresses-consort. First was Maria of Alania, consort to Michael VII Doukas (1071–78), who bore him a son and heir, the Kaisar Constantine (eventually betrothed to Anna Komnene, the historian author of the *Alexiad*). When Michael VII was deposed, Maria of Alania married Nikephoros III Botaneiates (1078–81), giving him legitimacy, and she adopted Alexios Komnenos before the Komnenian revolt in 1081 in an attempt to secure her son's safety.[39] After the revolt of the Komnenoi-Doukai, there was a rumour that Alexios intended to marry Maria himself, setting aside his wife Eirene Doukaina. Such an action would have alienated the Doukai faction on which the new regime relied for support, and Alexios Komnenos was forced to crown Eirene Doukaina as Augousta.[40]

The role and influence of Eirene Doukaina as consort of Alexios is clearly rendered in the *Alexiad*, but since the work was written by the daughter of the imperial couple and with an ulterior motive, it is not without bias. Reading between the lines it is clear that Eirene Doukaina was a woman of independent spirit. Even though Anna Komnene stresses that it was her devotion to Alexios that caused Eirene Doukaina to accompany him on military campaigns, there remains the clear suspicion that he compelled her to accompany him because she was too dangerous to be left alone in Constantinople at the centre of power.[41] Her role as a forceful power-broker was most apparent in her schemes to replace her son John Komnenos as heir with Anna Komnene, the historian, and her husband the Kaisar Nikephoros Bryennios, as Alexios lay dying in 1118.[42]

Less of an obvious danger to the *status quo* was Eirene, consort of John II Komnenos. Born Proska of Hungary, Eirene's foreign origin may have rendered her weak before native-born Byzantines with well-established networks of power and influence;[43] but it is more likely that her early death, before that of her husband

38 M. Mullett, 'The "Disgrace" of the Ex-Basilissa Maria', *Byzantinoslavica*, xlv (1985), 202–11.

39 Komnene, *Alexiad*, I.iv.1, II.i.5 (ed. Lieb, i, 45, 65). M. E. Mullett, 'Alexios I Komnenos and Imperial Renewal', in *New Constantines*, pp. 259–68.

40 Komnene, *Alexiad*, II.vii.7 (ed. Leib, i, 87).

41 *Ibid.*, XII.iii.2–3 (ed. Leib, iii, 60).

42 Contrast *ibid.*, XV.xi.4–20 (ed. Leib, iii, 231–40) with John Zonaras, *Epitome historiarum*, ed. M. Pinder, CSHB (Bonn, 1897), iii, 795–65. For recent interpretations, see Mullett, 'Alexios Komnenos and Imperial Renewal', pp. 263–7, and Hill, 'Alexios I Komnenos and the Imperial Women', pp. 39–40.

43 This was, after all, the inducement offered by the Kaisar John Doukas for Nikephoros III Botaneiates to marry the empress Maria of Alania, widow of Michael VII Doukas, 'because she was of foreign birth and had no crowd of relatives to embarrass the emperor' (Komnene, *Alexiad*, III.ii.3, ed. Leib, i, 107). The Kaisar John Doukas was probably also motivated by a design to protect the position of his nephew, Kaisar Constantine Doukas, son and porphyrogennitos heir of Michael VII Doukas. The final outcome of this concern for family – on the part of both male and female members – may be seen in the union of the Komnenoi and Doukai families, effected by the marriage of Alexios I Komnenos to Eirene Doukaina

in 1143, deprived her of the occasion to engage in succession plots.[44] In founding the monastic hospital complex of Christ Pantokrator in Constantinople,[45] however, she did participate in the standard run of Byzantine imperial activities, as her inclusion in the second imperial image in the south gallery of Aghia Sophia indicates.

The successive wives of Manuel I Komnenos (1143–80), Bertha-Eirene of Sulzbach and Maria of Antioch, are final examples of empresses-consort in the eleventh and twelfth centuries. Both were Westerners (broadly constructed) and their roles in the empire are less clearly representative of Byzantine ideas of empresses and empire. Bertha-Eirene was dispatched to Constantinople by her brother-in-law Conrad III, the Western emperor, in 1142 to cement the alliance conceived in 1140 between Byzantium and the Western empire. Political uncertainty delayed the solemnisation of the wedding until 1146. She died in Constantinople in about 1160. She remains largely a shadowy figure, in large part because of her failure to produce a male heir. Maria of Antioch was Manuel I Komnenos's second wife, whom he married in 1161 to strengthen his alliance with Antioch and further his Eastern policy.[46] She bore Manuel a son, Alexios, in 1169. After Manuel's death in 1180, Maria of Antioch served as regent for her young son, but her Latin affinities laid her open to intrigues by Andronikos Komnenos, which she was unable to stem by recourse to Hungarian aid, and she was condemned and executed in 1182 or 1183. The brief period of her regency might be held to merit her inclusion among the empresses-regnant, but its rapid and violent end would place that portion of her career more fittingly in the next section. However, her real importance – not least as provider of the long awaited porphyrogennite heir – means that her true place is as an empress-consort.

Empresses-*manquées*

Returning to the eleventh century, examples of the category of empresses-*manqueés* are more prevelant, and represent a more coherent Byzantine/Mediaeval

<hr>

in 1081 and the betrothal of Anna Komnene the historian to the Kaisar Constantine Doukas. This betrothal was never solemnised into marriage, and with the birth of John Komnenos in 1087, Anna Komnene's position as heir presumptive was weakened and finally lost in 1092. The Kaisar Constantine Doukas appears to have died about two years later, which seems to coincide with Maria's complicity in the plot against Alexios I Komnenos in 1094. In marrying her first husband's successor, surviving a *coup* against her second husband, tying herself to the new dynasty (the new emperor, Alexios I Komnenos, was her adoptive son and brother-in-law of her cousin), and plotting against the reigning emperor, it is clear that foreign origin did not prevent Maria of Alania from learning to play Byzantine court intrigue with consummate skill.

44 John Kinnamos, *Epitome*, ed. A. Meinke (Bonn, 1836), pp. 9–10, trans. C. Brand, *The Deeds of John and Manuel Comnenus* (New York, 1976), p.17.

45 'Typikon du Christ Pantokrator', ed. P. Gautier, *Revue des Études Byzantines*, xxxii (1974), 1–145. Its foundation is frequently ascribed to her husband, who merely completed what she had begun.

46 Magdalino, *The Empire of Manuel I Komnenos*, pp. 66–76.

view of the role of empresses and empire. The figure of Anna Dalassena, mother of Alexios I Komnenos, is presented vibrantly in *The Alexiad*. She is an empress-*manqueé*, but by the actions of her son she becomes in effect the vice-*reine* of the vice-gerent of God. According to the *chrysobul* recorded by Anna Komnene, her actions were to have the same authority as if they had been issued over Alexios's own signature. When his grasp on power was unsure, and when his presence at the front was a necessity, Anna Dalassena was a 'safe pair of hands' in which to place the empire;[47] but in the 1090s, when he was more frequently in the capital himself and his position was more secure, it was less necessary to have a vice-*reine*, and his mother was eased from power.[48] However, just as she had been the dynamo which had powered the Komnenian rebellion against Nikephoros III Botaneiates, so also she served as a model or at least an example of a woman wielding power, which her daughter-in-law (Eirene Doukaina) and her granddaughter (Anna Komnene) sought to emulate, though with a lack of conspicuous success.

From her own writings[49] it is clear that Anna Komnene felt cheated of what she felt to be her proper role in life: empress-regnant as first-born porphyrogennite of Alexios I Komnenos and Eirene Doukaina, and legitimator of her husband, Nikephoros Bryennios. Anna Komnene was born on 2 December 1083, the eldest child and first daughter of Alexios and Eirene Doukaina. Her birth was associated with a miraculous happening.[50] This self-conceptualisation as the eldest-born and heir of the Komnenoi-Doukai porphyrogennitoi was an expression of her goal in life: 'nämlich dereinst als Kaiserin den Thron zu besteigen'.[51] At an early age, Anna Komnene was betrothed to Constantine Doukas, the son of Michael VII Doukas and the empress Maria the Alan and she was brought up in the household of her future mother-in-law. Her prospects became less bright with the birth of her brother John in 1087, and in 1092 she lost her priority in the succession to him. Constantine Doukas died about two years later. By 1097 at the latest, Anna Komnene was married to Nikephoros Bryennios, prompted in part by the desire to tie the Bryennios family more closely to the Komnenoi-Doukai axis. The marriage produced two sons and a daughter, although they receive no mention in the *Alexiad*. Nikephoros Bryennios died in 1136 or 1137. After her husband's death, Anna retired to the monastery of Kecharitoumene, founded by her mother,[52] where she died in about 1153–54.

47 Komnene, *Alexiad*, III.vi–vii (ed. Leib, i, 119–24).
48 Hill, 'Alexios I Komnenos and the Imperial Women', pp. 50–2.
49 For the view that Anna Komnene was less than the author of the *Alexiad*, see J. Howard-Johnston, in *Alexios I Komnenos*, edd. M. Mullett and D. Smythe (Belfast, 1996), pp. 260–302.
50 Komnene, *Alexiad*, VI.vii.2 (ed. Leib, ii, 58).
51 H. Hunger, *Die hochsprachliche profane Literatur der Byzantiner*, i, *Philosophie, Rhetorik, Epistolographie, Geschichtsschreibung, Geographie* (Munich, 1978), p. 401.
52 'Le typikon de la Théotokos Kécharitôménè', *Revue des Études Byzantines*, xliii (1985), 5–166.

Conclusions

How far do these examples of Byzantine empresses enable us to see the reality behind the masks of empresses and empire in Middle Byzantium? In attempting a response, some qualifications must be set forth. Firstly, and perhaps self-evidently, there is no *one* Byzantine attitude to anything. It is necessary to note that the written sources derive from a very small part of the society which we study. There are many unanswered questions of the size of the writing and reading community in Byzantium, not to mention the further complication of the audience or hearing community.[53] All medievalists – in the Byzantine East, the Latin West and the Islamic South – share these problems. Although the extent of literacy was wider in Byzantium than in Western Christendom, at least in the eleventh and twelfth centuries, the principal narrative sources upon which I draw were written in the high-style atticising Greek of the period, the use of which Sevcenko has described as the conspicuous display of the badge of the élite.[54] These writings were the product of the educated élite, intended for that same élite. Nevertheless, they express ideas which would have been shared to some extent by all members of the society.[55]

Having blazoned my qualifiers, how are these women empresses viewed? In the *Chronographia* of Psellos there is considerable ambivalence. Psellos describes the Lady Helena in a purely patriarchal mode, but when he first described the government of Zoe and Theodora, he was approving. Having said that the two sisters had assumed power, and that for the first time the women's quarters had become the imperial council chamber, Psellos says that the two elements of the administration – the civil and the military – pulled together much better under the sovereign ladies than they would have done under an overlord issuing arrogant commands. The sisters did not introduce many new procedures, nor did they appoint many new ministers, but they removed only those who were of the tyrant's [Michael V] family, and retained the other ministers in their posts. For their part, these ministers were held in check by the fear that at some later date they would

---

[53] R. Browning, 'Literacy in the Byzantine world', *Byzantine and Modern Greek Studies*, iv (1978), 39–54; Cyril Mango, *Byzantium: Empire of New Rome* (London, 1980), pp. 125–48, 233–55; M. E. Mullett, 'Aristocracy and Patronage in the Literary Circles of Comnenian Constantinople', in *The Byzantine Aristocracy, IX to XIII Centuries*, ed. M. Angold (Oxford, 1984), pp. 173–201; *eadem*, 'Dancing with Deconstructionists in the Gardens of the Muses: New Literary History vs ?', in *Byzantine and Modern Greek Studies*, xiv (1990), 258–75; N. Oikonomides, 'Mount Athos: Levels of Literacy', *Dumbarton Oaks Papers*, xlii (1988), 167–78; N. G. Wilson, 'Books and Readers in Byzantium', in *Byzantine Books and Bookmen*, ed. N. G. Wilson (Washington, D.C., 1975), pp. 1–15.

[54] I. Sevcenko, 'Levels of Style in Byzantine Prose', *Jahrbuch der Österreichischen Byzantinistik*, xxxi (1981), 302.

[55] N. Abercrombie, S. Hill and B. S. Turner, *The Dominant Ideology Thesis* (London, 1980), pp. 1–2; M. N. Marger, *Elites and Masses: An introduction to Political Sociology* (New York, 1981), pp. 29, 307. The exact boundaries of this shared culture in mediaeval societies is one of the most interesting avenues of research.

be held accountable for their actions.[56] Psellos's exact attitude here is difficult to unravel. On the one hand, these ministers were 'most faithful, guarding an inherited goodwill towards [the sisters]', but that they were concerned that they might be called to account suggests that they recognised the situation as unstable. The result was that the government officials were very attentive to their duties, whether military or civilian, and furthermore showed due respect to the empresses as far as possible. On the whole, the personal government of Zoe and Theodora is seen as an improvement on the régimes of Michael IV and Michael V, but there is an unresolved question: how stable was the situation under women rulers? Psellos was unsure how to present these women governors: they were the legal heirs to the empire, yet since they were women their position as empresses-regnant was a perversion of the natural order. But attempts to replace them or to associate them with male rulers had been less than successful. With good officials, the Byzantine bureaucratic system under the sisters brings good government, but it is unnatural – the officials defer to the women only 'as far as possible', because the woman cannot command the same respect from officials (who are men) as could a *basileus*. Psellos emphasises that in the exercise of power and in their appearance before the people the sisters continued the customs of previous emperors:

> In the outward form of government the sisters did as previous emperors had done, for both sat before the imperial tribune in one line, slightly indented to Theodora's side, and near them were the Rods and Guards, and the race who brandish an axe at the right shoulder. Next stood the special favourites and those who organise things. Round [the women] on the outside came a guard, like a surrounding crown.[57]

Thus the bureaucracy and ceremonial of Byzantine government provided the shape and container for the female exercise of power (τό χράτος). The matters of government continued as before, and it made no difference whether it was an emperor or empresses at the centre of the web of power. It was against this backdrop that business was carried on, lawsuits judged, questions of public interest discussed or taxation levied, audiences with ambassadors and all other duties that occupy those who exercise power.[58] The sisters, recognised as empresses (βασιλίδες), gave necessary orders in a soft voice or replied, taking instruction from their advisers' experience or relying on their own judgment. Up to this point, Psellos's presentation of Zoe and Theodora has been largely positive. Whilst the situation was somewhat unusual, the complementary natures of the two sisters were working together in the best interests of the state in the imperial tradition. But Psellos goes on to say that 'neither one had sufficient intelligence to rule'. They knew neither how to administer nor were they able to reason solidly on matters of state; furthermore they confused the playthings of the women's quarters with serious imperial concerns. Here Psellos reverts to a patriarchal view of women

---

[56] Psellos, *Chronographis*, vi.2 (ed. Renauld, i, 117–18).
[57] *Ibid.*, vi.3 (ed. Renauld, i, 118).
[58] *Ibid.*, vi.10 (ed. Renauld, i, 118).

as belonging in the women's quarters, and Zoe and Theodora are faulted because they left the women's private realm to invade the public sphere of government.[59] This change in view could be ascribed to dual authorship, but it is better to say that Psellos, realising the positive attitude he was displaying to women ruling alone, retreated from it.

The attitude to women in positions of power in Anna Komnene's *Alexiad* is very different; but by the time that Anna was writing, the organisation of the Byzantine 'state apparatus' (if it is not too anachronistic to speak of such a concept in the mediaeval context) was becoming an extension of the family (defined in a specific way).[60] Thus to Anna Komnene it was natural that the concerns of women would include arranging dynastic marriages. The same is true of Psellos, but by the mid-twelfth century, such marriages had serious implications for the functioning of the Byzantine central bureaucracy. Furthermore, it must be recognised that Anna Komnene's positive view of these powerful women was coloured by her desire to be numbered among them, not exiled from power and influence for more than half her life by her detested brother, John.

Attempts to deconstruct the meaning of empresses-regnant, empresses-consort and empresses-*manquées* in the Middle Byzantine period are rendered difficult for a variety of reasons: the atticising, literary Greek of the written sources is frequently allusive if not elusive in meaning; the manner in which information is encoded in visual sources is a complex syntax and vocabulary that appears to be unchanging; Middle Byzantine society is understood from largely patriarchally inspired sources, frequently interpreted with patriarchal spectacles. Despite this bias, in the eleventh and twelfth centuries there were empresses who transmitted, held, and exercised political power. They provided access to power for men; they provided heirs; they served as regents; on occasion they reigned and ruled in their own right, though not without some patriarchal reservation. To a large extent, this apparently paradoxical situation, in which the sacred rule of the empire passed through or devolved upon women, was in part a reflection of the differing possibilities opened up by the development of the Byzantine state. Since the feudal principle (military service in return for land) was not the organising principle of Byzantine society, the person at the top of the chain of command was not expected to bear arms.[61] The increasing significance attached to birth in the porphyry chamber of the imperial palace meant that succession to the throne was not determined simply by primogeniture. And the bureaucratic government of New Rome, while not making of Byzantium a modern state, made it possible for the supreme office to be filled by a woman.

---

[59] *Ibid.*, vi.3–4 (ed. Renauld, i, 118).

[60] See above, n. 16.

[61] This is especially true of the eleventh century; a case can easily be made that under the Komnenoi in the twelfth century, this position was changing.

9

Queen or Consort:
Rulership and Politics in the Latin East, 1118–1228

Sarah Lambert

The necessity which every European dynasty felt during the medieval period of producing male heirs is neatly expressed in a letter written by Louis VII of France in 1165, on the birth of his first son, Philip Augustus:

> An ardent desire that God would give us progeny of the better sex inflamed us, for we had been terrified by a multitude of daughters.[1]

A response to this event was written by Bishop Arnulf of Lisieux:

> no one will be so arrogant or contumacious as to refuse to do the service owed to him whom he knows to have been begotten out of your flesh for the government of the realm.[2]

These remarks serve to introduce the central dichotomy which this paper will explore: how the perceived needs of dynasty – rulership handed down through successive generations from parent to child – conflict with the constructions of gender. The heir 'begotten out of your flesh' and bearing royal blood cannot fail to command respect and wield authority, unless that heir is one of the multitude of daughters. Two aspects of biology, descent and gender, are here being reconstructed by political society in ways which might be congruent, but which equally might conflict. Where there are only daughters, the demands of dynastic rule contradict the requirements of gender roles – and the questions are raised, can a daughter be an heir, can a woman inherit rulership?

Louis' contemporary, Baldwin II of Jerusalem, was, as the genealogical table demonstrates, presented with just such a 'multitude of daughters', and the problem of female succession was to recur with almost monotonous regularity in the dynasty which ruled the kingdom of Jerusalem from 1099 until 1228. Five women

---

1 *Monuments historiques*, ed. J. Tardif (Paris, 1866), p. 300 no. 588, 'nos quoque inflammaverat ardor iste, ut prestaret nobis Deus sobolem melioris sexus, qui territi eramus multitudine filiarum'. My thanks are due to Anne Duggan and Jinty Nelson for helpful advice and criticism.
2 *Letters of Arnulf of Lisieux*, ed. F. Barlow, Camden 3rd Series, 61 (London, 1938), p. 79, to Louis VII, 1165: 'Nullus enim erit adeo superbus aut contumax, qui illi debitum famulatum detractet impendere, quem de carne vestra ad regni noverit gubernacula procreatum.'

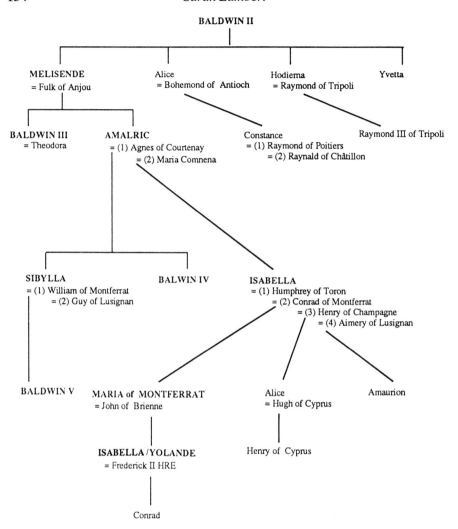

Figure 5 The succession to the throne of Jerusalem 1118–1228

inheriting the throne within less than sixty years presented the political classes of the Latin East with a series of monumental problems and contemporary male chroniclers with the task of recording female rule. How they attempted to reconcile the demands of dynasty and gender, amid the claims of factional politics; how facing up to the succession of female heirs shaped these politics; and how the situation was constructed to the advantage of baronial factions will be examined below.

Louis VII had divorced his first wife Eleanor in order to have a second try at producing a son. Much later, in the fourteenth century, when the Capetian dynasty finally ran out of direct male heirs, the solution imposed was a diversion of the succession and the retrospective outlawing of female succession to or transmission of the French crown, through an appeal to the 'ancient' Salic law.[3] However, in the Latin East, different strategies were developed to deal with that terrifying multitude of daughters and their ascent into queenship, and different texts, even different recensions of texts, reveal the diversity of views about the problem. It is important to bear in mind that there was no settled law on this point in Western Europe in the twelfth century. Ideas on succession to and transmission of political power, whether royal or noble, were in a state of flux. It is not clear either to what extent royal and noble succession were regarded as bound by the same principles or customs.[4]

The principle source for the kingdom of Jerusalem in this period is the chronicle of William of Tyre, undoubtedly one of the greatest historians of the twelfth century – perhaps of the whole medieval period.[5] His history of the ruling dynasty from 1099 to 1184 can be seen as an attempt to explain the decline of the kingdom from its heyday in the thirties and early forties to imminent disaster in the early 1180s. He was a client of the dynasty and owed his promotion to its patronage – but he also had an early taste of the legal education then available at the schools of Bologna and Paris, and so he tried to tell the story of the dynasty in legalistic terms, which sometimes clashed with the attempt to reflect accurately the politics of his 85-year history.[6] This was specially the case when he came to write about Queen Melisende. He depended on her as the lynch-pin in the dynasty; she provided the blood connection to those first crusaders who had established the kingdom, through her father Baldwin II and her uncle Baldwin I, but one can see that William was deeply uncertain about the role of the queen in political society and the nature of the relationship between succession and rulership for a queen.[7] He recorded her as heiress during her father Baldwin II's lifetime, and told how she was consecrated and crowned alongside her husband Fulk of Anjou. But after this he treated her inconsistently. He attributed conflicts between Melisende and

---

3   On French succession in the fourteenth century, see e.g. A. W. Lewis, *Royal Succession in Capetian France: Studies on Familial Order and the State* (Cambridge, Mass., 1981), *passim* and R. E. Giesey, 'The Juristic Basis of Dynastic Right to the French Throne', *Transactions of the American Philosophical Society*, li (1961), 3–42.

4   See for example J. Le Patourel, *Feudal Empires, Norman and Plantaganet* (London, 1984); J. Holt, 'Feudal Society and the Family in Medieval England', *TRHS*, xxxv (1985), 1–28; J. Martindale, 'Succession and Politics', in *England and her Neighbours, 1066–1453: Essays in Honour of Pierre Caplais*, edd. M. Jones and M. Vale (London, 1989), pp. 19–41.

5   *Willelmi Tyrensis Archiepiscopi Chronicon* [= William of Tyre], ed. R. B. C. Huygens, Corpus Christianorum continuatio Medievalis, 63–63a (Turnhout, 1986), xiv–xv (for Fulk's reign); xiii.24, rubric (for Melisende as heiress).

6   P. Edbury and J. Rowe, *William of Tyre, Historian of the Latin East* (Cambridge, 1988), p. 15; R. B. C. Huygens, 'Guillaume de Tyre, étudiant: un chapitre de son 'Histoire' retrouvé', *Latomus*, xxi (1962), 811–38.

7   For the contemporary and directly comparable case of Matilda of England, see M. Chibnall, *Empress Matilda: Queen Consort, Queen Mother and Lady of the English* (Oxford, 1993), p. 102. See also M. Facinger, 'A Study in Medieval Queenship: Capetian France 987–1237', *Studies in Medieval and Renaissance History*, v (1968), 3–47; H. E. Mayer, 'The Succession of Baldwin II of Jerusalem: The English Influence on the East', *Dumbarton Oaks Papers*, xxxix (1985), 139–47.

Fulk in the early years of their joint reign to what he admits were spurious
accusations of adultery. But Mayer has demonstrated that this supposedly domestic
quarrel was in fact a political conflict in which a party of the nobles, led by Hugh
of Jaffa, protested against Fulk's heavy-handed rule and his exclusion of the local
Latin nobility from office, and supported Melisende's closer involvement in
government. Although William said that after their reconciliation Fulk ruled
entirely according to Melisende's wishes, he made no further reference to her
political actions during Fulk's lifetime, although all the royal charters following
this conflict bear Melisende's name as well as Fulk's, testifying to her continued
role in political life.[8] Equally, when conflicts over her rulership arose later between
Melisende and her son Baldwin III, the barons of the king's council were clearly
divided about where royal power should lie. William reflected this uncertainty
without being able to resolve it.[9] These issues of power were fought out on the
battle field as well as at the level of text – Melisende was besieged in the citadel
of Jerusalem by her son Baldwin, who had been advised that his mother ought to
relinquish rule once he came of age. Nevertheless, after her defeat, and the
supposed withdrawal to the city of Nablus imposed on her by the victorious
Baldwin, Melisende appeared in William's chronicle, apparently more politically
active than before.[10]

When Melisende died in 1160, William reflected on her life in these words:

> Transcending the strength of women, the lady queen, Melisende, a prudent
> woman, discreet above the female sex, had ruled the kingdom with fitting
> moderation for more than thirty years, during the lifetime of her husband and
> the reign of her son.[11]

Despite his praise of her moderation and discretion there is an underlying confusion about her position. The 'thirty years' refers to the period from Baldwin II's
death in 1131 to Melisende's in 1160. At this point, William seems to be saying
that Melisende's reign dated from her father's death and that she was co-regnant
with Fulk throughout his lifetime: she *reigned* during the *lifetime* of her husband
and the *reign* of her son – Fulk is not described as reigning; but Baldwin III's reign
began during his mother's reign, so they were co-regnants as well – rather than
Melisende being regent in place of her child. William was trying to write a legally
clear and dynastically motivated account and to construct linkages between the

8   William of Tyre, xiv.15–18. For earlier studies on Queen Melisande, see H. E. Mayer,
    'Studies in the History of Queen Melisande', *Dumbarton Oaks Papers*, xxvi (1972), 95–182;
    idem, 'Succession of Baldwin II'. For the conflict, see *idem*, 'The Wheel of Fortune:
    Seigneurial Vicissitudes under Kings Fulk and Baldwin III of Jerusalem', *Speculum*, lxv
    (1990), 860–77. For the charters, *Regesta Regni Hierosolymitani* and *Additamentum*, ed. R.
    Rohricht (Innsbruck, 1893, 1904), nos 163, 179, 191.
9   William of Tyre, xiv.13–14.
10 *Ibid.*, xvii.18–19 (p. 785); xviii.1 (p. 809); xviii.1 (p. 809); xviii.20 (p. 840).
11 *Ibid.*, xviii.27, 32 (p. 850), 'domina Milissendis regina, mulier provida et supra sexum
    discrete femineum, qui regnum tam *vivente* marito quam *regnante* filio congruo moderamine
    annis triginta et amplius vires transcendens femineas, rexerat'.

image of a good wife, good mother, and wise and competent governor. Melisende was still defined by her relations with men, as wife, widow and mother, but her role as queen required her to transcend such gendered constraints, and William seems to have been presenting this as a real possibility.

Despite this evident uncertainty, William chose his words very carefully to articulate the indistinct position which Melisende held in his eyes. His carefulness is made particularly evident when his words are compared with those of the French translation of his work probably first made in the early thirteenth century.[12] This translation is for the most part so painstakingly accurate, that when it makes significant alterations to the picture of Melisende, these differences can be seen to reflect a genuinely different political perspective. For example, William recorded that Melisende had founded a convent at Bethany for her sister Yvetta, because 'It seemed unworthy to her that the daughter of a king should submit herself to a mother in the cloister like an ordinary person.'[13] I believe that he was using the expression *regis filia* consciously to echo Melisende's position as queen based on her own status as *regis filia*. However, when the translator came to this passage, he made no mention of the special position which Melisende thought was appropriate for a king's daughter, and omitted this sentence.[14] In the same way, the translator placed a very different interpretation on William's account of the young king's coronation. William recorded that after Baldwin III's consecration as king, he and Melisende were crowned together:

> After the death of his father, he was solemnly anointed, consecrated and crowned with his mother. For she was a most prudent mother, having full experience in almost all secular affairs, so entirely overcoming the condition of the female sex that she could extend her hand to forceful action. She ruled the kingdom with such industry and moderation, while her son was under the age of puberty, that she was rightly said to equal her progenitors in that regard.[15]

According to the French text:

[12] J. Pryor, 'The Eracles and William of Tyre: An Interim Report', in *The Horns of Hattin: Proceedings of the Second Conference of the Society for the Study of the Crusades and the Latin East*, ed. B. Z. Kedar (Jerusalem, 1992), p. 293.

[13] William of Tyre, xv.26, 9, 'Indignum videbatur ei ut regis filia tamquam una ex popularibus claustro alicui subesset matri.'

[14] 'Guilelmus Tyrensis Chronicon' in *Recueil des historiens des croisades: Historiens occidentaux*, i, 699 (French translation). For Melisende's title as *filia regis* see *Regesta Regni*, nos 121, 137a; Mayer, 'Succession'.

[15] William of Tyre, xvi.3, 1–17, 'Defuncto igitur patre . . . solemniter inunctus consecratus et cum matre coronatus est. Erat autem mater prudentissima, plenam pene in omnibus secularibus negotiis habens experientiam, sexus feminae plane vincens conditionem, ita ut manum mitteret ad fortia . . . Regnum enim, filio adhuc infra puberes annos constituto, tanta rexit industria, tanto procuravit moderamine, ut progenitores suos in ea parte aequare merito diceretur.'

> Baldwin II . . . was crowned on Christmas day . . . His mother wore the crown
> with him, because there was no queen as wife of this young king.[16]

Either not understanding or consciously misconstruing the situation, the translator
made Melisende's role directly comparable to that of a consort, standing in for,
and equivalent to, the future wife of her young son.

He also made additions to William's assessment of Melisende's reign. In the
routine translation of William's opinions about her political acumen and intelligence, quoted above, the translator interpolates that she was beautiful – 'de bone
contenance'[17] – and that she was virtuous in fact and in reputation:

> The good lady who was heir, Queen Melisende, held and governed the
> kingdom well, for she loved Our Lord greatly and guarded herself from sin
> for the sake of her conscience, and from all evil appearance, for the sake of
> her reputation.[18]

This introduction of 'private' virtues into praise of 'public' effectiveness may also
reflect a development in the containment of the feminine in a 'private sphere', in
contrast to public political functions, which could be seen to have taken place very
slowly in the course of the Middle Ages.[19]

There is a third source for the history of the twelfth century, which is rarely
mined for information, because of its evident inferiority to William's lengthy
account. This is the first section of the collection of texts published by Mas Latrie
under the title 'La Chronique d'Ernoul et de Bernard le Tresorier'. The section
dealing with the early years of the kingdom (hereafter cited as the *abrégé*,
following Morgan), is very short, possibly abridged, but it contains material not
included by William and has a very different emphasis.[20] Its significance in the
present context is that Melisende has been almost completely edited out of this
version. It describes the dying Baldwin II seeking the advice of the barons about
a husband for his eldest daughter, 'qui le regne puist gouverner apres lui'; but the
daughter, Melisende, is not named and is not accorded any political will of her
own.[21] The foundation of a royal monastery at Bethany, which in William of Tyre's

---

16 *Ibid.*, i, 707, 'Baudouin le tiers . . . le jour noel . . . fu coronez . . . Sa mére porta le jor corone
   avec lui, por ce qu'il n'avoit point de reine qui fust feme à ce jeune roi.'

17 *Ibid.*; cf. William of Tyre, xvi.23.

18 'Guilelmus Tyrensis Chronicon', p. 702, 'le roiaume tint molt bien et *governa* la bone dame
   qui estoit oirs, la reine Milisent, qui mout amoit Nostre Seigneur et bien se gardoit de pechié
   por sa conscience, *et de touz maus semblanz por sa bone renomee*'; cf. William of Tyre xv.27,
   lines 43–4: 'Reseditque regni potestas penes dominam Milisendem, deo amabilem reginam
   cui jure hereditario competebat.'

19 For the decline during this period of the public, formal role of the Capetian queen-consort,
   see Facinger, 'Medieval Queenship', pp. 4, 29.

20 *Chronique d'Ernoul et de Bernard le Trésorier*, ed. M. de Mas Latrie (Paris, 1871), pp.
   1–119. For the relationships between this compilation and the other translations and
   continuations of William of Tyre, see M. R. Morgan, *The Chronicle of Ernoul and the
   Continuations of William of Tyre* (Oxford, 1973), pp. 51–8 *et passim*.

21 Mas Latrie, p. 10.

original chronicle was Melisende's own project (a fact confirmed by charter evidence), is in the *abrégé* ascribed solely to King Baldwin II.[22] This version presents Baldwin III succeeding alone at Fulk's death, with no mention of Melisende's role at the coronation or of the subsequent disputes between her and her son.[23]

The succession in 1174 of Melisende's grandson, Baldwin IV, presented the dynasty with another crisis and William of Tyre with the difficulty of explaining the dynastic contortions which resulted from it. Baldwin IV was diagnosed as suffering from leprosy shortly before his accession, and his youth and illness meant that the succession was uncertain. As it was unlikely that the young Baldwin would marry attention must have focused on the position of his sister Sibylla and half-sister Isabella.[24] William made it clear that the question of the marriage of Sibylla, the elder sister, was of vital political importance, without ever explicitly stating that she was expected to succeed.[25] Several attempts were made to attract a suitable husband for Sibylla, but in William's account no promise was offered to any of the candidates that she would be allowed to succeed or transmit regnal power to her husband – unlike Melisende's contract with Fulk, which had included such a promise, and the contract later made between John of Brienne and Maria of Montferrat, which also included a promise of rulership. This uncertainty about Sibylla's future status may have contributed to putting off so promising a candidate as Count Stephen of Sancerre.[26] William's account of Sibylla's marriage to Guy of Lusignan implies that she was a potential heiress, since he reports that the match was hastily arranged by Baldwin IV, who feared a *coup* by Raymond of Tripoli. But her position was never clearly spelled out. In William's account of the succession crisis played out around Baldwin IV's death bed, no compromise was

---

[22] Mas Latrie, p. 5.

[23] Mas Latrie, p. 14.

[24] William of Tyre, xxi.1, lines 20–41. Most commentators have assumed that Baldwin's leprosy made it impossible for him to marry (e.g. R. C. Smail, 'The Predicaments of Guy of Lusignan, 1183–7', in *Outremere: Studies in the History of the Crusading Kingdom of Jerusalem*, edd. B. Kedar, H. Mayer, R. Smail [Jerusalem, 1982], pp. 159–76 at p. 161; H. E. Mayer, 'The Double County of Jaffa and Ascalon', in *Crusade and Settlement*, ed. P. Edbury [Cardiff, 1985], p. 183; J. Prawer, *Crusader Institutions* [Oxford, 1980], p. 336). But there seems to have been no canonical impediment implied by the disease: a decision of Alexander III (Mansi, xxii, 395: *Appendix Concilii Lateranensis*, xxxvii.3) emphatically allows lepers to marry, 'Leprosis autem . . . liberum est ipsis ad matrimonium convolare.' The *Livre au Roi*, however, certainly assumes that a knight who becomes a leper will immediately enter a monastery, and if he is married, the parties will be separated, 'celui mariages det estre partis' (*Recueil des historiens des croisades: Lois*, ed. M. le Comte Beugnot, i [Paris, 1841] 636c. 42), but this was not written until twenty-five years after Baldwin's time, and may record a more severe attitude to leprosy in an area where the disease was endemic.

[25] Her position as heiress was recognised in charters of the period: *Regesta Regni*, nos 545–6, 553, 553a, 559a, 570, 603, 614–5.

[26] William of Tyre, xiii.24; xx.25. For the proposed marriage to Henry of Burgundy, see *ibid.*, xxi.25, 29; cf. the successful negotiations with William of Montferrat and Guy of Lusignan (*ibid.*, xxi.12; xxii.1).

made between the claims of the heiress and the unpopularity of her husband –
between the demands of dynasty and those of government. The High Court agreed
– and William agreed with it – to by-pass Sibylla completely and crown her infant
son, Baldwin V. Even the role of regent for the child was denied to Sibylla and her
husband, because of Guy of Lusignan's unpopularity. Instead, a cousin, Raymond
of Tripoli, was appointed regent. This was not, in William's account, an overt
attempt to prevent the accession of a woman – William focused his account of
baronial opposition on Guy, even accusing him of plotting to seize the throne from
the sick king. There was no suggestion here that Sibylla might be allowed to
'transcend the strength of women' and rule in her own right (as in the case of
Melisende). Instead, in making Guy the principal object of this opposition, William
recognised the shift of power from dynastic ruler to 'king-consort', which takes
place when the inheritance devolved upon a queen. He accepted without question
the overturning of the 'normal' rules of succession – the by-passing of a generation
and the coronation of the baby Baldwin V in the last days of his uncle. For William,
this was the end of the story; he ended his chronicle with the succession assured
to Baldwin V, and the kingdom safe in the hands of the regent Raymond of Tripoli,
making a neat rounding off, having suppressed the very real dissension that
remained in the kingdom, and creating the appearance of consensus – a strategy
which underlies much his work.[27] This forms a marked contrast with the treatment
of the *abrégé*, which described Sibylla choosing a husband for herself.

The *abrégé*, having been extremely brief up to this point, now becomes much
fuller, giving more details about Sibylla's suitors than William himself. There are
two probable reasons for this. Firstly, as a partisan of the Ibelin family, the author
seems to have had access to family traditions beyond William's knowledge, and
secondly, he wanted to emphasise the role of Sibylla as an individual making her
own choice of partner – a role which he thought was quite inappropriate, and which
he and others blamed for the ultimate fall of the kingdom of Jerusalem in 1187.
This chronicle was written with hindsight about the eventual disposition of the
rump of the kingdom and the conflicts occasioned by Sibylla's succession.[28]
Sibylla is the only heiress in any of these accounts who seems to take any initiative
in the question of her own marriage. Accounts vary about the circumstances of her
eventual marriage to Guy of Lusignan, but Roger of Howden, who travelled to the
East with Richard I of England in 1191 and gathered much material for his
chronicle there, agrees with the *abrégé* that this was a match engineered by Sibylla
herself – a supposition supported by the way she later stuck to Guy in the teeth of
baronial opposition.[29]

Having devoted considerable space to the question of Sibylla's marriage,
accentuating her choice of partner as a crucial factor in political breakdown in

---

[27] *Ibid.*, xxii.20, xxiii.1.
[28] Mas Latrie, pp. 56–9.
[29] *Ibid.*, p. 60; *Gesta regis Henrici secundi Benedicti abbatis* [Roger of Howden], ed. W. Stubbs,
2 vols, RS 49 (London, 1867), i, 358–9; also in Roger of Howden, *Chronica magistri Rogeri
de Houedene*, ed. W. Stubbs, 4 vols, RS 51 (London, 1868–71), ii, 315–16.

1183, the *abrégé* presented Baldwin IV openly discussing the succession with the court. In this version, the baby Baldwin (V) was to be crowned because otherwise there might be dissension between the two sisters, Sibylla and Isabella. (Writing *c.* 1200, the author knew that there was indeed conflict between the sisters, or at least between their supporters. He was also able to acknowledge their claims to the succession, safe in the knowledge that the each reigned in turn.) This writer recognised that the sisters had claims to the succession, but saw the problems involved in choosing between them as critical to their exclusion from the throne. According to him, a regent was to be chosen for Baldwin V, 'qui le regne puist gouvrener, et qui nous croie de nos conseus'. Guy of Lusignan could not do the job because he was incapable of governing, so Raymond of Tripoli was chosen.[30]

The approach of this brief chronicle is particularly important here because, according to Morgan, it formed the introduction to the 'Chronicle of Ernoul', one distinct strand in the collection usually known as the *Continuations of William of Tyre*. Seen together, rather than as fragments, supplementary to William's work, this chronicle, which Morgan believes to have been one of the closest written sources to the events of 1184–97, deliberately constructed the politics of this period as a process by which the problem of the succession claims of the two sisters and the selection and role of the queen's husband was addressed by the political factions of the High Court.[31] It took as its central theme the relationship between dynasty and perceptions of fitness to govern.

According to 'Ernoul', the will of Baldwin IV, to which the nobles had assented, at first by-passed his sisters Sibylla and Isabella in favour of his infant nephew, and then, in the case of that nephew's death, offered the barons the chance to 'elect' Raymond of Tripoli. Raymond's connection to the dynasty as cousin of Baldwin III was very much emphasised in this account. Baldwin's will allegedly specified that if Raymond were not chosen, the rival merits of Sibylla and Isabella should be debated and the rulers of the West, Richard of England, Philip Augustus of France, and the Pope were to be invited to participate in the decision.[32]

Following on from suggestions in the *abrégé* about competition between the two sisters for the throne, 'Ernoul' interpreted the conflict which broke out between the factions which had formed around the two sisters, on the death of Baldwin V in 1185, to show how the failure of the dynasty to produce robust male heirs had encouraged the barons to attempt to establish control over the succession, through their claims to the right to consent to the queen's marriage. In enforcing these claims by a threatened withdrawal of service, they were establishing their say in the choice of a king – albeit a 'king-consort'. 'Ernoul' spoke for that party in the High Court which opposed Sibylla's marriage to Guy of Lusignan and engineered Isabella's divorce from Humphrey of Toron. He presented the queen as the means of transmitting the crown to her husband as king, and showed the

---

[30] Mas Latrie, p. 115.
[31] Morgan, *Chronicle of Ernoul*, p. 134 *et passim*, has tried to establish as closely as possible the original contents of this first version of the chronicle.
[32] Morgan, *Chronicle of Ernoul*, pp. 19–20.

high court struggling to establish control over the choice of marriage partner. In this way, the nobility could control access to the kingship and at the same time preserve its attachment to the dynasty and to hereditary principles.

In discussing these issues, 'Ernoul' described Guy as 'non profitable a maintenir le fait dou reaume', in other words, not fit to govern. This criterion was not applied to Sibylla, nor indeed to Isabella. The debate which 'Ernoul' described focused on the question of Sibylla's dubious legitimacy (her mother's marriage had been annulled), contrasted with her status as the elder sister, while Isabella had a possibly superior claim based on the concept of porphyrogeniture. The sisters' ability to govern was not brought into question.[33] The appeal of primogeniture was in the event strong enough to secure coronation for Sibylla, but she refused the demands to divorce Guy in favour of a more popular husband, and paid a heavy price for her loyalty. As king of Jerusalem, Guy had virtually no support from the barons, was mis-advised by them, possibly deliberately, and lost his kingdom at the battle of Hattin in 1187.[34] This demonstration of the force of opposition to a king imposed on the barons by the determined choice of Sibylla, is the symbolic centre of 'Ernoul's' account; for him, the internal strife and external dangers of the kingdom would only be dealt with when political dialogue between the factions in the High Court produced a suitable candidate who could be co-opted into the dynasty through marriage to the queen and who was 'profitable a gouverner'. He wrote his history as a process whereby the queen was gradually excluded from all political choices and became merely the figure-head for the dynasty, someone to whom the barons could attach their choice of king. This theme was continued in his treatment of the succession of Isabella, after Sybilla's death in 1191. According to 'Ernoul', the barons were justified in forcing Isabella to divorce her first husband, Humphrey of Toron, by threatening civil war, and her second husband (Conrad of Montferrat) was not a suitable king either, being too eager to seize the princess and the throne and indulging in bribery and corruption – but principally in not having been chosen by the barons.[35] Conrad's early death meant yet another search for a suitable man for attachment to the dynasty, who was fit to govern. An attempt was made to persuade Henry of Champagne to marry Isabella: the fact that he was reluctant and not covetous like Conrad were points in his favour. But

---

[33] *Ibid.* For the use of arguments from Porphyrogeniture, see Mayer, 'Succession of Baldwin II', pp. 139–47, with references to *Regni Ierosolimitani Brevis Historia*, ed. L. T. Belgrano, *Annali Genovesi de Caffaro ed de suoi continuatori*, i, Fonti di Storia Italiana (Rome, 1890), 136ff. Cf. J. Riley Smith, *The Feudal Nobility and the Kingdom of Jerusalem* (London, 1973), p. 104. For Henry I of England's claims against his brother Robert, see C. N. L. Brooke, *The Saxon and Norman Kings* (London, 1963), pp. 32, 143, 195–6. For Agnes's divorce from Amalric, see H. E. Mayer, 'The Beginnings of King Amalric of Jerusalem', in *The Horns of Hattin*, pp. 121–35.

[34] Morgan, *Chronicle of Ernoul*, p. 33; cf. R. Smail, 'Predicaments of Guy of Lusignan', pp. 159–76; B. Hamilton, 'Elephant of Christ', *SCH*, xv (London, 1978), 97–108; P. Edbury, 'Propaganda and Faction in the Kingdom of Jerusalem: The Background to Hattin', in *Crusaders and Muslims in Twelfth-Century Syria*, ed. M. Shatzmiller (Leiden, 1993), pp. 173–9.

[35] Morgan, *Chronicle of Ernoul*, pp. 105–7, 141.

in 'Ernoul's' account, Henry was made to express some of the problems associated with the position of male 'consort' to a queen. Says Henry, 'The lady is pregnant by the marquis [Conrad] and if she has a male heir, he will have the kingdom and I shall be encumbered with the lady.'[36]

Henry was not prepared to take on the protection of the kingdom and abandon his lands in Champagne for the sake of another man's son, who might oust him from power when he came of age, and who would stand in the way of the claims of his own children, while Isabella herself would prevent him looking for another profitable marriage. What is especially significant about Henry's objections is his assumption that Isabella's position would not be that of *queen-regnant*, but that he would share with her a quasi-regency, which would end when the child reached adulthood. Henry's objections were overcome by an extraordinary proposal from the barons and burgesses. 'They swore to Count Henry that they would make *his* heirs lords and kings of the kingdom, and that those who swore to him were in no way bound to the marquis [Conrad] and his heirs.'[37] In other words, they were prepared to disinherit Isabella's first child, posthumously born to Conrad, in order to get the candidate they wanted as king. Once again, 'Ernoul' was expressing a right to choose a king assumed by the barons, as they seized the opportunity created by the succession of a queen to police her choice of husband and king. The tension between the discourses of gender and of dynastic politics led them to claim the right to alter the ordinary path of succession, disinheriting a putative elder son in favour of any future half-brothers, in order to secure their own candidate as king.

The English account of the third crusade, the *Itinerarium peregrinorum et gesta regis Ricardi*, presented the circumstances quite differently. According to this source, having once been acknowledged as king, Sibylla's widower, Guy of Lusignan, retained his right to the kingdom, and King Richard backed this claim until it was clear that he lacked baronial support; but when Conrad, whose corruption the *Itinerarium* author emphasised, seized Princess Isabella, the barons asked Richard to decide between Guy and Conrad. The questions raised by 'Ernoul' about the precedence of the two sisters and the role of each in bringing a husband-governor to the throne as king were almost forgotten. The *Itinerarium* presented the dispute essentially as a conflict between the capable but wronged Guy and the wickedly ambitious Conrad, who had stolen Guy's crown and Humphrey's wife (Isabella), and was repeatedly cursed by the people for his failure to help them against Saladin at the siege of Acre in 1191.[38] For the writer of the *Itinerarium*, Conrad's sudden death demonstrated that he was rejected by God,

---

[36] *Ibid.*, p. 142, 'La dame estoit groce dou marquis [Conrad], et si ele avoit hoir mahle, il avroit le roiaume, et je seroit encombre de la dame.'

[37] *Ibid.*, p. 143, 'jurerent au conte Henri qu'il feroient de ses hoirs segnors et rois dou reiaume, et que c'il qui li jurerent n'estoient de riens tenu au marquis ne a ses hoirs'.

[38] *Itinerarium peregrinorum et gesta Regis Ricard*, in *Chronicles and Memorials of the Reign of Richard I*, ed. W. Stubbs, RS 38/i (London, 1864–65), 95, 97, 119, 334, 338.

and a third suitor, Henry of Champagne, appeared rather like a *deus ex machina* to pick up the pieces and the princess.[39] Henry was elected by popular acclaim:

> They chose him as prince and lord, as though he had been sent by God, and, approaching him, they began to urge most diligently that he accept the crown of the kingdom, without any contradiction or excuse, and that he should marry the Marquis's widow, to whom the kingdom was due by hereditary right.[40]

It is significant that in this account Henry of Champagne was chosen as ruler and only then urged to marry Conrad's widow; moreover, King Richard suggested that Henry could have the kingdom without marrying Isabella – indeed, he should not marry her, since she had committed adultery with Conrad:

> Concerning marriage with the Marquis's widow, I do not advise it, since the Marquis unlawfully abducted her in her husband's lifetime, and by polluting her committed adultery: indeed, the count should receive the kingdom . . .[41]

The leading citizens, on the other hand, urged that the marriage should take place, because Isabella's status as heiress would give Henry's rule more stability.

> Therefore the leading citizens persuaded the count to marry the heir to the kingdom. The count refused, lest he incur the displeasure of King Richard. The Franks and magnates of the realm urged that it should be done, arguing that things would be more firmly established by the marriage – so by their arrangement the marquise willingly came to the count and offered him the keys of the city.[42]

Henry's sudden death produced another crisis. The barons' discussions about a successor were set out in detail by 'Ernoul'. Resources of men and money were perceived to be the most important deciding factors in the choice of candidate. Isabella was therefore married to Aimery of Lusignan, now king of Cyprus, so that the resources of the island might be combined with what remained of the kingdom of Jerusalem, and she was finally crowned queen.[43] Despite having been acknowledged as 'plus dreit hoir' on her sister's death in 1192, and despite two previous marriages arranged with the intention of finding a worthy king, her position and

[39] *Ibid.*, p. 339.

[40] *Ibid.*, p. 342, 'tamquam a deo missum, elegerunt in principem et dominum, et ad ipsum accedentes cum omni diligentia supplicare coeperunt, ut patienter sui omni contradictione et excusatione *susciperet regni coronam, et viduam Marchisi duceret uxorem, cui regnum jure debebatur haereditario*'.

[41] *Ibid.*, p. 347, 'Super ducenda vero Marchisi relicta in conjugem non consulo; quoniam, vivente viro sua, Marchisus ipsam iniuste rapuit, et polluendo adulteriam commisit; regnum vero comes suscipiat.'

[42] *Ibid.*, pp. 347–8, 'Comitem itaque valentes persuadet heredem regni ducere uxorem, Comes renuit, ne incurrat offensam regis Ricardi, franci vero et regni magnates, alleganter rem fortius conjugio stabiliendam, urgent ita fieri, quibus ita procurantibus Marchisia ponte sua accedens ad comitem, obtuir ei claves civitatis.'

[43] Morgan, *Chronicle of Ernoul*, p. 199.

that of her husbands had not so far been formalised by coronation – and 'Ernoul' had been careful never to call her queen before this point. Even for 'Ernoul', the position of a queen did not depend solely on her status as heiress, but was indissolubly connected to her marriage to an *appropriate* king.

By insisting on the role of the political factions in choosing a husband for Isabella, and by openly making their support for the queen contingent on her acceptance of their choice, 'Ernoul' consolidated the barons' role as electors of the king through their choice of the queen's spouse. 'Ernoul' also attributed to them the right to determine the path of succession (as in the coronation of Baldwin V, the suggested election of Raymond of Tripoli, and the oath to Henry of Champagne).

The possibilities opened up by the repeated choice of consort for the queen also gave 'Ernoul' the opportunity to discuss the qualities necessary for a successful ruler. The questions of who was 'profitable a gouverner', who had the necessary resources and support of the barons, how that support was to be determined, and how much of it could be bought, could all be dealt with in isolation from the question of who was the 'plus droit heir'. Such open discussion of the issue of capability or fitness to govern had not been available to William of Tyre, writing during the reign of Baldwin IV, whose leprosy made it impossible for him to take an active role throughout much of his reign. Any discussion then of 'fitness' would have threatened the position of the legitimate king. 'Ernoul' never discussed the question of the women's basic fitness to rule, either, but he assumed that they transmitted the dynastic blood and no more; these women had no active role in the text. Thus in 'Ernoul's' chronicle, these two issues have become, as it were, 'gendered', in that fitness to govern was a practical attribute discussed only in relation to the king co-opted into the dynasty as husband of the queen, whereas she herself was judged according to genetic, dynastic criteria. At the same time, but in apparent contradiction, Isabella's connection to the throne was somewhat weakened, since despite acceptance as 'plus droit heir', she was not fully queen, not crowned, until united with someone who was 'fit to govern'.

By contrast, the writer of the *Itinerarium* suggested that the dynasty, in the shape of the polluted Isabella, could be abandoned altogether, and did comment on her abilities and those of women in general. Isabella, says this author, was easily persuaded, in a way typical of weak-willed women, to abandon one husband and embrace another:

> A woman easily changes her mind, "for woman is always fickle and change-able"; she is an inconstant sex with an excitable mind, and since she rejoices in new embraces, she lightly rejects the known ones and quickly casts them into oblivion. Indeed, the girl, easily schooled in wickedness, willingly takes up the foul doctrine of her advisers, and now does not blush to say that she was not abducted, but willingly followed the marquis.[44]

---

[44] *Itinerarium*, p. 121 (quoting Virgil, *Aeneid*, iv. 569), 'Facillime mulier mutat consilium, "nam varium et mutabilem semper foeminam", cui et sexus lubricus et mens mobilis et sicut novis gaudet amplexibus, sic notos leviter respuit, citius oblivioni contradit. Puella

Although not directly related to the question of female rulership, the pejorative tone of the whole passage reflects the writer's bad opinion of Isabella, and, by extension, a scorn for all women in political roles.

The principle of the election of a 'king-consort' and marginalisation of the hereditary queen was carried further in the *Livre au Roi* – a treatise on the succession to the crown and the relative obligations of king, queen and barons, sponsored by Aimery of Lusignan and Queen Isabella, in an attempt to settle the future succession in a legal way. The *Livre* specifically contemplates the future accession of queens regnant, and confirms their rights to inherit the throne. Although it assumes that almost all the normal duties of government will be carried out by the queen's husband as king, nonetheless he can act only with her formal consent, and under the strict scrutiny of the High Court; moreover, successive husbands will be chosen with the 'advice' of the High Court. 'Ernoul's' history had shown how that 'conseil' could be enforced by the barons' withdrawal of support.[45] The *Livre* also proposes a solution to the dilemma faced by Henry of Champagne. It states that the second husband of a reigning queen will not lose his position when she dies, but will have the right to be appointed regent for any under-age child who succeeds to the throne, whether his or his predecessor's. But the rights of children of the first marriage are protected from the kind of exclusion proposed to Henry by the barons, when they urged him to marry Isabella.

Three slightly different narratives carry the story of the monarchy to 1228: two versions of the *Estoire d'Eracles* – continuations of William of Tyre published by Beugnot in the nineteenth century (*A-Eracles* and *D-Eracles*) and the compilation known as the 'Chronicle of Bernard the Treasurer', containing a variant of the continuations and a version of the *abrégé*.[46] *A-Eracles* simply reports the death of Aimery in 1205, followed by the appointment at Queen Isabella's request of John of Ibelin as regent. *D-Eracles* records the deaths of Aimery, Isabella and Amaurion their infant son in one sentence, and then records the appointment of a regent for Maria of Montferrat, because she was not yet married – not because she was under age. (This was contrary to the principles expressed in the *Livre au Roi*, which declared that underage heirs required regents. Born in 1192/3, Maria would have been 12/13 years old in 1205.) As soon as she was old enough, a husband would be sought who could guard and maintain the land. This makes clear enough the absolute acceptance that the queen, whether Isabella or Maria of Montferrat, would

---

quidem in pravum docilis turpem monentium doctrinam libentius excipit et jam se non raptam, sed Marchisum secutam dicere non erubescit.'

[45] *Livre au Roi*, c. 4 (i, 609), 'S'il avient que li rois soit mors et est remese la royne de par cuy li reaumes meut, et puis avient que la dame priest autre mary aucun haut home, si come li afiert *par la conseil de ces homes liges* . . . nul don que celui roi done, ne doit estre tenu apres sa mort, see la royne sa moillyer ne l'otreis, par la guarantie de ces homes liges.' See also M. Greilsammer, 'Structure and Aims of the Livre au Roi', in *Outremere*, pp. 218–26.

[46] *A-* and *D-Eracles* variants are published in *Recueil des historiens des croisades. Historiens occidentaux*, ii; for *Bernard le Trésorier*, see n. 20. For a full discussion of the relationships between these texts, see Morgan, *Chronicle of Ernoul, passim.*

not be allowed to govern – and the barons' role in king-making was firmly entrenched in the text.

More uncompromising still is 'Bernard the Treasurer', which recorded simply that when Aimery died, the kingdom passed to the daughter of Conrad – and since she was unmarried the barons had to elect a regent. Although her succession was not questioned, 'Bernard' completely severed her connection with the dynasty – she was not called Isabella's daughter, but Conrad's.[47] Moreover, just as Isabella was not crowned and named as queen until 'properly' married (whether in the *A-Eracles* account, to Henry, or in the 'Ernoul' version, to Aimery of Lusignan), so in 'Bernard', Maria of Montferrat was not queen until married to the suitable candidate (John of Brienne), and seemingly not even crowned, since he 'porta Corone' alone.[48] From this point onwards, 'Bernard' is principally an account of the career of John of Brienne, and as such emphasises his importance. It says that he was unanimously selected by the barons of the High Court to marry Maria, that an embassy was sent to France to ask his consent, that he was promised the rulership of the kingdom before coming East, and that he was received at Acre with great celebrations. The couple were then married, and they proceeded to Tyre where John, alone, was crowned king. Thereafter 'Bernard's' text forgot about Maria completely. In both 'Bernard' and the *D-Eracles*, the queen regnant no longer even participated in the coronation – she was completely marginalised by the prominence of the king, so long as he had the political support of the barons.[49] The *A-Eracles*, on the other hand, reported that the barons sent an embassy to ask Philip Augustus to suggest a suitable husband, and that he nominated John of Brienne. This source also restored Maria to her place in the coronation, reporting that she and her husband were crowned together.[50]

'Ernoul' had organised the story of the succession and successive marriages of Isabella to represent the barons gradually finding a solution to the problem of choosing a king by marginalising the queen. This system culminated in the election of Aimery of Lusignan – who had money and men as well as the ability to govern and defend the kingdom – and who moreover was well known to the barons. The *A-Eracles*, by contrast, shows that system breaking down. The selection of a king had been handed over to Philip Augustus, and the barons had relinquished their control over the process. In this text, the barons were dismayed, when John of Brienne arrived, at the discovery that he was not rich, not even a count, merely regent for his nephew![51]

The death of Maria of Montferrat only two years later brought another female succession to be handled, since she too left only a daughter, Isabella/Yolande. *A-Eracles* noted the technical change of ruler, and said that John of Brienne

---

[47] Mas Latrie, p. 407.
[48] *Ibid.*, p. 409.
[49] *Ibid.*, pp. 409–55.
[50] *A-Eracles*, ed. Beugnot, pp. 307, 311; Mayer, 'Succession to Baldwin II', says that this is not likely because in 1209, Innocent III wrote to Philip Augustus urging him to let John go: *PL*, ccxvi, cols 36f no. 37.
[51] *A-Eracles*, ed. Beugnot, p. 308.

remained as regent for his daughter, who was under age (complying with the terms of the *Livre au Roi*). On the other hand, 'Bernard' continued to marginalise the queen by ignoring this; he simply reported Maria's death, and explained that since the king did not wish to remain without a wife, he married Stephanie of Armenia.[52]

The differing emphases of these texts continued when Isabella/Yolande came of age. According to *A-Eracles*, like her mother, she was not crowned until a suitable marriage was arranged, whereas in 'Bernard', Isabella was not crowned queen in Tyre at all, but was only crowned empress when she went to Apulia to marry Frederick II.[53] The marriage between Isabella/Yolande and the Emperor Frederick II, apparently arranged by Herman of Salza, Master of the Teutonic knights, marked the complete exclusion of the barons from the control of succession. Their system of electing a king had broken down. Isabella/Yolande died within a couple of years of her marriage, leaving a son, Conrad, and giving the Emperor Frederick a perfectly reasonable claim (according to the terms of the *Livre au Roi*) to rule as regent for this son. But instead of welcoming a male heir at last, unlike the joy at news of a son which led Louis VII to reward his messenger, cited above, the barons greeted the news of the birth of Conrad with consternation. No longer would they be able, as with an heiress to the throne, legitimately to choose a ruler by exercising control over the queen's marriage. Because of the 'success' of this marriage in finally producing a male heir, the barons effectively 'rejected the rule of their hereditary dynasty' and scrambled for a semblance of legality in so doing.[54] In the future, factions would strive for control of government through manipulation of the process of electing a regent and circumventing the attempts of the heir to acquire the throne.

The succession of four reigning queens had not confirmed women's role in the political culture of the Latin East, nor had it established an idea of queenship which could transcend the limits of gender, even though William of Tyre had hinted that such a transcendence had been possible in the case of Queen Melisende. The narrative accounts reveal a progressive diminution of the idea of queenship, from Melisende's transcendence of the role expected of her, as constructed by William of Tyre, through the by-passing of Sibylla in favour of her son, to the acceptance of Isabella as queen, and the repeated manipulation of the kingship through control of the choice of her husband. Finally, Maria of Montferrat's apparently silent inactivity marks a complete nadir in the portrayal of queenship by the continuators of William of Tyre.

Within this framework, however, there is also evident a lack of any real consensus about the way in which a reigning queen should be treated in political history and an inability fully to resolve the tensions between dynasty, gender, and the demands of politics. What remains evident is the flexible way in which people

[52] *Ibid.*, p. 320; *Bernard le Trésorier*, ed. Mas Latrie, p. 411.
[53] *Bernard le Trésorier*, ed. Mas Latrie, p. 451.
[54] P. Edbury, *The Kingdom of Cyprus and the Crusades, 1191–1374* (Cambridge, 1991); *idem*, 'John of Ibelin's Title to the County of Jaffa and Ascalon', *EHR*, xcviii (1983), 118.

might respond to a such tensions. In the kingdom of Jerusalem hereditary queenship was accepted out of political necessity, but also embraced as an opportunity for political manipulation. Queens were marginalised to a greater or lesser degree by contemporary historians, who demonstrated differing approaches to the problem of female rulership. They were also manipulated by members of the High Court, who pursued their own political agendas through the royal family. The existence of hereditary queenship was enshrined in the *Livre au roi* because the compilation was sponsored by King Aimery of Jerusalem and Cyprus, whose position in Jerusalem depended on his marriage to Isabella. Subsequent generations found it impossible to exclude women from the throne, as had once been threatened to Queen Sibylla. Instead, they excluded women more and more from political activity, through control of their marriages.

III

Images of Queenship

10

Maria *Regina*: Papal Symbol

Mary Stroll

Introduction

The guises of Maria *Virgo* are manifold.[1] She appears as the pious mother of Christ, as his bride, as an intercessory with God in heaven, as a symbol of the church, and as a queen. As Maria *Regina* she is portrayed alone, enthroned holding the Christ-child, or sharing a throne with the mature Christ. She is praised, venerated, and respected, but she is also manipulated to fulfil the goals of others. Popes used her to emancipate themselves from secular rulers or to identify themselves with Christ. Democratic leaders such as Cola di Rienzo (1313–54) championed her as an advocate of the people. The humble Mary of Nazareth, who bore her son in a stable, became an unlikely, but powerful instrument to convey the messages of popes. As Maria *Regina* she became the 'Madonna of the Popes' and a model for secular queens. The image had come full circle, for secular queens had also served as prototypes for Maria as *Regina*. By the middle of the thirteenth century Blanche of Castile, the mother of Louis IX, was portrayed in the likeness of Mary as the *sponsa* of Christ.

Four examples exemplify how popes used the Maria *Regina* image to transmit their messages. The Greek pope, John VII (705–07) used the image to emancipate the pope from Byzantine rule. Both Anaclet II and Innocent II found her to be an ideal medium for revealing their disparate conceptions of the papacy during the papal schism of 1130–38. Innocent III (1198–1216) skilfully used her to demonstrate that the papacy not only had won the struggle to free itself from secular authority, but also to authenticate its claim to be the highest authority in both *regnum* and *sacerdotium*. It requires no leap of imagination to see how such an image would be appropriate for a secular queen.[2]

Images of Mary other than the Maria *Regina*

Although dominant with the popes, the image of Mary as queen did not supersede all others. For example, the icon of the maternal Madonna of S. Sisto exemplifies

1 E. M. Jung-Inglessis, *Römische Madonnen: über die Entwicklung der Marienbilder in Rom von den Anfängen bis in die Gegenwart* (St Ottilien, 1989).
2 For a recent book on medieval queenship see *Medieval Queenship*, ed. Parsons.

the Virgin as advocate.[3] Of Byzantine origin, and probably painted earlier than the eighth century, the icon was brought to Rome and housed in the Benedictine cloister of S. Maria in Tempulo. According to legend, after Christ's ascension into heaven, the apostles decided that Mary's likeness should be painted because she was a woman of great beauty, and had borne the son of God. Portrayed by St Luke with the intervention of the Holy Spirit, she appears against a gold background with her hands in the advocate position.[4] Anyone could plead to her directly to intercede with her son in heaven. A copy of the icon was placed in the basilica of S. Maria in Aracoeli on the Capitoline where it gained phenomenal fame, especially when Cola di Rienzo singled it out in 1347 for special veneration as the advocate and true sovereign of the Roman people (pl. 11).[5]

Another icon especially beloved by the people was the Salus Populi Romani, housed in Santa Maria Maggiore, the first, and foremost Roman church dedicated to the Virgin. Probably created in the fifth century, Mary in this maternal pose was likened to the goddesses of the Roman Empire, who had the power to safeguard the wellbeing of the Roman people.[6]

After the declaration of St Ambrose that 'Maria est typus ecclesiae', Mary was so frequently portrayed as *Mater Ecclesia*, that the distinction between 'Mater' and 'Mary' became evanescent.[7] The images of *Mater Ecclesia* in the Exultet rolls, announcing Easter in joyous song, are often identified with Mary, and reveal the qualities attributed to her. One of the most famous is an illumination on a roll from the late eleventh century originating in southern Italy (pl. 13).[8] *Mater Ecclesia* is dressed in Byzantine ceremonial garb, wears pendant pearl earrings, and a crown with one point. Each hand is pressed against the wall of the arch in what seems to be the orant (praying) position, as though she is holding up the church through her intercession and prayer. The text states that in the lighting of the Easter candles *Mater Ecclesia* is adorned by the splendour of brilliant light. The resurrection of Christ signifying his victory over death is also a victory for the church, for Christ and *Ecclesia* are *Sponsus* and *Sponsa*.[9] The marriage metaphor is also a nexus

3　G. Wolf, *Salus Populi Romani: Die Geschichte römischer Kultbilder im Mittelalter* (Weinheim, 1990), pp. 161–70; Jung-Inglessis, *Römische Madonnen*, pp. 151–3.

4　*Ibid.*, pp. 162–3.

5　H. Belting, *Bild und Kult: Eine Geschichte des Bildes vor dem Zeitalter der Kunst* (Munich, 1990), p. 361; trans. E. Jephcott, *Likeness and Presence: A History of the Image before the Era of Art* (Chicago, 1994).

6　Wolf, *Salus Populi Romani*, pp. 3–9.

7　Ambrosius, *Expos. Ev. sec. Luc.*, ii.7 (*PL*, xv, 1555); Jung-Inglessis, *Römische Madonnen*, pp. 184–8; H. Toubert, 'Les Représentations de l'*Ecclesia* dans l'art des Xe–XIIe siècles', *Atti XIII Convegno di Studi 'Musica e Arte figurativa nei secoli X–XII'*, Todi, 15–18 ottobre 1972 (Todi, 1973), pp. 69–71; repr. *Un Art dirigé: Réforme grégorienne et iconographie* (Paris, 1990), pp. 37–63.

8　Vat. Barb. Lat. 592; Wolf, *Salus Populi Romani*, abb. 59, pp. 107–14. The text states that Christ's victory over death commemorated by Easter is also a victory for the church. *Christus* and *Ecclesia* are *Sponsus* and *Sponsa*, a metaphor arising from an exegesis of the Canticus Canticorum (*ibid.*, p. 111).

9　*Ibid.*, p. 111.

where *Ecclesia* and Mary intersect. Commentators sometimes refer to the bride in the Canticle of Canticles as *Ecclesia*, and sometimes as Mary.[10]

Reflecting the identification of Mary with the church, Honorius Augustodunensis, one of the most influential twelfth-century theologians, states, 'And all things that are said of the church can also be understood of this same Virgin, bride and mother.'[11] In sum, Mary became a symbol of the church as well as the advocate of the people.

Early representations of Maria *Regina*

The first premises of the transfer of imperial imagery to Mary seem to have originated in the early fifth century in a city outside Rome, possibly Ravenna or Aquileia.[12] In a small box (*pyxis*) found at Grado before 451 Mary appears enthroned like the pagan gods or emperors. Wearing a monogrammed nimbus, she holds the Christ-child and the astile cross – the sceptre as cruciform. The popularity of Mary as an individual object of devotion began in the same century. Apocryphal versions of her life, interests in her relics, and the first churches dedicated in her name sprang from this devotion. For the first time in Rome Mary appears as royalty in the annunciation and presentation at the temple scenes in the mosaics of the triumphal arch of Santa Maria Maggiore. She wears the clothes of a princess of the court of Constantinople with a diadem and pendant pearl earrings. In the annunciation scene she sits on a platform, and weaves with purple yarn, both signs of royalty (pl. 12).[13]

In the sixth century Mary is unequivocally portrayed as a queen in the basilica of Santa Maria Antiqua.[14] Transfigured into a celestial sovereign, but dressed in the garments of a Byzantine empress, she sits on a jewelled throne holding the

10 H. Coathalem, SJ, 'Le Parallélisme entre le Saint Vierge e l'Eglise dans la tradition latine jusqu'à la fin du XIIe siècle', *Studi Gregoriani*, lxxiv (1954); J. Huhn, *Das Geheimnis der Jungfrau-Mutter Maria nach dem Kirchenvater Ambrosius* (Würzburg, 1954); A. Müller, *Ecclesia–Maria. Die Einheit Marias und der Kirche* (Freiburg, 1954); F. Ohly, *Hohelied-Studien. Grundzüge einer Geschichte der Hoheliedauslegung des Abendlandes bis um 1200* (Wiesbaden, 1958); H. Riedlinger, *Die Makellosigkeit der Kirche in den lateinischen Hoheliedkommentaren des Mittelalters* (Münster, 1958); *idem*, 'Maria und die Kirche in den marianischen Hoheliedkommentaren des Mittelalters', in *Maria et Ecclesia. Acta congressus mariologici-mariani in civitate Lourdes anno 1958 celebrati*, iii, *De parallelismo inter Mariam et Ecclesiam* (Rome, 1959), pp. 241–89; Rupert of Deutz and Honorius Augustodunensis are among the commentators who sometimes refer to the bride in the Canticle as *Ecclesia*, and sometimes as Mary.
11 *Expositio in canticum canticorum*, *PL*, clxxii, 347–496 at col. 494c: 'Et omnia, quae de Ecclesia dicta sunt, possunt etiam de ipsa Virgine, sponsa et mater sponsi intellegi.' *Ibid.*, *Sigillum B. Mariae*, col. 499: 'Ideo cuncta quae de Ecclesia scribuntur, de ipsa [Maria] satis congrue leguntur.'
12 C. Bertelli, *La Madonna di Santa Maria in Trastevere* (Rome, 1961), p. 50.
13 These are the trappings of the *feminae clarissimae*, and do not clearly identify her as a queen. Wolf, *Salus populi Romani*, pp. 119–20; Jung-Inglessis, *Römische Madonnen*, pp. 34–6; C. Cecchelli, *I Mosaici della Basilica di S. Maria Maggiore* (Turin, 1956).
14 J. Hubert, J. Porcher, W. F. Volbach, *Europe in the Dark Ages* (London, 1969), p. 107.

Christ-child. From the right an angel presents a golden crown, and a corresponding figure stands on her left. The location of the fresco is key to its interpretation, for the basilica was attached to the imperial palace, where the officials of the Byzantine empire held court until the seventh century. The setting of the fresco is similar to the arches of Santa Sophia in Constantinople, and the decorative scheme similar to the basilica of the Arian king, Theodoric, in Ravenna.[15] Thus, the inspiration was Byzantine, and there is an unmistakable similarity between the prototype of Maria *Regina* and the portrait of the empress Theodora (Justinian's wife) in the mosaics in Ravenna (pl. 14).[16] In Santa Maria Antiqua the religious encountered the imperial, and their ideological similarities and differences were portrayed on its walls.[17]

While in the sixth century the Byzantine court in Constantinople had promoted the cult of the Virgin, in the seventh her popularity in Rome intensified. Under the Greek pope, Sergius I (687–701) the whole Marian liturgical cycle, Byzantine in origin, was integrated into the Roman calendar. The liturgy for the assumption of Mary into heaven, where she was exalted, especially affected the sphere of art.[18] In 609 the Pantheon became S. Maria ad Martyres, and the 'titulus Julii et Callisti' became S. Maria in Trastevere. The Madonna was frequently depicted seated on a throne holding Christ, who held a codex or scroll in his left hand, while blessing with his right.[19]

At the beginning of the eighth century another Greek pope, John VII (705–07), added a further thrust to the veneration of Maria as *Regina*. The mosaic in the oratory in St Peter's, and in all probability the encaustic icon of the Madonna della Clemenza in S. Maria in Trastevere, were created under his inspiration.[20] The Madonna della Clemenza is enthroned holding the Christ-child (pl. 15).[21] She wears Byzantine imperial apparel, and a crown similar to ones worn by Theodora and more contemporary empresses such as Irene. In her right hand she holds the astile cross. Angels flank both sides, and at her feet kneels a pope, no longer visible, but in all probability, John VII.

The oratory in St Peter's was destroyed in the seventeenth century, but the mosaic depicting Maria in the orant position has survived. Giacomo Grimaldi has

---

15 Bertelli, *La Madonna*, pp. 52–4.
16 J. Osborne, 'Early Medieval Painting in San Clemente, Rome: the Madonna and Child in the Niche', *Gesta*, xx (1981), 299–310 at p. 303. Osborne points out that some scholars see Byzantine elements in the portrayal of Mary's head in the Madonna in the Niche, and they conjecture that originally the work portrayed Theodora. Osborne demonstrates that the hypothesis is incorrect, but notes that it is interesting that the Madonna so closely resembled Theodora in the mosaics in Ravenna that the theory could be compelling.
17 Wolf, *Salus populi Romani*, pp. 120–1.
18 Bertelli, *La Madonna*, p. 58.
19 Osborne, 'The Madonna in the Niche', p. 303.
20 Wolf, *Salus Populi Romani*, p. 121 and n. 153, notes that some scholars date the Madonna della Clemenza to the sixth century. Dale Kinney dates it to the reign of Gregory IV in the ninth: 'S. Maria in Trastevere from its Founding to 1215' (Phil. Diss., New York University, 1975, Ann Arbor, 1982), pp. 60–70, 148–59.
21 Bertelli, *La Madonna*, remains the primary authority for the Madonna della Clemenza.

preserved a semblance of the whole mosaic in watercolor, including John VII as the donor (pl. 16).[22] John is portrayed as a small figure standing on Maria's right wearing the square nimbus of a living pope. Crowned and wearing the garments of a Byzantine princess, she is cast as a formidable figure standing on a platform holding centre stage.[23] No Christ-child accentuates her maternity, but an inscription on the periphery refers to her as the genetrix of God. In his inscription John declares himself to be her servant.[24]

What was his message? Since Byzantine emperors sometimes expressed their dominion through cult or the propagation of icons, it was a political act when the image of the Byzantine emperor was destroyed in Rome about 710, and replaced by the image of Christ the King. Conversely in Byzantium the image of Christ was destroyed in favour of the image of the emperor.[25] John, described as 'very learned,' was quick to adopt the technique of replacing imperial figures with religious figures cloaked in imperial trappings. By declaring himself to be the servant of the mother of God, he subtly asserted that the imperial figure to whom he owed obedience was not the Byzantine emperor, but the heavenly queen.[26] But why did John choose Maria *Regina* rather than, say, Christ himself? Possible reasons were the current Byzantine cult of the Virgin, and the reinterpretation of the Virgin as a symbol of the church.[27] He may deliberately have chosen the word 'genetrix' to emphasise Mary as the dominant creator, rather than as the maternal nurturer, not of Christ, but of God. Rather than the earthly mother of the human form of God, she is portrayed as a semi-deity.

Maria *Regina* in the twelfth century

Mary is entitled 'Maria *Regina*' for the first time in a fresco painted in Santa Maria Antiqua between 772 and 775. Dressed in royal attire, she is enthroned with the Christ-child.[28] During Carolingian times this model receded in importance as the papacy sought Frankish rather than Byzantine symbolism to convey its messages. With the resurgent papacy in the twelfth century there was need for a new symbol to encapsulate its ambitions. The Maria *Regina* image was resuscitated, and her royalty emphasised. Such epithets as *imperatrix et regina, regina mundi, regina*

---

22 Vat. lat. 6439, fols 260–1; the mosaic is in the church of S. Marco in Florence.
23 H. Belting, 'Papal Artistic Commissions as Definitions of the Medieval Church in Rome', in *Light on the Eternal City: Observations and Discoveries in the Art and Architecture of Rome*, edd. H. Hager and S. Scott Munshower, ii (Penn. State University, 1987), pp. 13–29 at p. 9. Belting emphasises that she wears the insignia of temporal power, which she never did in Byzantium.
24 *Beatae Dei Genitricis servus*; later popes will entitle themselves *Servus servorum Dei*.
25 Belting, 'Papal Artistic Commissions', p. 9.
26 *Ibid.*, p. 15. Belting asserts that the title, 'Servant of the Mother of God' implies that he was not a servant of anyone on earth; cf. Wolf, *Salus Populi Romani*, p. 74.
27 *Ibid.*
28 Bertelli, *La Madonna*, p. 59.

coeli et terrae imply that she was universally considered as the sovereign and queen of the entire world.[29]

Monks and theologians propagated her attributes as queen. In his sermon on the Assumption of the Blessed Mary, Bernard of Clairvaux speaks of Mary in her advocate role as queen of heaven, but also as queen of the world.[30] He asserted that having given Jesus his crown of flesh, Mary deserved the crown of glory and immortality.[31] Ernaldus, Bernard's biographer, described her as dressed in golden robes, reigning at Christ's right in heaven.[32] Odo of Morimond argued that since Jesus was a king from birth, Mary had to be a queen. The idea of a 'regni consortium' evolved in which Mary, the queen of the world, sits at the right side of her son, and reigns with him in heaven.[33] As such, she was thus the perfect vehicle for conveying the claims of universality of the *Ecclesia Romana*.[34]

Potentia is part of her glory and her elevation to the right of the king, for like him, she also possessed ruling attributes.[35] Guerric, abbot of Igny, and a contemporary of Bernard, speaks of her ruling power. He says that Mary is queen, and likewise the mother and bride of the king. To her is given *regnum et potestas*, and her bridegroom, Christ the King, desires to have an indivisible *imperium* with her.[36] Ernaldus asserts that she cannot be separated from the dominium and power

---

29 H. Barré, 'La Royauté de Marie au XIIe siècle en Occident', in *Maria et Ecclesia*, v: *Mariae Potestas Regalis in Ecclesiam* (Rome, 1959), pp. 93–119 at p. 94. Other titles were: *Domina, dominatrix, domina nostra, totius mundi domina, regina, regina omnium*.

30 *Sancti Bernardi Opera*, edd. J. Leclercq and H. Rochais, 8 vols (Rome, 1956–77), v, 230, 'In Assumptione Beatae Mariae': 'Sed et illud quis cogitare sufficiat, quam gloriosa hodie mundi Regina processerit, et quanto devotionis affectu tota in eius occursum caelestium legionum prodierit multitudo, quibus ad thronum gloriae canticis sit deducta, quam placido vultu, quam serena facie, quam divinis amplexibus suscepta a Filio, et super omnem exaltata sit creaturam, dum eo honore, quo tanta mater digna fuit, cum ea gloria, quae tantum decuit Filium?' There were four feasts in honour of Mary – the Purification, the Annunciation, the Nativity, and the Assumption, which was the highest.

31 *Ibid.*, p. 266; *Sermo Dominica infra Octavam Assumptionis*: 'Denique et coronavit eum, et vicissim ab eo meruit coronari. "Egredimini, Filiae Sion, et videte regem Salomonem in Diademate, quo coronavit eum mater sua." [Cant. 3:11] Verum hoc in diademate, quo coronavit eam Filius suus . . .'

32 *PL*, clxxxix, 727, 'Virgo sancta devenerit, ut cum Christo communem in salute mundi effectum obtineat, et a dextris eius regnans in coelestibus, circum amicta varietatibus, in deaurato vestitu astitit, inventa est Virgo ab angelo in Nazareth solitaria . . .' The themes are from the Canticle of Canticles as well as Psalm 41; Ernaldus was abbot of Bonaevallis; Barré, 'La Royauté', p. 97.

33 Barré, 'La Royauté', p. 98.

34 *Ibid.*, p. 95; Barré speaks of her unquestioned universality.

35 *PL*, clxxxiv, 1063: 'Regina, gloriae nomen et honoris, magnificentiae, sublimitatis et potentiae, gubernationis et iustitiae, defensionis et gratiae'. The words are attributed to Bernard of Clairvaux by the author of the sermons on the 'Salve Regina'.

36 *PL*, clxxxv, 195: 'Perge, Maria, perge secura in bonis Filii tui, fiduci aliter age tanquam regina, mater Regis et sponsa. Requiem quaerebas, sed amplioris gloriae est quod tibi debetur: regnum et potestas. Indivisum habere tecum cupit imperium, cui tecum in carne una, et uno spiritu indivisum fuit pietatis et unitatis mysterium: dum scilicet, salvo honore naturae, geminato munere gratiae iuncta est mater in matrimonium. Requiesce igitur, o felix, inter bracchia Sponsi. Replicabit tibi ni fallor, inter amplexus et oscula, quam suaviter

of her son.[37] Eadmer chimes in that God himself gives her a royal power that she exercises from the height of the heavens.[38] This image of a magisterial Maria *Regina* created by twelfth-century mystics and theologians was ripe to be plucked by popes seeking a symbol to encapsulate their own objectives. Let us examine their artistry.

The apse fresco in the chapel of St Nicholas in the Lateran palace

Anaclet II commissioned the fresco during the schism of 1130–38 when he reigned in Rome, and Innocent II was in exile (pl. 17).[39] After his return to Rome, Innocent expunged any identification of the fresco with Anaclet. It has recently been dubbed 'the apotheosis of the victorious papacy', marking the victory of the popes over the emperors in the Investiture Contest. To those who coined the title it represented an outmoded conception of ecclesiastical reform, focusing on the emperor as the enemy rather than embracing St Bernard's emphasis on spirituality.

In the lower level of the fresco popes of the reform plus two of their exemplars, Leo I and Gregory I, flank St Nicholas standing in a niche. In the upper level Mary sits enthroned on a platform within a star-studded heaven. Crowned, and dressed as a queen in the early Byzantine style, she holds the Christ-child, and in her right hand, an astile cross. Angels bearing torches rear back in wonder at each of her sides. Over her head the hand of God reaches down, extending the wreath of victory. As a young, beardless man wearing the square halo, Anaclet II kneels at the Virgin's left (pl. 18). Calixtus II, a bearded, older man wearing the square halo, kneels at her right. Silvester I, a much larger figure with a halo and a tiara, stands behind Calixtus; Anaclet I, bareheaded, but with a halo, stands behind Anaclet II. Two inscriptions separate this level from the lower. One concerns the builder of the chapel, and the other states that 'The Pious Virgin Mary presides in the heavenly spheres.'[40]

This complex painting scintillates with political symbolism, but here we are primarily interested in the image of Maria *Regina*. I suggest that rather than saluting a papal victory over the emperor, Anaclet II wished to associate the papacy with the palaeochristian church. By including Silvester I, the recipient of the rule of the West according to the Donation of Constantine, he accepts the temporal role

---

requieverit in tabernaculo corporis tui, quam suavis in cubiculo cordis tui.' Barré, 'La Royauté', pp. 96–7.

[37] Barré, 'La Royauté', p. 100.

[38] Eadmer, *Liber de excellentia B. Mariae*, *PL*, clix, 572: 'Stipatus itaque mille nullibus, immo innumerabilibus angelorum agminibus Deus ipse huic piisimae Matri suae de hoc mundo migranti occurrit, eamque super omnes coelos exaltatam, cunctae secum creaturae perenni iure dominaturam in throno collocavit.'

[39] Calixtus II (1119–24) rebuilt the chapel, but Anaclet II decorated it. Cf. M. Stroll, *Symbols as Power: The Papacy Following the Investiture Contest* (Leiden, 1991), pp. 132–49; *eadem*, *The Jewish Pope: Ideology and Politics in the Papal Schism of 1130* (Leiden, 1987), pp. 15–18; Wolf, *Salus Populi Romani*, pp. 122–3; U. Nilgen, 'Maria *Regina*: Ein politischer Kultbildtypus?', *Römisches Jahrbuch für Kunstgeschichte*, lxix (1981), 1–33.

[40] PRAESIDET AETHEREIS PIA VIRGO MARIA CHOREIS.

of the papacy. But he identifies Calixtus with this role, not himself. He aligns himself with Anaclet I, who reigned in the first century before the papacy's venture into the secular world. Anaclet I's bare head signifies his apostolic origin before Constantine granted Silvester his ruling headdress. Anaclet I is also identified with St Peter. Allegedly he was consecrated by St Peter, and constructed Peter's memorial after his death.

The similarity between the figure of Mary and the icon of the Madonna della Clemenza is not fortuitous, for Anaclet II had been cardinal priest of Santa Maria in Trastevere, and chose its treasured icon because it conveyed the message he wanted to transmit. Even though Mary is depicted as a queen, Anaclet II refers to her as 'the Pious Virgin'. He does not say that she 'reigns,' but that she 'presides' over the heavens. He very carefully demarcates himself and the other popes from her sphere in heaven, and significantly, he does not identify himself with her by placing himself in the niche below her throne. Rather, he allocates this spot to St Nicholas, the only non-pope below the heavenly sphere. He and the other popes venerate the Virgin as the keeper of the purity of the faith, but they do not share her power.

The apse fresco in Santa Maria in Trastevere

The Maria *Regina* in this fresco contrasts sharply with her image in the great apse mosaic in Santa Maria in Trastevere (pl. 19). After the schism Innocent rebuilt this church, arguably as a monument to his victory.[41] Eschewing the Madonna della Clemenza, he chose an image of Mary as the bride of Christ sharing the same throne. The scene was revolutionary. It was the first depiction of the coronation of the Virgin in heaven, and it was also the first time that she was portrayed enthroned without the Christ-child.[42]

By contrast with the Mediterranean features and colouring of the Madonna della Clemenza, she has delicate, almost northern European features. She and the bridegroom wear the nimbus, but while he is simply dressed, she wears the garments and jewellery of a Byzantine queen. Instead of the more traditional, mainly purple robes of the Madonna della Clemenza, she wears golden brocaded garments.[43] Innocent's reasons for this new image of Maria *Regina* are conjectural.

---

[41] Boso, *Liber Pontificalis*, ed. L. Duchesne, 2 vols (Paris, 1886–92), ii, 384: 'Hic beatus pontifex ecclesiam beate Dei genitricis Marie tituli Calixti totam innovavit et construxit'; *Liber Censuum de l'Eglise Romain*, ed. P. Fabre and L. Duchesne, 2 vols (Paris, 1910), ii, 169; Kinney, 'S. Maria in Trastevere', pp. 196–9; M.-L. Thèrel, *A l'Origine du décor du portail occidental de Notre-Dame de Senlis: le triomphe de la Vierge-église* (Paris, 1984); Nilgen, 'Maria *Regina*', pp. 28–30; Wolf, *Salus Populi Romani*, pp. 122–3; Stroll, *Symbols as Power*, pp. 169–79.

[42] Nilgen, 'Maria Regina', pp. 28–30; Belting, 'Papal Artistic Commissions', p. 17.

[43] Her garments may be inspired by Psalm 44:10: 'Astitit regina a dextris tuis in vestitu deaureato circumdata varietate.' In his sermon to the nuns of the Paraclete Abelard interpreted this verse as an announcement of the resurrection of the body and the glory of the Virgin at the right of Christ: *PL*, clxxviii, 541–3; P. Verdier, 'Suger a-t-il été en France le

He may not have wanted to use the icon associated with his bitter enemy, Anaclet, and he may have wanted a face similar to those he had seen in his wanderings in France or to the liturgically significant icon of Santa Maria Nuova.[44] With his right arm Christ embraces his bride, and with his left he holds an open book that states, 'Come, my elect, and I shall place you on my throne.'[45] She holds a scroll that reads, 'His left hand under my head, and his right shall embrace me.'[46] These verses from the Canticle of Canticles are used in the liturgy of the Feast of the Assumption of the Virgin.[47] Although the Feast was introduced into Rome as early as the seventh century, it became a subject of apse decoration only in the twelfth.[48] On either side of the bridal throne stand saints associated with the church. The exceptions are Peter, a saint, but not associated with the church, and Innocent, the donor of the church, but not a saint. Only Peter wears a light nimbus, possibly added later. The whole scene is set against a background of brilliant golden mosaics. From the sky above the hand of God extends a green and gold victory wreath over the head of Christ, the centre of the scene.

Some scholars have suggested a French inspiration for the mosaic.[49] Another focuses on an illustration accompanying a commentary by Honorius Augustodunensis on the text that Mary holds.[50] Honorius was the first of the great twelfth-century theologians to conceive of Rome as the spiritual capital of *Christianitas*, and he supported the papal and Roman position without reservation.[51] In the drawing Christ shares a throne with a crowned female figure. With his right hand he embraces her, and with his left a female figure kneeling at a lower level outside

créateur du thème iconographique du couronnement de la Vierge?', *Gesta*, xv (1976), 227–36 esp. p. 230.

44 E. Kitzinger, 'A Virgin's Face', *Art Bulletin*, lxii (1980), 6–20, believes that the model was the icon of Santa Maria Nuova, whch displays the same long nose and small mouth. He explains why Innocent would have adopted this model on liturgical grounds, and specifically the stop of the procession celebrating the Feast of the Assumption at Santa Maria Nuova. He also gives a political motive (p. 19) for demoting the Madonna della Clemenza, viz. that Anaclet had venerated the icon, and had used it as his model in the chapel of S. Nicholas.

45 'Veni electa mea et ponam in te thronum meum.'

46 'Leva eius sub capite meo et dexera (*sic*) illius amplesabitur (*sic*) me.'

47 *Canticus Canticorum*, 2:6; stated similarly, 8:3.

48 H. Belting, 'Icons and Roman Society in the Twelfth Century', *Italian Church Decoration of the Middle Ages and Early Renaissance: Functions, Forms and Regional Traditions*, ed. W. Tronzo (Bologna, 1989), pp. 27–41 at p. 39.

49 They point out that Bernard of Clairvaux and Suger of St Denis had great influence on Innocent, and that the scene of the enthronement became very popular in France in the second half of the twelfth century. É. Mâle, *L'Art religieux du XIIe siècle en France* (Paris, 1922), pp. 184–5; Stroll, *Symbols as Power*, p. 172 n. 35, for other sources.

50 G. A. Wellen, 'Sponsa Christi, Het Absis mozaiek van de Santa Maria in Trastevere te Rome en het Hooglied', *Feestbundel F. van der Meer* (Amsterdam/Brussels, 1966), pp. 148–59.

51 *Liber Duodecim Quaestionum*, *PL*, clxxii, 1182: 'Hinc est, quod Roma caput mundi Petro apostolo, non Michaeli archangelo primatum regiminis obtulit; et universa Ecclesia per orbem non solum in privatis locis, sed etiam in praecipuis urbibus episcopalem sedem Petro contulit.' M.-O. Garrigues, 'Honorius Augustodunensis et l'Italie', *Mélanges de l'Ecole Française de Rome. Moyen âge, tempes modernes*, lxxxiv (1952), 511–30. Honorius was probably an Irish monk. Italy was among his many travels.

the royal city under a tree. Honorius identifies this figure as the earthly church, and the figure on the throne as the heavenly church.

The illuminator probably could not imagine how Christ, sitting on a throne, could hold his left hand under the head of his bride and at the same time embrace her with his right. His solution was to draw two figures. I suggest that Innocent found another. While he had the artist portray Christ embracing Maria *Regina* as the image of the heavenly church with his right hand, he had himself portrayed holding a facsimile of the earthly church with his left.[52] Another interpretation of the mosaic supports this analysis. It concentrates on the figure of Christ, noting that he was the centre of the mosaic, and that the papal throne was directly underneath. An axis runs from the wreath, to Christ, to a pope sitting in the throne below. The configuration implies that while Christ was the lord of the eternal church, Innocent acted in his stead on earth.[53]

This identification of the pope with Christ is enhanced by the symbolism of the marriage of the bishop to his church, signified by his ring. The church of the pope is the *Ecclesia Romana*, identified in the twelfth century as the universal church, and symbolised by Maria *Regina*. The liturgy for the consecration of the pope sanctifies the marriage between the pope and the universal church.[54] The mosaic portrays the marriage of Christ with his church, and in a secondary sense, the pope with the *Ecclesia Romana*.[55]

The same scholar argues that the clue to Innocent's use of the unconventional enthronement scene lies in the second part of the apse inscription.[56] It reads:

---

[52] In the *Orthodoxa Defensio Imperialis*, written in the summer of 1112 at the imperial monastery of Farfa in the Sabina, the author (perhaps, Gregory of Catino) speaks of fomentors of schisms and dissensions, who cruelly strive to cut off the left hand of Christ from under the head of the church. *MGH, Libelli*, ii, 534–42 at p. 538: '. . . scismata et discensiones in eclesiae aperari videntur levamque Christi de sub capite eclesiae (*sic*) precidere crudeliter nituntur'.

[53] Kinney, *S. Maria in Trastevere*, pp. 325–34. G. Ladner states that after the Investiture Contest 'It is as if the Pope had not only now truly become the representative of Him who is not only *Rex Regum* and *Dominus Dominantium*, but who also rules *super gentes et super regna*, the King of Kings and the ruler of people and states.' 'The Concepts of "Ecclesia" and "Christianitas" ' in *Images and Ideas in the Middle Ages*, ii (Rome, 1983), pp. 486–515 at p. 491.

[54] M. Andrieu, *Le Pontifical romain au moyen-âge*, 4 vols, Studi e Testi, 86 (Rome, 1938–41), i, *Le Pontifical romain du XIIe siècle*, p. 149; ii, *Le Pontifical de la curie romaine au XIIIe siècle*, p. 374: 'Accipe anulum fidei scilicet signaculum, quatenus sponsam, Dei videlict sanctam UNIVERSALEM ecclesiam, intemerata fide ornatus illibate custodias.' See also Honorius Augustodunensis, *Gemma animae*, i.216 (*PL*, clxxii, 609): 'Pontifex, ergo anulum portat, ut se sponsum Ecclesiae agnoscat, ac pro illa animam, si necesse fuerit, sicut Christus ponat.' W. Imkamp, *Das Kirchenbild Innocenz' III. (1198–1216)*, Päpste und Papsttum, 22 (Stuttgart, 1983), pp. 302 and n. 193, 303 and n. 195.

[55] Nilgen, 'Maria Regina', p. 30. Nilgen notes that the other figures in the scene represent the orders of the Roman church. She asserts that 'It is the clergy of the *Ecclesia Romana* in all of its ranks under the leadership of Peter, which here accompany the unification of Christ and his church.'

[56] Nilgen, 'Maria Regina', *passim*.

In which [royal palace], O Christ, your seat remains forever
Worthy of his right hand is she whom the golden robe envelops[57]

This scholar reasons that Mary symbolises the church in the double sense as the basilica and as the *Ecclesia Romana*. By declaring that Mary is worthy of Christ's embrace, the opposite possibility is raised. What Innocent is implying is that Santa Maria in Trastevere was unworthy of Christ's embrace when Anaclet II was its cardinal, and the *Ecclesia Romana* was unworthy when Anaclet pretended to be pope. When the church in both senses was about to collapse, Innocent rebuilt it and made it worthy again unto eternity.

All of these theories have merit, but Innocent may have had a further message. Donors depicted in Rome at that time always diminished themselves in some way – by a square halo, small size, or humble posture. Innocent, by contrast, did not distinguish himself from the saints, even though he was still living, and was not a saint. How, then, could he appear in heaven with the enthroned Christ and Mary? His solution appears to have been to blur the imagery of heaven by setting the scene against a golden background, with the heavens above symbolised by coloured clouds. Although not depicted in the clouds, Christ and Mary were assumed to be in heaven.[58]

To see the difference between his conception of the papacy and Anaclet's, let us summarise how each of them used the Maria *Regina*. In the chapel of St Nicholas Mary, the Pious Virgin, appears in heaven, while Anaclet, a small figure, kneels at her feet outside. His square halo and youthful appearance immediately distinguish him from the popes wearing round halos and designated as saints. He primarily uses the Maria *Regina* image to identify with the palaeochristian church. In the apse mosaic Innocent utilises a revolutionary portrayal of Maria *Regina* to proclaim a bold, triumphant papacy. It was an audacious use of imagery to support his major theme of a victorious papacy that entered into a symbiosis with Christ and with Maria *Regina* symbolising the church universal.[59]

---

[57] Cited in Stroll, *Symbols as Power*, p. 165 n. 14; the whole inscription reads: 'HEC IN HONORE TVO PREFVLGIDA MATER HONORIS/ REGIA DIVINI RVTILAT FVLGORE DECORIS/ IN QVA CRISTE SEDES MANET VLTRA SECVLA SEDES/ DIGNA SVIS DEXTRIS EST QVA TEGIT AVREA VESTIS/ CVM MOLES RVITVRA VETVS FORET HIC ORIVVNDVS/ INNOCENTVS HANC RENOVAVIT PAPA SECVNDVS.'

[58] It is also significant that Innocent places himself on the sacerdotal side of the mosaic. *Orthodoxa Defensio Imperialis, MGH, Libelli*, ii, 534–42 at p. 536: 'Habet etiam sancta *eadem* eclesia (sic) singula membra propriis officiis deputata, habet levam, habet dextram. Ipsa enim dicit in canticis canticorum: "Leva eius sub capite meo et dextera illius amplexabitur me"; et per levam regnum, per dexteram vero intelligitur sacerdotium. Leva enim sponsi, id est Christi, sub capite eclesie dicitur, quia prelatis secularibus tuetur temporaliter et substentatur. Dextera autem eius amplexabitur, quia sacerdotali institutione ipsum novit auctorem, quo vitam eternam merebitur habere, sicut patri ipsi dicit . . .'

[59] Wolf, *Salus Populi Romani*, pp. 74–5; W. Ullmann, *Die Stellung des Papsttums im Mittelalter: Idee und Geschichte* (Graz/Vienna/Cologne, 1960), pp. 621–35; for references to Innocent's use of imperial symbolism in Santa Maria in Trastevere see K. Bull-Simonsen Einaudi, ' "Fons Olei" e Anastasio Bibliotecario', *Rivista dell'Istituto Nazionale d'Archeologia e Storia dell'Arte*, ser. 3, xiii (1990).

The apse mosaic of Innocent III in St Peter's

By the reign of Innocent III at the turn of the twelfth century, the papacy had evolved into a monarchy firmly ensconced in both the ecclesiastical and secular spheres.[60] From the vicar of Peter, the pope had become the successor of Peter, and the vicar of Christ.[61] Innocent's use of *Ecclesia Romana* in the form of Maria *Regina* in the apse mosaic of St Peter's illustrates this transition (pl. 20).[62]

The upper scene is rich in imagery, but we are mainly concerned with the lower. Here, the traditional lamb processions move towards the centre from Jerusalem and Bethlehem. In the centre Christ made flesh as the lamb of God stands on a mountain, his blood gushing into a chalice. Behind the lamb stands a throne on which a cross is erected under a baldachino representing the sacrament of the altar in the book of Revelation. On the left, wearing the tiara, Innocent inclines toward the centre with outstretched arms (pl. 21). On the right, wearing the jewelled crown and pearl earrings of an empress, *Ecclesia Romana* also reaches toward the centre (pl. 22).[63] In her left hand she holds a book, and in her right a *vexillum* displaying the keys of the kingdom of heaven, given to Peter by Christ. The *vexillum* is distinctively imperial, resembling the banner that St Peter gave to Charlemagne, depicted in the mosaics of Leo III in the Triclinium in the Lateran palace (pl. 23).

Although the scene does not specifically portray *Ecclesia Romana* as a bride, Innocent's great concentration on the marriage of the bishop with his diocese, and the pope with the *Ecclesia Romana* suggests that the marriage of Innocent with

---

[60] Innocent III writes to John of Constantinople, 'Petro [Christus] non solum universam ecclesiam, sed totum reliquit saeculum gubernandum' (*PL*, ccxiv, 759).

[61] The decretal, *Licet in tantum*: see *Die Register Innocenz' III.*, ii, *Pontifikatsjahr 1199/1200*, edd. O Hageneder, W. Maleczek, A. Strnad (Rome/Vienna, 1979), p. 517, '... sic et spirituale foedus coniugii, quod est inter episcopum et eius ecclesiam, quod in electione initiatum, ratum in confirmatione et in consecratione intelligitur consummatum, sine illius auctoritate solvi non potest, qui successor est Petri et vicarius Christi'. Cf. Imkamp, *Das Kirchenbild*, pp. 305, 307.

[62] The mosaic has been destroyed, but the busts of Innocent III and *Ecclesia Romana* still exist in the Museo di Roma. G. Grimaldi has depicted the mosaic in water colours, Archivio Cap. S Pietro, A 64 ter, Album, fol. 50r; for the *Ecclesia Romana* alone, Vat. lat. 5407, fol. 55v (103). A. Iacobini, 'La Pittura e le arti Suntuaries: Da Innocenzo III a Innocenzo IV (1198–1254)', in *Roma nel Duecento: L'Arte nella città dei papi da Innocenzo III a Bonifacio VIII*, ed. Angiola Maria Romanini (Turin, 1991), pp. 237–320; *idem*, 'Il Mosaico absidale di San Pietro in Vaticano', in *Fragmenta Picta Affreschi e Mosaici staccati del Medioevo romana*, ed. Maria Andaloro *et al.* (Rome, 1989); G. Ladner, *Die Papstbildnisse des Altertums und des Mittelalters*, 3 vols (Vatican City, 1941–84), ii, 56–68; T. Buddensieg, 'Le Coffret en ivoire de Pola, Saint-Pierre et le Latran', *Cahiers Archéologiques*, x (1959), 157–200; W. N. Schumacher, 'Eine römische Apsiskomposition', *Römische Quartalschrift*, liv (1959), 137–202; G. Matthiae, *Mosaici medioevale delle chiese di Roma*, 2 vols (Rome, 1967), ii, 327; J. Ruyschaert, 'Le Tableau Mariotti de la mosaique absidale de l'ancien St Pierre', *Rendiconti della Pontificia Accademia romana di Archeologia*, xl (1967–68), 295–317; Wolf, *Salus Populi Romani*, pp. 117–19.

[63] Iacobini, 'Il Mosaico', p. 126. Wolf, *Salus Populi Romani*, p. 117, describes her as being in the guise of a victor.

his church was the theme of the iconography.[64] Honorius Augustodunensis had already adumbrated that the bride – *Ecclesia Romana* – brings a rich dowry to the bridegroom, the pope. Enlarging upon this theme, Innocent states that she brings a *plenitudinem spiritualium* and a *latitudinem temporalium*. Others are called *in partem sollicitudinis*, he continues, but St Peter alone is called to *plentitudinem potestatis*. The mitre is the symbol of spiritual power, and the crown the symbol of temporal power.[65] He concludes that this spiritual marriage with the church brings to the pope the dowry of *plenitudinem potestatis*, and places him between God and man; less than God, but more than man.[66]

The apse mosaic alludes to this space between God and man, where Christ is made flesh. By wearing the tiara, Innocent symbolises the pope as ruler in the temporal world. Similarly, by wearing the ornaments of an empress and carrying an imperial banner displaying the keys to the kingdom of heaven, *Ecclesia Romana* symbolises the highest ecclesiastical and imperial authority. In his marriage to *Ecclesia Romana* Innocent assumes both the sacerdotal dignity and the regal power of Christ, thus exceeding the sovereignty of the emperor.[67] A papal throne below the mosaic designed either under the guidance of Calixtus II (1119–24) or of Innocent III is on a direct axis with Christ in the upper sphere and the lamb in the lower. In imitation of the throne of Solomon six steps lead up to a marble seat vermiculated in red and gold. There the pope rose above the altar to view the nave, and to be viewed by the worshippers.[68] If Innocent II were seen to imitate Christ while enthroned in Santa Maria in Trastevere, how much more did Innocent III appear in Christ's likeness while seated on the replica of Solomon's throne in St Peter's?

---

64 Imkamp, *Das Kirchenbild*, p. 322; for the marriage of bishops to their churches see K. Pennington, 'Innocent III and the Divine Authority of the Pope', *Pope and Bishops: The Papal Monarchy in the Twelfth and Thirteenth Centuries* (Philadelphia, 1984), pp. 13–42; repr. *Popes, Canonists and Texts, 1150–1550* (Variorum, 1993), ch. III, pp. 1–32 at pp. 3–4. He changed the equation from Christ and his church to the Bishop of Rome and the Roman church: Imkamp, *Das Kirchenbild*, p. 311.

65 Sermo III, 'In consecratione Pontificis', *PL*, ccxvii, 665: 'Ergo, qui habet sponsam, sponsus est. Haec autem sponsa non nupsit vacua, sed dotem mihi tribuit absque pretio pretiosam, spiritualium videlicet plenitudinem et latitudinem temporalium, magnitudinem et multitudinem utrorumque. Nam caeteri vocati sunt in partem sollicitudinis, solus autem Petrus assumptus est in plenitudinem potestatis. In signum spiritualium contulit mihi mitram, in signum temporalium autem dedit mihi coronam; mitram pro sacerdotio, coronam pro regno, illius me constituens vicarium, qui habet in vestimento et in femore sua scriptum: Rex regnum et Dominus dominatium.'

66 *Ibid.*, col. 658: 'inter Deum et hominem in medius constitutus, citra Deum, sed ultra hominem'; Imkamp, *Das Kirchenbild*, p. 320; Iacobini, 'La Pittura', p. 244; *idem*, 'Il Mosaico absidale', p. 126.

67 Iacobini, 'Il Mosaico absidale', p. 126.

68 S. de Blaauw, *Cultus et decor: liturgia e architettura nella Roma tardoantica et medievale: Basilica Salvatoris, Sanctae Mariae, Sancti Petri*, Studi e Testi, 355–6 (Vatican City, 1994), pp. 651–3. The top line of the inscription under the mosaic refers to the *Ecclesia Romana* as the Mother of all of churches: 'SUMMA PETRI SEDES EST HEC · SACRA PRINCIPIS AEDES · MATER CVNCTARVM DECOR ET DECVS ECCLESIARVM'.

Two mysterious illustrations

I suggest that two mysterious illustrations accompanying the thirteenth-century translation of *Liber Ystoriarum Romanorum*, written in the twelfth century, complement Innocent's message.[69] The illustrations of *Roma Caput Mundi* and *Ecclesia Romana* follow an exposition of the transference of power from the empire to the church through the Donation of Constantine.[70] The crowned figure of *Roma Caput Mundi* sits on a throne supported by two lions (pl. 24).[71] She holds a globe in her left hand, and a palm frond in her right, both symbols used by emperors beginning with Conrad I (911–18). Female figures representing India and Gallia present tribute. The face of the sun appears to her right near the palm frond, and the moon at her left, outside the arched setting below. Even though she has no nimbus, the depiction of the sun and the moon would suggest that she is reigning in heaven, were it not for the setting in a tripartate arch beneath a building. Even so, they bring to mind a sermon St Bernard wrote to commemorate the Assumption of Mary into heaven and her coronation.[72] Bernard speaks of the moon lying at her feet as a mediator of the sun, just as Mary is also a mediator. The topic of another sermon on the Assumption refers to Rev. 12:1: 'And there appeared a great wonder in heaven; a woman clothed with the sun, and the moon under her feet, and upon her head a crown of twelve stars.'[73] The contradictions in the symbolism defy a precise interpretation, but the sun/moon motifs and the juxtaposition with the Donation of Constantine suggest that *Roma Caput Mundi* is a version of Maria *Regina*, who rules the world from her throne both in heaven and on earth.

Ecclesia Romana is the final illustration (pl. 25).[74] The reverse of the image of *Ecclesia Romana* in the apse mosaic in St Peter's, she wears the nimbus, but not the crown. Dressed in the Byzantine style, she carries a model of the church in her left hand, and in her right a tripartite orb on which kneels an angel carrying a *vexillum*. She stands on the heads of a winged dragon and a serpent, clinging to the top of a lion. The accompanying legends declare that the globe is the world,

---

[69] *Storie de Troja et de Roma* (otherwise called *Liber Ystoriarum Romanorum*), ed. E. Monaci (Rome, 1920); Stroll, *Symbols as Power*, pp. 13–14.

[70] The exposition is illuminated by drawings taken from the Constantine legend, based upon frescoes in the chapel of S Silvester in the basilica of SS Quattro Coronati in Rome. They were painted under the direction of Innocent IV when he remodelled the church in the mid-thirteenth century, but they may be copies of frescoes created by Paschal II at the beginning of the twelfth century.

[71] Cod. Hamburg, C. 97 B; Monaci, *Storie*, p. li.

[72] 'Sermo infra Octavam Assumptionis', *Sancti Bernardi Opera*, v, 274: 'Iam te, Mater misericordiae, per ipsum sincerissimae tuae mentis affectum, tuis iacens provoluta pedibus Luna, mediatricem sibi apud Solem iustitiae constitutam devotis supplicationibus interpellat, ut in lumine tuo videat lumen, et Solis gratiam tuo mercatur obtentu, quam vere amavit prae omnibus et ornavit, stola gloriae induens et coronam pulchritudinis ponens in capite tuo.'

[73] *Ibid.*, p. 262: 'De verbis Apocalypsis: Signum magnum apparuit in Coelo, Mulier amicta sole, et Luna sub pedibus eius, et in capite eius corona stellarum duodecim.'

[74] Cod. Hamburg, C. 123 B.

that the angel symbolises the triumph of the clergy, and that the lion, dragon and serpent trampled under her feet signify the Roman empire.[75]

Although neither of these illustrations is entitled 'Maria *Regina*', they both would be recognisable as one of her guises. They suggest that the intention of their creator was to show that Constantine transferred imperial power to the Roman church. *Ecclesia Romana* then crushed the empire and became the *caput mundi*. The symbolism is more brutal than that of the apse mosaic in St Peter's, but both imply that *Ecclesia Romana*, whose bishop was the pope, had superseded the Roman empire.

From Maria *Regina* to secular queen

Around 1290 Nicholas IV (1288–92), the first Franciscan pope, commissioned Jacopo Torriti to create a mosaic in the apse of Santa Maria Maggiore (pl. 26).[76] A comparison of the mosaic with an almost contemporaneous illumination from a French Bible shows how the Maria *Regina* image had evolved into a model for the secular queen. Maria *Regina* shares a throne with Christ, but by contrast with Santa Maria in Trastevere, the scene is centred, and the focus is on both the bride and the groom. The heaven is precisely demarcated by a circle around the couple, making it clear that the donors and all other figures except the angels stand outside. Rather than the ornate garments and the pearl pendant earrings of a Byzantine queen, Mary is draped in flowing robes similar to those of Christ.[77] She unambiguously holds her hands in the advocate position. In his left hand Christ holds a book stating, 'Come, my elect, and I shall place you on my throne.' His right rests on the rim of Mary's crown indicating that he has just crowned her. The sun and the moon at their feet signify that they rule from the highest sphere of heaven. Small figures of the donors, Jacobus Colonna, archpriest of the basilica, and Nicholas IV, kneel to the right and the left below, far outside heaven. The pope no longer involves himself in the imagery of Maria *Regina* and Christ, the bride and groom.

---

[75] Monaci, *Storie*, p. lvii. The crushing theme is based upon Psalm 91:13, which was frequently commented upon in the Middle Ages. 'Super apsidem et basiliscum calcabis, conculcabis leonem et draconem'; cf. Stroll, *Symbols as Power*, pp. 13–14 n. 54.

[76] A. Tomei, 'La Pittura e le Arti Suntuarie: Da Alessandro IV a Bonifacio VIII (1254–1303)', *Roma nel Duecento*, pp. 321–404; M. R. Menna, 'Nicolo IV, i mosaici absidali di Santa Maria Maggiore e l'Oriente absidale', *Rivista dell'Istituto Nazionale d'Archeologia e Storia dell'Arte*, ser. 3, x (1987), 201–24; Wolf, *Salus Populi Romani*, pp. 176–96; M. Alpatoff, 'Die Entstehung des Mosaiks von Jacobus Torriti in S. Maria Maggiore in Rom absidale', *Jahrbuch für Kunstwissenschaft*, ii (1924), 1–19; H. Karp, *Die frühchristlichen und mittelalterlichen Mosaiken von S. Maria Maggiore zu Rom* (Baden-Baden, 1966); J. Gardner, 'Pope Nicholas and the Decoration of S. Maria Maggiore absidale', *Zeitschrift für Kunstgeschichte*, xxxvi (1973), 1–50; W. Tronzo, 'Apse Decoration, the Liturgy and the Perception of Art in Medieval Rome: S. Maria in Trastevere and S. Maria Maggiore absidale', in *Italian Church Decoration*, pp. 167–93; R. Krautheimer, *Rome: Profile of a City, 312–1308* (Princeton, 1980), pp. 217–25.

[77] Psalm 44:10 as in n. 43 above.

French cathedrals in the earlier thirteenth century had pioneered this theme, and in the late thirteenth century a French Bible illustrates a similar scene with a secular queen (pl. 27).[78] Blanche of Castile sits on a throne, separate, but adjoining the throne of her son, Louis IX (1226–70). She is crowned, and wears the contemporary robes of a queen. As the intercessor of the people, her hands are clearly in the advocate position toward her son. Just as the church had adopted motifs of the secular queen to create the image of Maria *Regina*, now the secular world reversed the process, adopting the image of Maria *Regina* as a model for the secular queen.

---

[78] Bible moralisée, New York, Pierpont Morgan Library, MS M. 240, fol. 8r; Wolf, *Salus Populi Romani*, p. 190. Wolf dates the illumination to the later thirteenth century. Other sources date it as early as 1230.

Plate 11 Madonna, Santa Maria in Aracoeli, Rome (photo: Fratelli
Alinari, Rome/ Art Resource, New York)

Plate 12 Maria, princess, triumphal arch, Santa Maria Maggiore, Rome (photo: Fratelli Alinari, Rome/ Art Resource, New York)

Plate 13 *Mater Ecclesia*, Exultet Roll: Vatican Library, MS Barbarini lat. 592 (by courtesy of the Biblioteca Apostolica Vaticana)

Plate 14 Empress Theodora, San Vitale, Ravenna (photo: Norman Roberson)

Plate 15 Madonna della Clemenza (photo: Bibliotheca Hertziana, Rome)

Plate 16 Chapel of John VII, St Peter's, Rome: Vatican Library, MS Vat. lat. 6439, fols 260–1 (by courtesy of the Biblioteca Apostolica Vaticana)

Plate 17 Apse fresco, chapel of St Nicholas, Lateran Palace, Rome: Vatican Library, engraving from Constantino Caetani, 1638 (by courtesy of the Biblioteca Apostolica Vaticana)

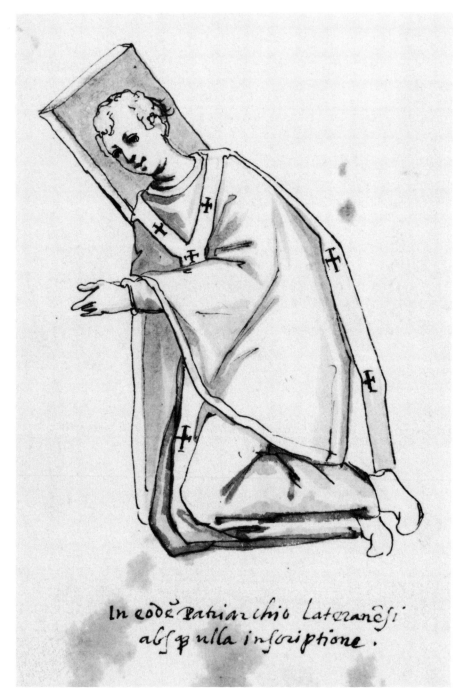

In eodě patriarchio Lateranēsi absq̃ ulla inscriptione.

Plate 18 Anaclet II: Vatican Library, MS Vat. lat. 5407, fol. 86 (by courtesy of the Biblioteca Apostolica Vaticana)

Plate 19 Apse mosaic, Santa Maria in Trastevere, Rome (photo: Anderson/ Art Resource, New York)

Plate 20

Plate 21

Plate 22

Plate 23 Triclinium, Lateran Palace: Vatican Library, MS Barbarini lat. 2738, fol. 13r (by courtesy of the Biblioteca Apostolica Vaticana)

Plate 20 (opposite top) Apse mosaic, old St Peter's, Rome: Vatican Library, MS Vat. lat. 5408, fols 29v–30r (by courtesy of the Biblioteca Apostolica Vaticana)

Plate 21 (opposite, bottom left) Pope Innocent III, apse mosaic, old St Peter's, Rome: Vatican Library, MS Vat. lat. 5407, fol. 60r (by courtesy of the Biblioteca Apostolica Vaticana)

Plate 22 (opposite, bottom right) *Ecclesia Romana*, apse mosaic, old St Peter's, Rome: Vatican Library, MS Vat. lat. 5407, fol. 55v (by courtesy of the Biblioteca Apostolica Vaticana)

Plate 24 *Roma Caput Mundi*: Cod. Hamburg, C. 97 B

Plate 25 *Ecclesia Romana*: Cod. Hamburg, C. 123 B

Plate 26 Apse mosaic, Santa Maria Maggiore (photo: Fratelli Alinari, Rome/ Art Resource, New York)

Plate 27 *Bible moralisée*: Blanche of Castile and Louis IX: New York, Pierpont Morgan Library, MS M. 240, fol. 8r

11

Queen and Patron

Diana Webb

It is well-known not only that the Italian city-states did not have kings, but that they went to great lengths to avoid having kings. It followed that they did not have queens. Between the death of Countess Matilda in 1115 and the appearance of princely courts in the north of the peninsula in the fifteenth century, which gave prominence to the womenfolk of the Gonzaga, Este, Sforza and Montefeltro, women were conspicuous by their virtual invisibility in the public (or perhaps more properly, political) life of the Italian cities. There were however queens, and sometimes even queens regnant, in the kingdom of Naples, and the consort of a foreign potentate such as an emperor would occasionally impinge on Italian consciousness. Several chroniclers, for example, recorded the death at Genoa in 1311 of Marguerite of Brabant, wife of the aspirant emperor Henry VII. She was, the Florentine Villani said, reputed a good and saintly lady; his fellow-townsman Dino Compagni recalled that she was 'a minister' to God's poor and 'had a very noble reputation for the great sanctity of her good life'.[1] The fact that neither chronicler gives Marguerite a name helps to make their remarks sound more generic than, perhaps, they were intended to be; but such descriptions hint that Italians no less than other Europeans were aware of the moral qualities that a queen was meant to exemplify.

Queens were far from absent from Italian culture; the popularity of courtly and Arthurian literature helped to ensure that. It was the undoing of Dante's Paolo and Francesca (*Inferno*, v) that they sat together reading stories of Lancelot and Guinevere. A little later, Boccaccio's young ladies and gentlemen took on the role of king or queen for the day as they presided over the story-telling and genteel diversions of the *Decameron*. There were kings and queens on Italian chessboards, and, from the later fourteenth century, their newfangled playing-cards. If city-state Italians rarely set eyes upon a living queen, they did not perhaps in that respect differ all that radically from the mass of their contemporaries elsewhere in Europe; but they too knew what queens were.

---

[1] G. Villani, *Nuova Cronica*, ed. G. Porta, 3 vols (Florence, 1991), ix.28 (ii, 233); D. Compagni, *Chronicle of Florence*, ed. and trans. D. Bornstein (Philadelphia, 1986), iii.30, p. 54. Earlier Compagni had recorded Marguerite in the classic queenly role of 'gift-giver' at great ceremonial occasions: 'The emperor held a large and honorable court in Milan; and on the morning of January 1, 1311, the empress presented many gifts to his knights' (*ibid.*, iii.26, p. 88).

There was no question but that the Virgin was understood, in Italy as elsewhere, to be a queen; and it was arguably she who presented rulers and ruled alike with their most familiar image of queenship. My interest here is in the ways in which perceptions of Mary's regality may have affected perceptions of the patronage which she exercised over many of the city-states. Patronage was a concept quite distinct from that of royalty, and as we shall see more fully in a moment, possessed its own vocabulary.[2] It is however arguable that precisely because the Italian cities eschewed monarchical government, their patron saints acquired a key importance in civic ceremonial as surrogate monarchs

In an age in which abstract conceptions of the state had a somewhat restricted academic public, it was the saint who on his or her principal feast-day conveniently received the visible demonstrations of homage that all governments needed to exact from their subjects, but which could not very easily or properly be paid to mere temporary magistrates. That was the saints' annual, routine function; but the patron also had the potential to intervene to save his or her city in an emergency. On 4 September 1260, the Sienese scored a victory over the Guelfs of Tuscany, headed by the Florentines, at the battle of Montaperti, which gave birth to a tradition which was elaborated during the next two centuries.[3] It was said that the Sienese, on the eve of a battle they could scarcely hope to win, handed over the government of their city to the Virgin and went out to receive victory under her auspices. Mary had long since been the patron of the church and commune of Siena. Some eight years before the battle of Montaperti, the design of the communal seal had been altered to depict the Virgin and Child.[4]

I shall be much concerned, in what follows, with words and images generated by this Sienese tradition, but it must be clearly understood that whatever unique features this particular civic cult may have possessed, Siena was by no means the only 'city of the Virgin' in medieval Italy. At Pisa (where she appeared on the city's coinage), at Parma, Spoleto, Orvieto and Cremona, to name only a handful, Mary had progressed naturally from being the patron of the cathedral church to being the patron of the city conceived as a political community. In all these places, as at Siena, the greatest of her four principal feasts, the Feast of the Assumption, was the central civic festivity of the year; it was the day on which both citizens and representatives of subject rural communities, as well as lords who recognised the authority of the commune, processed to the cathedral to make their offerings

---

[2] For a general survey of the subject outlined in the following paragraphs, and for further detail, see D. M. Webb, *Patrons and Defenders: The Saints in the Italian City States* (London, 1996). See also the summary observations in Webb, 'Saints and Cities in Medieval Italy', *History Today*, xliii (July 1993), 15–21.

[3] I discuss this tradition in detail in *Patrons and Defenders* (above, n. 2), ch. 6, to which the reader is referred for fuller references.

[4] The seal had hitherto represented the old fortress, the Castelvecchio. Both seals are illustrated by A. Middledorf-Kosegarten, 'Zur Bedeutung der Sieneser Domkuppel', *Münchener Jahrbuch der bildenden Kunst*, xxi (1970), 78. The 1252 seal was depicted in the lower border of Simone Martini's *Maestà* (for which see further below) in the palazzo pubblico: A. Martindale, *Simone Martini* (Oxford, 1988) pl. 8 and p. 206.

of wax tapers or pieces of fine cloth at her altar. In some other cities, Milan, Verona and Piacenza among them, a slightly different pattern obtained: the Virgin was patron of the cathedral, but shared the patronage of the commune with an ancient saint whose relics lay elsewhere in the city, the bishops Ambrose and Zeno at Milan and Verona respectively, the soldier-martyr Antoninus at Piacenza.

By the fourteenth or fifteenth centuries it is apparent that even where there was no old-established tradition of the Virgin's civic patronage, urban governments were taking steps to ensure that they were earning a share of her protection. In 1294, the Florentines decided to rebuild and rededicate their cathedral in the name of Santa Maria dei Fiori.[5] At Florence, as somewhat later at Bologna, official veneration of the Virgin was also focused on wonder-working images, for example that of the Madonna of Impruneta, which in the later fourteenth century began to be brought into Florence to be carried in procession at times of need or celebration.[6] In the middle of the fifteenth century the Sienese government gave instructions for the image before which, it was believed, their forbears had made their submission in September 1260 to be cut down for processional use.[7]

In many cities, the Virgin's four principal feasts (the Assumption, the Annunciation, the Nativity and the Purification), were public holidays on which no work was done, and many governments made an increasing point of celebrating one or more of them by sending official offerings to the urban church which was particularly associated with the feast in question. Mary's advance to virtually universal pre-eminence can be illustrated by the case of the Romagnol city of Faenza, where St Peter was, and remained, the traditional patron. Like all urban patrons, he received (together with St Paul, with whom of course he shared his principal feast-day) a solemn offering from all the officials and the citizen-body, and the day was also marked, as in many other cities, by a horse-race run in his honour for the prize of a piece of scarlet cloth. The early fifteenth-century statutes of Faenza, however, give precedence to the celebration of the Feast of the Assumption, which was marked by a similar solemn offering at the suburban monastery of Santa Maria Forisportam, and by a race run for a length of green cloth. In addition, the feast of the Annunciation was to be honoured at the Servite church by an offering made by the principal officials and the guilds.[8]

The wording of the statutes gives some clue to the rationale of the actions that were thus prescribed. SS Peter and Paul were the *patroni et singulares defensores hujus nostre civitatis*, and the veneration due to them was the veneration traditionally due to their cathedral church. The purpose of honouring the Virgin was 'so

---

5 Villani, *Nuova Cronica*, ix.9 (ii, 26).
6 Villani records miracles performed by an image of the Virgin at Or San Michele in Florence in 1293: *ibid.*, viii.155 (i, 628). For the Madonna of Impruneta, see R. Trexler, 'Florentine Religious Experience: The Sacred Image', *Studies in the Renaissance*, ix (1972), 7–41; for the Bolognese Madonna of St Luke, G. Lanzi and D. Ferrari, 'Le Processioni per la Madonna di San Luca in Bologna', *Il Santo*, xxiv (1984), 207–27.
7 E. Garrison, 'Towards a New History of the Siena Cathedral Madonnas', in *Studies in the History of Medieval Painting*, 4 vols (Florence, 1960–62), iv, 10.
8 *Statuta Faventiae*, ed. G. Rossini, *Rerum Italicarum Scriptores*, new edn, 28/v, 291–5.

that by the prayers and intercession of our lady, that same most glorious mother, to her Son, this city of Faenza and its people may continually be recommended and ever defended from all perils'. This, unsurprisingly in view of the Virgin's established reputation as the protector of the weak and the unworthy, is the leitmotiv of her urban patronage, as we shall see more fully.

The concept of the patron saint recalled that of the Roman *patronus*, the great man whose influence at court enabled him to defend and advance the interests of his clients, be they individuals or communities.[9] Four words were used more than any others, in the official language of the Italian cities, to describe the role of the patron saint: *patronus, defensor, advocatus, protector*. The ideas of defence, assistance, protection obviously underlie all four. Somewhat less commonly, but by no means rarely, terms were employed which implied headship, leadership or even executive power: *dux, caput, gubernator*. At Siena, where, as we have already noted, it came to be believed that the citizens had on the eve of the battle of Montaperti actually consigned the government of their city to the Virgin, she was first called *gubernatrix* in a document produced a few days after the battle which recorded the resubmission of Montalcino, a small town which had been in rebellion against the commune.[10] The title *gubernatores et defensores* was borne at Siena and some other cities, we may note, by the magistrates who actually ruled the commune. One unusual variant on the established range of terms was applied to the Virgin in a Sienese statute of about 1274, in which she is called not only *gubernatrix* but *receptrix* of the city.[11] This rather uncommon word was used *in malum sensum*, by Cicero and others, to designate a harbourer of criminals or receiver of stolen goods; St Ambrose, however, was more inclined to use it in a positive sense, in one place applying it to the Ark, in another to the soul as receiver of the Word.[12] All of these connotations can in some sense be regarded as applicable to the ever-merciful and sometimes even over-indulgent Virgin. In the vernacular recension of the Sienese statutes which was produced in 1309–11 she was designated, more conventionally, *capo et difendritice*.[13]

It was of course the Virgin's special relationship with her son which made her patronage so efficacious. This same special relationship with the King of Heaven entitled her to be regarded and represented as a queen. Odericus, canon of Siena,

---

9 For the early medieval development of this concept see A. M. Orselli, *L'idea e il culto del santo patrono cittadino nella letteratura latina christiana* (Bologna, 1965); reprinted in *L' immaginario religioso della città medievale* (Ravenna, 1985), pp. 3–182.

10 *Il Caleffo Vecchio del Comune di Siena*, ed. G. Cecchini, 3 vols (Siena, 1931–40), ii, 846–52 n. 628. The text is preceded by an invocation 'ad honorem et reverentiam omnipotentis Dei et beate Marie semper Virginis, que est defensatrix et gubernatrix civitatis ejusdem ...' The present writer has found no earlier instance of the use *gubernatrix* to describe Mary's role at Siena.

11 Siena, Archivio di Stato, Statuti di Siena 3, fols 1r–1v.

12 E. Forcellini, *Totius Latinitatis Lexicon*, ed. V. de Vit, 10 vols (Prato, 1858–87), v, 97; J. Facciolati, E. Forcellini and J. Furlanetti, *Lexicon totius latinitatis*, ed. J. Perin, 4 vols (Padua, 1864–90), iv, 23.

13 *Il Costituto del Comune di Siena volgarizzato nel MCCCIX–MCCCX*, ed. A. Lisini, 2 vols (Siena, 1905), ii, 361.

in the *Ordo Officiorum* he compiled in 1213 describing the liturgical year in the cathedral, in one place called her simply 'regina nostra'.[14] However, at Siena as elsewhere, the notaries and lawyers who drafted the statutes were almost invariably content to describe her patronage in the established terminology which was applied to other, lesser saints, as well, of course, as in the terms which were applied to her everywhere in Christendom: the blessed Virgin, the mother or *genitrix* of God, often further qualified by epithets such as *gloriosa*. The Pisan *Breve Communis* of 1286, prescribing the keeping of the Feast of the Assumption, was rather unusual in calling her 'our lady' in seigneurial fashion, *domina nostra*.[15]

The absence of the term *regina* from these texts, it might be said, simply preserves the analogy between the Virgin and other patrons. Male saints were never called *rex*, for the very good and obvious reason that there was only one *rex* in the court of heaven. Clearly, however, and precisely because of her unique relationship with the King of Heaven, Mary was not just a saint like any other. Several saints had been, or were believed to have been, kings or queens in their earthly lives, but Mary alone of patron saints was known to be a queen in heaven. Did that not give a particular quality to her patronage? I hope to be able to show that it did, in ways that did not always necessitate the use of the word *regina* in texts or the placing of a crown on the Virgin's head in images.

Siena was not the only 'city of the Virgin' to win a famous victory in the course of the thirteenth century with her assistance. In 1248 the women of Parma presented to her a model of the city, made in silver, in the hope of obtaining her help against Frederick II.[16] When the Parmigiani sallied forth and ransacked the emperor's stronghold of Vittoria, the credit therefore had to go to her, or so thought Pope Innocent IV, who in 1250 pointed out to them that they ought to be mindful of benefits received before they infringed clerical immunities. For Innocent too the Virgin was *patrona vestra*, and he envisaged her 'continually spreading the canopy (*umbraculum*) of her protection over you'.[17] To this particular image of protection we shall have to return.

A few years later, in May 1255, Humbert des Romans, general of the Dominican order, issued letters of confraternity to the congregations of the Virgin at Mantua and Bologna.[18] Both these societies of laymen were described as established *in honorem reginae caeli, matris Dei*. The members of such confraternities, the

14 *Ordo Officiorum Ecclesiae Senensis ab Oderico ejusdem ecclesiare canonico anno MCCXIII compositus*, ed. J. C. Trombelli (Bologna, 1766).

15 *Statuti inediti della Città di Pisa*, ed. F. Bonaini, 3 vols (Florence, 1854–57), iii, 263.

16 Salimbene di Adam, *Cronica*, ed. G. Scalia, 2 vols (Bari, 1966), i, 283. To Salimbene the Virgin was *mater misericordie*.

17 I. Affò, *Storia della città di Parma*, 4 vols (Parma, 1792–95), iii, 386–7.

18 For these brotherhoods, see G. G. Meersseman, 'Le Congregazioni della Vergine' in *Ordo Fraternitatis*, ii (= *Italia Sacra*, xxiv) (Rome, 1977), 921–1117. This study in its original form appeared as 'Les confréries de la Vierge', *Archivum Fratrum Praedicatorum*, xxii (1952; the Italian version incorporated further research on *laudesi* fraternities which appeared under the title 'Note sull' Origine delle Compagnie dei Laudesi (Siena 1267)', *Rivista Storica della Chiesa in Italia*, xvii (1963), 395–405. The texts of the letters issued to the confraternities of Mantua and Bologna are in 'Le congregazioni', pp. 1007–8, docs 5

establishment of which was an important part of the mendicant strategy for harnessing the pious energies of well-to-do townsmen, were accustomed to meet in the Dominican church for compline, where they would hear the brethren end the service with the singing of the *Salve Regina*.[19] The first verse of this hymn begins 'Salve, regina, mater misericordiae/ Vita, dulcedo et spes nostra, salve'; the second, 'Eja ergo, O advocata nostra,/ Illos tuos misericordes oculos ad nos converte.' An association of ideas which is of the greatest importance for our subject, between regality and mercy, was thus offered to the friars' hearers, while the 'pity' of the Virgin was also associated with her role as advocate.

The same terminology is developed in the statutes of the Dominican Marian confraternity of Arezzo in southern Tuscany, which were confirmed by the bishop in 1262.[20] The confraternity was itself named as that of 'holy Mary of mercy'. The civic dimension of her patronage is repeatedly emphasised. The bishop pronounces himself 'mindful of the pity of our advocate, the most blessed Holy Virgin, Mary mother of God, that she may always intercede for us with her son and promote and preserve the good state of our city'. Her four festivals were to be celebrated 'so as to commend to her the fraternity and the good state of our city'. The society was commended 'to the queen of mercy'; she was its *dux et caput*. The close kinship of this terminology with that which is used in the urban statutes is clear: what distinguishes the language of the confraternity statute is the appearance (albeit only once) of the word *regina*, in intimate association with the quality of mercy.

In a very short space of time confraternities came into being which had the special purpose of singing hymns (*laude*) in the vernacular before an image of the Virgin. Meersseman reckoned that the earliest of these was a Sienese confraternity which received confirmation of its statutes from Bishop Tommaso Fusconi, himself a Dominican, in 1267.[21] Various collections of *laude* survive: the only one certainly known to have been copied in the thirteenth century is of southern Tuscan provenance, the *Laudario di Cortona*.[22] In a number of hymns from this collection the familiar images and associations recur amidst a wealth of courtly epithets. One for example begins 'Come praise, and for love sing, of the amorous Virgin Mary: Mary glorious and blessed, for ever be highly praised; let us pray that you will be our advocate with your son, o pious Virgin. Piteous sovereign queen, strengthen the vain mind . . .'. It ends 'Vigorous, powerful, blessed, for you is this hymn sung; you are our advocate, the most faithful that could ever be.'[23] Another begins 'Hail,

and 6. In June 1261 Humbert issued a letter in similar terms for the benefit of a fraternity at Faenza (*ibid.*, pp. 1014–15, doc. 16).

[19] This custom was adopted at Bologna and in the Lombard province in 1221, and in 1233 was in use throughout the order: *ibid.*, p. 951.

[20] *Ibid.*, pp. 1015–27, doc. 17. There is an English translation in *Early Dominicans: Selected Writings*, ed. S. Tugwell OP (London, 1982), pp. 436–51.

[21] 'Note sull' origini', pp. 402–5; 'Le congregazioni', pp. 1030–2.

[22] The quotations that follow are derived from *Poeti del Duecento*, ed. G. Contini (Milan, 1960), ii, and *Poesia italiana del Duecento*, ed. P. Cudini (Milan, 1977).

[23] Contini, pp. 12–14; Cudini, pp. 258–9.

most holy lady, most powerful queen',[24] and another calls her 'resplendent queen above the angels'.[25] A hymn from a Pisan source imagines that Christ on ascending to heaven left Mary 'in his place' and when the angel came to announce her death, he said 'the Lord has sent me here, because the court demands you to fill the gap in their supreme joy'.[26] In other hymns the Virgin is told 'you exercised lordship (*signoreggiasti*) with great excellence, for you had licence to grant pardon' and is addressed as 'Great queen, who sways every kingdom'.[27] In an early Bolognese hymn associated with the order of the Servi di Santa Maria or Servites, she is 'Most powerful queen, exalted above the heavens . . . crowned before the king of glory'.[28]

Contemporary with these verbal images were of course a host of visual images in both two and three dimensions. Mary's royalty was most frequently expressed simply in her depiction enthroned with her infant Son; she might or might not also be shown crowned (significantly, crowns have often been added in more recent times to paintings which did not originally include them). Many images which showed her massive and frontal, the child on her lap, have a close affinity with the Romanesque representations of her as *Sedes Sapientiae*, which were familiar in Italy, and with her representation in the developing cathedral sculpture of northern France.[29] The sculpture of Benedetto Antelami and others working in the cities on the Via Emilia in northern Italy, the highroad from north-western Europe to Italy and Rome, furnishes striking examples already in the twelfth century. It is very much in this guise, for example, that the crowned Virgin, with her Son, receives the homage of the Magi in Antelami's relief over the north portal of the Baptistery at Parma.[30]

Such enthroned Madonnas embody a theological concept and a theological virtue, but it may not be too fanciful to allow for the possibility of associations of ideas set up in the minds of spectators by the visual resemblance of such images, and their more supple Gothic successors, to the crowned female figures of the virtues which are also to be found in Italian art of the period. In the celebrated

---

24 Contini, pp. 15–16; Cudini, p. 259.

25 Cudini, p. 264.

26 Contini, pp. 16–19.

27 *Ibid.*, pp. 24, 27.

28 *Ibid.*, p. 9.

29 For example a panel in the National Gallery, painted in the 1260s by Margarito of Arezzo, shows her crowned. For comments on the Byzantine style of the crown the Virgin is wearing in this and other images by Margarito, and also on the lion-headed throne, which resembles those in twelfth-century French wooden sculptures of the throne of wisdom, see M. Davies, *National Gallery Catalogues: The Early Italian Schools before 1400*, revised by D. Gordon (London, 1988), pp. 67–9; also J. Dunkerton and others, *From Giotto to Dürer: Early Renaissance Painting in the National Gallery* (London, 1991), pp. 212–13. The provenance of the panel is unknown, so there is no justification for connecting it with an Aretine Marian confraternity such as the one whose statutes are examined above, but it undoubtedly belongs to a contemporary and closely neighbouring environment. The iconography closely resembles that of two other signed panels by Margarito, now in Arezzo and in Washington.

30 A. C. Quintavalle, *Benedetto Antelami* (Milan, 1990), p. 120. Dating is difficult and the relief may be as late as *c.* 1220. For other related groups from the same region, and for the links of this sculpture with the Ile-de-France, see *ibid.*, pp. 83–95, 256–9, 356–8.

frescoes painted in the 1330s by Ambrogio Lorenzetti in the palazzo pubblico of Siena, a whole roster of crowned female figures exemplify the virtues, theological and temporal, in accordance with which the commune should be governed, while the (exclusively male) representatives of urban government obediently parade before them. One of the most recent of the innumerable commentators on these frescoes has suggested that we should not entirely overlook the emotional implications of this juxtaposition of female virtues with male earthly rulers.[31] The Madonna also possessed not only the affective power of femininity, but the potential to imply the virtues of rulership. In fact, as we shall see, Simone Martini had invested her with this explicit significance in an adjacent chamber of the Sienese *palazzo pubblico*, twenty years before the Lorenzetti frecoes were painted.

Urban governments, religious orders, confraternities, were all involved in commissioning Marian imagery. The visitor to the Uffizi gallery in Florence who begins at the beginning is confronted in one room by three enormous enthroned Madonnas, by Cimabue, Giotto and Duccio. The three, all painted for Florentine churches, are similar in that they portray the massive figure of the Virgin, her son on her lap, seated on a throne surrounded by adoring angels.[32] The contract for Duccio's so-called Rucellai Madonna survives: it was commissioned on 15 April 1285 by the officers of the confraternity which met at the Florentine Dominican church of Santa Maria Novella.[33] In 1308 Duccio received another Marian commission, for an altarpiece which was to stand on the high altar of the cathedral of Siena.[34] In this work, which was borne to the cathedral in 1311 amidst celebrations such as might have greeted the reception of a relic, Duccio developed the idea of the *Maestà* in such a way as to emphasise the Virgin's specifically Sienese role. Kneeling as suppliants on either side of the throne are four assistant patron saints of Siena, Ansanus, Savinus, Victor and Crescentius, all martyrs whose relics lay in the cathedral;[35] behind them, evoking the entire court of heaven,

---

31 R. Starn, *Ambrogio Lorenzetti: The Palazzo Pubblico, Siena* (New York, 1994), p. 60. See also p. 72, where Giotto's majestic crowned figure of Justice in the Arena Chapel at Padua, c. 1306, is illustrated for comparative purposes, and J. H. Stubblebine, *Giotto: The Arena Chapel Frescoes* (London, 1969), pl. 62. Such a figure might be compared with the monumental enthroned Virgin and Child executed by Arnolfo di Cambio in 1302 for the facade of Florence's new cathedral, 'one of the great hieratic images of Italian Gothic art': J. White, *Art and Architecture in Italy: 1250–1400* (Harmondsworth, 1966), p. 65 and pl. 28(a).

32 All three are reproduced in White, *Art and Architecture*, pll. 50, 63, 89. So too is one of the most noteworthy early examples of a *Maestà*, the *Madonna del Bordone* by the Florentine Coppo di Marcovaldo, painted for the Sienese Servite church in 1261; the painter was enlisted as a shield-bearer in the Florentine army and according to tradition painted the picture as a prisoner of war in Siena after the battle of Montaperti, although it is not clear that this was in fact his situation (*ibid.*, p. 108, and pl. 46). Here the Virgin and Child are attended only by a couple of small-scale airborne angels.

33 J. White, *Duccio: Tuscan Art and the Medieval Workshop* (London, 1979), pp. 185–7.

34 *Ibid.*, pp. 192–3.

35 For these saints and their iconography see *I Santi Patroni Senesi*, ed. F. M. Consolino (Siena, 1992).

are ranks of saints, among them the very great and recognisable such as Peter, Katherine and John the Baptist.

Altarpieces of the Virgin and Child painted in polyptych form presented what might be termed an abstract arrangement, in which a half-length image of the principal figures is flanked by half-lengths of selected saints. By contrast, the *Maestà*, executed in more and more elaborate forms by masters such as those we have named and their predecessors from the 1260s onwards, offered the spectator a three-dimensional scene of heavenly courtly life, and explicitly demonstrated the regality of the Virgin, whether or not she wore a crown on her head.[36] One art historian has suggested that 'Duccio's idea of representing the Madonna as liege-queen surrounded by her courtiers was certainly a new one in Italian painting', with the influence behind it of both French courtly art and the imagery of the *laudes*.[37] The *laudes*, we have seen, certainly envisaged her as a queen over angels. The idea of including among the courtiers saints especially associated with Siena was further elaborated by Simone Martini when, probably in 1315, he too painted a Maestà, this time in a secular setting, the main hall of the *palazzo pubblico* of Siena.[38] The four saints of Duccio's *Maestà* reappear, once again kneeling in supplication to the Virgin and her Son, while the Virgin is now represented as a worldly queen, an elegant Gothic figure wearing a crown.

A humanist chancellor of Siena, one hundred and forty years later, remarked that the Virgin had never been absent from the counsels of the republic.[39] Simone's Virgin was the visible embodiment of that belief. The saints evidently once presented verbal petitions, but the inscriptions in which these were recorded are now lost. The Virgin's own words, however, are preserved in the inscription on her throne:

> The angelic flowers, the rose and lily
> With which the heavenly fields are decked
> Do not delight me more than righteous counsel.
> But some I see who for their own estate
> Despise me and deceive my land
> And are most praised when they speak worst.
> Whoever stands condemned by this my speech take heed.

The 'reply of the Virgin to the speeches of the saints' is also recorded:

> My beloved, bear it in mind
> When your just devotees make supplication
> I will make them content as you desire,
> But if the powerful do harm to the weak
> Weighing them down with shame or hurt

36 For the formal development see White, *Duccio*, pp. 62–79.
37 E. T. de Wald, 'Observations on Duccio's *Maestà*', in *Late Classical and Medieval Studies in Honor of Albert Mathias Friend Jr*, ed. K. Weitzmann (Princeton, 1955), p. 366.
38 Martindale, *Simone Martini*, pp. 14–17, 204–9 and pll. 1–8.
39 Agostino Dati, *Opera* (Siena, 1503), p. 230v.

Your prayers are not for those
Nor for whoever deceives my land.[40]

The child sums up the message of the fresco, for he carries a scroll bearing the opening words of the Book of Wisdom: 'Love Justice, ye who judge the world.'

A couple of years later, Simone's brother-in-law Lippo Memmi executed an imitation of this *Maestà* in the palazzo pubblico of San Gimignano. Here however the omnicompetent Virgin was requested to intercede not for the earthly welfare of the community, but for the eternal welfare of the *podestà* who commissioned the fresco. St Nicholas on his behalf hails her 'Salve regina mundi, mater Dei', adding a petition that the lucky *podestà* be numbered among the angels and patriarchs.[41] The unusually specific political orientation of Simone's fresco for the Sienese *palazzo pubblico* is emphasised by the contrast; but it is important to remember that the intercession of the queen Virgin was at least as highly prized for its effectiveness in heaven as on earth.

There is a visual, though not a theological, ambiguity in these images of the Virgin in Majesty. The Child is, of course, always present, and his presence might be taken as a reminder that the Virgin's regality is totally dependent upon his: is it she, or she with him, who is enthroned? The theme of the Coronation of the Virgin dramatises this dependent relationship. One of the earliest representations of this subject to appear in an Italian civic context forms part of the stained-glass oculus designed for the cathedral of Siena in about 1287 and once attributed to Duccio. The Coronation is at the summit of the window, in a sequential relationship with the Assumption below it and the Death of the Virgin below that. Flanking the Assumption are images of saints specially venerated in the cathedral, including three of the four who were to appear in the *Maestà* of Duccio and Simone.[42] The oculus as a whole may be described as customised for its Sienese setting by their presence. Many subsequent versions of the Coronation of the Virgin, painted for both lay and ecclesiastical communities, were similarly trademarked. In 1372, the Florentine officials of the Mint, the *Zecca*, commissioned an altarpiece of the Coronation of the Virgin, which depicts a number of saints specifically associated with Florence as witnesses to the heavenly event, grouped before the dais on which Christ and his mother are enthroned. They include John the Baptist, supreme patron of the commune, St Matthew as patron of the Zecca, Reparata, the ancient patron of the cathedral, the fourth-century Florentine bishop-saint Zenobius, and

---

[40] Martindale, p. 207; translations in White, *Duccio*, p. 96.

[41] E. Carli, *La Pittura Senese del Trecento* (Milan, 1981), pp. 119–20. C. Frugoni, *A Distant City*, trans. W. McCuaig (Princeton, 1991), p. 88 and fig. 47.

[42] White, *Duccio*, pp. 137–40; *I Santi Patroni Senesi*, pp. 84–6 and figs 1–3. The group identity of the four *santi avvocati* as represented by Duccio and Simone was clearly established by c.1300, but not it seems very long before. Victor is missing from the *oculus*; Bartholomew, who had an altar in the cathedral, is represented instead. Miniatures of the four advocates as known after 1300 accompany the large miniature of the Assumption which serves as frontispiece to the register known, consequently, as the *Caleffo dell' Assunta*. See P. d'Ancona and E. Aeschlimann, *The Art of Illumination*, trans. A. M. Brown (London, 1969), p. 223 and pl. 103.

three saints who enjoyed special cults at Florence because they had brought the commune victory or deliverance on their feast-days: Barnabas, Anne (shown holding a model of the city) and Pope Victor I. Pope Victor had given the Florentines victory over Pisa as recently as 1364, so the witness list was very up-to-date.[43] As the queen-Virgin intercedes with her son, so the courtier-saints represent to her the specific interests of their city and, like ambassadors, register their respectful attendance at a great state occasion.

There were however modes of representation of the Virgin which showed her without her son. The composition known as the Madonna della Misericordia can be associated with the piety of the confraternities. This shows the Virgin with her mantle outspread, sheltering beneath it a horde of little folk, who are sometimes identifiable by their garb as confraternity members, but sometimes represent a cross-section of human society. The earliest record of this image is of the banner of a Roman confraternity which received its statutes from St Bonaventure in the 1260s, but the earliest surviving examples come from the fourteenth century.[44] In the thirteenth century Caesarius of Heisterbach told of the Cistercian monk who had a vision of paradise, but was distressed to see none of his brethren present until the Virgin lifted her cloak to disclose a multitude of them clustered underneath.[45] We may remember here also the letter of Innocent IV to the Parmigiani, quoted earlier, in which he evokes the image of the Virgin who 'continually extends the canopy of her protection over you'.[46] In the course of the century, the Dominicans appropriated the Cistercian vision, but the earliest Sienese representation of the motif of the Virgin's protective robe is in fact a panel in which Duccio shows her sheltering a little group of Franciscans.[47] In the immediate context of the thirteenth and fourteenth centuries, it seems as if a visual image developed in professional religious contexts was adapted for the use of lay society; but it had much earlier antecedents. Possession of the Virgin's robe itself had helped to protect Constantinople;[48] and Gregory of Tours tells the story of a Jewish boy who, having received the Eucharist with his Christian schoolmates, was protected from the rage of his

---

43 Frugoni, *Distant City*, p. 152 and fig. 44.

44 P. Perdrizet, *La Vierge de la Miséricorde* (Paris, 1908); C. Belting-Ihm, *'Sub Matris Tutela':* *Untersuchungen zur Vorgeschichte der Schutzmantelmadonna*, Abhandlungen der Heidelberger Akademie der Wissenschaften, philosophisch-historisch Klasse, iii (1976); G. Schiller, *Ikonographie der christlichen Kunst*, iv/2, *Maria* (Gütersloh, 1980), pp. 195–6. In northern Europe St Ursula is often represented in the same way, as on the famous reliquary painted by Hans Memling, in the Sint Jan's Hospital at Bruges; it may be relevant that she was supposed to be the daughter of a British king.

45 *Dialogus Miraculorum*, ed. J. Strange (Cologne, 1851), ii, 79–80.

46 Above, p. 209.

47 White, *Duccio*, pp. 46, 54–5.

48 On the Virgin as protector of Constantinople, see the studies of Averil Cameron: 'The Theotokos in Sixth-Century Constantinople', *Journal of Theological Studies*, xxix (1978), 79–108; 'Images of Authority: Elites and Icons in Late Sixth-Century Byzantium', *Past and Present*, lxxxiv (1979), 3–35; and 'The Virgin's Robe: An Episode in the History of Early Seventh-Century Constantinople', *Byzantion*, xlix (1979), 42–56, all collected in *Continuity and Change in Sixth-Century Byzantium* (London, 1981).

father, even to the extent of remaining unharmed in a furnace, when the Virgin covered him with her cloak.[49] In a vision experienced by Gherardesca of Pisa in the mid-thirteenth century, Mary delegated this role to the Magdalen with the words, 'Take Gherardesca under your mantle and cover her.'[50]

This was an image which obviously and explicitly celebrated the Virgin's merciful and protective aspect. The Madonna della Misericordia painted by Lippo Memmi for a fraternity in Orvieto cathedral shows her crowned,[51] but this is by no means always the case; nor, it may be argued, was it necessary for it to be so in order to evoke in the mind of the spectator the association between the merciful disposition which made the Virgin ever-ready to undertake the defence of the weak and the royal status, as the mother and spouse of Christ, which made her an effective protector. As we have seen, that association was abundantly documented in the language in which her devotees addressed her and on occasion supported by visionary experience. Gherardesca of Pisa was given to colourful visions of the afterlife: she once saw God placing the Virgin above all the choirs of angels and saints and declaring to her, 'Today I have placed you above the peoples and kingdoms and I shall divide my kingdom with you.' He proceeded, not to crown her (although it later appears that she has a crown on her head), but to bestow upon her a *nomen gloriosissimum*, that of *Mater misericordiae*. Addressing himself then to the Son, he declares that he will be called *Pater justitiae*; but (evidently turning back to the Virgin) his justice henceforth will yield to her mercy, and what she seeks *misericorditer* will be granted by him *de plena justitia*. 'Then the blessed Virgin sat on the throne of mercy and loving kindness, reigning with God the Father in glory for ever.'[52]

Such imagery has a clear kinship with the language of patronage as it was employed in the official pronouncements of the city states. The point is well made in the record of the proceedings of the general council of Siena on 12 August 1334. It was part of the annual routine which preceded the celebration of the Feast of the Assumption to propose certain prisoners for release from gaol. This was not a custom peculiar to Siena or to festivals of the Virgin: it was commonly done at Christmas and Easter, and at other patronal festivals such as that of the Baptist at Florence. The record of the decision taken at Siena in August 1334 included, as usual, a statement of the pious rationale of the custom. It was believed that this act

---

[49] *Gloria martyrum*, ix, ed. B. Krusch, *MGH, Scriptores rerum Merovingicarum*, ii/2 (Hanover, 1888; repr. 1957), 44; trans. R. van Dam (Liverpool, 1988), p. 30. The child identified his protectress as 'the woman who was sitting on that throne in the church where I received the bread from the table and who was cradling a young boy in her lap'. It is noteworthy that the boy's *mother* tried to save him and subsequently converted with him. It is interesting also that Gregory hoped that he would at the last be covered by Martin's *sacrosancto pallio*: *De virtutibus Martini*, ii.60 (ed. Krusch, p. 180); the phrase is translated as 'sacred shroud' by van Dam, *Saints and their Miracles in Late Antique Gaul* (Princeton, 1993), p. 259.

[50] *Vita*, in *Acta Sanctorum*, Maii 4, p. 528; trans. in E. Petroff, *Consolation of the Blessed* (New York, 1979), p. 110.

[51] Carli, *La pittura senese*, pp. 120–1.

[52] *Acta Sanctorum*, Maii 4, pp. 524–5; Petroff, *Consolation of the Blessed*, p. 104.

of mercy would be pleasing to the Virgin 'since the faith, hope and sincere devotion of the Sienese is and reposes especially in the most holy mother of God, ever virgin, perpetual and glorious, as in her who is truly head, leader and defender (*capud dux & defensatrix*) of the city, contado and jurisdiction of Siena, and [since] she is the most especial and singular queen of mercy and piety . . .'.[53]

The Virgin is simultaneously the patron of the Sienese polity and the merciful Queen of Heaven, but distinct terminology is employed for her two roles, the one particular and local (however many cities might claim a share in it), the other universal. Would it be possible to go further and say that the one is earthly, in the sense that the benefits of invoking the Virgin's patronage are to be experienced by the city on earth, and the other heavenly, in that the merits earned by performing acts of mercy that are pleasing to her as Queen of Heaven will redound to the spiritual credit of Sienese citizens in the hereafter?

In fact this seems to be not so much a distinction as a duality, which is well expressed in the last chapter of the Aretine confraternity statutes: 'May the Holy Spirit impress on our minds these ordinances which have been made for our salvation and for the comfort of the poor, particularly the embarrassed poor, and for the good and peaceful state of our city; may he also long preserve our fraternity and make it grow, at the prayers of the most glorious Virgin Mary, who is the head and leader of our fraternity, so that we may deserve to come to the meeting on high of the citizens of heaven . . .'.[54] Earthly and heavenly advantages are sought and obtained simultaneously, and varied emphases are discernible in the language of different texts which describe the Virgin's civic patronage.

At Arezzo, the communal statutes produced in 1337 laid down regulations for an official offering at the Feast of the Annunciation. The wax offered on this occasion was to go to the fraternity of blessed Mary of Mercy, 'for from this our lady the people of Arezzo both in ancient and modern times recognise that they have received many benefits'.[55] The *Ordinarium* of Parma cathedral, revised in 1417, states that the feast of the Annunciation is to be celebrated as devoutly as possible, 'to induce the people of Parma to contrition and to confirm them in the devotion of the said Virgin Mary, who undoubtedly protects all who devoutly invoke her from every danger; and in this church this can and must be done, since the church of Parma is dedicated to the Virgin and she is the patron of the city and people of Parma'.[56] In the statutes of Faenza at a very similar date the emphasis

---

53 Siena, Archivio di Stato, Consiglio Generale 115, fol. 114: 'tamquam in ea que vere est capud dux & defensatrix civitatis comitatus & iurisdictionis Senensis & ipsa specialissima et singularis sit regina misericordie et pietatis'.

54 *Early Dominican Writings*, ed. Tugwell, p. 450.

55 Florence, Archivio di Stato, Statuti di communità soggette 22, fol. 1v. Arezzo in 1337 was under Florentine control, although this did not become permanent until 1384. It had in fact already been stipulated in the earliest surviving communal statutes, ten years earlier, that the fraternity should receive a hundred pounds of wax offerings made at the cathedral at the feast of the Annunciation: *Statuto di Arezzo (1327)*, ed. G. Camerani (Florence, 1946), p. 99.

56 *Ordinarium Ecclesiae Parmensis e vetustioribus excerptum reformatum a. MCCCCXVII*, ed. A. Barbieri (Parma, 1866), p. 121.

is also, as we have seen, on the Virgin's capacity to deliver the city and citizens from danger.[57] The fourteenth century statutes of Piacenza, however, declare that the purpose of the civic celebration of the Assumption is 'for the salvation of the souls of the citizens of Piacenza and of all their dead'.[58]

In the closing months of the fourteenth century a virulent outbreak of plague began to spread across northern Italy. Even as it gathered force, a wave of penitential demonstrations accompanied it. The processions of the *Bianchi*, as the participants were called because of the white robes they affected, were supposedly carried out in obedience to the instructions of the Virgin herself. The legend of her apparition to a peasant who was taking his lunch in the fields was told in a number of variants, but all agreed that Christ was so enraged by the sins of the world that he was determined to destroy it. His Mother's hope was that if mankind did penance as she directed her Son's wrath could be averted.[59] The singing of *laude* formed part of these processions, and it seems that the Virgin was invoked in them above all as 'mother'.[60] 'We run to you, holy mother Mary, who is our advocate today and always before the father Saviour . . . You are our advocate, and will be, and have been; O thou our angelic mother, avert this wrath.' Christ himself, in dialogue with the Virgin, evokes the association of her protective role with her maternity: 'Mother mine, you have always been the advocate of sinners.'[61] In conformity with the general development of the genre, many of these *laude* take a more dramatic form than their thirteenth-century predecessors. One, for example, dramatises the Virgin's encounter with the lunching peasant.[62] When he realises the danger mankind is in, he exclaims 'O sweetest queen, give me some medicine, show me some teaching, with which I can content them', meaning his fellow-mortals whom he must persuade to do penance. She replies, 'Because I have always been their mother and advocate, and for them did I receive the annunciation, I want to teach you the way.' The *lauda* ends with the peasant addressing her as 'O gracious queen, o piteous empress'. The familiar vision of the Virgin enthroned among angels is evoked in one Florentine *lauda*: 'Honoured virgin, you are accompanied by the angels.' This *lauda* also invokes the Virgin's protection on the individual city: 'Mother full of pity, conserve Florence your city, which is God's servant, with liberty.'[63] The Virgin is sometimes addressed as queen, and may even be invoked in defence of specific urban liberties, but she is above all the merciful mother of God and of humankind.

It was at about this time that the story of what had happened at Siena on the eve

---

[57] Above, p. 207.

[58] *Statuta Varia Civitatis Placentiae*, ed. G. Bonora (Parma, 1860), p. 229.

[59] See in general D. Bornstein, *The Bianchi of 1399: Popular Devotion in Late Medieval Italy* (Ithaca, 1993).

[60] Bornstein discusses *bianchi* hymn-singing, pp. 120–45. The examples quoted here are to be found in *Le Laude dei Bianchi: edizione critica dal Codice Vaticano Chigiano L. VII. 266*, ed. B. Toscani (Florence, 1979).

[61] *Le Laude*, pp. 162–9.

[62] *Ibid.*, pp. 69–81.

[63] *Ibid.*, pp. 112–14.

of the battle of Montaperti approached its full development. According to an anonymous chronicle of the late fourteenth century, the Sienese solemnly gave their city to the Virgin, 'and by this means and through prayer made to the Mother of Mercy, she defended us from all danger'.[64] A generation or so later, another chronicler imagined the people processing around the city invoking the Virgin's aid and crying out 'misericordia, misericordia, Madre nostra reina del cielo'.[65] This is familiar terminology, and we now know where it came from. The language of the *laude*, of the statutes and of the chroniclers drew on a common stock. The chroniclers were also familiar with the visual imagery of the Madonna della Misericordia. In one incident, watchers from the city observe what is at first taken to be a pall of smoke hanging over the Sienese camp, but they soon come to understand that (as it is not moving) it is in fact the Virgin's protective robe.[66] For a hundred years, from the middle years of the fifteenth century until the death of the Sienese republic at the hands of the Florentines, the image of the Virgin hovering protectively over the city became a Sienese trademark, sometimes explicitly associated with the memory of Montaperti, sometimes celebrating the Virgin's continued protection of her city in the perilous present.[67]

According to the chronicler who gives the fullest account of what was believed to have happened at Siena on the eve of Montaperti, a pious layman called Buonaguida Lucari was appointed by the government to lead the people in their penitential exercises, and addressed them thus: 'You know, signori Sanesi, that we are commended to king Manfred; now it seems to me that we should give ourselves and all we have, all the city and contado of Siena, to the queen and empress of eternal life.'[68] This imaginary speech posits a contrast between Siena's conditional, temporal relationship with the leader of the Italian Ghibellines and a proposed act of total self-surrender to an eternal being. Writing in 1456/7 Agostino Dati, the humanist chancellor of Siena, preferred Romanist phraseology, but drew a not dissimilar contrast. He explained that Siena throughout its history had been pre-served from every peril because, although it had never known an earthly lord, it had equally never lacked a *princeps*, the unconquered Mother of God.[69] The Virgin, eternally royal in heaven, appears here in the role of surrogate monarch, moral and ideological defence against earthly defeat and tyranny.

Mary's royal status was a consequence of her motherhood. As Christ took on, in word and image, the attributes of emperor and king, so the mental picture entertained by Christians of the mother of Christ had come to incorporate elements

---

64 *Cronache senesi*, edd. A. Lisini and F. Iacometti, *Rerum Italicarum Scriptores*, NS xv/2, p. 58.

65 *Ibid.*, p. 202.

66 *Ibid.*, p. 207.

67 T. Burckhardt, *Siena: The City of the Virgin*, trans. M. M. Brown (London, 1960), pp. 94, 99, illustrates two early sixteenth-century examples: the woodcut frontispiece of a book about Montaperti and a fresco commissioned in 1528 to commemorate the repulse of Florentine forces from the Porta Camollia.

68 *Cronache senesi*, p. 201.

69 Dati, *Opera*, p. 230 v.

of the demeanour and activities of the mothers of earthly monarchs. The crowned or uncrowned figure seated on a throne surrounded by courtiers represents the externals of that development. The Pisan *lauda* which seems glancingly to envisage Mary as a regent for her Son, left behind *in sua vece*, or the picture, in another *lauda*, of the Virgin who ruled and had power to grant pardon, hint at its inner substance.[70] The verbal association, in the Italian sources which I have been quoting, of her queenship with her mercy, takes us to its heart.

The importance of works of charity and mercy to royal women who in a variety of medieval times and places came to be regarded as saints has often been remarked. In Merovingian Gaul, in Anglo-Saxon England, in Margaret's Scotland, in the emergent kingdoms of eastern Europe, the mothers, wives and daughters of kings were pictured as softening the harshness of the regimes presided over by their menfolk, civilising their courts, ensuring their almsgiving.[71] There was no such native Italian tradition of royal saintly women, although the fame of Elisabeth of Thuringia spread over the peninsula thanks to the Franciscans, and the *Ordinarium* of Parma unexpectedly testifies that St Radegund had done miracles in that city.[72] It was the late medieval urban bourgeoisie who embraced the penitential life which, certainly in east-central Europe, recruited women of royal blood.[73] Here too, Mary could enact for an Italian audience a royal role which was, as a model, perfectly well understood even if it lacked native flesh-and-blood exemplars.

I recall from the earliest history-book I ever possessed a coloured picture of a bloody, bold and resolute Edward III, gazing unforgivingly into the middle distance in his rage at the burghers of Calais, while at his feet Philippa of Hainault, hair and tears flowing, pleads for mercy. The Virgin who counters the seemingly implacable wrath of her offended Son, who in turn indulgently calls her 'ever the advocate of sinners', exemplifies this influential pattern. The Italian sources I have quoted carefully associate the word *regina* with two of Mary's aspects: her presence, surrounded by angels, in the court of heaven, and her never-failing exercise of mercy. In normal official parlance her patronage was described in terms which differentiated it little if at all from the patronage of other saints, but the eagerness of cities by the later Middle Ages to claim a special relationship with the Virgin, if they had not already done so, indicates clearly that, here as every-

---

[70] Above, p. 211.

[71] For some general observations on the changing role of charity in female sanctity, see J.A. McNamara, 'The Need to Give: Suffering and Female Sanctity In the Middle Ages', in *Images of Sainthood in Medieval Europe*, edd. R. Blumenfeld-Kosinski and T. Szell (Ithaca, 1991), pp. 199–221. On charitable activity as part of a programme of ascetic self-denial adopted by royal women, see G. Klaniczay, 'Legends as Life-Strategies for Aspirant Saints in the Later Middle Ages', in *The Uses of Supernatural Power* (Cambridge, 1990), pp. 95–110.

[72] *Ordinarium*, p. 181. Speaking of Radegund's altar in the cathedral the author remarks 'ut patet, multis claruit et claret miraculis'. The editor of the text was unable to trace any contemporary evidence of these miracles. It may be noted, however, that there was both a cult of St Hilary and a church of the Holy Cross in Parma.

[73] A. Vauchez, *La Sainteté en Occident aux derniers siècles du moyen âge* (Rome, 1981), p. 207; cf. Klaniczay (above, n. 69).

where in Europe, that patronage was well understood to be uniquely worth having. Among the rulers of the cities and the lawyers who drafted the statutes were men who stood at compline in the local Preachers' church and heard the *Salve Regina*, and who themselves perhaps joined in the singing of her praises as queen in confraternities of *laudesi*. They were familiar with images of her enthroned before a cloth of honour, or under a *baldacchino*, which betokened both sacrality and majesty; they saw her surrounded by saint and angel courtiers. Even when they envisaged her as the Mother of Mercy, the awareness that it was her regality which made her disposition to mercy effective can never have been far away, and her regality depended so immediately upon her motherhood of God that images of her as queen and as mother must have been profoundly interpenetrated in the consciousness of her worshippers. Triumphantly, and almost single-handedly, Mary represented to Italians the mercy and charity of queens.

12

Queens as Scapegoats in Medieval Hungary

János M. Bak

In a brief survey of eleventh- to fourteenth-century Hungarian queens, I called their becoming scapegoats for poor government or bad times one of their 'functions'.[1] This 'function' cost the lives of two medieval queens and the posthumous 'moral assassination' of a third. In comparison, during the same period of close to four hundred years, one king was murdered for obvious political reasons and another probably for personal ones.[2] The following discussion will explore the particular elements that made queens 'suitable' for this role, beyond the commonplace (medieval) Judeo-Christian prejudice that women – successors of Eve – were agents of Evil.

The chronologically first example is only partly pertinent to our topic, for the princely woman is only by implication regarded as guilty for things disapproved of by the author (and not by her subjects). I am thinking of Thietmar of Merseburg's negative image of Sarolt, wife of Grand Prince Géza and mother of King (St)

---

[1] 'Role and Function of Queens in Árpádian and Angevin Hungary (AD 1000–1386)', in *Medieval Queenship*, ed. Parsons, pp. 13–24.

[2] I wrote (*ibid.*) that no male ruler of Hungary died by an assassin's hand, while three queens were slain (the last being Elisabeth, queen of Franz Joseph, killed by an anarchist in Geneva in 1898) and a fourth suffered a *post mortem* moral assassination. In fact, two Hungarian kings, Ladislas IV, 'the Cuman', and Charles II, 'the Short', were murdered. Ladislas was killed in 1290 by one of his favourite Cuman warriors, either hired by magnates opposed to the king and his alleged maladministration of the realm or in consequence of some personal conflict or jealousy within the Cuman camp (we know nothing of the details). A century later, Charles of Durazzo, king of Hungary for about six weeks, was killed in February 1387 by men of the dowager queen Elisabeth Kotromanić – about whom later. Careless oversight on my part, no doubt, but I believe it is significant that I (and probably many others in Hungary) remember these two murders only when reminded, thus, in a way justifying them. Ladislas the Cuman had a miserably bad press in his time and for centuries afterwards, and Carolus Parvus was always seen as an evil usurper who had forced the widow and daughter of the highly regarded Louis of Anjou (the only Hungarian king called 'the Great' at least since the sixteenth century) to resign in his favour. In my mind, the killing of queens clearly overshadowed these two murders, to which might be added the poisoning of further male rulers, if we had sufficient evidence or were able to give credence to contemporary gossip. But the killing of women leaves a deeper impression in historical tradition and even in the mind of inattentive historians. It is, therefore, more correct to say that the real or moral assassination of queens as scapegoats was, even if not a numerically unique event in the ruling house, at least one that left a lasting imprint in the collective memory of the nation.

Stephen I. The colourful passage describing Beleknegi (her Slavic name) who drank heavily, rode like a *miles*, and once even killed a man, has oft been quoted.[3] Her husband, Géza, is reported to have been weak in adherence to the true faith and was supposed to have said that he was rich enough to venerate both his own pagan gods and the Christian one.[4] There is no express connection between the negative image of Sarolt and the less-than-perfect Christianity of her husband. But the opposite figure of the devoted and pious queen who converts her husband or strengthens him in the faith is all too well known[5] not to suggest that this passage is meant as a mirror image, as a bad example, not to be followed by princely wives.

The most interesting case is that of Sarolt's daughter-in-law, Queen Gisela of Bavaria, wife of St Stephen, the first Christian king of the country. Her case also has the advantage of not being connected with grisly details of a woman's murder. Near-contemporary sources know very little of her, and what they mention are all actions 'typical' of Christian queens assisting their evangelising husbands. There is some evidence about her almsgiving and pious foundations[6] and, of course, a tangible one too: the present-day coronation mantle of the kings of Hungary was originally a chasuble donated by Gisela to the royal collegiate church at Alba Regia (Székesfehérvár), with her own – and her husband's – portrait on it. It was probably embroidered by the queen's entourage or even by herself and her ladies.[7] The traditional Christian queen is also the image we receive in the early legends of her husband, written in the late eleventh century.[8] However, in the Hungarian chronicle – which survives only in fourteenth-century compilations, but which has been shown to go back in parts to the eleventh and twelfth[9] – Gisela suddenly appears in an entirely different light.

---

3 *Thietmari Merseburgensis episcopi Chronicon*, viii.4, ed. R. Holtzmann, *MGH SRG*, NS, ix (Berlin, 1935; repr. 1980), 498.
4 *Ibid.*, p. 497.
5 The examples abound: from Chlotilde and Chlovis of the Franks to Dubravka and Mieszko I of Poland, and so on. The biblical passage from I Cor. 7:14, '. . . sanctificabatur vir per mulierem fidelem' is explicitly quoted by the author of the *Chronicon Hungaro-Polonicum* à propos the missionary activity of the (legendary) Queen Adelheid; see *Chron. Hung.-Pol.*, c. 3, ed. J. Deér in *Scriptores rerum Hungaricarum tempore ducum regumque stirpis Arpadianae gestarum* [= *SRH*], ed. I. Szentpétery (Budapest, 1938), ii, 305.
6 That is what, e.g., Hermann of the Reichenau knew about her (*MGH SS*, v, 117). Several sources (e.g. the legends of St Stephen) regard Gisela as the founder of Veszprém cathedral. The nearby nuns' convent in Veszprémvölgy (completed in 1007) is also reputed to be founded by her. In fact, Veszprém (in western Hungary, north of Lake Balaton) seems to have been associated with the spouse of the ruler before the time of St Stephen, and remained so. The bishop of Veszprém had the right to crown the (non-reigning) queens and usually served as their chancellors. In fact, Alberic of Troisfontaines repeated the general statement that she was instrumental in baptising the pagan Magyars, before calumniating her (see below, n. 15).
7 Cf. É. Kovács and Zs. Lovag, *The Hungarian Crown and Other Regalia*, 2nd edn (Budapest, 1985), pp. 75–81.
8 *Legenda Maior S. Stephani*, c. 9, ed. E. Bartoniek, *SRH*, ii, 384–5.
9 The dating of the different original parts of the surviving text is one of the thorniest issues of Hungarian medieval scholarship; there is, however, consensus that the earliest parts were

The chronicler reports that after the death of his son, Imre (Henry), King Stephen was desolate. He suffered from pains in the leg and began to decline in bodily power. He, therefore, sent a messenger to Nitra, where his nephew (?) Vazul (Basil?) was incarcerated for some juvenile trespass, in order to make him his successor. The queen, so the story goes, upon hearing this, took council with an evil man named Buda and sent the latter's son, Sebus, to Nitra. Sebus blinded Vazul, poured hot lead into his ears and fled to Bohemia.[10] When the king's messenger arrived and saw the tragic condition of the man, he took him to Stephen, who *in nimias lacrimas erupit*, but was unable to punish the evildoer. However he warned the 'sons of László Szár' (whose relationship to Vazul is debated), Andrew, Béla and Levente, to escape abroad. The queen is then again mentioned after the death of Stephen as making – together with her accomplice Buda – 'her brother Peter the German or rather Venetian' king so that she might unimpeded pursue her own will and subject the kingdom to German rule.[11]

The motives for this interpretation – and thus the factors that made Gisela a scapegoat *post factum* – are relatively easy to establish. Assuming that the passages defaming Gisela originated in the later eleventh century (which is usually assumed by editors and students of the chronicles[12]), they were written at a time when the ruling monarchs, the aforementioned Andrew, Béla and their sons, were descendants of a relative of St Stephen, the enigmatic László Szár, or of Vazul himself. However, by that time, the saintly reputation of Stephen, the founder of the Christian kingdom, was considerable: in 1083 he and his prematurely deceased son, Imre, were inscribed in the catalogue of saints. The spiritual and political authority of St Stephen was part of the dynasty's legitimation; hence, the horrible deed against the progenitor of the ruling kings did not fit well into his saintly image. (Blinding as a mode of excluding an unwanted relative from succession, especially under unclear rules of inheritance, was a widespread method, especially in Byzantium, and it is recorded again, a century after the blinding of Vazul.[13] The reference to the hot lead seems to have been a later invention: the contemporary *Altaich Annals*[14] know nothing of it.) The conflicts with the German-Roman Empire, where King Andrew's son, Salomon, against whom the Hungarian lords seem to have supported his cousin (St) Ladislas, had enhanced anti-German (or in

---

composed in the later eleventh century, continued in the twelfth, extensively augmented in the later thirteenth and finally compiled in the fourteenth century. On these issues, C. A. Macartney, *The Medieval Hungarian Historians: A Critical and Analytical Guide* (Cambridge, 1953), although in parts challenged or refuted, is still useful.

10 'Audiens autem hoc Keisla regina iniit concilium cum Buda viro nephando et festinantissime misit nuncium nomine Sebus filium ipsius Buda ad carcerem . . . Sebus itaque preveniens nuncium regis effodit oculos Vazul et concavitates aurium eius plumbo obturaviet et recessit in Bohemiam', *Chronici Hungarici compositio saeculi XIV*, c. 69, ed. A. Domanovszky, *SRH*, i, 320.

11 'Keysla motus sue voluntatis pro libitu suo posset complere et regnum amisssa libertate Teutonicis subderetur sine impedimento', *ibid.*, c. 70 (*SRH*, i, 322).

12 See above, n. 9.

13 See below, at n. 16.

14 *MGH SS*, xx, 794.

general anti-foreigner) feelings in exactly the same decades. (It would depend on the exact dating of the original composition of the relevant passages, whether these attitudes might also have been informed by Hungary's frequent adherence to the papal side in the Investiture Contest.) Nothing seemed more 'logical' than to place the blame for the cruel deed on the queen, a 'German' and a 'scheming female'. Her being blamed for the support of the unpopular King Peter Orseolo, of Venetian origin, though in fact a nephew of King Stephen and only a remote relative of Gisela, was not unwarranted, as she found it appropriate to execute her late husband's will. The calumny stuck, so that, for example, Alberic of Troisfontaines reports centuries later that Gisela, *ut dicunt*, 'committed many evil things in the country' and wants us to know that she was duly killed after her holy husband's death.[15]

To keep the chronological order, it is appropriate to record the unhappy fate of Eufemia of Kiev, daughter of Prince Vladimir Monomach, second queen of King Koloman (1096–1116). The very incomplete record is only that a year or two after their marriage the queen was accused of adultery and sent back home – pregnant. She died in a Kievan monastery twenty-three years later. (Her son Boris, declared illegitimate, caused much trouble for decades, claiming a right to the throne.) What may have been the real background is not known.[16] Thus it cannot be decided whether she was made a 'scapegoat' for some mishap.

It was also in the twelfth century that – in contrast to some of her successors – a powerful queen 'got away with it'. Queen Ilona (Helena), the Serbian wife of King Béla II, 'the Blind' (together with his father, blinded in childhood by his uncle in order that he be excluded from succession), in co-operation with her able brother, ban Belosh, not only ran the realm with and for her husband successfully, but was instrumental in the bloody revenge they took on those lords who were supposed to have been involved in Béla's blinding. Contemporaries and national memory alike seem to have accepted the execution of some sixty-eight magnates at the meeting of 1131 (or 1132) in Arad, engineered by Queen Ilona.[17] Or, to be more cynical, no one was left alive to spread her bad fame.

The reconstruction of the murder of Queen Gertrude of Andechs-Merania, wife

---

[15] *MGH SS*, xxiii, 779. In fact, Gisela died as abbess of the convent of Passau-Niederburg, where she is buried. Her grave was for a long time a pilgrimage centre for Hungarians and she has been included in the *Acta Sanctorum* (2 May, p. 133), without having ever been canonised: see A. Uzsoki, 'Das Passauer Gisella-Grab im Spiegel der neuen Forschung' in *Gizella és kora* [G. and her age] (Veszprém, 1993), pp. 70–9; E. Boshof, 'Die bayerisch-ungarischen Kontakte zur Zeit Giselas', *ibid.*, pp. 80–8. (There were rumours that efforts were afoot to have her canonised for the 'millecentennarium' of Hungary in 1996, or some other suitable national festivity, with special reference to Hungary's hopes to join the European Union.)

[16] *Chron. Hung. comp. s. XIV*, c. 149 (*SRH*, i, 429); cf. A. Hodinka, 'Kálmánfi (Kolomanovics) Boris' in *Történelmi Tár* (Budapest, 1889).

[17] The chronicler (from the wording of the passage probably an author of the thirteenth century) has the queen address the meeting: 'volo audire cur dominus noster [vester] rex suis oculis sit privatum et quorum consilio hoc sit actum? modo mihi propalate et eos fideliter in hoc loco vindicantes, nobis de ipsis finem date.' *Chron. Hung. comp. s. XIV*, c. 160 (*SRH*, i, 447).

of Andrew II, is on the one hand quite simple, on the other quite difficult. She was assassinated in the course of a magnates' plot on 28 September 1213, after ten years' reign as queen of Hungary.[18] The motives of the conspirators are obscure and have been over-interpreted in the light of national historiography and romantic xenophobia. Domestic and foreign chronicles, donation charters for those who remained true to the king and queen – and then, twenty years later, King Béla's (Gertrude's son) actions after his accession to the throne against the conspirators – offer bits and pieces of evidence. They talk about a group of magnates (according to some sources including the highest officer of the realm, the count palatine, Bánk, himself) who, irritated by the queen's favouring her 'German' relatives – among whom Berthold of Andechs became archbishop of Kalocsa – attacked the encampment of Gertrude while her husband was waging war abroad, cruelly murdered her and cut her in pieces.[19] It was a typical palace revolt by the highest dignitaries of the realm who felt by-passed by the king's and the queen's favourites. However, by the end of the century the story became more colourful. Authors pretended to know that the motive of Bánk (whose actual role in the revolt is very doubtful, since he is listed among high dignitaries well after the event), was 'revenge for the sin committed against his wife'. Both versions of Hungarian chronicles – in their present form compiled in the following century – mention this motive. The seducer of the magnate's wife in the royal court is described as 'a guest relative of the queen'.[20] Henry of Mügeln, the Bavarian historical poet of the mid-fourteenth century – whose work is assumed to utilise texts since lost – wrote in so many words that the queen 'gave the wife of a magnate . . . to her brother, Bishop [Berthold] of Bamberg so that he could rape her. When the magnate heard this, he slew the queen.'[21]

---

18   On Gertrude and the Andechs-Meranians, see A. Kraut, 'Gertrud von Andechs, Königin von Ungarn, im Lichte der ungarischen Geschichtsschreibung und Literatur', *Lech-Isar-Land* (Weilheim, 1972), pp. 135–53; F. Hervay, 'Die Geschwister der heiligen Hedwig in Ungarn', *Archiv für schlesische Kirchengeschichte*, xl (1982), 223–40.

19   To this event, tradition connects an anecdote: Archbishop John of Esztergom (who may have resented the promotion of 'Meranian' clerks by the queen, but who otherwise does not seem to have been implicated in the plot) replied to the conspirators, when they asked his counsel, with the following message, 'Reginam occidere nolite timere bonum est si omnes consenserint ego non contradico'. The meaning of the sentence depends on the punctuation (before or after 'timere', and 'est', after 'consenserint' or after 'non') and was, supposedly, intended to be equivocal. The story was first recorded (if I am not mistaken) in Alberic of Troisfontaines (above, n. 15), but experts note that similar word-plays have been attributed to several other murders, such as those of Queen Joan (wife of Philip the Fair) of France and King Edward II of England, and were, anyhow, favourite games of medieval students (cf. B. Tóth, *Szájrul szájra . . .* [By Word of Mouth: Sayings of Hungarians], 2nd edn [Budapest, 1901], pp. 13f). At any rate, we all learned it in school and thus received a good lesson on necessary care in editing unpunctuated texts.

20   *Chron. Hung. comp. s. XIV*, c. 174 (*SRH*, i, 464f).

21   'Die selb kungin Gerdraud gab ein grossen fursten weib, der hiesz Banan, iren pruder, den pischoff von Bobenberg, das er sie beschlieff mit gewalt. Do der furst das erfür do slug er die kungin czu tode.' *Chron. Henrici de Mügeln*, c. 61, ed. E. Travnik, *SRH*, ii, 206. There is also an earlier (before 1285?) reference to the seduction story in the *Annales Austriae* (ed.

The incident raises a number of questions. First, it clearly repeats the xenophobic aspect of the Gisela-story. Queens were usually foreigners, almost by definition. Besides the political and diplomatic need for intermarriages, there was frequently open disapproval of a king marrying someone from his own country, a 'subject'.[22] Of course, such a marriage also carried the danger of a magnate family's getting too close to the throne. To avoid all that, most rulers of medieval Europe married from abroad, and in central Europe this might be called a rule. Charging 'foreigners' with harming the country's interests was as old as the emergence of more or less 'national' monarchies, if not older. Thus, even without an explicit implication of gender, queens, as highly visible and powerful 'foreigners' were logical choices for the role of a scapegoat.

The anecdotal detail of the seduction *topos* points to two additional aspects. The first, well-known to medievalists, is the assumption that women will succumb to seduction, if not closely supervised, and that men will always seduce (or rape?) women, if not hindered. The second is what I should like to call the 'cultural gap'. While we know little about the details, it can be assumed that the Hungarian-Bavarian (Andechs-Meranian) royal court of Andrew and Gertrude, to an extent 'westernised', was a milieu very far from the fairly simple way of life of Hungarian noble families, however rich or powerful. This was a time when the 'internationalisation' of European nobilities on crusades and similar joint enterprises had barely reached Hungary. The first rudiments of chivalric lifestyle, connected to changes in military organisation and technology, appeared in Hungary under Andrew II in whose court (*aula*) there is mention of *milites* and of noblemen who grew up together, hinting at the beginnings of courtly education of 'knaves'.[23] The cultural distance between poorly heated, rough country houses and castles, built of wood,[24] and the royal court must have been significant. Suspicion and dislike for the 'decadent' and 'sinful' life there could have travelled easily to the countryside and become enlarged en route. And finally, with due reverence to the honour of Mrs Bánk: it is not unthinkable – again in the context of 'cultural distance' – that a foreign knight or clerk, worldly wise and skilful with flattering words, might have easily won the favour of a somewhat naïve lady. (The topos of a girl seduced by the queen's entourage came up again – with exactly the same lack of any actual evidence to its truth – a century later, in the Záh episode.)[25]

The subsequent decades were characterised by holy princesses in Hungary and

---

Pertz, *MGH SS*, ix, 726), but the authenticity of the relevant continuation of the annals is debated and the passage may have been an interpolation of later date.

[22] Explicit criticism of a ruler who married 'a subject' was voiced in Poland, e.g. by the chronicler Jan Długosz in the fifteenth century and in a formal way at the diet of Piotrków 1548 (regarding Barbara of Radziwiłł); see A. Brzezińska, 'Political Significance of Love Magic Accusations at the Jagiellonian Court', M. A. thesis (Budapest CEU, 1995), pp. 74ff.

[23] Á. Kurcz, *Lovagi kultúra Magyarországon a 13–14. században* [Chivalric Culture in Hungary in the Thirteenth–Fourteenth Centuries] (Budapest, 1988), pp. 443, 445, 451.

[24] There were hardly any stone castles a generation later, when the Mongols attacked Hungary in 1241: see E. Fügedi, *Castle and Society in Medieval Hungary (1000–1437)* (Budapest, 1986), pp. 42–50.

[25] See below, at n. 28.

neighbouring states – Elisabeth of Hungary-Thuringia, St Margaret of Hungary, St Hedwig of Silesia and so on, about whom Gábor Klaniczay and André Vauchez have written extensively.[26] Certainly they were not made scapegoats by their contemporaries for failings in the realm, but in another sense they 'took the sins of the world upon themselves'. Thus, in a certain way, they did play what one might call the positive role of the biblical scapegoat. Margaret expressly spoke of her sacrificial life as a price for the peace which she helped to sponsor between father and brother.[27] But to include them here would be perhaps to strain the definition.

There is some scant evidence that the unsuccessful assassination attempt against King Charles of Anjou and his family in 1330 – foiled by the vigilance of bodyguards – had something to do with Queen Elisabeth Piast (in fact, it was the queen who suffered irreparable damage, losing four fingers in the attack). According to some sources, Elisabeth was accused by the attacker, a certain Felician Záh, of having assisted in the seduction of his daughter, Clare, by the queen's brother, Prince Casimir (later King Casimir the Great of Poland, 1333–70);[28] but this alleged motive resembles too closely the thirteenth-century story of Melinda Bánk to be taken at face value. However, chroniclers record the horrible punishment of Clare, who was expelled from the court and forced to ride around from place to place, half alive, with a cruelly mutilated face, proclaiming: 'Such punishment will reach all who betray the king!'[29] That she was a lady at court is thus proven, and this fragment of truth may have given rise to the rest of the story.

The tragic death of Elisabeth Kotromanić, widow of Louis I (1342–82), also exemplifies our subject. Since the records of the later fourteenth century allow a little more characterisation, we may risk outlining her personality and actions. A Bosnian princess, born in a region where powerful women played important roles in politics,[30] she must have suffered during the long years of powerlessness besides

---

26 See, among others, G. Klaniczay, 'Legends as Life-Strategies for Aspirant Saints in the Later Middle Ages', and 'The Cult of Dynastic Saints in Central Europe: Fourteenth-Century Angevins and Luxemburgs', *idem, The Uses of Supernatural Power*, trans. S. Singerman, ed. K. Margolis (Cambridge, 1990), pp. 95–128; A. Vauchez, ' "Beata stirps" sainteté et lignage en Occident aux XIIIe et XIVe siècles', *Famille et parenté dans l'Occident médiéval*, edd. G. Duby and J. Le Goff (Rome, 1977), pp. 397–406.
27 See T. Klaniczay and G. Klaniczay, *Szent Margit legendái és stigmái* [Legends and Stigmata of St Margaret] (Budapest, 1994), esp. pp. 141–75.
28 While the Hungarian chronicles (*Chron. Hung. comp. s. xiv*, c. 207 [*SRH*, i, 495]) do not mention anything of the seduction, Henry of Mügeln, who wrote his German chronicle *c.* 1365, added the seduction story (c. 71 [*SRH*, ii, 219]), and became the source for several later writers, such as Jan Długosz and others. There is evidence that the whole episode found its way into vernacular poetry or broadsheets, but the older studies on the subject remained too close to legal argumentation to be able to resolve the puzzle. It would also be important to explore whether there were strong feelings of animosity against 'the Poles' (the queen and her brother) that may have motivated the accusation.
29 *Chron. Hung. comp. s. xiv*, c. 207 (*SRH*, i, 495).
30 Her younger contemporary, Milica, widow of Prince Lazar who fell in the battle of Kosovo (1389), ruled Serbia alone for many years as regent for his son Stephen, and her sister-in-law, Mara Branković, was the leading spirit of the opposing camp among Serbian magnates. I

her mother-in-law (the lady who lost the fingers), whose presence in Hungarian-Polish politics was overwhelming until just a few years before her death in 1380. The younger Elisabeth became a widow soon after, with two daughters, Mary and Hedwig/Jadwiga, respectively promised the thrones of Hungary and Poland, though in both realms the resistance to a female ruler was considerable.[31] The question of the Polish succession was swiftly resolved by the election in Cracow of Hedwig/Jadwiga, quickly married to the pagan Lithuanian Grand Duke Jagiello (Jogaila) who – as the well-known formula goes – submitted to baptism at her request. She died early (1399), but her husband became the founder of Poland's second great dynasty.[32]

In Hungary, the regency automatically fell to Elisabeth, who, it seems, had been waiting for this chance for some time. She had her own following, especially the magnate clan of the lords of Gara (Garai), who were to play leading roles in Hungarian politics for several generations; but there were other groupings of magnates, and all of them had their own agenda and their own choice for the succession. Many supported the claims of Mary, while seeking to influence her marriage: some wanted a husband from the neighbouring Bohemia (Sigismund of Luxemburg), while others – including Queen Elisabeth – wished to revert to the French-Angevin connection; but a powerful faction, mainly of lords from the south, wanted to exclude Mary and elevate Charles of Durazzo, a relative of late King Louis and an Angevin from the Neapolitan-Sicilian branch of the family, who had been viceroy of Croatia-Slavonia a few years earlier. Elisabeth tried to play the various baronial cliques and suitors against one another, dropping and raising the one or the other aristocratic party to power, as medieval rulers often did, but she was unable to avoid disorder and bloodshed.

Despite Mary's marriage to Sigismund of Luxemburg, the struggles of the baronial factions led to ever deeper anarchy, reminiscent of the situation two

owe the 'portrait' of these formidable women to my colleague Ivica Prlender from Zagreb, who is going to publish his study on Katarina Branković (Mara's daughter) in the near future; until then, see I. Prlender, 'Kosovska bitva i obnova srpske drzave' [The Battle of Kosovo and the Renewal of the Serbian State], *Historijski zbornik* (1989), pp. 97–104.

31 Erik Fügedi had pointed out, from his inquiries into the history of the Hungarian noble family (e.g. in 'Kinship and Privilege: The Social System of Medieval Hungarian Nobility as Defined in Customary Law', *Nobilities in Central and Eastern Europe: Kinship, Property and Privilege*, ed. J. M. Bak, History and Society, 2/Medium Ævum Quotidianum, 29 (Budapest, 1994), pp. 55–76, esp. 62–4) that the political nation of that country, i.e. the noble commonwealth, was perhaps one of the most misogynist in a misogynist medieval Europe. Female inheritance of estates was virtually impossible, unless the king declared a daughter a male heir. And, characteristically, this was done by King Louis I, father of the two royal heiresses! Hungarian genealogical records fail even to mention the names of women in more than half of the cases, down to the end of the fifteenth century. Fügedi may have overstated his case, for conditions in the rest of Europe were not much better, but he has a point. Although no similar study is known to me from Poland, I venture to assume that women's status was not very different there either.

32 On her see the posthumous (and somewhat dated but very thorough) study of O. Halecki, *Jadwiga of Anjou and the Rise of East Central Europe*, ed. T. V. Gromada (Boulder, Col., 1991).

generations earlier, when only the strong hands of the two successive Angevin kings stopped the disorder. This time, the 'favouritism' of Elisabeth's regency and her young daughter's 'incapacity' were blamed. The so-called Neapolitan faction managed to lure Charles of Durazzo to Buda, where they forced the queens to abdicate and crowned him king of Hungary on the last day of 1386. As mentioned earlier,[33] Elisabeth's men cut him down and he died less than two months after his coronation. The rebellion now became more widespread. Nevertheless, Elisabeth, convinced that her royal dignity would calm the opposition, set out for Zagreb. Ambushed *en route*, her entourage – with the old palatine Gara at its head – fought courageously and was killed to the last man, while the two women fell into the hands of their enemies. Elisabeth is reported to have taken all blame for the factional strife upon herself and begged for the life of her daughter. They were incarcerated in a fortress on the Adriatic, and Elisabeth, still only in her mid-forties, was strangled in front of her daughter when her captors discovered that she had smuggled out plans for their relief to the Venetians.[34] Not long afterwards, Sigismund of Luxemburg managed to liberate his wife (Queen Mary), tricked the opposing party into submission, and finally executed some of its leaders, reigning as king of Hungary until 1437 (and emperor, 1410–37). Mary herself died in 1395, from an accident while pregnant, never having exercised power.

Although the dramatic story of Elisabeth Kotromanić is the last of its kind and no queen reigned in Hungary until Maria Theresa, the *topos* of the queen as a danger to the commonwealth did not vanish from the political arsenal. King Sigismund's second wife, Barbara of Cilly (Celje), who became very wealthy by lending cash to the almost always bankrupt king and acquiring in pledge a great number of castles, was seen by the Hungarian lords as an evil influence on the king-emperor. True, his foreign counsellors were also regularly blamed – even though several of them made important contributions to the country's administration and defence. But Barbara, again the mother only of a daughter, which made her position weak, came to be regarded as so dangerous, particularly for the succession of her daughter and son-in-law (another Elisabeth and Albert of Habsburg), that she was taken captive during the last weeks of her husband's life and released only after his death. Once the succession was secure enough to satisfy the barons, they 'merely' cancelled a good part of Barbara's totally legitimate financial claims. In Bohemia, where Barbara spent the rest of her life (to 1451) she was accused – not without good grounds – of supporting the claims of the Jagiellos of Poland, the royal candidates of the Hussite magnates.[35]

The attitude to Queen Beatrix of Naples, wife of Matthias I (Corvinus), was in

---

[33] See above, n. 2.

[34] The fifteenth-century chronicler, Johannes Thuróczy (*Chronica*, c. 196, edd. J. Galántai and J. Kristó [Budapest, 1985], pp. 205–6), reflecting upon her fate, regards the killing as lawful punishment for the murder of Charles of Durazzo (whose death, in turn, he interprets as divine retribution for his sins against the queens, among others), thus denying the 'scapegoat' character of Elisabeth, *ex post*.

[35] See E. Mályusz, *Kaiser Sigismund in Ungarn 1387–1437*, trans. A. Smodits (Budapest, 1990), p. 155.

some aspects similar: she, too, was suspected of hindering the succession in 1490. She may well been opposed to the accession of Matthias's bastard son to her late husband's throne and might have hoped for some role in government. Before that, however, the opposition to Matthias's strong government had included the queen among the alleged causes for lavish spending at court. The court historian, Bonfini, describes in detail the 'civilising' measures of Beatrix, from stressing the importance of formal royal ceremonial to introducing Latin cuisine to the sponsorship of foreign artists and authors. 'The Hungarians, insensitive to culture and enjoyment', continues the Florentine Bonfini, 'looked askance at all this, decried the boundless spending and defamed the royal majesty for ... abandoning the ancient mores.' The charges also included the claim that 'foreigners are stealing not only the country's gold but the entire country bit by bit, through the king's laxity'.[36] These grumblings may be milder than the violent attacks on foreign queens, but the *topoi* are there.

Finally, the last medieval queen of the country, Mary of Habsburg, may join this company insofar as the 'national party' of the early sixteenth century never wearied of blaming her for court intrigue (and also, later, of secretly supporting Protestantism), for favouring the south German capitalist Fuggers and their Hungarian allies, the Thurzó, and so on. Yet, as far as the record can be trusted, almost the opposite was true. Mary and her counsellors were well versed in royal finances and did their best to make good deals with the mining-banking consortia, which the Magyar magnates did not understand and merely regarded – to use the language of our day – 'as an international plutocratic conspiracy'. With little success, to be sure. The country's resources were too meagre for the task of defence, the devaluation of the currency could not be stopped, cancelling the 'privatisation' of the mines caused further decline, and so on.[37] But before the conflicts could become more violent, time ran out for Mary and her husband in the 1520s. Louis died fleeing the Ottomans after the lost battle at Mohács, and the queen left Hungary, only to become the unpopular representative of Habsburg absolutism in the Netherlands, but now in her own right.[38]

I am sure that if the sources for the Hungarian Middle Ages were richer, we would know more about accusations and abuses of queens and princesses. But that is what we have – or, more modestly, that is what I have found so far. What do these episodic, partly anecdotal details add up to? Queens were apt to be regarded as instigators of evil not only because of their sex but because they tended to be foreigners and, to boot, usually the highest ranking foreigners in the land.[39]

36 Antonio Bonfini, *Rerum Hungaricarum decades*, iv. 7, ed. I Fógel *et al.. (Leipzig/Budapest, 1941), pp. 99f.*

37 See A. Kubinyi, 'The Road to Defeat', in *From Hunyadi to Rákóczi. War and Society in Medieval and Early Modern Hungary* (Boulder, Col., 1982), edd. J. Bak and B. Király, pp. 159–78.

38 I understand that Elisabeth MacCartney (University of Iowa) is planning soon to present a monograph on her both as 'queen dowager of Hungary' and governor of the Low Countries.

39 In fact, some kings of non-native dynasties were also apostrophised as incapable rulers: in Hungary most explicitly Wladislas II (1490–1515). A noble confederation in 1505 explicitly

Moreover, when there was dissatisfaction with the government it was usual to blame not the king but the 'evil counsellors', and queens were regarded as having the ear of the sovereign more than anyone else. At the same time, it is also true that queens who did not content themselves with being pious intercessors and charitable benefactors in the shadow of their husbands were particularly liable to be charged with misuse of power – that is, if they transgressed their role model. Most, if not all, the accusations against Gertrude or Elisabeth Kotromanić – as tyrants or nepotists or evil influences on their men – were due to this 'usurpation'. They seem to have been neither better nor worse than their male contemporaries – but, by being active and forceful women, they drew the ire of their enemies on themselves. Had they followed the expected pattern of the unnoticeable, charitable, religious consort, they might have avoided their tragedies.

What we have also seen, even if only in apocryphal and fragmentary hints, was that a 'positive' function of queens in Hungary (and surely, elsewhere, too) could also turn into its obverse: their 'civilising' role. The dislike for the Neapolitan Beatrix's 'newfangled tastes' is an obvious example, but the more literary than historical accusations about 'sexual harassment' at court may be vaguely related to this aspect. Here again, the dislike for the court among the nobility of the countryside is a common feature throughout medieval (and later) Europe. Placing the blame for the 'alien customs' on the (foreign) queens combines the negative implications of their origin and their 'female' (non-warlike, not rough-and-ready) influence. All in all, the office of queen was not exactly an enviable job in those times and places.

maintained that 'the country never suffered greater losses . . . than when it was ruled by foreigners not of its own language': see J. M. Bak, *Königtum und Stände in Ungarn im 14.–16. Jh.* (Wiesbaden, 1973), p. 158.

13

The Image of the Queen in Old French Literature [1]

Karen Pratt

Although fictional evidence is problematic when assessing the role of queens in the Middle Ages, it can give us insights not only into contemporary reality but also into the ideologies of authors and their publics. In the following discussion, representations of queens in twelfth-and thirteenth-century male-authored literary texts will be compared both with the historical information available to us and with the queenly image evoked in a fifteenth-century didactic work by a female writer. In this way, we hope to arrive at a clearer understanding of the sort of 'mirror for princesses' Old French literature offers us.[2]

During the period which produced this literature there were no queens-regnant in medieval France or Anglo-Norman England[3] and this situation is reflected in the fictional texts, which provide few examples of the *rex femineus*.[4] Instead we

---

1   I am very grateful to all those who commented on my paper at the King's conference and at a Sheffield University French research seminar held respectively in April and May 1995. Special thanks are due to John Parsons for the numerous historical references, and to Janet Nelson and Simon Gaunt for their careful reading and generous suggestions.
2   While most of the literature under discussion was composed in France, some was produced in the Anglo-Norman regnum. Given the ease of cultural exchange between France and England after the Conquest, it seems appropriate to invoke historical evidence from both sides of the Channel.
3   See A. Poulet, 'Capetian Women and the Regency: The Genesis of a Vocation', *Medieval Queenship*, ed. Parsons, pp. 93–116; L. Huneycutt's contention that medieval churchmen could conceive of women as regents and consorts, but not as rulers, 'Female Succession and the Language of Power in the Writings of Twelfth-Century Churchmen', *ibid.*, pp. 189–201, at p. 191; J. Martindale, 'Succession and Politics in the Romance-Speaking World, c. 1000–1140', in *England and her Neighbours: Essays in Honour of Pierre Chaplais*, edd. M. Jones and M. Vale (London, 1989), pp. 19–41. S. Shahar does not include queens in her ground-breaking study of women in the Middle Ages (*The Fourth Estate* [London, 1983]) because 'in the High and Late Middle Ages no woman succeeded to the throne' (p. 9). Shahar's study of noblewomen in ch. 5 does however contain much of relevance to the present discussion.
4   Along with Dido, to be discussed below, a notable example from the *Roman d'Enéas* is Camille, queen of Vulcane. Yet despite her female sex, she is gendered masculine by the text: 'Lo jor ert rois, la nuit raïne' (*Enéas: Roman du XIIe Siècle*, ed. J.-J. Salverda de Grave (Paris, 1925), line 3977) and dies the death of a virgin knight in battle. She thus exemplifies what Huneycutt discusses in 'Female Succession', namely that medieval churchmen viewed queens-regnant only as honorary males; in the words of St Bernard to Melisende of Jerusalem, 'although a woman, you must act as a man', *op. cit.*, p. 199.

shall focus on female consorts, dowagers and regents, who acquired authority through their closeness to the king: their husband or minor son. However, despite possessing more power and influence than ordinary women, queens were still the victims of misogyny in literature and life.[5] Consequently, some of what follows will be relevant to the representation of medieval women in general, although the special, paradoxical position of queens will be the main focus of attention.[6]

Many queens in medieval literature are shadowy figures whose role is silently to support the king and who are subsumed under the concept of the ideal royal couple. However, when queens do figure prominently in a text, the image portrayed of them is, to say the least, ambiguous. This is because the epics and romances of the twelfth and thirteenth centuries which are to be considered here not only reflect the complex and diverse realities of royal life in the Middle Ages, but more importantly, they reveal the political and gender anxieties of their male authors and of the patriarchal society that produced them. The literature does yield up positive images of royal women, particularly in the laudatory portraits of worthy queens (offered no doubt as role models),[7] and in the depiction of a young woman's education for the role of ideal royal consort, exemplified by Chrétien de Troyes' *Erec et Enide*. However, a much more memorable, and more problematic image is conveyed by adulterous queens such as Iseut and Guinevere, whose expression of their own sexual identity leads to calamitous political consequences.

Since all women, even those destined eventually to be successful royal consorts, were viewed by clerical authors and the Church Fathers as daughters of Eve, possessing a sexual power that had to be contained and socially regulated, it is not surprising that the general ambivalence of medieval men towards women is discernible in male-authored fictional representations of queens.[8] As Christine de Pizan pointed out in her defences of women written during the 'Querelle de la Rose' in the late fourteenth to early fifteenth centuries, women had always received bad press because male clerics had for centuries held the monopoly on writing.[9]

---

[5] See R. Howard Bloch, *Medieval Misogyny* (Chicago, 1991).

[6] See P. Stafford, *Queens, Concubines and Dowagers* (Athens, GA, 1984); J. C. Parsons, 'Ritual and Symbol in the English Medieval Queenship to 1500', in *Women and Sovereignty*, ed. L. Fradenburg (Edinburgh, 1992), pp. 60–77, who refers (p. 60) to the paradoxical position of the queen as subordinate to her husband yet acquiring power through her influence over him in the bedchamber.

[7] The biblical role-models for queens were Esther and Judith, though they are rarely invoked in fictional works. Christine de Pizan (see below) does, however, mention Esther in her *Livre des Trois Vertus*, edd. C. C. Willard and E. Hicks (Paris, 1989), p. 53 (hereafter cited as *Livre*). The other exemplar of queenly behaviour, the Virgin Mary, could be emulated in her piety, gentleness and chastity only by those queen-dowagers and regents whose sexuality was no longer perceived as either a threat or a liability. See M. Warner, *Alone of all her Sex: The Myth and Cult of the Virgin Mary* (London, 1976).

[8] For medieval images of women, see *Woman Defamed and Woman Defended: An Anthology of Medieval Texts*, ed. A. Blamires with K. Pratt and C. W. Marx (Oxford, 1992).

[9] See for example her *Epistre au Dieu d'Amours*, edd. T. Fenster and M. Erler (Brill, 1990), lines 409–11. Yet women in the early Middle Ages often wrote in a masculine way (see P. Dronke, *Women Writers of the Middle Ages* [Cambridge, 1984]), Christine being the earliest 'feminine' author in French.

It is therefore to Christine that we shall turn for an unambiguously positive image of queens, before comparing it with the representations we find in earlier epic and romance.[10]

While mirrors for princes were a popular source of moral and political advice throughout the Middle Ages, didactic literature for women in the vernacular such as Robert de Blois' *Chastoiement des dames*, Philippe de Mézières' *Livre de la vertu du Saint Sacrement de mariage et du réconfort des dames mariées*, and the anonymous *Aiguillon d'amour divin* concentrated on moral teaching and were not specifically intended for royal ladies.[11] Christine's *Livre des Trois Vertus*, on the other hand, was written around 1405 for Marguerite de Bourgogne, recently married to the dauphin, Louis de Guyenne, and contains moral, political and practical advice for a young woman expecting to become queen of France.[12] It was subsequently translated into Portuguese at the request of Queen Isabel of Portugal. Women of royal birth played a role not only as readers of the *Livre*, but also as exempla within it, for Christine cites several queens from French history, including Jeanne of Evreux, wife of Charles IV, and Blanche of Castile in support of her arguments.[13] The moral teaching of the *Livre* is based on traditional sources such as Scripture, proverbial wisdom and medieval *florilegia*. On the other hand, much of the practical, political advice given by 'Prudence Mondaine' – 'worldly prudence'[14] – seems to be drawn from Christine's own experience of life at royal and ducal courts, and thus gives us interesting insights of a more personal, authentic nature.[15]

---

10 While acknowledging that the concept of queenship was not static in the Middle Ages and that the experiences of historical queens varied according to time and place, the fact that French queens from the twelfth to the fifteenth centuries operated in very similar court contexts seems to justify comparison of texts written more than two centuries apart. The dearth of women's writing from the period makes such chronological leaps inevitable if gendered readings are to be attempted.

11 The Chevalier de la Tour-Landry's book of instruction for his aristocratic daughters (*c.* 1371–2) contains mainly moral cautionary tales, while the *Ménagier de Paris* (1393) gives practical hints to his bourgeois wife. In Latin we find St Louis' advice for his daughter Isabelle of Navarre and Durand de Champagne's *Speculum dominarum* for Joan of Navarre, wife of Philip the Fair (see Poulet, 'Capetian Women', p. 96). See D. Bornstein, *The Lady in the Tower: Medieval Courtesy Literature for Women* (Hamden, Ct., 1983).

12 See n. 7 above. There is a modern English translation of the work by C. C. Willard entitled *A Medieval Woman's Mirror of Honor: The Treasury of the City of Ladies* (New York, 1989).

13 *Livre*, pp. 47, 88. On Blanche's powers as widow and regent during her son's minority, see Poulet, 'Capetian Women', pp. 109–10.

14 Although 'Prudence mondaine' represents a more secular authority than the three virtues, Christine points out that her advice is still consistent with God's teaching and in fact her admonitions 'en viennent et dependent' (*Livre*, p. 41).

15 While it is true that Christine's work has much in common with Bishop Turgot's *Life of St Margaret*, suggesting that many details may be topoi drawn from the lives of royal saints, the education she offers is not unlike the training which Parsons believes real queens gave to their daughters to prepare them for royal marriages (J. C. Parsons, 'Mothers, Daughters, Marriage, Power: Some Plantagenet Evidence, 1150–1500', *Medieval Queenship*, pp. 63–78 at pp. 75–8). Christine does, however, mention saintly queens (Clothilda, wife of Clovis; Bathilda, wife of Clovis II; and St Elizabeth of Hungary) in the *Livre*, p. 28, lines 65–7,

Christine's references to reading matter suitable for a young princess (saints' lives are particularly recommended) indicate that she is aware of the portraits of women promulgated by medieval romance and worried about their effect on female readers. Like other moralists, she fears the influence of negative exempla on her young pupil.[16] Thus, while concentrating on positive models of conduct, she also gives us glimpses of what was considered to be reprehensible behaviour in a queen, and it is interesting to note which of these positive and negative aspects are to be found in earlier male-authored fiction, and whether these writers differ from Christine in their ethical judgements on royal women.

Christine's earlier work, the *Cité des Dames* (1405), portrays the author being inspired by three allegorical figures to write her defence of women in response to the long tradition of clerical misogyny and slander. These three virtues, Reason, Rectitude and Justice (*Rayson, Droicture* and *Justice*), reappear at the beginning of the *Livre des Trois Vertus* to exhort her to continue her work.[17] The *Livre* is a mirror to teach women wisdom and virtue, and is divided into three parts, reflecting the three estates of medieval social organisation. The first part, which concerns us here, is addressed to 'roynes, princepces et haultes dames', women whose behaviour needs to be above reproach as they serve as examples to the lower classes.[18]

In broad terms, Christine's teaching falls into four overlapping, interdependent categories: religious and moral instruction; social behaviour at court; the politics of the realm; family life.[19] Her ethical advice is unremarkable: a princess is expected to lead a virtuous life, to attend religious services regularly, give alms to the poor, visit the sick, fast, go on pilgrimages and generally lay up her treasures in heaven. The required virtues are humility (even when faced with the reverence and respect shown her because of her high rank), pity, charity, chastity and 'patience'[20] (in the sense of being long-suffering, turning the other cheek and not insisting on the punishment of those who have offended her). Virtue, however, has

---

details of whose lives she may have known from clerical *vitae*. Her advice probably reflects both the teaching handed down orally from one generation of royal women to the next and the exemplary narratives of the *vitae*, whose rhetorical topoi nevertheless echoed reality.

[16] *Ibid.*, p. 94, lines 96–7; pp. 45–6, lines 129–50. More details of improving reading matter are given in the *Orders and Rules* of Cecily, duchess of York, a copy of which Jennifer Ward kindly provided prior to their publication in her *Women of the English Nobility and Gentry, 1066–1500* (Manchester, 1995). The description of Cecily's religious observances has much in common with Christine's *Livre* and Turgot's *Life of St Margaret*.

[17] *Livre*, pp. 45–6, lines 129–50. According to Willard's introduction to her translation of the *Livre* (p. 30), these three virtues are secular. In the *Cité* Reason holds a mirror which bestows self knowledge on the user; Rectitude carries a ruler with which to 'measure all things and to separate good from evil'; and Justice holds a measuring vessel with which to dispense equal shares of worldly fortune.

[18] *Livre*, p. 9, lines 65–6.

[19] As Parsons argues ('Mothers, Daughters', p. 75), the public and the private are artificial distinctions where the queen's sphere of influence is concerned. Her socio-political positioning is not marginal/liminal but interstitial (see Fradenburg's introduction to *Women and Sovereignty*, p. 5), moving easily between the private and public and bridging the gap between the royal family headed by the king and the people.

[20] *Livre*, p. 30.

a socio-political function, for the queen must, above all, protect the family's honour against slander.

Arrogance (*vaine gloire* or *boubans*),[21] avarice, *luxuria* or lechery, gluttony, sloth or idleness (*oiseuse*, which could take the form of staying in bed too long and taking naps after dinner)[22] are all to be avoided. Yet the pomp and ceremony of court life and the display expected of one of royal status are cleverly accommodated by Christine, who points out that a royal title and lifestyle did not prevent Louis IX from being canonised.[23] Indeed, Christine subtly manages to combine Christian moral teaching with the needs of court life. Thus, she says, a princess is allowed to accumulate money, provided she does not worship it. While scorning worldly fortune she will nevertheless show concern for her honour, and will use her money wisely to buy the clothes and jewels appropriate to her rank, and to provide food and entertainment necessary to impress visitors. While acts of charity should normally be secret, a queen should give publicly in order to encourage others to do likewise and to win their respect, behaviour the author calls 'juste ypocrisie'.[24]

Christine's advice on financial management is practical and detailed: a queen should take an interest in the running of her household (which was separate from the King's),[25] and treat tradesmen justly, paying a fair price for goods. A little clever self-interest is also encouraged, when the princess is told to be on good terms with the bourgeoisie in case she needs to borrow money from them, which must, of course, be repaid on time.[26] Christine, again combining practicality with morality, suggests dividing her revenue (which must be gained licitly, not through extortion) into five parts: for alms-giving (i); for housekeeping (for her *hostel* if her husband does not finance it) (ii); for servants' wages (iii); for gifts and rewards to strangers, to help foreigners impoverished by imprisonment, to provide the equipment necessary for knighthood, and to reward messengers (this is of course the *largesse* or generosity normally associated in romance with kings like Arthur) (iv);[27] for saving up and spending on jewellery and clothes as necessary (v).[28]

In contrast to the magnificent display of wealth presented largely uncritically by courtly romance, Christine preaches moderation in all things. She appears to be reacting to some of the commonplaces of anti-feminist literature when she advises modest dress, not taking too long over one's toilette, and speaking wisely

---

21 *Ibid.*, p. 28, lines 60–1.
22 *Ibid.*, p. 17, lines 100–07.
23 *Ibid.*, p. 27, line 57.
24 *Ibid.*, p. 67, line 53.
25 See Poulet, 'Capetian Women', p. 105, on a king's and queen's separate management of goods, especially the queen's dower.
26 *Livre*, p. 69.
27 However Guinevere's provision of a sword for Lancelot in the *Prose Lancelot* is an example of a queen's *largesse* (which is normally reserved for the clothing of *demoiselles*) being extended to a knight.
28 *Livre*, p. 76.

and briefly.[29] She even advocates the control of one's senses: a princess's gaze should not wander, nor should she indulge her sense of smell with very expensive perfumes and spices, or gesticulate wildly, grimace or laugh too much.[30] All of this is summed up in the words 'sobrece et chastete', for sensuous excess leads to sensuality, which medieval theology linked with the sin of pride:

> lecherie et friandise et superfluitéz de vins et de viandes est le nourissement de charnalité: c'est qui emflamme l'orgueil.

> (The sensual pleasures of fine foods, over-indulgence in wines and meats nourish lechery, which then inflames the ego.)[31]

Christine's moral teaching leads smoothly into castigation of court vices: envy, flattery, *covoitise*, and gossip, which, she claims, can all be counteracted by discretion, patience, and not over-reacting.[32] The princess's ability to keep her own counsel, to confide only in trusty servants and even to dissimulate on occasion is encouraged as a way of averting social, political and family strife. Female ingenuity (*engin*), verbal dexterity, and her exploitation of *semblant*, a term covering external appearance, facial expression, or even pretence, are often criticised in courtly romance as being the tools of the deceitful or adulterous wife.[33] In Christine's *Livre*, however, they are presented more positively as the instruments of diplomacy, especially effective in the political arena.

Here Christine has the queen playing an active role as mediator between the people and either her husband or her son if she is a widow. Her visits to the poor, the sick, women in childbed, her arranging marriages for poor girls and her sponsoring of christenings should win her the love and respect of the people, for whom she will be able to intercede.[34] To this end she must be well-informed, speak to her subjects or their representatives without making them wait too long, surround herself with reliable officials and trustworthy advisers, and listen attentively to all sides of the argument at council meetings.[35] It is for the queen to encourage negotiation rather than war, and here Christine cites recent historical

---

[29] *Ibid.*, p. 94. See *Woman Defamed* for many examples of such commonplace criticisms of women.

[30] *Livre*, p. 44.

[31] *Ibid.*, p. 18, line 121. All translations in this paper are my own.

[32] The court flatterer and gossip was a stock character in medieval romance and one whose origins were clearly not fictional.

[33] *Livre*, p. 62. An excellent example of these qualities at work in a court context is provided by the thirteenth-century short romance or *lai La Chastelaine de Vergi*.

[34] *Livre*, p. 88. The queen's intercessory role is modelled on that of the Virgin Mary, see Parsons, 'Ritual and Symbol', pp. 64–5, and *idem*, 'Mothers, Daughters', p. 64 (referring to the research of Huneycutt). However, R. Muir Wright, 'The Virgin in the Sun and the Tree', in *Women and Sovereignty*, pp. 36–59, shows that the iconography of the Coronation of the Virgin 'severs the connection with secular queenship' (p. 37). It would therefore be wrong to assume that an increase in Marian worship would necessarily produce more status and authority for historical queens.

[35] See Shahar, pp. 126–30, for some of the powers possessed by medieval noblewomen and the activities they undertook.

events to prove that it is the people who suffer during hostilities.[36] Although she concedes that the royal consort must be concerned for her husband's honour, she questions what she sees as the masculine system of revenge, and encourages queens, in the manner of Blanche of Castile, to prevail upon their husband or son to sue for peace:

> laquelle chose est le droit office de sage et bonne royne et princepce d'estre moyenne de paix et de concorde . . . Et ad ce doivent aviser principaulment les dames, car les hommes sont par nature plus courageux et plus chaulx, et le grant desir que ilz ont d'eulx vengier ne leur laisse aviser les perilz ne les maulx qui avenir en peuent. (p. 35: 52–8)

> (The proper role of a good, wise queen or princess is to bring about peace and harmony . . . In particular women should concern themselves with this, for men are by nature more rash and hot-headed, and the great desire they have to avenge themselves does not allow them to foresee the dangers and evil which can result.)[37]

Thus Christine, unlike St Bernard, who urged Melisende of Jerusalem to behave like a man in order to be a successful queen-regnant,[38] urges princesses to develop their traditional feminine qualities.

The queen's powers of diplomacy are also required within the family. Christine advises obedience to her spouse, from whom she derives her status, and patient suffering even if she discovers that her husband is unfaithful.[39] Nothing is achieved by bringing matters into the open, as she could be sent away and ultimately dishonoured.[40] Indeed, if the husband needs to be criticised in some way, especially if the salvation of his soul or his honour are in jeopardy, indirect methods are encouraged, such as asking his confessor to broach the matter,[41] or rebuking him herself, but apparently jokingly.

It is vital that the queen appear supportive of and loyal to her husband, even if this means defending him in public when she knows him to be in the wrong.[42] In his absence at war she should pray for him, and a wife should always be on good terms with her lord's relatives, advice Beroul's Iseut claims to have received from her mother.[43] If left a widow, she will pray for his soul, and defend her legal rights

---

[36] *Livre*, p. 34.

[37] *Ibid.*, p. 35, lines 52–8. As we shall see, this is the role played by Jocaste in the *Roman de Thèbes*.

[38] Huneycutt, 'Female Succession', pp. 199–200.

[39] The role-model for wifely obedience which Christine invokes (*Livre*, p. 53) is Esther, yet the queen's apparent subservience is clearly presented as a means of getting her own way and influencing her husband, at which the biblical prototype was very successful.

[40] *Livre*, p. 55. Chrétien de Troyes' heroine Enide, who will be discussed later, clearly believed that her criticism of her husband was to result in her banishment: 'Or m'estuet aler an essil' (*Kristian von Troyes Erec und Enide*, ed. W. Foerster [Halle, 1934], line 2596). She would no doubt have benefited from Christine's tactful advice here.

[41] *Livre*, p. 53.

[42] *Ibid.*, p. 54.

[43] See Beroul, *The Romance of Tristran*, ed. A. Ewert (Oxford, 1971), lines 73–7.

and inheritance (and her children's), something the author had experienced herself
after her husband's death.

On the matter of their children's upbringing, it is the king who finds a tutor for
his sons, but the queen supervises the moral education of all her children and
should show a personal interest in their development.[44] This is a good investment,
we are told, as children (by which she means sons) can protect women in
widowhood, staving off attack from enemies through the threat of revenge. While
she should make sure her sons are tutored in Latin and the sciences, her daughters
will be kept near her and taught by wise women, who will prevent them from
enjoying frivolous reading matter:

> ne nulz de choses vaines, de folies ou de dissolucions ne souffrera que devant
> elle soyent portéz. (p. 61: 64–5)

> (Nor will she allow worthless, foolish or dissolute subject-matter to be brought
> before them.)

No doubt they are to be discouraged from reading romances portraying so-called
courtly love, a phenomenon which Christine demystifies towards the end of her
Livre.

Christine's aim is to promote marital love, even if the husband is unfaithful.
She therefore describes how a governess should act as a go-between for newly
weds and should remind a young royal wife of her husband's good qualities when
he is away, thus stoking the fires of conjugal love.[45] Just as the governess will
protect her young mistress against other suitors, so a more mature queen will
discourage her ladies-in-waiting from responding to the wooing of fellow courtiers.[46] Moreover, young widows are advised not to re-marry unless their family and
friends agree, for they know best:

> si doit penser qu'ilz sauront mieulx congnoistre ce qui est bon qu'elle meismes
> ne feroit. (p. 90: 103–05)

> (And she should believe that they will be better able to recognise what is good
> for her than she herself could do.)

The penalties for royal ladies who succumb to the charms of courtly lovers are
great: they lose their honour and are ultimately deceived by their suitors. Govern-
esses have many exemplary stories to tell on this subject:

---

[44] *Livre*, p. 59. The literary queens to be discussed below are not depicted as mothers of young
children and therefore offer no points of comparison. In *Floire et Blancheflor*, a twelfth-century romance, it is the pagan king who chooses a tutor for his five-year-old son, but asks for
the queen's advice when Floire falls in love with the Christian girl, an attachment the king
is the first to note. On the theme of education, see P. Simons, 'The Theme of Education in
Twelfth- and Thirteenth-Century French Epic and Romance', unpublished Ph.D. thesis
(University of Sheffield, 1991).

[45] *Livre*, p. 97.

[46] *Ibid.*, pp. 98, 72.

Si lui dira de bons exemples du mal qui puet avenir et qui maintes fois avenu a pluseurs pour telz folies, la grant deshonneur et reprouches qui en sourdent, et les deceuvemens qui sont es hommes. (p. 102: 167–70)

(She will tell her exemplary stories of the evil that can come of it, and that has often befallen many a woman because of such folly, and the great dishonour and reproach which result, and the deception men are capable of.)

Christine ends this section of the *Livre* with a fictional letter quoted from her *Livre du Duc des vrais Amans* and written by the governess Sebile de la Tour to her mistress, warning her against courtly love.[47] The literary concept of illicit love, referred to as 'amer par amours', and the idealised relationship between the lady and her knight are here juxtaposed with harsh reality, which for the woman means deception, dishonour, her ruin and that of her children. It is impossible to keep such liaisons secret, despite the emphasis in courtly literature on *bien celer* (concealment) and it is politically disastrous if her children are thought to be illegitimate.[48] Interestingly, it is Christine, rather than the male authors under investigation, who mentions the problem of illegitimacy. As we shall see later, this is an anxiety which lurks behind the presentation of adulterous queens in romance, yet it is rarely voiced in their male-authored texts, and is indeed avoided by making these queens apparently barren.

In particular, Christine stresses the pain and dangers of love, which she considers to be 'par especial du cousté des dames' (especially serious for women).[49] Not only is it a sin against the sacrament of marriage, but the notion of the 'chevalier servant', whose prowess increases under the influence of the lady's love, a literary motif sometimes called the chivalry topos, is shown to be advantageous only to the man. For his reputation is enhanced, yet her influence goes unrewarded if it remains secret, and when the love is discovered, she is the one to be dishonoured. Through clever punning on the notion of 'service' Christine demonstrates how the lady who thought she was being served by her knight becomes subservient to her courtiers and confidantes who could reveal her shameful secret at any moment. Even the adultery of a husband is no excuse for such dalliances; weaving, sewing and time spent with the children are recommended as alternatives to taking a lover, which can only lead to the lady's downfall.

To those believing that courtly literature was written for and commissioned by ladies who enjoyed seeing themselves worshipped by their besotted male lovers, Christine's view of 'courtly love' may come as a surprise. While some female readers no doubt did take pleasure in the apparently flattering portraits of courtly ladies, Christine and some of her contemporaries clearly viewed such literature as potentially dangerous and misleading, for when read by young, impressionable

---

47 For Christine's views on courtly love, see C. C. Willard, 'Christine de Pizan's *Cent Ballades d'amant et de dame*: Criticism of Courtly Love', in *Court and Poet (Selected Proceedings of the Third Congress of the International Courtly Literature Society, Liverpool 1980)*, ed. G. S. Burgess (Liverpool, 1981), pp. 357–64.

48 *Livre*, p. 113.

49 *Ibid.*, p. 115, line 150.

females it gave them a false sense of security and superiority over their suitors. Christine's experience of court life enables her to point out the discrepancy between fiction and reality, and to reveal the seductive nature of courtly literature, which she demystifies by laying bare its androcentricity.[50]

Turning now to some examples of this literature we shall see if Christine's depiction of a virtuous, wise, diplomatic queen, active in the social, political and family spheres, is anticipated in twelfth- and thirteenth-century epic and romance.

Although Christine does not stress the point, some of the queens she mentions were foreign princesses, who left family and country in order to forge political alliances through their marriages.[51] This practice of exogamy, which results in the isolation and vulnerability of the queen, is reflected in several medieval texts, notably in Beroul's *Tristran*, where Iseut, an Irish princess, frequently laments the fact that she is alone and defenceless in Mark's kingdom, and has to ask for King Arthur's support when preparing to swear her ambiguous oath in defence of her virtue.[52] Fénice's rather vulnerable position in Chrétien's *Cligés* is similarly thought to reflect reality, probably echoing the situation of the Byzantine princesses used as marriage pawns in the twelfth century to cement relations between Germany and Byzantium.[53] Fénice is the daughter of the German emperor, promised to the duke of Saxony, but becomes the empress of Constantinople after the emperor's nephew wins her in combat. Having fallen in love, Iseut-like, with her husband's nephew, Cligés, she has to depend on her own wits and her resourceful nurse Thessala to extricate herself from this potentially tragic situation. However, while Iseut's vulnerability provokes pathos in Beroul's audience, Chrétien's comic treatment of Fénice encourages us to view her and her ingenuity with amused detachment.[54] Moreover, the ironic fate he gives her, to be remembered not for her loyalty to her lover, but for her deception of her husband, is representative of the ambiguity with which Chrétien treats many of his female protagonists. Thus a foreign princess, whose vulnerability mirrors that of many a twelfth-century lady, is transformed by clerical misogyny into a stock anti-feminist fictional character, whose antecedent is the wife of Solomon.

Other queens, while not actually foreign, also seem to lack family support when in need. This is the case with Guinevere, who finds herself in the *Mort Artu* first accused of murder, then almost forced against her will into marriage with Mordred (see below), Enide at the time of her marital crisis, and Athanaïs, in Gautier

---

[50] On female readers and the demystification of 'courtly love', see R. L. Krueger, *Women Readers and the Ideology of Gender in Old French Verse Romance* (Cambridge, 1993).

[51] See for examples, J. Gillingham, 'Love, Marriage and Politics in the Twelfth Century', *Forum for Modern Language Studies*, xxv (1989), 292–303. Parsons, 'Family, Sex, and Power: The Rhythms of Medieval Queenship', *Medieval Queenship*, p. 4, mentions the divided loyalties this might produce, and more positively the 'cross-cultural perspectives' of the queen, while *idem*, 'Ritual and Symbol', p. 61, discusses the means whereby a foreign bride might be 'naturalised'.

[52] See *Tristran*, lines 174, 3434–46.

[53] See L. Polak, *Chrétien de Troyes: Cligés* (London, 1982), pp. 9–11.

[54] A rather different view of female *engin* from that expressed by Christine, who of course never advocates witchcraft as a means of extricating oneself from tricky situations.

d'Arras's *Eracle* (*c.* 1176). The latter heroine is presented as an orphan, who is married to the Roman emperor after his adviser has failed to find a suitable wife for him in a bride-show (compare Esther). Her lack of relatives no doubt reflects symbolically the isolation of the bride in a political marriage, but may also contribute to the idealisation of this fictional character, whose family's interests cannot come into conflict with her husband's, as often happened in reality.

Deriving her power and authority from her husband rather than from her family, the queen in medieval literature is usually depicted, as in Christine's *Livre*, as a prominent figure at the royal court, surrounded by many noble ladies and sometimes holding court separately from her husband. Echoes of the separate domestic lives led by kings and queens are to be found in Arthurian romances, such as the *Queste*,[55] which evoke what Geoffrey of Monmouth in the Arthurian section of his *Historia regum Britanniae* calls the Trojan custom:

> The King went off with the men to feast in his own palace and the Queen retired with the married women to feast in hers; for the Britons still observed the ancient custom of Troy, the men celebrating festive occasions with their fellow-men and the women eating separately with the other women.[56]

More commonly though, the queen is present at feasts and court entertainments and takes an active part in them, as for example in Chrétien's *Yvain*, when she prevails upon Calogrenant to relate his chivalric adventures and then repeats the story to the king.[57] Festive occasions in romance are not, however, characterised by the moderation and avoidance of *superfluitéz* recommended by Christine, and fine clothes, such as those given to Enide by Guinevere, or bought by Ogrin for Iseut, are a mark of generosity or nobility rather than a sign of an excessive taste for luxury.[58]

An important role for a queen appears to have been her arrangement of marriages for young women.[59] While Christine talks of arranging marriages for the poor, most courtly literature emphasises aristocratic match-making. Iseut, for example, realises, once the love potion has waned, not only that she has sacrificed the luxury and privileges of court life, but also that she has failed in her duty to arrange marriages:

---

55 See *La Queste del Saint Graal*, ed. Albert Pauphilet (Paris, 1923), 10: 1.

56 Geoffrey of Monmouth, *The History of the Kings of Britain*, trans. L. Thorpe (Harmondsworth, 1966), p. 229. On gendered spaces, see R. Gilchrist, 'Medieval Bodies in the Material World', *Framing Medieval Bodies*, edd. S. Kay and M. Rubin (Manchester, 1994), pp. 43–61.

57 While Guinevere's role may be negative here, as she forces Calogrenant to tell a tale of his *honte*, more worrying is her ability to keep King Arthur from his knights: 'Mes cel jor einsi avint, / Que la reïne le detint, / Si demora tant delez li, / Qu'il s'oblia et andormi.' lines 49–52 (Chrétien de Troyes, *Yvain*, ed. T. B. A. Reid [Manchester, 1942; repr. 1967]).

58 On the other hand, anti-feminist, didactic literature of the period does castigate women for sartorial and gastronomic excesses.

59 For historical examples, see Parsons, 'Mothers, Daughters', p. 72, on the matrimonial politics of Eleanor of Castile.

> Les damoiseles des anors,
> Les filles as frans vavasors,
> Deüse ensenble o moi tenir
> En mes chanbres, por moi servir,
> Et les deüse marïer
> Et as seignors por bien doner.   (lines 2211–16).

(I should have had the young noblewomen of the realm, the daughters of noble vavassors around me in my chambers, to serve me and I should have arranged marriages for them and given them to suitable husbands.)

Similarly, in Chrétien's *Charette*, the young noblewomen of Arthur's realm, who

> desconseillees estoient,
> et distrent qu'eles se voldroient
> marïer molt procheinemant.   (lines 5363–5)[60]

(were dismayed and said that they would like to marry as soon as possible)

seem not to have been getting married during Guinevere's absence in Gorre, and are keen that she should preside over a tournament so that the backlog can be dealt with. Hence the tournament of Noauz, at which Lancelot proves his love for the queen by obeying her command to do his worst. Guinevere is also associated with marriage in other romances by Chrétien: in *Erec et Enide* she seems to supervise the wedding of the eponymous couple, and in *Cligés* she sets herself up as lecturer in matters marital, saying 'D'Amors andoctriner vos vuel, / . . . Por ce vos vuel metre a escole', and forcing the timorous Soredamors and Alexandre to declare their mutual love, then acting as marriage broker for them: 'Se vos en avez boen corage,/ J'asanblerai le mariage.'[61]

It is in *Eracle*, however, that we find an example of the empress arranging the marriage of poor orphans. This is mentioned in an idealising portrait of the empress Athanaïs which echoes many of the characteristics of Christine's ideal Christian queen (modelled on the Virgin Mary):

> vous dirai de l'empereïs
> con oevre en li sains Esperis,
> car loiauté aime et droiture,
> et Diu sour toute creature.
> Quanqu'ele emprent velt acomplir,[62]
> ce vous voel je por voir plevir,
> mais n'emprent onques nul rien

---

[60] Chrétien de Troyes, *Le Chevalier de la charette*, ed. M. Roques (Paris, 1981).

[61] Chrétien de Troyes, *Cligés*, ed. A. Micha (Paris, 1957), lines 2252–4, 2271–2.

[62] Compare Christine's *Livre*, p. 26, lines 23–4: 'Si ne doy entreprendre chose, ou perserverer je ne pense souffire.'

u il n'en ait raison et bien.
Dame a esté set ans de Rome
si c'onques Dius ne fist cel home
qui en puist dire vilenie,
s'il ne le sordist par envie.
Onques mais nule ne fu teus:
ele recuevre tous auteus,
messes fait canter et matines
et fait nourir ces orpehenines
por l'amour Diu et por Marie
et por l'amor Diu les marie;
de soi meïsme li souvient
si fait molt bien ce qui covient;
et quant ce vient c'on doit juner,
ces povres prent a gouvrener
de quanques onques ont mestier . . .
Ele establit maint abeïe
u Nostre Dame est obeïe.
Molt est ameë et proisie.   (lines 2927–55)[63]

(I shall tell you about the empress, how the Holy Spirit works in her, for she loves loyalty and rectitude, and God above all creatures. She wishes to accomplish all she undertakes, I can tell you truly, yet she never undertakes anything that is not wise and good. She has been empress of Rome for seven years such that no man alive could speak ill of her, unless he slandered her out of envy. There was never such a woman. She provides [cloths] for all altars, has masses and matins sung and supports female orphans for the love of God and the Virgin, and marries them for the love of God. And she remembers her own soul and does whatever is fitting, and when one is supposed to fast, she looks after the poor, giving them whatever they require. She founds many an abbey where Our Lady is obeyed. She is much loved and esteemed.)

In her religious observance, virtuous nature and good works Athanaïs is beyond reproach, although *envie*, that vice particularly rife at court according to Gautier and Christine, is an ever-present enemy. However, her virtue is eventually compromised by her husband's jealousy, for when the emperor Laïs goes to war he insists on locking her up in a tower against the advice of Eracle. The lady's imprisonment may be an echo of Eleanor of Aquitaine's treatment by her husband, Henry II, though the circumstances are very different.[64] Close-keeping is, however, a common feature of the jealous husband motif, and Gautier's aim here seems to be to criticise the emperor for his refusal to take pious Eracle's advice, rather

[63] Gautier d'Arras, *Eracle*, ed. G. Raynaud de Lage (Paris, 1976), lines 2927–55.
[64] See J. Martindale, 'Eleanor of Aquitaine', in *Richard Coeur de Lion in History and Myth*, ed. J. L. Nelson (London, 1992), pp. 17–50.

than to denigrate women.[65] Another positive portrait of Athanaïs, similar to Christine's ideal of the active queen, is given when Eracle describes what she would do in her husband's absence were she to remain free:

> 'il m'est vis que c'est raisons
> que me dame aut par ses maisons,
> par ses viles, par ses castiaus,
> par ses manoirs qu'ele a molt biaus;
> verra les terres et le gent,
> verra son or et son argent,
> si pensera en son corage
> qu'amer doit bien le signorage
> dont tele honors li est venue.'   (lines 3079–87)

('It seems to me that it is right that my lady should go around her houses, her towns, her castles, the splendid manors she has; and she will see her land and people, she will see her gold and silver, and she will think in her heart that she ought to love the husband from whom she has gained such honour.')

She could supervise her property, subjects and revenue, which she seems either to possess in her own right (perhaps received as dower as she was penniless on marriage) or to be responsible for as her husband's substitute.[66] Failure to heed Eracle's counsel leads to Athanaïs's adultery with a young nobleman, which her husband discovers. However, Laïs accepts some of the blame for his wife's infidelity, grants her a divorce (the verbs used are 'partir, departir, se consirer') and gives her in marriage to her lover, a solution never proposed in more famous French romances about the adultery of queens.[67]

The relatively positive image of a royal woman we gain from Gautier's *Eracle* is echoed by other early romances, notably the *romans antiques*. Yet as we have seen, this image is somewhat tainted by the queen's sexual misdemeanours. There can be no greater sexual crime, it would seem, than unwittingly marrying your own son, whom you know has killed your husband. However, Jocaste in the *Roman de Thèbes* soon casts off the shadow of incest, to emerge as a wise diplomat, struggling in vain to avert war between her sons. She epitomises Christine's 'queen as peace-maker', while her sons and the other men are vengeful, war-mongering,

---

[65] See K. Pratt, *Meister Otte's 'Eraclius' as an Adaptation of 'Eracle' by Gautier d'Arras* (Göppingen, 1987) for a study of this romance.
[66] See Poulet, 'Capetian Women', p. 104, on the emergence of the Capetian queen as the king's legal replacement. Indeed, because she swore no coronation oath her power was in a way less limited than her husband's, *ibid.*, pp. 105–6.
[67] *Eracle*, lines 5050–60. This may be because divorce was not an option from the late twelfth century onwards. I am grateful to Roy Wisbey for pointing out that divorce is however mentioned as a possibility in Eilhart's *Tristan*. For historical examples of divorced queens, see Poulet, p. 103, on Eleanor of Aquitaine; on divorce in general, see Shahar, p. 82 and C. N. L. Brooke, *The Medieval Idea of Marriage* (Oxford, 1989).

hot-headed males. Characteristic of this attitude which Christine defines as masculine is Eteocles's insistence on revenge:

> 'Mors sui, se n'em praing vengement . . .
> mout volentiers m'en vengeroie'   (lines 3874, 3880)

Jocaste is depicted playing an active role in councils, giving advice which is frequently heeded, and suggesting compromise solutions to avert disaster.[68] Most strikingly, it is Jocaste and her two daughters Antigone and Ismene who go as messengers to Polynices's camp, thus avoiding retaliation for the maltreatment of an earlier messenger. The queen, characterised as wise and brave by the narrator, says proudly:

> 'et pour soufraite de preudomes
> ert cist mesages fez par dames.'   (lines 4025–6)

('In the absence of worthy men, this message will be taken by ladies.')

To Polynices, the queen, representing 'senz et mesure' (line 4360, cf. line 4349), recommends moderation rather than pursuing even the rightful punishment of one's enemies:

> 'miex valt mesure
> que jugemenz ne que droiture.
> Cest felon a droit destruiroies,
> mes mout grant donmage y aroies.'   (lines 7983–6)

('Moderation is better than legal judgment and punishment. It would be lawful for you to kill this traitor, but great harm would befall you if you did.')

a diplomatic approach with which Christine de Pizan agrees.[69]

Jocaste's image is in no way tarnished by the display of pomp and wealth which attends her mission. The descriptions of the regal mother and daughters, with their luxurious clothing and splendid mounts, represent a rhetorical high point in the narrative and reinforce their royal status (lines 4040–106). Towards the end of the romance, having acted as marriage broker between Eteocles and the daughter of Daire (line 8040), Jocaste is praised by the narrator for her virtue:

> mout ert bone dame Jocaste
> et bonne aumosniere et bien chaste.   (lines 8067–8)

(Lady Jocasta was very virtuous, charitable and chaste.)

---

68 See Huneycutt, 'Female Succession', pp. 189–90, on the roles noble and royal women played at councils in the eleventh and twelfth centuries.

69 Similarly, in the *Roman de Troie*, Ecuba does all she can to bring about peace, turning to revenge only after her third son, Troilus, is killed by Achilles (Benoît de Sainte-Maure, *Le Roman de Troie*, ed. L. Constans, 6 vols [Paris, 1904–12], lines 21838–60). The narrator makes it clear that she departs from her usual role as peacemaker only under extreme provocation. I am grateful to Penny Eley for this reference.

It is Oedipus, not Jocasta, who is blamed by this author for the fratricide at Thebes.

A different emphasis is placed on the portrait of the queen in the almost contemporary *Roman d'Enéas*, for Dido is a young widow rather than a mother with grown-up children,[70] and as such becomes associated with an uncontrollable and fatal passion.[71] However, before her meeting with Eneas, she is presented as a clever and effective queen-regnant, who has, thanks to her wit and ingenuity, provided her subjects with a flourishing kingdom (lines 377–80). Dido's palace, temple and law courts are marvels to behold, and Carthage would have eclipsed Rome had not the gods willed it otherwise. The queen's hospitality and generosity to the exiled Trojans is exemplary. Yet her offer to share her land with Eneas (line 631), even before she has been struck by Cupid's arrow, seems excessive, and although there is no mention of marriage at this stage, Dido probably represents those royal widows, who, despite their resourcefulness, nevertheless needed the protection of a husband.[72] As with other medieval heroines who act on their desire, Dido is punished by the narrative for her lack of control, her *démesure*, and this is the image of her that passes into later antifeminist literature.[73] However, Christine de Pizan in her *Cité des Dames* stresses instead her positive achievements as a successful female ruler, and in a later chapter cites her as an example not of uncontrollable passion, but of loyalty in love. Christine depicts her as a victim, betrayed by Eneas, without dwelling on those details of her downfall which many male authors seem to have relished.

Turning now to the medieval epic, we find that queens usually play a rather minor part in what is essentially a masculine genre.[74] For example, the role of the

---

[70] According to Parsons, 'Family, Sex, and Power', p. 6, the royal woman's passage from wife to mother made her seem much less dangerous to the medieval male.

[71] Dido, though widowed, is not the wife of the late king of Carthage. She becomes queen in her own right having brought her followers to the land and won a kingdom by her ingenuity. There seems to be no historical parallel to this, though her literary treatment as a young widow open to remarriage does reflect contemporary anxieties. Poulet, p. 111, argues that Capetian kings preferred to nominate their mother as regent during their son's minority rather than their wife, who might remarry and thereby divert the throne away from the king's offspring.

[72] I am grateful to Simon Gaunt for pointing out the negative portrayal of Dido as a widow unfaithful to the memory of her husband. He reads her offer of only part of her kingdom as ungenerous (a desire to retain some power), in comparison with Lavine, whose acquisition will be accompanied by *all* her father's land. See S. Gaunt, 'From Epic to Romance: Gender and Sexuality in the *Roman d'Enéas*', *Romanic Review*, lxxxiii (1992), 1–27, at p. 11.

[73] The *vieille* in Jean de Meun's *Rose* presents Dido sympathetically as a victim of Eneas's treachery, yet mentions nothing of her qualities as ruler prior to the Trojan's arrival. Jean Lefèvre, in his *Lamentations de Matheolus*, is very critical of Dido, who, according to this version, commits suicide when pregnant (see *Woman Defamed*, p. 192). Huneycutt, p. 196, refers to John of Salisbury's use of Dido in his *Policraticus* as an *exemplum* of an effective female ruler nevertheless brought down by her lustful female body.

[74] An exception to this rule is Elisant in *Girart de Roussillon*. For a provocative discussion of the role of women in the epic, see S. Kay, *Political Fictions: The Chansons de Geste in the Age of Romance* (Oxford, 1995) and *eadem*, 'Kings, Vassals, and Queens: Problems of Hierarchy in the Old French and Occitan *Chansons de Geste*', *Journal of the Institute of Romance Studies*, i (1992), 27–47.

pagan queen Bramimonde in the *Chanson de Roland* is limited to rewarding the treacherous Ganelon with gifts for his wife, supporting her husband Marsile, even in defeat, railing against the ineffective pagan gods, and eventually being converted to Christianity.[75] Saracen princesses in other epics are shown disobeying their families in order to help Christian heroes and then converting to the true religion when they marry, actions thoroughly condoned by the epic authors. Sometimes though, the queen's role is problematic, especially if she becomes more than just a political helpmate. This is the case in Bertrand de Bar-sur-Aube's *Girart de Vienne*, dated *c.* 1180. The duchess of Burgundy is not a problem when she simply symbolises the fief of Burgundy, after her husband's death. She turns into, however, a source of real masculine anxiety, severely rocking the patriarchal boat, when she becomes simultaneously an object of desire and an actively desiring subject.

On learning that the duke of Burgundy is dead and that the duchess wishes the king to find her a new husband,[76] Charlemagne promises Girart the lady and the land:

> par la saiete dont il devoit berser
> li vet la dame et la terre doner.   (lines 1233–4)

> (with the arrow with which he was going to hunt, he goes to give him the lady and the land.)

However, on meeting the duchess 'a la chere façon' (an epithet which stresses her inflammatory beauty) Charles decides to marry her himself. While the emperor has no interest in Burgundy, the land goes with the lady, and Girart is therefore given another fief instead, Vienne. Although Charles's broken promise (a result of his unrestrained desire provoked unwittingly by the lady) is cause enough for war between the king and Girart's clan, the author chooses to introduce another *casus belli*, and this results directly from the duchess's wish to have the husband of her choice.[77] Thus female desire is shown by the text to be far more politically and socially disruptive than male desire. The duchess is pleased when she hears she is promised to young, attractive Girart, so when Charles claims her, she asks for Girart instead:

> 'Girart me done, a la chiere membree,
> a cui ge fui premiere presantee.'   (lines 1300–1)[78]

---

75 See S. Burch, 'Bramimunde: Her Name, her Nature', in *Roland and Charlemagne in Europe: Essays on the Reception and Transformation of a Legend*, ed. K. Pratt (London, 1996), pp. 67–81.

76 Cf. Laudine in Chrétien de Troyes' *Chevalier au lion*, another widow needing a protector quickly. On the widow's vulnerability, see H. Leyser, *Medieval Women: A Social History of Women in England 450–1500* (London, 1995).

77 See W. van Emden, 'The "Cocktail-Shaker Technique" in Two *Chansons de Geste*', in *The Medieval Alexander Legend and Romance Epic: Essays in Honour of David J. A. Ross*, ed. P. Noble *et al.* (New York, 1982), pp. 43–56.

78 I do not subscribe to Sarah Kay's argument ('Kings, Vassals, and Queens') that the duchess,

She subsequently attempts privately to persuade Girart to marry her, and when he rebukes her for being too forward, takes her revenge by forcing Girart, on the night of her wedding to the emperor, to kiss her foot rather than Charles's as a mark of gratitude for the fief of Vienne. Her later boasting about this insult triggers the war. What is noticeable both at the time of these fateful events and later when the duchess, now queen, speaks of them (lines 1780–928), is that men talk of women being given to them in marriage, while the queen talks of Girart being given to her as a husband: 'si me dona dant Girart le marchis' (line 1833). She makes the mistake of thinking she has a choice, that she can have the object of her desire, and the narrative punishes her for this subversive misapprehension.

Despite the narrator's denigration of the duchess, she is later credited with raising an army for the king in France, thereby echoing the support provided by Guibourc, the exemplary epic wife of Guillaume d'Orange in the *Chanson de Guillaume* and presumably reflecting the real-life behaviour of wives of warring barons and kings.[79] The queen is also present at the siege of Vienne, where she is captured from the king's tent in his absence and nearly killed, before being rescued by Charles. Just as kings are more active in the epic than they are in romance, so their spouses seem also to play a more active role. The queen, however, fades out of the narrative towards the end amid the general reconciliation, and it is Girart's good wife, another Guiborc, who is the last female to speak in the political arena (lines 6903–4).

Although the duchess does not take her revenge on Girart by claiming that he has seduced her, her behaviour is reminiscent of that of the wife of Potiphar, who seems to have been the model for other medieval queens with active libidos. This is the case with queen Eufeme in the thirteenth-century *Roman de Silence*, who not only falls in love with Silence, a woman disguised as a man, and then accuses him/her when rejected, but is also revealed to have a male lover disguised as a nun.[80] The image of the queen here is irredeemably negative, although Silence's marriage to the king at the end provides the promise of a virtuous royal consort.[81] The Potiphar's wife motif is used also by Marie de France in *Lanval*. Though not named, the queen who is rejected by Lanval and who then makes false accusations against him, is clearly Guinevere, and Marie is probably here invoking the tradition

---

in pointing out the potential 'mesalliance' between herself and the emperor, shares his ideology and supports hierarchical political organisation. The duchess's main motive is to find plausible, acceptable arguments for rejecting a suitor to whom she is not attracted. This common device is used also by the knight in the *Chastelaine de Vergi* and by the lady in *Equitan*, though in the latter case she is merely testing the king, not voicing her own objections.

[79] See Huneycutt, 'Female Succession', pp. 190, 194, where she refers to medieval queens' competence in warfare.

[80] *Le Roman de Silence*, ed. L. Thorpe (Cambridge, 1972) and *Silence: A Thirteenth-Century French Romance*, ed. S. Roche-Mahdi (East Lansing, MI, 1992).

[81] Our discussion of female speech will demonstrate that Silence, as her name implies, possesses the feminine virtue par excellence, namely verbal discretion. Her earlier success as a man may, however, suggest that the medieval ideal of queenship contained some masculine features.

of Arthur's wife's infidelity, which goes back at least as far as Geoffrey of Monmouth.

This brings us to the ambiguous image of the queen presented in Arthurian romance through the figure of Guinevere. As we have seen, she is presented quite positively in Chrétien's early romances *Erec et Enide* and *Cligés*, seeming to represent and promote an ideal of marriage. Equally important is her role as wise adviser to the king. In *Erec et Enide* she helps to defuse the potential conflict arising from Arthur's insistence on reviving the custom of the hunt for the white stag. Gawain points out that this could be divisive, and Guinevere suggests that Arthur delay bestowing the kiss on the most beautiful lady at court until Erec returns (lines 335ff). When Yder announces that Erec is bringing the most beautiful *pucele* with him, the queen points to the excellence of her advice:

> 'Mout vos donai buen consoil ier,
> Quant jel vos loai a atandre:
> Por ce fet il buen, consoil prandre.'   (lines 1220–2)

> ('I gave you very good advice yesterday, when I suggested you wait;
> that's why it is right to heed advice.')

Later Guinevere seems to function as a role model for Enide, whose education will be discussed presently.

Her role in *Cligés* is mainly as adviser to the lovers and promoter of *courtoisie*, but it is striking that Alexandre hands over the captured prisoners to her rather than to the king, as he fears Arthur will kill them (lines 1337ff). Guinevere is thus presented as a more merciful ruler, who can sometimes challenge the authority of the king, although after private discussions between the royal couple, Arthur prevails (lines 1403–12).

In Chrétien's later romances, Guinevere, though having an important social role at court, is mainly associated with abduction and adultery.[82] She is absent for much of *Yvain*, having been abducted by Meleagant (in another romance), and in *Perceval* she has been insulted by the Red Knight, in such a way as to question her chastity.[83] In the *Charrete*, she becomes a pawn in the negotiations between Arthur, Kay and Meleagant, who succeeds in carrying her off to what seems to be a Celtic Otherworld. Moreover, her influence on her lover Lancelot appears rather mixed: because of his love for her he succeeds in liberating the queen and Arthur's subjects from imprisonment in Gorre. On the other hand, love renders him ridiculous at times, makes him compromise his chivalric honour, and leads him to commit adultery. Guinevere, although idealised as the object of Lancelot's desire, is depicted as capricious and imperious.[84]

---

82 The abduction motif seems to have its origins in Celtic myth, the aggressor challenging the king's authority by removing the source of the king's heirs, hence the symbol of the kingdom's fertility.

83 The spilling of wine over Guinevere is reminiscent of chastity tests involving leaky goblets found in Breton lays.

84 The negative portrait of Guinevere becomes more explicit later in the *Queste*, in which she

Given this ambiguous presentation of the queen and the theme of love, the influence of Chrétien's patron, Marie de Champagne, the daughter of the king of France and of Eleanor of Aquitaine, may not have been as pervasive as the prologue suggests. For as Bonnie Krueger points out, Chrétien begins the *Charrete* with a transaction between a female patron and a male cleric, the poet portrayed as if he were the *chevalier servant* of his lady. However, the romance ends with a transaction between two male clerics, Chrétien and a certain Godefroi de Leigni, who supposedly finished the romance for him. The lady has vanished.[85]

Nor is it by any means certain that Marie de Champagne or her royal mother were great proponents of what modern critics call courtly love.[86] This idea is mainly promoted by Andreas Capellanus in his *De amore*, once thought to have been written for Marie, but now linked with the court of Philippe-Auguste of France.[87] His references to Eleanor, her daughter Marie, and other noble ladies presiding over courts of love and giving judgements on issues such as whether a young man with little moral fibre or an older, virtuous man would make a better lover, or whether consanguinity is grounds for terminating a love affair, are now viewed as humorous and ironic, and no longer accepted as evidence for the existence of such courts in reality.[88] Perhaps several hundred years before Christine's *Livre*, readers of romance were already aware of the subtle irony and misogyny of representations of royal women, despite the superficial attractions of the religion of love.

It has been argued recently that fictional adulterous queens, who indulge their own sexual desire, and who wield in many cases enormous influence over their lovers, are eventually punished within narratives by forfeiting what was in reality

---

tries to prevent Arthur's knights from seeking the Grail and is presented as the obstacle to Lancelot's spiritual fulfilment.

[85] R. Krueger, 'Desire, Meaning, and the Female Reader: The Problem in Chrétien's *Charrete*', in *The Passing of Arthur*, edd. C. Baswell and W. Sharpe (New York/London, 1988). Similarly, in prose continuations of the story culminating in the *Mort Artu*, the focus will eventually be on the relationship between Lancelot and Arthur, not on the lovers.

[86] Much has been made of the female patronage of romance, but it is unclear to what extent figures mentioned in dedications actually influenced the works in question. Of the works discussed in this paper, the following had aristocratic female patrons: the *Roman d'Enéas* was said by Layamon to have been written for Eleanor of Aquitaine; Marie de Champagne had Chrétien's *Charrete* and Gautier d'Arras's *Eracle* dedicated to her; and Christine de Pizan mentions several royal patrons.

[87] See A. Karnein, 'Auf der Suche nach einem Autor: Andreas, Verfasser von *De Amore*', *Germanisch-Romanische Monatsschrift*, xxviii (1978), 1–20; 'La réception du *De Amore* d'André le Chapelain au XIIIe siècle', *Romania*, cii (1981), 324–51; 'Amor est passio – a Definition of Courtly Love?', *Court and Poet*, pp. 215–21.

[88] P. G. Walsh, *Andreas Capellanus on Love* (London, 1982), points out (pp. 253, 256) that these specific cases may have been given to Eleanor because of their ironic relevance to her life. Her divorce from Louis VII was on the grounds of consanguinity and she then married a younger man. In this way Andreas may have been making fun of the queen as authoritative judge in a fictional court of love. Eleanor was also the object of satire, direct attacks and accusations of adultery from Occitan poets and French clerics after the queen's marriage to Henry II. See Martindale, 'Eleanor of Aquitaine', pp. 33–50.

a source of power for royal women, namely the production of legitimate heirs.[89] Iseut and Guinevere are barren; neither their husbands nor their lovers father children with them.[90] Fénice, on the other hand, goes to great lengths to avoid conception with her husband so as not to disinherit Cligés, yet there is no mention of children when married to Cligés later. This is in fact the only explicit reference in romances of adultery to paternity and succession, which must have been the focus of anxiety in medieval patriarchal society.[91] However, whereas childlessness, when viewed from the position of dynastic families headed by powerful fathers, would have been seen as a punishment, and these romances would consequently have had a dissuasive effect on some potential illicit lovers, childlessness would have been viewed rather differently by the young, unmarried males, whose fantasies were realised by courtly love literature. Indeed, it is likely that the very ambiguity of these texts would have led to a wide range of readings even amongst contemporaries.[92]

In the Middle Ages the most important symbolic meaning of a woman's body was its association with land.[93] In granting her love, the lady often used the terminology of land tenure as she handed over her body to her lover in return for his service. As we have seen, the duchess of Burgundy was synonymous with her late husband's fief. When Laïs divorces his wife in *Eracle* he makes the point that the empire does not go with the empress (line 5057), and that the couple will have to live off the land Paridés inherited from his father, now given to him free of all feudal service. Laïs's carefully worded conditions for the divorce suggest that his people might naturally expect the empress of Constantinople to confer sovereignty on her new husband (perhaps reflecting the powers of historical Byzantine

---

89 See P. McCracken, 'The Body Politic and the Queen's Adulterous Body in French Romance', *Feminist Approaches to the Body in Medieval Literature*, edd. L. Lomperis and S. Stanbury (Philadelphia, 1993), pp. 38–64. It is interesting that charges of adultery were levelled at two historical queens who remained childless, Edith, wife of Edward the Confessor and Kunigunde, married to the emperor Henry II. The lack of an heir was later explained as the consequence of chaste marriages; see Parsons, 'Family, Sex, and Power', p. 5, and Benoît de Sainte-Maure's *Chronique des ducs de Normandie*, ed. C. Fahlin, 3 vols (Uppsala/Geneva, 1951), pp. 54 and 67, line 36404, on Edward the Confessor's unconsummated marriage.

90 Celtic, French and German Arthurian traditions mention Arthur's son, Loholt, and some authors state that he was also Guinevere's child. Others name another mother or leave the maternal identity vague; see K. Busby, 'The Enigma of Loholt', *An Arthurian Tapestry: Essays in Memory of Lewis Thorpe*, ed. K. Varty (Glasgow, 1981), pp. 28–36. In the French texts treated here Guinevere is not presented as a mother.

91 See Shahar, *The Fourth Estate*, p. 137.

92 Whereas many critics emphasise gender as a source of divergent readings, age is a less frequently cited factor.

93 In the Celtic myth of the king's marriage with the Earth, the queen functioned as a metaphor for the kingdom and her abduction thus implied the loss of the king's sovereignty. Later this metaphoric function was replaced by the metonymic, as real queens became associated contiguously with their lands. See M. Herbert, 'Goddess and King: The Sacred Marriage in Early Ireland', *Women and Sovereignty*, pp. 264–75.

empresses).[94] Likewise, the widowed Jocaste in the *Roman de Thèbes* is expected to marry Oedipus, for her barons wish him to become king and see her marriage as a way of confirming this:

> 'Trestuit veulent qu'il ait le regne,
> et vous, dame, serez sa fame;
> le regne aiez ensemble o lui.'   (lines 455–7)

> ('Everyone wishes him to have the kingdom; and you, my lady, will
> be his wife; may you have the kingdom along with him.')

Owing to this symbolic connection between the queen's body and the kingdom, whether she has brought land to the marriage or not, the queen's adultery, sharing her body with two men, is bound to imply the lover's illicit claim to the political power tied to the land. This seems to be what the barons are saying in Beroul's *Tristran*, lines 606–9. Meleagant's abduction of Guinevere and his imprisonment of Arthur's subjects in the *Charette* are likewise a challenge to the king's power, a challenge to which the king fails to rise, leaving the young knights, Gawain and Lancelot to rescue the queen, the latter winning the prize – access to her body. The political consequences of this are not evident, however, until the later prose romance, the *Mort Artu*, which under the influence of the Tristan legend depicts the queen's adultery as a contributory factor in the downfall of Arthur's kingdom.[95] This motif was in fact already present in Geoffrey of Monmouth's *Historia* and Wace's *Brut*, where Guinevere's consent to adultery with Arthur's nephew Mordred leads directly to the men's fatal final battle. While the *Mort Artu* presents Guinevere in a more favourable light, showing her resisting with dignity Mordred's plan to seal his false claim to the throne by marrying the queen, the later romance nevertheless illustrates yet again the attitude that the queen is inextricably linked to the land, 'car sanz faille cil a cui Dex donra l'enneur de ce reigne ne puet estre qu'il ne vos ait a fame', Guinevere is told by a baron who believes Arthur to be dead.[96] Finally, we have an explicit expression of the land metaphor in *Cligés*, when Fénice, in refusing to become another Iseut, claims that Iseut's body 'fu a deus rentiers' (line 3114), i.e. there were two tenants deriving an income from it.[97]

While Christine and the male authors we have discussed would have agreed that in the interests of political stability the queen's sexuality needed to be

---

[94] See Liz James's article in this volume. On the perceived danger of a widowed queen transferring kingship to a future husband, see Poulet, 'Capetian Women', p. 110, who notes Philip IV's condition that his wife Joan could be regent during their son's minority only while she remained unmarried.

[95] For a discussion of the other factors involved, see my 'Aristotle, Augustine or Boethius? *La Mort le roi Artu* as Tragedy', *Nottingham French Studies*, xxx (1991), 81–109.

[96] *La Mort le roi Artu*, ed. J. Frappier (Geneva/Paris, 1964), p. 138, lines 13–14.

[97] I do not follow McCracken ('The Body Politic', p. 49) in her emphasis on 'metaphors of dismemberment'. More important than the splitting of the queen's body is its equation with land.

controlled and that her chastity was paramount,[98] there was another aspect of the queen's behaviour which was viewed rather differently by male and female writers, namely her use of speech. Much of Christine's advice is about developing one's powers of rhetoric to the benefit of everyone and averting those slanderous accusations which women have, according to Christine, suffered for centuries.[99] Chrétien's *Erec et Enide* is also, amongst other things, about the power of female speech, yet, as usual with Chrétien, the message which emerges is ambiguous.[100] Enide, newly married to Erec, son of King Lac, is destined to be queen. She has all the social and moral attributes appropriate to her new rank, but Erec loves her too much, spends too much time in bed with her, neglects chivalry and she unwittingly becomes the cause of his loss of reputation. However, when she laments their situation in bed one morning, and Erec, overhearing her, forces her to reveal the criticisms against him, she provokes her husband's anger and spends most of the rest of the romance regretting her *parole*. Moreover, Erec forbids her to utter a word during their adventures, thus implying that he too thought she was wrong to criticise him in that manner.

What is interesting about the thematic of speech in this romance is that it is linked to sexuality; Enide speaks out in bed,[101] conjugal relations are suspended during the same period that Enide's speech is prohibited, and Erec's *amour propre*, perhaps his sense of his own virility, is wounded by his wife's verbal challenge. Moreover, though the protagonists seem to concur that Enide was rash to criticise her husband (and one suspects that Christine, given her advice on the subject, might have agreed too) the narrative itself demonstrates the effectiveness of female speech. Queen Guinevere's advice, discussed above, Enide's *parole*, which instigates Erec's chivalric rehabilitation, her clever use of speech to save herself from lecherous counts or to protect Erec from Guivret's attack, all suggest that silence is not always golden.[102]

The implication at the end of *Erec et Enide* is that Enide has learned obedience and respect for her husband, and that Erec has learned to moderate his lust and to

---

98 Interestingly though Fradenburg, *Women and Sovereignty*, p. 2, argues that the sovereign's need to be exclusive, different from his/her subjects, can lead to an 'extraordinary body or sexuality'.

99 For a discussion of Christine's attitude towards the power of woman's words, see L. Dulac, 'The Representation and Functions of Feminine Speech in Christine de Pizan's *Livre des Trois Vertus*', in *Reinterpreting Christine De Pizan*, ed. E. J. Richards (Athens, GA, 1992). On the ambivalence of churchmen towards woman's speech and on the model of the pious wife, see S. Farmer, 'Persuasive Voices: Clerical Images of Medieval Wives', *Speculum*, lxi (1986), 517–43.

100 See my 'Adapting Enide: Chrétien, Hartmann and the Female Reader', in *Chrétien de Troyes and The German Middle Ages*, edd. M. Jones and R. Wisbey (Cambridge, 1993), pp. 67–84.

101 Clearly the bedchamber is a site of anxiety because of a woman's potential sexual influence over her husband. It is for this reason that a queen's bed (where her other sources of power, legitimate male heirs, were conceived) became symbolic of her authority, hence her hearing of petitions in bed, see Parsons, 'Family, Sex, and Power', p. 10.

102 Though Chrétien has his heroine, in a speech of self-criticism (ll. 4630–1), invoke this type of proverbial wisdom, his narrative seems to prove the opposite.

take his wife's feelings into consideration. They therefore deserve to be crowned together by Arthur,[103] in a coronation scene which manages both to imply their equality, in that they are seated on identical thrones (lines 6713–15), and to suggest Enide's inferiority, in that after a detailed description of Erec's crowning (mentioning the anointing, the crown and the sceptre) the narrator simply says, 'puis ra Enide coronee' (line 6887, 'then he crowned Enide'). Whereas in reality the coronation of a queen was modelled on the wedding ceremony, for frequently the woman became queen on her marriage and her most important function was to be the king's spouse,[104] Enide's coronation with Erec takes place a long time after her wedding, and serves as confirmation of her own and her husband's right to rule in the mould of Arthur and Guinevere. Chrétien seems to depart from historical practice in that Enide is not provided with a lower throne than her husband's, yet this may be explained by the fact that it serves first as Arthur's throne, which he vacates in order that Enide might be seated while being crowned (lines 6733, 6833–4). The sceptre, the symbol of the king's authority, is given only to Erec.[105] Thus, despite the romancer's attempts to imply an idealised equality between the royal pair, Chrétien nevertheless maintains the idea, conveyed by contemporary coronation ritual, that a queen's power is both superior to the masses' but subordinate to her husband's.[106] Furthermore, although Enide's unwitting challenge to Erec's authority and masculinity seems to have been contained, and neutralised, her role as adviser to, even critic of her husband, remains problematic. No doubt this was a role which needed to be carried out by historical queens with all the tact and diplomacy they could muster.

Given that the factor distinguishing queens from ordinary women is their power, authority and political influence, as well as their ability to cross the boundaries between the private and the public, it is not surprising that negative images of queens in medieval literature are associated with enhanced sexual power and an independence of spirit not normally granted to women. Christine de Pizan, though encouraging a more active and influential role for royal women than we find in even the most flattering fictional representations, does not challenge the queen's subordinate role, nor offer anything more positive than Christian patience to princesses disappointed in marriage. The authors of epics and romances, written at a time of ever-shifting political boundaries and wars over land and sovereignty,

---

[103] Enide's suitability for queenship seems to rest on her beauty, corroborated by her mother's charms, which Arthur admires, lines 6616–23. Arthur's claim that beautiful trees bear beautiful flowers and fruit echoes a favourite topos of chroniclers defending the choice of a particular royal bride; see Parsons, 'Family, Sex, and Power', p. 3.

[104] See Parsons, 'Ritual and Symbol', pp. 62–3.

[105] Interestingly in the edition by Mario Roques, based on the Guiot manuscript, King Arthur says before the coronation that Erec and Enide will both carry the royal insignia: 'la porteront roial ansaigne, / corone d'or et ceptre el poing' (ll. 6496–7); Foerster's critical edition in my view again demonstrates its superiority in giving the reading 'porteroiz', line 6554 (referring to Arthur), instead of 'porteront'. Perhaps by the time of Guiot in the thirteenth century the carrying of sceptres by queens was more acceptable.

[106] See Parsons, 'Ritual and Symbol', pp. 62–4.

reveal more disturbing royal tensions and anxieties, perhaps symbolised by the medieval game of chess.[107] For while Chrétien in his *Cligés* celebrates Alexander's marriage to Soredamours by claiming that his beloved had become the queen on the chessboard of which he was king:

> . . . s'amie fu fierce
> De l'eschaquier don il fu rois.   (lines 2334–5)

Gautier d'Arras remarks, when the empress commits adultery, that the king had been checkmated by his queen:

> Li rois ert matés par se fierge
> mais ce n'ert mie par l'aufin
> par autrë ert li jus a fin.   (lines 4388–90)

If it is symbolic systems which are most revealing of a society's psyche, then perhaps the medieval chessboard with its vulnerable king needing the protection of a more mobile queen underlines most clearly the real king's dependence on his consort's co-operation for effective rule.[108] This somewhat resented, yet reluctantly acknowledged dependence is one explanation for the ambiguous presentation of queens in medieval French literature.

---

[107] The parallel between chess and the role of queens in medieval German literature is the subject of R. N. Combridge's 'Ladies, Queens and Decorum', *Reading Medieval Studies*, i (1975), 71–83.

[108] Although the queen on the medieval chessboard was not as powerful and flexible a piece as it is today, she replaced the vizir (hence 'fierce') as second-in-command when the game was transported from the Arab world to the Christian West. The decision to include a female within the king's army of protectors is indicative of the important political role played by queens in the Middle Ages. The potential treachery of the royal consort must though have been a source of greater anxiety than the possible betrayal of his male supporters, for I know of no example of the verb 'mater' being used metaphorically in connection with the king's defeat by other chess pieces on his side. On chess in general, see R. Eales, 'The Game of Chess: An Aspect of Medieval Knightly Culture', in *The Ideals and Practice of Medieval Knighthood*, edd. C. Harper-Bill and R. Harvey (Woodbridge, 1986), pp. 12–34. On 'mater' and its possible sexual connotations, see Tobler-Lommatzsch, v, 1250–3; on 'fierce/fierge', see *idem*, iii, 1826–7. Godefroy, iii, 788, gives the following quotation from the *Salut d'amor*, which makes explicit the dependence of the king on his queen:

> Quar je sui mas en l'eschequier
> Dont vous estes fierge establie
> S'au deschiquier n'ai vostre aie.   (Richelieu 837, fol. 267)

IV

Queens and Culture

14

The Architecture of Queenship: Royal Saints, Female Dynasties and the Spread of Gothic Architecture in Central Europe

Paul Crossley

The church of St Elizabeth in Marburg on the Lahn, begun in 1235 and consecrated in 1283, occupies a special position in the history of medieval architecture. Modest in scale, repetitive in detail, it was, nevertheless, the *'Schöpfungsbau* of German Gothic',[1] the earliest example in the Empire of a fully-fledged Gothic church. Its impact on local opinion can be measured by the famous passage in Burchard of Hall's chronicle of St Peter at Wimpfen-im-Tal, where the small church of Wimpfen, begun in about 1270 in the 'French style' (*opere Francigeno*) by an architect 'who had recently come from the city of Paris', was such a brilliant curiosity that crowds flocked to see it: its 'columns and windows, fashioned in the manner of precious metalwork' with 'much labour and expense', excited the admiration of visitors who 'came from all quarters' and 'praised it'.[2] A generation earlier, and a little over a hundred miles to the north, the people of the Lahn valley must have been struck with equal force by the unfamiliar modernity of St Elizabeth's church. Here, for the first time in Germany east of the Rhine, was true, new-minted, *opus francigenum* (pll. 28–31). Its attenuated proportions and diaphanous screens of windows provided the setting for quotations from the most modish elements of Ile-de-France Gothic. The transept chapels of Laon cathedral, the choirs of St-Yved of Braine or St-Léger at Soissons, the radiating chapels of Chartres and Le Mans cathedrals – these are some of the sources on which the Marburg architect seems to have drawn for his polygonally-apsed choir, with its exterior passages running through the buttresses in front of the windows. Marburg's most distinctive feature, its double window system (here used as a unifying motif round the whole building) recalls collegiate and parish churches in the Laonnois and Parisis (Mons-en-Laonnois, Larchant); while the windows themselves are quotations from no less a source than Reims cathedral, which also provided the model for the giant *piliers cantonné* of the nave, with their four attached shafts. Within this French vocabulary there is, of course, a German syntax.

1 J. Michler, 'Die Langhaushalle der Marburger Elisabethkirche', *Zeitschrift für Kunstgeschichte*, xxxii (1969), 104–32 at p. 125.
2 For the church of Wimpfen and the chronicle of Burchard von Hall, see H. Klotz, *Der Ostbau der Stiftskirche zu Wimpfen im Tal. Zum Frühwerk des Erwin von Steinbach* (Berlin, 1967).

The trefoil plan of its choir and transepts may have drawn on a distinguished tradition of Romanesque churches in the lower Rhine; while its nave of three equally tall aisles adopted a hall church format favoured in contemporary West-phalia and Mecklenburg. It may have been precisely this admixture of familiarity and modernity that guaranteed Marburg's success. The anonymous architect of the choir was probably the *magister operis* of the church of Our Lady at Trier, begun just a few years earlier in or soon after 1233[3] in a similarly precocious Laonnois and Remois style. But, whereas Trier's unique centralised plan provoked virtually no imitation,[4] Marburg's influence in central and northern Germany in the second half of the thirteenth century was profound and immediate. Right across central Germany, from Westphalian Minden in the west to Werden and Hamburg in the north, from Mainz in the Middle Rhine to Mühlhausen and Arnstadt in the Thuringian east, Marburg became a point of reference for cathedrals (Minden), parish churches (Wetzlar), Cistercian buildings (Haina) and the more ambitious enterprises of the mendicant orders (Franciscan churches of Munster, Trier and Cologne).[5] No building in thirteenth-century Europe associated so directly with a queen or royal princess had played a more decisive part in the spread of French-inspired Gothic architecture.

This paper makes no claim to be another history of St Elizabeth's church and its 'artistic followers'.[6] In any case, Marburg's impact on the course of German Gothic – the subject of intense research in Germany in the last fifty years – is not in doubt. Instead, it concentrates on the figure of St Elizabeth herself, and on the aristocratic and regal female patrons – many of them a part of her family network – who copied her mausoleum as a model of modernity. For these benefactors architectural quotation from St Elizabeth's church meant a number of things: it paid homage to her memory, it evoked her example of Franciscan (but also

---

3   The starting date for the church is controversial. N. Borger-Keweloh, *Die Liebfrauenkirche in Trier. Studien zu Baugeschichte*, Trier Zeitschrift für Geschichte und Kunst des Trierer Landes und seiner Nachbargebiete, 8 (1986), pp. 127f. put it to soon after 1233; N. Nussbaum, *Deutsche Kirchenbaukunst der Gotik* (Darmstadt, 1994), p. 341 n. 117, puts it at 1227. It was certainly begun before Marburg. The Marburg architect used Trier feet: see A. Tuczek, 'Das Masswesen der Elisabethkirche in Marburg und der Liebfrauenkirche in Trier', *HJL*, xxi (1971), 1–99.

4   For Trier's meagre following see W. Götz, *Zentralbau und Zentralbautendenz in der gotischen Architektur* (Berlin, 1968), pp. 45ff.

5   For Marburg's influence see, still, R. Hamann and K. Wilhelm-Kästner, *Die Elisabethkirche zu Marburg und ihre Künstlerische Nachfolge*, i (Wilhelm-Kästner), *Die Architektur*, ii (Hamann), *Die Plastik* (Marburg, 1924–9); H.-J. Kunst, 'Die Elisabethkirche in Marburg und die Bischofskirchen', in *Die Elisabethkirche. Architektur in der Geschichte*, ed. H.-J. Kunst, in *700 Jahre Elisabethkirche in Marburg 1283–1983* (exhibition catalogue, Philipps-Universität Marburg, 1983), i, 69–75; *idem*, 'Die Elisabethkirche in Marburg und die Kollegiatsstiftskirchen', *ibid.*, pp. 77–80; W. Schenkluhn, 'Die Auswirkung der Marburger Elisabethkirche auf die Ordensarchitektur in Deutschland', *ibid.*, pp. 81–101; R. L. Auer, 'Landesherrliche Architektur. Die Rezeption der Elisabethkirche in den hessischen Pfarr-kirchen', *ibid.*, pp. 103–23

6   A term derived from the title of Hamann and Wilhelm-Kästner's classic study, *Die Elisabethkirche*.

aristocratic) piety, and it gave to patrons something of the kudos of her Franco-Hungarin connections. To underline the importance of St Elizabeth in the shaping and success of her own church might seem to labour the obvious; but the tendency of recent research has been to submerge the historical Elizabeth in the *Realpolitik* of her times; to see her lavish shrine church as antithetical to her Franciscan poverty and *caritas*; and to concentrate on the posthumous exploitation of her cult by her confessor Konrad of Marburg, by the Teutonic Knights, by the Landgraves of Thuringia, and by the German Emperor Frederick II. As a result, St Elizabeth herself, and her well-connected Andechs-Meranien family, have become shadowy presences, having only a titular influence on the form and meaning of her church.[7] To examine this position critically we have to remind ourselves of St Elizabeth and her history.[8]

Born in 1207, the daughter of King Andrew II of Hungary and of Gertrud of Andechs-Meranien, Elizabeth of Hungary was betrothed to the Landgrave Henry IV of Thuringia, moved to his castle on the Wartburg near Eisenach at the age of four, and married him in 1221. At Henry's death on crusade with Frederick II in 1227, Elizabeth, already under the dubious influence of her confessor, the papal Inquisitor Konrad of Marburg, determined on a wholesale rejection of secular life. She vowed perpetual widowhood and embraced a regime of extreme fasting – what Caroline Bynum has diagnosed, with some reservations, as a kind of holy *anorexia nervosa*[9] – combined with food-relief and hospital care for the sick and poor. Her uneasy relations with her two brothers-in-law, the new Landgrave Henry Raspe, and his brother Konrad, and the domineering influence of Konrad of Marburg, persuaded her to escape from the Wartburg and settle in Marburg, a town where she possessed property as part of her dowry. Already a Franciscan tertiary, in 1228 she founded a Franciscan hospital in Marburg for the poor and sick, and here, dressed in the grey penitential tunic (*tunica grisea*) supposedly sent her by

---

7   Especially U. Geese, 'Die Reliquien der Elisabeth von Thuringen im Interesse des Ketzer-predigers Konrad von Marburg', in *Bauwerk und Bildwerk im Hochmittelalter*, edd. K. Clausberg, D. Kimpel, H.-J. Kunst, R. Suckale (Giesau, 1981), pp. 127–40, and *idem*, 'Die hl. Elisabeth im Kräftefeld zweier konkurrierender Mächte', in *Die Elisabethkirche*, ed. Kunst, pp. 55–67. Michler in his monumental study, *Die Elisabethkirche zu Marburg in ihrer ursprünglichen Farbigkeit*, Quellen und Studien zur Geschichte des Deutschen Ordens, 19 (Marburg, 1984), does not mention the Andechs-Meranien connection, while the catalogue of the Andechs-Meranien exhibition, held in Andechs in 1993, included no serious discussion of architecture. See *Herzöge und Heilige. Das Geschlecht der Andechs-Meranier im europäischen Hochmittelalter*, edd. J. Kirmeier and E. Brockhoff, Veröffentlichungen zur Bayerischen Geschichte und Kultur, 24/93 (Regensburg, 1993).

8   The following account of St Elizabeth's life is based on A. Huyskens, 'Der Hospitalbau der heiligen Elisabeth und die erste Wallfahrtskirche zu Marburg', *Zeitschrift für hessische Geschichte und Landeskunde*, xliii (1909), 130ff; contributions by P. Schmidt and H. Beumann in *Sankt Elisabeth, Fürstin – Dienerin – Heilige, Aufsätze, Dokumentation Katalog* (Sigmaringen, 1981), pp. 45–69, and 151–66; and essays in *Die heilige Elisabeth in Hessen*, ed. W. Heinemeyer, in *700 Jahre Elisabethkirche in Marburg*, iv, 15–85.

9   *Holy Feast and Holy Fast: The Religious Significance of Food to Medieval Women* (Berkeley, 1988), pp. 135–6, 204–7.

St Francis,[10] she lived out the rest of her short life in works of mendicant charity, until her premature death, brought about directly by her mortifications, in her own hospital on 17 November 1231.

Like all medieval cults, the memory of St Elizabeth was soon hijacked by the interests of those who promoted it. In his letter of petition for her canonisation sent to Pope Gregory IX on 11 August 1232, Konrad of Marburg presented her less as the sister of charity than as the wondrous miracle-worker and the scourge of German heretics.[11] The new, self-contained, and finger-shaped church (the so-called *basilica*) which Konrad built in 1231-2 around her grave in her hospital chapel (pl. 28) may well have been a deliberate attempt to cordon off the saint's remains, physically and symbolically, from the confines of the hospital and its modest chapel (*capella modica*) where she had been buried.[12] With Konrad's murder, a year later, on 30 July 1233, the rich political assets accruing from Elizabeth's sanctity now became the bone of contention between, on the one hand, Archbishop Siegfried II of Mainz, who was quick to claim ownership over her hospital as part of an aggressive policy to annex the whole of the duchy of Hesse, and, on the other hand, a powerful alliance, backed by the Emperor Frederick II, between the Landgraves of Thuringia and the Teutonic Knights.[13] In the event, Konrad and the knights prevailed. After intense personal lobbying from Konrad at the papal curia, Gregory IX transferred the hospital from the Franciscans to the knights on I July 1234; and in Perugia, less than a year later, on 27 May 1235, in the presence of Konrad and Hermann von Salza, the Grand Master of the knights, he officially canonised St Elizabeth, thus setting the seal of her sanctity on the alliance between the Thuringian landgraves and the Teutonic Order. Her canonisation and her new church were clearly inseparable projects, for three days later the pope issued an indulgence for the building of the new (present) church 'in honour of St Elizabeth . . . where her tomb shines with the multiplicity of her miracles, and where a church has been begun in a sumptuous style (*edificare*

---

[10] For the so-called penitential tunic see *Die Zeit der Staufer. Geschichte-Kunst-Kultur*, ed. R. Haussherr, 4 vols (exhibition catalogue, Stuttgart, 1977), i, no. 779, p. 620, pl. 570. Caesarius of Heisterbach said that she received the tunic *de manu magistri Conradi de Marburg*; see A. Huyskens, 'Des Caesarius Schriften über die Heilige Elisabeth', *Annalen des Hist. Vereins für den Niederrhein*, lxxxvi (1908), 1–59 at p. 23; and E. Keyser, 'Das Gebiet des Deutschen Ritterordens in Marburg', *Zeitschrift der Vereins für hessische Geschichte und Landeskunde*, lxxiii (1962), 71–91 at p. 79 n. 10.

[11] Geese, 'Die Reliquien', p. 137; A. Wyss, *Hessisches Urkundenbuch. Erste Abteilung. Urkundenbuch der Deutschordensballei Hessen von 1207 bis 1299* (Leipzig, 1879), no. 28.

[12] The term *capella modica* comes from Caesarius of Heisterbach's life of the saint; see Geese, 'Die Reliquien', pp. 134–5.

[13] The alliance between the Thuringian landgraves and the knights is set out in E. Keyser, 'Untersuchungen zur Geschichte des Deutschen Ordens in Marburg', *HJL*, x (1960), 16–43; Keyser, 'Das Gebiet', pp. 84–5; H. Boockmann, *Der Deutsche Orden* (Munich, 1981), pp. 139–44; the competing claims are discussed by W. Schenkluhn and P van Stipelen, 'Architektur als Zitat. Die Trier Liebfrauenkirche in Marburg', in *Die Elisabethkirche*, ed. Kunst, pp. 19–21.

ceperini opere sumptuoso).[14] On 14 August the official foundation stone was laid,[15] and on 1 May 1236 the relics were translated into a new tomb (probably still in the old *basilica*) in the presence of Hermann von Salza, the archbishops of Cologne, Trier, Mainz and Bremen, an estimated crowd of over a million pilgrims, and the Emperor Frederick II, who placed a crown on the head of the saint. The whole ceremony dramatically exemplifies the power of sanctity in the service of high diplomacy. The crown on the corpse gave to Frederick's office the dignity of a *sacrum imperium*, and bound the alliance between the landgraves and the knights – and their conquests east of the Elbe – to the ambitions of the Hohenstaufen.[16] Konrad was elected Grand Master of the knights after the death of Hermann von Salza in 1239.[17] By 1243 the three apses of the choir were complete and the old *basilica* demolished; by 1248 the eastern bays of the nave were being roofed, and in 1249 there was a second translation of the relics, perhaps into the eastern choir apse. By 1283, when the whole church was consecrated, the nave and the first two stories of the west facade were complete.[18]

Like the legends that embroidered her early *vitae*,[19] the political opportunism that overlays the early history of St Elizabeth's church has persuaded us that the key to the building's 'programme' – its general shape, its liturgical dispositions, and its stylistic alliances – has little to do with the saint herself, and almost everything to do with the landgraves, the Teutonic Knights, and even Frederick II.[20] Certainly

14 For the canonisation and its lavish charities see J. Leinweber, 'Das kirchliche Heiligspre-chungsverfahren bis zum Jahre 1234. Der Kanonisationsprozess der hl. Elisabeth von Thüringen', in *Sankt Elisabeth*, pp. 128–36. For the indulgence see Wyss, *Hessisches Urkundenbuch*, no. 53, Keyser, 'Untersuchungen', p. 22, and Keyser, 'Das Gebiet', p. 85.

15 Wyss, *Hessisches Urkundenbuch*, no. 649; Keyser, 'Untersuchungen', p. 22; Schenkluhn and van Stipelen, 'Architektur als Zitat', p. 21.

16 Huyskens, 'Des Caesarius Schriften', p. 56. Frederick's part in the translation is discussed at length by H. Beumann, 'Kaiser Friedrich II und die heilige Elisabeth. Zum Besuch des Kaisers in Marburg am 1 Mai 1236', in *Sankt Elisabeth*, pp. 151–66, and by M. Frase, 'Die Translation der heiligen Elisabeth am Mai 1236. Überlegungen zur Teilnehmerzahl des Festes und zur Problematik des Ölwunders', in *Elisabeth, der Deutsche Orden und ihre Kirche. Festschrift zur 700 Jährigen Wiederkehr der Weihe der Elisabethkirche Marburg 1983*, edd. U. Arnold and H. Liebing, Quellen und Studien zur Geschichte des Deutschen Ordens, 18 (Marburg, 1983), pp. 39–51, where he estimates the numbers attending as 1,200,000!

17 Keyser, 'Das Gebiet', p. 86; Boockmann, *Der Deutsche Orden*, p. 144.

18 For the chronology see Michler, *Die Elisabethkirche*, pp. 29–37; Schenkluhn and van Stipelen, 'Architektur als Zitat', pp. 21–8.

19 There are lives by Caesarius of Heisterbach, ed. Huyskens, 'Des Caesarius Schriften', by Konrad of Marburg (as part of his petition to Gregory IX for the canonisation), ed. Huyskens, *Quellenstudien zur Geschichte der heiligen Elisabeth, Landgrafin von Thüringen* (Marburg, 1908), and the *Libellus*, containing the testimony of witnesses before the papal commission, also ed. A. Huyskens, *Der sog. Libellus de dictis quatuor ancillarum S. Elisabeth confectus* (Kempten/Munich, 1911).

20 K. E. Demandt, 'Verfremdung und Wiederkehr der Heiligen Elisabeth', *HJL*, xxii (1972), notes an early 'alienation from the original ideals of the hospital'; Michler, *Die Elisabethkirche*, p. 10, points to the absence of any spirit of asceticism in the church, and to the limited access given to pilgrims visiting the shrine.

the Teutonic Knights' chapel at Ramersdorf (now in the old cemetery of Bonn), built c. 1225–30, just a few years before the beginning of the Marburg church, suggests a direct knowledge of the most sophisticated Burgundian High Gothic architecture.[21] And its hall church format provides a convenient precedent in their use of this system in the nave at Marburg. There are also good reasons for assuming that the choice of the architect of Our Lady's church at Trier to design the new Marburg choir served the interests of the Thuringian landgraves. The Trier archbishop, Dietrich von Wied, was an early supporter of the Teutonic Order, and an ally of the landgraves against the archbishops of Mainz. At Mainz cathedral in the early 1230s Archbishop Siegfried II was completing a large trefoil-planned western choir, consisting of three polygonal apses, in a grandiose but 'conservative' late Romanesque manner. Schenkluhn and van Stipelen have convincingly argued that Marburg's adoption of a similar system, but in the very different language of modern French Gothic, and in pointed and specific imitation of Trier, was a gesture calculated to underline the triple alliance between knights, landgraves, and Trier electors.[22]

But the international connections of the Knights, and the high politics of the landgraves have also led to far-fetched explanations for the Marburg programme. Attempts to derive its trefoil plan from the knights' four-conch castle church of Tartlau in remote Transylvania[23] have foundered on the recent discovery that Tartlau was begun at least four years after Marburg, in the 1240s.[24] To see Marburg's east end as another version of the church of the Nativity in Bethlehem, the archetype of all trefoil choirs, may tally with the knights' first-hand knowledge of the architecture of the Holy Land, but the credentials of the Bethlehem church as a functionally appropriate model are undermined by the fact that it never served as a mausoleum.[25] Equally unconvincing has been the recent attempt to explain the Reims-style columns of the nave of Marburg in terms of the political ideology of the landgraves. The issue is too detailed to be argued at length in this context; suffice it to say that no evidence from the fabric of the building unequivocally supports the thesis that these columns were originally intended to be plain round cylinders, like those opposite the side chapels in Our Lady at Trier, nor that in 1246 or soon thereafter they were re-designed in the form of the present giant *piliers cantonné* (pl. 29) in order to celebrate Henry Raspe's election in 1246 to the

[21] H.E. Kubach and A. Verbeek, *Romanische Baukunst an Rhein und Maas. Katalog der vorromanischen und romanischen Denkmäler* (Berlin, 1976), i, 119–20. The closest similarities are with the ambulatory and axial chapel of the cathedral of Auxerre, begun in c. 1217; see R. Branner, *Burgundian Gothic Architecture* (London, 1960), pp. 39–47.

[22] Schenkluhn and van Stipelen, 'Architektur als Zitat', pp. 36–44.

[23] The Bethlehem connection is advanced by F. Möbius, 'Baukunst', in *Geschichte der deutschen Kunst 1200–1350*, edd. F. Möbius and H. Sciurie (Leipzig, 1989), p. 230. Tartlau was introduced to the problem by Götz, *Zentralbau*, pp. 26–7.

[24] E. Marosi, *Die Anfänge der Gotik in Ungarn. Esztergom in der Kunst des 12.–13. Jahrhunderts* (Budapest, 1984), pp. 163–4.

[25] R. Milburn, *Early Christian Art and Architecture* (Aldershot, 1988), pp. 98–100; R. Krautheimer, *Early Christian and Byzantine Architecture* (Harmondsworth, 1965), pp. 89–90.

German kingship by quoting from the pillars of the coronation church of the Capetians. In fact, there are strong reasons for concluding that the Reims-style piers at Marburg were not conceived as subsequent gestures of parity with the French monarchy and its *Königskathedral*, but were planned from the start.[26] The concentration on the political imperatives of the knights and the landgraves leaves out of the reckoning a critical factor in the programme of all medieval shrine churches: the need to devise a setting for a saint that was, in every sense, appropriate, both in relation to her earthly memory and her celestial status. Considerations of saintly decorum must have exercised the minds of Hermann von Salza and Konrad of Thuringia as they pondered on the programme of the new church in the critical year between their acquisition of the hospital on 1 July 1234 and the canonisation on 27 May 1235. The virtues presented to the papal commission for her canonisation, and those urged by Hermann and Konrad on the papal court in Rieti in the summer of 1234, and in Perugia a year later, did not include questions of architectural taste; but it would be difficult for patrons who so obviously shared the values of Elizabeth's aristocratic background to ignore the cultural interests of Elizabeth herself, and the francophile tastes of her Andechs-Meranien family. Speculative though this argument must be, I want to advance the hypothesis that the style of St Elizabeth's church directly reflected the reputation of her family as one of the most powerful forces in the introduction of French Gothic architecture into central and eastern Europe.

Elizabeth's extreme asceticism suggests that in the later years of her life she would, along with St Francis, have rejected the *vanitas* of all permanent architecture, at least for her own church. Caesarius of Heisterbach mentions the 'modest chapel' (*capella modica*) in the Marburg hospital where her remains were first consigned.[27] But as the daughter of King Andrew II of Hungary, her Hungarian

---

26 Schenkluhn and van Stipelen, 'Architektur als Zitat', pp. 26–8, 42ff, argue that the awkward junction of the thin arcade arches of the nave with the thicker respond system of the south-west crossing pier implies that originally the arcade arches of the hall were to have been wider, indeed as wide as those of the crossing. This system is also found at Our Lady at Trier. Moreover, the nave aisle responds, with three shafts of equal gauge, were originally to support transverse arches of the same profile as the diagonal ribs (i.e. the same system as in the straight bays of the transepts). These two changes they adduce as evidence that the original pillars of the nave were planned to be simple round columns, like those at Trier, not the present Reimsian pillars. The 'subsequent' adoption of the High Gothic cathedral *piliers cantonné* system necessitated the thickening of the transverse arches to match the pillar's aisle-facing shaft, and produced an arcade arch which is too narrow for the respond system on the west face of the south-west crossing pier. These 'changes', however, admit of other explanations: the need to differentiate the arcade arches of the nave from the more important crossing arches, and the need to maintain the aisle bay divisions with thicker transverse arches. Schenkluhn and van Stipelen admit that the 'Trier' columns of their 'plan 1' would have been supports for a hall church, but this ignores the fact that their proposed thicker arcade arches would have occupied so much of the column's width that there would have been no room for the springing of the diagonal ribs at the same level, a problem not encountered at Trier since it is a basilica, and the ribs spring not from the columns but higher up, from the vault responds.

27 Huyskens, 'Des Caesarius Schriften', p. 50.

family connections would have exposed her to the most advanced, French-inspired Gothic art and architecture anywhere east of the Rhineland.[28] From the 1180s to the 1220s/30s, under King Béla III and his successors, a steady stream of Mosan and French architects and sculptors, – first in the cathedral at Esztergom, and then, from Esztergom to other royal commissions – brought to Hungary the latest Gothic ornaments and techniques directly from Paris and the north east of France.[29] The destruction of so much Hungarian early Gothic makes it impossible to reconstruct what Elizabeth might have been familiar with in Hungary in the critical years around 1220, but fragments of two key monuments of that decade, both connected with her family, and both by the French-trained Esztergom workshop, the cathedral of Kalocsa and the Cistercian church at Pilis, show just how closely King Andrew and his court maintained their connections with the Ile-de-France. Kalocsa was begun under Elizabeth's uncle, Archbishop Berthold of Andechs-Meranien, and its French-inspired chevet (the earliest in Europe east of the Rhine) (pl. 32) as well as its surviving capitals and responds, show a knowledge of Parisian and Chartrain fashions in the decades either side of 1200.[30] The architectural fragments from the destroyed Pilis exhibit similar affiliations, but its most spectacular tribute to France was the tomb, now in fragments, of Elizabeth's mother, Queen Gertrud of Andechs-Meranien, constructed by a Chartres-trained sculptor at Pilis probably in the 1220s (pll. 33–4). Gerevich has convincingly shown how the tomb's leaf carving, heads, drapery and foliage forms match, detail for detail, the sculpture of the slightly earlier (c. 1210–20) south transept portal at Chartres, while the architectural details of the tomb imply a direct knowledge of the choir of Reims cathedral.[31]

[28] Although Elizabeth left Hungary for Thuringia at the age of four, she maintained good contacts with the Hungarian court and her Hungarian branch of the Andechs-Meranien family. A few months after her marriage at the end of 1221 she returned with her husband, Landgrave Ludwig IV, to Hungary. Her uncle, Bishop Ekbert of Bamberg, tried to persuade her in 1228 to re-marry. And in 1228 Elizabeth was in Bamberg to receive the body of Ludwig on its journey from the Holy Land, leaving to accompany it to its final resting place in the Ludowinger's Hauskloster at Reinhardsbrunn in May 1228. Ekbert was a key figure in negotiating the size of Elizabeth's widow's income and entitlements with the landgraves in 1228. The saint also regularly received Hungarian delegations and visitors in Marburg. Indeed, Konrad of Marburg was worried lest Elizabeth backslide from her Franciscan regime to her older aristocratic habits. See A. Schütz, 'Elisabeth, Landgrafin von Thüringen', in *Herzöge und Heilige*, pp. 131–44 at pp. 133–9.

[29] Marosi, *Die Anfänge der Gotik in Ungarn, passim.*

[30] *Ibid.,* pp. 122, 152, 154–65, 170. Some of the cathedral's sculpture is a crude and conservative paraphrase of Burgundian models of the 1160s–80s (see p. 130). But its leaf carving and respond systems (pll. 249–52), clearly related to Esztergom, have the same Parisian and Chartrain background. For Bishop Berthold see A. Schütz, in *Herzöge und Heilige*, pp. 84ff.

[31] The parallels with the Chartres Confessors Portal are especially close. See L. Gerevich, 'Ergebnisse der Ausgrabungen in der ungarischen Zisterzienserabtei Pilis', *Acta Archaeologica*, xxxvii (1985), 128–30; *idem,* 'Ausgrabungen in der ungarischen Zisterzienserabtei Pilis', *Analecta Cisterciensia*, xxxix (1983), 291–3; P. C. Claussen attributes the tomb to a sculptor from the north porch of Chartres; see *Chartres Studien. Zu Vorgeschichte, Funktion und Skulptur der Vorhallen* (Wiesbaden, 1975), pp. 112f, pl. 75a; *Herzöge und Heilige*, p. 225 no. 52; Marosi, *Die Anfänge der Gotik in Ungarn*, pp. 135–6.

If this was the kind of precocious French Gothic taste that Elizabeth, through report or direct experience, would have been acquainted with by her Andechs-Meranien family, it comes as no surprise to find her as a generous benefactor, in the last years of her life, of the new choir of Cambrai cathedral, begun sometime before 1231. 'She helped by gold and by money to complete the choir', and in 1232 the chapter, in gratitude, endowed a yearly Mass in her honour, and a few years later, in 1239, in recognition of her canonisation, dedicated one of the radiating chapels to her.[32] Why Elizabeth singled out Cambrai for her generosity is not certain, though her Andechs-Meranien French connections may lie behind the choice. Her aunt, sister of her mother Gertrud, was Agnes, the disputed queen of King Philip Augustus of France; and Agnes's son Philip Hurepel was made count of Boulogne after Bouvines.[33] In any event, the object of Elizabeth's gifts, the earliest parts of Cambrai choir, the radiating chapels, although no longer surviving, were constructed in a style deriving directly from the last word in French High Gothic architecture in the later 1220s – the choir of the French coronation church of Reims cathedral (pl. 35).[34]

---

32 Our information on the plan and chronology of Cambrai choir, destroyed in the French Revolution, comes from A. Le Gray, *Recherches sur l'église métropolitaine de Cambrai* (Paris, 1825). In it, Le Gray reproduces a 1797 plan of the transept and choir by Boileaux, and gives to each of the chapels a date, without specifying if this refers to the foundation or the consecration of the chapel. The usual date given for the beginning of the new choir at Cambrai is 'circa 1227', but this refers to the chapel of SS Peter and Paul 'built *c.* 1227', which opens eastwards from the south transept of the 1180s and stylistically belongs to it. Its construction, and that of the corresponding chapel of Notre-Dame de la Grande in the north transept, 'fondée vers l'an 1232', mark – for H. R. Hahnloser, *Villard de Honnecourt. Kritische Gesamtausgabe des Bauhüttenbuches ms fr 19093 der Pariser Nationalbibliothek*, 2nd revised edn (Graz 1972), p. 386 – the end of the transept construction and not the beginning of the new choir. Certainly the first mention of work on the choir is the foundation of the chapel of St Nicholas (westernmost on north side) 'in 1230 or 1231' – see Le Gray, *Recherches*, p. 34, cited in Hahnloser, *Villard de Honnecourt*, p. 386. The sixteenth-century historian of the cathedral, Julien de Ligne, in his *Sommaire des antiquités de l'église archiépiscopale de Cambrai*, records that 'Sainte Elisabeth . . . ayda par or et par argent à achever le dit choeur', and Le Gray, basing his information on now-lost documentary evidence, adds that the gold was a considerable sum, and that St Elizabeth took a lively interest in the work – 'cet edifice auquel elle prenoît le plus vif intérêt': see Le Gray, *Recherches*, pp. 19, 137, cited in Hahnloser, *Villard de Honnecourt*, p. 386. All this means that the choir must have been begun before her death in 1231, but whether it was begun in 1230/31, and not in the late 1220s, as Hahnloser argues, is impossible to confirm. Certainly the dates for the other chapels belong to the 1230s or 1240s, the next one after the chapel of St Nicholas being the chapel of St Elizabeth, dated to 1239 and given the place of honour to the south of the axial chapel (of the Holy Trinity, dated 1240). On 19 November 1232 the chapter endowed a yearly Mass (*festum duplex*) in St Elizabeth's honour. But we cannot infer that the gap between the 1230/31 chapel and the 1239 one means a break in the work which slowed construction down. The Reims tracery of the chapel windows looks more like the 1220s than the 1230s. To identify the radiating chapels with Amiens, as Hahnloser, *Villard de Honnecourt*, p. 386 does, is not convincing.

33 E. Hallam, *Capetian France 987–1328* (London, 1983), p. 132. Philip Hurepel married Matilda, the daughter of the count of Flanders.

34 For Cambrai and its debts to Reims see P. Heliot, 'Le nef et le clocher de l'ancienne cathédrale

The Cambrai connection raises intriguing possibilities for the sources of Marburg. The long-acknowledged debts which Marburg owed to Reims cathedral, could by the same token, also be debts to Cambrai: all three share the same heavy *piliers cantonné*, and the same east ends marked out by polygonally-apsed chapel spaces dominated by the repetitive leitmotif of large bar tracery windows composed of two lights beneath an oculus. Marburg even adopted in its (original) nave roof the system of cross-placed saddle roofs used, rather awkwardly, in the Cambrai chapels, but avoided at Reims. And if Cambrai can be included in the Marburg sources, then its curved transept ends, dating to the previous phase of the cathedral's construction, in the 1180s, take on a new significance. Although of a more complex, aisled, form than Marburg's they transform the east end of the cathedral into a trefoil plan which in outline anticipates the Marburg solution by combining, albeit as an historical accident, the older triconch system with advanced High Gothic Remois forms.[35] And this in turn raises the question of whether Cambrai was singled out by the devisors of the Marburg 'programme' because of its special associations with St Elizabeth. Elizabeth's church may not have registered her taste in architecture, but it certainly could evoke one of her most favoured buildings; and in its quotations from some of the most advanced Ile-de-France churches of the first third of the thirteenth century Hermannn von Salza and Konrad of Thuringia provided a setting for her that properly reflected the precocious tastes of her Andechs-Meranien family.

A postscript to these far-flung exchanges, which may throw further light on Elizabeth's architectural connections, is the famous Hungarian journey of Villard de Honnecourt, the early thirteenth-century Picard architect, or architect *manqué*, who left behind a priceless 'sketch'- or pattern-book, begun probably in about 1220 and finished by other architects a decade or so later. In it he often proudly refers to a journey he made to Hungary; and the similarity between a tiled pavement which he drew and captioned with the remark 'I saw such in Hungary', and the almost identical fragments of tiling excavated in the Cistercian church at Pilis, proves that Villard had been to Pilis.[36] Villard hardly needed an introduction to Hungarian sites, since by the time he was travelling eastwards, probably in the later 1220s, northern French masons and artists had been regularly arriving in Hungary for nearly forty years.[37] But if he needed any encouragement, St

de Cambrai', *Wallraf-Richartz-Jahrbuch*, xviii (1956), 91–110. Despite its destruction in 1796–7 we know its appearance from a seventeenth-century drawing of the exterior by van der Meulen, Boileaux's plan, and a model of 1695, formally in Berlin. See also Hahnloser, *Villard de Honnecourt*, pp. 226–8, 356–7, 386–7.

[35] R. Branner, 'The Transept of Cambrai Cathedral', in *Gedenkschrift Ernst Gall*, edd. M. Kuhn and L. Grodecki (Berlin/Munich, 1965), pp. 69–86. The debt Marburg may have owed to Cambrai was first fully spelt out by A. von Stockhausen, 'Zur ältesten Baugeschichte der Elisabethkirche in Marburg a.d. Lahn', *Zeitschrift für Kunstgeschichte*, ix (1940), 175–87.

[36] On fol. 15r, 'J'esoie un fois en Hongrie la u ie mes maint jor la vi io le pavement d'une glize de si faite maniere'. Hahnloser, *Villard de Honnecourt*, pp. 73–5, 358; F. Bucher, *Architektor: The Lodge Books and Sketchbooks of Medieval Architects*, i (New York, 1979), p. 100.

[37] Marosi, *Die Anfänge der Gotik in Ungarn*. Villard's journey to Hungary is dated by Hahnloser, *Villard de Honnecourt*, pp. 395–7 to the mid-1230s, and by Bucher, *Architektor*,

Elizabeth, or someone in her circle, might have provided it.[38] For we know that Villard had an exceptionally close knowledge of the plans for the new choir of Cambrai cathedral (he drew an initial, unrealised design for it in his book) (pl. 36), and was probably there at the start of operations, when Elizabeth's 'considerable gifts of gold and money' were pouring in.[39] And although we cannot reconstruct with any certainty his itinerary eastwards through Germany it is possible that he stopped off at Lausanne (where he drew a version of its southern transept rose window),[40] and at Bamberg in Franconia, roughly half way between Cambrai and Pilis. Villard was fascinated by the towers of Laon cathedral – he drew their elevations and their ground plan – and in the early 1230s the Laon towers found their earliest imitators in both Lausanne and Bamberg – indeed the western towers at Bamberg and the south-western tower at Lausanne share idiosyncrasies which prove that they knew, not only Laon, but each other's versions of Laon.[41] Now the bishop of Bamberg at the time of the building of the towers was none other than Elizabeth's uncle, Ekbert of Andechs-Meranien, the brother of Queen Gertrud and of Bishop Berthold of Kalocsa, and a man who took a sympathetic interest in Elizabeth's future after the death of her husband in 1227.[42] Ekbert's stay in Hungary between 1208 and 1211, and his participation in Andrew II's crusade in 1217/18, may have acquainted him with the latest French-inspired architecture of the Hungarian court, or that experience may, in turn, have fixed his attentions directly on the Ile-de France.[43] Certainly by the mid 1230s Ekbert and his chapter were importing a group of sculptors who had come directly from Reims to decorate

---

pp. 20–3 to the later 1220s. R. Bechmann, *Villard de Honnecourt. La pensée technique au XIIIe siècle et sa communication* (Paris, 1993), p. 22, places it 'sometime before the Tartar invasion of Hungary'.

38 A suggestion first advanced by Hahnloser, *Villard de Honnecourt*, p. 233, and P. Frankl, *The Gothic. Literary Sources and Interpretations through Eight Centuries* (Princeton, 1960), p. 36, and expanded by P. Kidson in a review of Bucher, *Architektor*, in *Journal of the Society of Architectural Historians*, xl (1981), 329–33.

39 Villard's reference to Cambrai cathedral, in his caption to his drawing of a radiating chapel of Reims cathedral, 'in such a manner those of Cambrai must be (made) if done correctly', implies that he knew of designs for the uncompleted Cambria chapels. See Hahnloser, *Villard de Honnecourt*, pp. 1o2–5; Bucher, *Architektor*, p. 164.

40 Hahnloser, *Villard de Honnecourt*, pp. 76, 388; Marosi, *Die Anfänge der Gotik in Ungarn*, p. 136.

41 The Bamberg towers were begun in c. 1230 and finished by 1237. They are modelled, specifically, on the south transept tower at Laon, the Tour de l'Horloge; but footings for screens of columns across the whole tower face have parallels with Lausanne. See D. von Winterfeld, *Der Dom in Bamberg*, i: *Die Baugeschichte bis zur Vollendung im 13. Jahrhundert* (Berlin, 1979), pp. 132–40, 156–7. See also the very Laon-like miniature towers in the baldachine over the Mary of the Annunciation inside Bamberg cathedral.

42 For Ekbert's career see Schütz in *Herzöge und Heilige*, pp. 72, 89ff, 136ff. He gave her shelter in his castle in Pottenstein, oversaw the funeral commemoration for Ludwig's body in Bamberg cathedral in 1228, and probably negotiated with Henry Raspe and his brother Konrad the terms of Elizabeth's settlement.

43 Marosi, *Die Anfänge der Gotik in Ungarn*, p. 170. The baldachine above the figure of the angel flanking the Mary Annunciate in Bamberg has been identified by Marosi as a 'toy' version of the apse of Berthold's Kalocsa cathedral.

the portals and interior of the cathedral. Villard's notional presence in Bamberg at about the same time would not, therefore, have been anything out of the ordinary. It would have provided a convenient half-way stop in his progress eastwards ; and his connections with Ekbert's niece via Cambrai would have given him an extra claim on the attention of the bishop's household. Nothing from this tissue of connections suggests that Villard was the substantial cause of the Swiss and German imitations of Laon, or that he was the executant of anything at Pilis, including Gertrud's tomb; his journey is simply a 'trace element' of the networks which bound St Elizabeth and her Andechs-Meranien family to the spread of Gothic architecture from France to central Europe in the last years of her life. Not to commemorate them, a few years later, in the Champenois and Laonnois style of her mausoleum church might have seemed like a breach of architectural decorum.

A second tendency in recent scholarship on the Marburg church is to subsume the physical and devotional importance of St Elizabeth's cult in the tensions between those who organised it. As relations between the landgraves and the knights deteriorated in the second half of the thirteenth century so St Elizabeth's physical presence in her own church became (it is argued) increasingly compromised. Much of the evidence produced to support this case centres around the sacred topography of the choir. The initial function of the church, to provide a modern setting for St Elizabeth's cult, was demoted by the competing liturgical interests of the two parties. Sometime before 1274 the southern apse of the east end, whose original liturgical status is still uncertain, was turned into the mausoleum of the new counts of Hesse-Thuringia – a wholesale occupation of a sacred space that stood out in sharp and aggressive contrast to the self-contained choir space of the knights, which cordons off the whole crossing with its large rood screen and high-backed stalls. The knights' own liturgical measures (it is argued) also tended to detract from the presence of St Elizabeth, in this case by emphasising their own patron, the Virgin Mary, along the prominent west-east axis of the church: at its western extremity, where a standing figure of the Virgin and child dominates the centre of the tympanum of the western portal (pl. 37), and at its eastern end, with a similar figure in the central panel of the high altar (pl. 38).[44]

How convincing is this image of liturgical competition as a symptom of political aspiration? Certainly relations between the landgraves and the knights came under strain in the 1260s and 1270s, though they never deteriorated into serious conflict. And it is true that the original prominence given to St Elizabeth at the start of the building of the church – a prominence registered in Gregory IX's indulgence of 30 May 1235 'for the honour of the Holy Elizabeth' (*in honorem sancte Elysabeth*)[45] – shifts in favour of the Virgin Mary as the principal patron of the church, and, after 1260, to the emphasis on the church as simply 'the church of the Brothers of the German House in Marburg'.[46] But to interpret the segregation of separate

[44] Geese, 'Die Reliquien', pp. 127–30; *idem*, 'Die hl. Elisabeth'.
[45] Wyss, *Hessisches Urkundenbuch*, no. 53.
[46] Geese, 'Die Reliquien', pp. 127–30, who quotes Matthias Werner's conclusion that

interests as signs of tension and conflict is to misread legitimate liturgical differentiation as a symptom of political animosity – a tendency to underestimate
liturgical imperatives in favour of ideological interests which underlies much of
recent neo-Marxist interpretations of medieval architecture.[47] In fact, St Elizabeth
remained a powerful force in the choir at Marburg, a figure who, far from being
subsumed by the liturgical interests of knights and landgraves, gave them meaning
and distinction.[48] As the south transept began to take shape as the landgrave
mausoleum in the 1270s[49] a new mausoleum for St Elizabeth was constructed over
her tomb as a balancing accent in the north transept, thus – literally over the heads
of the knights – invoking St Elizabeth as the titular saint and principle intercessor
of the Hesse landgraves (pl. 31). On feast days the head reliquary of the saint was
exhibited from the upper platform of the mausoleum.[50] In turn, but now in an
west-east direction, the knights terminated their choir with a new high altar,
consecrated in 1290, behind which a raised platform (begun but never finished)
was intended to support Elizabeth's shrine. If ever realised, this scheme would
have elevated the shrine as the climactic point of a long vista that started at the
western end of the nave, and was framed, at the choir screen, by a large arched
opening, once placed at ground level (like the doorway of the contemporary
screen at the nearby Cistercian church at Haina) but now raised above the later,

indulgences up to 1257 refer to the building as the church of St Elizabeth, but increasingly
after 1260 refer to it as church of 'the Brothers of the German Order in Marburg'; see M.
Werner, 'Die Heilige Elisabeth und die Anfänge des Deutschen Ordens', in *Marburger
Geschichte. Rückblick auf die Stadtgeschichte in Einzelbeiträgen*, ed. Magistrat der Stadt
Marburg (Marburg, 1979), p. 160.

47 See particularly M. Warnke, *Bau und Überbau. Sociologie der mittelalterlichen Architektur
nach der Schriftquellen* (Frankfurt, 1976), pp. 153ff, and especially pp. 73ff: 'indulgences
and relics appear in medieval building operations as fictive rights to dispense authority, as
symbolic mechanisms of regulation which allow different social interests to define their
claims and aspirations. They are the media through which the representational and functional
aims of a building can be generalized.' A similarly ideological (in the Marxist sense) and
conflictual interpretation, centred specifically around Reims cathedral, has been advanced
by B. Abou-el-Haj, 'The Urban Setting for Late Medieval Church Building: Reims and its
Cathedral between 1210 and 1240', *Art History*, xi (1988), 17–41.

48 For Elizabeth's 'return' as a legitimate figure-head for her daughter's, Sophie of Brabant's,
claims to Hesse-Thuringia, see Demandt, 'Verfremdung und Wiederkehr'.

49 When the south transept was designated as a mausoleum for the landgraves is a contested
and uncertain issue. Geese, 'Die hl. Elisabeth', pp. 62, 67 n. 31, and J. A. Holladay, 'Die
Elisabethkirche als Begräbnisstätte – Anfänge', in *Elisabeth, der Deutsche Orden und ihre
Kirche*, pp. 323–38, reject the idea that it was to be a mausoleum from the start. But Michler,
Die Elisabethkirche, pp. 10–11, 232–7, argues that the present tomb of Landgrave Konrad
(died 1240) was placed in its present position immediately after the return of his body from
Rome – a date which is consistent with the Remois style of its effigy and the date for the
completion of the south transept to *c.* 1241–3. What is certain is that no other tomb was
placed here until that of his wife, Aleydis von Braunschweig, who died in 1274.

50 For the mausoleum see Michler, *Die Elisabethkirche*, pp. 220–5; and E. Leppin, 'Die
Elisabethkirche. Ein Wegweiser zum Verstehen', in *Die Elisabethkirche*, ed. Kunst, pp. 25–7
no. 8. For the exhibition of the relics from the mausoleum see E. Dinkler-von Schubert, *Der
Schrein der hl. Elisabeth zu Marburg* (Marburg, 1964), p. 152.

fourteenth-century screen (pl. 29).[51] Why the scheme was abandoned we do not know; what is clear is that both the knights' and the dukes' private spheres in the east end of the church were at some time designed to find their public and visible climax, as well as their sacred legitimation, in the bones of the saint.[52]

Once we admit to St Elizabeth's intended prominence, her relationship with the Virgin Mary in the church can also be seen as a sign of co-operation and enhancement rather than demotion. Since the patron of the knights was the virgin (their full title was 'the Brothers of the German Hospital of Mary in Jerusalem') it was inevitable that she should displace St Elizabeth on the central axis of the building. But St Elizabeth was the Teutonic Knights' 'second patron', and her statue in the right panel of the high altar, and her coronation by the Virgin in the oculus of the St Elizabeth medallion window in the choir (s II), again directly to the right of the central axis of the choir window programme, identify her with the Mother of all charity, the archetype of all female virtue, just as St Francis, her mentor, is shown, in the same oculus of the same window, beneath the figure of Christ.[53] The reconciling power of St Elizabeth's cult, drawing together different interest groups in a single sacred topography, not only unified the apparently disparate functions and spaces of her choir, but also made her church such a sympathetic model for very different classes of patron. The use of Marburg forms in central Germany cuts across disparate institutions, and unites churches with very different functions: they are, not surprisingly, favoured by the Teutonic Knights (St Blaise in Mühlhausen), but they also appear in a Cistercian church recently appropriated by the Landgraves of Hesse (the abbey of Haina) and in the dynastic burial hall of a Benedictine monastery (Nienburg an der Salle).[54]

Given this power to recommend its forms to different institutional needs, it is surprising that a central aspect of the Marburg church – its ideal of aristocratic female sanctity – figured hardly at all in its central German followers. The prestige of St Elizabeth must have played a part in the popularity of her church, but it remained an allegiance scarcely recognised by its imitators in any overt form. The

---

51 For the screen see Michler, *Die Elisabethkirche*, pp. 225–32; Geese, 'Die hl. Elisabeth', p. 61.

52 From the early fourteenth century the shrine was kept in the north-west corner of the sacristy, where it acquired the status of a treasure, to be brought out and exhibited in the more public spaces of the church. See Geese, 'Die hl. Elisabeth', p. 64; Dinkler-von Schubert, *Der Schrein*, p. 154.

53 For the glass see A. Haseloff, *Die Glasgemälde der Elisabethkirche in Marburg* (Berlin, 1907), pp. 9f, 12–17, tables 9–12; and Leppin, 'Die Elisabethkirche', pp. 31–4. Note the anonymous French Franciscan who transcribed a collection of stories of St Elizabeth, and who cast St Francis and St Elizabeth according to gender: 'Francis was the father of the Friars Minor and [Elizabeth] was their mother. And he guarded them like a father, and she fed them like a mother.' See Huyskens, *Quellenstudien*, p. 70 no. 3, quoted in Bynum, *Holy Feast and Holy Fast*, p. 102.

54 For Mühlhausen and Haina see W. Schenkluhn, 'Die Auswirkungen der Marburger Elisabethkirche auf die Ordensarchitektur in Deutschland', in *Die Elisabethkirche*, ed. Kunst, pp. 81–101, with further literature; for Nienburg see W. Schenkluhn, 'Die Elisabethkirche als Zitat', *ibid.*, p. 186; and Hamann and Wilhelm-Kästner, *Die Elisabethkirche*, pp. 214–20.

principle exception to this trend is to be found much further east, in the Piast duchy of Lower Silesia on the western fringe of the kingdom of Poland. Here the creation by the local dukes of an aristocratic female saint as a patron of their dynasty and symbol of the political unity of their territory – a sort of *Landesheilige* – has close parallels with the promotion of St Elizabeth by the Landgraves of Thuringia. And once more, the Andechs-Meranien family are at the centre of the story. St Hedwig of Silesia (1170s/80s–1243) was the daughter of Count Berthold IV of Andechs-Meranien, the sister of Bishop Ekbert of Bamberg, and the aunt of St Elizabeth.[55] In 1186 she married Henry I (the Bearded), future duke of Silesia, and in 1203, in the presence of her uncle Otto, dean of Bamberg, and of her brother Ekbert, she founded a new Cistercian nuns' church at Trzebnica, thirty miles north of Wrocław (Breslau), with a community brought from St Theodore in Bamberg.[56] From here she cultivated the cult of St Elizabeth in Silesia, preserving in the church a rib of the saint and a black veil. Hedwig died in 1243, and was canonised on 26 March 1267, after vigorous promotion from her grandchildren Bolesław of Legnica, Konrad of Głogów, and particularly Władysław, prince of Wrocław, who had been elected archbishop of Salzburg in 1265. On 25 August 1267 she was translated into a new shrine at Trzebnica in the presence of Władysław, Ottokar II Přemyslid, numerous Silesian princes and 'an almost uncountable mass of people from various parts of the world'.[57] The parallels between this history and the promotion and translation of St Elizabeth, the close family ties between Hedwig and the Thuringian princess, and the presence of her relics in the church, might lead us to expect that the large new shrine-space begun at Trzebnica in 1268 or 1269[58] to contain and display the relics of St Hedwig should follow closely the design of St Elizabeth in Marburg. But it does not. It takes the form of a polygonally-apsed and brilliantly glazed chapel, opening off the south transept of the earlier thirteenth-century church and intended as the southern section of a total rebuilding (never realised) of the old choir, in which the new chapel was to be joined to a corresponding chapel on the north side by an extended, straight-ended sanctuary, vaulted at the same height as the chapels (pll. 39–41). Clearly a new generation of architectural thinking separates St Elizabeth's church from the Trzebnica chapel,

55 Fundamental for St Hedwig is J. Gottschalk, *St Hedwig, Herzogin von Schlesien*, Forschungen und Quellen zur Kirchen- und Kulturgeschichte Ostdeutschlands, 2 (Cologne/Graz, 1964); a useful summary, with further literature, is given by A. Schütz, 'Hedwig, Herzogin von Schlesien', in *Herzöge und Heilige*, pp. 145–64.
56 For the Romanesque Cistercian church at Trzebnica see *Sztuka Polska Przedromańska i Romańska do Schyłku XIII Wieku*, ed. M. Walicki (Warsaw, 1971), i, pp. 179–80, ii, pp. 767–8, 827–8; M. Kutzner, *Cysterska Architektura na Śląsku w latach 1200–1330* (Toruń, 1969), pp. 22–30.
57 *Legenda maior*, c. 12, pp. 153ff; and Schütz, 'Hedwig, Herzogin von Schlesien', pp. 159–60.
58 The sources give either 28 April 1268 or 1 May 1269; see M. Kutzner, 'Der Gotische Umbau der Klosterkirche in Trzebnica. Künstlerische Beziehungen Sachsens und Thuringens in Schlesien', in *Kunst des Mittelalters in Sachsen. Festschrift Wolf Schubert* (Weimar, 1967), pp. 107–16 at pp. 108 and n. 5, 114; E. Walter, 'Zur Baugeschichte der gotischen Grabkapelle der hl. Hedwig in Trebnitz', *Archiv für schlesische Kirchengeschichte*, xxxii (1974), 21–43, argues for a beginning of the chapel just a little before the official foundation.

a change from an allegiance to Remois and Champenois forms in the 1230s and '40s to an increasing fascination with the Parisian architecture of the Sainte-Chapelle and its derivatives.[59] But the new aesthetic alignment at Trzebnica does not expunge all references to St Elizabeth's building and its followers; nor does it ignore St Hedwig's Andechs-Meranien connections. It recasts both allegiances in a new (for Silesia) stylistic language, a language that is predominantly Bohemian.

Marian Kutzner convincingly established Archbishop Władysław as a driving force behind both the canonisation and the building of the new chapel, and suggested that his background may well have given him a special knowledge of contemporary Austrian, Bohemian and Hungarian chapels using a similar elegant and attenuated Rayonnant vocabulary.[60] Władysław's intervention was clearly critical at Trzebnica – he laid the foundation stone of the new chapel and placed his own brickworks at the disposal of the masons – but the Austrian and Hungarian parallels for the chapel are less convincing than the Bohemian, partly because the stylistic orientation of the chapel may owe as much to Wladyslaw's political ally, King Ottokar II of Bohemia.[61] In the *Legenda maior* of St Hedwig, Ottokar takes pride of place immediately before Władysław as the most important of the glittering figures attending her translation.[62] The Bohemian king made Władysław his chancellor, as well as dean of the Vyšehrad in Prague,[63] and relations between the two remained close after Władysław's move to Salzburg. The central Silesian dukes, Władysław and his brother Henry III, were vital allies in Ottokar's opposition to the Hungarian kings and the German princes; and they played a modest but necessary part in grander plans to extend his central European and Balkan empire into East Prussia. In this context of friendship and high alliance it is not surprising that one of the closest precedents for the Hedwig chapel's style and function was the most up-to-date royal foundation in Bohemia: the chapel choir

---

[59] The stylistic allegiances of the chapel and its archaeology are discussed in Kutzner, 'Der Gotische Umbau'; J. Jarzewicz, 'Architektura Kaplicy św Jadwigi w Trzebnicy', *Sprawozdania Poznańskiego Towarzystwa Przyjaciół Nauk*, ci (1983), 83–92; J. Rozpędowski, 'Opactwo Pań Cysterek w Trzebnicy', in *Historia i Kultura Cystersów w dawnej Polsce i ich Europejskie Związki*, ed. J. Strzelczyk (Poznań, 1987), pp. 263–81.

[60] M. Kutzner, 'Śląsk', in *Architektura Gotycka w Polsce*, edd. T. Mroczko and M. Arszyński, 4 vols (Warsaw, 1995), i, 128.

[61] R. Wagner-Rieger, 'Gotische Kapellen in Niederösterreich', in *Festschrift für K. M. Swoboda* (Vienna, 1959), pp. 273–96, identified a series of what she called *Stifterkapellen* in Austria from the late thirteenth century onwards. The problem is that few, or perhaps none (?) of her examples (apart from the Capella Speciosa at Klosterneuburg) pre-date Trzebnica. One of the earliest of them, and close stylistically to the Silesian chapel, the Leechkirche in Graz, owned by the Teutonic Knights, is usually given a starting date of 1275, too late to have been of any influence in Silesia. See however G. Brucher, *Gotische Baukunst in Österreich* (Salzburg/Vienna, 1990), p. 62, who suggests that it might have been begun earlier.

[62] *Legenda maior*, p. 153.

[63] For the alliance between Ottokar II and the central Silesian princes see Schütz, 'Hedwig, Herzogin von Schlesien', p. 159, and E. Randt, 'Politische Geschichte bis zum Jahre 1327', in *Geschichte Schlesiens*, i, edd. L. Peter, J. J. Menzel, W. Irgang (Sigmaringen, 1988), pp. 73–156 at pp. 91ff.

of St Saviour in the Agnes monastery in Prague, founded by King Ottokar II and Queen Agnes Přemyslid in 1261 to serve as a Sainte-Chapellian state treasury and burial choir for the Bohemian royal family (pl. 42). Both chapels share the same Sainte-Chapellian format – a tall cross-rib vaulted space illuminated by large tracery windows, and some telling similarities of detail: their attenuated vaults responds (tripartite in the Prague apse like those at Trzebnica), their naturalistic leaf carving on capitals and roof bosses and, most noticeably, a rare and identical tracery motif: a doublet of un-enclosed trefoiled lancets supporting an un-enclosed cinquefoil oculus – an idiosyncratic motif first appearing in the apse of St Saviour and then used as one of the alternating window designs for the Hedwig chapel.[64]

Like the tributes to St Elizabeth embodied in the stylistic language of her Marburg church, these Bohemian references at Trzebnica may not have been conceived without reference to St Hedwig and her Bohemian family alliances. Queen Agnes, the mother of Ottokar II, and the joint founder of the St Saviour chapel, was related to St Hedwig by marriage, and her life has striking parallels to St Elizabeth of Marburg. The daughter of Princess Konstancia, the sister of Andrew II of Hungary, Agnes was drawn into the Andechs-Meranien family via her aunt Gertrud, her mother's sister-in-law. St Hedwig was therefore her aunt's sister, and her cousin was St Elizabeth.[65] Like Elizabeth, she showed a precocious devotion to the Franciscans, and to Franciscan *caritas*. Like her cousin, Agnes became a Franciscan tertiary, and in 1231, only three years after the Marburg foundation, she set up her own hospital in Prague attached to the Agnes monastery, the first convent of Poor Clares north of the Alps.[66] By looking to Agnes's latest foundation in Prague, Władysław, along with Hedwig's other grandchildren, could combine their grandmother's old family associations with their present grand alliance with one of the most successful of the Přemyslid kings.

But St Elizabeth's church is not forgotten in this Bohemian entente. Both Marburg and Trzebnica were princely mausolea conceived around the body of a female family saint. In both, altars were crowded round the shrine: Marburg had at least three in the north choir arm, Trzebnica's chapel had no less than six. And in both a polygonally-apsed chapel space, placed to the side of the main choir, contained the tomb. According the *Legenda maior*, Hedwig herself, in the last year of her life, had insisted to the nuns and the abbess, her daughter Gertrud, that the only way to avoid the disturbance of pilgrims was to bury her in a side chapel – precisely the solution that seems to have worked so successfully at Marburg.[67] The connections between Marburg and Trzebnica extended, however, beyond matters of general programme to particular architectural detail. Marburg's most obvious

---

64 Some of these Prague connections were first noted by H. Soukupová-Benáková, 'Přemys-lovské Mauzoleum v Klášteře Blahoslavené Anežky na Františku', *Uměni*, xxiv (1976), 193–217, esp. pp. 205–6; and *eadem, Anežsky Klášter v Praze* (Prague, 1989), pp. 127–74, esp. pp. 170–3.

65 See the family tree in *Herzöge und Heilige*, p. 272.

66 Soukupová, *Anežsky Klášter*, pp. 43–4.

67 *Legenda maior*, c. 8, pp. 114f.

imprint is the other tracery design of Trzebnica's windows: a single oculus crowning two lancets. This basically Remois form is given a peculiarly Marburg inflection: an uncusped oculus whose profile merges with the surrounding window arch (as in the western bays of the Marburg nave) and whose size is kept small by pronounced stilting of the lancets (pl. 31, 42). To use such an archaic tracery design, at a time when Marburg's other followers in central Germany were employing more complex and fashionable forms,[68] and to alternate it pointedly with an advanced Bohemian pattern amounts to a self-conscious quotation: a posthumous tribute paid on behalf of one Andechs princess to another. A more oblique tribute may lie in the similarities (noted by Kutzner) between the architectural details of the chapel and the exactly contemporary choir of the church of Our Lady in Arnstadt. With its hall choir and attenuated Remois pillars, Arnstadt exemplifies the elegance of many of Marburg's central German followers of the last quarter of the thirteenth century.[69] To look to Arnstadt, therefore, may amount to an invocation of Marburg through the lens of one of its most sophisticated architectural 'copies'.

More direct references to Marburg may be found in the sculpture of the double-sided portal which joins the chapel to the old sanctuary, its choir-facing tympanum carved with a crucifixion, its chapel-facing tympanum with a Coronation of the Virgin (pl. 43). The crucifixion is usually identified as a cruder version of the choir screen crucifixion at Naumburg, while the naturalistic leaf carving on both faces of the portal, and throughout the chapel, is compared to that in the choir and choir screen of Meissen cathedral (begun 1259–60, in use by 1268).[70] But two features of this portal suggest a direct contact not just with Thuringia and Upper Saxony but with Marburg; and although the Marburg parallels – all coming in the western bays of the nave and the portal of the west facade – are too vaguely dated (*c.* 1265–83) to establish their definite priority it is most unlikely that influences went from remote Silesia to centrally-placed Hesse.[71] One Marburg reference is the symbolic alternation of naturalistic leaf patterns. In the west portal at Marburg

---

[68] For example, the piled up trefoils in the nave at Haina (Hesse) *c.* 1265, and in the collegiate church of Wetter (Hesse) 1263–80; or the triple oculi in the choir of St Blaise in Mühlhausen (Thuringia) *c.* 1270.

[69] Kutzner, 'Der Gotische Umbau', p. 111, first noted the similarities with Arnstadt, and attributed both buildings to the same workshop. The uncertain dating of the choir at Arnstadt (*c.* 1260–70? or begun in 1275?) makes it difficult to know which way the influences travelled.

[70] *Ibid.*, pp. 111ff; and E. Lehmann and E. Schubert, *Der Meissner Dom. Beiträge zur Baugeschichte und Baugestalt bis zum Ende des 13. Jahrhundert* (Berlin, 1968), p. 33.

[71] The Marburg work belongs to Michler's 'third campaign', to whose first phase ('*c.* 1265') he attributes the aisle walls up to the towers, and to whose second (sometime before 1283) he gives the westernmost four nave pillar-pairs and all their vaults. See Michler, *Die Elisabethkirche*, pp. 36–7. But Hamann, *Die Elisabethkirche*, ii, 86, was wary of giving too precise dates to this sculpture, most of it by the so-called 'Amiens Master'. Stylistically there is no reason why it could not have been carved in the 1260s, especially since naturalistic leaf carving had appeared as early as the early 1240s in the tomb of Konrad of Thuringia – see *ibid.*, ii, 66, pl. 86 – and in Michler's 'first phase' of campaign three (see responds of nave, Wilhelm-Kästner, *Die Elisabethkirche*, i, 16, fig. 19b). Also the steeple-like baldachin above

the tympanum is covered with a carpet of leaves, vine on the left side (symbolic of the Eucharist) and roses on the right (the Virgin's emblem) (pl. 37). At Trzebnica the alternation distinguishes the two faces of the portal, rather than its halves: vines surrounding the Crucifixion, and therefore (appropriately) facing the choir and the high altar, and oak and roses surrounding the Coronation of the Virgin, the roses (on the lintel) conforming closely to the Marburg variety. The second Marburg reference lies in the Coronation iconography itself – a rare Marian motif in central German sculpture of this period but prefigured in the a roof boss in the central aisle of the nave of Marburg (fourth bay from east) (pl. 44).[72] Both coronations identify their respective saints with Marian virtue, just as the author of the *Legenda maior* uses Marian motifs and comparisons, and draws on St Elizabeth's *Libellus* as a source for his Hedwig narrative.[73]

What we find at Trzebnica is exactly what we would expect of patrons and architects in the late 1260s looking for the kind of architecture, and architectural decoration, suitable for St Hedwig herself – concentrating on Marburg's recent sculpture, quoting pointedly from Marburg's old fashioned repertory, but finding their real architectural models both in Marburg's own more fashionable followers and in contemporary royal mausolea chapels. This international range of reference gave the St Hedwig chapel a unique status in Silesia. It had no predecessors and no real followers, although Hessian-Thuringian patterns reappear sporadically in the late thirteenth-century parish churches of Złotoryja (Goldberg) and Lwówek (Löwenberg).[74] But St Hedwig's, and the Piasts', promotion of St Elizabeth's cult put down deep roots in the province. In 1255 Duke Konrad I of Głogów, a grandson of St Hedwig, endowed the collegiate church of Głogów in Lower Silesia. In *c.* 1300 standing figures of himself and his wife Salomea were set up around the choir. The manner of their posthumous commemoration derives from the *Stifter* figures in the west choir at Naumburg, or the choir at Meissen, but the style of the Salomea figure is directly indebted to the figure of St Elizabeth on the Marburg high altar.[75] A generation earlier, in Wrocław, St Hedwig's family was preserving the memory of St Elizabeth's in two mid-thirteenth-century foundations: the St Elizabeth hospital founded in about 1253 within the enclosure of the ducal palace by Duke Henry II, the son of St Hedwig, and his wife Anna, a cousin of St Elizabeth, and the parish church of St Elizabeth in the new town, founded in 1253

---

the statue of the Virgin and Child on the west portal is earlier in style than that above Aleydis's tomb of 1274; compare Hamann, *Die Elisabethkirche*, ii, 74, pl. 103; ii, 82, pl. 118.

72 Wilhelm-Kästner, *Die Elisabethkirche*, i, 19, pl. 25; for illustrations of all this sculpture see *ibid.*, pp. 10–25.

73 Schütz, 'Hedwig, Herzogin von Schlesien', p. 152; and *Libellus*, p. 18, and *Legenda maior*, c. 4, p. 82. For the Marian comparisons see *Legenda maior*, c. 1, pp. 73ff.

74 For Złotoryja and Lwówek, see Kutzner, 'Der Gotische Umbau', pp. 114ff, and H. Kozaczewska-Golasz, T. Kozaczewski, 'Trzynastowieczny kościół N. Panny Marii w Złotoryi', *Prace Naukowe Instytutu Historii Architektury, Sztuki i Techniki Politechniki Wrocławskiej*, xxii (1989), 113–39.

75 M. Zlat, 'Schlesische Kunst des Mittelalters in den polnischen Forschungen seit 1945', in *Kunst des Mittelalters in Sachsen. Festschrift Wolf Schubert* (Weimar, 1967), p. 167; and J. Kębłowski, 'Posąg Księżny Salomei Głogowskiej', *Studia Muzealne*, v (1966), 19–48.

by Duke Bolesław II, Anna's son and another of St Hedwig's grandsons.[76] But Wrocław's most dramatic identification with Marburg came with the foundation in 1288 by Hedwig's great-grandson, Duke Henry IV (the Honourable), of the church of the Holy Cross, on Ostrow Tumski, just to the east of the perimeter wall of the ducal castle (pll. 45–6). Few scholars have failed to recognise the similarities between Marburg and this imposing, brick-built mausoleum, with its prominent cross-shaped plan, and its polygonally-apsed choir and transepts giving on to a spacious hall nave. The traditional ties between the Silesian Piasts and the Hessian Landgraves seem only to confirm the visual connections.[77] Henry IV's motives are laid out explicitly in the foundation charter of 11 January 1288: to honour the Holy Cross, to expiate an uncompleted promise to visit the Holy Land, and to commemorate his parents Judith of Masowia and Henry III, his guardians Archbishop Władysław of Salzburg and King Ottokar II, and his uncle Duke Bolesław the Shy. Like Marburg, St Cross is a monument to dynastic memory. But it was not intended by Henry to act as his permanent burial place; he planned a Cistercian nuns' church for the purpose in the neighbouring castle. The paradox of founding a dynastic church with specific reference to the necropolis of the dukes of Hesse, indeed with all the hall-marks of a mausoleum, but with no intention of actually using it for that purpose, has recently been resolved by Stanisław Stulin's re-dating of the whole enterprise. It now seems that the building founded by Henry in 1288, and mentioned as consecrated in 1295, was not the present two-storied church, but a more provisional structure, parts of which were incorporated into the existing building when it was begun, at the east end, in *c.* 1320. Between about 1320 and 1330 the lower church and the choir were constructed, together with parts of the transepts and the lower parts of the nave; while a second campaign, from *c.* 1340–71, saw the nave's completion.[78] It was therefore only under Henry the Honourable's successor, Duke Henry III of Głogów (the commemorator of Salomea and Konrad at Głogów) or, more plausibly, under Henry VI, duke of Wrocław in the critical years of the 1320s and 1330s, that Henry IV's original

---

[76] For the Elizabeth hospital see T. Jacobi and F. Scherf, 'Zur Rezeption der Elisabethkirche in Schlesien', in *Die Elisabethkirche*, ed. Kunst, pp. 128–30; *Wrocław. Jego Dzieje i Kultura* (Warsaw, 1978), ed. Z. Świechowski, pp. 52–3. For the parish church see *Architektura Gotycka w Polsce*, ii (catalogue), 226, with full bibliography. Princess Anna's Bohemian contacts are underlined by M. Kutzner, 'Społeczne Uwarunkowanie Rozwoju śląskiej Architektury w Latach 1200–1330', in *Sztuka i Ideologia XIII wieku*, ed. P. Skubiszewski (Wrocław/Warsaw/Kraków/Gdańsk, 1974), p. 222 as one channel for the widespread penetration of Bohemian ideas into Wrocław in the third quarter of the thirteenth century.

[77] Wilhelm-Kästner, *Die Elisabethkirche*, i, 49; H. Tintelnot, *Die Mittelalterliche Baukunst Schlesiens* (Kitzingen, 1951), p. 71; Jacobi and Scherf, 'Zur Rezeption', pp. 125–8. For further literature on St Cross see A. Grzybkowski, 'Die Kreuzkirche in Breslau. Stiftung und Funktion', *Zeitschrift für Kunstgeschichte*, li (1988), 461–78, and *Architektura Gotycka w Polsce*, ii (catalogue), 264–5.

[78] S. Stulin, 'Drogi kształtowania się stylu regionalnego architektury sakralnej na Śląsku w 1 połowie XIV wieku' (manuscript, Instytut Historii Architektury Sztuki i Techniki Politechniki Wrocławskiej, Wrocław, 1982). His manuscript was unavailable to me. I am relying on a short summary in *Architektura Gotycka w Polsce*, ii (catalogue), 264–5.

intentions were expanded around the figure of the founder himself, and a grandiose brick version of Marburg was chosen as the most appropriate setting for a full-scale commemoration of the most powerful and successful of the Wrocław dukes, and the nominees of his foundation charter.[79] Henry IV's tomb (*c.* 1300? *c.* 1320?) was set up in the new church;[80] his kneeling figure, holding a model of the church with its trefoil choir, decorates the Holy Trinity tympanum of the nave's north portal; the five roof bosses of the transept in the lower church commemorate, by their heraldry, the figures of his 1288 charter,[81] and the altars of the lower church are dedicated to the Holy Trinity, St Hedwig, and St Bartholomew – the latter a key saint for the Silesian Piasts, for St Hedwig's first burial site was in front of the saint's altar at Trzebnica and her relics were translated on his feast day (25 August 1267).[82] Thanks to his successors' need to identify with his heroic reputation, one of the last of the great Silesian Piasts finds his resting place surrounded by memories of St Hedwig and his (and her) family, in a setting that evokes, in the grand and simplified language of *Backsteingotik*, the ancestral glamour of St Elizabeth at Marburg.

A retrospective and oblique light on the St Elizabeth associations of the St Cross plan is cast by the smaller church of St Matthias in Wrocław, situated to the north of the town on land belonging to the Wrocław dukes. In 1253 it came into the hands of the Wrocław St Elizabeth hospital, but it was not until the very end of the fourteenth century that its original square nave (*c.* 1270) was expanded by three polygonally-ended conches to form a plan clearly modelled (in the greater length given to the choir) on St Cross.[83] A more complex ideological and historical relationship with St Cross is embodied in the small and compact triconch burial chapel added by Duke Bolesław III of Legnica-Brzeg (Leignitz-Brieg) to the Cistercian church of Lubiąż in Lower Silesia (pll. 47–8). Founded in 1311 as the mausoleum for the duke's Legnica branch of the Silesian Piasts, and in use by 1329, it falls naturally into the Marburg-influenced circle of St Cross in Wrocław, though it may have been built by a ducal workshop active in Legnica.[84] The

---

79 S. Skibiński, *Pierwotny kościół Franciskanów w Krakowie* (Poznań, 1977), p. 76 is right to attribute the centralised cross-plan of St Cross to the church's memorial function, but I am not convinced by Grzybkowski's attempt to find a source for St Cross's plan in the Dominican churches of Wrocław and Cieszyn; see *idem*, 'Die Kreuzkirche in Breslau', p. 472.

80 K. Bauch, *Das mittelalterliche Grabbild. Figurliche Grabmaler des 11. bis 15. Jahrhunderts in Europa* (Berlin/New York, 1976), pp. 135–6, fig. 217; *Wrocław*, pp. 155–6, figs 228, 229.

81 According to Grzybkowski, 'Die Kreuzkirche in Breslau', p. 478, they are his mother Judith of Masowia and also his father Henry III, Władysław, Ottokar II, Bolesaw the Shy, and perhaps the imperial eagle (in the crossing).

82 Trzebnica was founded on that day, which was also the day of the death of Duchess Adelheid, wife of Bolesaw I, father of Henry I (the Bearded). For Hedwig's burial see Gottschalk, *St Hedwig*, pp. 213f.

83 Götz, *Zentralbau*, p. 38, who sees (unconvincingly) influences from St Apolinaris in Sadzka in Bohemia; Jacobi and Scherf, 'Zur Rezeption', p. 130; *Architektura Gotycka w Polsce*, ii (catalogue), 272, and ii (plates), nos 1159–60.

84 Götz, *Zentralbau*, p. 38; Kutzner, *Cysterska Architektura*, pp. 84–7; *Architektura Gotycka w Polsce*, ii (catalogue), 141–2.

identical size of its apses recalls Marburg, their five-sided polygonality parallels St Cross. In addition, Stulin has pointed to the Upper Rhenish and Swabian derivation of some of the decorative details and to workshop connections with the Wrocław church, notably in tracery and mouldings.[85] But the simultaneous chronologies of St Cross and the Lubiąż chapel now make it difficult to establish which way the influences went, just as they now exclude any clear 'ideological' reading of the Lubiąż chapel as Bolesław III's attempts to support his claims to Wrocław by identifying himself with the mighty reputation of Henry IV.[86] At issue here is not the St Cross of Henry IV but its reincarnation under Henry VI, who was also Bolesław III's brother; if anything, the new St Cross may be a response to Lubiąż and not vice versa. What cannot be doubted are the tensions and rivalries between Bolesław III and his brother for the Wrocław dukedom in the first quarter of the fourteenth century, expressed as forcefully in their near-identical seals as in the close similarities between their trefoil-choir mausolea.[87] Clearly the relationship between St Cross and the Lubiąż chapel, however defined, was played out against the background of dynastic rivalry; and the model of Marburg still impressed itself on the protagonists as a legitimising archetype for a Silesian Piast mausoleum.

The final Piast genuflection before the shrine church of St Elizabeth came from a more unexpected quarter, from the Cistercian nuns' church of St Mary in Old Brno, in Luxembourg Moravia (pll. 49–50) Klára Benešovská has recently untangled, in exemplary fashion, the circumstances of its foundation.[88] Its benefactor, Queen Elizabeth Richenza (Eliška Rejčka) of Bohemia, was a Piast princess, the daughter of Přemysl II, king of Great Poland, and (from 1300) the wife of the Přemyslid king, Wenceslas II of Bohemia. A Přemyslid only by marriage, Elizabeth never settled comfortably into the cliquish and intensely Přemyslid court in Prague. On Wenceslas's death in 1305 her presence became a source of mounting tension. Her hasty marriage to Rudolf of Hapsburg in 1306 ended disastrously with Rudolf's premature death less than a year later. Elizabeth's influence was further compromised with the election of Anna Přemyslid's husband, Duke Henry of Carinthia, to the Bohemian throne, and soon afterwards, accompanied by her daughter Agnes, she left Prague for Austria, to live in exile with her brother-in-law, Frederick the Fair, in Klosterneuburg. By 1310, the year John of Luxembourg succeeded to the Bohemian throne, she was back in Bohemia,

---

[85] Stulin, 'Drogi kształtowania się stylu regionalnego architektury', cited in *Architektura Gotycka w Polsce*, ii (catalogue), p. 142.

[86] Jacobi and Scherf, 'Zur Rezeption', pp. 130–3.

[87] For the seals see Z. Piech, *Ikonografia Pieczęci Piastów* (Kraków, 1993), pp. 31 nos 48 and 57, 225 and 230, pll. 43 and 52. For the political divisions of Silesia around 1300 see Randt, 'Politische Geschichte', pp. 73–156, esp. 137ff.

[88] Most of the material on this church is drawn from Kuthan, *Die Mittelalterliche Baukunst*, pp. 265–72, and K. Benešovská, 'Das Zisterzienserinnenkloster von Altbrunn und die Personlichkeit seiner Stifterin', in *Cystersi w Kulturze Sredniowiecznej Europy*, ed. J. Strzelczyk, Poznań Uniwersytet im. Adama Mickiewicza, Seria Historia, 165 (Poznań, 1992), pp. 83–100.

setting up her court in the north-western city of Königgrätz. Rich, well-connected and ambitious, she and her life-long paramour, Henry of Leipa, Lord Chamberlain to King John, led the opposition of the Bohemian nobles to the monarchical and centralising policies of her namesake, Elizabeth Přemyslid, daughter of Wenceslas II by a previous marriage, and wife of King John. Elizabeth Přemyslid, brought up in the dazzling international court of Wenceslas, among memories of her grandfather Ottokar II's spectacular central European Empire centred in Prague and stretching to the Adriatic, resented the growth of magnate power under King John's young and inexperienced leadership. She even secured Henry of Leipa's imprisonment between 1315 and 1318. In the long struggle that ensued, King John was at first too weak or too uninterested to adjudicate, though he became increasingly suspicious of his wife, and was eventually forced to lend his support, and much financial aid, to Henry and Elizabeth Richenza. In 1319 the reinstated Henry, now the vice-roy of Moravia, set up a semi-permanent court with Elizabeth in Brno; and in 1322–23 their alliance was finally vindicated with the exile of Elizabeth Přemyslid to Bavaria. She returned to Bohemia only in the last decade of her life, but never again played a leading role in Bohemian politics

It was during this critical period of success, when Elizabeth Richenza had seen off her rivals and secured the support of King John, that she founded, on I June 1323, a convent of Cistercian nuns in Old Brno, and set aside its church as the mausoleum for herself and her family. Ten years later, in 1333, the church was ready for services. To favour the Cistercians as their dynastic mausolea was entirely in line with Přemyslid policy in Bohemia for at least half a century. Even the title of the convent in the foundation charter, 'Aula S. Maria' must consciously refer to the greatest of the Přemyslid burial churches, the now completely destroyed Cistercian church of Zbraslav just outside Prague, founded in 1297 by Wenceslas II with the royal title of 'Aula Regia'. This sumptuous *Königskirche* was still under construction when the Brno church was begun. But in at least two respects – the prominent use of brick with stone dressings, and the trefoil east end – Brno looks like no other Bohemian Cistercian church; indeed, the contrast with Zbraslav could not be more pointed, particularly in the design of the choir. Where Brno uses a polygonally-apsed triconch, the Zbraslav choir, as revealed in a nineteenth-century plan and in recent excavations, followed the second church at Cîteaux in having cellular chapels opening off a square-ended ambulatory – the whole configuration in the shape of a three-aisled hall church.[89] Is this refusal to adopt any aspect of Zbraslav another indication of Elizabeth Richenza's suspicion of the Přemyslid past, and in particular her opposition to Elizabeth Přemyslid? The question might seem fanciful were it not for the fact that Zbraslav – the St Denis and Royaumont of the Přemyslid royal family – was the object of the special

89 For Zbraslav see K. Benešovská, H. Ječný, D. Stehlíková, M. Tryml, 'Nové Prameny k Dějinám Klášterního Kostela Cisterciácků na Zbraslavi', *Umění*, xxxiv (1986), 385–409; and P. Crossley, 'Kraków Cathedral and the Formation of a Dynastic Architecture in Southern Central Europe', in *Polish and English Responses to French Art and Architecture*, ed. F. Ames-Lewis (Birkbeck College, London, 1995), pp. 31–46, esp. p. 38.

generosity of Richenza's bitter rival, Elizabeth Přemyslid, after the latter's return from exile to Bohemia. In the political turmoil that followed Wenceslas II's death in 1305 the pace of construction on the large church had slowed down. Elizabeth Přemyslid's donation of nine new chapels and altars in 1329 to this mausoleum of her father, mother and sisters hastened the completion of its nave and showed her to be the single legal inheritor and guardian of Přemyslid tradition under a hostile Luxembourg rule. Given the rivalry between the two queens, and Elizabeth Richenza's status as an 'outsider' in the old Přemyslid court, her 'Aula' at Brno may simply be referring to the Zbraslav 'Aula' in order to deny, in its plan and materials, everything that Zbraslav stood for.

If not Bohemian, what sources lie behind Elizabeth's church? The trefoil plan of its choir, expressed in elevation by a tall apsidal sanctuary and two similarly apsed dwarf transepts; the burial of Henry of Leipa in the church in 1329, probably in one of these small transepts; and the burial of Elizabeth Richenza herself in front of the altar of the Holy Cross, at the centre of the eastern crossing, in 1335 proves that we are dealing with yet another example of the long tradition of cross-shaped mausolea. St Elizabeth at Marburg is often cited as a specific source, especially since Elizabeth Richenza and her daughter Agnes visited the Rhineland in 1333, venerated the relics at Trier and Cologne (sites rich in trefoil or quatrefoil plans), and just may have visited Marburg on the way. It is worth noting that the Brno foundation lay close to a new hospital founded by Elizabeth at the same time. But the Marburg connection is pure conjecture, and Elizabeth's journey could have had no outcome on the design of the church, whose trefoil choir was laid out as part of the original plan of 1323, ten years before the Rhine expedition.[90] The other most-cited source for the Brno choir is St Cross in Wrocław, though Benešovská, even on the basis of the old chronologies, is sceptical of any connection.[91] The new dating for the east end of the Wrocław church, '*c.* 1320–30', makes it a parallel phenomenon, not necessarily a precedent or an inspiration. But some connection between the two buildings would be difficult to deny, given the rarity of their ground plans and the nature of their patronage; and all the evidence still points to a Silesian and Piast inspiration in Brno, rather than a Moravian intervention in Wrocław. Brick was not a favoured material in Bohemia or Moravia in the early fourteenth century. To combine it with the kind of tall, chapel-like choir (the so-called long choir) seen in Brno points only to one source: Wrocław and Lower Silesia, where the mendicant orders were precocious in marrying this type of polygonally-apsed choir with an overall brick construction using stone dressings.[92] And it is surely no coincidence that Elizabeth Richenza's other surviving church foundation, the parish church (now cathedral) of her town in Hradec Králové

---

[90] Benešovská, 'Das Zisterzienserinnenkloster von Altbrunn', has convincingly established the chronology of the construction and also dismissed any direct influence from Marburg.

[91] *Ibid.*, pp. 95 and 99.

[92] See P. Crossley, *Gothic Architecture in the Reign of Kasimir the Great: Church Architecture in Lesser Poland 1320–1380* (Kraków, 1985), pp. 59, 79, 126, 128–32; and A. Grzybkowski, 'Das Problem der Langchöre in Bettelorden-Kirchen im östlichen Mitteleuropa des 13. Jahrhunderts', *Architektura. Zeitschrift für Geschichte der Baukunst*, xiii (1983), 152–68.

(Königgrätz) in northern Bohemia, begun in 1307 also has an imposing brick long choir, having some similarities of detail with the Brno mausoleum.[93] Politically and territorially Elizabeth's history and interests centre on Silesia and Lesser Poland. Between the coronation of her husband Wenceslas as king of Bohemia and Poland in 1300 and her coronation as queen in 1303 she had spent three years in the Kraków household of Griffina, former duchess of Kraków, widow of Leszek the Black and sister of Wenceslas's mother Kunigunda of Hungary. In 1316 she married her daughter Agnes to the Silesian duke Henry of Jawór (Jauer), thereby extending her own power in Lower Silesia, and consolidating it with Henry of Leipa's control of the Lower Silesian/border territory around Kłodzko. She might even have known the ducal chapel at Lubiąż, since her stepdaughter by her marriage to Wenceslas was the wife of its founder Bolesław III. If the ideal model behind her burial church at Brno was her namesake's shrine church in Marburg, the language of its realisation spoke, not of the counts of Hesse-Thuringia, nor certainly of the Přemyslids, but of the vigorous Silesian Piast dukes who, under Henry IV and his successors, had so nearly united the kingdom of Poland under their suzerainty.

Elizabeth Richenza's burial in the crossing of her new church in 1335 marks an exact century since the foundation of her namesake's church in Marburg. Between those two events, the ideal image of St Elizabeth's mausoleum, refined by stylistic advance and modified by local custom, continued to haunt the imagination of some of the greatest architectural patrons of central Europe. The inspiration of no other queen or royal princess had done so much for Gothic architecture.[94]

---

93 The date of Königgrätz cathedral is, as far as I know, obscure. Although funded by Elizabeth in 1307, how much of the present building survived the town fire of 1339 is uncertain. See K. A. Cechner, *Topographie der Historischen und Kunst-Denkmale im Königsreiche Böhmen*, xix, *Der Politische Bezirk Königgrätz* (Prague, 1915), pp. 74ff. However, the use of large hollow chamfers in the chancel arch and nave pillars, a feature singled out by Benešovská, as typical of the second phase of building at Brno ('Das Zisterzienserinnenkloster von Altbrunn', p. 98), may be an additional link between the two buildings.

94 Since the writing of this article, Achim Timmermann has kindly drawn my attention to Andreas Köstner's new investigation into the cult of St Elizabeth in Marburg and the liturgical history of her church and its furnishings, *Die Ausstattung der Marburger Elisabethkirche. Zur Ästhetisierung des Kultraums im Mittelalter* (Berlin 1995). Nothing in this important study substantially undermines my own conclusions; in fact its emphasis on liturgical presentation rather than ideological meaning lends them some support, and his suggestive concept of 'aestheticising' the church space (denying close access to relics and reliquaries, but, by way of compensation, giving them increasing visual emphasis) tallies with my own suggestions about the re-emphasis on the visual presence of St Elizabeth from 1270s onwards. Köstner, however, follows Geese and others in seeing the supplanting of St Elizabeth's importance in the second half of the 13th century in favour of the Knights and the Landgraves, and he also argues that her cult never became popular.

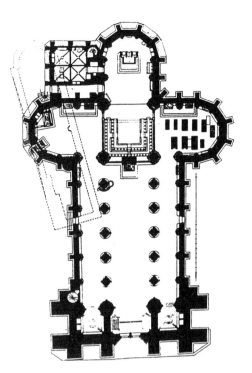

Plate 28 St Elizabeth at Marburg: ground plan (after Köstner)

Plate 29 St Elizabeth at Marburg: interior of nave looking east (photo: Bildarchiv Marburg)

Plate 30 St Elizabeth at Marburg: exterior from the east (photo: Courtauld Institute of Art)

Plate 31 St Elizabeth at Marburg: interior of choir and north transept (photo: Bildarchiv Marburg)

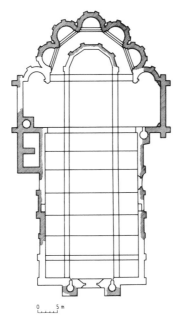

Plate 32 Kalocsa cathedral: ground plan (after Marosi)

Plate 33 Pilis, Cistercian church: reconstruction of the tomb of Gertrud of Andechs-Meranien (after Gerevich)

Plate 34 Head from the tomb of Gertrud of Andrechs-Meranien (photo: Lájos Sugar)

Plate 35 Cambrai cathedral: drawing by A. van der Meulen (Paris, Musée des Gobelins)

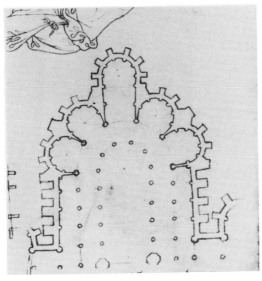

Plate 36 Villard de Honnecourt, plan of the choir of Cambrai cathedral (photo: Courtauld Institute of Art)

Plate 37 St Elizabeth at Marburg: tympanum of west portal (photo: Courtauld Institute of Art)

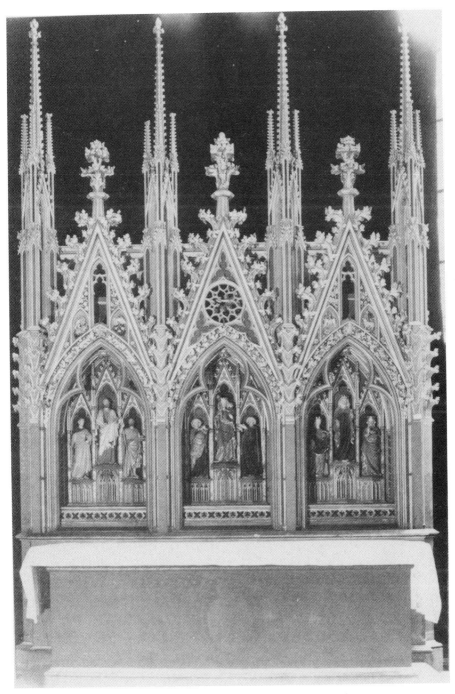

Plate 38 St Elizabeth at Marburg: high altar, figure of St Elizabeth

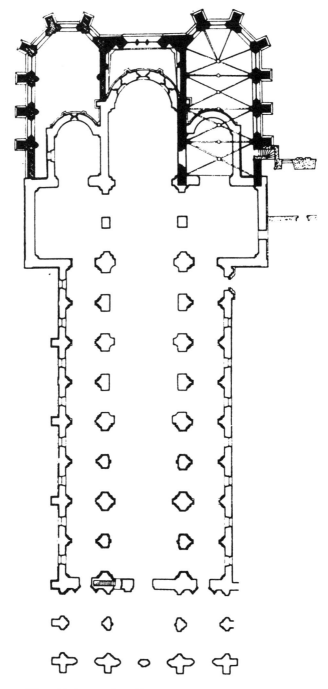

Plate 39 Trzebnica, Cistercian church: ground plan
(after Kutzner)

Plate 40 Trzebnica, Cistercian church: interior of St Hedwig's chapel
(photo: Courtauld Institute of Art)

Plate 41 Trzebnica, Cistercian church: exterior of St Hedwig's chapel from the south (photo: PAN Warsaw)

Plate 42 Prague, Agnes monastery, St Saviour's choir: interior (photo: A. Paul)

Plate 43 Trzebnica, St Hedwig's chapel: portal from the chapel to the choir (south side) (photo: Courtauld Institute of Art)

Plate 44 St Elizabeth at Marburg, roof boss: Coronation of the Virgin (photo: Bildarchiv Marburg)

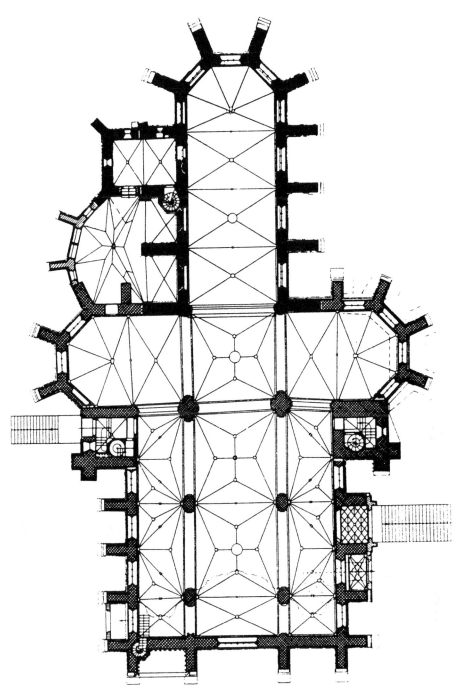

Plate 45 Holy Cross church, Wrocław: ground plan (after Burgemeister)

Plate 46 Holy Cross church, Wrocław: view from east (photo: Courtauld Institute of Art)

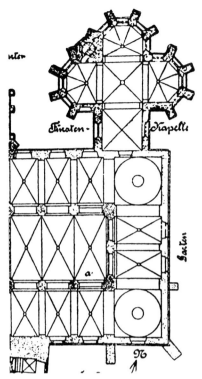

Plate 47 Cistercian church, Lubiąż, burial chapel: ground plan (after Jacobi and Scherf)

Plate 48 Cistercian church, Lubiąż, burial chapel: general view (photo: PAN, Warsaw)

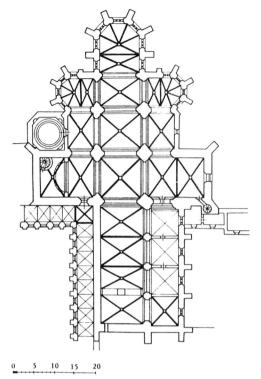

0 5 10 15 20

Plate 49 St Mary, Old Brno:
ground plan (after Chadraba,
Denkstein and Krasa)

Plate 50 St Mary,
Old Brno: exterior
from south-east
(photo: author)

15

Early Medieval Rites of Queen-Making and the Shaping of Medieval Queenship

Janet L. Nelson

'We wish you to know, brethren, that our *dominus et senior* the glorious king Charles besought the devotion of our humility, that, through the authority of the ministry conferred on us by God, just as he has been anointed and consecrated king by episcopal authority with sacred unction and blessing, just as we read that the Lord commanded in the Scriptures that kings be anointed and consecrated to royal power, in the same way we should bless (*benedicamus*) his wife our lady in the title of queen (*in nomine reginae*), as we have learned has previously been done by the apostolic see and by our predecessors for other [queens] (*de aliis*).'[1]

Thus Hincmar and colleague[2] in August 866, presenting, a shade self-

---

1   I translate from the edition of R. A. Jackson, *Ordines Coronationis Franciae: Texts and Ordines for the Coronation of Frankish and French Kings and Queens in the Middle Ages*, i (Philadelphia, 1995), Ordo VI, pp. 80–6, at pp. 82–3. Among recent historiography on Carolingian coronations, I would signal in particular G. Lanoë, 'L'*ordo* de couronnement de Charles le Chauve', in *Kings and Kingship in Medieval Europe*, ed. A. J. Duggan, King's College London Medieval Studies, x (London, 1993), pp. 41–68 (noting, p. 52 n. 40, that 'le couronnement des reines pose dès l'origine bien des problèmes', and promising to return to this subject). See also R.-H. Bautier, 'Sacres et couronnements sous les Carolingiens et les premiers Capetiens', *Annuaire-Bulletin de la Société d'Histoire de la France* (1987), pp. 7–56 (repr. in Bautier's collected papers, *Recherches sur l'histoire de la France médiévale* [London, 1991], ch. 2), an important study which does not deal very fully with queens' consecrations, and regrettably cites no recent anglophone historiography. Neither do many contributors to *Le Sacre des rois: Actes du Colloque international d'histoire sur les sacres ... Reims 1975* (Paris, 1985), nor R. Folz, 'Les Trois couronnements de Charles le Chauve', *Byzantion*, lxi (1991), 93–111.

2   Archbishop Herard of Tours was the colleague. Two different manuscripts were apparently available to J. Sirmond in the seventeenth century: in one, containing a dossier of material on the Council of Soissons, printed in Sirmond's edition of *Concilia antiqua Galliae* (Paris, 1629), and reprinted by Mansi, xv (Venice, 1770), cols 703–60, the *adlocutio*, preceding Ermentrude's consecration, at 725–8, was attributed to Herard and tacked onto a longer speech on another topic; the other, a now-lost Liège manuscript, edited by Sirmond in *Capitula Caroli Calvi* (Paris, 1623), and repr. by A. Boretius, *MGH, Capitularia regum Francorum*, edd. A. Boretius and V. Krause, 2 vols (Hanover, 1883–97; repr. 1957), ii, 453–5 no. 301, attributed the *adlocutio* to 'duo episcopi', evidently Hincmar and Herard; cf. Jackson, p. 82 n. 5. Ermentrude's *ordo* was preserved in the Liège manuscript alongside Hincmar's *ordines* for Judith, see below, pp. 306–8, for Charles the Bald (869) and for Louis the Stammerer (877), the four treated here as a set: see J. L. Nelson, *Politics and Ritual in*

consciously, the justification for what was clearly a rather unexpected performance – the consecration of Ermentrude, who had been Charles the Bald's wife for nearly twenty-four years and borne him eleven children. The particular circumstances of her consecration are not my prime concern here.[3] Instead I would stress the intimate linkage of king and queen in Charles's and Hincmar's wider and longer-term concerns with monarchic representation. The anointing of kings could be, and had been, justified by appeal to Scripture; but, as Hincmar acknowledged, there were no queenly equivalents to David and Solomon and Josiah. Hincmar had to invent a tradition, claiming precedents for the making of Carolingian queens and empresses by popes and bishops. Real enough though these precedents were, and important sources of inspiration, they had left little trace in the written record; they lacked continuity and hence formal stability; and their dependence on modern history rather than Scripture left some ideological spadework to be done. These drawbacks were mitigated, if not overcome, when queenly consecration found an anchorage in liturgy between the mid-ninth century and the early tenth. The aim of the present paper is to assess the significance of these developments in reflecting, and perhaps engendering, a firmer delineation, or institutionalisation, of the queen's function.

Queenly consecration in context

Queens had indeed been blessed before the mid-ninth century. Yet the evidence goes back no further than the advent of the Carolingian dynasty in 751. According to what is probably the most nearly-contemporary source, 'Pippin . . . by the consecration of bishops and by the subjection of lay magnates, together with the queen Bertrada as the rules of ancient tradition require was elevated into the kingdom.'[4] Three years later, Bertrada was consecrated at St-Denis along with her husband and two sons, by Pope Stephen II.[5] Consecration or coronation is possible,

Early Medieval Europe (London, 1986), pp. 138, 343. I think that the Liège manuscript's version should be preferred to that of the Soissons dossier, and that the 866 *adlocutio*, with the *ordo* itself, bears the stamp of Hincmar's authorship. I hope to return in a future paper to Sirmond and his work.

3 See now the wide-ranging study of F.-R. Erkens, ' "Sicut Esther regina": Die westfränk-ische Königin als *consors regni*', *Francia*, xx/1 (1993), 15–38, plausibly suggesting, pp. 33–7, Charles's intent to contrast his own marital rectitude with the scandal of Lothar II's 'two wives'. Ermentrude's anointing represented a strengthening of marriage as well as 'a sacral elevation of the queen' (p. 35). Lotharingia was certainly in Charles's sights in 866.

4 Continuator of Fredegar, c. 33: *The Fourth Book of the Chronicle of Fredegar and its Continuators* , ed. J. M. Wallace-Hadrill (London, 1960), p. 102. See now R. Collins, 'Deception and Misrepresentation in Early Eighth-Century Frankish Historiography: Two Case Studies', in *Karl Martell in seiner Zeit*, edd. J. Jarnut, U. Nonn and M. Richter (Sigmaringen, 1992), pp. 227–47, at 243–6, arguing convincingly that Count Hildebrand's section of the Continuation was presented to Pippin at his accession, and is a highly tendentious work.

5 Codex Carolinus, no. 11, ed. W. Gundlach, *MGH Epp.*, iii (Berlin, 1892), 505. The arguments of A. Stoclet, 'La "Clausula de unctione Pippini regis": mises au point et nouvelles hypothèses', *Francia*, viii (1980), 1–42, stressing the tenth-century date of the manuscript,

if perhaps improbable, for Charlemagne's wife Fastrada in 783.[6] Louis the Pious's first wife Irmengard was crowned with a golden crown at Reims by Pope Stephen III in 816,[7] and Louis' second wife Judith was probably crowned by Louis himself and 'acclaimed by all as empress (*augusta*)' in 819.[8] In place of all these possibilities, we reach certainty, at last, when we come to the mid-ninth century.

It is no coincidence that the history of queenly *ordines* begins and flourishes at this point. The Carolingian family, even before 751, had been keen patrons of church reform. They encouraged clergy and monks to perform their sacramental and intercessory functions correctly, and be seen to do so.[9] Key agents were bishops, and a key instrument was liturgy. Thanks to regular and relatively frequent synodal meetings, and the multiplication of the means to produce and distribute liturgical books,[10] the bishops became increasingly active, collectively self-conscious and self-propelled. Hincmar, archbishop of Reims from 845 to 882, was perhaps their most articulate and loquacious spokesman, an exemplary if not quite representative figure.[11] Few traditional forms of liturgy escaped his attention, and he pioneered several new ones.[12] He was not alone, however. Many other bishops took an active interest in reform, liturgy, and the written word. The archbishops of Sens, in particular, rivalled their confrères for the leadership of the church in the West Frankish realm; and the role of Archbishop Walter (887–923), almost as long in post as Hincmar, merits special attention.[13] Furthermore, the Carolingian rulers themselves were increasingly interested in the ideology of rulership, as articulated in texts but also as represented in symbolism and public ritual. Here a

have persuaded me that the *Clausula* cannot be accepted as unproblematic evidence for what happened in 754. Stoclet's work is not cited by G. Wolf, 'Königinnen-Krönungen des frühen Mittelalters bis zum Beginn des Investiturstreits', *Zeitschrift für Rechtsgeschichte, Kan. Abt.*, lxxvi (1990), 62–88, at p. 63.

6 *Annales regni Francorum*, ed. F. Kurze, *MGH SRG*, vi (Hanover, 1895), 66.
7 Thegan, *Gesta Hludowici imperatoris*, c. 17, ed. G. Pertz, *MGH SS*, ii (Hanover, 1829), 594; cf. Ermold, *In Honorem Hludowici Pii*, ed. and trans. E. Faral, *Ermold le Noir: Poème sur Louis le Pieux* (Paris, 1964), lines 1101–5. Ermold's evidence seems to me to be accepted too enthusiastically by Wolf, 'Königinnen-Krönungen', pp. 81–2.
8 *Annales Mettenses Priores*, ed. B. Simson, *MGH SRG*, x (Hanover, 1905), 95–6.
9 As explicitly stated in Charlemagne's capitulary *de litteris colendis*, ed. A. Boretius, *MGH, Capitularia*, i, 79 no. 29: '. . . ut quicumque vos propter nomen Domini et sanctae conversationis nobilitatem ad videndum expetierit, sicut de aspectu vestro aedificetur visus, ita quoque de sapientia vestra, quam in legendo seu cantando perceperit, instructus . . . redeat'. For the wider context, see W. Ullmann, *The Carolingian Renaissance and the Idea of Reform* (Cambridge, 1969), R. McKitterick, *The Frankish Church and the Carolingian Reforms* (London, 1977), and G. Brown, 'Introduction: The Carolingian Renaissance', in *Carolingian Culture*, ed. R. McKitterick (Cambridge, 1994), pp. 1–51.
10 R. McKitterick, *The Carolingians and the Written Word* (Cambridge, 1989), pp. 135–64, discusses book-production in general.
11 J. M. Wallace-Hadrill, *The Frankish Church* (Oxford, 1984), pp. 292–303, is the classic account. See now also the fine monograph of M. Stratmann, *Hinkmar von Reims als Verwalter von Bistum und Kirchenprovinz* (Sigmaringen, 1991). Cf. Bautier, 'Sacres', pp. 42–3.
12 Nelson, *Politics and Ritual*, esp. chs 7 and 15.
13 Below, p. 310.

crucial figure was Charles the Bald (840–77).[14] During his reign, there was increasing stress, in a battery of media, on the active functions of the king, as provider of justice and equity as well as war-leader, and as protector and regulator of the church in his realm. At the same time, the dynastic element of kingship came to be amplified. It was hardly surprising that alongside this enhanced concern with the king's function went an increased interest in the queen's.

Already in the 820s, the *de Ordine Palatii* described the queen's centrally important roles.[15] She was responsible for the 'good order of the palace' (*honestas palatii*), and in particular for the *ornamentum regale*, that is, the *regalia*, the royal insignia and cemeronial equipment, also the annual gifts for the *milites*, the king's military household. It was also the queen's job, with the help of the chamberlain, to supervise the provisioning of the court, so that all would be made ready for a royal visit in good time (*tempore congruo, opportuno tempore*). Finally, while the chamberlain normally arranged the giving of gifts to foreign envoys, sometimes the queen might involve herself there too, should the king command it. Here then, in the palace, the queen operated as the materfamilias, 'the lady with a mead-cup', perhaps with a certain ritualised role to play at royal feasts.[16]

The West Franks by the mid-ninth century were certainly very familiar with the position and status of queen. The ruler's wife was routinely called queen in letters and in charters.[17] Sedulius Scottus ('the Irishman'), in his *Liber de rectoribus*

---

[14] See the fundamental study of the late and much lamented R. Deshman, 'The Exalted Servant: The Ruler Theology of the Prayer-Book of Charles the Bald', *Viator*, xi (1980), 385–417; also L. Nees, *A Tainted Mantle: Hercules and the Classical Tradition at the Carolingian Court* (Philadelphia, 1991); N. Staubach, *Rex christianus: Hofkultur und Herrschaftspropaganda im Reich Karls des Kahlen, Teil II: Die Grundlegen der 'religion royale'* (Cologne/Weimar/Vienna, 1993); J. L. Nelson, *Charles the Bald* (London, 1992), and *eadem, The Frankish World* (London, 1996), especially chs 5–7, and 9.

[15] Edd. T. Gross and R. Schieffer, *MGH Fontes*, NS (Hanover, 1980), pp. 72–3, c. 22. A form of this work was written in the 820s by Adalard of Corbie, but the extant version is as revised by Hincmar of Reims in 881. See B. Kasten, *Adalhard von Corbie: Die Biographie eines karolingischen Politikers und Klostervorstehers* (Düsseldorf, 1986), pp. 72–84, arguing that Adalard's Italian experience influenced his writing. The section on the queen could, it seems to me, refer equally to the 820s and the 870s.

[16] Cf. M. J. Enright, 'Lady with a Mead-Cup: Ritual, Group Cohesion and Hierarchy in the Germanic Warband', *Frühmittelalterliche Studien*, xxii (1988), 170–203.

[17] E.g. Lupus of Ferrières, *epp.* 6 (referring to Judith), 89 and 95 (written for Ermentrude), ed. P. Marshall (Leipzig, 1984), pp. 16, 88, and 93; Nithard, *Historiarum Libri IV*, i.3, 3rd edn, ed. E. Müller, *MGH SRG*, xliv (Hanover, 1907), 4; *Annales de Saint Bertin*, edd. F. Grat, J. Vielliard and S. Clémencet (Paris, 1964), *s.a.* 840, p. 36: *augusta* (Judith); *s.a.* 857, p. 74: *regina* (Theutberga); Hincmar, letters to queens and empresses, summarised in Flodoard, *Historia Remensis Ecclesiae*, iii.27, edd. I. Heller and G. Waitz, *MGH SS*, xiii (Hanover, 1881), 547–50. For the charter evidence, see the convenient summary in Erkens, ' "Sicut Esther regina" ', pp. 18, 24–5. Worth noting, therefore, are cases where a queenly title is not accorded. That Nithard calls Judith queen only once, for instance, and elsewhere refers to her simply as Louis' wife or Charles the Bald's mother, could suggest personal hostility to her. That in a series of letters, *epp.* 50, 90, 96, 102, 149 (?), 150, 190, 197, ed. E. Dümmler, *MGH Epp.*, iv (Berlin, 1895), 94, 134, 140, 149, 244, 246, 317, 326, Alcuin never calls Liutgard queen or refers to her as such could suggest some doubt about her status; cf. *ep.* 62

christianis, written in 869 for Charles the Bald, devoted practically a whole chapter (c. 5) to the queen.[18] First in relation to her husband: he performs his royal office (*regendi ministerium gerit*) in ruling himself, then his wife, his children and the *domestici* of his household. But it was not enough for the king alone to be virtuous, his wife too had to be so: indeed she had to be 'adorned with purity'. 'And as the moon shines with the splendour of the stars around it, so the king adorns himself with his entourage, and, above all, with the queen. 'It is for her to concern herself *disciplinariter* with whatever is necessary, it is for her to regulate *pacifice* the children and the household, with modest face and cheerful words (*humili facie hilarique sermone*). She must be the beauty of the *familia*; at the same time she must have the prudence of the good counsellor. If the bad wife was characterised by *persuasio*, the good one had *consilium*. Notwithstanding feminine frailty, the husband of a prudent queen should be grateful for her advice. St Paul had said, 'the pagan husband (*infidelis*) will be sanctified (*sanctificatus erit*) by his believing wife'.[19] Sedulius's version has: 'the husband will be saved (*salvabitur*) by his wife'. Beside her husband, the wife should flourish in her prudence, like Queen Esther of old:

> Princeps et rectrix, populum si rite gubernant, suam regant prosapiam.

> (If king and queen govern the people justly, they will rule their own off-spring.)[20]

Note here that the queen has the title of *rectrix*. Even in a poetic text, this counts for something: alongside the prince, the queen 'governs' and 'rules'. Furthermore, ruling the people, and ruling the children, were indeed two intimately linked spheres of queenly activity. The troubles of Louis the Pious's reign had shown some possible drawbacks in this area.[21] Charles the Bald's wife Ermentrude, on the other hand, performed her queenly roles, apparently with discretion and success.[22]

where he does call Cynethryth of Mercia *regina* (though in *epp.* 101, referring to Cynethryth, and 122, he seems to avoid using the term queen for an Anglo-Saxon king's wife too).

18 Ed. S. Hellmann, *Sedulius Scottus*, Quellen und Untersuchungen zur lateinischen Philologie des Mittelalters, i/1 (Munich, 1906), 35–7. I am very grateful to my colleague Evelyn Cornell for tracking down King's College Library's long-lost copy of this book. On the significance of Sedulius's work, Staubach, *Rex christianus*, supersedes earlier studies, and argues cogently that Charles was Sedulius's addressee, the Lotharingian succession the context.

19 I Cor. 7:14.

20 Ed. Hellmann, pp. 35–7.

21 E. Ward, 'Caesar's Wife: The Career of the Empress Judith 819–29', in *Charlemagne's Heir: New Perspectives on the Reign of Louis the Pious*, edd. P. Godman and R. Collins (Oxford, 1990), pp. 205–27; cf. *eadem*, 'Agobard of Lyons and Paschasius Radbertus as Critics of the Empress Judith', *SCH*, xxvii (1990), 15–25.

22 J. Hyam, 'Ermentrude and Richildis', in *Charles the Bald: Court and Kingdom*, edd. M. T. Gibson and J. L. Nelson, 2nd rev. edn (London, 1990), pp. 154–68. For the telling argument that ninth-century accusations of queenly adultery were symptomatic of queens' increased

The *ordines*

The case of Judith, daughter of Charles the Bald, in 856 is the first queenly consecration for which there is not only relatively full contemporary documentation but a surviving *ordo*.[23] This was not, strictly speaking, a West Frankish queen-making, for the occasion was Judith's marriage to King Æthelwulf of the West Saxons and hence Judith's becoming a West Saxon queen. Nevertheless, the setting was a West Frankish royal palace, Verberie on the Oise, and one officiant a West Frankish prelate. According to the *Annals of St-Bertin*:

> Æthelwulf . . . received Judith in marriage, and after Bishop Hincmar of Reims had consecrated her and placed a diadem on her head, he [Æthelwulf] formally conferred on her the title of queen, which was something not customary before then to him or to his people.[24]

Four points can be noted here. First, the conferring of the queenly title is done by the king, not the bishop. Second, however, the bishop's acts precede the king's conferring of the title, thus strongly suggesting that Judith's becoming queen depended on her consecration and coronation: these made the queen, and the king set the seal on what has been done; in other words, Æthelwulf did not simply declare his wife queen without a prior change in her status. Third, although the Latin *benedicere* need not mean consecration, it clearly does so here, for the central *benedictio* was accompanied by a prayer, 'Deus electorum', derived from the blessing of holy oils and borrowed directly – as a glance at the parallel texts will show – from an equivalent prayer for the anointing of a king.[25] Hence Judith's consecration was clearly envisaged by those who designed and witnessed it as a status-changing rite. Fourth, the *nomen* of 'queen' was something already familiar to the West Franks and borrowed from them in 856 by Æthelwulf. Judith thus had to be made queen before leaving her father's kingdom.[26] A king's wife could of course bear the title 'queen' without having been consecrated. The fact that Hincmar had to adapt a king's *ordo* for Judith suggests that no queen's *ordo* was available to him.

---

political significance, see G. Bührer-Thierry, 'Les reines adultères', *Cahiers de civilisation médiévale*, xxxv (1992), 299–312.

[23] See Appendix, Text A. Earlier editions are now largely superseded by that of Jackson, *Ordines*, pp. 73–9 no. V. Unfortunately Wolf, 'Königinnen-Krönungen', pp. 66–7, discusses Judith's consecration without citing any historiography in English.

[24] *The Annals of St-Bertin*, s.a. 856, trans. J. L. Nelson (Manchester, 1991), p. 83. The Latin reads: 'Ediluulf . . . Iudith . . . in matrimonium accipit, et eam, Ingmaro Durocortori Remorum episcopo benedicente, inposito capiti eius diademate, reginae nomine insignit, quod sibi suaeque genti eatenus fuerat insuetum', ed. Grat, p. 73.

[25] See below, p. 313. I think I established this derivation and this borrowing in 'The Earliest Royal *ordo*', in *Authority and Power: Studies in Medieval Law and Government presented to Walter Ullmann*, edd. P. Linehan and B. Tierney (Cambridge, 1980), pp. 29–48, reprinted in my *Politics and Ritual*, pp. 341–60.

[26] Pointed out already by W. Stevenson in his editorial notes to Asser, *De Rebus Gestis Ælfredi* (Oxford, 1904; repr. 1959), p. 201.

This contrast between Frankish and West Saxon treatment of the king's wife deserves to be explored a little further. It is attested not only by the *Annals of St-Bertin* but by the *Life of Alfred*, whose author, Asser, claimed to be writing in 893, and, as regards this very issue, on evidence supplied by Alfred himself. The coincidence of these two sources here seems to me to support the argument for the *Life*'s authenticity as a ninth-century work.[27] It may be that the West Saxons' 'custom' was not of very long standing. The one-year reign, in 672, of King Cenwalh's widowed *cuen*, Seaxburh, was retained in the social memory of some late-ninth-century West Saxons.[28] Further, the West Saxons' neighbours and rivals, the Mercians, certainly had queens in the later eighth and ninth centuries; and while it is not certain that Eadburh, daughter of the Mercian king Offa was also daughter of Offa's wife Queen Cynethryth,[29] it seems quite likely that when Eadburh married the West Saxon king Beohrtric in 789, she too received the title of queen. Yet the new dynasty established by Egbert, Beohrtric's successor, in 802, seems from the outset to have downplayed the status of the king's wife.[30] Hence the need for a special enhancement of Judith's position, a declaration of her *nomen*, at Verberie in 856, and her further honouring in Wessex by being publicly accorded a seat 'beside her husband on a royal throne'.[31]

What light does the 856 *Ordo* throw on the nature of Judith's honourable *nomen*? She was anointed with chrism, like the king. Borrowing and modifying the king's anointing-prayer 'Deus electorum', Hincmar omitted references to 'the people subjected to [him]', to 'attaining the height of the kingdom in the counsels of knowledge and the equity of judgement', and to 'presenting a face of joy to the whole people'. In place of these phrases, Hincmar inserted two biblical allusions to explain the meaning of the anointing:

> [God] who by this unction made joyful the face of your maidservant Judith
> for the liberating of your servants and the confounding of their enemies, and
> who so made radiant the face of your handmaiden Esther by this spiritual
> anointing of your mercy that by her prayers you inclined the fierce heart of

27 A. P. Smyth, *Alfred the Great* (Oxford, 1995), pp. 149–367, takes the contrary view.

28 *Anglo-Saxon Chronicle 'A'*, ed. J. Bately (Cambridge, 1985), p. 31: 'Seaxburg an gear ricsode his cuen æfter him'. See further the comments of Nelson, 'Reconstructing a Royal Family: Reflections on Alfred from Asser, ch. 2', in *People and Places in Northern Europe, 500–1600: Essays in Honour of P. H. Sawyer*, edd. I. Wood and N. Lund (Woodbridge, 1991), pp. 47–66, at 55–6, 65.

29 For Cynethryth as *regina* on coins issued in her name, see M. Archibald, 'The Mercian Supremacy: Coins', in *The Making of England: Anglo-Saxon Art and Culture, AD 600–900*, edd. J. Backhouse and L. Webster (London, 1991), pp. 245–6, and for Alcuin addressing Cynethryth as *regina*, see n. 17, above.

30 P. Stafford, 'The King's Wife in Wessex, 800–1066', *Past and Present*, xci (1981), 3–27.

31 Asser, *De Rebus Gestis Ælfredi*, c. 13, p. 11. For differing interpretations of the political context of this episode, see Stafford, 'Charles the Bald, Judith and England', in *Charles the Bald*, edd. Gibson and Nelson, pp. 139–53; M. J. Enright, 'Charles the Bald and Æthelwulf of Wessex: The Alliance of 856 and Strategies of Royal Succession', *Journal of Medieval History*, v (1979), 291–302; Nelson, *Charles the Bald*, p. 182. For Judith's 'liberating' role, see the Vulgate book of Judith, 13:20.

the king to mercy and to the salvation of those who believed in you, we ask
you, omnipotent God, . . . to make her fittingly lovely[32] with chastity.

Through these changes, Hincmar gendered the function and qualities of the queen.
The reference to the 'face' of both the Old Testament women, and the final
reference to the 'beauty of chastity', suggest the importance of the queen's physical
appearance and demeanour in the representation of monarchy. Where the king was
to show 'equity of judgement', the queen was characterised by 'mercy': two
distinct if complementary aspects of justice.[33] While mentions of the *populus* and
the *plebs* were dropped, Esther's role as intercessor with her husband was spelled
out, and the concluding phrase highlighted chastity as the queenly virtue *par
excellence*. Gender played a key part in the stories of both Judith and Esther: each
traded on her feminity to defeat or sway a powerful man.[34] There is nothing about
fertility in this prayer, however. Neither Judith nor Esther would have been an apt
model of maternity. The choice of these two biblical women was of course
determined on the one hand by the name Charles's daughter bore (she had been
named for her grandmother),[35] on the other by the fittingness of a queenly
exemplar. Yet both Judith and Esther were women imbued with power, and
Hincmar's prayer is explicit on the significance of their divinely-inspired interventions: the *liberatio* and *salvatio* of the chosen people. Their individual 'private'
actions had the most public of consequences.

In 866, before a great assembly in a major Carolingian cult-site, Hincmar's
claims about the historicity of queen-making rites had implications also for the
role and functions of the queen. He stated explicitly that there was a queenly
nomen.[36] In the coronation-prayer itself, that idea was amplified: the queen was
to remain stalwart *in hoc seculo* 'in merits, in *nomen* and in *virtus*', that is, in
official title and in necessary attributes. The queen was 'crowned with a crown of
justice, crowned with glory'. Like Charles the Bald himself, his wife surely wore
a crown, now a prime symbol of royalty, and among the insignia handed on by
Charles on his deathbed to his son and heir. In Charles's own inauguration-rite as
king of the (Lotharingian) Franks in 869, the coronation-prayer drew on that
composed for Ermentrude three years before. The inspiration, to be sure, was
biblical: Pss. 8:7; 20:4; 44:8, and Heb. 1:9. But it is surely significant that the

---

[32] The adjective *decora* combines the senses of appropriateness and beauty. See Appendix,
Text A.

[33] See for illuminating comment on the implications of this for later ritual practice, J. C.
Parsons, 'Ritual and Symbol in the English Queenship to 1500', in *Women and Sovereignty*,
ed. L. O. Fradenburg (Edinburgh, 1992), pp. 60–77.

[34] The Vulgate sources are Judith, chs 10–13, and Esther, 2:15–18; 5:1–8.

[35] For this widespread naming-practice, see C. Bouchard, 'Patterns of Women's Names in
Royal Lineages: Ninth–Eleventh Centuries', *Medieval Prosopography*, ix/1 (1988), 1–32.

[36] Appendix, Text B; Jackson, *Ordines*, p. 83. For the same expression already applied to Judith
in 856 by the author of the *Annals of St-Bertin, s.a.* 856, see above, p. 306. Whether the
author of this passage was Prudentius, responsible for the annals between 835 and 861, or
Hincmar, who continued the annals down to 882, and may have made interpolations in the
earlier annals, must remain for now an open question, on which more work needs to be done.

formula 'Coronet te Dominus' was first used for a queen (and last used for a queen too, since the amplified 869 version of the prayer, translated into English, was used in 1953 for Elizabeth II)[37] – significant because the virtues here specified are not *gender*-specific.[38] Queen and king alike need faith manifested in good works. For queen and king alike, virtues that accompany an earthly crown prefigure the wearing of a heavenly crown (*in futuro*; in the *regnum perpetuum*). The notion of co-rulership in heaven[39] is equally applied to the queen and king, only the queen will sit at the right hand of another, heavenly, king. Important though the theme of fertility was in the 866 *ordo*, Ermentrude's consecration was, after all, more than a piece of fertility-magic.[40] One important difference between the officiants in the act of coronation nevertheless signalled the queen's ancillary position as consort: whereas Charles was consecrated by clergy, he himself joined the clergy in crowning the queen. Did he have a Byzantine model in mind?[41]

In Hincmar's *ordines* queenly status was high, but imprecise. Another queen's *ordo*, produced apparently at Sens, intimated the conferment of a more clearly functional authority. This *ordo*, the so-called Erdmann *Ordo*, is the first queen's *ordo* to be presented in a liturgical book alongside that of the king.[42] There is no continuity with Hincmar's *ordines*: instead the composer[43] had turned to another source. The prayer to be said over the newly-anointed queen is clearly taken almost word-for-word from the prayer over the newly-ordained abbess. Here, although the phrase *regimen animarum* from the abbess's rite is not used, a queenly office

---

37 E. C. Ratcliffe, *The Coronation Service of Queen Elizabeth II* (Cambridge, 1953), p. 49.
38 Cf. also the *ordo*, dating from the third quarter of the ninth century, recently published by R. Elze, 'Ein karolingischer Ordo für die Krönung eines Herrscherpaares', *Bullettino dell'Istituto Storico Italiano per il Medio Evo e Archivio Muratorio*, lxxxviii (1992), 417–23.
39 P. E. Schramm, 'Mitherrschaft im Himmel: ein Topos der Herrscherkults in christlicher Einkleidung', in Schramm, *Kaiser, Könige und Päpste, Gesammelte Aufsätze*, i (Stuttgart, 1968), 79–85.
40 The interpretation of Ermentrude's consecration as a *Fruchtbarkeitszauber* was first offered by E. H. Kantorowicz, 'The Carolingian King in the Bible of San Paolo Fuori le Mura', in *Late Classical and Medieval Studies in Honour of A. M. Friend* (Princeton, 1955), pp. 287–300, at 290 (cf. also A. Wintersig, 'Zur Königinnenweihe', *Jahrbuch für Liturgiewissenschaft*, v [1925], 150–3 at p. 152: 'eine Weihe der Thronfolgermutter'), and has recently been taken up again by Erkens, ' "Sicut Esther regina" ', p. 28.
41 Cf. Wolf, 'Königinnen-Krönungen', pp. 81–2, with reference to 816.
42 Appendix, Text C. Cf. Jackson, *Ordines*, no. XIII, pp. 151–2. Schramm named the *ordo* after Carl Erdmann (d. 1944), and although Erdmann himself objected, the name has stuck: Jackson, p. 143. The older of the two manuscripts, a pontifical from Sens, has generally been dated to *c.* 900, but for the still unpublished arguments of P. Konakov and G. Lobrichon for a date 'about 875 or even from the middle of the century', see Jackson, p. 26, with some further general remarks ('that there was no generally accepted coronation rite in ninth-century Francia, that each coronation ceremony was an *ad hoc* ceremony, that a rite was devised for each coronation and used on that occasion alone . . . [and that] Louis the Stammerer's *Ordo* [of 877] would play a crucial role in standardizing the ceremony'). The mid-ninth century should, however, be highlighted as the period during which a continuous tradition took shape, and the importance of Hincmar's *ordines* as a group deserves emphasis too: see above, p. 301, n. 2.
43 See below, p. 310.

is evoked in the idea of the queen's being 'instituted' and remaining 'worthy' (*digna*). The position of abbess was the most authoritative one available to women, not least in the Carolingian period when abbesses, like abbots, were subject to the institutionalised demands of the realm, owing military service, for instance, holding military strongpoints, and sometimes being summoned to assemblies.[44] Abbesses were also *magistrae*, female-teachers.[45] This combination of functions likewise characterised the later Carolingian queen.

The prayer for the conferring of the ring in this same queen's *ordo* has struck some modern commentators as anomalous (Appendix, Text D). Walter Ullmann argued that the ring here 'has the function of a knuckle-duster'.[46] It has been claimed, too, that this prayer must have been borrowed from a rite for a king, or even for a bishop.[47] This ring is not a wedding-ring, but an amulet, a charm, not necessarily conceived as gender-specific, that is, for men only. Avoiding heresy and summoning barbarous *gentes* to acknowledgement of the truth of the faith could be queenly functions. Patronage of missionaries, support for the church, care for the spiritual wellbeing of the household, were characteristic responsibilities of powerful women, and of queens par excellence.[48] Thus by the tenth century, here again a queenly office is being outlined.

If the 'Erdmann' composer should be located at Sens, as the earliest manuscript might suggest, there is a problem in supplying a plausible occasion for the first use of the king's and queen's *ordines* as a pair. The contemporary evidence for the consecration of Odo (Eudes) by Archbishop Walter of Sens on 29 February 888 makes no mention of Odo's queen Theodrada. Further, an *ordo* for Odo's consecration is extant, and it is not 'Erdmann'.[49] Similar problems surround a second possibility: King Ralph was consecrated at St-Médard, Soissons, by Archbishop Walter on 13 July 923, but Ralph's wife Emma was consecrated later in the year by Archbishop Seulf at Reims. My tentative solution is that since the extant *ordo* for Odo clearly represents only a part of what took place, 'Erdmann' too might have been used for the royal couple in February 888.[50] I would stress the likelihood

---

[44] Nelson, *Politics and Ritual*, pp. 122–4, and cf. *eadem, The Frankish World*, pp. 19–29, 209.

[45] Nelson, 'Les Femmes et l'évangelisation', *Revue du Nord*, lxviii (1986), 471–85.

[46] *Principles of Government and Politics in the Middle Ages* (London, 1961), pp. 181–2.

[47] C. A. Bouman, *Sacring and Crowning* (Groningen, 1957), p. 131, and cf. pp. 129–30.

[48] See Nelson, 'Les reines carolingiennes au XIe siècle', in *Femmes et pouvoirs des femmes à Byzance et en Occident*, edd. A. Dierkens, J. M. Sansterre, S. Lebecq and R. Le Jan (forthcoming).

[49] Jackson, *Ordines*, Ordo XI, pp. 133–8. Cf. also Schramm, *Könige*, ii, 211–14.

[50] Cf. the fundamental study by O. Guillot, 'Les Etapes de l'accession d'Eudes au pouvoir royal', in *'Media in Francia . . .': Recueil de mélanges offert à Karl Ferdinand Werner* (Maulévrier, 1989), pp. 199–223. Cf. also Bautier, 'Sacres', pp. 47–8. I cannot wholly share the view of Jackson, p. 142, that 'the king's and queen's *ordines* have nothing to do with each other either in the Erdmann *Ordo* or in other early *ordines*, and their juxtaposition in no way reflects a joint coronation or implies that the two were to be used for a joint coronation'. These propositions may be true at some times and places, but do not hold universally. They reflect the situation once pontificals had assumed more generalised, standardised form and function. In the ninth and tenth centuries, when royal *ordines* were

of Theodrada's consecration alongside her husband: a clear statement of dynastic intent.[51] The twin 'Erdmann' *ordines* might then have been reused for Ralph and Emma, even though they were consecrated separately, Ralph at Soissons in July 923, and Emma at Reims later that year.[52] Again I think Emma's consecration was very significant: Ralph's acceptability to the *primates* of West Francia had much to do with the fact that his wife was 'the daughter of King Robert', his immediate predecessor.[53]

A fourth and final queen's *ordo* to consider briefly here is that associated with the 'Seven Forms' king's *ordo*.[54] It may have been used for Gerberga, wife of Louis IV 'd'Outremer'. Gerberga, sister of Otto I, and widow of the recently-dead Duke Giselbert of Lotharingia, married Louis in 939, and was consecrated by Archbishop Artold of Reims.[55] The hypothesis of use for Gerberga, given the

still at an early stage of formation and diffusion, the presence of a queen's *ordo* does seem to me a potentially important indication of historical context.

51 A hagiographer writing before 894 called Theodrada *regina*: *Vita Rignoberti*, ed. W. Levison, *MGH, Scriptores rerum Merovingicarum*, vii (Hanover/Leipzig, 1920), 55.

52 The suggestion of Bautier, 'Sacres', p. 50 n. 152, that a set of blessings for a king's investiture with ring, sword, crown, sceptre and staff, which follows the queen's *ordo* in the Sens Pontifical, Jackson, Ordo XIIIB, was used for Ralph's *Festkrönung* on the occasion of Emma's consecration, deserves further consideration, if the date of the manuscript does not preclude it (see above, n. 42). It does not seem to me implausible that Seulf of Reims would have used a queen's *ordo* emanating from Sens: Robert was consecrated by Walter of Sens (Bautier, 'Sacres', p. 49 n. 50) as Seulf's predecessor Harvey of Reims lay dying (Flodoard says 'he died three days after Robert was made king', *Historia Remensis Ecclesiae*, iv.17, p. 577), and as Seulf was a firm adherent of Robert and Ralph, he might well have been willing to signal this, and the continuity of the two regimes, by re-using for Ralph the *ordo* used for Robert. Reims-Sens rivalry was not a constant, and other factors affected particular situations, as in this case. The prayer-texts of Ordo XIIIB are brief, but I do not see any evidence to support Jackson's idea, p. 144, that their content represents 'a primitive . . . survival . . . from the early ninth or even the late eighth century'. *Pace* Jackson, p. 143 n. 2, Bautier, 'Sacres', pp. 49–50, did *not* suggest that 'Erdmann' was composed for a 'double coronation' of Robert and Ralph in 923.

53 Flodoard, *Annales*, ann. 923, ed. P. Lauer (Paris, 1906), p. 17, notes the relationship. For the importance of the consecration of the Anglo-Saxon King Edgar's wife Ælfthryth in 973, see Nelson, *Politics and Ritual*, pp. 296–303, 370–4.

54 Jackson, Ordo XIV, pp. 159–67, suggesting, p. 154, renaming as 'the Ordo of Eleven Forms', in order to signal the presence of the queen's *ordo*, of four formulae, following the king's. Yet it is clear that the queen's *ordo* sometimes travelled independently of the king's, and *vice versa*. Moreover, Carl Erdmann's original name of 'Seven Forms Ordo' is now well established: I therefore retain it here while using Jackson's edition. This is the place to observe that while I much admire the ingenuity of Lanoë, 'L'ordo de couronnement' (cf. above n. 1), arguing that an abbreviated, five-form, version of the king's *ordo* preserved in a Leyden manuscript of *c*. 1000 represents the *ordo* used for Charles the Bald in 848, I am not convinced, chiefly because (a) the 877 form of the consecration prayer, 'Omnipotens sempiterne deus creator' seems to me older than that of the Leyden manuscript, and (b) the original form of the 'two peoples' mentioned in the Leyden consecration prayer were, in my view, the Angles and Saxons (rather than the Franks and Aquitanians), and so derive from an Anglo-Saxon model which travelled to the Continent in the tenth century (see my *Politics and Ritual*, pp. 361–6, a discussion not cited by Lanoë in this context).

55 Flodoard, *Annales*, ann. 939, p. 74 (suggesting that the location was in Lotharingia);

importance of the Ottonian connection, would help explain why the 'Seven Forms' queen's *ordo* was incorporated into the Romano-Germanic Pontifical and other Ottonian pontificals in Italy as well as in Germany.[56] Artold had also consecrated Louis himself,[57] and may have composed new *ordines* for both king and queen, or used *ordines* which he found already at Reims, rather than continue following the Sens tradition embodied in 'Erdmann'. The queen's *ordo* (like the king's) clearly picks up on a Reims tradition. References to both Judith and Esther models are recapitulated, and amplified. God 'once willed to entrust the triumph of [his] glory and strength into the hands of a woman, Judith, for the sake of the Jewish people';[58] and brought about Esther's marriage 'for the sake of Israel's salvation from its captivity'.[59] The queen's crown is said to be 'of royal excellence', its outward glitter the sign of wisdom as well as virtues within. More important still, blessing is sought for 'your servant whom we have elected to be queen'; and God is requested 'for the sake of the salvation of your Christian people, to make [the queen] enter into worthy and sublime union with our king'. There are, moreover, several strong parallels in wording between this *ordo* and the king's.[60] All this adds up to a representation of the queen as involved in 'a partnership of [the king's] realm (*regni sui participium*)', even if, at the same time, the prayers differentiated clearly between the king's office of ruling and the queen's supporting role.

In the tenth-century narrative and charter evidence, queens and empresses are conspicuous for their political activities in all the kingdoms of Latin Christendom for which adequate documentation survives. Theophano, coming from Byzantium as Otto II's bride, and later seizing the opportunies of a regency, found a position and a status ready-made.[61] If her high profile was exceptional, her impact as a consort was typical.[62] The composers and performers of queenly *ordines* were

---

Flodoard, *Historia Remensis Ecclesiae*, iv.35, p. 585, quotes the letter of Artold to the Council of Ingelheim in 948: 'Postquam Ludovicum regem, favente Hugone cunctisque regni principibus, Gerbergam quoque reginam benedixeram et sacro perfuderam chrismate'; cf. also Richer, *Historiarum Libri IV*, 2nd edn, ed. G. Waitz, *MGH SRG*, li (Hanover, 1877), ii.19, p. 49: 'Ludowicus rex Gislebertum extinctum comperiens . . . in Belgicam profectus, eius uxorem Gerbergam, Ottonis sororem, coniugio duxit eamque secum reginam in regnum coronavit.'

[56] *Ordines coronationis imperialis: Die Ordines für die Weihe und Krönung des Kaisers und der Kaiserin*, ed. R. Elze, *MGH Fontes*, ix (Hanover, 1960), *Ordo III*, pp. 6–9; *Le Pontifical romano-germanique du dixième siècle*, edd. C. Vogel and R. Elze, 3 vols, Studi e Testi, 226–7, 269 (Vatican City, 1963–72), i, 246–63.

[57] Flodoard, *Annales*, pp. 63–4; Richer, *Historiarum Libri IV*, ii.4, p. 42.

[58] Appendix, Text E. The prayer continues with allusions to the fertility of Sarah, Rebecca, Leah and Rachel. The examples of Sarah, Rebecca and Rachel were also invoked in the *Ordo* of Ermentrude (866).

[59] Cf. above, n. 34.

[60] Note the notion of 'election into being queen/king' in prayer 1; and repeated references to the mediation of the officiating bishops in prayers 3 and 4.

[61] See *Kaiserin Theophanu: Begegnung des Ostens und Westens um die Wende des ersten Jahrtausends*, edd. A. von Euw and P. Schreiner (Cologne, 1991), and *The Empress Theophano*, ed. A. Davids (Cambridge, 1995).

[62] The literature on tenth-century queens and empresses is now extensive: see *Frauen im*

responding to the real world about them: queens were not only mothers of future kings, but acted in partnership with their husbands, and perhaps did so because they knew themselves to have been consecrated to that end. In incorporating allusions to such roles and functions into the most solemn formulae of the queen's inauguration, formulae used from the tenth-century onwards in much of Latin Christendom, the queen-makers were also giving shape – and permanent shape – to medieval queenship.

Appendix

EARLY *ORDINES* FOR KINGS AND QUEENS

A. The earliest king's *ordo*

Deus electorum fortitudo et humilium celsitudo, qui in primordio per effusionem diluvii crimina mundi castigare voluisti et per columbam, ramum olivae portantem, pacem terris redditam demonstrasti, iterumque Aaron famulum tuum per unctionem olei sacerdotem sanxisti, et postea per huius unguenti infusionem ad regendum populum Israeliticum sacerdotes, reges et prophetas perfecisti, vultumque ecclesiae in oleo exhilarandum per propheticam famuli tui voce David esse praedixisti: ita, quaesumus, omnipotens pater, ut per huius creaturae pinguedinem hunc servum tuum sanctificare tua benedictione digneris, eumque in similitudinem *columbae pacem simplicitatis* populo sibi subdito praestare, et exempla Aaron in Dei servitio diligenter imitari, regnique fastigia in consiliis scientiae et aequitate iudicii semper assequi,*

The Judith *Ordo* (856)

Deus electorum fortitudo et humilium celsitudo, qui in primordio per effusionem diluvii crimina mundi purgari voluisti et per columbam, ramum olivae portantem, pacem terris redditam demonstrasti, iterum Aaron famulum tuum per unctionem olei sacerdotem unxisti et postea per huius unguenti infusionem ad regendum populum Israeliticum sacerdotes, reges et prophetas perfecisti, vultumque ecclesiae in oleo exhilarandum prophetica famuli tui voce David esse praedixisti: qui hoc etiam unguento famulae tuae Iudith ad liberationem servorum tuorum et confusionem inimicorum vultum exhilarasti et ancillae tuae Hester faciem hac spiritali misericordiae tuae unctione adeo lucifluam reddidisti, ut efferatum cor regis ad misericordiam et salvationem in te credentium ipsius precibus inclinares: te *quaesumus, omnipotens Deus, ut per huius*

Frühmittelalter: Eine ausgewählte, kommentierte Bibliographie, edd. W. Affeldt, C. Nolte, S. Reiter and U. Vorwerk (Frankfurt, 1990), Section 9, pp. 225–66. T. Vogelsang, *Die Frau als Herrscherin im hohen Mittelalter* (Frankfurt, 1954), still provides a valuable starting-point; and P. Stafford, *Queens, Concubines and Dowagers* (Athens, Ga/London, 1983) is indispensable. See further J. Verdon, 'Les Femmes et la politique en France au Xe siècle', in *Economies et sociétés au moyen âge: Mélanges offerts à E. Perroy* (Paris, 1973), pp. 108–19. See now also R. Collins, 'Queens-Dowager and Queens-Regent in Tenth-Century León and Navarre', in *Medieval Queenship*, ed. Parsons, pp. 79–92; Stafford, 'The Portrayal of Royal Women in England, Mid-Tenth to Mid-Twelfth Centuries', *ibid.*, pp. 143–68; and *eadem*, in the present volume, with further references. For tenth-century Italian queens, see the perceptive analysis of P. Buc, 'Italian Hussies and German Matrons: Liutprand of Cremona on Dynastic Legitimacy', *Frühmittelalterliche Studien*, xxix (1995), 207–25; and for the most recent comment on Ottonian queenly consecration and its implications, H. Keller, 'Widukind's Bericht über die Aachener Wahl und Krönung Ottos I', *Frühmittelalterliche Studien*, xxix (1995), 390–453, at 418–19.

vultumque hilaritatis per hanc olei unctionem tuamque benedictionem, te adiuvante, toti plebi paratum habere facias.

creatura pinguedinem, columbae pace, simplicitate, ac pudicitia decoram efficias.

B. *Ordo* of Queen Ermentrude (866)

. . . *Corona* eam, *Domine, corona iustitiae,* corona eam *fructibus* sanctis et operibus benedictis. Sit meritis et nomine atque virtute regina adsistens in hoc seculo *fide recta* et operibus *bonis,* et in futuro honore et *gloria coronata* a dextris regis, in vestitu bonorum operum, circumdata virtutum varietate. . . . *Coronet te Dominus gloria* et honore et sempiterna protectione. Qui vivit et regnat.

Ordo of Charles the Bald (869)

Coronet te Dominus corona gloriae atque *iustitiae,* ut cum *fide recta* et multiplici bonorum operum fructu, ad coronam pervenias regni perpetui.

C. Eighth-Century Gelasian Sacramentary of Gellone

Oratio quando abbas vel abbatissa ordinatur . . .

O.s.d. divinum *tuae benedictionis spiritum famulæ* tuae N. nobis *propitiatus infunde, ut quae per manus nostrae impositionem hodie* abbatissa constituitur *sanctificatione tua digna* a te *electa permaneat* . . .

'Erdmann' *Ordo* (c. 875/c. 900)

Ordo ad ordinandam reginam

O.s.d. affluentem *spiritum tuae benedictionis* super *hanc famulam tuam* nostra oratione *propitiatus infunde, ut quae per manus nostrae impositionem hodie* regina instituitur *sanctificatione tua digna* et *electa permaneat* . . .

D. 'Erdmann' *Ordo* (c. 875/c. 900)

Ordo ad ordinandam reginam . . .

Tunc summus episcoporum accipiens anulum et digito illius imponens dicat.
Accipe anulum fidei, signaculum sanctae Trinitatis, quo possis omnes hereticas pravitates devitare, barbaras quoque gentes virtute tibi praestita ad agnitionem veritatis advocare.

E. Ordo of Seven Forms (early tenth century)

Queen's *Ordo*

Incipit benedictio regine in ingressu ecclesie

Omnipotens eterne Deus, fons et origo totius bonitatis, qui feminei sexus fragilitatem nequaquam reprobando aversaris, sed dignanter comprobando potius eligis, et qui infirma mundi eligendo fortia queque confundere decrevisti, quique etiam glorie virtutisque tue triumphum in manu Iudith femine olim Iudaice plebi de hoste sevissimo resignare voluisti, *respice, quesumus, ad preces humilitatis nostre, et super hanc famulam tuam N. quam supplici devotione in reginam eligimus,*

King's *Ordo*

Ordo qualiter rex ordinari debet

O.e.D. creator omnium, imperator angelorum, rex regnantium dominusque dominantium, qui Habraham fidelem famulum tuum de hostibus triumphare fecisti, Moysi et Iosue populo prelatis multiplicem victoriam tribuisti, humilemque David puerum tuum regni fastigio sublimasti,

respice, quesumus, ad preces humilitatis nostre, et super hunc famulum tuum N. quem suplici devotione in regem eligimus, be+nedictionum tuarum dona multiplica, eamque dextera tua potentie semper et ubique circumda, ut umbone muniminis tui undique secus firmiter protecta, *visibilis seu invisibilis hostis* nequitias triumphaliter expugnare valeat, et una cum Sara atque Rebecca, Lia et Rachel, beatis reverendisque feminis, fructu uteri sui fecundari seu gratulari mereatur ad decorem totius regni statumque sancte Dei ecclesie regendum necnon protegendum. Per Christum . . .

Item alia oratio eiusdem ante altare

Deus qui solus habes immortalitatem lucemque inhabitas inaccessibilem . . . qui superbos equo moderamine de principatu deicis atque humiles dignanter in sublime provehis, ineffabilem misericordiam tuam supplices exoramus, ut sicut Hester reginam Israhelis causa salutis de captivitatis sue compede solutam ad regis Assueri talamum regnique sui consortium transire fecisti, ita hanc famulam tuam N. humilitatis nostre be+nedictione christiane plebis gratia salutis ad dignam sublimemque regis nostri copulam regnique sui *participium* misercorditer transire concedas, et ut in regalis federe coniugii semper manens pudica proximam virginitati palmam continere queat, tibique Deo vivo et vero in omnibus et super omnia iugiter placere desideret, et te inspirante que tibi placita sunt toto corde perficiat. . . .

Corone inpositio

Officio indignitatis nostre seu congregationis in reginam bene+dicta, *accipe coronam regalis excellentie, que licet ab indignis episcoporum tamen manibus capiti tuo imponitur* . . .

benedicti+onum tuarum dona in eo multiplica eumque dextera tue potentie semper et ubique circumda, quatinus predicti Habrae fidelitate firmatus, Moysi mansuetudine fretus, Salomonis sapientia decoratus, tibi in omnibus placeat et per tramitem iustitie inoffenso gressu semper incedat, ecclesiamque tuam deinceps cum plebibus sibi annexis ita enutriat ac doceat, muniat et instruat, contraque omnes *visibiles et invisibiles hostes* eidem potenter regaliterque tue virtutis regimen administret et ad vere fidei pacisque concordiam eorum animos te opitulante reformet, ut horum populorum debita subiectione fultus, cum digno amore glorificetur, et ad paternum decenter solium tua miseratione conscendere mereatur, tue quoque protectionis galea munitus et scuto insuperabili iugiter protectus armisque celestibus circumdatus, optabilis victorie triumphum fideliter vel feliciter capiat terroremque sue potentie infidelibus inferat et pacem tibi militantibus letanter reportet, per dominum nostrum . . .

Corone regalis impositio

Accipe coronam regni, que licet ab indignis episcoporum tamen manibus capiti tuo imponitur. . . . et per hanc te *participem* ministerii nostri non ignores . . .

16

'Never was a body buried in England with such solemnity and honour': The Burials and Posthumous Commemorations of English Queens to 1500 *

John Carmi Parsons

A queen-consort of England after 1066 rarely, if ever, exercised in her own right either of the central royal functions of warrior or lawgiver. Her role in the life of the realm was thus represented, or constructed, chiefly through such formalised ritual displays as her coronation, childbearing, intercession, pious exercises, or her reception by ecclesiastical or civic dignitaries. The most consistent theme evident in the acts or utterances that characterised such performances is the frequency and subtlety with which they emphasised the queen's subordination to the king, her isolation from his authority and the de-centring of her sexuality, especially her role as perpetuator of the royal lineage. The queen's coronation *ordo*, for example, exalted her as wife and mother, but at the same time implied certain controls over her intimate relationship with the king; when she arrived at an episcopal town, bishop and clergy met her in procession with incense and reverence, but the antiphon sung while she made her devotions in the cathedral implicitly inscribed woman's compliant dissociation from male authority. By the mid-fifteenth century, even the couple's chapel offerings were minutely graduated.[1]

I was therefore taken aback by the directions for the burial of an English queen-consort found in the *Liber regie capelle*, an account written in the late 1440s of the ritual and ceremonial of the English chapel royal. The *Liber* contains elaborate directions for preparing an anointed king's body for burial and the secular

* My thanks to Anne Duggan, Janet Nelson and David Carpenter for their invitation to participate in the King's College conference, and for a generous travel grant which allowed me to attend the conference.

1 J. C. Parsons, 'Ritual and Symbol in the English Queenship to 1500', in *Women and Sovereignty*, ed. L. O. Fradenburg, *Cosmos*, vii (1991) (Edinburgh, 1992), 60–77; 'The Queen's Intercession in Thirteenth-Century England', in *Power of the Weak: Studies on Medieval Women*, edd. J. Carpenter and S. B. Maclean (Urbana, IL, 1995), pp. 147–77; and 'The Pregnant Queen as Counsellor and the Medieval Construction of Mothering', in *Medieval Mothering*, edd. J. C. Parsons and B. Wheeler (New York, 1996), pp. 39–61. On the chapel royal, *Liber regie capelle: A Manuscript in the Biblioteca Publica, Evora*, ed. W. Ullmann, Henry Bradshaw Society, 92 (London, 1961), p. 61.

ceremonies that followed: his lying-in-state, the makeup of the funeral procession, the formalities at his burial. The passage tersely concludes: 'Now the exequies of a queen who leaves this world are entirely carried out in the form noted above, whereby anyone can easily understand from the one the form of the other. And so it would be useless to write more fully of this.'[2] Even supposing that a tired scribe simply wanted to save himself some work, it is striking that a queen achieved ritual equality with the king only in death. Curiosity as to why this was so, and what it might signify, led me to ponder the death of queens.

Until very recently, studies of medieval royal ritual have focused primarily upon the king. His wife is ignored, or at best honoured with a brief note that she will *not* be considered, either because she has no share in the king's dignity or because she has no real constitutional importance. True, medieval kings' funerals did serve to mark the transmission of authority from one male to another, a moment of social and political tension that required a reassuringly awesome display, a function admittedly not shared by queens' burials, however grand they might be.[3] In recent years, however, Janet Nelson, Michael Enright, Louise Fradenburg, John Parsons and others have elucidated queens' integral role in royal ritual, their contribution to the image of male sovereignty and to the affirmation of hierarchial social relationships.[4] Though queens' death rituals did not mark the transmission of power, then, they could still enter forcefully into representations of sovereignty, and thus merit attention in their own right.

Another frame of reference is suggested by works of Patrick Geary, Frances Yates, Mary Carruthers, and Jacques Le Goff on the medieval stimulation and manipulation of memory, especially (in the present context) the role in that process

---

2   *Liber regie capelle*, ed. Ullmann, p. 115: 'Exequie autem Regine de hoc seculo migrantis modo et forma superius annotatis totaliter quasi fiunt, unde per unum potest faciliter aliquis formam alterius intelligere. Et ideo frustra de hoc esset amplius conscribendum.' Liturgical services would, of course, have been the same for husband or wife.

3   E.g. U. Borkowska, 'The Funeral Ceremonies of the Polish Kings from the Fourteenth to the Eighteenth Centuries', *Journal of Ecclesiastical History*, xxxvi (1985), 513–34, esp. p. 513 n. 1; A. Erlande-Brandenburg, *Le Roi est mort: Étude sur les funérailles des rois de France jusqu'à la fin du XIIIe siècle* (Paris, 1975), p. 23, takes a narrow view of burials of non-reigning Capetians. The role of such rites in signifying the transmission of power is concisely stated in C. Gittings, *Death, Burial, and the Individual in Early Modern England* (London, 1988), pp. 166, 178–9; see also R. E. Giesey, 'Models of Rulership in French Royal Ceremonial', in *Rites of Power: Symbolism, Ritual, and Politics since the Middle Ages*, ed. S. Wilentz (Philadelphia, 1985), pp. 46–51, and E. A. R. Brown, 'The Ceremonial of Royal Succession in Capetian France: The Double Funeral of Louis X', *Traditio*, xxxiv (1978), 227–71.

4   J. L. Nelson, 'Inauguration Rituals', in *Early Medieval Kingship*, edd. P. H. Sawyer and I. N. Woods (Leeds, 1977), pp. 50–71, repr. in Nelson, *Ritual, Politics and Power in Early Medieval Europe* (Ronceverte, 1986), pp. 283–308; M. E. Enright, 'Lady with a Mead-Cup: Ritual, Group Cohesion and Hierarchy in the Germanic Warband', *Frühmittelalterliche Studien*, xxii (1988), 170–203; L. O. Fradenburg, ed., *Women and Sovereignty*, and *City, Marriage, Tournament: The Arts of Rule in Late Medieval Scotland* (Madison, WI, 1991), esp. pp. 67–149; J. C. Parsons, 'Ritual and Symbol', pp. 60–77, and 'Queen's Intercession', pp. 147–77.

of commemorative services for the dead and of visual images on their tombs: an authoritative past was made accessible to the present as the illustrious dead were honoured through manipulation of the spoken (or sung) word and objects (or images).[5] Such ideas might apply in particular ways to a limited group like the queens of medieval England. Gábor Klaniczay, for example, has studied women of the Hungarian royal lineage who took earlier female members of that house as life models in a quest for personal sanctity. Klaniczay focuses on written lives and the iconography of royal Hungarian female saints as the chief means by which the memory of these women was made available to their later relatives – much as Lois Huneycutt thinks St Margaret of Scotland's *vita* influenced the life of Margaret's daughter Edith-Matilda, queen of Henry I of England. But Klaniczay acknowledges that as others adopted such life models, they drew upon a much wider range of sources, from which (as Geary posits) posthumous remembrances, liturgical or monumental, cannot be excluded.[6] I therefore address here the prospect that queens' death rituals created socially acceptable images of queenship, while affording successive queens access to traditions of queenship that were created and perpetuated in part by just such rites and monuments.

As these topics have not previously been treated in a very systematic fashion, the responses suggested here are bound to be preliminary in nature. I consequently treat death rituals in a very broad sense that includes funeral observances, the symbolic language of tombs, and later commemorations.[7] Extant evidence is not copious, but I hope to offer some answers to the questions posed above, and to indicate avenues for future research. In essence, I shall pursue for death rituals much the same sort of inquiry Dr Karen Pratt follows for literature – examining medieval English queens' death rituals, suggesting contexts for their depictions of queens and queenship, and inferring something about the kind of royal mirror they afford.

My first task is to recount what is known of English queens' burials in the Middle Ages. Here I distinguish between rituals surrounding death and burial, and the mere facts of burial – when, where, and whether a monument once existed or now survives. For the moment, I am concerned with the latter, and despite the time

---

5 Geary, *Phantoms of Remembrance: Memory and Oblivion at the End of the First Millennium* (Princeton, 1994), and *Living with the Dead in the Middle Ages* (Ithaca, NY, 1994); Carruthers, *The Book of Memory: A Study of Memory in Medieval Culture* (Cambridge, 1990), pp. 221–57; Yates, *The Art of Memory* (Chicago, 1966), pp. 82–104; Le Goff, *History and Memory*, trans. S. Rendall, E. Claman (New York, 1992).

6 Klaniczay, 'Legends and Life-Strategies for Aspirant Saints in the Later Middle Ages', in idem, *The Uses of Supernatural Power: The Transformation of Popular Religion in Medieval and Early-Modern Europe*, trans. S. Singerman, ed. K. Margolis (Princeton, 1990), pp. 95–110. Cf. L. L. Huneycutt, 'The Image of a Perfect Princess: The *Life of St Margaret* in the Reign of Matilda II', *Anglo-Norman Studies*, xii (1991), 81–97, and 'Intercession and the High-Medieval Queen: The *Esther* Topos', in *Power of the Weak*, edd. Carpenter and MacLean, pp. 126–46.

7 On the need to observe broad definitions in these matters, and the cultural factors influencing such definition for the medieval period, Gittings, *Death, Burial and the Individual*, pp. 19–20.

span indicated, this bids fair to be the easiest part of my task. Of the burials of Anglo-Saxon kings' wives we know little before the tenth century, save for isolated cases in which they were buried in churches with which they had some particular link: the missionary Bertha of Kent in Augustine's monastery at Canterbury, or St Æthelthryth of Northumbria and her sister Sexberga of Kent, both in the convent at Ely where they ended their lives as abbesses.[8] Tenth-century politics of royal succession and the chequered marital careers of the kings of the house of Wessex favoured the emergence of royal monastic foundations as burial places for women of the royal house, among them the convents at Shaftesbury and Wilton to which several of them retired as widows. This tradition appears to have been strong; despite the evolving links between the royal house and the see of Winchester diligently nourished by Edgar's second wife Ælfthryth, she was buried at Wherwell, a house to which she had shown personal favour. Save for Edward the Martyr (d. 978) and Æthelred II (d. 1016), Winchester did serve as a royal necropolis in later reigns, receiving the bodies of Cnut in 1035, Harthacnut in 1042, and Ælfgifu-Emma in 1052. Perhaps because of Winchester's links to the Danes, Edward the Confessor (d. 1066) restored Westminster abbey and was buried there; his wife Edith (d. 1075) probably meant to be buried at Wilton, a house she personally enriched, but because William the Conqueror was unwilling to see Wilton emerge as a centre for adherents of the house of Godwin, Edith was buried in 1075 at Westminster – one indication that queens' burials in the eleventh century could already assume significant political overtones.[9]

Elizabeth Hallam has charted the processes by which kings' burials were elaborated in England and France from the eleventh century, and the emergence of the monastery of St-Denis near Paris as a Capetian dynastic necropolis has been studied by E. A. R. Brown and Alain Erlande-Brandenburg, among others. English kingship's political and dynastic contexts, of course, differed greatly from those in France, and Emma Mason shows that as a result, Anglo-Norman and early Angevin kings of England did not adopt a single burial church; instead they sought individual intercession through the personal monastic foundations where they were buried, the locations of which were frequently determined by prevailing geopolitical axes within the Anglo-Norman *regnum*.[10] One consequence was that the first Anglo-Norman queens were not buried with their husbands. Matilda of

---

[8] On Bertha, Bede, *Historia Ecclesiastica Gentis Anglorum*, ed. J. Stevenson, English Historical Society (London, 1838), ii.5 (p. 110); on Æthelthryth and Sexberga, P. Stafford, *Queens, Concubines, and Dowagers: The King's Wife in the Early Middle Ages* (Athens, GA, 1983), pp. 177–8, 180, 182, 190.

[9] Stafford, *Queens, Concubines, and Dowagers*, pp. 178–9, 188–90; E. Mason, ' "*Pro statu et incolumitate regni mei*": Royal Monastic Patronage, 1066–1154', in *Religion and National Identity*, ed. S. Mews, SCH, 18 (1982), pp. 99–117, esp. 103; B. Yorke, 'Anglo-Saxon Royal Burial: The Documentary Evidence', *Medieval Europe 1992: A Conference on Medieval Archaeology in Europe*, pre-printed papers vol. 4, 'Death and Burial' (York, 1992), pp. 41–5.

[10] E. Hallam, 'Royal Burial and the Cult of Kingship in England and France, 1066–1300', *Journal of Medieval History*, viii (1982), 359–80; E. A. R. Brown, 'Burying and Unburying the Kings of France', in *Persons in Groups: Social Behavior as Identity Formation in*

Flanders (d. 1083) was interred in her foundation at La Trinité in Caen; Edith-Matilda (d. 1118) hoped to be buried in her foundation at Holy Trinity Aldgate, but died at Westminster while Henry I was in Normandy, and the monks there buried her in the abbey church.[11] Henry I's second queen, Adelicia of Louvain (d. 1151), was probably buried in the convent at Afflinghem where she died. Matilda of Boulogne (d. 1152), however, was buried with Stephen (d. 1154) in their foundation at Faversham – evidently meant as their burial church – and Eleanor of Aquitaine (d. 1204) at Fontevrault in Poitou, where Henry II (d. 1189) already rested.[12]

Thereafter only exceptional circumstances accounted for an English queen's interment apart from her husband: Eleanor of Provence's (d. 1291) religious profession at Amesbury and her burial there rather than at Westminster with Henry III (d. 1272), Isabella of France's (d. 1358) burial in the London Franciscan church rather than at Gloucester with Edward II (d. 1327), or Margaret of Anjou's (d. 1482) burial in France. One further development requires comment. Eleanor of Aquitaine, Eleanor of Castile (d. 1290), and Philippa of Hainaut (d. 1369) were buried in the same churches as their husbands and near them, but not in the same tombs with them. While double monuments for aristocratic couples appeared in England around the mid-fourteenth century, it was only with Anne of Bohemia (d. 1394) and Richard II (d. 1400) that a double royal tomb was commissioned; this fashion prevailed for the surviving royal monuments of the later medieval period – Henry IV (d. 1413) and Joan of Navarre (d. 1437) at Canterbury, and Henry VII (d. 1509) and Elizabeth of York (d. 1503) at Westminster abbey.[13]

Medieval and Renaissance Europe, ed. R. C. Trexler (Binghamton, NY, 1985), pp. 241–66; Erlande-Brandenburg, *Le Roi est mort*; Mason, ' *"Pro statu et incolumitate"* ', pp. 99–117.

[11] On Matilda of Flanders, Mason, *ibid.*, p. 105; on Edith-Matilda, *The Cartulary of Holy Trinity, Aldgate*, ed. G. A. J. Hodgett (London, 1971), nos 12–13, 997, and *Regesta Regum Anglo-Normannorum*, edd. H. W. C. Davis, R. J. Whitwell and C. Johnson, 3 vols (Oxford, 1913–68), ii, nos 1240, 1249, 1315, 1316*, 1377, 1514, 1529.

[12] For Faversham, Hallam, 'Royal Burial', p. 369; on Fontevrault, T. S. R. Boase, 'Fontevrault and the Plantagenets', *Journal of the British Archaeological Association*, 3rd ser., xxxiv (1971), 1–10. Despite the generally-agreed precocity of English *kings'* burial practices, elaboration of English *queens'* burials appears to have lagged behind Capetian practice. French queens were customarily buried with their husbands at St-Denis only from the thirteenth century, but their burials were already associated by the mid-twelfth with sites of importance to Capetian kingship (noted by Dr Kathleen Nolan in a paper read at the Thirtieth International Congress on Medieval Studies at Western Michigan University, May 1995). Reasons for the differing significance attached to queens' burials in England and France at this period need investigation; on differences in queenship in the two kingdoms, J. C. Parsons, 'Family, Sex, and Power: The Rhythms of Medieval Queenship', in *Medieval Queenship*, ed. Parsons, p. 7.

[13] Katherine of Valois (d. 1437) lies in Henry V's (d. 1422) chantry in Westminster abbey, but not in the same tomb. Anne Neville's (d. 1483) Westminster burial implies Richard III (d. 1485) expected to be buried there, but events did not favour such plans. Elizabeth Woodville (d. 1495) and Edward IV (d. 1483) lie together in St George's chapel at Windsor Castle, with no tomb. In general, H. M. Colvin, R. A. Brown and A. J. Taylor, *The History of the King's Works: The Middle Ages*, 2 vols as one (London, 1963), pp. 477–90. E. Panofsky, *Tomb*

Earlier royal tombs were rarely iconographically explicit. The graves of Edith, Matilda of Flanders, and Edith-Matilda were unmarked or distinguished only by flat slabs and lamps; Matilda of Flanders' surviving slab bears a Latin inscription which would have been incomprehensible to most observers unless some literate person identified the queen. The early thirteenth-century Angevin tombs at Fontevrault are the first funerary effigies of English kings and their wives; Berengaria of Navarre's (d. 1230) effigy, originally in her foundation at L'Epau, survives at Le Mans and effigies figure on all later tombs of English queens. Of those now lost but of which description survives, Isabella of France's alabaster monument in the London Franciscan church was especially elaborate, with statues of the archangels at its corners.[14] Among themselves, the extant tombs show significant evolution. All the queens' effigies are crowned, but at first sceptres were lacking; Eleanor of Aquitaine's effigy holds a book, Berengaria's a reliquary, and Isabella of Angoulême's (d. 1246) at Fontevrault merely folds the hands upon the breast. In contrast, the effigies of Eleanor of Castile and Philippa of Hainaut held one sceptre each, Joan of Navarre two; Elizabeth of York (like Henry VII beside her) sheds the ensigns of royalty and clasps her hands in prayer. Eleanor of Castile's and Philippa's tombs, moreover, prominently evoked their ancestry and family connections, to which I will return. As queens came to share kings' tombs, however, such displays were combined with, and by implication subordinated to, those of the king; Elizabeth of York's heraldic identity is entirely subsumed in Henry VII's as they both bore the royal arms, she by birth and he by conquest and coronation.[15]

Sculpture: Four Lectures on its Changing Aspects from Ancient Egypt to Bernini, ed. H. W. Janson (New York, 1964), p. 57, pll. 222, 247, thinks the first conjugal tombs were the early thirteenth-century monuments of Henry II and Eleanor of Aquitaine at Fontevrault (not really a single tomb, nor certainly next to each other in their original placement), and the *c.* 1240 tomb of their daughter Matilda (d. 1189) and Henry the Lion of Saxony (d. 1194) in Germany. Conjugal aristocratic tombs existed in the empire by the late thirteenth century but were evidently adopted by noble English couples only at the mid-fourteenth; their use by royal couples followed (P. Coss, *The Knight in Medieval England, 1100–1400* [Stroud, 1993], pp. 92–4). A closely argued chronology of such tombs in England is needed, but cannot be attempted in this article.

[14] Erlande-Brandenburg, 'Les Gisants de Fontevrault', in *The Year 1200: A Symposium*, edd. J. Hoffeld and T. Hoving (Dublin, 1975), pp. 561–77; M. Mitchell, *Berengaria: Enigmatic Queen of England* (Burwash Weald, 1986); C. L. Kingsford, *The Grey Friars of London: Their History with the Register of their Convent and an Appendix of Documents*, British Society of Franciscan Studies, 6 (Aberdeen, 1915), p. 74; and F. D. Blackley, 'Isabella of France, Queen of England (1308–1358), and the Late Medieval Cult of the Dead', *Canadian Journal of History*, xv (1980), 23–47, esp. pp. 29–32. Adelaide of Maurienne (d. 1154), Louis VI of France's widow and Eleanor of Aquitaine's mother-in-law, had a tomb with visual representation of the deceased (see n. 12). That effigies first appeared for both English kings and queens only in the thirteenth century, however, means that their appearance for queens was not a separate phenomenon linked to the resurgent English queenship of the thirteenth century (J. C. Parsons, *Eleanor of Castile: Queen and Society in Thirteenth-Century England* [New York, 1995], pp. 71–4, and 'Queen's Intercession', pp. 149–50).

[15] P. G. Lindley, ' "Una grande opera per il mio re": Gilt-Bronze Effigies in England from the Middle Ages to the Renaissance', *Journal of the British Archaeological Association*, cxliii

As the facts of burial are not plentiful, it would appear unlikely that we can find anything more about the ritual contexts of queens' burials. It is difficult, in fact, to say much about royal funerals in England before 1290, as no English chronicler noted them in detail – probably because until then, most English kings and queens rested in France. For the most part we are told simply that a queen was buried fittingly, with clergy and nobles present; as with the well-known story of Richard II laying out the earl of Arundel at Anne of Bohemia's funeral,[16] such details as the chroniclers do record are rarely helpful in reconstructing the solemnities. The first exception, remarkable in its evident novelty, is Eleanor of Castile's funeral in 1290. During the journey southward from Lincoln, her body was exposed to view in royal robes, crown and sceptre; she was buried with her regalia – likely gilt copper substitutes like those seen in Edward I's tomb in 1774 – and so lavish was her Westminster abbey funeral that the Barnwell annalist said that 'never was a body buried in England with such solemnity and honour'.[17] Eleanor's was the first royal funeral to be deliberately and extensively exploited in England to exalt monarchy, and in dealing with the processes that shaped the *Liber Regie Capelle*'s prescription, it is significant that a queen's burial provided the opportunity. David Cannadine notes the twentieth century's (re)discovery of queens' funerals for royal pageantry, but it was the thirteenth that first did so, and later kings followed Edward I's example. Isabella of France's last progress through London in November 1358 was prepared with the cleansing of streets in Bishopsgate and Aldgate. The months that had elapsed since her death meant that her embalmed body was borne in a closed coffin; the cortège included forty torchbearers and paupers to pray at the bier, and alms were given to convents and the poor along the way. Isabella's son Edward III walked with his retinue to her elaborate funeral service in the London Franciscan church, with many magnates and ecclesiastical lords. Her magnificent burial, and the religious commemorations Edward laid on for her, were presumably meant to rehabilitate her memory and by implication confirm his legitimacy as Edward II's son, or to stress the claim to the French throne he derived through her. Philippa died in August 1369 and was buried in January 1370, so a closed coffin was again used; hearses, well lighted with candles, were set up in the five churches in which her body rested between Windsor and Westminster, and magnates were officially summoned to her funeral. At Anne of Bohemia's 1394 funeral even more

(1990), 112–30; J. C. Parsons, 'Ritual and Symbol', pp. 62–5. I avoid debate on 'standing' vs 'reclining' effigies, or on open vs closed eyes – i.e. whether effigies are 'lifelike' or 'deathlike'. Of those noted here, all queens are recumbent though 'standing' and 'open-eyed' except Elizabeth of York, the drapery of whose garments shows her reclining (but open-eyed). For orientation to these themes, P. Ariès, *The Hour of Our Death*, trans. H. Weaver (London, 1981), pp. 240–3, and P. G. Lindley, 'Ritual, Regicide and Representation', in *idem*, *Gothic to Renaissance: Essays on Sculpture in England* (Stamford, 1995), pp. 108–9.

16 Thomas Walsingham, *Annales Ricardi Secundi et Henrici Quarti*, in *Johannis de Trokelowe et Henrici de Blaneford . . . Chronica et Annales*, ed. H. T. Riley, RS 28 (London, 1865), iii, p. 424.

17 *Liber memorandorum ecclesie de Bernewelle*, ed. J. W. Clark (Cambridge, 1907), p. 226.

candles were used than at Philippa's – more than for any earlier queen of England – and again, the magnates were officially summoned.[18]

Several points may be suggested from this necessarily brief survey of recorded ceremonial.[19] First, queens' funerals could be used as effectively as kings' burials to mark royal 'centres': Westminster abbey, long recognised as the coronation church, by 1290 had been rebuilt by Henry III around the shrine of the royal patron Edward the Confessor, and Eleanor of Castile's interment there was a significant step in the abbey church's evolution into a royal mausoleum. Queens' funerals also created precedents for kings' burials: Edward I's 1307 funeral procession followed the same route through London as his wife's had done in 1290.[20] The few details we have of Isabella's, Philippa's, and Anne's burials further indicate that like the royal tombs, such events became increasingly elaborate over time, highlighting their importance well before the chapel royal's rituals were written out in the fifteenth century. And even for a queen like Isabella whose past was anomalous, a grand funeral and religious commemorations were not out of place even though she was not buried in a church that sheltered the remains of earlier male rulers. A full history of English royal burial practices has yet to be written; but even if they cannot be closely observed before the *Liber Regie Capelle*'s compilation in the mid-1440s, some elements were evidently in place well before

[18] D. Cannadine, 'Splendor out of Court: Royal Spectacle and Pageantry in Modern Britain, *c.* 1820–1977', in *Rites of Power: Symbolism, Ritual, and Politics since the Middle Ages* ed. S. Wilentz (Philadelphia, 1985), pp. 206–43, esp. p. 229. On Isabella, Blackley, 'Isabella of France', pp. 30–2; on Philippa, *The Anonimalle Chronicle, 1333 to 1381*, ed. V. H. Galbraith (Manchester, 1927), p. 58 (she rested at Windsor, Kingston, St Mary Overy, St Paul's and Westminster); on Anne, Jean Froissart, *Oeuvres*, ed. J. M. B. C. Kervyn de Lettenhove, 25 vols (Brussels, 1867–77), xv, 136–7. Little is known of Joan of Navarre's 1437 Canterbury funeral; she outlived Henry IV and her stepson Henry V (in whose reign she was imprisoned on suspicion of sorcery), and seemingly Henry VI was careless of the burial of a dowager who was neither his mother nor grandmother (cf. the rich burials of Edward I's and Edward III's mothers).

[19] It was only accidental that the burials of 1358 and 1370 were not contemporary with the queens' deaths (cf. Gittings, *Death and the Individual*, pp. 19–20). The months between Isabella's and Philippa's deaths and burials evidently resulted from decisions to finish their tombs before the funerals. Eleanor of Castile's burial three weeks after death was made possible by the existence of an empty royal grave in Westminster abbey, first occupied by Edward the Confessor (1066–1163) and then by Henry III from November 1272 to May 1290, when he was moved to his present tomb; Eleanor was buried in the grave that December, and there awaited completion of her tomb (J. C. Parsons, *Eleanor of Castile*, p. 279 n. 203).

[20] E. Mason, ' "The site of king-making and coronation": Westminster Abbey and the Crown in the Eleventh and Twelfth Centuries', in *The Church and Sovereignty: Essays in Honour of Michael Wilks*, ed. D. Wood (Oxford, 1991), pp. 57–76; E. Hallam, 'The Eleanor Crosses and Royal Burial Customs', in *Eleanor of Castile, 1290–1990: Essays to Commemorate the Seven Hundredth Anniversary of her Death, 28 November 1990*, ed. D. Parsons (Stamford, 1991), pp. 14–15. On Edward I's procession, *Flores historiarum per Matthaeum Westmonasteriensem collecti*, ed. H. R. Luard, 3 vols, RS 95 (London, 1890), iii, 71–2; *The Chronicle of Walter of Guisborough*, ed. H. Rothwell, Camden Society, 3rd ser., 89 (1957), p. 379.

that, including perhaps something approaching equality of ceremonial for the burials of kings and their wives.

As the first queen's tomb to be so elaborated in medieval England, Eleanor of Castile's monument in Westminster abbey is deserving of careful attention. This stately and beautiful tomb has been described often, and no details need be repeated here. In the present context it need only be remarked that the effigy appears to represent a queen at the moment of coronation: as the *ordo* prescribes, her hair is let down on her shoulders, she wears only a simple tunic and flowing robe, and she bears the crown and sceptre. Her tomb thus juxtaposes and compresses royal beginnings and endings – coronations and funerals – just as the abbey church itself was coming to do as the Plantagenets adopted it as a place of burial as well as a coronation church.[21] It is significant too that Eleanor's effigy shares what Paul Binski calls the official restraint of the kings' effigies at Westminster: her tomb is, so to speak, appropriated to share in the monumental legitimation of monarchy.[22] Here, then, one answer appears to questions posed by the *Liber regie capelle*'s prescription. The queen's funeral was a matter of royal prestige: just as a living queen was received by bishops or civic worthies with pomp and ceremony,[23] honouring her in death honoured the king and with him, the kingship.

A second reason for burying a queen with the same ceremony used for a king is implied by the work of Ralph Giesey and E. A. R. Brown on kings' burials as marking the legitimate transfer of power.[24] A queen's funeral would not serve the identical purpose, but it is not out of place to look for similar resonances in her burial. It has become a commonplace of the history of medieval queenship, for example, to observe that the custom of anointing and crowning queens was linked to the evolution of hereditary succession: the king's wife was consecrated to designate her as his legitimate spouse and the mother of his lawful heir. I have suggested elsewhere that it was to strengthen a weak hereditary principle in English kingship that the births of English royal children were developed as

---

[21] J. C. Parsons, *Eleanor of Castile*, p. 207; I disagree here with P. Binski, *Westminster Abbey and the Plantagenets: Kingship and the Representation of Power 1200–1400* (London/New Haven, CT, 1995), p. 110, on whether Eleanor is shown in coronation robes. Admittedly the first rubricated English coronation *ordo* dates from the 1380s, but clearly a number of its prescriptions were observed long before its composition (J. C. Parsons, 'Ritual and Symbol', pp. 62–3).

[22] On legitimising royal dynasties by tombs and other behaviours, Erlande-Brandenburg, 'Les Gisants de Fontevraut', pp. 563–4; P. Metcalf and R. Huntingdon, *Celebrations of Death: The Anthropology of Mortuary Ritual*, 2nd edn (Cambridge, 1991), pp. 144–51, esp. p. 149. On 'official' restraint in the Westminster effigies, Binski, *Westminster Abbey*, pp. 110, 112. Cf., however, Philippa's anomalous tomb in alabaster (Binski, pp. 179–80), which elicits notice of individual queens' aims and situations. Philippa had commissioned her tomb before death, and on her deathbed begged Edward III to promise to be buried with her even if he took a second wife; yet she was buried in a separate tomb that is a particularly strong evocation of identity expressed through the foreign connections she brought her husband and children.

[23] J. C. Parsons, 'Ritual and Symbol', p. 68, and *Eleanor of Castile*, pp. 32–3.

[24] Giesey, 'Models of Rulership', pp. 46–51; Brown, 'Ceremonial of Royal Succession', 227–71.

occasions to display Marian imagery, affording Christological resonances to the birth of a king's son and heir – another example, like that in Dr Stroll's article, of how males could exploit the Marian cult.[25] In the present context, the question naturally arises whether a queen's death rituals, including her tomb, might not serve a like end.

Suppose for a moment that kings alone were ceremoniously interred and monumentalised; the result would be churches full of only male monuments, resembling the royal galleries on cathedral façades. John Steane posits that these horizontal galleries' exclusively male population notwithstanding, they would, like the biblical 'begats', have implied vertical lineages to medieval observers, a theory supported by André Vauchez' discussion of the power of familial models in medieval thinking, as seen in the depiction of celibate religious on a pedigree, as if descended from their orders' founders.[26] But I suggest here that kingship's genetic continuity would be made unmistakably clear to observers only when the king's wife was monumentalised and commemorated: links between royal generations would be clearly manifest only upon visualisation of the conjugal and biogenetic factors a queen alone could (literally) embody. It would follow that monumental evocation of a queen next to or near the king, with the implied emphasis on her dynastic motherhood, would afford her (or her successors) means to assert that maternity as a virtually unchallengeable claim to power. So much is implicit in Alain Erlande-Brandenburg's idea that it was Eleanor of Aquitaine who commissioned the Fontevrault tombs, echoed by Andrew Martindale's study of aristocratic women's and queens' manipulation of their tombs' imagery to import secular motifs into sacred spaces.[27] Scrutiny of queens' tombs and their representation of the deceased may thus tell us something about queens' collective awareness of their office, or even of their self-image.

Eleanor of Castile was planning in the mid-1280s for her burial at Westminster abbey; nine months before her death, she provided for her heart burial in the London Dominican church, and her treasury records suggest at least a possibility that she may have ordered her Westminster tomb-chest before she died. Given Eleanor's well-attested interest in heraldry and the personal nature of armorial bearings, attention is at once drawn to her tomb-chest's strong heraldic identity,

---

[25] J. C. Parsons, 'Family, Sex, and Power', pp. 8–9; 'Ritual and Symbol', p. 66; and 'Queen's Intercession', p. 161.

[26] J. Steane, 'Symbols of Power: Changing Perceptions of the English Monarchy through the Middle Ages', in *Medieval Europe 1992: A Conference on Medieval Archaeology in Europe*, vii: *Art and Symbolism* (York, 1992), pp. 35–6; A. Vauchez, '*Beata stirps*: Sainteté et lignage en occident aux XIIIe et XIVe siècles', in *Famille et parenté dans l'occident médiéval: Actes du colloque de Paris (6–8 juin 1974)*, edd. G. Duby and J. Le Goff (Rome, 1977), pp. 405–6.

[27] Erlande-Brandenburg, 'Les Gisants de Fontevraut', pp. 563–4; A. Martindale, 'Patrons and Minders: The Intrusion of the Secular into Sacred Spaces in the Late Middle Ages', in *The Church and the Arts*, ed. D. Wood, SCH, 28 (Oxford, 1992), pp. 143–78. Undoubtedly the Fontevrault tombs were also a reminder to the Capetian monarchy of Plantagenet presence and power; but if Eleanor did order them – including one for herself – she may ironically have followed Capetian practice (see n. 12).

unprecedented for an English royal tomb.[28] Her gilt latten effigy (certainly cast after her death) presents a stylised image of queenship, but the tomb-chest's visual display conspicuously individualises Eleanor. The presence of her maternal Ponthevin arms in particular asserts her identity as countess of Ponthieu in her own right – a dignity she had previously advertised in England neither on her seal nor in the intitulation of her documents. The arms of Castile and León, lozenged and diapered on the plate of her effigy, moreover, recall the identical arrangement of those arms on the royal sarcophagi in the convent of las Huelgas near Burgos, where Eleanor wed Edward I – a link which, Elizabeth Hallam suggests, influenced the English abbey church's emergence as a Plantagenet cemetery.[29] It could be argued that the Ponthevin arms appear on Eleanor's tomb simply because she was countess there; but that no one else in England could bear the same combination of Castilian-Leonese, Ponthevin, and Plantagenet arms preserves her tomb's individuality. It should be noted too that Eleanor was the third successive countess of Ponthieu, after her grandmother Marie Talvas and her mother Jeanne de Dammartin. The implications for her self-image were surely profound, and as I show elsewhere her personal, and individual, experience as a Castilian infanta wed to an English king equipped her to sponsor a quite sophisticated literary articulation of her role as countess of Ponthieu, based on both the Castilian and English elements in her background.[30]

Philippa's tomb-chest and effigy were quite certainly commissioned before her death. The latter's realism strongly implies an attempt at portraiture, and just as her effigy showed a trend toward individuation, Philippa's tomb-chest abandoned Eleanor's symbolic evocations of ancestry to display individual statuettes of parents and relatives, heraldically identified. Significantly, these images were placed on the tomb's south side, facing outward to the ambulatory where they could be seen by a greater number of people; figures of Edward III's kin were on

---

[28] B. F. Harvey, *Westminster Abbey and its Estates in the Middle Ages* (Oxford, 1977), pp. 31–2. On Eleanor's preparations for burial, J. C. Parsons, *Eleanor of Castile*, pp. 83, 206–7, 214, 323 n. 4, and for her interest in heraldry, p. 53.

[29] Hallam, 'Eleanor Crosses', pp. 14–15; Henry III's plate diapers the Plantagenet arms identically. On las Huelgas, M. Gómez-Moreno y Martínez, *El panteón real de las Huelgas de Burgos* (Madrid, 1946). For Eleanor and Ponthieu, J. C. Parsons, 'The Beginnings of English Administration in Ponthieu: An Unnoticed Document of 1280', *Mediaeval Studies*, i (1988), 371–403; and *Eleanor of Castile*, p. 47.

[30] J. C. Parsons, 'Of Queens, Courts and Books: Reflections on the Literary Patronage of Thirteenth-Century Plantagenet Queens', in *The Cultural Patronage of Medieval Women*, ed. J. H. McCash (Athens, GA, 1996), pp. 174–201. Another case of matrilinear influence in royal patronage is argued by M. Shadis, 'Piety, Politics and Power: The Patronage of Leonor of England and her Daughters Berenguela of León and Blanche of Castile', *ibid.*, pp. 202–27. On matrilineal links in the medieval aristocracy, J. C. Parsons, 'Mothers, Daughters, Marriage, Power: Some Plantagenet Evidence, 1150–1500', in *idem*, *Medieval Queenship*, pp. 63–78; on medieval matrilinies in general, P. Sheingorn, 'The Holy Kinship: The Ascendancy of Matriliny in Sacred Genealogy of the Fifteenth Century', *Thought*, lxiv (1989), 269–86.

the tomb's north side, facing inward toward St Edward's shrine and the other Plantagenet tombs there.[31]

The consciousness of ancestry and kin implied by the tombs of Eleanor and Philippa echoes the nobility of a queen's descent, her chief qualification as a royal wife and mother, and the importance of the international connections her marriage brought the king. It also suggests reference to the new blood queens alone could bring a royal house, as Edith-Matilda carried the Anglo-Saxon royal blood to the Normans, and Isabella of France gave Edward III his claim to the French throne. That Eleanor and Philippa portrayed or heraldically evoked their mothers on their tombs[32] also recalls the links of training and education, silent and often ignored, that evolved as queens raised their daughters as a new generation of diplomatic brides. (As noted regarding Eleanor of Castile's marriage as a means by which Castilian royal burial practices reached England, these brides' migrations quite often transplanted customs that might influence royal burial.) Aristocratic women, moreover, had long been the chief remembrancers of ancestral dead, however that role might be de-valorised by male ecclesiastical writers. As churchmen became solely responsible for religious services for the dead, however, noblewomen evolved new ways to continue their commemorative function – literary patronage, for example, allowed them to extend and glorify royal ancestry, as Eleanor of Castile did for her Ponthevin forebears. Tombs were another and very natural means for noblewomen and queens to display such dynastic awareness.[33]

Queens' consciousness of ancestry and office, and their tendency to represent their ancestry on their tombs, suggest as well some fundamental differences in

---

[31] Binski, *Westminster Abbey and the Plantagenets*, pp. 179–80; Martindale, 'Patrons and Minders', p. 157; Lindley, 'Ritual, Regicide and Representation', p. 109. The figures are now lost, save for one on the north side; a partial nineteenth-century reconstruction, the figures arranged differently to the original as described by Martindale, is in the Victoria and Albert Museum, London (T. Cocke, *Nine Hundred Years: The Restorations of Westminster Abbey* [London, 1995], cat. no. 46).

[32] Binski, *Westminster Abbey and the Plantagenets*, pp. 113–18, 177–9, notes Isabella of France instigated creation of the tomb of her son John of Eltham, whose 'weepers' recall the images heraldically identified as kinsmen on the tombs of Henry III's son Edmund and the latter's wife Aveline. Might Isabella have had similar images on her tomb, which Binski thinks came from the same shop as John of Eltham's?

[33] For the queen attending commemorations, *Liber Regie Capelle*, ed. Ullmann, p. 60. On links between noble burial foundations and genealogy, G. Duby, 'Remarques sur la littérature généalogique en France aux XIe et XIIe siècles', in *Les Hommes et les structures au moyen âge* (Paris, 1973), trans. C. Postan as *The Chivalrous Society* (Berkeley, CA, 1977), p. 155. For women's association with such expressions in a funeral context, Geary, *Phantoms of Remembrance*, pp. 51–73. Such roles might be intensified by coronation ritual's emphasis on royal women's place in dynastic structures (J. C. Parsons, 'Ritual and Symbol', pp. 66–7; on the resulting cultural and political networks, *idem*, 'Mothers, Daughters, Marriage, Power', and 'Queens, Courts, and Books'). The maternal links noted here recall the late-medieval imagery of the Holy Kindred, which stressed relationships among St Anne's daughters and their offspring (Sheingorn, 'Holy Kinship', 268–86); cf. P. Stirnemann, 'Women and Books in France: 1170–1220', in *Representations of the Feminine in the Middle Ages*, ed. B. Wheeler, Feminea Medievalia, 1 (Cambridge, 1993), pp. 247–52.

kingly and queenly thinking. If Eleanor and Philippa recalled their ancestry on their tombs, their husbands are on record, in clean contrast, as having drawn attention to the number of children they fathered – Edward I often delighting to speak of the sixteen Eleanor bore him, Edward III putting on his tomb statuettes of Philippa's twelve. In essence, a queen's children were appropriated by the king, as was her tomb itself.[34] Such appropriation highlights what is often represented as medieval women's transience in the families that exchanged and received them, a factor likely more acute for queens than for other women. Queens were not only consigned to new families upon marriage; they had to negotiate loyalties to natal and affinal families in often forbiddingly politicised contexts, and they had to adjust to new languages or customs. The imagery of Eleanor's and Philippa's tombs, however, hardly implies they were overcome by any sense of impermanence. Rather, they were clearly cognizant of their membership in paternal and maternal lineages as well as of affinities acquired by marriage, and of all the benefits these relationships could bring them. Their tombs thus celebrate their capacity to exploit the connections acquired in their lives.[35] Exalting her children's maternal lineage, moreover, profited and in a sense reclaimed them for the queen.

Even allowing for appropriation of so many of the queen's dynastic and formal functions, then, we can justifiably regard the tombs of Eleanor of Castile and Philippa – separate from their husbands' and certainly in the one case if not both, commissioned in the woman's lifetime – as evocations of a distinct queenly identity. Edward II's widow Isabella may have meant her burial too as such a statement: evidently as a personal choice, she was interred in the mantle she wore at her wedding, and her alabaster effigy, again commissioned in her lifetime, held in its breast the heart of the husband at whose deposition (and perhaps murder)

---

[34] For Edward I, *Opus chronicorum*, ed. H. T. Riley in *Johannis de Trokelowe et Henrici de Blaneford . . . Chronica et Annales*, RS 28 (London, 1866), iii, 48; on Edward III's tomb, Binski, *Westminster Abbey and the Plantagenets*, pp. 195–9. All tombs showing children in Martindale, 'Patrons and Minders', p. 163, are of noble males, but the first to depict ancestry and kin at pp. 157–60 are of women; Philippa did have the Black Prince shown on her tomb (p. 157). Thibaut III of Champagne's tomb depicts kin, wife, and children – but his wife ordered it after his death (M. Bur, 'Les Comtes de Champagne et la "Normanitas": Sémiologie d'un tombeau', *Proceedings of the Battle Conference on Anglo-Norman Studies*, iii [1980], 22–32; Stirnemann, 'Women and Books', p. 251, calls this tomb a 'commanding statement of power and position by a courageous woman'). On males arrogating children, A. Newton, 'The Occlusion of Maternity in Chaucer's *Clerk's Tale*', in *Medieval Mothering*, edd. Parsons and Wheeler (New York, 1996), pp. 63–75, esp. 66–7. Appropriation can also be linked to Aristotelian ideas on the female's passive role in conception, on which cf. in this context J. C. Parsons, 'Pregnant Queen as Counsellor', *ibid.*, pp. 48–9.

[35] For the impact of women's transience on their thinking, B. J. Harris, 'Property, Power, and Personal Relations: Elite Mothers and Sons in Yorkist and Early Tudor England', *Signs*, xv (1990), 606–632. On queens' divided loyalties between natal and affinal families, C. T. Wood, 'The First Two Queens Elizabeth', in *Women and Sovereignty*, ed. Fradenburg, pp. 121–31. A useful case study of a woman's manipulation of natal and affinal relationships is K. A. LoPrete, 'Adela of Blois as Countess and as Mother', in *Medieval Mothering*, edd. Parsons and Wheeler, pp. 311–31.

Isabella had connived.[36] The emphasis on marriage implied by this burial, more-over, resonates with extant information on those of Eleanor of Castile and Philippa. The dying Philippa asked Edward III to promise to be buried with her, and she too was buried in her wedding mantle.[37] Eleanor was buried in 'royal vestments', not certainly those worn at her coronation; a wedding mantle was not mentioned, but the candle buried with her, its penitential and apotropaic evocations apart, was also redolent of wedding and fertility imagery and, like Isabella's and Philippa's mantles, recalled Eleanor's roles as a dynastic wife and mother.[38]

Such gestures, common to the burials of several consorts, suggest a kind of group identity among queens in the sense Lois Huneycutt discusses regarding Henry I's wife Edith-Matilda, who patterned herself on the virtues of her mother St Margaret of Scotland, as expounded in the *vita* of Margaret that Edith-Matilda commissioned between 1104 and 1107. The ways in which royal women were assimilated to, and reproduced, such relationships among themselves have been argued from their endeavours in such areas as diplomatic marriage,[39] and their burials could well be viewed in the same light. The paucity of foundations dedicated to the Holy Trinity in twelfth-century England, for example, suggests that Edith-Matilda's foundation at Holy Trinity Aldgate, where she meant to be buried, was inspired either by her mother's like foundation and burial at Dunferm-line, or by Matilda of Flanders' foundation at La Trinité in Caen, where she and at least three of her daughters rested. Edith-Matilda's niece, Matilda of Boulogne, linked herself with her aunt by patronising Holy Trinity Aldgate, burying two of her children there, and taking its prior as her confessor, as Edith-Matilda had done. A similar link can be seen in the *vita* of Matilda of Boulogne's paternal grand-mother St Ida, probably commissioned by Matilda between 1130 and 1135 and very likely inspired by her aunt's *vita* of her mother, St Margaret.[40]

That such female royal networks could be advertised through queens' burials is also suggested by the interments of several royal women in the London

---

36 Blackley, 'Isabella of France', p. 30; Kingsford, *Grey Friars*, pp. 70, 74, 170. Certainly Edward II's heart was reserved after his embalming (S. A. Moore, 'Documents Relating to the Death and Burial of King Edward II', *Archaeologia*, l [1887], 215–26; T. F. Tout, 'The Captivity and Death of Edward of Caernarvon', *Bulletin of the John Rylands Library*, vi [1921–22], 92–3, references I owe Dr Phillip G. Lindley).

37 Froissart, *Oeuvres*, ed. Kervyn de Lettenhove, vii, 429; W. H. St John Hope, 'On the Funeral Effigies of the Kings and Queens of England, with specific reference to those in the Abbey Church of Westminster', *Archaeologia*, lx (1907), 544.

38 For Eleanor's funeral, J. C. Parsons, *Eleanor of Castile*, pp. 59–60; on candle symbolism, E. Panofsky, 'Jan van Eyck's "Arnolfini Portrait" ', *Burlington Magazine*, lxiv (1934), 117–27, repr. in *Modern Perspectives in Western Art History*, ed. W. E. Kleinbauer (New York, 1971), p. 200.

39 Huneycutt, 'Image of the Perfect Princess', and 'Intercession and the High-Medieval Queen'; J. C. Parsons, 'Mothers, Daughters, Marriage, Power'.

40 My thanks to Lois Huneycutt for discussion on Holy Trinity sites. On Matilda of Boulogne and Holy Trinity, *Cartulary of Holy Trinity*, ed. Hodgett, p. 3 no. 14, and p. 192 nos 975–6; for St Ida's life, R. Nip, 'Godelieve of Gistel and Ida of Boulogne', in *Sanctity and Motherhood: Essays on Holy Mothers in the Middle Ages*, ed. A. B. Mulder-Bakker (New York, 1995), pp. 212–13.

Franciscan church. Most of these women were Franciscan patrons, but significantly, a number of them were 'displaced', their status in the family anomalous, so that burial in a dynastic setting was unnecessary or inappropriate. Eleanor of Provence died as a Benedictine, but she was a devoted patron of the Franciscans and her heart lay in their London church near the tomb of her daughter, Countess Beatrice of Richmond. Nearby lay Edward I's second wife Margaret of France, the great royal patron of the house, and her granddaughter Duchess Margaret of Norfolk. Edward II's widow Isabella lay there with her daughter Queen Joan of Scotland (who abandoned David II), and Edward III's daughter Countess Isabella of Bedford, deserted by Enguerran de Coucy.[41] Reminiscent of the burials at La Trinité in Caen and Holy Trinity Aldgate's appeal to Matilda of Boulogne, this female Plantagenet cemetery suggests that even when events made conjugal burial unlikely, a sense of identity among royal women was strong enough to induce them to gather themselves together in death.

Death rituals allowed queens to inscribe themselves in this evolving tradition of glorious and glorified royal consorts by attending their predecessors' commemorations, as is most clearly evident in Margaret of France's 1306 appearance with Edward I at a sumptuous Westminster service for Eleanor of Castile. Queen Margaret's presence was arguably a matter of Christian charity, and presumably of consideration for Edward's feelings too; but by appearing as queen on such an occasion, Margaret openly asserted a claim to the deference owed one who held the same office as the dead woman who merited such commemoration. By the mid-fifteenth century, the queen attended regularly the chapel royal's services for the ancestors and predecessors of the king and herself.[42] If the conduct of these services was by then the exclusive province of male clerics, the intimate and indissoluble relations between the living and the dead in the Middle Ages meant that such rites could assure that past queens remained very much a part of the face of queenship. In Mary Carruthers' view, moreover, even a medieval queen faced the world with a ' "self" constructed out of bits and pieces of great [people] of the past', and remembrance of queens past could indeed shape that self. Previous queens' articulation of their experience as they taught their daughters sharpened their sense of self as it prepared the daughters' self-realising choice to accept their diplomatic marriages; tombs and commemorations visualized and perpetuated that experience for later queens, figurative 'daughters' thus enabled to incorporate it into their practice of queenship.[43]

But as Carruthers implies, a remembering audience is also an inescapable

---

41 Kingsford, *Grey Friars*, pp. 70–1, 74–5, 75, 165, 167.

42 *Annales Paulini*, ed. W. Stubbs in *Chronicles of the Reigns of Edward I and Edward II*, 2 vols, RS 76 (London, 1882–83), ii, 225; *Liber regie capelle*, ed. Ullmann, p. 60. Eleanor of Castile kept her natal family's obits in her own chapel (J. C. Parsons, *The Court and Household of Eleanor of Castile in 1290* [Toronto, 1977], pp. 95, 100); removal of such services to the chapel royal brought more closely under male control any claims to power the queen might derive from her ancestry.

43 J. C. Parsons, 'Mothers, Daughters, Marriage, Power', pp. 76–8; Carruthers, *Book of Memory*, pp. 179–80.

necessity to the performance of queenship if it is to have any meaning. A queen's actions require some ground in common to herself and those who witness them.[44] In the present context, the question raised here is obvious: if we can deduce something of queenly attitudes toward death rituals, what effects had such pageantry and monuments on those meant to absorb the lessons thus offered? Eleanor of Castile's tripartite burial was unique among those of English queens in England; Eleanor of Provence's heart rested at the London Franciscans, but though Isabella of France had a 1345 dispensation for tripartite burial, it was not used.[45] Others did imitate Eleanor's burials, however, and by the mid-fourteenth century the Eleanor crosses, erected by Edward I in her memory, were influencing her evolving reputation. But however grand her monuments and commemorations, it is an untenable notion that her burials alone shaped the evolution of such customs in late medieval England, especially chantry foundations; it is much more likely that such usages were stimulated by successive royal deaths over time, as witness the splendid commemorations accorded Isabella of France and Philippa.[46]

Such indications of popular awareness of queens' death rituals in medieval England do elicit enquiry into the messages these rituals and tombs conveyed to the realm at large. The queen was, ironically, a stranger to the notions of dynastic continuity her death rituals helped articulate; she did not enter her office in the same way as the king, nor did one queen succeed another as a king does.[47] The king's appropriation of their children, those living tokens of the very continuity the queen assured, and the ritual de-centring of the sexual side of her motherhood, touch upon the negative side of her biogenetic role – specifically that she, an alien, was the king's sexual partner. That her sexual role was both revered and feared is clearly shown by the variety of ways in which medieval society addressed the implicit threat her body was seen to pose to the king's ability to meet his obligations to the realm and, by implication, to a male-ordered social hierarchy.[48] The desire to obscure her sexual role, and the king's appropriation of it, would seem at first glance to negate any reading of her tomb as an assertion of power based on her biogenetic role in monarchy's continuity. Yet her tomb could perpetuate the formalities of an intermittent office. Beginning with her coronation, royal ritual persistently reiterated a close link between the queen's functions as dynastic mother and intercessor, effacing her sexual maternity and instead stressing a nurturing intercession. Some queens, like Eleanor of Provence, evidently substituted intercession for biological maternity as they ceased to bear children and faced widowhood; others, like Margaret and Isabella of France, exploited intercession

---

[44] Carruthers, *Book of Memory*, pp. 181–2.

[45] Blackley, 'Isabella of France', p. 28 n. 30.

[46] J. C. Parsons, *Eleanor of Castile*, pp. 216–20.

[47] There are resonances here with what L. O. Fradenburg calls queenship's 'special periodicity' ('Rethinking Queenship', in *eadem, Women and Sovereignty*, pp. 8–9).

[48] Discussed variously in J. C. Parsons, 'Ritual and Symbol', 'Queen's Intercession', and 'The Pregnant Queen as Counsellor'.

to win popular favour or to create the image of a mutually supportive marriage.[49] A queen's biological maternity was limited in time by natural physiological processes, but her nurturing intercession was not so bounded and was susceptible to identification with her office's timeless formalities.

In a sense, then, we may say that the queen had two bodies, if not in the exact sense Ernst Kantorowicz argued for a king. Her 'official' body was exalted by unction and coronation; to become a model of proper female regal behaviour, however, that body had to be abased to the intercessor's submissive posture. Her physical body, like that of any woman, was impugned as a site of sin and pollution and, in the queen's case, feared especially as a means whereby she might sway her husband. Her reproductive function was of crucial importance to the realm, but that aspect of her maternity was secreted and its nurturing side emphasised by association with her intercession. The importance ritually assigned to a queen as a nurturing mother-intercessor thus echoes Kantorowicz's ideas on the combinative yet distinguishing function of kings' tombs, which mask a decaying physical body while perpetuating the official body with a rich effigy: by visualising an 'official' body, a queen's tomb realised ritual emphasis on her ageless nurturing-intercessory function, in contrast to the temporal limits of her biogenetic-sexual body, secreted by ritual and hidden within her tomb.[50]

The dead queen – or more properly, her tomb – thus became a blank canvas on which an 'official' image could inscribe accepted gender-power relations possibly menaced by her behaviour in her lifetime. This tendency is most evident in the conjugal tombs that implicitly subordinate wife to husband, but even in the tombs of Eleanor of Castile and Philippa, such 'official' images can be seen to function in this way. The images of Eleanor on tomb and Eleanor crosses, for example, distanced her memory from an unhelpful reality by depicting a submissiveness, grace, and generosity patently constructed by an appeal to Marian imagery,[51] echoing the Marian allusions that constructed and represented the queen's office to medieval English society. Many events in the lives of English medieval queens were occasions to display Marian imagery: their intercession and childbearing were taking on such overtones by the thirteenth century, when petitioners and clerics already used Marian imagery to seek or extol queenly mediation,[52] and the fifteenth-century chapel royal's rituals linked queen and Marian cult on a daily

---

49 I treat these questions in 'The Intercessionary Patronage of Queens Margaret and Isabella of France', to appear in *Thirteenth Century England VI: Papers from the Durham Conference 1995*, edd. M. C. Prestwich, R. H. Britnell and Robin Frame (Woodbridge, 1997).

50 This material is argued in my 'Pregnant Queen as Counsellor'. Cf. E. Kantorowicz, *The King's Two Bodies: A Study in Medieval Political Theology* (Princeton, 1957), pp. 419–36; Metcalf and Huntingdon, *Celebrations of Death*, pp. 162–90; Lindley, 'Ritual, Regicide and Representation', pp. 97–112.

51 In general, E. T. Hansen, 'The Death of Blanche and the Life of the Moral Order', *Thought*, lxiv (September 1989), 287–97, esp. p. 292. My *Eleanor of Castile*, pp. 61–7, 113–17, 149–56, 211–13, 248–53, considers how queens might challenge such relations and the improvement of their posthumous reputations by monumental evocation.

52 J. C. Parsons, 'Queen's Intercession', pp. 152–5. A late-medieval desire to think of Christ, the Virgin and the saints in corporeal ways could have further tightened associations between

basis.[53] It seems worthwhile, then, to ask if death rituals also played a part in Marianising the queenly office in England.

Philippa's death on the vigil of the feast of the Virgin's Assumption in 1369 allowed her former clerk Jean Froissart to describe the event in patently Marian language, with clouds of angels bearing her spirit to Heaven; as her funeral was in late January 1370, chroniclers dated it by reference to the feast of the Purification on 2 February.[54] Eleanor of Provence died in June 1291 and was buried on the feast of the Assumption, with all its echoes of the Virgin's coronation and her physical presence at her Son's side, where she might intercede with Him on behalf of sinful humanity. Eleanor's funeral was delayed as her son was in Scotland when she died; but the choice of 15 August for her burial cannot have been haphazard. (The assimilation of events in royal women's lives to Marian feasts was not limited to England; as Dr Conklin notes, Queen Isambour's 1193 marriage and coronation in France coincided with the Assumption, the liturgy for which uses Vulgate Ps. 44's coronation imagery.[55]) Long before their deaths, indeed, royal pageantry implied that English queens in death would be linked with Marian imagery. Margaret of Anjou's 1445 London entry included a pageant prophesying her coronation by Christ in Heaven after death; this was, of course, the end of any Christian who died in a state of grace, but in this case, resonances with the Virgin's coronation were made unmistakable by the pageantry's Marianising references to the Sponsa of Cant. 3:1 and 7:12 and the Woman of Apoc. 12:1, the latter closely juxtaposed with Margaret's heavenly coronation.[56] The Virgin's coronation, with its obvious echoes of earthly queenly ritual, could have broadcast an exalted yet submissive queenly image to multiple effect. The wedding imagery that was part of queens' burials and was implied by conjugal tombs, for example, suggests parallels with Georges Duby's idea that the image of the Virgin's coronation enhanced the dignity of the married state, and with Louise Fradenburg's views on royal marriage as a model of loving community and compliant submission for the realm. The imagery of queens' tombs can be cited too: Eleanor of Castile's effigy

celestial and terrestrial rulers; M. Rubin, *Corpus Christi: The Eucharist in Late Medieval Culture* (Cambridge, 1991), pp. 302–6.

[53] J. C. Parsons, 'Ritual and Symbol', pp. 65–7, and 'Queen's Intercession', pp. 152–9; *Liber regie capelle*, ed. Ullmann, p. 60.

[54] Froissart, *Oeuvres*, ed. Kervyn de Lettenhove, vii, 429; *The Brut or The Chronicles of England*, ed. F. W. D. Brie, 2 vols, Early English Text Society, Old Ser., 131 (London, 1906–08), ii, 321; *The Anonimalle Chronicle*, ed. Galbraith, p. 58.

[55] *The Chronicle of Lanercost, 1272–1346*, ed. H. Maxwell (Glasgow, 1913), pp. 81–2, notes the delay of Eleanor's burial. There are parallels in the life of Edward I's daughter Mary, so named as she was born near the feast of the Annunciation 1279; she was dedicated at Amesbury on the feast of the Assumption 1285, and probably professed on the feast of the Virgin's Conception 1291 (J. C. Parsons, 'The Year of Eleanor of Castile's Birth and her Children by Edward I', *Mediaeval Studies*, xlvi [1984], 264). For Assumption liturgy's links to rituals honouring English queens, J. C. Parsons, 'Ritual and Symbol', p. 68.

[56] G. Kipling, 'The London Pageants for Margaret of Anjou: A Medieval Script Restored', *Medieval English Theatre*, iv (1982), 5–27.

has been directly compared to an image of the Virgin, and bears obvious stylistic affinities to a Marian painting in South Newington church, dated to the 1330s.[57]

With these evocations may be compared the numerous petitions to Edward I and his officials after Eleanor of Castile's death, seeking favour or pardon 'for the good of the late queen's soul'. By granting such petitions, Edward of course showed a Christian husband's proper concern for his late wife's spiritual welfare, but from a petitioner's viewpoint, such requests suggest a certain extension beyond the tomb of a queen's capacity to sway her husband. Michael Prestwich has, moreover, noted Edward's intensified celebration of Marian feasts during his widowhood, observances that declined after he remarried in 1299 and all but vanished by the last years of his life.[58] The contexts here hint that ritual association of the earthly and heavenly queens, at a queen's death and burial as well as in her lifetime, resonated in popular awareness strongly enough that, on the one hand, the Virgin could emerge as a kind of proxy queen when there was no living consort – rather as Dr Webb suggests for Italian city-states – and on the other, that a queen might almost continue mediating from (we assume) on high after her death. Later queens were thereby encouraged to adopt acceptable models of submissive and gracious behaviour, and that such traditions indeed influenced popular expectation is made explicit in the Londoners' address to Anne of Bohemia upon her arrival in 1382: 'Since it pertains to your most benign piety to assume . . . the role of mediatrix between your most illustrious prince . . . our lord the king, just as did our other lady Queens who preceded your most excellent highness . . . , may it be pleasing to your most clement and preeminent nobility to mediate with our lord the king in such wise with gracious words and deeds.'[59] Here, as Carruthers would

---

[57] J. C. Parsons, *Eleanor of Castile*, pp. 207, 323 n. 3; P. G. Lindley, 'Romanticizing Reality: The Sculptural Memorials of Queen Eleanor and their Context', in *Eleanor of Castile*, ed. D. Parsons, pp. 69–92, esp. p. 73. See also G. Duby, *The Knight, the Lady and the Priest: The Making of Modern Marriage in Medieval France*, trans. B. Bray (Chicago, 1983), p. 207; L. Fradenburg, 'Sovereign Love: The Wedding of Margaret Tudor and James IV of Scotland', in *eadem, Women and Sovereignty*, pp. 78–100, and *City, Marriage, Tournament*, pp. 67–83. A long tradition existed of representing royal marriage as mediating divine models of community: see Sedulius Scottus, *Liber de rectoribus christianis*, in *Sedulius Scottus*, ed. S. Hellmann (Munich, 1906), p. 37; Angelomus of Luxeuil, 'Epistola Lotharium Imperatorem de obitu conjugis', ed. E. Dümmler in *MGH, Epp.* v, suppl., pp. 625–30, esp. p. 625.

[58] *Select Bills in Eyre, AD 1292–1333*, ed. W. C. Bolland, Selden Society, 30 (1914), p. lviii; M. E. Fenwick, 'The Inquiry into Complaints against the Ministers of Eleanor of Castile, 1291–92', M.A. thesis (University of London, 1931), p. xxiii. On Edward I's Marian devotions, M. C. Prestwich, 'The Piety of Edward I', in *England in the Thirteenth Century: Proceedings of the 1984 Harlaxton Symposium*, ed. W. M. Ormrod (Harlaxton, 1985), pp. 120–8, esp. p. 121; *idem, Edward I*, p. 112.

[59] The address to Anne of Bohemia is quoted and translated from an unpublished source by P. Strohm, 'Queens as Intercessors', in *idem, Hochon's Arrow: The Social Imagination of Fourteenth-Century Texts* (Princeton, 1992), p. 105. D. Loades, *The Tudor Court* (Totawa, NJ, 1987), pp. 4–5, suggests the living queen was perhaps seen as an intercessor with Heaven for the entire realm.

anticipate, a remembering audience indeed provided meaning – and direction – for a future consort's performance.

The living queen's subordination was closely linked to the preservation of a male hierarchy to which, as a woman, she was an outsider,[60] and death rituals could perpetuate this vital social role. The crowds of magnates who attended queens' burials made such occasions natural moments at which to observe and reinforce precedence and hierarchy. Subsequent commemorations very often included banquets; it is unclear whether Eleanor of Castile's yearly service did so, but certainly those of Isabella of France, Philippa of Hainaut and Anne of Bohemia did.[61] As integral elements of royal ritual, banquets reinforced hierarchy, and Michael Enright in particular has shown how queens' actions on such occasions contributed significantly to that support.[62] A queen's posthumous commemorations, including banquets, can surely be seen, then, to have allowed her (or her office) in a sense to continue performing gestures suitable to such appearances during her lifetime. Indeed, the hierarchical aspects of royal women's obits were sometimes made explicit: John of Gaunt's mother-in-law, Duchess Blanche of Lancaster, specified sums to be given to each city officer attending her anniversary, beginning with the mayor and sheriffs and including the chamberlain, swordbearer and lesser officials. And such occasions could be turned to overtly political purposes, as Gaunt used his first wife's 1381 obit to mark a recent reconciliation with the Londoners.[63] Queens' commemorations might thus sustain their social functions as well as preserve individual memory: as in life, a deceased queen remained an instrument of lordship and order.[64]

As Elizabeth Ward notes, queenship was a nebulous concept in the Middle Ages and, as Pauline Stafford stresses, queens had to deal with many variables. Queens of England lost many avenues to direct or official authority and had to develop informal ways of demonstrating influence and power. One self-evident result was that a queen had to avail herself of any likely buttress to her position. Funerals, monuments, and commemorations were just as important to the portrayal and construction of the queenly office as the coronations Janet Nelson discusses, and they offered means by which queens could gain access to those traditions of queenly activity Dr Stafford emphasises. In life, each queen adapted traditions shaped in part by earlier queens' death rituals, and her own death rituals assisted

---

[60] J. C. Parsons, *Eleanor of Castile*, pp. 62–3, and 'Queen's Intercession', pp. 159–61.

[61] Blackley, 'Isabella of France', pp. 35–7; E. H. Pearce, *The Monks of Westminster, being a Register of the Brethren of the Convent from the time of the Confessor to the Dissolution* (Cambridge, 1916), pp. 18–19; N. B. Lewis, 'The Anniversary Service for Blanche, Duchess of Lancaster, 12th September, 1374', *Bulletin of the John Rylands Library*, xxi (1937), 9.

[62] Enright, 'Lady with a Mead-Cup', pp. 170–203; J. M. Hill, *The Cultural World in Beowulf* (Toronto, 1995), pp. 100–04, reads Wealtheow's behaviour at Heorot differently from Enright but still acknowledges her actions' impact on relationships among the males gathered there. On royal banquets and hierarchy in general, B. Lincoln, *Discourse and the Construction of Society* (Oxford, 1989), pp. 75–88.

[63] R. Grafton, *Grafton's Chronicle, or, History of England*, 2 vols (London, 1809), i, 409; Lewis, 'Anniversary Service for Blanche', p. 7.

[64] On queens as such instruments, J. C. Parsons, 'Queen's Intercession', pp. 160–1.

the evolution and preservation of those same traditions. This process could, however, increase the power or influence of later queens – or they could preserve ambiguous aspects of a queen's life. Individual heraldic display, for example, advertised her nobility and the value of her foreign connections; but they also stressed her foreignness, so trying for the English throughout the Middle Ages (and for other peoples too, as János Bak shows).

However her exaltation served the interests of kingship, a queen's distinct and individual presence, and any tokens of her independent power, were out of place, and so the individual tombs of the thirteenth and early fourteenth centuries gave way to conjugal monuments that more explicitly manifested the queen's subordination to her husband. That such tombs also implied the intimacy of their relationship and the queen's ease of access to her spouse suggests reference to an analogous development. The queen's intercession with the king had grown in importance from the early thirteenth century and offered royal consorts a highly visible, and socially acceptable, way to bolster her position and her influence; at the same time, it implicitly demonstrated the superiority of the king's authority and his wife's subordination to it. But intercession could be exploited to the extent that a queen's popularity might outstrip that of her husband. The barren Anne of Bohemia, for example, virtually staked her career on her ability to mediate with Richard II and was exceptionally beloved in consequence by his subjects, who made their expectations so clear upon her arrival in England in 1382.[65] It is appropriate – and perhaps now, more understandable – that it was their tomb that first visualised both the intimacy and the subordination implied in the queen's intercessionary role.

Individual or conjugal, a queen's tomb concretised her office's innate tensions – between the value of her international ties and the problems they could pose to the realm, between the need to continue the royal line and the threat of her sexual sway over the king, between a submissive Marianising effigy and the individuality asserted by heraldry. Notwithstanding the equality of ceremony inscribed in the *Liber regie capelle* in the 1440s, then, queens from the late fourteenth century were subordinated to kings in the imagery of death. They were, after all, the most visible of women and their ritual or figurative portrayals were bound to reverberate in observers' awareness. Living queens were diplomatic, political, and moral necessities to their male kin; their death rituals were vital to the creation of an image of the queen as a 'paradigmatic figure of the completely perfect and totally absent woman upon whom the moral and social order depend[ed]'.[66] In short, it was easier (and safer) to exalt a deceased consort than to praise the king's living bedfellow.

[65] Strohm, 'Queens as Intercessors', pp. 105–19.
[66] A. Crawford, 'The King's Burden? – the Consequences of Royal Marriage in Fifteenth-Century England', in *Patronage, the Crown and the Provinces in Later Medieval England*, ed. R. A. Griffiths (Gloucester, 1981), pp. 33–56; Hansen, 'Death of Blanche', p. 293.

Index

Abbreviations: dk = dk; dr = daughter; f. = founded; kg = king; qn = queen